The Macedonian Empire

The Macedonian Empire

THE ERA OF WARFARE UNDER PHILIP II
AND ALEXANDER THE GREAT,
359–323 B.C.

by James R. Ashley

McFarland & Company, Inc., Publishers
Jefferson, North Carolina, and London

> *The present work is a reprint of the library bound edition of* The Macedonian Empire: The Era of Warfare Under Philip II and Alexander the Great, 359–323 B.C., *first published in 1998 by McFarland.*

LIBRARY OF CONGRESS CATALOGUING-IN-PUBLICATION DATA

Ashley, James R., 1948–
　The Macedonian empire : the era of warfare under Philip II and Alexander the Great, 359–323 B.C. / by James R. Ashley.
　　p. cm.
　Includes bibliographical references and index.

　ISBN:13: 978-0-7864-1918-0
　softcover : 50# alkaline paper ∞

　1. Philip II, King of Macedonia, 382–336 B.C. — Military leadership.　2. Alexander, the Great, 356–323 B.C. — Military leadership.　3. Macedonia — History — To 168 B.C.
4. Greece — History — Macedonian Expansion, 359–323 B.C.
5. Military art and science — Greece.　I. Title.
DF233.2.A84　2004
938'.07 — dc21　　　　　　　　　　　　　　　　　97-40332

British Library cataloguing data are available

©1998 James R. Ashley. All rights reserved

No part of this book may be reproduced or transmitted in any form or by any means, electronic or mechanical, including photocopying or recording, or by any information storage and retrieval system, without permission in writing from the publisher.

Cover image ©2004 Art Today

Manufactured in the United States of America

*McFarland & Company, Inc., Publishers
　Box 611, Jefferson, North Carolina 28640
　www.mcfarlandpub.com*

Table of Contents

List of Maps by Subject ix
Preface 1
Introduction 5

Part I: Ancient Warfare

1. The Armies 13
    Athens 15
    Boeotia 16
    Illyria 17
    India 18
    Macedonia 22
    Persia 55
    Phocia 64
    Scythia 65
    Sparta 67
    Thessaly 71
    Thrace 71

2. Siege Operations 73

3. Logistics 80

4. Naval Operations 83
    The Trireme 83
    Naval Tactics 86
    Athenian Navy 87
    Macedonian Navy 91
    Persian Navy 104

Part II: The Reign of Philip II

5. Campaigns of Philip II 111
    Illyria 111
    Third Sacred War 115
    The Macedonian Coast 126
    Chalcidice 126

Thessaly 130
Thrace 133
Epirus 144
Euboea 145
Scythia 148
Fourth Sacred War 149
Phocis 151
Peloponnesus 158
Asia Minor 160

PART III: CAMPAIGNS OF ALEXANDER THE GREAT

6. Greece 165
Thessaly 165
The Balkans 166
Central Greece 175
The Peloponnese 181

7. The Western Persian Empire 184
Asia Minor 185
Cilicia 219
Phoenicia 235
Egypt 251
Mesopotamia 255
Susiana 270
Persis 271
Media 279

8. The Eastern Persian Empire 282
Hyrcania 282
Areia 285
Drangiana 287
Arachosia 289
Parapamisadae 289
Hindu Kush 289
Bactria 289
Sogdiana 294
Pareitacae 302
Scythia 303

9. India 306
Bajaur 309
Swat 311
Upper Punjab 317
Lower Punjab 333

10. The Southern Persian Empire 342
Gedrosa 342
Carmania 351

11. Return to Babylon 352
Persis 352
Susiana 352
Media 353
Babylonia 355

12. Arabia 357

Appendices

A. Peace of Philocrates 361
B. Assassination Attempts Against Alexander 365
C. Macedonian Army Mutinies 369
D. Hephaestion's Funeral 374
E. Mileage of Alexander's Campaigns 376
F. Alexander's Income and Expenses 377
G. Alexander's Funeral Train 383
H. Kings and Satraps 385
I. Chronology of the Macedonian Empire 392

Glossary 407
Notes 441
Bibliography 467
Index 471

List of Maps by Subject

Campaigns of Philip II
1. Greece 112
2. The Balkans 113
3. Central Greece 116
4. Chalcidice 127
5. Thessaly 131
6. Thrace 134
7. Epirus 145
10. The Peloponnesus 160
11. Northwest Asia Minor 161

Battles of Philip II
8, 9. Chaeronea. 154–5

Campaigns of Alexander the Great in Greece
12. Greece 166
13. The Balkans 168
14. Central Greece 176

Campaigns of Alexander the Great in the Western Persian Empire
16. Alexander's Western Asian Empire 186
17. Northwest Asia Minor 187
20. Southwest Asia Minor 204
22. South Central Asia Minor 211
23. North Central Asia Minor 214
24. Eastern Asia Minor. 216
25. Cilicia 218
28. Phoenicia. 236
30. Egypt. 250
32. Mesopotamia 256
36. Susiana/Persis. 272
37. Media. 278

Campaigns of Alexander the Great in the Eastern Persian Empire
38. Alexander's Eastern Asian Empire 284
39. Hyrcania. 286

40. Areia 288
41. The Northwest Frontier 290

Campaigns of Alexander the Great in India
42. Kabul Valley 308
44. Upper Punjab. 316
48. Lower Punjab. 334

Campaigns of Alexander the Great in the Southern Persian Empire
49. Gedrosa. 344
50. Return to Babylon 354

Battles of Alexander the Great
15.   Thebes 178
18, 19. Granicus River 194, 196
26, 27. Issus. 224, 226
33, 34. Gaugamela 260, 262
46, 47. Hydaspes River 322, 324

Sieges of Alexander the Great
21. Halicarnassus. 208
29. Tyre. 241
43. Rock of Aornos. 314

Cities
31. Alexandria 253
35. Babylon. 270

Other Maps
45. Hydaspes River Crossing 320
51. Persian Royal Road 430

Preface

From the moment I read Major-General J.F.C. Fuller's *The Generalship of Alexander the Great*, I became interested in Alexander's military campaigns. As I read book after book on the subject, I found that the political and cultural aspects of the era were stressed, while the military operations were relegated to a secondary role, frequently being recounted virtually verbatim from Arrian's *Anabasis of Alexandri* and his *Indica*. It seemed to me that there must be more to be said about the military operations of a man who, without doubt, was the greatest conqueror of the ancient world. Fuller's work seemed to be an excellent jumping off point for this effort and therein began this book.

Aristobulus, Callisthenes, Marsyas of Pella, Nearchus, and Ptolemy (who had obtained Alexander's journal) all accompanied Alexander on a number of his campaigns and wrote individual histories about Alexander's reign. Cleitarchus, who was in Greece studying philosophy when Alexander was campaigning in Asia, also wrote a history after Alexander's death, based on the stories he had obtained from the returning Greek mercenaries who had served in Alexander's army. Interestingly enough, none of these primary sources survived beyond the ancient era, but they were available to several historians of the Roman Empire, who incorporated them into their own histories of Alexander. These secondary sources form the basis of my book. Arrian, or more properly Flavius Arrianus Xenophon, drew heavily upon Ptolemy and Aristobulus for Alexander's campaigns in the Persian Empire and upon Nearchus for Alexander's campaigns in India. Diodorus Siculus drew heavily upon Aristobulus, the "mercenary source," up to the battle of Issus, and Cleitarchus for Alexander's campaigns in India. Curtius, or more properly Quintus Curtius Rufus, drew upon Ptolemy, Cleitarchus, and the "mercenary source." Finally, there is the account of Justin, or more properly M. Junianus Justinus, notable more for its extreme brevity than anything else.

It is important to bear in mind that Alexander died in 323 B.C. Curtius and Diodorus wrote their histories about three centuries later; Arrian, about five centuries later, and Justin, about seven centuries later. All the works, even Arrian at times, are filled with inconsistencies, exaggerations and omissions. I rounded out these standard Roman Empire sources on the era with Herodotus who, although having died about a century before Alexander, gives a highly detailed look at the Persian Empire; Polybius, who provides details on the Macedonian phalanx; Plutarch, who wrote a non-military biography of Alexander; Strabo, an ancient geographer; and Xenophon, whose legendary march of the 10,000 out of the heart of the Persian Empire revealed many strengths of the Greek army and many corresponding weaknesses of the Persian.

For Philip II, Alexander's father, Diodorus and Justin are the primary ancient sources used. Unfortunately, being overshadowed by his more renowned son, Alexander, he was given little attention by both ancient historians and modern ones.

This covers most of what has survived from the ancient world on Alexander the Great and his father Philip II. It is useful to keep in mind that the ancient historians were not well trained in their undertaking, at least not by today's standards. There were frightfully large gaps in their histories and much misinformation. Ptolemy sought to exaggerate his own importance at the expense of others, Cleitarchus and Herodotus gathered their information from stories told to them, and Cleitarchus was a renowned panderer. Because much of the primary source information of the era was corrupted by bias and selectivity, many events therein remain in dispute. Consequently, even many dates, particularly in Philip's reign, can only be approximated. The 20th century scholarship used in this book for Philip II includes works by Bradford, Cawkwell and Ellis; and for Alexander the Great, works by Bosworth, Bury, Delbruck, Fuller, Green, Hammond and Tarn.

In structuring the book I have deliberately excluded from the main body of the text anything not directly related to the military campaigns, battles and sieges, confining such information to the appendix and glossary. This focused the main body of the book on the military accomplishments of Philip and Alexander and how they were achieved. The personalities and accomplishments of other individuals of the era are the subject of a future book.

Having had an extensive historical wargaming background in my youth, I have approached this book a bit differently from others on the subject. A historical wargamer is most interested in recreating as accurately as possible a historical battle, then introducing variously "what-ifs" in order to gauge the impact of different events upon the outcome of the battle. Many of these "what-ifs" are discussed in detail in the battle analyses.

While attempting to follow the progress of Alexander's various campaigns, I often could not find various locations mentioned in the text of the book I was reading, and it was usually difficult to correlate ancient strategic maps with current geography. In an attempt to resolve this, I made diligent efforts to locate every geographical reference discussed in the text on a map (and was usually but not always able to do so); designed the strategic maps to be sequential (i.e., at the point one ends the next begins); and included a number of composite maps, which indicated the relationship of the various strategic maps not only to one another but to current geography.

I exercised considerable care in drawing the tactical battle maps. Philip's battle at Chaeronea and each of the major battles Alexander fought have an order-of-battle map and an operations map, showing the major tactical movements. The order-of-battle map is a carefully researched initial disposition of forces for both opponents, which includes both the combat strength and commanders of individual units that were either known or could reasonably be extrapolated. As the

Macedonian, Greek and Persian armies each had standard space deployments for individual soldiers and standard unit formations of files and ranks, it did not prove difficult to determine the battlefield frontage of a unit. I used this information to construct a precisely scaled deployment of all units. This is critical information if one is attempting to analyze not only how the battle unfolded but the effect of alternate strategies. It also puts into clear perspective the sheer impossibility of deploying the ridiculously high combat strength attributed to the Persian army by many ancient and contemporary writers.

Most books on Alexander the Great focus almost exclusively on his reign, and all but ignore that of his father, Philip II. Philip was the most famous and successful commander of his time, and Alexander as a youth despaired that Philip would leave his generation with anything significant to achieve. Had Philip not been assassinated on the eve of his Persian campaign, it is not unlikely that Alexander would have stood in his shadow as a talented subordinate. Because Philip had set the stage for Alexander and could rightly be credited in superbly training Alexander in the art of war, I considered a detailed look at Philip's military campaigns necessary for a comprehensive understanding of Alexander's and, therefore, included them in this book.

Unlike Alexander's campaigns, however, which fall into a relatively orderly sequence, Philip's are an almost incomprehensible jumble. This was because Philip often conducted several campaigns simultaneously. The Sacred War waxed and waned over most of Philip's reign, and during it he frequently had to intervene on the side of the democrats in Thessaly or conduct incursions into Thrace in order to reassert his control there. To bring some logic to this complexity of events, I have divided Philip's campaigns geographically, according to the various city-states/nations. Although this may put events of one city-state/nation slightly out of synchronization with another, it enables the reader to comprehend more clearly the scope of Philip's military operations against the individual city-states/nations over a frequently extended period of time.

Because historians disagree over many aspects of this era, I have made a far more extensive use of footnotes than merely to document and explain the source information used in the body of the text. They also serve to present alternative interpretations of facts originating in either the ancient or modern period. This approach, I feel, gives the reader a way to put in proper perspective my choice of facts and figures for the text.

Introduction

The Macedonian Empire endured only 36 years, beginning with Philip II's assumption of the throne in 359 B.C. and ending with the death of his legendary son, Alexander the Great, in 323 B.C. When Philip was declared king, the Macedonian army had just been heavily defeated by the Dardanians, a Balkan tribe led by Bardylis. Macedonia had sustained 4,000 casualties and its king, Perdiccas III, lay dead on the battlefield. Northwest Macedonia was occupied by the Dardanians, and it was obvious that they were preparing for a full-scale invasion deep inside the state. The Paeonians to the west of the Dardanians were also preparing to take advantage of Macedonia's weakness by again raiding across its frontier. The Macedonian army had been so demoralized by its recent defeat that it feared to face the Dardanians in the field again. If this wasn't bad enough, both the Athenians and the Thracians were supporting pretenders to the Macedonian throne. Neither Philip nor Macedonia had any friends they could turn to in their supreme crisis. The Greeks contemptuously looked upon the citizens of Macedonia as uncouth barbarians still dressed in bearskins. Also, it had not been forgotten that the Macedonians had allied with Persia during its invasions of Greece. It was clearly one of the bleakest periods in Macedonian history.

This gloomy situation took no account, however, of Philip II, a Macedonian who was shortly to prove himself to be one of the great kings of ancient history. Philip's first task was to secure his throne against those who would take it from him. Only after this was done would he be able to proceed against his external enemies. Through bribery and treaties, Philip was able to neutralize the support the pretenders to his throne depended upon, allowing him to dispose of them quickly. With his position now secure, Philip was able to turn his full attention to rebuilding the Macedonian army.

While being held hostage at Thebes, Philip lived with General Pammenes, who was a close friend of Epaminondas, the great Theban general whose army dominated Greece while he lived. From Epaminondas, Philip learned the importance of training, planning, combined arms, and battlefield mobility. He incessantly watched the drills of the "Sacred Band" (Thebes' elite hoplite force), and its soldiers made such a great impression on him that upon his return to Macedonia he organized its infantry along similar lines. Philip also added large numbers of peltasts (skirmishing infantry) and psiloi (missile infantry) to his army's roster in support of his newly organized heavy-infantry phalanx. He then steadily expanded the ranks of the Companion cavalry through the creation of numerous estates for their support in the territories he had conquered. Philip would develop his Companions into an offensive arm that would decide most of the battles he and Alexander would fight.

Philip believed that victory went to the side that had trained the hardest, and he drilled his army both day and night. His soldiers were regularly force-marched up to 37 miles a day during all seasons of the year.[1] Unlike most other Greeks, Philip's soldiers carried their supplies on their backs. They became used to enduring hardship as a matter of routine. They were even forbidden the comfort of a warm bath, that luxury being reserved only for women in labor. Philip's close personal leadership of his troops gave him a control over the evolutions of his army theretofore unknown in the ancient world. This allowed him to take full advantage of mistakes his opponents frequently made on the battlefield. Philip also vigorously pursued a beaten foe whenever possible, thereby usually ensuring that his victory would be decisive. His use of the localized attack, the echelon formation, a combined-arms doctrine, and tactical deception forever ended the highly stylized mode that had characterized Classical Greek warfare. Not only did Philip introduce fluidity to the Greek battlefield, he saw the necessity of competent leadership for any successful military action.

At last, Philip had the instrument that would enable him to deal with the Balkan tribes. He secured Macedonia's northern border by decisively defeating the Dardanians. Then, by a combination of bribery, statesmanship and successful military actions, he extended his eastern border by ejecting Athens from the Chalcidice and subjugating Thrace. Philip's conquests in the Balkans and Thrace doubled Macedonia's territory and tripled its population.[2] This, in conjunction with the increased wealth from the Crenidas mines, allowed him to triple the size of his army.[3] In the south, Philip imposed Macedonian rule on Thessaly, and then used that state as a springboard to project his power into central Greece. In 338 B.C., at Chaeronea, Philip decisively defeated the largest army that the Greeks were able to field against him. Macedonia was now elevated to the status of an empire.

Philip's conquest of Greece spelled the death of the city-state, although this was not recognized by the Greeks at the time. Unlike Macedonia and Rome, which granted citizenship to entire communities, in Greece only the sons of a citizen father and a citizen mother could obtain that status. As a result, the citizen population of Greek city-states tended to grow slowly. This led to a situation where a Greek city-state frequently had to rely on shifting alliances to prevent being overpowered by larger city-states or city-state coalitions. In an era of constant political and economic instability, alliances were frequently made and dissolved to suit the particular circumstances faced at the time. Then too, internal struggles of the Greek city-states were highly destructive to their military effectiveness. Revolutions and bloody reprisals were commonplace, and there was often more dissent between rival political factions and economic classes within a city than between other city-states. The resulting widespread political instability largely prohibited a collective consciousness developing between the Greeks, except in rare circumstances, such as the wars against Troy and Persia. This led to an almost continual state of discord and warfare throughout Greece during its classical period as each city-state fought unrelentingly to maintain its independence.

At the beginning of Philip's reign, Macedonia had been divided into several centrifugal areas, each seeking to retain its own independent identity. Philip, however, broke this tendency down by redistributing populations throughout his kingdom. This not only developed the country's resources much more rapidly than would otherwise have been the case but served to diffuse regional animosities. Universal citizenship bound together the various cities to the higher responsibilities of the state, and the national army Philip created served to increase the dependency of the lower nobility on the king. Philip attempted to use strong political persuasion to induce the various independent Greek city-states to begin thinking as a national entity. Being convinced, however, that their very separateness was a guarantee of their freedoms, the city-states viewed his attempt to unify them as a foreign intrusion into their internal affairs and for that reason largely rejected it. Philip was left with no choice but to compel their unwilling participation in his federation by force of arms. In the aftermath of the battle of Chaeronea, he was able to force Greek cooperation through the League of Corinth. This organization supported existing governments, protected the city-states against internal revolts, established peace throughout Greece, and gave everyone a forum to adjudicate disputes. In return, the Greeks were forced to relinquish control of both their foreign policy and military forces to Philip. Compliance to the peace was enforced by Philip as hegemon (military leader) of the military levy raised from among the League members. Just after receiving the rubber-stamp approval of the League to conduct his long-cherished campaign against the Persian Empire, however, Philip was assassinated.

Philip had bequeathed to Alexander three critically important things. First, his appointment of Aristotle as his son's tutor gave the youth a breadth of vision transcending the narrow confines of Macedonia. It imbued him with the glorious history of Greece and the profound respect for the achievements of great men. The fanatic mysticism of Alexander's mother, Olympias, imparted to him the greatness of his lineage and the favor of the gods to any great enterprise he should undertake. Both these combined to give Alexander a driving force during his short life, the almost overwhelming desire to gain the favor of the gods by surpassing the deeds of mortal man.

Second, the army that Philip had created was far superior in both size and fighting effectiveness to anything in Greece, the Persian Empire, or India. At the time of Philip's death, the Macedonian army included 4,000 cavalry, 24,000 infantry, and large numbers of supporting troops.[4] In comparison, Athens in the fourth century was only able to field an expeditionary force of 12,000 for service in the Peloponnese, and the great Theban victory over Sparta at Leuctra in 371 B.C. was won by an army numbering only 6,000.[5] In point of fact, no single Greek state was able to field an army even half the size of the Macedonian army. The military strength of the state was such that in 340 B.C. a number of military operations could be conducted simultaneously: Philip's sieges of Perinthus, Selymbria and Byzantium; Alexander's invasion and defeat of the Maedi; and Parmenio's suppression of revolts in Thrace.[6]

The army developed by Philip was an extremely well-balanced force of shock combat, missile power and mobility. In combat effectiveness only the Thebans appear to have been its equal. The archers and slingers in Philip's army were far more numerous than they were in the army of any single Greek city, and his peltasts excelled in dominating skirmishes and in supporting his Companion cavalry. Philip led his army into battle for over two decades in operations ranging from field battles to siege assaults. At Philip's premature death, he bequeathed to his son Alexander a virtually invincible army. It was led by experienced officers and battle-hardened veterans equal to any and all demands Alexander would make of them. The army would triumph in field battles, guerrilla actions, and sieges with equal ease, despite facing disadvantageous tactical situations and usually being outnumbered by its opponents.

Lastly, Philip left Alexander a secure homeland with his subjugation of the Balkans, central Greece and Thrace. Only Sparta would attempt to throw off Macedonian domination, and it would fail largely because a fearful Greece would refuse to support its revolt. This relative political tranquility allowed Alexander to focus exclusively on his destiny in Persia and India rather than having to divide his attention between those areas and Greece.

It took Alexander a little more than a decade to conquer the Persian Empire and western India. During his 12-year reign, he never failed to vanquish his opponent, whether he engaged him in a field battle; besieged him in an impregnable position on an island, a sand dune or a mountain-top; assaulted him in fortified mountain passes; or fought him aboard ship. Alexander defeated mountain tribes, nomads, fanatics, chariots and elephants with seemingly equal ease. He fought and won his actions under a wider variety of circumstances than probably any other general in history and excelled in his ability to master them all. It became axiomatic with Alexander's opponents that no position could withstand him and no single state could defeat him. His mere approach was often sufficient to compel surrender. At the end of Alexander's reign, Greek rule extended over portions of three continents, encompassing Greece, the Persian Empire, and western India. Alexander's intention was to surpass all the conquerors who both proceeded and followed him, and in this he was successful.

Alexander is widely held to be the greatest military commander of all time. He won every field battle he fought, despite the fact that his opponent always chose the battlefield and usually heavily outnumbered him. Any lesser general would have withdrawn under such unfavorable circumstances and fought the battle another day, but not Alexander. He took his battles where he found them and overcame the disadvantage of his position by the excellence of his tactical plan and the superior fighting ability of his army. His field battles were not highlighted by grand flanking operations or surprise night attacks but were fought out in the open along his opponent's line. His sheer intellect and unflinching perseverance controlled the battlefield, and none of his opponents were able to stand against him.

Although Alexander's military successes were nothing short of astounding, his careless statesmanship all but ensured that his empire would not endure. After conquering such a huge and diverse territory, Alexander appears to have had little interest in actually ruling it. He administered his conquests much as the Persians had and with little better results. This lack of attention to administration and his failure to provide a successor resulted in decades of civil war and unrest in both Greece and Asia after his death. The generals who succeeded to Alexander's rule had never agreed with his visionary ideas of sharing rule with the Persians. Upon Alexander's death they immediately divided up his empire among them, removed the remaining Persians from any office of authority, and proceeded to campaign against each other. The continued rule of Alexander's line was fabricated by establishing a joint reign of Alexander's infant son, Alexander IV, and Alexander's mentally impaired half-brother, Arrhidaeus. A little more than a decade later both would be murdered. Also slain would be Alexander's illegitimate son, Heracles; his mistress, Barsine; his wives, Roxane and Stateira; his mother, Olympias; and his sister, Cleopatra. At their demise, the Argead line of Philip and Alexander came to an end.

Somewhat ironically, although Alexander is widely recognized as the greatest military conqueror of all time, his legacy was more economic, cultural and political. Economically, the eastern Persian Empire was given its first impetus in moving from a largely agrarian economy to one based on trade and commerce. Many of the new cities Alexander established there were intended to be key focal points for trade and his massive settlement of them by Greeks was to provide the impetus for such activity.[7] The enormous gold and silver reserves of the Persian treasury were freely circulated throughout his newly won empire. This tremendously stimulated trade, giving ambitious Greeks the opportunity to make fabulous riches in Asia. Alexander's conquest allowed the Greeks to extend their culture into Asia and be modified by the best of the Asian culture. Politically, Alexander was associated with attempting to unify Asia under the brotherhood-of-man concept. It was somewhat romantically portrayed that he had intended to fuse the Greeks and Persians into a common social structure. Although Alexander did attempt this to a degree, it proved an abject failure because the Macedonians and Greeks did not want it to succeed. Nevertheless, observing the practice of Greek political democracy first-hand from the cities that Alexander had established in their midst, the various peoples in the eastern Persian Empire developed a national consciousness, which would be broadened and deepened during the era of the Hellenistic kingdoms. Alexander had undoubtedly hoped to enable the various peoples to realize that their national aspirations could best be achieved under the umbrella of his empire. Towards the end of his reign, however, being convinced that the old guard Macedonians would be detrimental to this development, Alexander decided to dispense with them and rule his new empire with a small core of loyal Macedonians and a largely Persian army.

Alexander's impact on history was nothing less than astounding. The provincial outlook of both Greece and Asia was forever shattered by the Macedonian era.

It was a time of rising expectations and continual change. The upper classes on both continents began to feel that a Greek education was an indispensable part of civilization. This promoted Greek culture, speech, literature and philosophy in many of the cities Alexander had conquered. The barriers of isolation were quickly broken and replaced by an outlook giving free scope to the development of the individual. Although the resulting Hellenistic culture was heavily Greek in outlook, it was greatly influenced and modified by Asiatic ideas in science, religion and philosophy. So strong did Hellenism become that when Rome finally conquered the Hellenistic kingdoms, it fully absorbed their superior culture. Everything Greek, from their gods to their architecture to their philosophy, was readily adopted by Rome, and no affluent citizen of its empire considered himself well educated unless he had assimilated Greek culture. It is ironic that a nation thought by the Greeks to consist of uncouth drunkards dressed in bearskins should have raised Greek culture up to perhaps its highest level in the ancient world.

Part I
Ancient Warfare

1. The Armies

The military doctrine, composition and armament of ancient armies were largely determined by the type of government they adopted, the social conventions they practiced, the terrain of their homeland, and the enemies they had to face. In the Balkans, covered with heavy woods and mountainous terrain, the peltast predominated. Mobility was ensured by light armament, and adaptability was achieved by the open-order fighting formation used. In Macedonia and Thessaly, where broad plains supported the raising of horses and the monarchial system of government produced a land-holding nobility used to riding and fighting from childhood, the heavy cavalry prevailed. Also, the large number of hardy and intelligent peasants in Macedonia made practical the development of the phalanx, a formation inexpensively armed and easily trained. Warfare in central and southern Greece revolved around the heavy infantry hoplite. Terrain, economics and military doctrine in this area had largely precluded the extensive development of cavalry and the use of light troops.

Persia had an aristocratic class whose members were overly fond of the ostentatious display of wealth the decorations of their horses offered them. The numerous large plains of Persia led to the development of heavy cavalry as its primary arm. Because the Persian leaders feared revolt, their infantry remained untrained and unarmed and was only levied in extreme emergencies. As a result, the Persians did not develop a heavy infantry force, instead preferring to hire Greek mercenary hoplites to meet their needs for such troops. The Indian army revolved around the elephant, its supporting bowmen and the chariot force. Cavalry in the Indian army was a secondary arm attracting only inferior leaders and recruits. Although the Indian bowmen were heavily armed, they were only lightly armored and consequently were unable to stand up against even the lightly armed Greek peltasts in hand-to-hand combat.

Warfare in classical Greece had developed into a highly stylized affair, with the elements of surprise and unpredictability being eliminated almost by mutual agreement. The Greeks had developed heavy infantry shock armies that were intended to shatter their opponents upon the impact of the charge. If this did not occur, the battle devolved into a massive pushing contest, with an attempt being made to shove the front ranks of the hoplites through an enemy formation in order to break its cohesion. Missile fire was negligible for Greek armies, and the small number of cavalry available were relegated to protecting the vulnerable flanks of the hoplites.

The democracies of central Greece were usually comprised of peasant farmers. Because of the mountainous terrain of much of the country, agriculture there was usually at a subsistence level, even in the best of times. As a result, the peasant had to farm a relatively large area of land to feed his family, which required a considerable amount of his time and effort. Being so closely tied to the land, the peasant had to be home to plant his crops in the spring and to harvest them in the fall. This schedule had several implications for the development of Greek armies. This restricted the peasant's military service to the summer months between the planting and harvest seasons. Because of the hardships of movement and logistics imposed by mud and snow, military campaigns were normally not conducted during the spring, fall and winter months by Greek armies. As the citizens of a Greek democracy considered military service part of their civic duty, it was relatively easy to raise the full levy of the city-state. The short campaigning season, the difficulties of supply, and the large wage expense usually precluded, however, any protracted military operations. Lengthy sieges were only rarely conducted both because of the time factor and because Greek siege techniques were not well developed at this time. As the catapult was not then in use, the Greeks had no means of directly breaching a masonry wall from a distance or any effective way of suppressing enemy defensive missile fire. This made any assault against a heavily defended wall often prohibitive in terms of casualties because of the long exposure of the attacker on open ground. Consequently, the Greeks were usually forced to adopt the passive siege technique of contravallation, whereby a city was enclosed by a counter wall in an attempt to starve it out. This was both a lengthy and costly operation, only affordable by the wealthiest of Greek city-states.

A city had two strategic possibilities upon being attacked: to meet the enemy in the field or to shelter its population within its walls. Greek campaigns tended to be relatively straightforward, the armies usually marching directly to their objective. If the defender remained behind the protection of the city walls, the invader's soldiers would usually ravage the surrounding countryside, and then withdraw back to their homeland with all the loot they could carry. If the defender, however, decided to engage the attacker in the field, a single battle would usually decide the war, the loser then immediately opening negotiations for ending hostilities. This occurred because Greek hoplite armies were typically comprised of the city's most influential citizens and any defeat was usually catastrophic on morale. The army's overriding concern in the event of defeat was to recover its dead — a proper burial of the dead was extremely important throughout Greek ancient history — and any prisoners held by the enemy. The loser of the battle might be forced to ransom its prisoners, surrender some land, or pay an indemnity to the victor. That being settled, the attacking army would return home.

Almost by mutual consent a level battlefield would be chosen for the battle. This was needed by both sides for the deployment of their arm of decision, the close-order infantry hoplites. There was usually little strategic or tactical maneuvering for position by either side. Both the approach to battle and the battle itself were straight-up affairs containing few, if any, surprises. Consequently, classical

1: THE ARMIES 15

Greek warfare devolved into highly stylized campaigns, with battles rarely being decisive. During the Peloponnesian War, the inability of a Greek hoplite army to force a decision against its opponents in the field became quite clear. As any defeats were usually the result of the operations of light cavalry or light infantry, the Greeks tended to relegate those two arms to the close support of the hoplites rather than to use them offensively.

The second effect Greek society had on the development of its armies was in their armament. Since the peasants had neither the time to be extensively trained nor the income to outfit themselves with expensive arms, Greek armies were organized into spearmen, whose armament was relatively inexpensive and whose training was easy to acquire in a relatively short period of time. The use of the spear as a jabbing weapon was easy to master, and tactical battlefield maneuvering was almost nonexistent, there being no complicated drills to learn. All the hoplites had to do in general was to march straight ahead and crash into the enemy line.

Athens

Athens was the second most powerful military power in Greece, being eclipsed only by Macedonia. At its point of supreme power, just prior to the outbreak of the Peloponnesian War in 431 B.C., Athens was able to deploy 1,200 cavalry, 13,000 hoplites, 1,600 foot-archers, 16,000 garrison troops and 300 triremes.[1] But although its military forces were sizeable, Athens was only a second-class land power, its relatively undisciplined hoplite militia being frequently outclassed by the more effective forces that Boeotia, Macedonia, and Sparta fielded. Nevertheless, under the leadership of Demosthenes, Athens waged an unrelenting war against Macedonia, significantly delaying the latter's conquest of Greece. Heavily defeated at the battle of Chaeronea, the Athens gave only grudging and minimal support to the campaign against the Persians, merely biding their time until the death of Alexander the Great allowed them to attempt a revolt from Macedonian rule.

Cavalry Athenians were generally reluctant to serve in the cavalry because of the required time commitment and expense. As a result, although 100 cavalry were supposed to be provided by the wealthiest citizens of each of the city's 12 tribes, this was really never done and the arm was always considerably under strength.[2] Such cavalry that existed was usually deployed on each wing of the hoplites in a depth of 10 ranks.[3] Further details on the armament of the Athenian cavalry appear later in this chapter.

Heavy Infantry The Athenian army was organized on the basis of 10 tribes at first and then 12 tribes, each providing a 1,000-strong hoplite taxies.[4] The Athenian hoplites were little better than citizen militia. Although enthusiastically responding in an emergency, they were not particularly well trained or highly disciplined, as was typical of militia levies. This made their performance on the battlefield extremely uneven and subject to uncontrollable emotion rather than sound military discipline. This was clearly demonstrated at the battle of Chaeronea, where their impulsiveness lost the battle for the Greek army. On remote campaigns Athens preferred to employ the expendable Greek mercenaries in place of its valuable citizenry. When Athens itself was directly threatened, however, as by Philip II's arrival into central Greece, it was able to mobilize a force of 10,000 citizen hoplites, each accompanied by a servant.[5] Additional details on the Greek hoplites, appear later in this chapter.

Light Infantry   Athenian light infantry troops were few in number and indifferently trained. Most of the poorer classes that normally would have provided the manpower for the light infantry preferred service as rowers with the fleet. Thus the Athenians usually either hired mercenaries or relied on their allies for their light infantry needs.

Boeotia

The cities of Boeotia were organized into the Boeotian League by Thebes during the middle of the third century. For the purpose of mobilization, Boeotia was divided into 11 districts (Thebes accounting for four of them), each required to provide to the League a force of 100 cavalry, 1,000 hoplites and 1,000 light infantry.[6] It appears that the Boeotian League was able to mobilize only two-thirds of the full force of its army at any one time.[7] Field armies serving outside Boeotia thus rarely exceeded 6,000 hoplites.[8]

Epaminondas, who commanded Thebe's army in the 370s, revolutionized hoplite warfare in Greece. His two great innovations — the attack in echelon (a refused left flank and advanced right flank) and concentration of force at the point of attack (increasing the number of ranks at the point of impact to a depth of 50 or more) were instrumental in defeating the heretofore invincible Spartan army at Leuctra (371 B.C.) and again at Second Mantineia (362 B.C.). His death at Second Mantineia, however, brought an end to the Theban attempt to dominate Greece.

During the Third Sacred War (355 B.C.–346 B.C.), which Thebes had instigated in an attempt to gain control over central Greece, the Boeotian army had been defeated as often as they were victorious. Suffering severe financial hardship during the war, at one point the Boeotians had been forced to hire their army out to a revolting Persian satrap in Asia Minor for badly needed income. At the conclusion of the war, Thebes believed that Philip of Macedonia, whom it had called upon for assistance, had denied the city its rightful fruits of victory. Consequently, in the Fourth Sacred War against Amphissa (338 B.C.), Thebes allied the Boeotians with Athens and against Macedonia. Badly defeated in the subsequent battle of Chaeronea by Philip, the Boeotian army took heavy casualties. Its legendary Theban Sacred Band was virtually eliminated on the battlefield by Philip's son, the future Alexander the Great. A Macedonian garrison was installed in the Cadmea, and the city's government was purged of all factions hostile to Macedonia.

In 335 B.C., believing that Alexander had died while campaigning in the

Balkans, Thebes decided to revolt and throw off Macedonian rule. Although Alexander gave the Thebans a chance to reconsider their actions, they were resolved to settle the issue by battle. The Thebans deployed their army outside of Thebes, opposite the Cadmea, for a field battle. Their cavalry manned the first line and their hoplites the second, each being protected by a stockade. Although Alexander's phalanx was able to penetrate the first line, it was unable to make any headway against the second line. Even when the Macedonian reserves were thrown into the battle, the Theban hoplites were able to offset the superior numbers, weaponry, and formation of the phalanx by their greater body strength.[9] Alexander, having observed that the Thebans had largely stripped the garrison from their city behind them to augment their field army, sent a force through an unguarded gate in their walls. Seeing the Macedonians enter their city behind them, the Thebans broke up in disorder and withdrew back into the city. There, their army separated into small groups and was virtually eliminated in the subsequent fighting in the narrow streets. The survivors were sold into slavery, and the city was razed. Alexander had destroyed one of the most ancient and powerful city-states in Greece.

Cavalry Boeotian cavalry had the reputation of being among the best in Greece.[10] In constant action against the cavalry of Boeotia's northern Thessalian neighbor, the Boeotian cavalry was able to develop into a highly effective combat force. The cavalry was organized into squadrons commanded by a hipparch.[11]

Heavy Infantry The mainstay of the Boeotian army was its hoplites, considered to be among the best in Greece in both fighting ability and morale. This was clearly evidenced by their ability to stand up to Alexander's phalanx in the battle outside of Thebes. The hoplites were organized into lochoi 300–400 strong.[12] The Cadmea was garrisoned by an elite Theban hoplite unit known throughout Greece as the Sacred Band, a formation believed to be invincible.[13] The formation consisted of 150 pairs of homosexual lovers who had vowed to die rather than surrender.[14] At the battle of Chaeronea they did just that, only 42 surviving the encounter.[15] Details on Boeotian army hoplite armament appear later in this chapter.

Illyria

The Illyrian tribes inhabited the area of modern Albania and Yugoslavia. The various tribes there rarely combined for any action, each preferring to be at war with its neighbors for the loot and slaves to be acquired. The warriors usually fought alongside of their slaves, some nobles being able to field several hundred slaves.[16] As Illyria was a land and sea raiding people, the supply of slaves available to them for war would have always been considerable. The largest Illyrian army raised from a single tribe during the Macedonian era was that of the Dardanians under Bardylis. In 358 B.C., he was able to raise a force of 500 cavalry and 10,000 infantry.[17]

Cavalry As the Illyrians typically had only small numbers of light cavalry, they were vulnerable to harassing and flanking attacks by such troops.[18] Their cavalry, such as existed, was usually unarmored and shieldless; javelins were its primary weapon.[19]

Infantry The typical Illyrian warrior was undisciplined and poorly armed and fought independently, his main objective being to demonstrate military prowess.[20] This placed him at a severe disadvantage when facing the close-order formations of the Macedonians, where each man supported those alongside and in front of him. Although the Illyrians would sometimes make rash charges, they preferred to weaken their opponents at a distance with missile fire rather than closing to engage them in hand-to-hand combat. If charged, they frequently fled, it being considered no particular disgrace to do so.[21] The Illyrians panicked easily and were highly susceptible to surprise because they usually did not deploy sentries and could not be induced to fortify their encampments.[22] Illyrian infantry troops were typically armed with spears or javelins, a short curved sword with the cutting edge on the inside, a light axe and a small, round convex shield.[23] Their preferred tactic was to occupy a commanding wooded hill. This gave the infantry a defensive advantage over enemy light skirmishing troops and cavalry and an offensive advantage against close-order heavy infantry troops, who were usually disordered by such terrain.

India

Unlike the Persian Empire, which the Great King alone ruled, India was fragmented into numerous independent kingdoms, each with its own king and army. An Indian army was usually led in battle by its king, the troops either being provided by his nobles or recruited as mercenaries.[24] It was an army constructed along similar lines to that of the Persians, originating from the tip of the manpower pyramid rather than from the base, as was common for Greek armies. The peasants were prohibited from bearing arms not so much out of fear of their revolt as out of the belief that warfare was the exclusive prerogative of the nobility.[25] Indian warfare was usually conducted according to a code of chivalry in which a defeated enemy was made a subject ally rather than being deprived of his lands by the conqueror. This was because the main objective in Indian war was the exercise of military prowess and the acquisition of tribute in preference to subjugation.[26] The armies made it a point only to fight each other, generally leaving the peasants undisturbed.[27]

An Indian army would assemble for war in a large and strongly fortified encampment of the peacetime garrison. Because the army generally carried all its supplies and systematically occupied all strategic positions along the route of march, its advance tended to be slow and methodical. The actual fighting was a highly stylized and gentlemanly affair, the combatants meeting at an agreed time and place. Ambushes, battlefield surprises, the use of poison weapons and direct attacks on horses and elephants were frowned upon. Pride required that the various arms of an Indian army only fought each other, that is, chariots only fought chariots, cavalry only fought cavalry, etc. Although many of these courtly rules were frequently violated, they nevertheless formed an ideal code of conduct for righteous Indians to live up to and many did so.

The usual tactical deployment of an Indian army was in "mixed array" formation, the infantry and chariots deployed in the center, cavalry on the flanks, and elephants on the wings.[28] This was an all-purpose formation used to penetrate the enemy center with the chariots or break its flanks with the elephants. In "breaking array" formation, the elephants would be deployed in the center, chariots on their flanks, and cavalry on the outer wings.[29] This formation was intended to penetrate the enemy center with an attack by the elephants, which were supported by the chariots As was typical with all ancient armies of the period, no reserves were deployed in either formation, all units being deployed in the front line.

Cavalry The cavalry held a low status in Indian armies, attracting neither the best leaders or the best recruits.[30] As a result, its discipline was lax and its combat effectiveness low. Indian cavalry was not particularly proficient at scouting and seems to have been used mostly for raiding, for attacking the flank and rear of troops unable to defend themselves, and in the pursuit of a disordered and beaten enemy.[31] When used on the battlefield, the Indian cavalry was typically deployed in a deep formation to give it greater cohesion.[32]

Indian cavalry troops were armed with two javelins, a small shield and a small composite bow.[33] Because of their low status, it is unlikely that they were armored, except possibly for the royal cavalry.[34] As with all other ancient cavalry of this era, Indian horses did not have saddles or stirrups, neither of which had yet been invented. This made it difficult for the rider to control his horse and nearly impossible for him to keep his seat during the impact of a charge.

Infantry India had no heavy infantry or any access to it. Their infantry was actually only light infantry armed with a six-foot-long bamboo bow[35]; a four-and-a-half-foot-long, two-handed, wide-bladed broadsword[36]; and a long, narrow shield of untanned hide.[37] A number of the Indian infantry were armed with the javelin in place of the bow.[38] The archers were usually screened by a line of javelin men whose lack of armor precluded them from directly engaging either the phalanx or peltasts.[39] The unwieldy bow of the Indian infantry, its slow rate of fire, and general inaccuracy rendered the users only marginally effective as missile troops.[40] Thus they were usually deployed in support of the elephants in the hope that the animals would subject the opposing enemy infantry forces to such heavy casualties as to break their morale and give the Indian infantry the opportunity to pursue a routing enemy to advantage, being heavily armed but only lightly armored. Although they were unencumbered by any armor, the Indian infantry troops' close-order formation, their long and unwieldy swords and huge bows made them unsuitable for use on rough ground or in woods.[41] Typically, Indian infantry deployed in a deep close-order formation occupying a three-foot frontage, with only one foot separating files.[42]

The Indian bow was said to be so powerful that its three-foot-long arrow could penetrate any shield or cuirass.[43] However, the six-foot length of the bow made it unwieldy and difficult to fire, and the long and heavy arrows used sacrificed both accuracy and rate of fire.[44]

The density of the Indian infantry formation also severely limited the effective use of the weapon. Although under normal circumstances an archer required a minimum lateral area of six feet for unimpeded use of the weapon, the dense Indian formation usually only provided its users half that much room. Indian bows were generally not strung until the archers deployed on the battlefield.[45] Because of the large size of the bow, it was necessary to brace it on the ground with the left foot in order to string it.[46] In the event of a rapid deployment from column to line or if inclement weather had made the ground wet and slippery (as at the battle of Hydaspes River), the inability to string the bows quickly could make Indian missile fire negligible.[47]

The broadsword of the Indian infantry was used for delivering powerful two-handed blows, the force of which could shatter a shield.[48] As it was swung well above the head with both hands, however, the wielder was all but defenseless to a quickly delivered counterthrust.[49]

Chariots The chariot force was one of the prestige arms of the Indian army and attracted its best warriors. Initially, each chariot was accompanied by a force of five cavalry and fifteen infantry. Nine chariots made up a tactical unit and five such units, or forty-five chariots, a division.[50] In earlier Indian history, the accompanying cavalry and infantry were probably personal retainers of the nobly born charioteer. Later, however, they were probably organized as separate military units. Chariots were usually deployed on the wings of the army in advance of the cavalry. Indian chariots were big and heavy, being drawn by four horses and manned by large crews — usually consisting of two armored drivers, two men-at-arms, and two archers.[51] The vehicles were, in effect, little more than large wagons whose usual tactic was simply to crash their way through an enemy line. Being slow and relatively unmaneuverable, the chariots were likely to bog down quickly if the ground was muddy or rough and would frequently overturn upon hitting large potholes.

The Indians attempted to use chariots twice against Alexander in a field battle. When Alexander crossed the Hydaspes River, Porus sent his son Aristobulus against him with a force of 60 chariots and 2,000 cavalry.[52] The chariots quickly bogged down in the muddy ground, and many had to be abandoned before Alexander's line was ever reached. A short time later, at the main battle of Hydaspes River, Porus was able to deploy perhaps as many as 300 chariots against the Macedonian army.[53] The chariots on the Indian left wing were quickly decimated, however, by massed missile fire from Alexander's mounted archers while still in their deployment area and appear to have played no part in the ensuing battle. Those on the right wing of the Indian line were blocked from charging by the redeployment of the Indian cavalry there to the left flank. By the time that the cavalry had cleared the chariot's charge lanes, Alexander's infantry was already locked in close combat with the Indian army and the vehicles were unable to intervene in the battle.

Elephants Elephants in the ancient world were obtained from either Africa or India. The African elephant was typically larger than the Indian elephant, having longer tusks, larger ears, and a concave back in contrast to the convex back of the Indian elephant.[54] An African bull elephant would weigh from five to seven tons compared to the four-ton weight of a rhinoceros or hippopotamus.[55] The life span of an elephant normally was from 60 to 80 years.[56]

Because elephants' digestion is so poor, they must eat twice as much food as they actually need.[57] An African elephant requires a daily minimum of 100 pounds of hay or 300–350 pounds of vegetation and up to 50 gallons of water, whereas the smaller Indian elephant is able to get by on half as much.[58] An elephant's eyes are relatively small, making for poor eyesight in sunlight. In the shade of the forest, however, an elephant can see clearly for a considerable distance.[59] To compensate for their poor eyesight, elephants have excellent hearing.[60] Although elephants can swim across rivers, they generally prefer to walk along the bed.[61] An elephant can move along on land at a steady six miles per hour but is able to charge at twenty miles per hour.[62] The construction of the elephant's leg and its bulk precluded it from leaping across ditches but not from climbing up slopes and sliding down ramps.[63] The elephant will build up a deep affection for its mahout, or trainer/driver, and in his absence may become ill-tempered, confused, and unmanageable. An elephant's skin is one inch thick in places, making its body almost impervious to arrows, javelins, or sword thrusts. Elephants are not warlike by nature and are easily panicked, especially if their driver is killed or if the lead elephant of the herd is injured. A mouse, barking dogs, or a squealing pig can quickly stampede a herd.[64] Although generally peaceful, an elephant will fight an opponent for leadership of a herd by pushing its opponent's head aside and then goring it with its tusks.

As a rule, elephants were used to neutralize enemy cavalry, whose horses usually became unmanageable in their presence, or to disorder opposing infantry formations by inflicting heavy casualties on them. Elephants were usually deployed from 50 to 100 feet apart along the center of the army in advance of the infantry.[65] Individual elephants required a minimum frontage of about 15 feet to fight effectively.[66]

The elephants were organized in a similar manner to the chariots, a unit being composed of nine elephants and five such units forming a division.[67] Elephants were frequently supported by light infantry, usually eight being assigned to an individual animal.[68] At the battle of Hydaspes River, however, the Indian light infantry supported the elephant line from the rear rather than being intermixed with them. Had the nonarmored Indian bowmen attempted to engage Alexander's peltasts in a stand-up fight, they would have been quickly overpowered both because of their lack of defensive armor and their clumsy weaponry.

An elephant would typically carry a mahout riding on its neck and sometimes a soldier on its back, who was armed with either a javelin, spear, or bow.[69] Towers atop elephants were not in use until after Alexander's time.[70] A mahout sat behind the head of the elephant, but being completely unarmored, he was extremely vulnerable to any enemy missile weapons.

The elephants were always terrifying in battle. The confusion and devastation an elephant attack produced was guaranteed to shake the morale of any troops they confronted. Alexander's infantry did have a hard fight against the elephants at the battle of Hydaspes River, but was able to defeat them, though not without sustaining heavy casualties in the process. The broadswords and axes Alexander equipped his peltasts with were effective in hamstringing the elephants and severing their trunks. Light arrows had little effect against the elephants, and it was difficult to wound them with either javelins or sarissas.[71] If the objective of the elephant attack could be determined, light catapults could be set up to fire on them or caltrops could be used to disable them. This, however, almost never happened because the movement of the animals was rarely that predictable. Although Alexander's preparations at the Hydaspes River would in time master the elephants, nothing could mitigate the ferocity of their initial charge. Men were crushed, gored and thrown through the air as if they were feather pillows.[72] It was clearly one of the most horrifying ordeals that the Macedonian infantry had ever faced. Interestingly enough, although Alexander later fought numerous Indian tribes throughout the Punjab, there was no record of any elephants being fielded against him. This would indicate that only the wealthiest of Indian kings could afford the expense of training and maintaining the huge animals.

Mercenaries Mercenaries were a major source of manpower for Indian armies. In general, they were the best disciplined troops in the army.[73] They were usually of the warrior nobility but their ranks sometimes included fugitive nobles and Brahmins. Mercenaries were typically armed and equipped identically to the Indian infantry with which they usually served.

Macedonia

Leadership

Philip II Through one of the ironies of history, Philip II of Macedonia had been forced to spend part of his youth as a hostage in Thebes to ensure that Alexander II, then king of Macedonia, did not again invade Thessaly.[74] While there, Philip had the opportunity to associate closely with Epaminondas, probably the greatest general of his age and an innovator of several new concepts in warfare. Although Epaminondas had retained the hoplite formation as the decisive arm in Greek combat, he deepened its ranks at the critical point of impact, making it a focused battering ram rather than a mere across-the-board pushing force. Opposing generals found, much to their consternation, that they could no longer predict with certainty where Epaminondas' blow would fall because he attacked at almost any point along the battle line. The great Theban had also developed the echeloned attack, an oblique advance with one wing thrown forward and the other refused. Previously, Greek warfare had consisted of parallel lines engaging. That made it easy to align comparable fighting units against each other and for a broad front advance to be made in a straight line against the enemy. Now, however, a battle could be fought and won by only a portion of the line being engaged and not necessary directly across from where they were deployed in the line but at any point along it where a weakness was perceived. Tactical mobility had been introduced on the battlefield and never again would the Greeks be able to confidently fight a predictable set-piece battle.

Philip spent many hours watching the drill of the elite Theban "Sacred Band." When he returned to Macedonia as king, he implemented many of Epaminondas' tactics as well as developing several of his own. He drilled his army to be totally responsive to his command, an unusual discipline in ancient armies of the time. This allowed both Philip and Alexander to execute complicated maneuvers and take advantage of battlefield opportunities that other armies of the era were incapable of duplicating. The training and discipline Philip imposed on his troops gave both him and Alexander a tremendous advantage on the tactical battlefield. At Chaeronea, Philip was able to conduct a successful feigned retreat to draw the Athenians out of line and defeat them, while at Gaugamela, Alexander was able to take advantage of a gap in the Persian line and turn a stalemated battle into an overwhelming victory.

The overriding ambition of both Philip and Alexander was to conquer the Persian Empire. The battle of Cunaxa in 401 B.C. had clearly demonstrated three things to the Greeks. First, that the Persian infantry could not stand up to Greek hoplites. The significantly higher combat effectiveness of the Greek hoplites compared to the Persian infantry arose from their superior discipline, weaponry, protection and morale. Second, without an adequate cavalry and light infantry force, the Greeks would be unable to defeat the Persians decisively. Heavy infantry formations were notoriously reluctant to advance against enemy cavalry and were almost defenseless to reply to missile fire from enemy light infantry. Thus the Greek hoplites would probably be unable to exploit any victory they might gain over Persian infantry. Lastly, the Greeks learned the value of logistics. The 1,500 miles the Greeks traveled from Sardis to Cunaxa under Cyrus' supply system could readily be compared to their haphazard return trip under Xenophon. It was evident that there was no substitute for an efficient supply net, and both Philip and Alexander were always to give logistics a high priority.[75]

One of the most important tactics Philip developed, which Alexander was also to use in three of the four field battles he fought, was to make the cavalry the major offensive arm of the army and relegate the phalanx to its support. This concept was a radical reversal from previous Greek military doctrine, which relied exclusively on the heavy infantry as the arm of decision. In the battles Philip and Alexander were to fight, the Companion cavalry usually clinched the victory, the only exception being the battle of Hydaspes River. The phalanx usually formed an irresistible wall to pin the enemy line in place and ensure that the Companions were able to execute their attack without interference. The ranks of the Companions were steadily expanded during Philip's reign by the enfranchisement of the cavalrymen with land conquered in the Balkans, the Chersonese and Thrace. The acquisition of Thessaly also effectively doubled the number of heavy cavalry Philip was able to field. Large numbers of light infantry were recruited from the Balkans, as well as a substantial force of mercenary light cavalry and mercenary hoplites.

Missile troops — which included archers, javelin men and slingers — had played a relatively small role in Greek combat up to Philip's time.[76] They were frequently undisciplined and indifferently trained in the use of their weapons. Philip, however, greatly expanded his force of light troops, being able to recruit extensive numbers of javelin men from the tribes he had conquered in the Balkans, to enlist large numbers of archers from the frontier areas of northern Macedonia, and to hire mercenaries from the mountainous areas of Crete, Greece and Rhodes. The light infantry soldiers were then intensely trained in the use of their weapons and in the performance of their military duties. When Philip was finished, his missile troops had become a highly effective military force.

Philip also dispensed with the time-honored Greek practice of engaging in set-piece battles, instead preferring the use of battlefield deception whenever possible. This was graphically illustrated at Chaeronea, where he executed a feint retreat to lure the Athenian hoplites into a precipitous attack that disordered their ranks and set them up for a devastating counterattack. Philip set up an intelligence service that scouted ahead of the army to discover feasible routes, gather food supplies, and reconnoiter the enemy. He also took precautions to screen his army from observation and deceive his opponent as to his intentions. The Greeks largely considered these activities underhanded and generally refused to engage in them. Philip, however, excelled in them and took pride in doing so.

Although Philip doubtless fought numerous battles throughout his reign, only a few have been documented and only one, Chaeronea, in any detail. From what we know of his battles, however, it is evident that they formed the basis of Alexander's tactics. Philip made excellent use of battlefield deception, enemy weaknesses, and surprise attacks. He developed an invincible heavy-infantry phalanx, trained a large and effective missile force, and made the Companion cavalry his arm of decision. Strategically, the Macedonian army's mobility and an efficient reconnaissance network allowed Philip to make frequent use of the element of strategic surprise and to capture objectives long before his opponent ever suspected he was in the vicinity. The numerous battles Philip's army fought during his reign formed a solid core of highly proficient leaders and soldiers who were able to execute whatever he or Alexander would demand of them.

Alexander the Great Alexander's great tactical innovation was the effective use of combined arms on the battlefield, the Companions almost always being supported by skirmishing infantry. At Granicus River, the hypaspists fought alongside the Companion cavalry and greatly disordered Memnon's stationary cavalry, while at Gaugamela they provided a screen for the Companions and overwhelmed Darius' chariot attack by the heavy missile fire they were able to deliver. Acting in concert, Alexander's combined force not only gave the Companions great staying power but allowed him the flexibility to conduct operations not available to opposing commanders. In India, Alexander restructured his Companion cavalry to incorporate light missile-firing cavalry. This allowed them the flexibility to engage at advantage both the heavy Persian cavalry in shock combat and the missile-firing Scythians.

Alexander also introduced the use of reserves on the battlefield that could take advantage of unforeseen opportunities.[77] Typically, ancient armies of that era did not maintain reserves, their entire effective force being deployed in close-order and in great depth along their front line. This tactic all but precluded any redeployment during a battle and restricted the troops to executing rigidly the battle plan developed prior to the beginning of hostilities. At both Issus and Gaugamela, Alexander kept his Companion cavalry in reserve in the hope of being able to exploit any favorable situation that developed. This occurred at Issus, when the hypaspists disordered the Cardaces, and at Gaugamela, when a gap developed in Bessus' wing. In both cases, Alexander's Companions were able to exploit the opportunity that developed during the fighting and win the battle because of it.

Like Philip, Alexander clearly saw the need for ever greater numbers of light infantry for use against the expected large numbers of Persian missile troops. As the Persians had, however, reoriented their infantry doctrine from missile fire delivery to shock combat, Alexander's missile troops proved far more useful against Persian and Indian cavalry, chariots, and elephants, all of which were highly susceptible to disruption from either the presence of light infantry or the heavy missile fire they were able to deliver. At the end of his reign, Alexander had planned to convert the middle 12 ranks of his phalanx to Persian missile-firing troops in an attempt to give his phalanx intrinsic missile fire support. This would have allowed the phalanx the flexibility to engage in missile fire on its approach and shock combat upon contact with an enemy formation.

Alexander was one of the first commanders in ancient history to use catapults tactically on the battlefield. (Onomarchus, commander of the Phocian army, first used them in that manner against Philip II of Macedonia during the Third Sacred War.[78]) At Pelium, in the northwest corner of Macedonia, Alexander lined the catapults up hub-to-hub along a riverbank to cover the crossing of his withdrawing troops against a Balkan attack, while at the Jaxartes River he used them to drive the Scythians away from the riverbank so that he could conduct an amphibious assault against them.

The army that Alexander inherited from Philip simply could not be beaten in a field battle by any army in the central or eastern Mediterranean at that time, provided, of course, it was led by a competent commander. Alexander, however, was much more than a competent commander, he was clearly a military genius who was always able to anticipate the plans of his opponent and quickly devise effective countermeasures against them. The result was that no matter who his opponent was or under what circumstances he fought, Alexander never lost a field battle, guerrilla action, or siege during the 12 years of his reign. Considering the natural and man-made handicaps Alexander often fought under, it is easy to understand why he is widely considered to be history's greatest military commander.

Alexander fought several battles in the Balkans but only one in central Greece, that being against Thebes. That city-state's defeat, however, was so decisive that all Greece, except Sparta, was intimidated by it throughout Alexander's reign. Just after the battle of Issus, Sparta made a bid to revolt against Antipater, Alexander's regent in Greece. At the subsequent battle of Megalopolis, the Spartans were so heavily defeated that their military power was permanently broken, relegating them to the status of a second-class power unable to cause any further trouble for Alexander.

Alexander would only fight three great field battles to conquer the western Persian Empire. His victory at each would place large areas of Persian territory under his control: the battle of Granicus River gave him Asia Minor; the battle of Issus gave him Cilicia, Phoenicia and Egypt; and the battle of Gaugamela gave him Babylonia, Mesopotamia and Susiana. As a rule, except for Halicarnassus, Tyre and Gaza, all of which had to be taken by siege, the Persian defeats in the field battles induced cities to surrender to Alexander upon his mere approach.

Alexander would fight one great field battle in India, at the Hydaspes River. This, however, would only give him Porus' kingdom of Gujrat. Each of the large number of independent kingdoms there had to be conquered separately. All operations in India involved sieges or the storming of cities or mountain passes.

Mobility

Greek armies were quite small by modern standards, usually marching in a single column, led by the right flank. At the head of the column was the psiloi, or light infantry, who also acted as flankers. They were followed by the cavalry, peltasts, and phalanx. Behind them marched the baggage train. Bringing up the rear were the forces of the left flank, formed in an identical manner to the right flank force. Under normal circumstances, Alexander's army was able to sustain a march of 13 miles a day, roughly double that of the Persian army.[79] When required, however, the Macedonians could force-march 19 miles a day.[80] For short marches of four to five days in duration, a specialized force of cavalry and light infantry could force-march up to 50 miles a day.[81] This was only done when it was imperative to achieve strategic surprise against an enemy. Time after time Alexander simply astounded his opponents by the speed of his march, and on more than one occasion they promptly surrendered upon his unexpected appearance.

One of the major reasons for the Macedonian army's exceptional mobility was that Philip had severely limited the use of carts, instead relying on the more mobile pack horses. Oxen, which normally pulled the carts, could travel no faster than two miles per hour and were limited to a five-hour work-day.[82] This resulted in a daily march rate of only 10 miles, at best. A horse or mule, on the other hand, was able to transport 300 pounds on its back an average of 32 miles a day.[83] Horses, of course, could be used to pull up to 1,000 pounds in a cart, but there was a severe disadvantage to using the animals in that manner. The soft leather throat harness used for carts at that time progressively choked the animal the harder it pulled. Across rough ground or up elevations the animal would be required to pull increasingly harder with the result that it would be quickly fatigued because of oxygen depravation. Thus the horse or mule had to be rested frequently to recuperate from this strain. Failure to do so might incapacitate the animal and render it useless for further work. As a result, both Philip and Alexander were more than willing to forego the additional carrying capacity of carts for the increased mobility that pack animals gave the Macedonian army.

Most ancient roads where Alexander marched were little more than dusty dirt tracks. At the first rains they quickly turned into muddy quagmires in which the carts would quickly become stuck. Any attempt by carts to leave the main road and go cross-country would usually result in a breakdown, the frames of the carts being unable to stand up to the additional jostling. The widespread use of carts would, therefore, have greatly restricted Alexander's line of march to a reasonably well-maintained road network, which did not always exist, especially in the eastern Persian Empire. Also, most ancient generals were convinced that carts only encouraged soldiers to accumulate excessive and unnecessary baggage. When Alexander allowed the soldiers to use carts in India, they took along so much loot that the mobility of the army was compromised. He doubtless tolerated this because the pace of the army in India was generally leisurely and travel was frequently along or on large rivers, where the fleet was able to transport a large portion of the excess baggage, much of which consisted of loot.

Philip also severely limited the number of servants in his army. While Spartan hoplites had as many as seven servants each, Philip only allowed one servant for every ten of his phalangites and one for each heavy cavalryman.[84] This allowed Philip a much smaller noncombat support component than other Greeks used and yielded a greater operating range for his army. Fewer mouths to feed meant that the supplies that were carried lasted longer. Also, since the Macedonian army contained a far higher ratio of combat to support troops, its combat strength was considerably higher than a comparably sized Greek army, giving both Philip and Alexander a considerable battlefield advantage.

Order of Battle

Pages The pages were the adolescent sons of prominent Macedonian nobility and were personally selected by the king to attend him.[85] Constantly in the presence of their king, the pages soon developed a close attachment to him. The pages brought the king his horse and assisted him in mounting it, accompanied him on the hunt, ran errands for him, waited on his table, and fought alongside him in battle.[86] At night, they guarded the king while he slept.[87] Only the king was allowed to discipline a page. Although a beating was the usual punishment for a breach of discipline, Philip was alleged to have once killed a page for disobeying a military order.[88] As the career of each page was dependent upon the favor of the king, competition among the boys was intense. The king alone decided the future of each page, and there was no appeal to his decision.

Within the school of pages, homosexual attachments frequently developed, usually being centered around heirs to the throne.[89] One such "attachment" revolved around Alexander and allegedly included Erigyius, Harpalus, Hephaestion, Laomedon, Nearchus and Ptolemy. When Alexander's friends were exiled by Philip in 337 B.C. for supporting his involvement in the Pixodarus intrigue, it appeared that their political and military careers had ended. When Alexander became king, however, he not only restored his exiled friends to high office but personally saw to their advancement.

Pages entered the service at the age of 14, and during the next four years their education was personally supervised by the king. By the time they left the service at age 17 or 18, the pages had been thoroughly trained in both war and civil government, many of them going on to join the king's Companions. It would be from their ranks that many of the military commanders and civil administrators for Alexander's newly won empire would be recruited. On the battlefield the pages usually fought with the hypaspists.[90]

Bodyguards (Somatophylakes) The bodyguards were eight officers from the Companions appointed by Alexander to guard his person and act as his aides-de-camp. They were frequently appointed to command large detachments of troops on independent commands. The following Companions held the position of bodyguard at one time or another.[91]

- Aristonous, son of Pisaeus (Arrian VI:28).
- Arrhybas. Died of a disease (Arrian III:5).
- Balacrus, son of Nicanor. Appointed satrap of Cilicia (Arrian II:12).
- Demetrius. Arrested for complicity in Philotas' conspiracy against Alexander (Arrian III:27).
- Hephaestion, son of Amyntor. Died in Ecbatana from overindulgence in wine (Arrian VI:28; Diodorus XVII:61).
- Leonnatus, son of Anteas (Arrian III:5; IV:24; VI:9, 22, 28).
- Lysimachus, son of Lysimachus (Arrian V:13, 24; VI:28).
- Menes, son of Dionysius (Arrian II:12).
- Nicanor, son of Parmenio. Died of an illness in Areia (Arrian III:25).
- Peitho, son of Crateuas (Arrian VI:28).
- Peucestas, son of Orontes (Arrian VI:28, 30; Diodorus XVII:99).
- Ptolemy, son of Lagus (Arrian I:24; III:6, 27; IV:8,15; VI:28; VII:4; Curtius IX:8).

Companion Cavalry (Hetairoi) Lying on the northern frontier of Greece, Macedonia had never become part of the highly stylized Greek hoplite method of warfare. Its dominant military arms had been the heavy cavalry of the nobility and the elite hypaspist infantry. An effective heavy-infantry force of the peasants had not been effectively organized before Philip. The peasant troops under his predecessor, Perdiccas III, were so ineffective that even the lightly armed peltasts of the Balkans tribes were able to defeat them.

Cavalry was generally most effective against the undefended flanks and rear of an infantry formation. Its presence on a battlefield would frequently inhibit all forward movement of the heavy infantry unless equal numbers of friendly cavalry were in direct support. Frontally, a well-ordered, heavy-infantry formation had little to fear from cavalry, it normally not being possible to force a horse to charge through a steady wall of spears. Even had that been possible, the rider would have experienced considerable difficulty in withstanding the effects of any shock charge. Without a saddle or stirrups, neither of which had yet been invented, he was likely to be unseated on contact by the impact he would have sustained. If a cavalryman rode up to throw a javelin or fire some other missile weapon, he took the risk that when he wheeled his horse away, the enemy infantry would close with him and through missile fire or a spear thrust would wound his horse or him. If the infantry was disordered, in open-order, or was wavering, however, it was possible for the cavalry to break into the infantry's formation and cause heavy casualties. Although cavalry was effective in pursuit, this was a tactic rarely used in Greece before Philip's time. Inadequate cavalry strength and a defensive doctrine usually restricted the operations of the cavalry to merely protecting the flanks of the advancing hoplites.

The Companion cavalry derived its name from the personal closeness of its members to the Macedonian king. They held their land directly from the crown, in return for which they were required to provide personal military service to him. Lowland Macedonia, with one of the few level plains in Greece, was ideal cavalry country. In Greece, only Thessaly and Macedonia had open plains with enough room and sufficient quantities of fodder and water to support the raising of horses. However, because of limited quantities of feed there, even in the best of times, Greek horses were always significantly smaller than their much better fed Persian counterparts and were unable to bear the weight of armor for both horse and rider. The Greek horses partly compensated for this disadvantage by having greater maneuverability and endurance than the Persian horses. As the members of the Macedonian aristocratic landowning class usually went about mounted, they were distinguished by their horsemanship. In earlier days, they formed the king's royal standing army, a mobile force of troops highly trained to ride and fight. These were the men who lived, drank and hunted with the king in peace and fought by his side in war. It was from this pool of Companions that the king largely drew his military commanders and civil administrators, and they formed part of the inner council that advised him in all pertinent matters of state.

The Companions were armed with either a 14½-foot-long sarissa or a nine-foot-long spear, as the occasion required, and a long, slightly curving slashing sword.[92] The steel points on both ends of the sarissa made it unusable in a close-order formation.[93] The weapon could only used in open-order or in a linear line that would not endanger any riders coming up behind. In most engagements, the Companions used the nine-foot-long spear gripped slightly back from the middle.[94] As the Companions carried only a single spear into battle, it could not be thrown but had to be retained for hand-to-hand combat.[95] The usual tactic of the Companions against infantry troops was to attempt to ride them down; against cavalry they sought to dismount the riders by killing or wounding their horses. For their defense, the Companions wore a bronze cuirass and a helmet.[96] Shields were not carried until sometime later, where they were used only when fighting on foot.[97]

The small horses of the Companions were unarmored because they were unable to bear the additional weight.[98] Although the Companion only sat on a simple padded cloth, his balance and horsemanship were superb. So skillful was he that despite the absence of a saddle and stirrups, he was able to keep his seat during the impact of a charge and continue to use his weapon effectively. No cavalry in the ancient world could compare to the Companions in this regard. The Companions were said to have compensated for their unsteady seat by using their sarissas in an overhand stabbing motion rather than holding them underhandedly and rigidly straight, as medieval knights were later to do with their lances.

The Companion cavalry occupied the far right position of the line, the hypaspists usually being deployed on their left. Their general objective was to punch a hole in the enemy line through which the accompanying hypaspists could then advance. Alexander always took position on the right flank and personally led the Companion cavalry in the attack. The usual tactical formation of the Companions was the wedge, a trianglelike configuration so tightly aligned as to preclude any penetration between the horses by enemy cavalrymen. The narrowness of the wedge tip made it ideal for piercing the enemy line, while its steadily expanding base served to quickly widen the penetration. The formation also facilitated alignment of the ranks, as all eyes could be constantly trained on the squadron leader at the point position. The compactness of the wedge largely precluded any lateral movement, however, except for a gradual incline to either the right or left.[99] Philip was said to have adapted the wedge from the Thracian rhomboid.[100] By eliminating the usually superfluous men on the flanks and rear of that formation, he increased the combat effectiveness of the wedge, largely sacrificing lateral maneuverability for frontal penetration power.

The basic Companion unit was an ilai, a formation of 64 men.[101] Eight ilai formed a hipparchy under a hipparch. In close-order formation with necessary gaps between the ilai to enable the horses to wheel freely and maneuver laterally, the average frontage of an individual horse was about six feet.[102] In wedge formation, with the boots of the rider of each horse touching those of his neighbors on either side, the frontage of the horse shrank to only 40 inches.[103] Typically, the Companions were deployed from four to six ranks deep.[104]

For Alexander's expedition into Persia, the Companions were organized into eight ilai: seven with a strength of 215 and one at 300, for a total strength of about 1,800.[105] The larger ilai was designated as the Royal Agema and was Alexander's personal guard when he fought mounted. It was comprised of nobles personally selected by the king. The other six ilai were recruited territorially.

In 331 B.C., during his stay in Babylon, Alexander formed four Companion lochoi, each with a strength of 500, by pairing two ilai together.[106] The additional manpower necessary to bring the command up to their new authorized strength of 2,000 was obtained from incorporating the Scouts into the formation. Just before entering India in 327 B.C., Alexander reorganized the Companions by grouping each of the Macedonian lochoi with a Persian lochoi. This formed four hipparchies, each about 1,000 strong.[107] The Persian lochoi included Areians, Arachosians, Bactrians, Parthyaeans and Sogdians.[108] A fifth Companion hipparchy was raised exclusively from eastern Persian cavalry but was probably officered by Macedonians.[109] The hipparchies now contained a mixture of heavy and light cavalry, allowing them to engage in shock charges or missile fire with equal effectiveness.[110] When Alexander concluded his Indian campaign, he sent most of his eastern Persian cavalry back to their homes.[111] Upon his arrival back at Susa, each hipparchy contained only one Macedonian lochoi. For the first time, eight Persian nobles, Roxanne's brother among them, were taken into the Agema, which an Achaemenid was now designated to command. This reorganization was greatly resented by the Macedonian Companions because of the inclusion of "barbarians," that is, Persians and Medes, into its ranks. As a result of the Opis mutiny, Alexander largely replaced the Macedonian Companions with western Persians.

Alexander's Companion cavalry was always stationed on the right flank which, in the three field battles he fought with the Persians, was always the offensive wing. The discipline and agility of the Companions would allow Alexander to closely control their evolutions in the midst of a battle, unlike most other ancient cavalry commanders, who usually lost control of their units at the beginning of the battle. Alexander was thus able to penetrate the Persian line on the right flank with the Companions at both Granicus River and Issus and then redirect them to attack the Persian center, while at Gaugamela he was able to use them to exploit a gap that opened in Bessus' line during the course of the battle.

The Companion cavalry was originally commanded by Philotas (son of Parmenio). The eight initial ilai commanders under him were Ariston, Cleitus, Demetrius, Glaucias, Hegelochus, Heracleides, Meleager and Sopolis.[112] When Philotas was convicted and executed in an alleged plot against Alexander's life, the Companions were divided into two commands: one under Cleitus the Black (son of Dropidas), who had saved Alexander's life at the battle of Granicus River, and the other under Hephaestion, Alexander's "special" friend.[113] The division was made to reduce the possibility of the Companions being used in a plot against Alexander. Also, it was a chance for the king to give Hephaestion a prestigious command. In India, the army's Companion hipparchies were commanded by Coenus, Demetrius, Perdiccas and Hephaestion.

Thessalian Cavalry Thessaly was the most renowned horse-breeding area in Greece. Its cavalry was superb and comparable in numbers, training and morale to the Companions.[114] The country was governed by a feudal aristocracy and was therefore much closer to Macedonia in its institutions than to the democracies of the Greek city-states. Consequently, Philip was extremely eager to gain control over that state. During the Third Sacred War, the leaders of Thessaly called upon Philip to lead their divided country against the Phocians. For the subsequent services rendered to them, they made Philip archon and gave him control over their army and economy, but only for the duration of the Sacred War. When Philip refused to relinquish both the office and the areas within Thessaly that he held, an uncoordinated revolt broke out that was quickly suppressed. Thessaly had now become, for all practicable purposes, a tightly controlled province of Macedonia.

The Thessalians fought in a diamond-shaped formation called the rhomboid.¹¹⁵ This was a highly maneuverable, star-shaped formation able to turn quickly in any one of four directions and still conduct a wedge attack. The commander rode at the point of the formation facing the enemy, while subordinate officers were stationed at the other three points. The rhomboid formation was well adapted for breaking an enemy line, as the best cavalrymen could be concentrated at the spearhead of the penetration that was focused across a narrow front. The Thessalian cavalryman wore a helmet and a breastplate and carried two six-foot-long javelins.¹¹⁶ Usually one of the javelins was thrown, while the other was retained as a hand-held weapon. The Thessalian cavalrymen also carried a curved slashing-sword.¹¹⁷ The protective armor worn by the Thessalians was similar to that of the Companions.¹¹⁸

The left flank of the army was the permanent station of the Thessalian cavalry. Unlike the offensive right wing, the left was always given the unenviable job of fighting a defensive action against the bulk of the Persian cavalry. That the Thessalian cavalry never broke under such heavy odds was a clear testament to their superior combat effectiveness. When Alexander invaded the Persian Empire in 333 B.C., the Thessalian heavy cavalry numbered eight ilai of 225 each, for a total combat strength of about 1,800.¹¹⁹ Their cavalry was reinforced by another 200 troopers at Gordium, topping off its numbers at the full mobilization strength of 2,000 heavy cavalry.¹²⁰ One ilai, the "Pharsalians," was considered to be elite and comparable to the Agema of the Companions. It formed the personal guard for Parmenio, who was second-in-command to Alexander and usually led the left wing of the Macedonian army. Calas commanded the Thessalian cavalry at Granicus River.¹²¹ At Sardis, when he was promoted to the office of satrap of Hellespontine Phrygia, Alexander (son of Aeropus) was designated to replace him. Upon the latter's execution for treason, however, Philip was appointed to lead the Thessalians, commanding them at the battles of Gaugamela and Hydaspes River.¹²² At Ecbatana, in Media, the Thessalian cavalry was mustered out. Upon being offered the opportunity of reenlisting as mercenaries, however, many of them chose to do so.¹²³ At the Oxus River, in Sogdiana, Alexander dismissed the remaining Thessalian cavalry from service with his army.¹²⁴

The Scouts (Prodromoi/Sarisophori) The Scouts were Macedonians who were frequently referred to as "Lancers" because of the long lancelike sarissas they carried.¹²⁵ They were light cavalry who reconnoitered in advance of the army when it was on the march. On the battlefield, they functioned in a shock role to protect the right flank of the Companion cavalry, frequently serving with the Paeonians.¹²⁶ At Gaugamela, the Scouts, led by Aretes, played a pivotal role in defeating the Persian cavalry who, although heavily outnumbering them, were clearly afraid of the Scouts' long lances.¹²⁷ Four ilai of Scouts were known to have served in Alexander's army, each 150 strong.¹²⁸ The Scouts do not appear to have been very effective in the scouting role because the Greek cavalry had not yet developed effective reconnaissance techniques. When Persian light cavalry troops were recruited, they assumed the reconnaissance duties of the Scouts, who were then integrated with the Companions and relegated exclusively to a heavy cavalry shock role.

The main weapon of the Scouts was a shorter 14-foot-long version of the infantry sarissa that could be held with one hand.[129] The cavalry sarissa vibrated at the charge and frequently shattered on contact. Having pointed metal tips at both ends, the weapon could not be used in a close-order formation without posing an extreme danger to friendly troops approaching from the rear. It was, however, ideal for use in open or linear formations against enemy light cavalry armed with spears or javelins. The rear point of the weapon also could be used on an enemy coming up from behind. The cavalry sarissa could also be reversed if the tip on the front of the weapon was broken off in combat, and thus it could continue to be used effectively. Although the Scouts were sometimes called Lancers, the sarissa could not be used as a lance in the medieval manner. Lacking a saddle or stirrups, any rider attempting to use the weapon in that way would quickly find himself unseated from his horse and thrown to the ground. Instead, it was gripped in an underhanded manner and jabbed upwards or downwards against a man on the ground or the head of a horse.

Allied Greek Cavalry In the rough country of southern and central Greece, cavalry was of limited use. The hazards for horses operating in such terrain without either a saddle or stirrup, neither of which had yet been invented, frequently lamed them. As a result, the reconnoitering duties of cavalry there were usually more efficiently performed by light infantry. In Greece, the expense of maintaining a horse restricted their ownership to the wealthy, who were usually the landowning nobility. This class was more typical of the warrior-aristocracy of the monarchies of northern Greece than the peasant-farmers of the central Greek democracies, who had neither the inclination, time, or income necessary to assume the burdens of a cavalryman. As a result, the Greek democratic city-states usually recruited mercenaries. Although light cavalry might be able to charge peltasts successfully, they would be almost totally ineffective against the front of well-ordered hoplites.[130] If they caught the hoplites on the flank or rear, however, they could be deadly against them. So fearful were the hoplites of this possibility that they generally refused to advance against enemy cavalry. An allied Greek light cavalryman was typically armed with javelins, a sword and a shield. Most light cavalry units deployed with an interval of three feet between horses.[131]

Light cavalry was initially largely recruited from eastern Macedonia and then the Balkans, after Philip had subdued several tribes there. The Greeks, as part of their obligation under the terms of the League of Corinth, provided a contingent of 600 light cavalry.[132] Strategically, Greek allied light cavalry was used primarily for escort and garrison duty in Media and India. The allied Greek cavalry appears to have been kept in reserve during major battles, being only used in the pursuit in order to ride down disordered Persian and Indian infantry.

At Gaugamela, the allied Greek cavalry proved disappointing to Alexander because it was unable to hold the Persian cavalry attacks on either flank. As a result, at Ecbatana, in Media, Alexander mustered out the Greek allies. When offered the opportunity of reenlisting as mercenaries, however, many chose to do so.[133] Thereafter they were assigned to garrison duty. When Alexander entered the eastern satrapies of the Persian Empire, he began heavily recruiting light cavalry from Bactria and Sogdiana because they had proved themselves to be more effective light cavalry than their Greek counterparts. At the battle of Granicus River, Philip (son of Menelaus) commanded the allied Greek cavalry. Erigyius commanded them at the battle of Gaugamela.[134]

Paeonian Cavalry The Paeonian cavalry was levied from the Balkan tribe of that name in compliance with its treaty with Philip. On the battlefield the Paeonian cavalry usually served with the Scouts and was deployed on the flank of the Companions.[135] The Paeonians were involved in the opening of the battles at both Granicus River and Gaugamela, alongside Alexander's Companion cavalry. Although they were initially able to field only one ilai, 150-strong, it was augmented by 500 reinforcements in Egypt and an additional 600 at Susa.[136] The Paeonian cavalry appear to have been left behind as a garrison in Persia. The Paeonians were armed with both missile weapons and side arms.[137] Although they did not wear a breastplate, they did carry a shield.[138] At Issus, the Paeonians were under the command of Antiochus.[139]

Thracian Cavalry The Odrysian Thracians carried out an identical role to the Scouts on the battlefield, but in support of the Thessalian cavalry on the left flank of the army.[140] The Thracians, although initially raising only one ilai, 150-strong, were able to recruit three more by Gaugamela.[141] Thracian cavalry strength quickly grew to 500, then to 1,000 by Egypt, and to 1,600 by Susa.[142] The Thracian cavalry fought alongside the Greek allied cavalry at the battles of Granicus River and Gaugamela. Upon reaching Media most of the Thracian cavalry was assigned to garrison duty with Parmenio.[143] The remainder accompanying the army was left behind with Philip in India.[144]

The Thracians were armed with both missile weapons and side arms.[145] Their basic attack formation was the wedge.[146] Calas (son of Harpalus) commanded the Thracian cavalry when Alexander crossed into Asia Minor. Upon being appointed satrap of Hellespontine Phrygia, he relinquished command of the Thracians to Sitalces, who commanded them at the battles of Issus and Gaugamela.[147]

Greek Mercenary Cavalry Greek mercenary cavalry were professional soldiers who hired out for pay. They were normally used by Alexander on secondary missions. The one time that Alexander used them in his battle line at Gaugamela, a mercenary cavalry unit under Menidas was defeated by the Saca cavalry on Alexander's right flank, while another under Andromachus was unable to hold Mazaeus' Cappadocians on Parmenio's left flank. Alexander is not known to have used Greek mercenary cavalry on frontline operations after this. Observing the superior effectiveness of Bactrian and Sogdiana light cavalry in Spitamenes' operations against him, Alexander began to recruit light cavalry from these areas and use them in tasks he had formerly assigned to the Greek mercenary cavalry. Those Greek mercenary cavalry Alexander had with him when he departed India were left behind with Leonnatus in southeast Gedrosa, while he marched through the Makran desert. Menidas commanded the Greek mercenary cavalry at the battle of Gaugamela.[148]

Horse Archers   In 329 B.C. at Sogdiana, Alexander created a 1,000-strength hipparchy of horse archers. They were comprised primarily of Bactrian, Sogdiana and Scythian light cavalry. Firing their bows while mounted, the horse archers were highly effective in delivering a heavy missile fire against enemy formations. At the battle of Hydaspes River, for instance, they were able to both disorder the Indian cavalry and decimate the Indian chariots.

Mounted Javelin Men   These troops were believed to have been recruited in late 330 B.C. from the Persians or the Paeonians.[149] As the name implies, they were armed with a javelin that they typically threw upon closing with the enemy.

Foot Companions (Pezhetairoi)   The Foot Companions were frequently referred to as the phalanx, the word meaning "finger." They trace their origins to Alexander I of Macedonia, who organized them to keep his nobles in check. His phalanx, however, was not a very formidable force. Although the peasants who formed its ranks were robust, they were undisciplined. Under Philip all that changed; he transformed them into one of the most effective fighting units in the ancient world, dominating the battlefield until broken by the Roman legions at Pydna in 168 B.C.[150] The Persian infantry and cavalry could make no impression upon the front of a well-ordered phalanx, and although the elephants of India could disorder the formation and inflict heavy casualties on it, they were unable to break it. Of the Greeks, only the Thebans were able to fight the phalanx to a standstill. Nevertheless, the phalanx was the most deadly shock momentum formation of the heavy infantry in the ancient world, and even the Romans faced it with great fear.

The Foot Companion was armed with a sarissa; a javelin,[151] when it was not practical to use the long sarissa; a short sword[152]; a light, concave, bronze-faced shield about two feet in diameter[153]; and a bronze helmet. When not involved in a field battle, the phalanx soldier would usually carry a javelin. This would occur on forced marches through rough country, in the storming of cities, and in naval combat. Since the mobility of the phalanx was similar to the peltasts, it is generally assumed that they were not encumbered by the weight of armor. With the long sarissa engaging the enemy at a safe distance, strategists probably thought the defensive armor superfluous and an unnecessary impediment to movement.[154] Besides, it is not likely that the peasants of the Foot Companions could have afforded the cost of the armor. It is likely, however, that the men in the front rank wore breastplates and greaves.[155] As the strongest men with the best endurance would likely have formed the first rank of the phalanx, the weight of armor may not necessarily have hindered their movement. However, this would have proved extremely useful against enemy missile fire.

The sarissa introduced by Philip was a 21-foot-long pike.[156] This compared with the normal nine-foot-long spear carried by the Greek hoplite and the six- to seven-foot-long javelin carried by the Persians. The additional length of the weapon gave the Macedonians the confidence that when meeting enemy troops in battle they would always be able to deliver the first strike. The sarissa was made of cornel wood and was attached to the point by a socket.[157] It was divided into two halves for carrying on the march, being assembled just before battle by sliding an iron sleeve down over the two parts.[158] Much training and discipline was required to handle the weapon properly, and Philip drilled his phalanx incessantly.

The extreme length and 14-pound weight of the sarissa required the use of both hands to wield the weapon.[159] It had to be held about six feet up from the butt of the shaft for proper balance.[160] Thus it projected 15 feet in front of the holder. As the close-order ranks of the phalanx usually occupied a depth of three feet, the sarissas of the second rank would project 12 feet out in front of the first rank; those of the third rank, nine feet out; the fourth rank, six feet out; and the fifth rank, three feet out.[161] The front rank of the phalanx was thus protected by a wall of sarissas from the first five ranks, all held at varying heights and constantly being jabbed rather than merely held stationary.[162]

If the enemy got close enough to engage in hand-to-hand combat, soldiers in the phalanx would be at a hopeless disadvantage because the long length of their sarissas would preclude them from being brought to bear in a close-in fight. Any enemy would first make contact with the sarissa a full 15 feet from the first rank of the phalanx, long before its six-foot-long javelins or nine-foot-long spears could make contact. Then, every three feet from the outer sarissas, another rank of them would be encountered. This wall of spears projecting from the phalanx ensured that the opponents would sustain heavy casualties on their approach without being able to inflict any themselves. The phalanx was also capable of presenting a much denser formation than its opponent. Because the effectiveness of the phalanx was achieved by literally crashing into an enemy formation and then pushing its front rank through the enemy line, its soldiers did not require any lateral room to wield their weapons. They merely marched straight ahead. This allowed them to use a closed-shields formation that gave each man a frontage of only 18 inches and made possible a far higher concentration of weapons to be projected than any enemy formation was capable of, each front-rank opponent of the phalanx being targeted with up to 10 sarissas.[163]

The phalanx delivered its frontal attack by impact and momentum over a short distance. The formation's combat effectiveness depended almost solely on the sarissa. To be successful in its attack, the phalanx had to create a gap in the enemy's line and push troops through it to break the cohesion of the enemy formation. The long sarissa gave the phalanx a superior weapon to penetrate an enemy formation and cause heavy casualties, while the phalanx's momentum and depth allowed it to push troops irresistibly into the breach that was inevitably made. Taxies of the phalanx usually closed up on each other to prevent the enemy from penetrating any gaps between them. The Thessalian cavalry would be stationed on the left flank of the phalanx and the hypaspists on the right flank. The front of the phalanx was usually screened by the peltasts.

It is interesting to note that although the unengaged ranks of the phalanx might have been used to extend the formation's frontage in an attempt to outflank an enemy that they were in contact with, the tactic was never employed. This was probably partly because the phalanx was trained to maneuver by file, not rank, and partly because the formation's overriding concern was its pushing power, which would be increased by the inclusion of the additional ranks. The phalanx had a fear of rough ground that might disorder its ranks and allow enemy penetrations.[164] In order for the formation to deploy properly, a level battlefield of two to three miles in width that was free of any obstacles had to be selected. In Greece, where mountainous terrain predominated, such ground was sometimes difficult to locate. Then, the opponents of the phalanx also had to agree to deploy on the open ground. If they instead chose to move through woods or over rough ground or to assault a city directly, the phalanx was helpless to intervene. The surrender of the strategic initiative to its opponent whether to engage the formation or not was a fatal weakness of the phalanx. In his campaign against the Taulantians in the Balkans, Alexander was to find that he was unable to attack the tribes there either in the woods or on the slopes of the hills. Only when he was able to trick them into coming down onto the plain was he able to engage them successfully.

Against enemy missile fire, the phalanx had two primary defenses. Because only the front rank of the formation was heavily armored, it was able to close rapidly with an enemy. In fact, it took the formation a little over one minute to contact an enemy formation from the time it first came into missile range, which was typically at about 150 yards.[165] Both the rapid movement of the phalanx and the heavy defensive armor of its first rank greatly diminished the effectiveness of any enemy missile fire against it. For this reason, the Persians pursued the same tactics against the phalanx as they had against the hoplites, meeting it with the shock impact of the Greek mercenaries rather than attempting to disorder it by missile fire. A secondary defense of the phalanx against incoming missile fire was the sarissa itself. Held at varying levels by the unengaged ranks — all ranks after the fifth who had not leveled their sarissa's horizontally — from just above horizontal all the way to vertical, the resulting "wall of wood" proved surprisingly effective at deflecting incoming missile fire for a time.

Although the phalanx was clearly superior to any other heavy infantry formation of its time, it did have several notable weaknesses: it was particularly vulnerable to sustained missile fire, flank attacks, hand-to-hand combat, and movement over rough ground. When a phalanx was able to close quickly with an enemy formation, the effects of enemy missile fire were normally negligible. However, if the formation was subjected to a sustained missile barrage, it would begin to take heavy casualties. Because the rear ranks of the phalanx were unarmored, any enemy arrows finding their mark there would inevitably result in a wound or a death.

Having the problem of all linear formations, the phalanx had vulnerable flanks. Although a phalanx was trained to execute a turn to the rear, it had no procedure to wheel to the flank. This was because the formation's core tactical unit, the file, was trained to move vertically, not laterally.[166] Any redeployment to the flank had to be made by first withdrawing the file straight back out of the formation, then marching across its rear to realign itself to the flank. When making the move, the file exposed the entire formation to danger because the resulting gap created by its withdrawal allowed penetration by an enemy. In any case, it might not be possible to execute such a maneuver if the sarissas were already lowered and engaged to the front. Any attempt to do so would disorder the entire formation. Since the sarissa was held from six to seven feet up from the end, that part of the shaft protruding to the rear of each rank made any attempt to turn to the flank virtually impossible without dislocating adjacent files or rear ranks, both of which were only three feet distant. The rear of a phalanx was not quite as vulnerable as a flank in an emergency because the unengaged back ranks—files were segmented by quarters, that is, in units of four soldiers—were able to face about without too much trouble. However, since the phalanx was trained to operate as an intact offensive formation whose effectiveness was achieved by its forward momentum, the facing of the formation in two directions at the same time would relegate it to a stationary defense. This would have been an unfamiliar formation to the phalanx that would have clearly caused confusion and subsequent disorder.

The phalanx was unable to engage in hand-to-hand combat because the long sarissas were all but useless in arm's length fighting. The formation was designed to engage an enemy at a distance, where the first few ranks of the projecting weapons would contact their opponents without the possibility of an initial reply. The secondary weapon of the phalanx troops was a short sword that was only used for thrusting and stabbing, placing its user at a serious disadvantage against the Spanish cutting sword of the Roman legionaries or the heavy broadswords of the Balkan tribes.[167] Because the soldiers of the phalanx were largely untrained in the use of these swords, lacked the proper room in which to use the weapons, and, except for possibly the first rank, had no defensive armor or shield that could protect them against any blows delivered by their opponents, the phalanx was all but defenseless in any close-in fight.

When in open-order formation, each soldier of the phalanx occupied six feet of frontage; in close-order formation, three feet; and in the "locked-shields" formation, one and a half feet.[168] The basic tactical unit of the phalanx was the file, consisting of sixteen ranks under Philip and eight ranks under Alexander.[169] The front-ranked man, a lochagos, commanded the file; a half-file leader, a hemilochites, commanded the last eight ranks; and quarter-file leaders, enomotarchs, commanded at the fourth and twelfth ranks.[170] This theoretically made the file highly flexible by units of fours. The frontage of a taxies could only be expanded by marching the last four or eight ranks of the file straight back out of the formation. Once clear of the rear rank, the file then either marched to the left or right. Lanes could be created in the line for chariots to pass through in much the same way, except that the entire file would make the move. Alexander typically fought with a phalanx depth of eight ranks both because this was the normal depth of the Greek mercenary hoplite units at the time and because he was usually heavily outnumbered by the Persians and needed the extended frontage that the shallower formation gave him. A file of 16 men comprised a lochos under a lochagos; four files, a tetrarchia, totaling 64 men, under a tetrarch; two tetrarchia, a taxiarchia, totaling 128 men, under a taxiarch; two tarxiarchs, a syntagma, totaling 256 men, under a syntagmatarch; six syntagma, a taxies, totaling 1,500 men, under a strategos or taxies; and six taxies, a phalanx, totaling 9,000 men, under a phalangiarch.[171]

When Alexander invaded Asia, he took six veteran taxies of the phalanx units with him.[172] Another eight taxies of younger and less experienced soldiers were left behind in Macedonia with Antipater.[173] A seventh taxies of the phalanx was later created somewhere between Susa and India.[174] The Asian field army's seven taxies were commanded by the following strategos, or generals:

1st taxies	Craterus, who was left behind in Bactria; then Gorgias
2d taxies	Meleager
3d taxies	Ptolemy (son of Seleucus), killed at Issus; then Polysperchon (son of Simmias)
4th taxies	Amyntas, who died in Drangiana; then Simmias, in temporary command; then Attalus
5th taxies	Coenus, who died in the Punjab; then Antigens (son of Coenus)
6th taxies	Perdiccas, who was promoted to staff at Sogdiana; then Philotas, who was promoted to satrap of Cilicia; then Alcetas
7th taxies	Cleitus the White, who was promoted to command a cavalry hipparchy; then Antigonus, who was promoted to satrap of Phrygia; then Peithon[175]

In all four of Alexander's great field battles, his phalanx troops fought with their ranks disordered—by river-bank obstacles at Granicus River and Issus, by both a chariot and cavalry charge at Gaugamela, and by elephants at the Hydaspes River. In each case, Alexander's phalanx troops were so well trained that despite their disarray they maintained their basic formation. The Macedonians were really superb infantrymen, and it is almost regrettable that they were usually relegated to a secondary role on the battlefield. The only exception to this was at the battle of Hydaspes River, where the presence of elephants precluded any approach by the Companions, who usually spearheaded the attack. This left the infantry to fight it out alone with the elephants.

With Alexander's return to Babylon, the phalanx was reorganized. The first three ranks of the formation were to be comprised of Macedonians and the next twelve of Persians; a Macedonian was to be the file closer.[176] The Macedonians were to be armed, as usual, with the sarissa, but the Persians were to carry either the javelin or bow.[177] Alexander believed that the enemies he was now likely to meet would be more mobile and would be armed largely with missile weapons. Thus he thought that his new phalanx formation would be more effective against them than the current pure shock formation. Upon Alexander's death soon after the announcement of the new formation, its implementation was canceled by his successors, who had obviously preferred the weight of shock impact over that of combined arms flexibility.

Hypaspists The hypaspists derived their name from the king's squire who initially carried his shield into battle.[178] In the Macedonian army, a unit of hypaspists was formed from the ranks of the nobility and became the bodyguard of the Macedonian king. The hypaspists were the counterpart of the Companion cavalry, and although their full name was "hypaspists of the Companions," they were usually known simply as the "Guards." Just prior to Alexander's entry into India, he allowed the hypaspists to carry silver shields and assume the title of "Argyraspids" (silver-shields). After Alexander's death, the Argyraspids fiercely insisted on that title to distinguish them from all other hypaspists raised by the successors.

The hypaspists were extremely versatile troops and were used for a great number of difficult assignments requiring exceptional endurance. They frequently found themselves in the company of the Agrianians, who were also routinely relegated to such roles. The hypaspists were selected both for their skill with weapons and their exceptional endurance. Their position in the battle line was on the vulnerable right flank of the phalanx, where they maintained a link with the Companion cavalry, which was trained to support.[179] When the Companions broke through the enemy line, it was the responsibility of the hypaspists to cover their flank and rear. They could also double as shock troops to support the phalanx, should the need arise. Strategically, the hypaspists were frequently sent on night raids and forced marches of more than 30 miles a day, despite the fact that many of their number were over 60 years old.[180] Age was apparently no impediment to their ability to carry out the strenuous duties that Alexander frequently assigned them.

There is considerable disagreement and confusion over just what classification of infantry the hypaspists were because they appear to have been used at various times both as heavy infantry and peltasts. It is likely that when the hypaspists were serving with the phalanx they used the sarissa and when they assumed the duties of a peltast they used the javelin.[181]

The hypaspists were organized into three battalions of 1,000 men each.[182] One of these was the royal battalion, or Agema, which acted as Alexander's personal guard when he fought on foot.[183] The hypaspist taxies were always kept at full strength by drawing on recruits from the phalanx and were consequently able to maintain their high morale and combat effectiveness throughout the campaigns in Asia, despite the continual losses they incurred.[184] Their reputation for toughness and endurance excelled all other troops in the army. The hypaspists were originally commanded by Nicanor, who led them at the battles of Granicus River, Issus and Gaugamela.[185] Upon his death by illness, Nicanor was replaced by Seleucus, who commanded the hypaspists at the battle of Hydaspes River.[186]

Greek Allied Hoplites The hoplite formation was the basic Greek organization of heavy infantry from the Persian invasions up through Alexander's time. It was a close-order formation, with each man occupying a frontage and depth of three feet.[187] Although the hoplite unit was theoretically able to fight in any multiple of four ranks, its normal formation depth was eight ranks during the Macedonian era.[188] The hoplite's effectiveness depended upon the impact momentum of the first rank and on the push support of all ranks behind. The formation was like a gigantic battering ram, with most of its manpower being used to add the hoplite tactic was to head straight for the enemy, closing as quickly as possible. The heavy armor and large shield of the hoplite effectively protected him against enemy missile fire during the minute or so that it took to make his charge within the 150-yard range of missile fire.[189] Opposing hoplites would always countercharge their attackers, both sides literally crashing into each other.[190] The first two ranks of the hoplites would project their weapons out in front of the formation, but usually the impact of contact would shatter both the spears and shields of those ranks.

If the hoplites were unable to break into the enemy line on impact, the issue would settle into a pushing match, each side attempting to penetrate its opponent's line by literally pushing its front ranks through the opposing formation. To increase the forward momentum, the rear ranks used their shields and the force of their shoulders to push against the backs of those ranks in front. Eventually, one side or the other first experienced a slowing in its forward movement. This was the first indication that the unit might soon be experiencing the dreaded "pushback." The hoplite formation was offensive by nature and was only effective in the momentum of an advance. If thrown on the defensive, its line would become quickly fragmented, as the stationary hoplites in the front ranks struggled to keep their footing while being pushed off balance by the still advancing ranks behind them. In the resulting confusion, hoplites in the rear ranks would begin to put their personal safety above that of the group, giving serious consideration to deserting the formation. Their departure would steadily decrease the pushing pressure on the ranks in front. Since the formation was so tightly compressed, any hesitation or doubt would be instantly transmitted among the ranks by many subtleties that the men had grown accustomed to recognize — a lessening of pressure, a hesitancy of action, a trembling of fear. It is at this time that the formation faced its greatest danger because an instantaneous collapse of morale might shatter its cohesion. The result would be a breakup of the formation, with each man now being only concerned with his own survival.

Hoplite formations were reluctant to advance if enemy cavalry was present and they were unsupported by equal numbers of comparable friendly cavalry. They greatly feared being attacked on their vulnerable flanks or rear. If surrounded by enemy cavalry or if the situation lent itself to a surprise attack, the hoplites would march in a hollow square with the baggage train, camp-followers, and light troops in the center.

The hoplite was a heavy infantryman carrying an estimated 50–70 pounds of equipment.[191] He was protected by a breastplate,[192] a bronze helmet with hinged cheek-protectors,[193] bronze greaves,[194] and a large, round bronze shield.[195] The main weapon of the hoplite was a nine-foot-long thrusting spear;[196] his secondary weapon was a two-foot-long thrusting sword.[197] The spear took little specialized training or skill to use in the tightly packed hoplite formation, the main requirements being bravery and endurance rather than extensive weapons training or drill proficiency.[198] The difficulty for the hoplite was in striking his opponent a fatal blow. As the hoplite closed with the enemy, he thrust his spear down from the shoulder.[199] Although a hoplite had a better chance of incapacitating or killing his opponent by passing the spear underneath the shield into his groin instead of over the shield through his heavily armored neck, arms, or shoulders, the overlapping shields in the hoplite close-order formation usually precluded this.[200] The first two ranks of the hoplites were able to project their weapons out front of their formation.[201] Since the hoplite shield was held by the left arm, its size, shape, and the manner in which it had to be held only allowed the user to cover his left side. For the protection of his right side, the hoplite had to close up to his neighbor's shield on that side. This led to a noticeable slide to the right of most hoplite units as the hoplite on the far right attempted to move his vulnerable right side up into friendly shield support or beyond the enemy's left flank.[202] In the tightly packed hoplite formation, there was no room for maneuverability or individual combat.[203] Any attempt at heroics by an individual would leave a gap in the line that would not only endanger the man on his left but threaten the entire formation.

Cities did not normally issue the hoplites their equipment.[204] Instead, each hoplite brought along his own weaponry that varied according to the individual's comfort and preference. This would result in a hodgepodge of different equipment being used; some was decades old and had been passed down from grandfathers. Because of the weight and general discomfort of his heavy equipment, the hoplite generally did not arm himself until just before the actual fighting.[205] His servant, who carried and cared for the equipment, would stand close by him and at the last minute before the hoplite was to engage in combat the servant would assist his master in arming himself.

The various Greek allied hoplite formations were frequently under the command of Parmenio. Although Alexander crossed into Asia with 5,000 hoplites and subsequently acquired several thousand more, he never used them as frontline troops in any of his field battles.[206] The hoplites were either hired mercenaries or impressed Greek allied troops. The allies were less than enthusiastic soldiers, being, in effect, unwilling hostages to guarantee their home city's continued good behavior. In addition to their questionable loyalty, neither the hoplites' training or weapons were compatible with those of a soldier of the phalanx, and there would have been significant difficulties in integrating the two formations. Also, as there were so many different contingents from the various cities, it would have been difficult to organize them into a single homogenous unit.[207] As a result, on the battlefield Alexander usually relegated the hoplites to the reserve. Off the battlefield, they were mainly used for secondary missions in which sheer numbers rather than military skill were called for. Many of the hoplites were kept busy at various miscellaneous duties such as road building and escort missions. Eventually, most of the hoplites were assigned to garrison duty along the army's line of march. Alexander had no interest, it appears, in prematurely sending any of them home, where they might stir up trouble. When Alexander reached Media, he discharged most of the Greek allied troops, while the Argives remained behind to garrison Sardis. Most of the other allies eventually returned to Greece.[208] The allied Greek hoplites were initially commanded by Antigonus (son of Philip).[209] When he was appointed to conduct the siege of Celeanae, in Asia Minor, Balacrus then assumed command of them.[210] Left behind in Egypt as one of the generals in command of the army there, Balacrus was replaced by Calamus.[211]

Greek Mercenaries The mercenaries were usually Greek soldiers of fortune. Some of them had been exiled and others were out for the adventure and loot professional soldiering offered. There was an almost inexhaustible supply of mercenaries available, and both Darius and Alexander made extensive use of their services.[212] When Alexander crossed the Hellespont, he enlisted about 5,000 mercenaries as infantry; at the end of his reign as many as 60,000 mercenaries had been in his employ at one time or another.[213] After Alexander's death, the Greek mercenaries who had been settled in the eastern satrapies revolted and made their way west, sometimes in groups numbering in the thousands.[214] They had little desire, it seems, to act as lynch pins for the economic development of a people they despised. Although Alexander's successors initially drove the mercenaries back to the cities that they had been settled in, they soon changed their minds and began to enlist them en masse into their armies.

Mercenaries worked for pay and were usually nonpolitical, not especially caring if they were employed by a tyrant or a democracy. Many were professional soldiers and thus were more highly trained than any part-time citizen-soldier could ever hope to be. Although mercenaries were expensive, there were several advantages to using them. Mercenaries like Rhodian/Balaeric slingers, Cretan archers, or Rhodian engineers provided specialty skills that might not be otherwise available to an army or were in short supply because of extensive training requirements and/or high weaponry costs. Mercenaries were usually already highly trained, professionally officered, and well armed. In ancient times, a unit's proficiency on the parade ground often indicated its battlefield effectiveness.[215] The mercenaries' discipline was usually achieved only with long and hard training. They were available for campaigning all year long, not having to go back home during the planting or harvesting season or any other time.[216]

The mercenaries were generally more maneuverable than their citizen counterparts, their effectiveness on the battlefield higher, and they were less susceptible to panic.[217] They were also expendable, unlike the citizens of a city-state. Contrary to other periods in time, the morale of mercenaries was generally higher than that of the rest of the army and they were more likely to serve loyally, as long as they were paid promptly. If they were not paid, they could refuse to advance, could march off the battlefield, or could actually change sides during a battle. Their leaders were usually men of wide and varied experience, who were resourceful and inventive and had learned a great many tricks of the trade from the school of hard experience. They were, however, difficult to control at times, especially when loot was within easy reach, and if they were not paid promptly, they were not above pillaging friendly territory.[218] Also, since their objective was to grow rich without getting injured, mercenaries were sometimes reluctant to engage in a battle that could result in a large number of casualties.

Menon was initially in command of the Greek mercenaries. When he was appointed satrap of Lydia, however, Clearchus replaced him. Cleander commanded the so-called "old guard" mercenaries at Gaugamela.[219]

Like the allies serving in the Macedonian army, the mercenaries seem to have played the part of the odd man out. In battles they were, with few exceptions, usually placed in reserve to sit it out as mere spectators. Upon reaching Ecbatana, in Media, all the mercenaries except those recently enlisted as cavalry under Erigyius were left behind under the command of Parmenio.[220] After his murder they soon rejoined Alexander but found themselves frequently assigned to secondary operations of garrisoning eastern settlements already established or being posted to the various satrapal armies that were created. In Areia, Erigyius was given command of a force of 600 mercenary cavalry and 6,000 mercenary infantry and ordered to engage Satibarzanes.[221]

This was done, and Satibarzanes' force was not only defeated but he himself was killed in single combat with Erigyius. In Sogdiana, Pharnuches was sent to relieve Maracanda, then being besieged by Spitamenes. Pharnuches' force included 800 mercenary cavalry and 1,500 mercenary infantry.[222] Incompetent leadership, faulty force composition, and shaky morale all combined to produce a disastrous defeat for the mercenary force. Because of the large number of mercenaries garrisoning the east, Alexander believed that he could rule the former Persian Empire with an army consisting of a small core of loyal Macedonians augmented by Persians.

When Alexander marched out of the Makran, he issued a decree for the Asian satraps to disband their mercenary armies. Alexander perceived that the satraps were expanding their military strength to prepare for a future revolt against him. From his point of view, the only thing that could be done was to return the mercenaries to Greece. Because the mercenaries' loyalty was almost always to the highest bidder, their continued presence in Asia would always be destabilizing. Although great turmoil would be created by the return of the exiles, this would largely work to Alexander's advantage because the cities would be forced to concentrate their energies on suppressing local unrest and litigating the numerous lawsuits that were sure to be filed rather than planning any revolt against him. As the returning exiles would also owe everything to Alexander their loyalty to him would be absolute. The Exile's Decree announcing the new policy was duly sent to the various Greek cities, but Alexander died before it could be implemented. His successors promptly shelved the decree, correctly foreseeing that they would soon be needing the services of the mercenaries for their own armies in the upcoming struggle for power.

Peltasts/Javelin Men The peltasts took their name from the pelte, a light, crescent-shaped shield that they carried.[223] They operated in the midrange between psiloi, or light infantry, and the heavy infantry hoplites. Peltasts were recruited generally from the poorer peoples of the mountainous areas of southern and western Greece and from the Balkans.[224] Since most of the troops serving in this capacity were poverty-stricken, the regular pay and opportunity for looting were powerful enlistment inducements. The Balkan tribes conquered by both Philip and

Alexander were also required to provide troop levies upon request, thus ensuring the availability of a large number of peltasts for the Macedonian army.

Peltasts could function as skirmishers, who engaged enemy skirmishers in hand-to-hand combat, or as psiloi, who attempted to disorder enemy formations with missile fire. Although the peltasts were unable to stand up to equal numbers of hoplites frontally, they could, under favorable circumstances, attack the flanks and rear of hoplite formations. Peltasts were much more versatile then either the hoplites or psiloi, being able to deliver a heavy missile fire, move quickly across the battlefield, and engage in limited hand-to-hand combat. Whereas skirmishers would typically evade a charge by heavier troops, the peltasts could form a line and hold it against light cavalry in the open or against heavy infantry in rough or wooded terrain. The peltasts frequently supported the heavy cavalry by killing dismounted enemy riders or causing confusion in an enemy cavalry formation by their presence.[225] When the occasion demanded it, the peltasts could also fight in field battles as phalanx troops. In this regard, they had common combat characteristics with the hypaspists, being able to operate either as light or heavy infantry.

The peltasts were armed with throwing javelins, usually carrying two or three of them; a sword; and a shield.[226] Lacking any specialized training to operate a bow or sling effectively, most peltasts were quickly trained in the relatively simple function of throwing a javelin or fighting hand-to-hand with it.[227] At the battle of the Hydaspes River, some of the peltasts were given axes and broadswords that they used to hamstring the Indian elephants. The peltasts wore a broad metal belt that served to protect the abdomen.[228] Their wicker shield was usually crescent-shaped and covered with goatskin or sheepskin. A strap made it possible for the shield to be supported by the user's shoulder, while a single handle either at the rim or in the center allowed it to be held up in front of the body to deflect blows. As a secondary weapon, the peltasts carried a sword.[229]

The peltasts usually fought in an open-order formation, probably eight deep, although at times they might not have fought in any formation at all. Their organization would be adapted to the terrain they were confronted with and the need to screen the phalanx from enemy missile fire or skirmish attack. At Gaugamela, there were two units of peltasts with the field army and a third with the baggage train. Each appears to have had a strength of about 500 men. By the time of Alexander's campaign in Swat, a number of the javelin men had been mounted on horses.[230]

Agrianians The Agrianians were an elite body of peltast javelin troops recruited from the personal "shield-bearers" of the Agrianian king. The Agrianians were a Balkan tribe residing along the foothills of the mountainous Strymon Valley, south of Sofia.[231] At the beginning of the Persian campaign, Alexander crossed over into Asia Minor with 500 Agrianians.[232] Just before Issus, another 500 joined his army.[233]

The Agrianians were always one of the units selected by Alexander for a strategic forced march or a rapid tactical movement over rough terrain. They frequently served with both the hypaspists and the phalanx, and in battle they usually formed part of the screening forces operating in front of the Companions.[234] The Agrianians were always in close proximity to the archers. Once the battle started, the Agrianians would usually operate with the Companions in a combined-arms function to disorder enemy cavalry by their presence or to kill enemy horses and any dismounted riders. The armament of the Agrianians was similar to that of the peltast. They carried a large shield, a long spear and a sword. Body armor was worn that was light enough not to hinder their exceptional mobility. Attalus commanded the Agrianians at battles of Granicus River, Issus and Gaugamela.[235]

Balkan Levies Both Philip and Alexander were able to levy peltasts from the conquered tribes in the Balkans as mercenaries because of their successful campaigns there. Alexander took more than 7,500 levies from the Balkans into Asia with him: 3,000 from Illyria, 1,000 from the Triballians, and 3,000 from Thrace.[236] They were mostly undisciplined troops.[237] On the battlefield the Balkan troops were used as peltast skirmishers or, in emergencies, as missile-support troops. Their lack of discipline and resulting instability, however, largely precluded their continued use for frontline duty.

Thracian Javelin Men The Thracian javelin men supported the Thessalian cavalry on the left of the line in the same manner as the Agrianians supported the Companions on the right of the line.[238] Off the battlefield, they were usually assigned to mountain warfare, garrison duty, or detached secondary missions. Most of the Thracian infantry was assigned to garrison duty in Media and Parthyaea, the remainder being left in India.[239] The Thracian infantry was under the command of the Odrysian prince Sitalces. He led them at the siege of Telmissus and in the battles of Issus and Gaugamela.[240]

Light Infantry (Psiloi) Light infantry played little part in the heavy infantry battles of classical Greece. They were restricted to support roles such as scouting, screening heavy infantry, and protecting the army's flank. The few Greek operations where light troops had proved decisive were dismissed as aberrations. During the Peloponnesian War, for instance, the loss of an Athenian army at Syracuse was seen by the Greeks as resulting from the more open terrain of Sicily rather than from any structural deficiency in their army.

Before Philip, light infantry had been generally held in low esteem. Being raised from the poorer segment of the population, it was usually relatively undisciplined, unreliable in battle, and poorly armed. Virtually the only effective light infantry missile troops in Greece were hired mercenaries, who had achieved their weapon proficiency through intensive training. Both Philip and Alexander saw that to offset the typically heavy missile fire of the Persian army, Greek missile support troops would have to be improved and greatly expanded. The Agrianians, archers, javelin men, and horse archers were eventually organized into huge 1,000-strength units and were frequently assigned offensive missions in support of the main battlefield assault. The heavy missile fire of light infantry was successfully used by Alexander to decimate chariots, disorder cavalry, and kill the unprotected mahouts atop the Indian elephants. Other duties of light infantry included scouting, protecting heavy infantry on the march, participating in ambushes, storming cities and mountain passes, and making forced marches to achieve strategic surprise.[241] Under Alexander's careful training, Greek light infantry had finally come unto its own as a powerful offensive arm.

The psiloi was comprised of foot-archers and slingers. They were without any defensive armor, and neither their training or weaponry allowed them to engage in hand-to-hand combat.[242] Nevertheless, they usually carried a short sword to offer at least some deterrent to an attacker.[243] The method of fighting was based on audacity and opportunism rather than mastery of any complicated drill. Their usual tactic was to skirmish in front of the phalanx, either to disorder opposing enemy close-order troops or to screen the deployment of friendly heavy infantry against a similar attack by the enemy. They would stand and fire their missile weapons against opposing light infantry, but if heavier troops advanced on them, they would usually fall back and take position on the flanks of the phalanx.

Light infantry typically operated in a loose formation that allowed them either to skirmish in open ground or to operate effectively in rough terrain and woods. Typically, a light infantryman would have a frontage and depth of six feet. The Greeks considered this the minimum distance necessary to operate a missile weapon without interference from adjacent troops. Light troops generally fought eight ranks deep, despite the fact that four ranks would seem to have been a more effective depth for them.[244]

Archers Archery was not highly regarded in Greece, the arm being thought of as more appropriate for the effeminate barbarians — the Persians.[245] Cretan archers, however, were widely respected throughout the Mediterranean for their skill with a bow and were heavily recruited by Alexander as mercenaries.[246] Smaller numbers of archers were obtained from Macedonia and the Balkans. When Alexander invaded Persia, he took a single 500-man archer unit with him into Asia Minor.[247] Another archer unit of the same size joined him just prior to the battle of Issus.[248] The strength of the archers was steadily expanded, probably by recruiting Cretans, until they numbered about 2,000 at the time of Alexander's death.

Arrows were made of reed and had 4.25-inch bronze heads.[249] Bronze was undoubtedly used because of the ease of casting. The effective range of Greek bows was 80–100 yards. Because the Cretan archers drew their bowstring to their ear, in contrast to the Greek archers, who only drew theirs to their chest, they were able to achieve higher trajectories and thus had a greater range than their Greek counterparts.[250] Persian archers, however, were usually able to outrange the Cretans, probably because they used a longer arrow that allowed them to pull the bowstring back farther.[251] All Greek archers carried swords, but it appears that only the Cretans also carried shields.[252] This would indicate that they were prepared to fight hand-to-hand to defend themselves and may be one of the reasons why Greek commanders preferred them.[253]

Euryotas the Cretan commanded the archers at the siege of Halicarnassus, where he was killed.[254] He was replaced by Cleandrus, who was killed at Sagalassus, in Asia Minor.[255] Antiochus then led the Cretans, commanding them at Issus. Dying in Egypt, he was replaced by Ombrion (or Brison as he is otherwise known), who commanded the archers at Gaugamela.[256]

After the Hydaspes River was crossed, Tauron succeeded to Ombrion's command.[257] Just before the battle of Hydaspes River, however, Tauron was assigned to command one of the taxies of the phalanx. It is not known who was then assigned to command the archers.

Slingers The Rhodians and the Balaeric islanders were usually unsurpassed in the Greek world for their expertise with the sling. Their services were thus always in high demand. Several hilly areas in the Peloponnese also produced slingers: notably Achaea, Acarnania and Elis.[258] Good slingers could outrange most archers.

The sling was a leather pouch attacked to two thongs. It was operated in a similar manner to the staff sling, but it required less room to use and had a shorter range. The staff sling was a leather pouch attached to a six-foot-long pole swung with both arms. When one of the two thongs of the pouch was released, the lead bullet contained inside it was discharged. Slingers needed a lot of room to work their weapon properly and avoid injuring their neighbors. Typically, a slinger carried as many as three slings of different lengths, the longest of which was swung round in the greatest arc to achieve the highest velocity and greatest range. The one-ounce oval lead bullets typically used by the Rhodian slingers had twice the range of the fist-sized stones used by their Persian counterparts.[259] Persian slingers would typically carry a few heavy stones, while the Rhodians could carry up to 50 one-ounce lead bullets. Slingers were unarmed except for the sling. They wore no defensive armor, nor did they carry a shield, both of which would have hindered the use of their weapon.

Persians The Macedonian army had evolved from a wholly Greek army at the time Alexander crossed the Hellespont to a heavily Oriental army as he lay dying 12 years later. In 328 B.C., Alexander first recruited Persians from Arachosia, the Parapamisadae, Bactria, Sogdiana and Scythia to form separate cavalry units. During the campaign, the Persians were brigaded with the Companions, although they were still in separate lochoi. When Alexander concluded his Indian campaign, he sent most of his eastern Persian cavalry back to their homes. His four Companion hipparchies, being now only comprised of one Macedonian lochoi, shrank to half their former size. In 324 B.C., Alexander added a fifth Companion hipparchy raised exclusively from western Persian cavalry but probably officered by Macedonians.

When Alexander left Bactria in 327 B.C., he issued an order that 30,000 Persian youths were to be recruited from the northeast satrapies and trained to fight in the style of the Macedonian phalanx.[260] In 324 B.C., this Persian force completed its training and presented itself to Alexander at Susa. He was suitably impressed with their drill proficiency on the parade ground, although his army was generally contemptuous of them. At Babylonia, Peucestas arrived with 20,000 Persian bowmen that Alexander planned to integrate into his phalanx for the Arabian campaign. Macedonians armed with sarissas would form the first three ranks of a phalanx file, Persians armed with missile weapons the next twelve, and a Macedonian file closed the last rank. This new phalanx was intended to combine shock with missile fire support and was thought by Alexander to be more effective for fighting the more lightly equipped enemy missile troops he was now likely to encounter. The Macedonian troops, feeling that they had now been demeaned to the level of the "barbarian" Persians, mutinied at Opis. (For additional details on the Opis Mutiny, see Appendix C.)

In reaction, Alexander proceeded to recruit a wholly Persian army under Persian officers. Convinced that he was serious about reorganizing them out of the army, the Macedonians relented in their demands and begged his forgiveness. After a tearful reconciliation on both sides, Alexander mustered 10,000 Macedonians out of the army without further incident.[261] Alexander had become the king of Asia and had been distancing himself from the Macedonians for some time. They had observed this with distaste and bitterly resented their subsequent loss of privileged status. Alexander's intention was to eventually rule Asia with an Asian rather than a Macedonian army, a situation the Macedonian army clearly perceived at Opis. The sudden death of Alexander at Babylon, however, brought a sharp halt to his Orientalization policies. All the remaining Persians holding high military and political office were removed by Alexander's successor generals, who then proceeded to recruit heavily Greek armies whenever they could for their upcoming struggle for power. They clearly wanted no part of sharing power with a people that they so thoroughly despised.

Elephants Although Alexander had acquired 200 elephants in India, he never used them in battle, preferring, instead, to use them as pack animals or to commemorate ceremonial occasions.[262] He no doubt made this decision because elephants were slow, clumsy, difficult to control when angered, apt to be confused when the leader of the herd or their vulnerable mahout was killed, and easily frightened by mice, barking dogs and squealing pigs. As a result, although the elephants were terrifying in battle and could cause heavy casualties, Alexander probably concluded that their unstable temperament made them about as dangerous to friendly troops as to the enemy, and he saw little advantage in using them on the battlefield.

Engineers Although little has been written about Alexander's engineers, they performed some of the most spectacular construction feats in the ancient world. At Tyre, his engineers built, repaired, and maintained the 200-foot-wide, half-mile-long mole and erected the four largest siege towers of their day, each over 70 feet tall. They constructed, and perhaps also designed, the floating rams and amphibious assault ships used at Tyre. At the siege of the Rock of Aornos, Alexander's engineers built a suspension bridge between two ridges and later a boat bridge spanning the Indus River. These were only the spectacular things that Alexander's engineers built. There were also the day-to-day tasks which, although not as glamorous, were nevertheless as critical to Alexander success. The rebuilding of roads and the construction of ships, catapults and bridges allowed Alexander to overcome all natural and man-made obstacles standing between his army and its enemies and contributed significantly to many of his successes.

Catapults The use of catapults had previously been restricted to besieging enemy cities. Alexander was the second commander in history to use them tactically in a field battle.[263] In Illyria, he lined the catapults up hub-to-hub along the bank of a river outside of Pelium to lay down an effective missile barrage to cover his retreating troops. At the Jaxartes River, he used the catapults to clear the Scythians away from the far river bank in order to cover an amphibious landing against them.

When catapults were transported, only their essential parts were carried by pack mule. Any wooden pieces were usually cut and fitted by the engineers at the site of assembly. Although this dramatically increased the mobility of the siege train, it did mandate that a sizeable stand of usable timber be nearby the siege site for use in constructing the siege engines.

Reinforcements

Alexander received a large number of reinforcements during his campaigns in Asia. They are documented here by references from Arrian, Curtius and Diodorus. Multiple references to the same reinforcement are listed to enable the reader to see how the various ancient writers interpreted Alexander's orders.

Asia Minor At Halicarnassus, Ptolemy (son of Seleucus), Coenus (son of Polemocrates), and Meander (son of Neoptolemus) were sent to Macedonia to recruit cavalry and infantry. Cleander (son of Polemocrates) was also sent to the Peloponnese to hire mercenaries. (Arrian I:24)

At Halicarnassus, Alexander sent Coenus (son of Polemocrates) and Meleager (son of Neoptolemus) to Macedonia in command of all the recently married men. They were to return in the spring with any levies recruited there. (Curtius II)

At Gordium, Ptolemy (son of Seleucus), Meleager (son of Neoptolemus), and Coenus (son of Polemocrates) returned, bringing with them 400 Macedonian cavalry, 3,000 Macedonian infantry, 200 Thessalian cavalry and 150 Eleans. (Arrian I:29; Curtius III:1)

At Ancyra, an unspecified number of troops arrived from Macedonia. (Curtius III:1)

At Miletus, Alexander took the 300 Greek mercenaries into service who had taken refuge on a small island outside the city's harbor. (Arrian I:19)

At Miletus, Alexander took the Greek mercenaries into his service. (Curtius II)

At Pamphylia, Alexander sent Cleander to the Peloponnese to hire mercenaries. (Curtius III:1)

Aegean Islands At Tenedos, the 3,000 Greek mercenaries and oarsmen captured there were used to reinforce the Macedonian fleet. (Curtius IV:5)

Phoenicia At Sidon, Cleander (son of Polemocrates) returned from the Peloponnese with 4,000 Greek mercenaries. (Arrian II:20)

1: THE ARMIES 51

At Tyre, Cleander arrived with soldiers recently transported to Asia. (Curtius V:13)

At Gaza, Amyntas (son of Andromenes) was sent to Macedonia with 10 triremes to enlist soldiers. (Curtius IV:6; Diodorus XVII:49)

Egypt At Memphis, Menidas (son of Hegesandros) arrived with 400 Greek mercenaries and Asclepiodorus (son of Eunicus) with 500 Thracian cavalry. (Arrian III:5)

Babylonia On the road out from Babylon, Amyntas (son of Andromenes) arrived with a large force of 500 cavalry and 6,000 infantry from Macedonia, 600 cavalry and 3,500 infantry from the Peloponnese, a Greek mercenary force of 100 cavalry and 4,000 infantry, and 50 sons of the Macedonian nobility. (Diodorus XVII:65)

On the road out from Babylon, Amyntas (son of Andromenes) arrived with a large force of 500 cavalry and 3,500 infantry from Macedonia, 600 cavalry and 3,000 infantry from Thrace, 380 cavalry and 4,000 infantry mercenaries from the Peloponnese, and 50 sons of the Macedonian nobility. (Curtius V:1)

At Babylon, Amyntas (son of Andromenes) arrived with a force of cavalry and infantry from Macedonia. (Arrian III:16)

Susiana At Susa, Amyntas (son of Andromenes) arrived from Macedonia with a cavalry and infantry force of unrecorded strength. (Arrian III: 16)

Media At Media, Platon, an Athenian, arrived from Cilicia with a force of 1,000 cavalry and 5,000 infantry. (Curtius V:11)

At Ecbatana, Alexander mustered out the Thessalian cavalry and the remaining Greek allies. They were allowed to reenlist as mercenaries and many did so. (Arrian III:19)

Hyrcania At Hyrcania, 1,500 Greek mercenaries surrendered to Alexander. He recruited into his army only those who had been in Persian employ before the Greek alliance with Macedonia, established at the League of Corinth. (Arrian III:24)

Bactria At Bactria, Philip (son of Menelaus) arrived from Media with a force of mercenaries and some Thessalian volunteers under Andromachus. (Arrian III:25)

At Bactria, Nearchus arrived with a Greek mercenary force and Asclepiodorus (son of Hegesandros) with an army. (Arrian IV:7)

Sogdiana Ptolemy and Melanidas arrived from Greece with 1,000 Greek mercenary cavalry and 4,000 Greek mercenary infantry; Asander, from Lycia, with 500 cavalry and 4,000 infantry; Asclepiodorus, from Syria, with 500 cavalry and 4,000 infantry; and 600 cavalry and 7,400 infantry arrived from Antipater. (Curtius VII:10)

Alexander ordered 30,000 Persian youths to be trained as soldiers. (Curtius VIII:4)

Pharasmanes, the king of the Chorasinians, arrived with 1,500 cavalry. (Arrian IV:15)

Sopolis and Epocillus were sent to Macedonia to bring back troops. (Arrian IV:18)

Bajaur   At Nautaca, Sopolis, Epocillus, and Menidas were sent to Macedonia to bring back an army. (Arrian IV:18)

At Nysa, 300 local cavalry were recruited as hostages. (Arrian V:1)

At Massaga, Alexander recruited the surviving Indian mercenaries, who submitted to him. When they attempted to desert and return home, however, he massacred them. (Arrian IV:27)

Swat   At Dyrta, Alexander took into his service 25,000 Indian troops and 15 elephants previously in service with Aphrices. He then proceeded to round up other elephants wandering around the countryside. (Diodorus XVII:86)

Near Dyrta, along the Indus River, Alexander rounded up a number of elephants pasturing there. (Arrian IV:30)

Areia   At Artacana, 500 Greeks arrived with Zoilus, 3,000 Illyrians arrived from Antipater, 130 Thessalian cavalry from Philip, and a force of 300 cavalry and 2,600 foreign infantry from Lydia. (Curtius VI:6)

Arachosia   Parmenio arrived with 6,000 Macedonians, 5,000 Greeks, 600 cavalry, and 200 nobles. (Curtius VII:3)

Alexander ordered the natives to furnish him with 2,500 cavalry. (Curtius IX:7)

Upper Punjab   At the Indus River, Taxiles sent 30 elephants on ahead as a gift to Alexander. He then arrived himself, accompanied by 700 Indian cavalry who took service with Alexander. (Arrian V:3)

Taxiles provided Alexander with 30 elephants and 700 cavalry. (Arrian V:3)

At the Indus River, Alexander rounded up elephants that Abisares had left behind to pasture. (Arrian IV:30)

At the Indus River, Taxiles sent Alexander 25 elephants. (Arrian IV:22)

At Taxila, Taxiles and the governor of the district arrived with 5,000 Indians. (Arrian V:8)

At Taxila, Omphis (Taxiles) presented Alexander with 56 elephants. (Curtius VIII:12)

At Glausae, Phrataphernes, satrap of Parthyaea and Hyrcania, arrived with the Thracians Alexander had left behind with him. (Arrian V:20)

Alexander received 40 elephants from Abisares as a gift. (Arrian V:20)

At the Acesines River, Porus was sent back to his kingdom to recruit the most warlike Indians and any elephants there. (Arrian V:21)

At Sangala, Porus arrived with 5,000 Indians and a number of elephants. (Arrian V:24)

At the Beas River, Memnon arrived from Thrace with 5,000 cavalry. A force of 7,000 infantry and 25,000 suits of armor also arrived from Harpalus. (Curtius IX:3)

Upon Alexander's return from the Beas River, he was met by a force of 6,000 Greek cavalry and 30,000 Greek allied infantry under their own commanders. They brought with them 25,000 suits of armor for Alexander's infantry. (Diodorus XVII:95)

At the Acesines River, Arsaces, a governor of a territory next to Abisares, presented Alexander with 30 elephants. (Arrian V:29)

Lower Punjab   The Malli and Oxydracae were ordered by Alexander to provide him with 2,500 cavalry. (Curtius IX:7)

1: THE ARMIES

A force of 1,000 Oxydracae were enrolled in Alexander's army as hostages. Although not requested to do so, the Oxydracae also provided Alexander 500 chariots. Alexander soon returned the hostages but, interestingly enough, kept the chariots. (Arrian VI:14)

Alexander was presented with 2,800 Indian cavalry and 1,030 chariots. (Curtius IX:8)

Indian envoys presented Alexander 300 cavalry and 1,030 chariots. (Curtius IX:7)

Carmania Cleander and Sitalces arrived with a combined force of 1,000 cavalry and 5,000 infantry. (Curtius X:1)

Babylonia At Opis, Alexander requested Antipater to send from Macedonia drafts equal in number to the 10,000 Macedonian infantry dismissed from service. (Arrian VII:12)

At Babylon, Peucestas arrived with 20,000 Persian bowmen and slingers and forces from Cossaea and Tapuria, Philoxenus arrived with an army from Caria, Meander arrived with forces from Lydia, and Menidas arrived with a cavalry force. (Arrian VII: 23; Diodorus XVII: 110)

At Babylon, Peucestas arrived with 20,000 archers and slingers. (Curtius X:4; Diodorus XVII:110)

In 324 B.C., Alexander ordered Antipater to recruit additional Macedonian troops for service in Asia and to accompany them to Babylon. Neither Antipater nor the reinforcements ever arrived. (Arrian VII:12)

Demobilizations

Alexander demobilized troops on several occasions throughout his reign. He also assigned numerous permanent garrisons at various strategic locations throughout his newly won empire. The Athenian mercenaries Alexander had captured at Granicus River were the first to be released. Alexander's so-called Greek allies had been coerced into providing troops for his campaigns in Persia, allegedly to free the subject Greeks there and to exact revenge for the earlier Persian desecrations to the temples of Greece. With the death of Darius, Alexander's justification for his Persian campaign had been fulfilled and he released all the Greek allies. A large number of them, however, chose to reenlist in his army as mercenaries. Macedonians unfit for further duty were the next to be demobilized. They were followed by the veteran Macedonians who stood in opposition to Alexander's Orientalization policies.

Assignment of garrison troops occurred throughout Alexander's reign. In the west, the garrisons included a percentage of Macedonian troops, but in the east they consisted almost exclusively of mercenary troops. The demobilizations are documented by references from Arrian, Curtius and Diodorus. Multiple references to the same demobilization are listed to enable the reader to see how the various ancient writers interpreted Alexander's orders.

Asia Minor At Gordium, an embassy from Athens requested that Alexander release the 2,000 Athenians captured at Granicus River and those held under arrest in Macedonia. Although Alexander denied the release, fearing that to grant it might increase the ability of the Greeks to take action against him, he told the ambassadors to renew their request at a later date, when circumstances were more favorable for it. (Arrian I:29)

Alexander instructed the Athenian embassy to approach him again on the subject of returning their troops, when the situation might be more promising. (Curtius III:1)

Phoenicia When Alexander returned to Tyre from Egypt, he released all the Athenian captives taken at the Granicus River. (Arrian III: 6)

Egypt At Memphis, Alexander granted the Athenian request for the return of all Greek prisoners. (Curtius IV:8)

Media At Ecbatana, Alexander dismissed his Thessalian cavalry and the rest of his Greek allies. (Arrian III:19)

At Ecbatana, Alexander dismissed the Greek allies. (Diodorus XVII:74)

Hyrcania Of the 1,500 Greek mercenaries who had surrendered to him, Alexander demobilized those who had been in Persian employ after the Greek alliance with Macedonia established at the League of Corinth. (Arrian III:24)

Bajaur At Argaeum, Alexander demobilized any of the army who were past fighting to provide a garrison for the city. (Arrian IV:23)

Bactria Before crossing the Oxus River into Sogdiana, Alexander dismissed the elder Macedonians who were no longer fit for service, as well as the Thessalian volunteers. (Arrian III:29; Curtius VII:5)

Sogdiana At Alexandria-Eschate, Alexander mustered out the Greek mercenaries unfit for further service. (Arrian III:24)

The Punjab At Taxila, Alexander left behind a garrison consisting of invalid soldiers. (Arrian V:8)

At Sopithes' kingdom, Alexander dismissed 300 cavalry who had been recruited at the city of Nysa. (Arrian VI:2)

At the junction of the Acesines and Indus rivers, Alexander left the Thracians and other troops in garrison with Philip. (Arrian VI:15)

At Taxila, Alexander left behind invalid soldiers as a garrison. (Arrian V:8)

At the Acesines River, Alexander garrisoned the city that Hephaestion had been instructed to fortify with mercenaries unfit for further service with his army. (Arrian V:29)

At Sangala, Porus was ordered by Alexander to garrison the cities recently captured with the 5,000 Indian troops he had recently brought with him. (Arrian V:24)

At Mallus, Alexander dismissed the 1,000 Oxydracae hostages he had demanded of the tribe. (Arrian VI:14)

At the kingdom of Sopithes, the 300 cavalry recruited from Nysa were demobilized. (Arrian VI:2)

Babylonia At Opis, Alexander demobilized 10,000 Macedonian infantrymen unfit for service because of old age or disability. (Arrian VII:12; Curtius X:4)

1: THE ARMIES   55

Persia

Leadership

Although the Great King was the command control focus of a Persian army, this function was never completely or effectively exercised by Darius III. He tended to make incredibly bad tactical military decisions or proved indecisive at making them at all. As a result, the Persian army was never well coordinated and was usually unable to take full advantage of its large numbers. Darius was indecisive in his actions. The Greeks despised this approach as indicating cowardice and an inability to take the initiative. Strategically, Darius was uneven, demonstrating both competence and incompetence at virtually the same time. Having an army consisting largely of cavalry, which was most effective on the attack, and superior numbers, which allowed him to turn either or both of the Macedonian flanks, Darius was well positioned to impose his strategy on Alexander. He chose instead to assume a passive defense, no doubt thinking that the advantages of choice of battlefield, a larger army, and a defensive posture would give him the highest probability of winning any encounters against the smaller Macedonian army. This turned out to be about the worst strategy he could have pursued because it surrendered the initiative to Alexander, who was then free to develop his own plan without interference. Unfortunately for Darius, Alexander's brilliance in devising both strategic and tactical plans and his army's unfailing ability to carry them out always proved fatal to the Great King.

Despite the demonstrated effectiveness of the Greeks at Cunaxa and as mercenaries in Persian employ, Darius seriously underestimated the threat that Alexander posed. Instead of commanding the Persian army in the initial confrontation against Alexander, he delegated it to his none too competent civilian satraps in Asia Minor. The result was that the Persians chose an infantry battlefield unsuited for their largely cavalry army and fought an ill-advised and disjointed battle, virtually handing Alexander a victory he badly needed. At Issus, Darius threw away the strategic advantage in movement he had achieved against Alexander by selecting a battlefield much too small for his large army. The result was that the Persian cavalry was jammed into such a constricted frontage that its superior numbers were largely negated and their fighting effectiveness seriously compromised by the lack of maneuvering room.

At Gaugamela, Darius again threw away his strategic advantage of an open battlefield by assuming a passive defense. This allowed Alexander to approach his position in the most advantageous manner and fight the overwhelming numbers of the Persian cavalry on Bessus' wing to a standstill with only a portion of his cavalry. When Alexander's center was pierced, the Persian cavalry proceeded under Darius' orders to execute the political objective of attempting to rescue his family from captivity instead of pursuing a military objective of rolling up the exposed flanks of the phalanx. When Bessus created a gap in his line, Alexander charged into it with his yet unengaged Companions and won the battle. Again, as at Issus, Darius had a disturbing propensity to take to his heels during the battle whenever he was personally threatened with harm. This was hardly the way to inspire his army. Because Darius was unwilling to give much independent authority to his generals, for fear that they might use it to revolt against him, they tended to exercise little, if any, military initiative on the battlefield.[264] As they only proceeded under Darius' direct orders, the Persian commanders allowed disasters to unfold and simply ignored opportunities because they were unwilling to put their lives in jeopardy by exceeding their authority. This rigidity in Persian leadership contributed in no small measure to the poor showing of the Persian army in the two battles that Darius personally fought against Alexander.

Mobility

The enormous Persian baggage train was in large part responsible for the slow march rate of their army, which typically averaged about 6.5 miles a day, roughly half the speed of Alexander's army. On Darius' campaigns his baggage train usually contained his entire family, who were comfortably transported in 15 wagons, 300–400 ladies of the court, 30,000 camp followers, a portion of the royal treasure, and all the royal trappings of comfort, including a solid gold bathtub.[265] The baggage train also carried enough grain to supply the large Persian army for several months. The enormity of the train can be gauged by the estimated 7,000 pack animals it was said to require, all of which also had to be fed.[266] A supply and equipment wagon was frequently allocated to every 30 soldiers, which meant that a Persian army of 100,000 men might require over 3,000 wagons.[267] Rivers were generally not bridged, except occasionally by boats, and roads were primitive dirt tracks that became mud sinkholes at the first rain. Baggage train wagons would frequently get stuck in soft sand and mud, halting the entire marching column while soldiers attempted to extract them. It is little wonder that the Persian baggage train moved so slowly.

Strategy and Tactics

The Persian army usually formed a long line in an attempt to outflank its opponents. The chariots were placed in the first rank, the infantry deployed behind them in the center, and the cavalry on the wings. Units were drawn up by the various nationalities in dense squares. The bravest troops were placed at the front of the formation, inferior troops stacked in succeeding ranks. Formations were necessarily deep in order to provide stability through mass to the large number of unstable troops. All Persian frontline strength was deployed along the combat line, with none being held in reserve. Persian success on the battlefield frequently depended on sheer numbers either to wear their opponents down or to encircle them on one or both wings.

The chariots would usually open the battle by a charge against the enemy line to throw it into disorder. After this, the main infantry line would advance to the attack but not to engage the enemy immediately. Upon reaching effective missile range, the infantry troops would push their shields into the ground and from their protection begin a missile barrage against the opposing line. At some point, the enemy would close with the Persians to escape the unremitting missile fire and attempt to decide the issue by hand-to-hand combat. Against the untrained mobs fielded by internal rebels, the heavy missile fire usually proved successful. Either the low morale of the rebels broke before contact was ever made or they were simply overwhelmed by the sheer volume of fire. If the Persian attack was being conducted by the cavalry, wave after wave of cavalrymen would be dispatched in an attempt to overwhelm their opponents by sheer numbers or exhaust their ability to resist effectively. The deep Persian formations were usually too unwieldy to control properly, and because of their lack of homogeneity and discipline, they were subject to sudden panic at any unexpected turn of events. If the Persian line was broken, the battle was usually regarded as lost and the army fled the field, frequently led by its commander. Once routed, the Persian army's lack of discipline would largely preclude any attempt at rallying.

In a field battle against the heavy infantry of the Greeks, the crude force the Persians fielded was almost incapable of winning a stand-up fight against them. The heavy armor protection and the Greek tendency to close rapidly to combat greatly reduced the effectiveness of the Persian missile fire. This was undoubtedly why by Alexander's time the Persians largely abandoned this tactic in preference to the reliance on the shock combat value of the hired Greek mercenaries. Since Darius neglected, however, to hire enough of the mercenaries and made poor use of those that he had on the battlefield, their potential decisiveness was never achieved.

The Persian army usually began marching after sunrise, taking a midday halt during the heat.[268] They seldom marched at night. A march of 25 miles a day — which must, obviously, have been made without the inhibiting presence of the baggage train — was strenuous and would necessitate a rest for as long as three days. With the approach of evening, the Persians looked for a campsite on an open plain near water. They disliked camping near an enemy and preferred a distance of seven to eight miles from their opponents as a buffer against a surprise attack. As the heavy cavalry hobbled their horses at night to prevent them from wandering off or being led away by the enemy, the Persian offensive arm was virtually defenseless in the event of an unexpected enemy attack during darkness.

Combat Strength

With few exceptions, the writers of antiquity attributed incredible numbers to the Persian army, at times in excess of one million. Propaganda purposes were obviously behind most of the wild overestimates, for it pleased the Greeks to think that their army was able to defeat several times their number. The reality was, however, that the Persian army was always considerably smaller than ancient historians have indicated, and during Alexander's time it was unlikely to have ever exceeded 90,000 in strength. Nevertheless, the Persians significantly outnumbered the Macedonians in the two battles Darius himself fought against Alexander; by almost four to one at Issus and about two to one at Gaugamela.

Because of the huge territory and large population of the Persian Empire, compared to Greece, most ancient writers assumed that Persia could raise and field enormous armies. The fact of the matter was that the combined city-states of Greece could theoretically field a far larger military force than the Persians.[269] This was because the Persian army was not composed of the citizenry at large but of the small core of the nobility. Consequently, the overwhelming mass of Persian subjects were not part of the empire's military force pool. In this regard, Persia's army was very similar to the feudal armies of the Middle Ages, being comprised of a small select force. In times of national emergency, however, infantry could be levied from among the empire's peasants. Unfortunately, the force raised was almost totally ineffective militarily, being untrained, poorly armed, low in morale and reluctant to fight. In Greece, however, the entire male population was highly trained and superbly equipped for war, and men considered its pursuit to be an important part of their civic duty. As a result, while the Persian Empire drew its effective soldiery from the aristocracy at the tip of their manpower pyramid, the Greeks drew theirs from the citizenry at the base of theirs. Thus the size of the effective military contingents of both armies was actually much closer than the size of their respective populations would indicate.

In numerical terms, the Persians could mobilize 40,000–50,000 cavalry at any one time, recruited largely from central Persia and the northwest frontier.[270] Except for a select group of 2,000 aristocrats who formed the king's bodyguard, there was really no effective Persian infantry.[271] Although the infantry levies may have numbered as many as 60,000 at any one time, they were an insignificant military asset, always deployed well to the rear on any battlefield. Ironically, the mainstay infantry troops in the Persian army were the Greek mercenaries, approximately 20,000 being in Persian employ when Alexander crossed into Asia Minor. Because they were committed by Darius piecemeal, however, only a fraction of these were present on a battlefield at any one time.

The maximum force the Persians put in the field usually tended to be lower than their full mobilization because the raising of the forces for the army was largely left in the hands of the local satraps, who, for reasons of self-interest, neither mobilized their full levy nor arrived with any punctuality. The Persian king never knew ahead of time exactly how many troops would be mobilized by his decree or exactly when they would be available. When the Persian army finally did assemble, it would be composed of numerous tribes, each speaking different languages and armed according to local custom.[272] The troops had probably never operated together before, and their leaders were more used to giving orders then taking them. The commanding satraps were usually civilian administrators whose lack of military skill and delusions about their own military abilities would at times imperil the army by their rash actions. With such a force, the Persians stood little chance of defeating the battle-hardened Macedonian army.

Order of Battle

The Persian army was normally organized on the basis of 10.[273] Each division of 10,000 men was divided into 10 battalions of 1,000 men each, each battalion into 10 companies of 100 men each, and each company into 10 platoons of 10 men each.²⁷⁴ With the large number of low morale troops in the Persian ranks, however, formations at times tended to be considerably denser in order to strengthen their generally loose cohesion. The Persian choice of narrow battlefields at Gaugamela and Issus also made it necessary to deploy units of their army in much deeper formations.

Royal Guards The Royal Guards consisted of two 1,000-strong units: a cavalry unit known as the royal kinsmen, recruited from the Great King's relatives, and an infantry unit known as the "Apple Bearers," for their apple-shaped spearbutts.²⁷⁵ Although these were elite units recruited exclusively from the Persian nobility, they were clearly inferior to the Companions, being unable to protect Darius against their advance both at Issus and Gaugamela. The Royal Guards were armed with a spear, bow and a shield.²⁷⁶

Heavy Cavalry Unlike classical Greece, whose military development was centered around the heavy infantry hoplite, in Persia the heavy cavalry became the elite striking arm. The huge horses raised on the Nisaean Plain made their close-order charges almost irresistible, while the heavy defensive armor of both man and horse made them almost invulnerable. The aristocracy provided a large pool of manpower trained from youth to fight on horseback. The heavy cavalry force that the Persians were able to mobilize was at least four to five times the force that Alexander was ever able to field. For all its numbers, however, the Persian heavy cavalry was never really an effective force against the Greeks. The arm was not particularly well led on either the strategic or tactical level, was haphazardly trained, and was equipped for the most part with inferior weaponry. Despite the bravery of the Persian heavy cavalry troops, they were unable to stand up to their Thessalian or Companion counterparts in a field battle, no matter how favorable their tactical situation or how heavily they outnumbered them.

There were several reasons for the relative ineffectiveness of the Persian cavalry troops. They had acquired their reputation in Asia largely as a result of successes against revolting satrapal cavalry and infantry levies. These victories were not won on the basis of any particular military skill but usually resulted from the larger Persian horses and the low morale of the untrained satrapal infantry. Soldiers of the Great King's cavalry used the greater size and strength of their horses to overpower those of their opponents or simply overwhelmed them by sheer numbers. These tactics usually prevailed against internal disorders in their empire, where their opponent was apt to be an undisciplined scratch force likely to waver and break before contact was ever made. In such a situation, the only skill necessary for the soldiers of the Persian cavalry was to keep from falling off their horses during the charge. Against the Companions, however, with their superior morale and close-in fighting skills, these crude tactics proved to be largely ineffective. Instead of breaking on the initial charge, the Companions rapidly closed and began conducting a combat of maneuver and close-in fighting that the heavily encumbered Persians were unable to deal with effectively. The weight of armor on the Persian horse all but precluded maneuverability, while its weight on the rider adversely affected his range of vision and ability to wield his weapons effectively. The result was that although the Persian cavalry could inflict heavy casualties on the Companions in its initial charge, when the fighting became hand-to-hand, the Companions and Thessalians soon predominated, regardless of how heavily they were outnumbered. At Granicus River and Issus, the Persian army had clearly chosen unsuitable battlefields. At Gaugamela, however, Darius finally had a large plain and overwhelming numbers of cavalry. The initial Persian cavalry charges wreaked great havoc on Greek allied and mercenary cavalry units, which were unable to withstand their assault. When the engagement then became hand-to-hand, however, the Lancers and Thessalians were able to fight the Persian cavalry to a stand-still, despite the disparity in numbers.

In studying the various battles that the Persian cavalry fought with Alexander, it is clear that poor strategic leadership also seriously hindered its combat effectiveness. At Granicus River, the Persians forced their cavalry to hold a defensive position behind a stream with steep, muddy banks. This not only precluded the use of their one effective weapon, the cavalry charge, but relegated them to a static defense in which they could easily be thrown into disorder. At Issus, an incredibly faulty deployment not only largely precluded the use of the Persian cavalry's superior numbers but greatly hampered them in the effective use of their weapons. In both battles, the Persians allowed the Macedonians to wage the kind of cavalry battle they were most skilled at and the Persians were least skilled at — hand-to-hand combat.

Persian cavalry troops were extremely susceptible to night attack because of their practice of hobbling their horses at sunset, a practice resulting from the shortage of effective infantry that could establish a secure defense perimeter around the cavalry. If the Persian army could not encamp several miles away from its enemy at night, as was the case at Gaugamela, all its soldiers were ordered to remain under arms all night on guard against a surprise attack.

The Persian heavy cavalry troops carried two five- to six-foot-long javelins and a sword.[277] Against opposing enemy cavalry, one javelin was usually thrown during the advance, while the other was retained for thrusting in the ensuing hand-to-hand combat.[278] Against enemy infantry, both javelins would be thrown and the sword used for any close combat.[279] In an attempt to counteract the Macedonian lance, which had been used with such noticeable effect at the battle of Issus, Darius reequipped his Guard Cavalry with long spears just prior to the battle of Gaugamela. A lack of time, apparently, precluded any more of his cavalry from being similarly equipped.[280]

Persian heavy cavalrymen were fully armored, wearing helmets, chain mail coats and greaves. Because of the protection afforded by the armor, shields were not normally carried. The heads of the heavy cavalry horses were protected by a frontlet and their neck and chest by a breastpiece. The sides and flanks of the horse had individual coverings, and a cuirass protected the thighs. The weight sustained by the horse was considerable, making its movements both slow and deliberate.

1: THE ARMIES

Light Cavalry The Persian light cavalry was widely known for its maneuverability. It operated in a loose formation that hung on the flanks and rear of an enemy column in large numbers and endlessly repeated the cycle of attacking, withdrawing and rallying. Even when retiring, Persian light cavalry was formidable because the soldiers continued firing their arrows over the rear of their horses at any pursuing enemy.[281] In Alexander's time, however, it seems that most Persian light cavalry units had discarded the bow in favor of the javelin to enable them to engage the Greeks in hand-to-hand combat.

Greek Mercenaries The only effective heavy infantry the Persians had at their disposal was the 20,000 or so Greek mercenaries in their employ.[282] In morale, training and leadership, the mercenaries were the equal of the Macedonian phalanx. Only in weaponry and formation were they inferior, but then only in a field battle on open ground. Behind an obstacle like a bluff or a river, the mercenaries were at little, if any, disadvantage in fighting a phalanx whose ranks were certain to be disordered by crossing the obstacle. In siege operations, where the phalanx had to forgo their usual weaponry and close-order formation, the Greek mercenaries were every bit their equal.

The Greek mercenaries were preferred by Darius because as foreign troops they were not likely to revolt against a paymaster who had almost unlimited funds at his disposal. Darius also greatly appreciated their combat effectiveness, the mercenaries being largely responsible for his victories over rebel satraps and for his recent conquest of Egypt. They stood up well to the Macedonians but unfortunately were used piecemeal by Darius and were often poorly supported on their flanks. The Greek mercenaries always gave Alexander a hard fight, however, and he sustained his highest casualties whenever he engaged them.

Initially, the Persians used their entire force of 20,000 Greek mercenaries as marines aboard their fleet. Although 5,000 of them were recalled to serve with the satrapal army in Asia Minor upon Alexander's appearance there, they were deliberately held out of the battle at the Granicus River by the commanding satraps. Prior to the battle of Issus, the remaining mercenaries serving with the fleet were called into service with the field army and 12,000 of them were available for the battle. After the Persian defeat, however, most of the surviving mercenaries in Persian employ departed for Crete, Asia Minor and Egypt. Alexander's advance through Asia Minor and Phoenicia had cut the Great King off from the mercenary recruiting areas in Greece, and by the time of Gaugamela, Darius would only have 2,000 Greek mercenaries left to serve him, a relatively insignificant force in an army of 75,000.

Cardaces The Cardaces were Persian youths of noble birth who were given special physical training.[283] They usually accompanied the king on the hunt or were used as a police force. At the age of 20, the Cardaces received training as either cavalrymen or archers.[284] They were armed with two five- to six-foot-long javelins, a four-foot-long bow and a battle-axe.[285] As protection, they usually carried a wicker shield. Some, however, chose to carry a heavier hoplite shield, doubtless leading to the misconception that the Cardaces were heavy infantry.[286] The Cardaces wore a simple padded jerkin which gave them no protection.

The Cardaces were originally thought to have been organized by Darius in an attempt to develop a Persian heavy infantry force to support the flanks of the Greek mercenaries.[287] The Cardaces appear to have been more of a peltast force, however, being lightly armed and armored. So desperate was Darius for trained infantry that he put the Cardaces into his front line at Issus in support of the outer flanks of the Greek mercenaries. Their poor showing there was such a disappointment to him that he did not use them in combat again.

Levy Infantry The Persians had never developed a native heavy infantry force. Their land-owning aristocracy, which constituted the bulk of the empire's trained forces, formed the cavalry arm. There, individual prowess could be demonstrated and wealth openly displayed in the richness of the various accoutrements of the horse. The peasant class, which typically comprised the heavy infantry, did not form a standing military force in Persia as it had in Greece. This was because the Persian leaders feared that if they trained, armed and organized the peasants, they would be more likely to revolt and would stand a better chance of success if they did so. Therefore they were kept untrained and unarmed, being only called up in times of national emergencies. The attitude of the Persian aristocracy was that it was better to be safe than sorry, and anyway there were always tens of thousands of highly effective nonpolitical Greek mercenaries for hire by a Persian king who had almost unlimited funds with which to pay their wages. The levy infantry was typically comprised of serfs with little discipline, inferior armament and low morale. Being conscripted frequently under duress, they had little interest in risking their lives in any fighting.

As with its cavalry, the army's levies were probably reasonably effective when fighting other levies within the Persian Empire. In that case, it was usually a battle between two largely untrained and unskilled mobs ineffectually flailing away at each other. The forces of the Great King would prevail only because they were usually able to overwhelm their opponent by sheer weight of numbers. Against the phalanx or even the Greek mercenaries, the Persian levy infantry simply did not stand a chance. Darius clearly recognized their ineffectiveness by always deploying them well back of the front line in any battle with the Greeks, apparently using them only after the Macedonians were seriously disordered or in flight from the battlefield.

Soldiers in the Persian levy infantry typically wore a soft hat, a leather tunic with long sleeves, and leather trousers as protection for their legs. They carried a full-body wicker shield,[288] a short spear,[289] a stabbing sword,[290] a battle-axe, and a four-foot-long bow[291] slung over the shoulder. During the Macedonian era, however, it became common for the levy infantry to be armed only with a javelin because the bow had proved largely ineffectual against the heavily armed Greek hoplites.

In sieges and mountainous terrain, Persian infantry were somewhat more effective, although it appears that Alexander never had much trouble in regularly defeating them. The most difficult aspect of such an engagement was to overcome the difficulties of terrain in order to close physically with the Persians. Once this was done, the issue was rarely in doubt. Mountain tribes that had successfully defied the Persians for over 100 years were thoroughly defeated by Alexander in a matter of weeks. These undisciplined troops were usually lightly and poorly equipped and were extremely susceptible both to surprise and deception. When faced with an unexpected situation, their unstable temperament usually precipitated flight. More often than not they broke before ever becoming engaged.

Archers Persian archers were quite often mounted. Those archers who were afoot had little discipline and were usually combined with the slingers to give them some stability.[292] Foot-archers were used to screen cavalry deployments, outflank an enemy, or harass his line of march through rough terrain. When fighting Alexander, the Persians replaced their usual tactic of disordering their enemy by missile fire and a cavalry charge with a tactic that subordinated both archers and cavalry to the support of the Greek mercenaries.

Persian bows were of composite construction and were quite large. The arrows were light and long, allowing the Persians to draw their bowstrings to their ears, in comparison to the Greeks whose shorter arrows only allowed them to draw their bowstrings back to their chests.[293] Thus the Persian archers were usually able to outrange their Greek counterparts.[294]

Slingers The Persian slingers had only half the range of their Rhodian counterparts because they used fist-sized stones for ammunition.[295] The Rhodians used the smaller lead bullets that usually weighed about an ounce each.

Chariots The chariot was a shock weapon whose momentum was used to disorder a close-order infantry formation. The vehicles needed a level field and a long, straight run to work up to their maximum speed. Chariots were rarely used against enemy cavalry because the horses could easily maneuver out of the fixed path to which the charging vehicles were restricted. The scythed chariot used by the Persians had the additional terror of rotating scythes — razor-sharp blades mounted on the hubs. Anyone coming into contact with them would suffer horribly debilitating injuries that were frequently followed by an agonizing death.

For those who kept their nerve and discipline, chariots could be dealt with effectively. The vehicles were restricted to level ground that had to be carefully chosen and prepared. This was because rough ground could cause the driver to lose control of the horses or could subject the vehicle to high-speed damage. The final run of the chariot had to be delivered in a straight line at maximum speed. Once in motion the chariot was unable to deviate from its line of attack, regardless of what occurred in front or to the sides. Because of this rigidity and the length of the run required to work up the proper charge speed, it was relatively easy to determine accurately the point of impact of the vehicles and then to open a lane for them to pass harmlessly through.

Both horse and chariot driver were extremely vulnerable to concentrated missile attack.[296] A wounded horse or one not under the driver's control could frequently be turned back towards its own start line. Many times at the mere approach of the chariots, however, an enemy line of low morale infantry levies would dissolve before contact was ever made. At other times, the chariots would smash through the line, causing horrible mutilations that would not only severely shake the integrity of the formation they contacted but adversely affect the morale of any nearby troops witnessing the carnage the vehicles wrought. Against highly disciplined troops, however, the chariot was to have almost negligible value, because these troops opened lanes for the vehicles to pass through. As the chariots moved through the lanes, their crews would be attacked from the sides with spears, javelins, and even swords. Emerging in the rear of the enemy line, the chariot would be forced to slow down to allow the horses to catch their wind or to enable the vehicle to turn around. At that point, the chariot was extremely vulnerable to attack by the light infantry soldiers, who would either stab its crew or pull them off the vehicle from behind.

Darius' single use of chariots against Alexander was at the battle of Gaugamela. None of the 50 chariots directed against the Macedonian right flank were able to close with its line, virtually the entire force being eliminated by heavy missile fire on its approach. On Parmenio's left flank, many chariots were turned back to their own lines by loud noises. Those few that did reach his lines suffered heavy casualties from the troops stationed alongside the lanes through which they passed. Upon slowing down, the survivors were largely overcome by light infantry. Despite the fact that both Persian chariot horses and drivers were heavily armored, Alexander's missile fire appears to have been highly effective against them.

Scythed chariots were pulled by four armored horses and were usually manned by a driver, a warrior armed with a bow, and an attendant.[297] The driver wore a cuirass above the waist, arm-pieces and a helmet. He relied on the chariot itself to protect his lower body.[298] The chariots at Gaugamela had 27-inch blades at the end of the yoke and broader curved blades on the axle ends that turned with the vehicle's wheels.[299]

Elephants Although Darius reputedly had 15 elephants with him at Gaugamela, they were not used in the battle, probably because the Persian cavalry troops were not trained to operate with them.[300] After the battle, the elephants were captured with the baggage train. In no other encounter with Alexander did the Persians use elephants.

Camels Camels affected horses in much the same way as elephants did; at the smell and sound of them horses became frightened and unmanageable. Although the Persians had used camels to disorder cavalry of their opponents in the past, there is no evidence that they ever used them on the battlefield against Alexander.[301]

Engineers The Persians do not seem to have had a specialized corps of trained engineers similar to that of the Macedonian army. Any engineering work was usually assigned to army troops who were in general directed by one or two professionals trained in engineering.

Phocia

The Phocian army was relatively small, the state only being able to field a citizen force of 500 cavalry and 3,000 hoplites.[302] Shortly after the Phocians captured the oracle of Delphi in 355 B.C., however, they began appropriating the enormous funds stored there and were able to raise a large force of Greek mercenaries. Later during the war, after offering double the normal wage, the Phocians were able to field a force of about 17,000 mercenaries at any one time.

During the Third Sacred War, the Phocians campaigned with varying success until they were badly defeated by Philip of Macedonia at Crocus Field in Thessaly. In 352 B.C., the Delphi treasury became exhausted from the cost of maintaining the huge Phocian mercenary force, and Phayllus, their commander, treacherously betrayed the state to Philip in return for safe passage of himself and 8,000 mercenaries to the Peloponnese.[303] What remained of the Phocian army after his departure was dissolved, and the state was occupied by Philip and the forces of the Amphictyonic Council. All weapons of the Phocians were destroyed, and they were prohibited the ownership of horses until the 10,000 talents that they had taken from the Delphi treasury were repaid.[304]

The Phocian army appears to have been no different than the typical Greek hoplite army of the time, and Phocian soldiers would have been armed in that fashion. The Greek mercenary force would have also been armed in a similar manner. The mainstay of the Phocian army consisted for the most part of hoplites, with only small numbers of lightly armed infantry or cavalry being in evidence.

Scythia

The Scythians were a number of nomadic tribes extending across the northern border of the Persian Empire and Thrace. They led Spartan lives and fought continuously. The barbaric nature of the Scythian warrior was such that he would drink the blood of the first person that he killed and sever the heads of all those that he had slain as a demonstration of his prowess to his king.[305] He would make a drinking cup out of the skulls of his victims and use the skin of their corpses for a towel or as a decoration for his horse. Although the Scythians fought with barbaric savagery, they were extremely sensitive to any slur against their "so-called" honor. Body tattooing for a Scythian was considered a distinction of high birth and the lack of it an indication of inferiority.[306]

Although the Scythian army was widely known throughout the ancient world for its mercenary horse archers, it was able to field a sizeable infantry force.[307] In 310 B.C., one Scythian army was said to consist of 10,000 cavalry and over 20,000 infantry.[308] While Alexander was in Hyrcania, a force of 100 so-called Amazons were brought before him, apparently desiring to serve in his army. They appear to have been Scythian women trained from youth to fight on horseback with the bow, axe and javelin, similar to the legendary Amazons. Alexander politely dismissed them, fearing that they would eventually come to harm at the hands of his soldiers. The legend persisted, however, that he had been paid a visit by the Amazons.

The usual Scythian noble cavalry formation was a wedge, which was designed to penetrate an enemy line on a deep but narrow front. The light cavalry used skirmishing tactics, firing bows at a stationary or retreating enemy, then falling back when charged, all the while firing over the rear of their horses. In delivering their offensive missile fire, the Scythians typically split a unit into two forces, each circling in the opposite directions across an enemy front and continually firing arrows. If the circling formation was penetrated, however, its normal circling movement would be interrupted and the resulting confusion would throw the formation into disorder.

The main weapon of the Scythians was a short composite bow. The light arrows used had the advantage of a high rate of fire, but at the sacrifice of range.[309] This was somewhat offset, however, by the use of a longer arrow that allowed the bowstring to be drawn to the ear or even the right shoulder.[310] The Scythian bow thus had an effective range of about 160 yards and a maximum range of about 380 yards.[311] The proficiency of the Scythians with the bow was such that they were able to achieve remarkable accuracy with it no matter which hand they fired it with.[312] Arrows were frequently poisoned with snake venom.[313] Within an hour of being struck by a Scythian arrow, a victim would usually go into shock and respiratory arrest. If he survived this, gangrene would set in after a day. Quivers held up to 200 of the smaller arrows.[314] Usually a spear, javelin and axe were also carried.[315] Shields were small and were made of hide or wicker and strengthened by an iron hoop that was sometimes covered with iron plate.[316] The nobles wore scale armor, while the body of the typical warrior was protected by leather.[317]

Darius' Invasion In 513 B.C., Darius began a campaign against the Scythians. He advanced deep into the Scythian territory but was unable to engage them in battle. The Scythians pursued a scorched-earth strategy, managing to keep just out of contact with Darius' army. Darius was finally forced to concede defeat and withdraw from their territory, losing most of his army in the process.

Philip's Invasion In 339 B.C., upon the Scythian refusal to provide him with economic support in his siege against Byzantium, Philip invaded their territory on a pretext of being denied the right of placing a statue of Heracles at the mouth of the Danube River. The Scythians were brought to battle on the plain of Dobrudja in southeast Rumania and defeated, the Scythian king being one of the casualties. The tribe was forced to surrender 20,000 of its children and women to Philip and 20,000 of its mares.

Alexander's Invasion As Alexander was building walls around the city of Alexandria-Eschate, in Sogdiana, in 329 B.C., a large force of Scythian cavalry gathered opposite him on the northern side of the Jaxartes River, daring him to cross over and see what he could make of men like themselves. Alexander accepted the challenge, crossed over the river, broke into the Scythian cavalry circles, and disordered their formations. When Alexander's reserves exploited the resulting confusion, the Scythians fled from the battlefield. The Scythians were widely considered to be invincible at that time, and Alexander's victory over them convinced many that it was impossible for any one nation to defeat him.

Sparta

For nearly two centuries, the Spartan army dominated the battlefields of Greece. The reputation of the Spartan soldiers was such that their enemies were often afraid to face them in the field. The Spartan predominance, however, was dangerously flawed because it was based solely on courage and discipline to the exclusion of innovation, experimentation and adaptability. Consequently, when faced by new tactics, the Spartans were unable to adapt to them and were twice defeated by a Theban army under Epaminondas: once at Leuctra, in 371 B.C., and again at Second Mantineia, in 362 B.C. As a result of those defeats, Sparta lost its historic domination over the Peloponnese. The crippling casualties Sparta sustained in its defeat by Antipater at Megalopolis in 330 B.C. forced it to assume the status of a second-class power, thus ending its ability to again play any significant role in Greek affairs during the Macedonian era.

Unlike any other state of Greece, Sparta was geared solely for war. Serfs farmed the land and supported a warrior class that did nothing but engage in military operations. When not actually fighting, the Spartans trained unceasingly in weapons drill and tactics. Sparta was the only state before Philip's rise in Macedonia to maintain a standing army all year round. The state's sole reason for existence was to train unbeatable soldiers.

The Spartan elders determined at birth which babies were to live and which were to die. Deformed, unhealthy, abnormally small, or female babies were frequently abandoned to die in a chasm at the foot of Mt. Taygetos.[318] This brutal screening process was intended to maintain the integrity of a population intolerant of the slightest weakness. Spartan training began as early as age seven. At that time, the male child was taken from his mother and assigned to a group of his peers with whom he would live in barracks for the next six years. Obedience, discipline, conformity and courage were beaten into the youth by a brutal education system. Bravery was considered the greatest ideal and cowardice the ultimate disgrace. He was toughened by physical hardships, constant exercises, and outdoor activities in all weather. Fighting among the boys was encouraged, but not to the point of serious injury. The quantity of food given to the youths was intentionally insufficient, and they were expected to resort to theft to make up the difference. If caught, they were punished for their failed attempt rather than for the act of stealing.

At the age of 19, the Spartan entered another class and became liable for military service. Although eligible for combat, he was not yet considered a full soldier.[319] At the age of 24, the Spartan became qualified to assume the responsibilities of a frontline soldier.[320] The most promising candidates were inducted into the field army, while the others, who were considered inferiors, formed a replacement pool. The Spartan was allowed at this point to grow his hair long for the first time, indicating that he had at last come into manhood.[321]

At the age of 30, the Spartan became a candidate for the Assembly.[322] This was the most critical juncture of the Spartans' life, for only as a citizen could he live a relatively normal life. Marriage could then be considered, as could the raising of a family. Any member of the Assembly could veto his application, however, and once that occurred there was no second chance. If unsuccessful in his candidacy, he could only look forward to a life of ostracism by a society totally committed to its rigid social conventions. If accepted, he could now leave the barracks and establish residency on the farm he had received from the state.[323]

Most Greek battles were set-piece in tactics, making them ideally suited to the highly disciplined method of Spartan training. The close-order hoplite formation, which formed the basis of every Greek city-state's army, could only be used on open ground that was relatively free of obstructions. Therefore, almost by mutual consent, such terrain would be selected for the battlefield. Because the Greeks had little cavalry, few missile troops, and disdained trickery, battles tended to be completely predictable, frontal, stand-up fights between opposing heavy infantry. The Spartans' superior training, exceptional physical endurance, higher morale, greater maneuverability, and professional leadership ensured that such a battle most often went in their favor. It is well to remember that most Greeks received little, if any, military training at this time, and their generals and officers, more often than not, tended to be politicians whose experience was in the assembly rather than on the battlefield. In such a static environment, it is not surprising that Spartan military supremacy went unchallenged for over two centuries.

One of the most critical military problems Sparta faced was the continuing decline in its military force pool. A Spartan hoplite was not allowed to engage in any labor, being supported solely by the farm allocated to his use and the helots made available to work it. Since the mountainous terrain in Laconia and Messenia contained only a small amount of arable land, new farms could only be created by conquering additional lands or forming them from already existing ones. In the latter case, any significant downsizing of farm size would reduce the tenants below a subsistence level. When Messenia achieved its independence, almost half the farmland that had supported its hoplites was removed from Spartan control. This, in conjunction with the rise of wealthy Spartans who had amassed large estates consisting of numerous individual farms, drastically reduced the number of hoplites able to meet the required property qualification for citizenship. The size of the Spartan army thus steadily fell, from 5,000 in 479 to 2,500 by 418 to 1,050 by 371.[324] And although Sparta was the preeminent military power of Greece during the Peloponnesian War, it dropped to a second-class power by Philip's reign and became a virtual nonentity after the battle of Megalopolis.

In order for Sparta to wage war beyond its borders, its small population mandated that it would have had to enlist the aid of mercenaries. They were expensive, however, and since Sparta was barely a subsistence state with a barter economy and no coinage of its own, it was unable to generate any significant revenues for the purpose.[325] Sparta was thus forced to hire its army out for revenue, which it frequently did in Italy and the Persian Empire, or to go helmet-in-hand to beg a stipend from the Persian king.[326] During Alexander's reign, the Spartans were able to accumulate enough income from campaigning in Italy to employ a mercenary army for the conquest of Crete and to support the Spartan army at the battle of Megalopolis.

Cavalry The mountainous terrain of the Peloponnese and the narrow valleys there made the use of cavalry largely impracticable.[327] The Spartan cavalry force thus remained small, being no more than 600 strong in the best of times.[328] The arm was divided into 12 oulamoi of 50 troopers each.[329] Spartan cavalry was generally of poor quality because the wealthy Spartan nobles who would normally have constituted the arm instead purchased untrained substitutes to serve in their place.[330]

These novice cavalrymen frequently rode their horses for the first time on the eve of battle, and their performance was generally so abysmal that the Spartans were eventually forced to hire mercenary cavalry.

Sciritai The Sciritai was an elite guard unit of 300 hoplites recruited from the mountainous area of northern Laconia.[331] It was a great distinction to be selected for this unit, service being for the duration of one year. By the battle of Mantineia (418 B.C.), the Sciritai had grown to the size of a 600-man lochoi.[332]

On the battlefield, the Sciritai were always stationed on the vulnerable far left wing of the army, participating in both the opening and closing of the battle. Off the battlefield, they were frequently employed by the Ephors for difficult missions of a dangerous or highly confidential nature, usually functioning in the role of secret police.[333]

They also performed scouting functions for the army when it was on the march. The Sciritai were armed offensively in a similar manner to the hoplite but were lightly armored to increase their mobility.[334]

Heavy Infantry Spartan infantry was based upon the hoplite, and for many decades these soldiers were unbeatable on the battlefield. Sparta's entire social structure was based on the development and maintenance of its hoplite formation. Any change in its military structure would have required Sparta to pay troops, which its crude barter economy did not enable it to do, or to mobilize its landless class, which would have resulted in a collapse of the state. This situation led to the development of a military structure highly resistant to change. About the time of the Peloponnesian War, innovations in the conduct of warfare began to be introduced on the battlefield, but Spartan rigidity virtually precluded any adoption of them. The Spartan victories over the years were almost solely the result of their maneuverability and discipline, while their defeats were the result of tactical innovations used by their opponents that the Spartans were unable to respond to effectively.

The rigorous Spartan training produced a core of professional officers and noncommissioned officers capable of executing maneuvers within certain limits. The availability of this large pool of professional officers allowed the Spartans to break their army down into tactical units as small an enomotia, a formation of only 32 men.[335] By contrast, the smallest tactical unit most other Greek states fielded was a lochos of 300 men.[336] This placed the Greeks at a decided disadvantage in maneuvering against the Spartans. The typical Spartan tactic was to pin the enemy frontally and then maneuver against his left flank in an attempt to roll up his line. Whereas most Greeks in an advance rushed forward in disorder, the Spartan marched with precise alignment to the sound of flutes.[337] When the Spartans engaged an enemy line, their frontline cohesion largely compensated for their lack of momentum.

The Spartans were armed similarly to other Greek hoplites of the period, who were equipped with a spear, a sword, a breastplate, a shield, a helmet and greaves. The single exception was that instead of the usual Greek sword, the Spartans carried a long dagger.[338]

This was undoubtedly because of the Spartan tendency to fight at close quarters. As time went by, the Spartans tended to reduce their armor considerably in an attempt to further increase their mobility.

At the height of their power during the Peloponnesian Wars, the Spartans were able to field seven lochoi, later known as Mora, each at a strength of 512 men.[339] Each lochoi was divided into four pentecostyes, and then into four enomotia, each consisting of 32 men.[340] The Spartan hoplites usually maintained a formation depth of eight ranks.[341] Their tactics mandated that they always turned clockwise, that is to the right, so that the shield on the left side of the hoplite would always be facing the enemy.

Perioeci When the Spartans completed their conquest of Laconia and Messenia during the ninth through seventh centuries, they established an agreement with the Dorian villages there to supply perioeci services to the Spartan army as hoplites. At the battle of Plataea in 479 B.C., the number of hoplites provided by perioeci service was equal to the number the Spartans were able to mobilize.

Helots The helots were serfs of the state assigned to farm the land of the Spartan warriors, who were then able to concentrate exclusively on improving their military proficiency. The helots were required to turn about half their produce over to their masters.[342] A large number of helots routinely accompanied their Spartan masters on their campaigns, attending them as servants. On occasion, the helots also served as light infantry and in emergencies, even as hoplites.

Being greatly outnumbered by the helots, the Spartan warriors always lived in fear of a revolt by them. As a result, it was dangerous for the helots to excel on the battlefield. To do so would only heighten the Spartan warriors' suspicion of them that had led to widespread massacres of the helots several times in the past.

In 424 B.C., for example, the Spartan leaders promised 2,000 of the bravest helots their freedom.[343] Perceiving the large number of the helots gathered together in one place as a threat to the state, however, they instead massacred them.

Light Infantry The Spartans largely recruited light infantry from among their Peloponnesian allies.[344]

Archers The Spartans regarded the bow as a woman's weapon. They apparently did raise some archers in 424 B.C., but only a very small number.[345]

Thessaly

Cavalry The traditional military arm of Thessaly was heavy cavalry. Although under Jason, Thessaly was capable of fielding a force of 6,000 cavalry and 10,000 hoplites, during Alexander's reign the state was only called upon to field 2,000 heavy cavalry.[346] In training, fighting proficiency and morale, the Thessalian cavalry were virtually identical to the Companions. Whereas the Companions anchored the offensive right flank of the Macedonian army, the Thessalians anchored the defensive left flank. The result was that they were frequently heavily outnumbered, having to engage a disproportionately large number of the Persian cavalry to facilitate Alexander's attack on the right flank. It was a tribute to the fighting ability of the Thessalians that despite this frequent disparity in numbers they always managed to hold their position, although at times, especially at Gaugamela, it was difficult to do so.

The Thessalian cavalry ilai from Pharsalus was widely considered to be superior to all others in Thessaly's cavalry force.[347] During Alexander's reign the Pharsalus formed the personal escort of Parmenio, who was second in command after the king and always led the left wing of the Macedonian army. The Thessalian cavalry troops were typically armed with either javelins or spears. Details on the Thessalian cavalry appeared earlier in this chapter, in the Macedonia section.

Infantry Neither the Thessalian peasants of the plain nor the mountain tribes were organized into effective infantry. The nobility of the plain had decided not to train or arm a peasantry which might then be inclined to revolt against them in the future.

Thrace

The various Thracian tribes rarely united for any concerted action. Their soldiers tended to serve more often as auxiliaries to other armies than to constitute a standing army. Thracian troops were undisciplined and savage.[348] They were unpredictable and unreliable and would frequently break off a battle in search of loot. The Greeks viewed them as little better than barbarians, and they were generally assigned rear-echelon duties, which included executions, massacres, foraging, and garrison duty. So indifferent to killing were the Thracians that they would indiscriminately butcher women, children, and even animals when their battle frenzy was aroused.[349] During the Peloponnesian War, for example, the Thracians broke into the Boeotian town of Mycalassus and killed all the children at a boys' school there.[350]

Cavalry The Thracian cavalry was comprised of lightly armored noblemen. Being relatively undisciplined, they were usually only used for skirmishing or raids.[351] Their traditional formation was the wedge.[352] A Thracian cavalry unit was in frontline use in the Macedonian field army at both Granicus River and

Gaugamela. After that, they appear to have been assigned to garrison duties in Media, along with the Thracian infantry. When Alexander left India, the Thracian cavalry was left behind as part of the garrison for the satrapy in the upper Punjab ruled by Philip (son of Machatas).

Infantry The Thracian infantry soldiers, who were basically peltasts, were more at home in heavily wooded terrain where they could launch surprise attacks from the cover of the forest. Whenever they were involved in hand-to-hand combat with disciplined heavy infantry, the Thracians were usually defeated. Their infantry troops were armed with a thrusting spear or javelins, a sword or a dagger, and a small shield.[353] The Thracian javelin men served on the battlefield of Issus under command of Sitalces.

2. Siege Operations

Prior to Philip's reign, the Greeks had been notoriously unsuccessful at prosecuting siege operations. Their usual siege technique was contravallation — surrounding a city by a parallel outer wall to isolate it from outside assistance in the hope that either starvation or some traitorous faction within would deliver it into the attackers' hands. This was a fairly passive approach, mandating a long siege of several months, sometimes years, and even then there was no guarantee of success. If the city was a port, the besieging force also had to have naval superiority for an effective blockade; otherwise the city could be easily reprovisioned by sea. Cities were rarely stormed because of the high number of casualties the attackers would usually incur by their long exposure to enemy missile fire out in the open. All the Greek states, except for Sparta, mobilized the citizenry for their armies when needed. The length of service was usually of short duration because there were no funds available to pay the army's wages over a protracted period of time or because the soldiers had to work their farms. Military operations were essentially limited to the summer months because severe weather in the winter and the need to plant and harvest the crops during the spring and fall made those seasons impractical for military campaigns. Under such restrictions Greek armies rarely conducted sieges, instead merely looting and burning nearby areas in an attempt to draw out the enemy army sheltering inside a city. If the defenders refused to leave the shelter of their walls to fight a field battle, the invading force would usually then return home with all the loot it could carry.

The Besiegers

Dionysus I of Syracuse   The first significant advance in Greek siege warfare occurred in 399 B.C., when Dionysus I (ruler of Syracuse) laid siege to Motya, a Carthaginian city in western Sicily.[1] He built a mole to gain access to the island city, used arrow-firing catapults and mobile six-story towers to suppress enemy missile fire from the walls, and employed battering rams to breach the city's walls. The result was that Dionysus was able to take the city by storm. The innovations in technique and weaponry that he used against Motya would become the standard elements in most successful ancient sieges.

Philip II   When Philip II assumed the Macedonian throne, the siege techniques developed by Dionysus I were commonly practiced in Greece. Contravallation of cities with a counter wall had been largely abandoned in preference to the use of rams, wheeled towers, mines to weaken the walls, and arrow-shooting catapults to clear the walls of defenders. Throughout his reign Philip conducted 11 sieges, and although he was not always successful at every one he undertook, he always learned something from every one of them and became progressively more skilled at conducting them. All Philip's sieges were undertaken with the same basic components available to any other city in Greece. The difference was that his approach was superior in large part because of the careful and analytical methods used by his engineers, who were specially commissioned to study siege craft and recommend continuing improvements to its technique. Towards the end of Philip's reign, his chief engineer invented the arrow-firing torsion catapult, which could engage enemy defenders on a wall at a greater distance than Dionysus' flexion catapults. Philip became so proficient at conducting sieges that it took him only one month to conclude the siege of Olynthus and three months to set up siege engines, construct siege towers, and breach the walls of Perinthus. In comparison, it had taken the Athenians, who were acknowledged throughout Greece as successful besiegers, 10 months to besiege and capture Samos in 366–65 and over two years to besiege and capture Thasos.[2]

Philip's lack of success in conducting siege operations at both Perinthus and Byzantium resulted, in large part from the lack of a stone-throwing catapult. Having only arrow-shooting catapults, Philip was able to clear walls of defenders but was unable to breach them. Only the stone-throwing torsion catapults could do this, and they did not make their appearance until later in Alexander's reign. However, when Alexander assumed the throne, Philip had provided him with the tools, skilled experts, and doctrine he would need to conduct successfully some of the most difficult sieges of antiquity.

Alexander the Great It is under Alexander the Great that siege warfare in the ancient Greek world reached its height. Sometime in the 330s B.C., the torsion catapult was further developed to throw one-talent (57-pound) stones.[3] Called the stone thrower, the newly developed catapult was typically used at a range of from 150 to 200 yards against walls and up to 400 yards at other targets.[4] It was now possible not only to lay down an intensive missile barrage to clear the walls of enemy defenders but to batter down the masonry of walls and towers. This allowed the assaulting troops to pass through the wall rather than laboriously attacking up and over it, considerably minimizing the number of casualties incurred by enemy missile fire.

Alexander conducted six great sieges in the Persian Empire, three in the western area and three in the eastern. The siege at Halicarnassus lasted two months and denied the Persian fleet its major naval base in the southern Aegean Sea, while the siege at Tyre, which lasted seven months, resulted in the breakup of the Persian fleet and led to the loss of Persian naval domination in the Aegean. Alexander's last great siege in the western Persian Empire at Gaza gave him control of Egypt. At Halicarnassus, the Persians and the Greek mercenaries evacuated the position as untenable because of the heavy losses they had sustained in an unsuccessful sortie against Alexander while Alexander carried both Tyre and Gaza by storm.

In the eastern Persian Empire, Alexander persecuted three great sieges against mountain tribes who had taken refuge in almost impregnable positions. In each instance, Alexander could have easily isolated the positions by a small force. He appears, however, to have been intrigued with the difficulty of taking the positions and to have decided to prosecute the sieges more for mystic reasons than military logic. He won the Rock of Sogdiana by a clever trick, the Rock of Chorienes by surrender, and the Rock of Aornos by abandonment. Had Alexander been forced to assault the latter two positions, he would probably have carried them, but only after paying a heavy price in casualties.

Alexander successfully tackled some of the most difficult siege operations in the ancient world with a relentless determination and innovation unmatched throughout history. Each position he took by siege was considered impregnable at the time, ranging from being half-a-mile offshore, in the middle of a sand dune, to being atop a mountain. He was undoubtedly one of the most successful of ancient besiegers. No position was able to withstand him, and any resistance to a siege he imposed was widely considered to be futile.

Demetrius Poliorcetes (the Great Besieger)   Probably the greatest siege ever undertaken in the ancient world was Demetrius' siege of Rhodes in 305 B.C., conducted only 18 years after Alexander's death. The siege, however, was more notable for the gigantic scale on which Demetrius conducted it than for its success. Ironically, although his siege was completely unsuccessful, Demetrius nevertheless became known as the "Great Besieger."

Demetrius besieged Rhodes because it refused to join him in an attack on Egypt. He landed on the island with an army 40,000-strong.[5] A gigantic catapult bombarded the city's walls with three-talent (171-pound) stones.[6] Demetrius constructed a huge siege tower on the hulls of six galleys, but it capsized in a storm while being towed into position.[7] The rams he constructed were 180 feet long and took 1,500 men to operate in relays.[8] A total of 600 horses were required to transport them.[9] His siege tower was 150 feet high (nine stories) and took 3,400 men to move and 1,000 men to operate.[10] Having little to show for his gigantic effort, Demetrius finally abandoned the siege and sailed away. He later built a gigantic floating siege tower at Thebes that was so heavy that it could only be moved a quarter of a mile in two months. The war engines that Demetrius left behind at Rhodes were sold, and the proceeds were used to finance the construction of the 100-feet-high Colossus of Rhodes in the city's harbor.[11] The gigantic statue later became known as one of the seven wonders of the ancient world.

Siege Techniques

Siege Assault   The objective of the attacker in a siege was usually to capture a city by assault without incurring excessive casualties in the process. If this were not possible, the attacker would surround the city to cut it off from outside assistance so that it might be starved into submission. A typical siege assault would commence with a bombardment by stone-throwing catapults in an attempt to breach the walls. If this was successful, bolt-shooting catapults and siege towers would be brought up to begin a missile-fire bombardment to clear the defenders off the walls or draw their missile fire to the towers. Under cover of the missile fire, the rams would be brought up to widen the breach, if that was necessary. If not, an immediate attempt would be made to pass troops through the opening. A siege tower would be rolled up and a drawbridge dropped, providing a means of debarking the assaulting troops into the breach. Upon overpowering the defenders, the assault troops would fight their way to a nearby gate and open it, allowing the main body of the besieging army to enter the city and defeat the remaining garrison. If the attacking assault was thrown back, a renewed bombardment of the stone-throwing catapults might widen the current breach or begin a new one. A lack of success might result in the undertaking of mining operations to collapse a section of the wall or one of the towers.

Mining Operations Although mining was one of the most effective ways to weaken or collapse a wall, it was also one of the most time consuming. A tunnel would be dug some distance from the wall to be undermined. The dirt would be laboriously hauled away and the tunnel shored up by wooden beams. When the tunnel had progressed far enough to lie beneath the wall, it was filled with combustible material and ignited. The supporting beams would then burn through, and the tunnel ceiling would cave in. This would usually weaken the foundation under the wall enough to collapse a section of it, forming a deep and wide breach.

Countermining operations might locate the tunnel, and assault troops could be sent into it in an effort to prematurely burn it out. Terrain and weather largely determined the practicality of mining operations. Rocky or sandy ground or an elevated position might preclude any attempt at mining, while winter weather or heavy rain might significantly delay its progress.

Moles A mole was simply a causeway built over water. Its purpose was to enable an army to conduct a land assault against a city located on a nearby island. As Alexander found out at Tyre, however, a mole can be extraordinarily difficult to construct across the open sea because violent storms can easily pound it to pieces and enemy naval superiority can seriously interfere with its construction. Alexander's mole at Tyre was one of the greatest such projects in history, being over a half-mile long and 200 feet wide. It involved a tremendous initial construction effort and no less a maintenance effort because continuing and extensive repairs had to be made to counteract the battering it took from storms and the burning damage from the highly successful Tyrian sortie from the city. Ironically, Alexander's mole proved to be almost totally ineffective because the reinforced wall opposite it was too strong to be breached. Tyre actually fell through an assault by sea at the southern part of the city. In effect, the tremendous effort it took to construct the mole was hardly justified by the results, although it may have proved useful in diverting the defender's attention away from the main assault delivered by sea. Later sieges against islands rarely used moles, instead relying on seaborne breaching and assault.

Mounds A mound might be built against an elevated position by a besieger to enable siege artillery and siege towers to be deployed against the walls. A tremendous construction effort involving hand-carrying countless tons of dirt to the site in baskets was usually necessary to raise a mound high enough to reach the walls. The only siege in which Alexander is known to have used a mound was at Gaza, in Phoenicia, but the nature of the soft and sandy ground there made it virtually impossible to push the siege towers and rams up to the wall. As a result, the first three assaults against the city were thrown back because without the towers it was not possible to suppress the heavy defensive missile fire from the city walls. The city was finally taken as a result of a mining operation that collapsed a section of the wall and provided the breach necessary for a successful assault to be made.

Siege Equipment

Sieges were prosecuted with a wide variety of equipment. Light catapults and siege towers were used to clear the defenders from the walls, while the heavy catapults and battering rams were brought up to breach them.

Catapults In classical Greece, siege assaults were rarely undertaken because an attacker would incur heavy casualties in his exposure to enemy missile fire over the long stretch of open ground approaching the wall and then in climbing up ladders placed against the wall. Two things were needed for a successful assault: a way to breach the wall to enable an attack to advance through it rather than over it and a way to drive the defenders from positions on the walls nearby the point of assault. The catapult met both these requirements.

The catapult appears to have been invented by Dionysus of Syracuse about 400 B.C. for use against the Carthaginians. This so-called "belly bow" catapult was, in effect, a large crossbow too powerful to be drawn back by a single arm. The belly bow allowed the use of a bow with a pull of 150 pounds to 200 pounds compared to the usual 40-pound to 60-pound pull of a hand bow. The belly bow was categorized as a flexion catapult because it derived its low torque from the bending of wood, that is, the bending of the bow itself. The first such weapon was braced against the stomach, both hands being required to draw back the bowstring along a ratcheted shaft. The bowstring was locked in place by one of the ratchets. The further the firer pulled back the bowstring the greater the range of the arrow fired. Later, even more powerful belly bows had to be braced against the ground or a wall to arm them. The effective range of the belly bow was about 250 yards, roughly 25 percent greater than that of a conventional bow.[12] The belly bow could, of course, shoot further, but only with a corresponding decrease in accuracy. The weight and slow rate of fire of the belly bow generally precluded its use in field operations.[13]

The next development in catapults was made in the latter part of Philip II's reign. His chief engineer, a Thessalian named Polyidus, in all likelihood invented the torsion catapult, which was first used in Philip's sieges of Perinthus and Byzantium in 340 B.C.[14] This catapult was commonly called the shield piercer because the arrow it fired was able to penetrate an enemy shield at a distance of a quarter of a mile.[15] The use of twisted hair or sinew resulted in a much higher torque than could be achieved with the flexion catapult. The catapult was now mounted on a swivel frame. As the bowstring was too powerful to be pulled back with the hands, a winch was used. The torsion catapult proved to be more complicated to operate than a flexion catapult, requiring significantly more maintenance. The skeins of hair or sinew would slacken from prolonged use or in wet weather and would periodically have to be tightened or replaced.[16] The shield piercer was to prove deadly against the individual defenders but was ineffective against the masonry of their defenses. This was rectified, however, by the next advance in catapult design.

Early in the reign of Alexander the Great the stone-throwing catapult was invented. This was a torsion catapult configured to throw a stone rather than to shoot an arrow. The stone throwers during Alexander's time could fire a one-talent (57-pound) stone up to 200 yards against a wall and 400 yards at a group of individuals.[17] Eighteen years after Alexander's death the size of the catapult had progressed to the extent that Demetrius Poliorcetes was able to fire three-talent (171-pound) stones against Rhodes. At long last the Greeks were able to batter down the masonry of walls. The first recorded use of the stone-throwing catapult was at Alexander the Great's siege of Tyre, in 332 B.C.

Siege Towers Siege towers were movable wooden structures built to overlook a wall. Their purpose was to allow missile troops to drive the defenders from their position along the stretch of the wall to be assaulted or to draw the defensive missile fire to the tower and away from the point of attack. The tower was usually covered by animal hides as protection against both missile fire and combustion. At each level in the tower, there were openings for discharging missile weapons. A number of catapults were usually stationed at intermediate levels throughout the structure. Most towers had a drawbridge attached that could be lowered directly onto the walls or into any breach made.

Assault and missile troops would occupy the various floors of the tower, passing between the different levels by inside ladders. The wheeled tower was pushed up to the wall by troops sheltering behind it. The troops in the tower would then begin an intensive missile barrage against the defenders on the wall. When the defenders began to suffer an unacceptable number of casualties in their relatively unprotected position below the higher tower, they would invariably be forced to withdraw from their position. This would allow the rams to advance and begin their battering operations against the wall, hopefully unimpeded by enemy missile fire. When a breach was subsequently made, the tower would drop its drawbridge into it, allowing the assault troops to pass from the tower through the breach. If the top of the wall was cleared of defenders, the tower might drop its drawbridge there to gain a position for the assault troops.

Defenders fought a siege tower in several ways. Wide and deep moats were frequently constructed around the walls that would have to be filled in before a tower could move across the area. When the tower was under construction or awaiting assault, the garrison of a besieged city might sortie out in an attempt to burn it. Wooden structures could also be built atop of the walls in an attempt to gain a height advantage over the tower. Pikes could be used to prevent a drawbridge of the tower from properly deploying, while grappling hooks could tear it down altogether.

2: SIEGE OPERATIONS

Battering Rams   The typical battering ram was a pointed tree trunk armored on one end and suspended by chains from an overhead frame; it was usually covered in hides as protection against both missile fire and combustion. Wheels would be attached to the frame to allow it to be pushed into position against that part of the wall weakened by catapult bombardment or mining. The pointed log would be repeatedly swung against an area, and the resulting concentration of force was usually enough to cause the masonry to give way, forming a small hole. The penetration would be progressively widened until a section of the wall gave way and a breach was made. The ram would then be withdrawn, and the assaulting troops would move up to attack through the breach.

An important preliminary step to be taken before advancing the battering ram was to clear the walls of enemy defenders by concentrated missile fire. If the defenders were able to return to the walls while a battering ram was operating against their position, they might drop a rock on the ram to collapse the frame or swing a grappling hook down to overturn it. Intact adjacent towers might also bring the ram under catapult fire to damage it or destroy it with large stones. Walls could also be buttressed or a crescent wall quickly built behind the damaged wall to localize any breakthrough. Counterattacking reserves could be brought up to throw back any assaulting troops entering the breach, who would probably be disadvantaged by the resulting climb over the rubble.

Siege Train   The siege train typically only consisted of the essential parts for assembling the siege engines, rams and towers. Most of the wood required to complete the construction was procured at the site of the siege. Because of the large transport requirements of siege equipment, the siege train was usually carried by sea whenever possible. On land, siege equipment was generally carried on wagons pulled by slow-moving oxen. This meant that the siege train either quickly fell behind a fast-moving army or dramatically slowed its rate of march. Special attention had to be paid to the accumulation of vital supplies for the siege, and careful training was necessary for the effective deployment of the siege train.

3. Logistics

Alexander had crossed the Hellespont with an army of 5,000 cavalry,[1] 30,000 infantry,[2] 5,000 cavalry servants,[3] 3,000 infantry servants,[4] and 12,000 camp followers.[5] With a daily dry feed requirement of 10 pounds per horse and three pounds per man, his army would consume about 750 tons of dry provisions each week. At an average yield of 160 tons of produce per square mile on productive land, a one month's stay of the army in an area would require the agricultural production of almost 19 square miles, or a distance of about two miles out from a city in all directions.[6] It is readily apparent why in the ancient world any prolonged stay by an army in an area would quickly deplete local supplies.

During the winter the Macedonians always tried to make camp in populated regions in Asia having easy access to navigable rivers or the seashore. When this could not be done, the army was divided up into smaller forces to ease the supply problem. Because of overland transport limitations, agricultural production only occurred in close proximity to populated centers.[7] Thus, whenever possible, Alexander's army marched through areas of high population density in preference to uninhabited areas. This usually ensured that adequate provisions could be impressed from the local area along the way, so long as the stay was not prolonged.

Under normal circumstances a soldier would require a minimum daily ration requirement of three pounds of grain and two quarts of water, for a total weight of eight pounds.[8] Like the Roman army, the Macedonian army's basic staple was the grain ration of wheat, barley, or millet. The ration would not spoil in hot weather like meat, fish, vegetables, or fruit and was easy to transport in bulk. Water, however, was a unique problem for all armies. It was the heaviest part of the ration, and its bulk and viscosity made for difficulties in transport. While the soldier's solid ration might be reduced for a short time without noticeable effect, a reduction in the water ration could have immediate and serious consequences. Dehydration would quickly result, with its debilitating effect on stamina and marching ability. On marches into rough country or dry climates, increasing amounts of water were necessary. A desert march, for instance, would require as much as nine quarts of water daily per individual.[9] With the increase in temperature or roughness of ground, water usage increased significantly. Marches were usually made from river to river, as the limited capacity of overland transport usually precluded supplies being carried overland in any significant quantities.

Assuming that sufficient forage and water was readily available, a 1,500-man phalanx taxies might get by with 2.25 short tons of dry rations a day and a Companion cavalry ilai of 215 men might get by with 1.4 short tons for both men and horses per day. Of course, marches through the desert, across barren mountain passes, over rough areas, or through uninhabited territory could affect the logistics of water by reducing the supply available and/or increasing the quantity required. In marching through a desolate mountain pass like the 47-mile Khawak Pass over the Hindu Kush Mountains, for instance, all parts of the ration might have to be carried, including the water. In this situation, a phalanx taxies' daily logistical requirement would increase to six short tons and a cavalry ilai's to 11.6 short tons.[10] This would, of course, place a crippling burden on the supply train, usually resulting in the army going on either short or starvation rations, an event which was to occur several times during Alexander's campaigns in the eastern Persian Empire.

Over an extended distance, a horse or mule can carry 200 pounds; a light cart with two animals, 1,000 pounds; and a large merchant ship of the period, about 400 tons.[11] Because of the low overland carrying capacities of animals, waterborne supply was always preferable to that carried overland. When this was not possible, however, Alexander's army usually relied on pack animals in preference to carts. There were several serious drawbacks to using carts in antiquity. The most obvious was related to the rudimentary throat and girth harness, which, as we have seen in Chapter 1, tended to choke the animal pulling a cart.[12] The later invention of the rigid shoulder harness would largely rectify this situation. Carts also had the tendency to break down frequently when operating off well-maintained roads, of which there were very few in the eastern Persian Empire. Then, too, most ancient generals were convinced that carts unduly restricted an army's speed and mobility and only encouraged soldiers to accumulate excessive and unnecessary baggage. In this regard, they were, undoubtedly, quite correct. Philip II had all but prohibited the use of carts in the Macedonian army, and Alexander appears to have adopted the same policy, at least up until the time that he reached India. Only a few carts were retained to carry some of the siege equipment and to provide ambulances for the wounded. This greatly increased the mobility of the Macedonian army and enabled it to regularly outmarch Greek, Persian and Indian armies.[13]

It is unlikely that the Macedonians ever had more than 20,000 pack animals available to them at any one time.[14] This would have given them a maximum overland lift capacity of around 2,000 tons. Assuming an army the size that Alexander crossed over the Hellespont with and 20,000 pack animals traveling in fair weather over relatively level ground with water readily available, the daily dry ration requirement would be about 100 tons. This would allow the army a 20-day marching range before all dry rations supplies carried were exhausted. Of course, it should be remembered that the supply train was constantly renewing itself. As supplies were consumed, the now unloaded pack animals would be sent out with foragers who were continually collecting supplies along the army's line of march.

Most Greek armies traveled with a minimum of one servant per hoplite, but the Spartans traveled with as many as seven.[15] The use of large numbers of servants would add significantly to the number of men to be fed but do nothing to augment the combat effectiveness of the army. The effect of this huge number of servants was to decrease dramatically the striking range of an army, which was usually limited to the length of its overland supply line. The more supplies that were consumed, the shorter the operational range of the army. Philip therefore limited servants to one for each cavalryman and one for every 10 infantrymen.[16] He also required his soldiers to carry 30 days of grain rations on their back.[17] Thus his "logistics tail," or the number of support troops, was always significantly smaller than that of any other Greek army. This resulted in a higher percentage of combat troops in Philip's army, a faster rate of march, and an increase in his army's operating range to more than 400 miles from a supply source, a distance about one-third greater than that possible for any other Greek army.

The Persian army traveled at about half the speed of the Macedonian army. This was the result, in large part, of the enormous supply train with which the Great King burdened his army. Among other things, it contained his 365 concubines, his children, and their governesses carried in 15 wagons, 200 of his relatives, 30,000 camp followers, a portion of his treasury carried by 600 mules and 300 camels, and several weeks' supplies for his army.[18] Altogether, the supply train was estimated to require over 7,000 pack animals.[19] In addition, with one wagon being used to carry supplies and equipment for every 30 men, a Persian army of 100,000 would require over 3,000 wagons.[20] The Indian army also had a large supply train, usually preferring to carry its own supplies rather than forage for them.

It can readily be seen how critical it was for ancient army commanders to give proper attention to logistics. A failure to do so could easily result in an army sustaining a greater number of casualties from inadequate supplies than from fighting a major field battle. Alexander was to learn this painful lesson at least twice on his campaigns, at Khawak Pass, in the Hindu Kush mountains, and again in the Makran desert, in Gedrosa. In both cases, faulty planning on his part forced the Macedonians on starvation rations. In the Makran, this proved disastrous, and many lives were lost as a result.

4. Naval Operations

The Trireme

In the age of Homer, Greek ships were used primarily as transports, merely serving to convey an invading army or a force of raiders to their destination and back. Each ship during this era contained 20 rowers, who were the soldiers being transported.[1] After the Trojan War, however, naval tactics began to evolve that stressed the use of the ram. Ships became lighter and narrower to achieve greater speed and maneuverability, both important factors in successful ramming. Crews became specialized rowers, and the number of soldiers was limited. Ship development continued with the introduction of the bireme and pentecounter, but boarding continued to remain the most common naval battle tactic. With the development of the trireme by either the Phoenicians or the Corinthians about 650 B.C., however, ramming tactics were refined. The larger number of rowers in the trireme increased the ship's speed, while its small compliment of soldiers increased its stability.

The trireme was developed exclusively as a warship, obtaining its name from the fact that the rowers sat in three levels. Since there was a limit to lengthening ships to accommodate additional rowers because of the stress it would place on the ship's keel, rowers were stacked in levels: two to a bireme, three to a trireme, four to a quadrireme, and five to a quinquereme. Boarding ability and missile volume were sacrificed for the greater speed and maneuverability of the vessel. This was done by greatly reducing the deck and increasing the number of oarsmen from 50 in the pentecounter to 170 in the trireme.[2]

The trireme was a long narrow ship about 121 feet long and 20 feet wide.[3] The narrowness of the vessel was designed to minimize the hull's resistance to water, while its long length distributed bow and wave pressure away from the bow and stern to the sides. The low freeboard of the vessels also minimized wind resistance.[4] The trireme's shallow four-and-a-half-foot draft and displacement of only 80 tons made it susceptible to being easily swamped by high waves and tossed about in strong winds.[5] Because the ship was not ballasted, it would float even when its hull was pierced.[6] These factors made the ship highly maneuverable and greatly increased the effectiveness of its main weapon, the ram.[7] As the trireme's deck did not extend to the sides of the ship, the ends of the long and narrow vessel were prone to sagging.[8] To prevent this, strong cables about one and a half inches in diameter, called hypozomata, ran twice through the interior length of the ship.[9]

They were carefully tightened when the trireme was in the water and loosened when the ship was in dry dock. In later Greek and Roman ships, the use of a complete deck eliminated the need for these cables.

The proper seasoning of wood was extremely important for the construction of a ship. If green wood was used that still contained moisture, it would not expand enough to prevent gaps from occurring between the hull planks. Ancient Greek ships were not generally caulked, relying instead on the swelling of the wood to seal the joints between the planks.[10] As the wood dried out, it would develop cracks that could greatly endanger the integrity of the ship, the hull sometimes literally coming apart at the seams.[11]

Older triremes that were no longer serviceable for ramming could be converted to either troop or horse transports, although it was usually better to build specially designed transports with broader hulls and a deeper draft to increase their seaworthiness.[12] In either case, only the top level of rowers was retained to propel the ship. This made available the lower two levels formerly occupied by rowers to accommodate either 30 soldiers or 30 horses.[13] A horse transport would be about eight tons heavier than a trireme fully manned by rowers.[14]

Although the trireme carried a sail, it was only used to move strategically. When entering a battle, the sail was taken down and stored ashore whenever possible.[15] The sail was usually made of linen, the ends being bound by leather.[16] The skin of a hyena was strongly preferred by sailors for the binding because they believed that it deflected lightning.[17] In a good wind, the trireme could proceed under sail at a speed of about eight knots per hour.[18] Normal cruising speed under oars was four knots an hour, while a ramming speed under oars of up to 11 knots an hour could be achieved within 30 seconds but only for a short duration of five to ten minutes, depending upon the conditioning and experience of the crews. To sustain this pace for any extended period of time would quickly exhaust the rowers. At a speed of four knots, a trireme could turn completely around in the space of two and a half times the ship's length.[19]

A rowing crew of 170 were arranged in three levels.[20] The lowest level was named the thalamites because they sat in the hold, or thalamos, of the ship. Their oars projected through ports only one and a half feet above the water line.[21] The zygites, who sat on the zyga, formed the middle level. The top level was occupied by the thranites. All oars were 14 feet long, each bank slanting downward at different angels, becoming progressively steeper in angle at the higher levels.[22] This configuration allowed the blades of the oars to be aligned behind each other as they swept down on the water. Although the thranites were somewhat protected overhead by the two gangways, they were completely exposed above the gunwale to enemy missile fire.[23] To help mitigate this vulnerability, a leather screen extended down from the deck gangway to the gunwale.[24] The poop deck of the ship was three feet above the level of the thranites and was the normal station of the complement of 14 marines the trireme usually carried.[25] A small number of seamen were also aboard the ship. Their duties were navigation, handling of the sail, and docking of the ship. Each trireme had two rudders, one on each side. The helmsman was able to control both of them from a small platform on the quarter deck. To turn the ship to starboard, the helmsman pulled the rudder oar in his right hand towards him and pushed the rudder oar in his left hand away from him. To turn to port, he pulled the rudder oars in the opposite direction.[26]

Although the trireme was a powerful warship, it did have some severe limitations.

- The trireme was crowded and was thus unable to carry enough food for voyages lasting longer than five days. Lack of space also precluded meals being cooked on board the vessels; the crews usually beached their ships and cooked and ate their meals ashore. There also had to be a market ashore where the crews of the ships could purchase their food and wine. Triremes did not normally carry drinking water, even on a short trip.[27]
- Because of the lack of space aboard ship, the crew of a trireme had to sleep ashore.[28] This made it necessary for the fleet to have a secure base on land each night where its ships could be beached and the crews could be bedded down in safety
- A trireme lay low in the water and was easily swamped by even moderately rough seas. It was unable to endure rough weather and, therefore, seldom sailed out of sight of land.
- Each trireme only carried a small number of marines aboard, who might easily be overpowered if forced to land on a hostile shore. The rowers were unarmed and untrained in hand-to-hand combat.
- Because of the trireme's long length and narrow beam, the ship was a relatively unstable firing platform. More than a few men moving around on deck would cause the ship to begin to roll, thereby putting the oarsmen off their timing and reducing the ship's top speed.[29] The effect of any weapon thrown would only exacerbate the situation. As a result, javelin men were instructed to throw their weapons from a sitting position.[30] Had all the crew moved to one side of the ship, the shift in weight would probably have capsized the narrow vessel, so sensitive was its trim.[31]
- A trireme's crew was highly skilled and trained. When a ship sank and its crew was lost, the seamen and rowers were difficult to replace.
- A trireme was not very effective against merchant ships. The sturdy construction of the merchant ship and the fragile nature of the trireme sometimes mitigated against the trireme's survival after a successful ramming. Under sail with a fair wind, a merchant ship might make for the open sea and expose the fragile trireme to severe wave damage or swamping if either the winds should increase or a storm brew up.
- The maximum daily range of the trireme was about 30 miles from its home base.[32] At that distance, it became extremely difficult to conduct an effective blockade against a port. This limit was determined by the sailing time needed from its land beachhead, where crews ate their meals and slept at night, to their patrol station and back. The voyage had to be made during daylight because triremes did not sail at night. Under normal circumstances a round trip at extended range might consume twelve hours of daylight, during which time enemy naval forces could freely enter or exit the so-called "besieged" port.
- Triremes refrained from active operations at night, even in known waters.

Therefore merchant ships were not hindered from running into or out of a blockaded port after dark.

- The trireme rapidly deteriorated unless it was protected from the elements when not on active service. Extensive dry-dock facilities and storage sheds were therefore required, and the ship had to undergo continuing maintenance to remain seaworthy. Otherwise, the timbers of the ship would continue to soak up water. This would increase the ship's weight and, over time, waterlog the ship and increase leakage. It was estimated that one ton of water soaking into the timbers would result in seven additional tons of displacement.[33] This extra weight would decrease acceleration by as much as 15 percent.[34] The 6 percent increase in the ship's draft caused by the additional weight would expand its turning radius by 8 percent and reduce the crew's pulling effectiveness by 18 percent to 32 percent.[35]

Triremes were costly to maintain. Rhodes rented triremes at a cost of 10,000 drachma per month.[36] For an eight-month sailing season, the cost of the construction and maintenance of a trireme averaged over the vessel's useful life was about 13 talents. It was clear that only the wealthy city-states could provide the manpower and afford the cost of constructing and maintaining a trireme.

- Although a trireme was extremely maneuverable, the vessel was too crowded for extended sailing. To maximize a trireme's speed, as many crew as possible were crammed into the vessel. As a result, the crew were so closely packed together that their noses virtually touched the rowers in front of them.[37] This cramped condition led to extreme fatigue of the crews, even on a short journey.

Naval Tactics

During the Peloponnesian War, the ram became the principal weapon of a Greek warship, with the seamanship skills of the crews being indispensable to victory. The Athenians perfected ramming techniques relying on speed, maneuverability, experience and judgment. A tactic called circumnavigation, or periplous, was used to sail around a ship or line of ships so as to be able to attack the enemy ship from the stern or beam. Another tactic, named diekplous, called for breaking through an enemy line by rowing between two opposing ships and then circling round to ram one of them before either could react to the attack. These tactical maneuvers called for high speed, an outstanding steersman and skillful oarsmanship. It was understood in the ancient world that Athenian naval skill could only be rivaled by copying their technique. This was, however, beyond the capabilities of all but a few maritime powers.

No longer was it possible to hastily assemble a navy crewed by land troops with any reasonable chance for victory. Only highly trained crews were likely to win naval battles, which now depended on nautical skill rather than overpowering numbers. In the eastern Mediterranean, sizable forces of this nature only came from five locales: Athens, Carthage, Cyprus, Egypt or Phoenicia. Any large and effective battle fleet had to be recruited from one of these areas.

When Alexander recruited his navy for service in Asia, it contained only 20 Athenian triremes. The remainder of the fleet was recruited from other parts of Greece, notably the Peloponnese and Macedonia, areas not particularly noteworthy for their expertise in seamanship. The Greek fleet was much inferior in effectiveness to that of the Persians, whose fleet was comprised of highly skilled Phoenician and Cyprian crews. Also, when fully mobilized the Persian fleet was probably two to three times the size of Alexander's allied Greek fleet. This largely explains Alexander's extreme reluctance to engage the Persian fleet in open combat and the ease with which he made the decision to dissolve his none too reliable crews at Miletus.

In the naval actions of the eastern Mediterranean, Alexander was forced to revert back to the crude boarding tactics of earlier generations because his crews lacked nautical skills.[38] It was always easier for him to find well-trained infantry than to recruit skilled oarsmen. In this regard, he had much in common with the traditionally land-bound Romans, who were also forced to attempt to turn every naval action into a land battle on water. Despite the unsuitability of the use of pentecontars and triremes for boarding actions, Alexander nevertheless crammed them full of troops whenever he was about to fight a naval battle. Interestingly enough, it seems that the Persians and Tyrians also followed suit. We are given few tactical details on the ship-to-ship naval battles during this era, but it would appear that although ramming was sometimes used, boarding actions were at least as common, if not more so.

The inability of ancient warships to maintain station over a wide area increased the element of strategic surprise by an aggressive naval power. This was rarely put to effective use, however, because of the inferior reconnaissance abilities of the fleets at that time. Little attention was paid to intelligence gathering, and the necessary information from which an operational plan could be devised was rarely available in time to plan a strategic surprise.

Athenian Navy

Reign of Philip II

The Athenians were unable to accomplish anything significant against Philip. It was beyond their ability to prevent him from conquering the Chersonese because they were unable to affect either his overland line of communications or the operations of his army by sea and they were too weak to field an effective force against him on land. Although the Athenians were able to frustrate Philip in extending his power into central Greece, they were unable to prevent him from doing so. When Athens with other Greeks attempted to make an all-out stand against Macedonia on the mainland, they were heavily defeated by Philip at Chaeronea.

Social War (357–55 B.C.)   Chios, Rhodes and Cos, being strongly encouraged by Mausolus, the king of Caria, revolted from their Athenian alliance. Byzantium, which had already been in revolt for several years, came to the support of the rebels. Chabrias was sent with an Athenian fleet of 60 triremes to Chios, where the rebels had raised a combined navy of 100 triremes.[39] Chares accompanied Chabrias as the commander of a ground force of mercenaries. While the Athenians were besieging Cos, the rebel garrison troops sortied out against Chares, who managed to fight them to a standstill. Chabrias then led the Athenian naval force into the harbor in an attempt to land forces along the shore to assist Chares. Recklessly pushing out ahead of his battle line without support, Chabrias was defeated and killed. After the battle, Chares embarked the Athenians on the ships and departed from the area.

The rebel navy turned to plunder the Athenian-held islands of Imbros and Lemnos, and then laid siege to Samos. The Athenians, meanwhile, sent out another force of 60 ships under Iphicrates and Timotheus.[40] It combined with Chares' force and besieged Byzantium in an attempt to draw the rebel navy into the Hellespont. Upon hearing of the Athenian presence there, the rebel navy immediately lifted its siege of Samos and sailed north to Byzantium's assistance. As the opposing fleets were about to engage in battle, a storm blew up. Iphicrates and Timotheus refused to fight in such rough seas, much to the objection of Chares.[41] He later denounced both of them as cowards and traitors in a letter sent to the Athenian Assembly.[42] The enraged Athenians heavily fined the two generals and deprived them of their offices, leaving Chares in sole command of the expeditionary force.

Revolt of Artabazus, Satrap of Hellespontine Phrygia (359–58 B.C.)
In an attempt to reduce the possibility of revolt in his empire, Artaxerxes Ochus commanded his satraps to disband their mercenary armies.[43] The 10,000 Greek mercenaries who were subsequently dismissed took employment with Chares. When Artabazus, the Persian satrap of Hellespontine Phrygia, revolted from Artaxerxes, he requested the support of Chares' mercenary army, promising lucrative compensation. Upon hearing of the offer, the mercenaries insisted that Chares either immediately settle accounts of their back wages or accompany them in service to Artabazus. Not being provided by Athens with sufficient funds to meet the mercenaries' wages, Chares took service with Artabazus in Asia Minor in 356 B.C.[44]

Artaxerxes sent out an army against Artabazus commanded by Tithraustes. Although it outnumbered Chares' force, especially in cavalry, he nevertheless defeated it and then proceeded to sack the towns of Lampsacus and Sigeum.[45] The Athenians initially approved of Chares' action because of the generous subsidy that they had received from Artabazus. When the Persian king threatened to wage war against Athens with a fleet of 300 ships, however, the Athenians reluctantly negotiated a peace recognizing the independence of Byzantium, Chios, Cos, and Rhodes.[46] Athens then withdrew its support from Artabazus.

Upon Chares' departure, Artabazus sought Theban support, offering to pay them handsomely for it. Thebes at that time was desperately short of money as a result of the severe financial drain caused by the protracted Third Sacred War. Believing the war to be over with the Phocian defeat at Neon, Thebes decided it was safe to send out an army of 5,000 hoplites under the the command of Pammenes in order to generate some badly needed revenue for the city.[47] The Theban army subsequently won two battles for Artabazus against Artaxerxes. Artabazus, however, suspecting Pammenes of disloyalty, had him arrested and imprisoned. Upon his release, Pammenes and his Theban army returned to Greece. Being deserted by the remaining mercenaries in his employ, Artabazus found himself unable to contend with the Great King's troops alone and was forced to flee into exile to Philip's court in Macedonia.

Olynthus Olynthus sent a delegation to Athens to propose that a treaty of alliance be established between them. Although the city had formerly been hostile to Athens, Philip's successful campaign along the west coast of the Chersonese had convinced it of its future peril. Athens signed a treaty with Olynthus and sent out a force of 30 triremes and 2,000 peltasts to the city's defense under the command of Chares.[48] Before Olynthus came under attack, another Athenian force was mobilized, consisting of 18 triremes, 150 cavalry, and 4,000 peltast mercenaries.[49] Chares was appointed to command it but was reluctant to do so, being at the time under public examination for his conduct during the first expedition to Olynthus. The Assembly had apparently not allocated adequate revenue to enable him to pay the wages of his troops at the time, and to make up the deficiency, he was forced to resort to piracy and to enforce levies of money from cities friendly to Athens along the Chersonese/Thracian coast. Although Chares had insisted on being cleared of the charges against him before he would sail, when the inquiry dragged on, he decided to go out with the expedition.

Arriving at the Chersonese, Chares combined forces with the Olynthians and began conducting operations in Philip's rear. At some point, he was recalled to Athens, and Charidemus took over command of the Athenian force. At first he conducted a successful campaign, overrunning Pallene and devastating Bottice on the west side of the Chersonese. Instead of capitalizing on his successes, however, Charidemus appears to have given himself up to debaucheries, and he accomplished nothing further. When Philip captured Torone and cut Olynthus off from the sea, Olynthus sent a third delegation to Athens. In response to a request for additional aid, the Athenians sent out a force of 17 triremes, 300 cavalry, and 2,000 hoplites.[50] The Etesian winds delayed the arrival of the force, however, until after Olynthus had fallen to Philip, either in August or September. Seeing that nothing further could be accomplished, the force returned to Athens.

Macedonia Chares was in command of a force of 20 ships at Neapolis, across from the island of Thasos.[51] He attempted to blockade ports in Macedonia, but his force was probably too small to accomplish anything significant.

Sestos The Athenians sent a force of 60 ships under the command of Chares to the Hellespont. In subsequent operations, he captured Sestos. His brutal murder of all the adult males and enslavement of the remainder of population so frightened Cersobleptes, the king of eastern Thrace, that he again allied himself with Athens.

Heraion Teichos When Athens received word that Philip was besieging the fort at Heraion Teichos in Thrace, the Assembly made plans to send a fleet of 40 triremes manned by its own citizens against him.[52] When Philip became seriously ill, however, and it appeared that he might die, the Athenians equivocated, now seeing little justification for such a response. Instead, in September 351 B.C., Athens sent out a small force of only 10 ships to the Hellespont under command of Charidemus to determine if anything might be accomplished by a larger force. The reconnaissance did not lead to any further action.

Neapolis Philip embarked his infantry and siege train at Maronea on his small fleet and began sailing back to Macedonia. Chares, however, was lying in ambush for him with 20 triremes at Neapolis.[53] Upon receiving intelligence of this, Philip drew the Athenian force off with his four fastest ships while his slower transports evaded the trap by sailing close along the coast. Philip's entire force arrived safely in Macedonia without loss.

Thermopylae Phocian ambassadors arrived in Athens, promising they would deliver to it the cities of Alponus, Thronium and Nicaea if the Athenians would send a force to occupy them. Athenian possession of these strategic cities, which controlled the pass at Thermopylae, would deny Philip overland access into central Greece. As the Athenians were mobilizing a fleet of 50 triremes, they sent Proxenus, one of their generals, on ahead to make arrangements for the occupation of the cities.[54] Upon his arrival, however, he was told by Phalaecus, who had just been reinstated in command of the Phocian army at Thermopylae, that the agreement made with Athens would not now be honored and that he should return home. When the Athenians were informed of this event, they promptly canceled their intended expedition.

Byzantium A merchant fleet carrying corn from the Black Sea region gathered annually in the Hellespont at Byzantium to await escort by the Athenian navy to Athens. As Philip was currently besieging that city, however, the so-called "corn ships" anchored across the strait from the city along the shore of Asia Minor. Philip suspected the corn ships of supplying the city of Selymbria, which he was currently besieging. In the temporary absence of Chares, he landed his troops on the Asiatic shore and boarded the 230 corn ships.[55] After releasing 50 non–Athenian corn ships, Philip sold the cargoes of the remainder for 700 talents and then broke up their hulls and used the wood to construct siege engines for use against Byzantium.[56] The Persian king decided not to intervene in the conflict, rightly concluding that Athens would declare war against Philip over the seizure of its corn fleet.

When Chares became aware of Philip's seizure of the corn ships, he immediately sailed against the Macedonian fleet with 120 ships.[57] He was able to drive the Macedonian ships into the Bosporus and then, with the assistance of the Byzantine fleet, into the Black Sea. Chares then established a blockade base at the entrance to the Bosporus. To extricate his fleet, Philip sent a false dispatch to Antipater from Thrace, requesting the Macedonian king's immediate presence there to suppress a revolt that had isolated several Macedonian detachments. Chares fell for the ruse and immediately sailed with the Athenian fleet for the coast of Thrace. This allowed the Macedonian fleet to escape from the Black Sea and then, in the company of Philip's army, sail safely back to Macedonia. The Athenian fleet, being unable to engage Philip's fleet successfully along the treacherous Thracian coastline, soon returned to Athens.

Reign of Alexander the Great

There were some 350 triremes in the Athenian naval arsenal.[58] Although not all of them were seaworthy, Athens in a crisis could put at least 100 triremes out to sea at any one time. The limitation in Athens' deployment of its navy was not so much in the number of ships as in its ability to pay the wages of its crews. Athenian naval support to Alexander was negligible. The city provided him with a mere 20 ships and then only under duress.[59] The marital ardor of its crews was tempered by the fact that Alexander clearly considered them untrustworthy hostages for the continued good behavior of Athens. They took no noteworthy action on Alexander's behalf and appear to have been used for little more than transporting the Macedonian siege engines.

Macedonian Navy

Mediterranean Sea

The Balkans A small force of Macedonian ships sailed to Byzantium and up the Danube to join Alexander at Peuce Island, where Triballians and free Thracians had taken refuge. They participated in his unsuccessful attempt to make an amphibious assault against the island. Alexander then used them to carry a portion of his army across the Danube so that he could engage and defeat the Getae.

The Hellespont Alexander used the 160 triremes of his allied Greek navy to transport his army across the Dardanelles from Sestos to Abydos.[60] As the Persian fleet had not been mobilized at the time, the operation proceeded without interference. Alexander took another 60 smaller ships on a sightseeing excursion to the nearby fabled city of Troy.

Miletus The 160-ship allied Greek fleet under Nicanor arrived at Miletus three days in advance of the Persian fleet and anchored at the island of Lade, directly across from the city.[61] The anchorage was promptly fortified and strongly garrisoned by 4,000 Thracian troops and Greek mercenaries.[62] Thus when the 400-ship Persian fleet arrived, it was forced to base itself nine miles away at Mycale, the nearest usable anchorage that was available.[63]

Although the Persian fleet sailed out daily to challenge Alexander to battle, he could not be provoked to engage the enemy ships with his outnumbered, untrustworthy, and partly trained fleet. When Alexander launched his final attack on Miletus, Nicanor was ordered to block the harbor entrance with the Greek fleet to prevent the Persian fleet from reinforcing the city. When reaching the harbor, the Greeks, whose ships were heavily loaded with troops, formed in a line across the harbor mouth, bows facing outward. Upon its arrival, the Persian fleet declined to force the strongly held harbor entrance, and the city quickly fell to Alexander by assault.

Disbanding the Fleet   After the Persian fleet withdrew from Miletus, Alexander decided to disband his fleet, except for 20 Athenians triremes.[64] His allied fleet had transported the Macedonian army across the Hellespont, provided initial supplies for his army until he could establish a functioning land-based supply net in Asia Minor, and assisted in conquering the coastline of Ionia and the outlying islands as far south as Miletus. In the immediate future, however, the fleet was likely to be more a strategic and economic liability than an asset. The following rationale probably played a part in Alexander's decision.

- The 160 triremes of Alexander's navy were inferior both in numbers and seamanship to the 400 triremes of the Persian navy. The Greek fleet did not stand a reasonable chance of winning a battle against the Persian fleet, and its inferiority at sea would doubtless adversely influence Alexander's strategy on land because he would be continually forced to take steps to protect it.
- The cost to maintain the Greek fleet was 160 talents a month.[65] Alexander crossed over into Asia with a mere 60 talents in his treasury and his campaign in Asia Minor had not resulted in the acquisition of much revenue to this point because the main Persian treasury reserves were not stored there, but in the central Persian Empire.[66] The cost of the fleet was a continuing and heavy drain on his already meager resources and was probably imperiling his ability to meet the wage expenses of his large army.
- The navy was no longer needed for supply transport. Alexander now controlled enough Persian grain-producing areas in Asia Minor to be able to dispense with his waterborne supply pipeline to Greece.[67]
- The 32,000 seamen of the fleet were an unnecessary burden on his supply net. There were almost as many men in the fleet as in his army, but their strategic value was small. The 50 tons of grain they consumed daily was disproportionate to their current usefulness.
- The loyalty of the various contingents of the allied fleet was suspect. Alexander believed that in a sea battle large elements of his allied fleet would probably either desert back to their home city or join the Persians.
- Alexander judged that it was not possible for the Persian fleet to induce Greece to revolt. Athens would be reluctant to make any overt moves as long as he continued to hold hostage her 20 triremes and thousands of its citizens captured among the Greek mercenaries at the battle of the Granicus River. Sparta was too unpopular in Greece to form a focus of any revolt, its imperialist ambitions having alienated most of its neighbors. Any attempt by Sparta to extol Greek liberty was likely to be greeted with derision for its duplicity. Outside of these two powers, only Thebes could have served as a focus of Greek discontent, and Alexander had destroyed the city.

Phoenician Campaign   Although Alexander had disbanded his fleet, he could not safely ignore the ability of the Persian fleet to cause him serious harm. Under the circumstances, the Persians were clearly capable of interdicting the Hellespont to cut him off from Greek reinforcements or fomenting and supporting revolts in southern Greece. Alexander's solution was to deprive the Persians of all their naval bases in the eastern Mediterranean by conquering Phoenicia. This would achieve four objectives.

- Alexander would place himself between the Persian fleet and Darius, its paymaster. As soon as the fleet's pay moved into arrears, many crews who were only serving as mercenaries for wages would promptly desert the Persians.
- Naval contingents whose home city was threatened or conquered would probably desert a Persian fleet that had failed to protect their family, relatives and friends. Alexander's restoration of democratic government to the cities in Asia Minor that submitted to him would also be a powerful inducement for desertion by many of the Greeks serving with the Persian fleet.
- The main source of recruitment for skilled seamen would be denied the Persian navy. It would find it difficult or impossible to obtain trained seamen to operate its ships because many of them had been obtained from Phoenicia.
- The Persians would lose the ability to maintain their ships. Without the extensive docking and repair facilities of the Phoenician ports, the Persian navy would be unable to maintain existing ship hulls or construct new ships. The result would be a continual diminishing of the Persian fleet as older ships became unseaworthy from lack of proper maintenance and new ships were no longer available.

Tyre After several reverses at Tyre, it became clear to Alexander that it would not be possible to take the island city without a navy. The Tyrian naval supremacy allowed them to launch highly destructive raids against his mole at will, undoing much of the construction that had been so laboriously undertaken. Only a strong navy could protect the mole until its completion.

In hopes of being able to recruit a Phoenician navy, Alexander went to Sidon. Luck was with him because he arrived at the city in the aftermath of the breakup of the Persian fleet. The kings of Byblos and Aradus, being informed that their home cities had recently fallen to Alexander, deserted the Persian navy and sailed for home. Making their way to Sidon, they immediately offered their ships to Alexander. Byblos, Aradus and Sidon together provided him with a navy of 80 ships.[68] During the next few weeks, 20 ships arrived from Rhodes and Soli, one from Macedonia, and 120 more from Cyprus.[69] Alexander's combined fleet of 221 ships now considerably outnumbered the ships at Tyre's disposal, giving him naval supremacy in the eastern Mediterranean.

Alexander crammed as many of his hypaspists as he could aboard the ships of his allied fleet and set sail in close-order formation for Tyre. His deployment indicated that he intended to force the Tyrian navy into a hand-to-hand infantry fight rather than engage in any naval maneuvering. Alexander commanded the right wing of the fleet; Craterus and Pnytagoras, the king of Cyprus, jointly commanded the left. At the approach of Alexander's fleet, the Tyrians began to withdraw. Upon seeing that the Tyrian ships were crammed with soldiers, Alexander thought that if he could beat them back to their harbors and prevent them from reentering the city, it might quickly fall to him.[70] A desperate race now began. Three Tyrian ships managed to hold off the leading ships of Alexander's fleet just long enough for their fleet to reach the safety of the city's harbors, although they were sunk one after the other. When the Tyrians aligned their ships across the narrow harbor entrance, bows facing outward and packed full of soldiers, Alexander saw that nothing more could be accomplished there and sailed to the mole, where he anchored his fleet. The next day his navy began the blockade of Tyre. The Cyprian fleet under Andromachus took station opposite Sidon Harbor in the north, while the Phoenicians, whom Alexander accompanied, blockaded Egyptian Harbor in the south.[71] The Macedonian and Rhodian ships stayed back to cover the mole.

After some time had passed, the Tyrians devised a plan to attack the Cypriot fleet blockading Sidon Harbor. Extending their sails in front of the harbor to screen their operation from observation, the Tyrians manned three quinqueremes, one quadriremes, and seven triremes with their best crews and marines.[72] The plan was to overwhelm quickly the picket squadron on station and then to inflict a crushing defeat on the remainder of the Cypriot fleet, which would be forced to fight a battle in the confusion of having to board their ships and set sail in haste while in the unexpected presence of the enemy. The sortie force left the harbor in single file, rowing out in absolute silence so as not to disclose its presence prematurely. When in sight of the Cypriot picket squadron, the Tyrians raised their war cry, increased to ramming speed, and engaged in battle.

Although Alexander, who had his headquarters with the Phoenician fleet blockading the Egyptian harbor, normally took relief from the noon-day heat by napping ashore, on this day, for some unknown reason, he had returned to the ships earlier than usual. Receiving word of the Tyrian sortie, most likely by a signal from the mole, Alexander ordered all the ships that were manned at the time — five triremes and some quinqueremes — to accompany him in assisting the hard-pressed Cypriot fleet.[73] Defenders on Tyre's wall desperately tried to warn their sortie force of Alexander's approach, but their efforts were apparently neither seen or heard, no doubt because of the noise and confusion of the raging battle.

The Tyrian sortie force had run ashore or wrecked the Cypriot picket ships, while their marines had landed ashore and fought their way to the beached Cypriot ships, managing to set several afire. The Tyrians afloat were waging a winning battle against the Cypriots, who were fighting with partially crewed ships in haphazard and fragmented formations. Although Alexander arrived at the scene of battle 45 minutes after setting out, he still managed to take the Tyrian sortie force by surprise, falling on them from the rear while they were still locked in combat with the Cypriots. Subsequently sinking or wrecking several of the Tyrian ships, Alexander chased the remainder back to their base, sinking a quinquereme and a quadrireme just outside the entrance of Sidon Harbor. Although most of the ships in the Tyrian sortie force were sunk, their crews largely escaped by swimming back into the harbor. The disappointment at the tragic result of its sortie must have severely demoralized the Tyrian navy because it remained confined to its ports for the remainder of the siege.

Without the continual harassment from the Tyrian navy, Alexander's mole was able to reach the walls of Tyre. He now constructed ram ships — two large merchant ships with a platform suspended over them on which was placed a ram — and assault ships that had the same basic configuration as the ram ships, except that the platform suspended over the ships held assaulting troops in place of the ram. The first attempt by the ram ships to breach the walls near Sidon Harbor was unsuccessful. Moving to the south end of the island, Alexander was able to make a small breach in the wall, but an assault against it was thrown back. Another breach was then made near the initial one. The ram ships renewed their attack against that breach and widened it. This time an assault carried the position, and the city fell. While Alexander was assaulting through his breach in the south, the Phoenician fleet dismantled the boom across Egyptian Harbor and forced its way inside the harbor. The Cyprian fleet managed to gain Sidon Harbor despite the presence of the remaining Tyrian navy there. The ships' crews had doubtless been called away to help man the walls in an attempt to stem Alexander's successful attack in the south.

The Hellespont Although Alexander ordered the officers in command at the Hellespont to attack Memnon's force at Mytilene immediately, this could not be done because sufficient ships were not available. Alexander thus instructed the League of Corinth to send a fleet to hold the Hellespont and provided 500 talents to meet the expected costs of mobilizing it.[74] He also gave Antipater 600 talents to raise another fleet to hold the eastern coast of Greece should Memnon move in that direction.[75]

Siphnos Proteus (son of Andronicus) had assembled ships from Euboea and the Peloponnese, as ordered by Antipater, to guard Greece against a Persian invasion. Learning that Datames was anchored near Siphnos with 10 ships of the Persian fleet, he sailed from Chalcis that night with 15 ships.[76] Arriving at the island of Cythnus at dawn, Proteus lay at anchor all day to obtain intelligence of the Persian disposition. When Proteus attacked just before dawn on the following day, Datames was taken completely by surprise and had eight of his ships sunk in rapid succession. He then fled back to the Persian fleet with the remaining two ships of his force.[77]

Tenedos Hegelochus captured Tenedos after it had revolted from the Persians. He then besieged Chios.

Chios A faction of citizens at Chios made plans to turn the city over to the Macedonians but were betrayed to the Persians by Apollonides before they could do so. Hegelochus continued to maintain the siege. The continuing friction between the remaining Macedonian supporters and the Persians soon provided another opportunity for the Macedonian partisans still remaining inside the city to rise up. In the resulting confusion, Hegelochus' ships were able to force their way into the city's harbor. The Persian garrison was eliminated in the subsequent fighting, and Apollonides, the ruler of Chios, and Pharnabazus, the commander of the Persian fleet, were both captured. The spoils taken by the Macedonians included 12 triremes with crews, 30 triremes without crews, 50 pirate ships, and 3,000 Greek mercenaries.[78] Aristonicus, the despot of Methymna, unknowingly sailed into the harbor of Chios after its fall with five pirate ships, having been misled into believing that Pharnabazus still retained possession of the harbor.[79] The pirates were subsequently all killed, the rowers were conscripted into the Macedonian fleet, and Aristonicus was brought before Alexander in chains.

Mitylene Mitylene was held by Chares, an Athenian general, with a garrison of 2,000 Persians.[80] Upon determining that he could not withstand a siege, Chares negotiated a withdrawal, and the Macedonians occupied the city. With the fall of Mitylene, other cities on the island of Lesbos willingly surrendered.

Cos Amphoterus was sent to Cos with 60 ships in response to a request from its citizens loyal to Macedonia. He occupied the city without incident. All the prisoners captured by Hegelochus were ordered to be brought to the city. Pharnabazus, however, managed to escape custody shortly after his arrival there.

Sparta Learning that Sparta was planning to revolt, Alexander sent Amphoterus to the Peloponnesians with a number of ships. The Phoenicians and Cypriots were also instructed to send 100 additional ships in support of Amphoterus.[81] Alexander then gave Menes—the satrap of Cilicia, Phoenicia and Syria—3,000 talents to be divided with Antipater and used for prosecuting the naval war against Sparta.[82]

India

Indus River Upon completing the siege of the Rock of Aornos in Swat, Alexander marched on Dyrta, a city lying along the Indus River. Building a number of ships from the nearby woods, he embarked his force and sailed down the Indus to the bridge Hephaestion had built over the river at Attock. While waiting for Alexander, Hephaestion had constructed a fleet of triaconters and smaller boats.

Hydaspes (Jhelum) River On learning that Porus had deployed for battle on the far side of the Hydaspes River, Alexander sent Coenus (son of Polemocrates) back to the Indus River to dismantle the boat bridge spanning that river, cut the boats into sections, and transport them overland to the Hydaspes River for reassembly. The small boats were cut in two sections, the triaconters into three.[83]

The boats were reassembled in secret opposite Alexander's intended crossing of the Hydaspes River at Admana Island, 19 miles upstream from Porus' main camp. When Alexander arrived with the assaulting force, he loaded as many of his hypaspists as possible aboard the ships and rowed across the river at night. The remainder of his army crossed on straw-filled floats. Alexander had mistakenly disembarked his force on the island of Admana, however, rather than on the opposite mainland shore. After a frantic search, a usable ford was found, and Alexander's force safely crossed over to the mainland, although not without some difficulty.

Acesines (Chenab) River Alexander crossed the Acesines River using boats and straw-stuffed hide floats. Although the swift current, sharp rocks, and almost two-mile width of the river wrecked several boats, the floats crossed safely.[84]

Hydraotes (Ravi) River The Hydraotes River was as wide as the Acesines, but the current was much weaker. Alexander was thus able to cross this river with little difficulty.

Hydaspes (Jhelum) River (second campaign) Alexander embarked the hypaspists, archers, Agrianians, and the Agema aboard ships at Haranpur, while the remainder of his army marched along both sides of the shore.[85] Nearchus was made admiral of a fleet that consisted of 80 triaconters and 2,000 service ships— horse transports, grain barges, etc.[86] Most of the ships had been built during the previous two months on the river or commandeered locally. Onesicritus was designated as Nearchus' second-in-command.[87] A total of 32 ship captains were appointed as trierarchs, or rear admirals, including 24 Macedonians, eight Greeks, and one Persian, the eunuch Bagoas.[88] In early November 326 B.C., 8,000 troops embarked aboard the fleet at Jalalpur, including the hypaspists and the Companion cavalry.[89] Craterus marched along the west bank of the river with a portion of the cavalry and infantry, while Hephaestion moved down the east bank with the remainder of the army, which included the elephants.

The fleet traveled no more than five miles a day because of the frequent stops made along the shore. The Hydaspes was said to be two and a half miles wide along the route traveled.[90] Alexander reached the junction of the Hydaspes and Acesines rivers in five days, all the tribes along the way submitting to him without incident. Because of the rapid flow of water resulting from the convergence of two wide streams into a narrow one, violent whirlpools had formed at the junction. Many of the longer ships were damaged or wrecked in collisions with one another or from being thrown against the rocks. Alexander's flagship sank in the rough waters, and being unable to swim, he came close to drowning. Although the wide merchant ships spun uncontrollably, much to the terror of their crews and passengers, they sustained relatively little damage. As the river broadened out, the whirlpools disappeared. This allowed the damaged ships to pull up on shore in order to make much needed repairs.

Acesines (Chenab) River Nearchus sailed down the Acesines River with the undamaged portion of the fleet to the borders of the territory of the Malli. Alexander marched alongside the river, rejoined Nearchus, and then divided up his army into several forces. While Alexander conducted his campaign against the Malli and Oxydracae, Nearchus sailed the fleet down to the vicinity of Multan and established a base camp nearby to await Alexander's arrival there at the conclusion of his campaign.[91] While in camp, Nearchus ordered the construction of a number of additional boats.

Alexander received a serious wound in the assault on the citadel just north of Multan, and the army's rank-and-file believed that he had died and their officers were concealing the fact from them. To demonstrate that he was still alive, Alexander was floated down river to the base camp on a platform suspended between two merchant ships.

When Alexander had sufficiently recovered from his wound, he embarked 1,700 Companions and 10,000 infantry, including some light infantry and a portion of the phalanx, and sailed down the Acesines River to the Indus River.[92] Here he camped until he was joined by Perdiccas, who was moving down the bank of the Hydraotes with the remainder of the army. While Alexander was at the camp, Xanthrians arrived, bringing with him a number of triaconters and transports.

The junction of the Acesines and Indus rivers was established as the southern boundary of Philip's satrapy, and Alexander ordered that a city and dockyards be built on the site. When Craterus arrived, Alexander ferried him over to the left bank of the river.

Indus River (second campaign) Alexander left the junction of the Acesines and Indus rivers and sailed down to the city of Sogda. Here he built a new fortified city and dockyards and repaired the damaged ships of the fleet. He then sailed down to the kingdom of Musicanus because that king had neglected to send any envoys to him. The voyage was made so quickly that Musicanus was literally stunned into submission. Alexander reinstated Musicanus after he had acknowledged his error in failing to submit to him.

Alexander then sailed down to Pattala, subduing several tribes along the way. On the third day of his voyage, he received word that the king of Pattala had fled the territory with most of its inhabitants. Sending out his light troops, Alexander persuaded the greater number of those who had run off to return to the city. At Pattala, the Indus River separates into an eastern and western branch. Alexander built a harbor and dockyard there and then sailed down the western branch of the Indus.

As all the Indians in his vicinity had run off, Alexander was without a pilot familiar with the local stretch of the river, and his fleet experienced great difficulties in its voyage to the sea. The day after he set sail, a fierce storm blew up and the accompanying high winds severely damaged the fleet, even wrecking a number of the triaconters. The fleet was forced to take shelter from the storm by running up on the shore. Damaged ships were repaired, new ships built, and light troops sent out to capture some Indians familiar with the river who could serve as navigators for the fleet. The troops were successful in their mission, and the Indian prisoners guided the Greek fleet for the remainder of its journey down the Indus.

The fleet finally arrived at the delta, where the river is reputed to have been over 2.5 miles wide.[93] The wind, however, blew so strongly from the ocean that the oars became difficult to lift, and Alexander was forced to put into a side channel. As the fleet lay at anchor there, the tide flowed rapidly out, leaving the ships stranded on the shore, much to the amazement of the Greeks, who had never experienced anything like this in the Mediterranean. Several hours later, however, the tide flowed in just as rapidly and the ships were refloated, although several were damaged or wrecked in collisions from the sudden onrush of water.

Alexander anchored at the island of Chilluta, from where he could see another island off the coast, 25 miles away. He sent a force in fast boats to reconnoiter it. Upon the return of this force, Alexander offered a sacrifice to the gods as he indicated he had been instructed to do at Siwah.[94] He then sailed back to Pattala up the eastern branch, which provided some shelter from the monsoon winds. Arriving back at the city, Alexander ordered the construction of a great harbor and dockyards there and began gathering four months' supplies in preparation for his upcoming Gedrosian campaign. A fleet of several ships was stationed at Pattala. Alexander now sailed down the eastern arm of the Indus River. Reaching a lake near the delta, Alexander left behind his lighter ships, and accompanied by troops under command of Leonnatus, he sailed down to the sea. Exploring the coast with light cavalry about three days' distance from his anchorage, Alexander concluded that the eastern branch of the Indus was an easier passage and returned to Pattala.

Arabian Sea

Alexander underwent considerable indecision in appointing a fleet admiral for the Arabian Sea exploration. Because of the unknown dangers inherent in the voyage, he considered the assignment to be extremely hazardous. Some candidates for the position were rejected because they were unwilling to take the required risks, others because they were obsessed by the desire to return home safely. Finally, Nearchus prevailed on Alexander to appoint him fleet admiral, despite the king's obvious reluctance to place one of his close personal friends in such obvious peril. When the selection became known, both the fleet and army were pleased, as in their opinion Alexander would never have exposed one of his close friends to a mission where there was extreme danger.

Where the western arm of the Indus delta met Lake Samarah, Alexander ordered a harbor constructed that would serve as a base of operations for the naval expedition into the Arabian Sea. Nearchus' orders were to determine the feasibility of a seaborne trading route between the Indus and Euphrates rivers. The coast, all islands, any gulfs, and all cities along the way were to be explored. Nearchus was to make detailed notes of land fertility and all water supplies.

The Macedonian fleet assembled for the Arabian Sea exploration consisted of 34 triremes, 80 triaconters, and 400 merchant ships.[95] The naval crews totaled 12,400.[96] The force was a transport, not a war fleet, but a contingent of archers and mercenaries was brought along to cover any landings the fleet might be required to make. Alexander designated that an additional 8,000 soldiers be transported aboard the fleet, including the peltasts, archers and Companion cavalry.[97]

Alexander was greatly concerned with the length of Nearchus' proposed voyage in the Arabian Sea and the possibility of the fleet encountering a long stretch of desert coastline that might preclude the availability of either food or water. As the onshore summer winds and strong tides frequently caused dangerous surf conditions along the coast, the heavier ships would have to remain at sea, leaving only the light ships able to land ashore to gather supplies. In the event of a storm or gale, however, the heavier ships of the fleet could ride it out at sea, whereas any lighter ships attempting to do so would likely incur excessive damage or be sunk.

In an attempt to mitigate the difficulties of the fleet in obtaining food and water, Alexander decided to start out in advance of their sailing. He would march along the coast to dig wells for water and gather food inland for the fleet, leaving depots with appropriate recognition markers along the shore. Soon after starting out, however, Alexander was informed that the Taloi Mountains ran right down to the coast. This would force him to march inland and largely abandon the fleet to its own devices. Even had he been able to proceed along the coast, his army would have consumed the bulk of the meager supplies there, leaving the fleet with little, if anything. Also, it would have been quite likely that the local natives would have obliterated any markers he left behind, filled in any wells that were dug, and taken any food stored in the depots.

Winds from the southwest monsoon, which normally began blowing around mid-July, were delayed in 325 B.C. until August. Sailing would only be possible again on the high seas after the setting of the Pleiads, about November 5.[98] When Pattala was besieged by the local natives who rose up in revolt in October, Nearchus was still able to weigh anchor and sail 19 miles to the Indus River delta.[99] The monsoon winds, however, made the waves so rough in the Arabian sea that Nearchus was forced to dig a half-mile-long channel to ease his ships out into the gulf. Nearchus then sailed another 19 miles down the coast to the island of Crocala, which formed a barrier against the increasing roughness of the sea.[100] About a quarter of a mile away, he put into the shelter of another island named Bibacta.[101] As the sea had now become too rough for sailing, Nearchus built a fortified camp and was forced to wait a month for the monsoon winds to abate.[102]

Early in November the monsoon winds finally died down, and Nearchus was able to sail 210 miles along the coast to Crocala, which was held by Leonnatus.[103] Here Nearchus landed the crews on shore and built a fortified camp. The Oreitans, numbering 400 cavalry and 8,000 infantry, attacked but were defeated by Leonnatus in a hard-fought battle.[104] In the fighting, over 6,000 Oreitans were killed, including virtually all their high-ranking leaders.[105] Leonnatus' losses were only 15 cavalry and a few infantry, but among the dead was Apollophanes, Alexander's satrap of Gedrosa.[106] Damaged ships of the fleet were beached and repaired. Nearchus took 10 days' rations on board and left a number of malingering crew members with Leonnatus in exchange for some of his more reliable infantry.[107]

When the fleet obtained a favorable wind, it left Crocala the next day and sailed 63 miles to the Tomerus River.[108] Here it came upon what appears to have been one of the last pockets of the Neanderthal. They had hairy bodies and claw-like fingernails that they used to rip apart the fish they ate. Since they had no iron, all their cutting tools were made of stone. Animal skins were worn for clothing. A force of 600 fighting men of the tribe massed on the beach to repel any landing attempted there.[109] They were armed with nine-foot-long spears, the wooden tips of which had been hardened by fire.[110] Nearchus initially stayed offshore and bombarded them with long-range missile fire. When this proved to be relatively ineffective, he ordered members of his light infantry who were strong swimmers to swim for shore in their armor, form up in battle order three ranks deep, and charge the Neanderthals at a run. Their attack broke the Neanderthals, who quickly fled into the hills. Nearchus then beached his ships and over the next five days made needed repairs.

After sailing for another 38 miles, Nearchus left the territory of the Oreitans and entered that of the Gedrosians.[111] Continuing his journey along the coast, Nearchus sailed another 538 miles and anchored at Cyiza in the territory of the fish-eaters, so named because they existed almost exclusively on a diet of fish.[112] Interestingly enough, they appear to have had little skill at actually catching fish. Nets made from the bark of date palms, some as long as a quarter of a mile, were laid out along the shoreline for the tide to wash over. When the water receded, the fish-eaters merely gathered the fish trapped in the nets. They ate the smaller fish raw and pounded the larger and tougher ones into a flour from which they made bread. What animals they had were fed fish dried out in the sun because their territory contained no meadows on which grass could be grown. Their shelters were made from the bones of whales that had died at sea and then washed up on the shore.

At this point, the fleet was experiencing its first shortage of provisions.[113] Arriving at a small town, Nearchus thought that it was unlikely that the fish-eaters would willingly part with any of their feed supplies unless forced to do so. As he did not have the time to besiege their walled town, he decided to use a stratagem on the inhabitants. He ordered the fleet to prepare as if it was going to put out to sea, while a single ship was hidden near the town. With a handful of soldiers, Nearchus went to visit the fish-eaters and was politely invited inside their town. As Nearchus entered, he stationed two archers to occupy the posterns of the gate while he, the interpreter, and another two archers climbed the walls and signaled to the crew of his nearby ship. The interpreter with Nearchus told the fish-eaters to give them their corn if they wanted to save their city. The fish-eaters replied that they had none to give, went for their weapons, and attacked the small Greek force. Nearchus, however, easily held them back with his archers until the rest of his crew entered the city. At that point, the fish-eaters begged him to spare the city and take whatever corn he found. Although the fish-eaters had only a small amount of corn and barley, they did have a larger supply of fish flour. Nearchus took everything they had.

At midnight the next day, the fleet sailed another 175 miles to Canasis, a deserted town. The shortage of food was now severe, and Nearchus was afraid to disembark his crews for fear they would desert. Only small quantities of corn and palm dates were found ashore. During the next 369 miles, Nearchus' fleet was able to obtain only small quantities of corn from the poverty-stricken villages along the coast. So desperate for food were his men that they immediately slaughtered and ate some camels they came across.

The fleet now came ashore in the satrapy of Carmania, anchoring at Badis. The area was wooded and contained plentiful supplies of drinking water and various fruits.[114] From there the coast inclined towards the northwest, indicating the entrance to the Red Sea. Sailing another 200 miles, the fleet reached an uninhabited place along the coast named Harmozia. There the fleet anchored and disembarked. Encountering a Greek, they were informed that Alexander's camp was five days' journey inland. Nearchus beached his ships to repair damages and surrounded his camp with a double stockade, a mud wall and a trench.

When the satrap of Carmania heard of Nearchus' landing in his territory, he thought that Alexander would generously reward the first person to bring him information of his admiral's safe arrival. Instead, when the anxious Alexander sent out search parties who were unable to find Nearchus, the governor was arrested for spreading false rumors. One of Alexander's search parties, however, had passed right by Nearchus' group but was unable to recognize them because of their disheveled condition. They were all covered in tattered rags, had long hair, were unwashed, covered with brine, and pale from sleeplessness. When Alexander's search party passed them a second time, Nearchus inquired of them whether they knew of Alexander's whereabouts. After identifying himself, Nearchus was immediately taken to the Macedonian king. When Alexander first saw Nearchus and his party, he thought that they were the sole survivors of the fleet and wept, both for the safe arrival of his friend and for the loss of the fleet. He then asked Nearchus how the fleet was lost, and on being told that it was all safe, he wept all the more as the news seemed too good to be true.

Persian Gulf

At the end of the festivities celebrating Nearchus' safe return from the Arabian Sea exploration, Alexander expressed his wish to appoint another admiral over the fleet so that Nearchus' life would not be placed in further danger by the hazards of sailing the fleet to Babylon. Nearchus, however, vigorously objected, stating that the hardships of his command on the most dangerous part of the voyage would be eclipsed by the greater glory to be acquired on the final and easier part. Alexander relented on the forcefulness of Nearchus' request and reluctantly allowed him to continue as admiral of the fleet.

Alexander gave Nearchus a small escort back to his fleet. Because Carmania's satrap had been executed, however, and Tlepolemus, his successor, had not yet established his authority, anarchy prevailed throughout the satrapy. Although Nearchus' party fought with the local natives on three separate occasions, they were able to reach the coast and safely rejoin the fleet.

Nearchus then weighed anchor and after sailing 38 miles anchored at Organa, a 100-mile-long island.[115] Its governor, Mazenes, volunteered to act as his navigator as far as Susa. Continuing its journey, the fleet reached an island said to be sacred to Poseidon. As they put out to sea at dawn, the inbound tide came in so quickly and with such force that it swept three ships unto the beach. The next day, however, all the ships were safely refloated.

After a long but relatively uneventful voyage, the fleet arrived at Cataea, a small island said to be sacred to both Hermes and Aphrodite. It marked the boundary between Carmania and Persis. Much of the Persian coast consisted of shallows, dangerous surf and lagoons. The Susiana coast, by contrast, was marshy with breakers, a good anchorage only being found with considerable difficulty. As a result, for most of the remaining voyage the ships had to remain out in the open sea.[116]

Tigris River

When he arrived at the mouth of the Euphrates, Nearchus received reports that Alexander was headed towards Susa with his army. Determined to meet the king, Nearchus sailed 75 miles up the Pasitigris and Eulaeus rivers to a pontoon bridge the army would be using to cross the river.[117] Upon meeting Alexander, Nearchus accompanied him to Susa. At their departure from that city, Alexander ordered Hephaestion to embark a large number of infantry, the Agema, and a small number of Companions and sail with him down the river to the Persian Gulf.[118] Alexander then took the faster and more seaworthy ships and sailed out into the open sea and up the mouth of the Tigris River, while the remainder of his navy under Hephaestion, which included some damaged ships, sailed across a canal cut between the Eulaeus and Tigris rivers. Rejoining Hephaestion on the Tigris, the combined force sailed up the river to Opis. As Alexander proceeded up the river, he removed the "weirs" the Persians had installed there. These damlike obstructions were emplaced to prevent any hostile navy from navigating the Tigris. Alexander was obviously far more concerned with free navigation in support of trade than he was in securing himself against any remote possibility of invasion along the river. From Opis, Alexander marched overland to Ecbatana, the capital of Media.

Caspian Sea

Alexander wanted to determine if the Caspian Sea was connected to the Black Sea by a waterway and was part of the ocean forming the eastern border of Asia or if it was merely an inland sea. Upon his return to Babylon, he ordered Heracleides of Argos, a Macedonian officer, to begin building a war fleet on the Caspian coast of Hyrcania. It was evident that Alexander thought it quite likely that Heracleides would be forced to fight unfriendly tribes during the course of his exploration. The fleet was partially completed in 323 B.C. when Alexander arrived in Babylon. His subsequent death there, however, brought an end to any plans for the exploration of the Caspian.

Arabia

Now that Alexander had explored the Arabian Sea and the Persian Gulf, he wondered if he could sail around Arabia to the Gulf of Egypt, that is, the Red Sea. Knowing little of Arabia's size, he sent four ships on separate voyages to explore round the peninsula. Three of the voyages originated from the Indian Ocean and were to explore the eastern coast of Arabia: Archias, exploring the island of Tylus, or Bahrain; Androsthenes, exploring both Tylus and the Gerrhaean coast; and Hieron of Soli, exploring the coast of Arabia as far down as Ras Mussendam. Archias did not sail further south than Tylus, but Androsthenes sailed west from the Gulf of Egypt as far as Yemen before being forced to turn back because of a lack of water. As a result of these voyages, Alexander learned that Arabia was about as large as India and was believed to be rich in natural resources.

The docks of Babylon were expanded to accommodate 1,000 ships for the Arabian expedition.[119] Nearchus was again appointed to command the fleet. It comprised ships that had come up the Euphrates from the Red Sea; some ships that were cut into sections and carted overland from Phoenicia to Thapsacus, where they were reassembled and sailed down to Babylon (two quinqueremes, three quadriremes, 12 triremes, and 30 triaconters); and other ships constructed from the cypress trees cut down near Babylon.[120] Miccalus of Clazomenae had been given 500 talents and sent to Phoenicia to recruit crews.[121] Impressed by the reports of the richness of Arabia, Alexander was determined to conquer and colonize its coast. He believed the area to be as potentially prosperous as Phoenicia. Tylus was a primary objective of the expedition, both because of its soil fertility and its location astride one of the main distribution points for the spice trade with Arabia. It appears that Alexander's intention was to campaign as far south as Yemen and to conquer the spice lands themselves. It is quite likely that he wished to annex the south coast of the Persian Gulf and use it as a springboard to invade the interior of Arabia. Alexander contracted his fatal illness just prior to the departure of the Arabian campaign. Upon Alexander's subsequent death, his successors canceled the Arabian campaign and concentrated their efforts on holding those portions of his empire they had acquired.

Persian Navy

Although the Persians were primarily a land power, they recognized the importance of a large navy in the eastern Mediterranean and spared no expense in assembling the largest fleet in antiquity. The conquest of Phoenicia, the Greek islands, Cyprus and Egypt provided the skilled seamen, shipbuilding facilities, and dockyards necessary to build and maintain the fleet. Each national contingent or city-state commanded its own forces, although the fleet commander was always a Persian or a Persian appointee. The Phoenicians not only furnished the largest number of ships but were said to have the best constructed vessels and the most skilled seamen. The Egyptians usually provided the next largest contingent, followed by the Cypriots, Cilicians, Carians, Lycians and Pamphylians, respectively. From 30 to 40 marines were stationed aboard each ship.[122] Initially, they were either Persians or Medes, but later they were primarily Greek mercenaries. It is thought that since the main weapon of the trireme was the ram, the purpose of the large number of marines on the ships might have been to prevent the desertion of their crews.[123] As many of the naval contingents of the Persian fleet had been impressed into service or served as mercenaries, their loyalty was always in doubt. This suspicion was to be borne out during Alexander's siege of Tyre, when the Persian navy suffered heavy desertions from the Phoenician and Cyprian contingents. The one and a half to two and a quarter tons of additional weight of the large number of troops on their decks made the Persian triremes top-heavy and difficult to handle and doubtless adversely affected their seaworthiness. To rectify this situation, the Persians started constructing their triremes with broader hulls and higher sterns.[124] The resulting weight and size of the Persian trireme caused greater wind resistance, reduced speed, and sluggish handling, making them considerably less maneuverable than their Greek counterparts although a more suitable platform for boarding actions.

Tactics

Persian naval tactics were relatively simple. Because it usually heavily outnumbered any potential enemy, the main concern of the Persian fleet was the escape of its opponent. This led to an advance on the enemy by the main body of the Persian fleet in a crescent formation in an attempt to collapse its flanks, driving them into the center to create demoralization and mass confusion. A secondary naval force was often detached to cut off any enemy escape to the rear. The Persian ships were normally deployed several lines deep, their tactic being to rush upon their opponent in such numbers so as to preclude any naval maneuvering. If the initial Persian attack was held at arm's length, however, the numerous and tightly packed ships of the fleet could easily be thrown into disorder and become entangled with one another by an unexpected enemy reaction or a change in either the direction or intensity of the wind. When this occurred, an opponent like the Athenians could pick the struggling Persian ships off as easily as shooting ducks in a barrel. Any heavy losses in Persian ships were usually accompanied by equally heavy manpower losses. The crews of all Persian vessels were fully armed and were unable to swim; they frequently drowned even when only just offshore.[125] A Persian fleet could avoid naval combat, however, simply by running its ships up on a beach and constructing a wall round them which could easily be defended by their heavily-armed crews.

Persian Naval Operations

Hellespont When Alexander crossed over into Asia in 334 B.C., his passage across the Dardanelles was not contested by the Persian fleet.[126] Typically, it was as time consuming for the Persians to mobilize their navy as their army, the process usually taking several months. Although Darius began raising the fleet as early as 336–35 B.C., he was seriously hampered in his efforts by the need to prosecute an immediate campaign against Egypt, which had revolted from his empire in 338 B.C. Darius was finally able to subdue Egypt about the time of Alexander's Balkan campaign. Immediately thereafter, the Persian fleet went into a required maintenance refit. The time this took and the need to synchronize the fleet's mobilization with the agricultural harvests largely precluded its availability to dispute Alexander's crossing of the Hellespont in May 334 B.C.[127]

Miletus By midsummer of 334 B.C., Darius had appointed Memnon commander of the 400 ships of the Persian fleet that had been mobilized.[128] Memnon took the fleet to Miletus, which was being besieged by Alexander, arriving there only a few days after the 160-ship allied Greek navy had occupied and fortified a base at Lade, an island just across from the city's harbor.[129] The Persians were forced to establish their base at the next closest anchorage at Mt. Mycale, nine miles from Miletus. Each day the Persians would sail to Miletus in an attempt to provoke a battle with the Greek fleet, but Alexander would always refuse to commit his unreliable and untrained navy to battle. When Alexander sent a strong land force under Philotas to Mycale, however, the Persian fleet was deprived of its only water supply and was forced to withdraw to Samos.

Halicarnassus   From Samos, Memnon sailed with the Persian fleet to Halicarnassus, the main Persian naval base in the southern Aegean and one of the most heavily fortified cities in the Persian Empire. As Alexander had demobilized his fleet at Miletus, the Persian navy did not have to concern itself with a possible fleet action. Instead, it picketed the nearby waters in an attempt to interdict individual Greek ships. The majority of its ships anchored in Halicarnassus' harbor to provide their crews as additional support for the defense of the city, should that prove necessary.

At Myndus, the Persian fleet frustrated Alexander's attempt to take the city by supplying seaborne reinforcements to it. Alexander had hoped to capture the city by treachery and then land his siege artillery there. After a siege of two months, Halicarnassus' harbor was rendered usable, and the Persian fleet evacuated what troops and stores they could and sailed to Cos. For additional details on the siege of Halicarnassus, see Chapter 7.

Mytilene   After leaving Halicarnassus, Alexander proceeded to march southeast along the Lycian coast. Memnon now began a campaign to reconquer the northern Aegean islands held by the Greeks. With a Persian fleet of 300 ships and 60,000 men, he captured Chios by treachery and all of Lesbos except Mytilene. Around that city he built a double wall.[130] Part of the fleet was used to blockade Mytilene harbor, while the remainder was sent to Sigeum, a promontory of Lesbos. There the ships intercepted cargo ships bound to Mytilene and generally patrolled the coast. While prosecuting the siege of the city, however, Memnon became ill and died.[131] Pharnabazus was appointed to command the Persian fleet the month after Memnon's death.

Mytilene was successfully blockaded and fell, being again forced to ally with Persia under the terms of the Peace of Antalcidas. Upon their return, the city's exiles were to receive back half the property of which they had been deprived. A Persian garrison was established in the city under Lycomedes of Rhodes. Diogenes, one of the exiles, was appointed to rule Mitylene.

Lycia   Instead of keeping the fleet concentrated, Pharnabazus dispersed it to undertake simultaneously four separate operations: besieging Mytilene, besieging Tenedos, assisting the Spartans in their revolt, and attempting to reconquer the cities along the Carian and Lycian coast that had been lost to Alexander. Although this strategy effectively interdicted Alexander by sea along the coast of Asia Minor, it was largely a wasted effort because Alexander's successful land campaign had already established a solid supply base in Asia. His critical line of communications at the Hellespont, however, was never attacked by the Persian fleet. Cutting him off here from Macedonian and Greek reinforcements could have done serious harm to his campaign because he had continuing manpower needs for the conquest and retention of the Persian Empire.

Pharnabazus sailed to Lycia with the Greek mercenaries, while Autophradates went to the other islands. Darius now recalled the Greek mercenaries for service with his army because they were the only effective heavy infantry troops available to him who were able to stand up against the Macedonian phalanx. Their departure forced the demobilization of some 200 ships, with the result that the Macedonian navy was now able to reach a rough parity in numbers with the Persian fleet. Pharnabazus then sailed to join Autophradates.

Cyclades Ten ships were sent to the Cyclades under Datames, while a hundred went on to Tenedos.[132] Although the city was strongly inclined towards Alexander, it was forced to submit to Pharnabazus upon his arrival there, Alexander being unable to send a fleet to support them. The walls of Tenedos were destroyed and its citizens forced to resume the Peace of Antalcidas with Darius. The Persian fleet immediately sailed to the island of Andros and then to the island of Siphnos to meet with Agis, the king of Sparta. He had arrived there in a single trireme to request both funds and ships for his campaign against Crete.

Dissolution of the Fleet As the Persian fleet lay at anchor at Siphnos, it heard the news of Darius' loss of the battle of Issus and the beginning of Alexander's Phoenician campaign. The fleet again separated, Pharnabazus going to Chios with 12 triremes and 1,500 mercenaries to suppress unrest there, 10 triremes accompanying Agis, and the remaining ships of the fleet sailing to Phoenicia to suppress expected uprisings there.[133] Unfortunately, the Phoenician rebellions there were too far advanced, and the Persian fleet was unable to contain them. Agis, after dispatching the 10 ships and 30 talents he had received to his brother Agesilaus on Crete, joined Autophradates at Halicarnassus. The Persian fleet then reunited and sailed to Crete to assist the Spartans in conquering the island.

As Alexander's Phoenician campaign progressed, the Persian navy was systematically deprived of its naval bases and recruiting areas for its ships' crews and was cut off from its source of wages at Susa. When Alexander began to besiege Tyre, the Persian fleet finally broke up with the desertion of naval contingents from Byblos, Aradus and Cyprus. These immediately offered their services to Alexander and were soon joined by ships from Lycia, Mallus, Rhodes and Soli. Alexander now possessed naval supremacy in the Aegean and eastern Mediterranean, and from that point on the remaining Persian navy was the heavily outnumbered defender. Chios, Cos, Lesbos and Tenedos were subsequently retaken by the Macedonian fleet, one after the other, and the remnants of the once mighty Persian fleet were eventually run to ground, with Pharnabazus suffering the indignity of being captured.

Part II

The Reign of Philip II

5. Campaigns of Philip II

Philip inherited a kingdom whose northern frontier was occupied by marauding Balkan tribes. This was the result of the Dardanians' shattering victory over the Macedonian army under Philip's predecessor, Perdiccas III. After thoroughly rebuilding his army, Philip proceeded to subdue the Balkan tribes and eject them from northern Macedonia. Upon securing the eastern coast of Macedonia, he then subdued the Thracian coast to secure his line of communications to Asia Minor, and he removed the Athenian threat to his eastern route by ejecting them from the Chersonese. After safeguarding Macedonia's western border by turning Epirus into a client state, Philip secured Thessaly to the south by becoming involved in the Sacred War in its behalf. This made it possible for him to project his power into central Greece. At the battle of Chaeronea, Philip's overwhelming defeat of an allied Greek army allowed him to bring central Greece and the Peloponnese under his control. He was now master of all Greece and stood poised to begin his long dreamed of campaign against Persia. Philip's untimely assassination, however, left this glorious task to his son, Alexander III, better known to history as Alexander the Great.

Illyria

Paeonians

In the aftermath of Perdiccas' defeat in 359 B.C. by the Dardanians, the Paeonians began regularly raiding and pillaging northern Macedonia. When their king, Agis, died, Philip saw an opportunity for successful military action against them in early 358 B.C. The death of a Balkan king usually precipitated confusion in the tribe, temporarily weakening its cohesion and ability to react effectively to external threats. In the subsequent campaign, Philip quickly defeated the Paeonians. The treaty imposed on them required acknowledgment of the Macedonian frontiers and the raising on demand of troops for Philip's use. A fortified line constructed along the Axios River in Paeonia provided northern Macedonia with an effective buffer against any further attacks from that tribe.

Dardanians

The Dardanians were one of the three most powerful Illyrian tribes. Perdiccas III, king of Macedonia, humiliated by the indignity of having to pay tribute

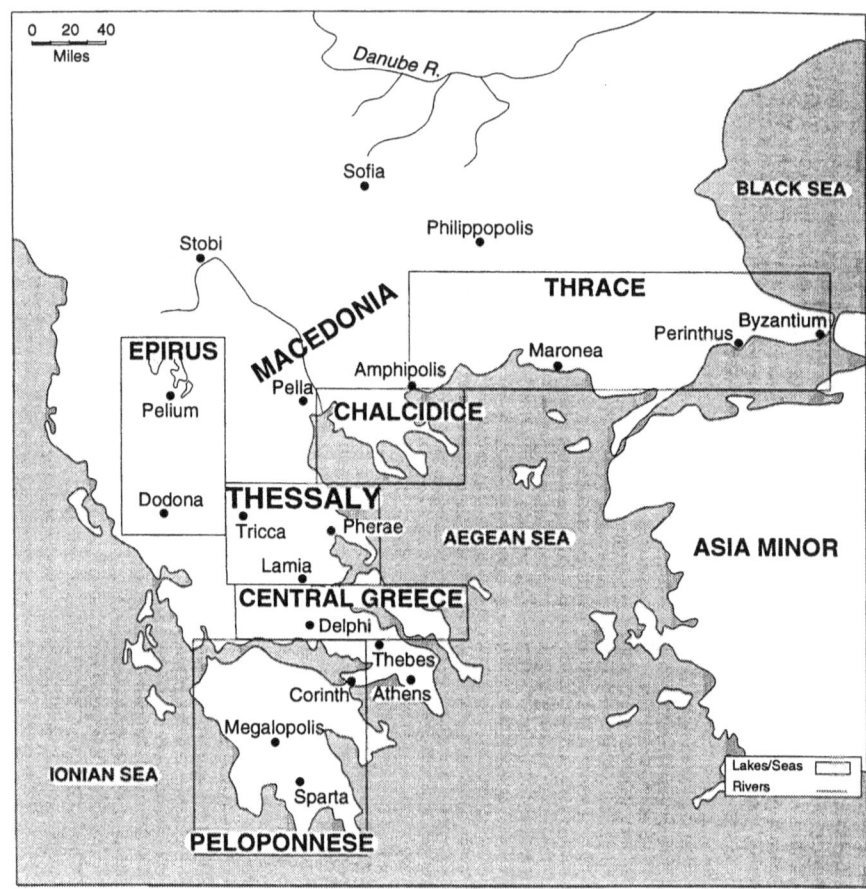

Map 1: Greece

to the Dardanians, marched north in the spring of 358 B.C. at the head of the Macedonian army to resolve the issue by battle. The Dardanians, under their king Bardylis, heavily defeated the Macedonians. Among the 4,000 Macedonian dead was their king, Perdiccas III.[1] The Dardanians followed up their victory by expanding their control southward to Lake Lychnitis and westward into upper Macedonia.

When Philip assumed the Macedonian throne, substantial areas of upper Macedonia remained in control of Bardylis. In order to concentrate on the internal struggle necessary to secure his crown, Philip reaffirmed the treaty the Dardanians had imposed on Macedonia by force of arms and sealed the alliance by his marriage to Audata, probably a niece or daughter of Bardylis. This action undoubtedly deterred a full-scale Dardanian invasion of Macedonia at a time when the country was most vulnerable.

Battle of Erigon Valley By the spring of 358 B.C., Philip had at last secured

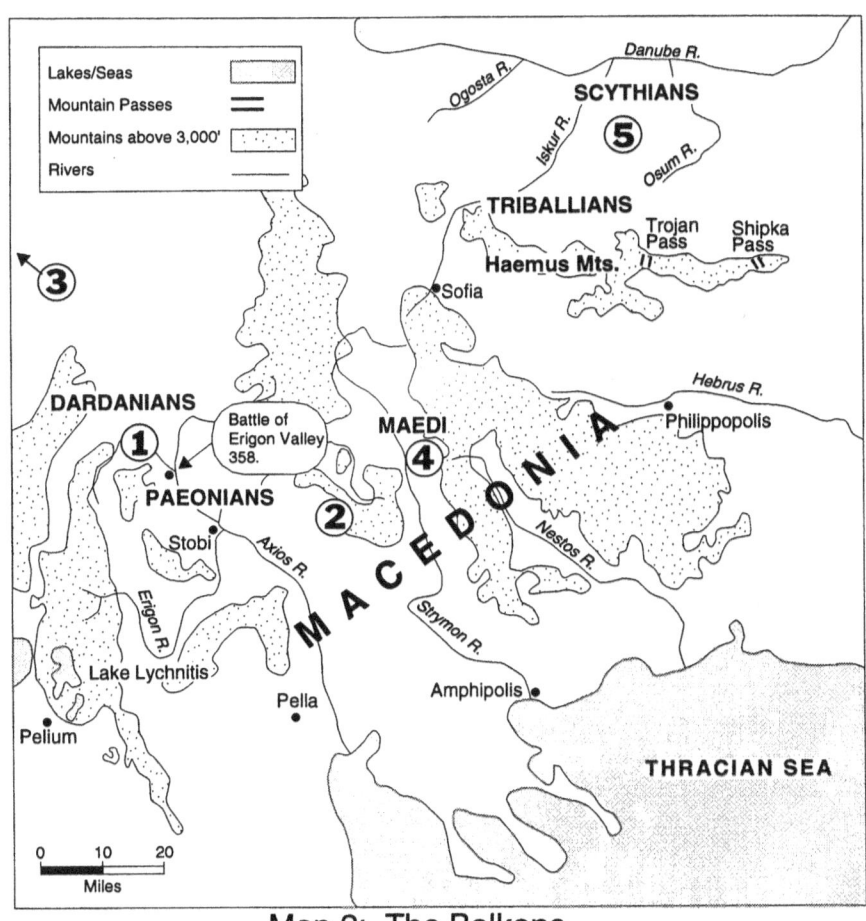

Map 2: The Balkans

1. In 358 B.C., Philip campaigns against the Dardanians. 2. In 358 B.C., Philip campaigns against the Paeonians. 3. In 345 B.C., Philip campaigns against the Ardiaioi. 4. In 340 B.C., Alexander defeats the Maedi. 5. In 339 B.C., Philip defeats the Scythians. Refusing to part with any of his Scythian booty while passing through the territory of the Triballians, Philip is attacked and wounded by them, and has his booty taken from him.

his throne and was now able to address the occupation of northwest Macedonia by the Dardanians under their king Bardylis. When word of the mobilization of the Macedonian army came to Bardylis' attention, he proposed to Philip that they sign a treaty to maintain the status quo. This was, of course, unacceptable to Philip, because he was not prepared to consider any terms other than a full Dardanian withdrawal from northwest Macedonia. Bardylis, however, was not inclined to give up his occupation without a fight. Philip mobilized every able-bodied soldier in Macedonia for the battle. The Dardanians, as before, were not likely to take any prisoners, so any defeat at their hands would probably result in crippling casualties for the Macedonians. Philip, however, never lacked courage and marched his army northwest from Macedonia.

Although the two armies were almost equal in numbers — Bardylis fielding 500 cavalry and 10,000 infantry against Philip's force of 600 cavalry and 10,000 infantry — Philip's force was by far the better trained and equipped.[2] The armies met in battle on a plain in the Erigon Valley, near Lake Okhrida, just south of Dardanian territory.[3] Bardylis initially deployed in a linear formation with his strongest troops in the center. Philip concentrated his best troops, the hypaspists, on his right flank. As Philip advanced to engage Bardylis, his cavalry turned one or both of Bardylis' flanks, forcing him to redeploy into a square formation. Philip's hypaspists then achieved a penetration into the right corner of the Dardanian square that the Companions were able to widen.[4] This threw Bardylis' entire formation into disorder, after which it was quickly broken by the phalanx and routed off the battlefield.

The battle had cost the Dardanian 7,000 casualties, almost three quarters of their army.[5] Philip secured Macedonia's northwest frontier by annexing Dardanian territory as far as Lake Lychnitis. This would form an effective buffer against any future Dardanian raids attempted through the Drilon Valley.[6]

Generalship It was clear that the superiority of Philip's Companions played a key role in forcing Bardylis to adopt the square formation and then in exploiting the penetration made by the hypaspists. The echeloned formation Philip used in his attack and his concentration of the superior hitting power of his hypaspists along a narrow front all but ensured a breakthrough. Also telling was the inferiority of Bardylis' peltasts compared to both the phalanx and hypaspists, the Illyrian infantry clearly being no match for the well-trained and heavily armed Macedonians.

Ardiaioi

In 345 B.C., Philip conducted a hard-fought campaign against the Ardiaioi, under their king Pleuratus. He ruled the territory in the lower valley of the Drilon, which corresponds roughly to modern northern Albania. The influence of the Ardiaioi had gradually spread southward, and realistically it was probably only a matter of time before they would attack northwest Macedonia. Philip's strategic options were to await the event or to launch a preemptive strike. He unhesitatingly decided to march against them. In the course of the resulting battle, Philip was seriously wounded in the lower right leg, being saved from death only when one of his "favorites" jumped in front of him at the sacrifice of his own life. Philip's campaign against the Ardiaioi was, however, highly successful, and he returned to Macedonia with much booty.

Triballians

In the spring of 339 B.C., Philip was returning to Macedonia loaded down with the booty of over 20,000 prisoners and 20,000 mares he had taken in the Scythian campaign.[7] When he reached the territory of the Triballians in the Mount

Haemus area, they demanded a share of his loot before allowing him to pass on. Although they were reputed to be the fiercest tribe in the Balkans, Philip refused to part with any of his spoils. He was subsequently attacked and during the fighting was severely wounded in the thigh, a javelin penetrating his leg with enough force to kill his horse. Philip's army, believing him to be dead, panicked, and in the resulting confusion the Triballians were able to make off with most of their booty. Philip, however, recovered sufficiently to conduct a fighting withdrawal of his army safely back to Macedonia.

Because the Triballians refused to acknowledge his sovereignty, Philip again invaded their territory. The details of the campaign are unknown, but Philip was apparently victorious over them. The terms of the resulting treaty forced the Triballians to acknowledge Macedonia's sovereignty over them.

Generalship

Philip embarked on a punitive campaign in Illyria not only to provide some realistic training for his new army but to secure the northern frontier of Macedonia against occupation or raids of bordering Balkan tribes. The campaign gave Philip the opportunity to fine-tune the army's new tactical doctrine against light opposition from the largely undisciplined and poorly armed Illyrian tribes, who usually suffered heavy casualties in all their encounters with the Macedonians. The tribes' sole success occurred in the confusion of the Macedonian army's mistaken belief that Philip had been killed in battle with the Triballians. Strategically, Philip's campaigns successfully secured the northern frontier of Macedonia during his lifetime. Although the Illyrian tribes were not completely pacified by him, their power was temporarily broken by a straight-up military defeat and it was not until Alexander's reign that they again presented a threat to Macedonia.

The Third Sacred War

The so-called "Third Sacred War" broke out between the Amphictyonic League and Phocis in 355 B.C. It supposedly began because of Phocian cultivation of a portion of the Cirrhan plain, which had been consecrated to the god at Delphi. The underlying cause of the war, however, was a Theban attempt to dominate central Greece. The Thebans, who controlled the Amphictyonic Council, convinced it to impose a heavy fine on the Phocians for the sacrilege.[8] When the Phocians protested that to pay the fine would ruin them, the Council promptly doubled the amount and stated that unless it was discharged the entire Phocian state would be confiscated and dedicated to the gods.

Philomelus

Philomelus, one of Phocis' leading citizens, vowed that if the Phocis would appoint him its general with absolute powers he would successfully conclude the upcoming war. On the strength of this promise, he was elected to the position.

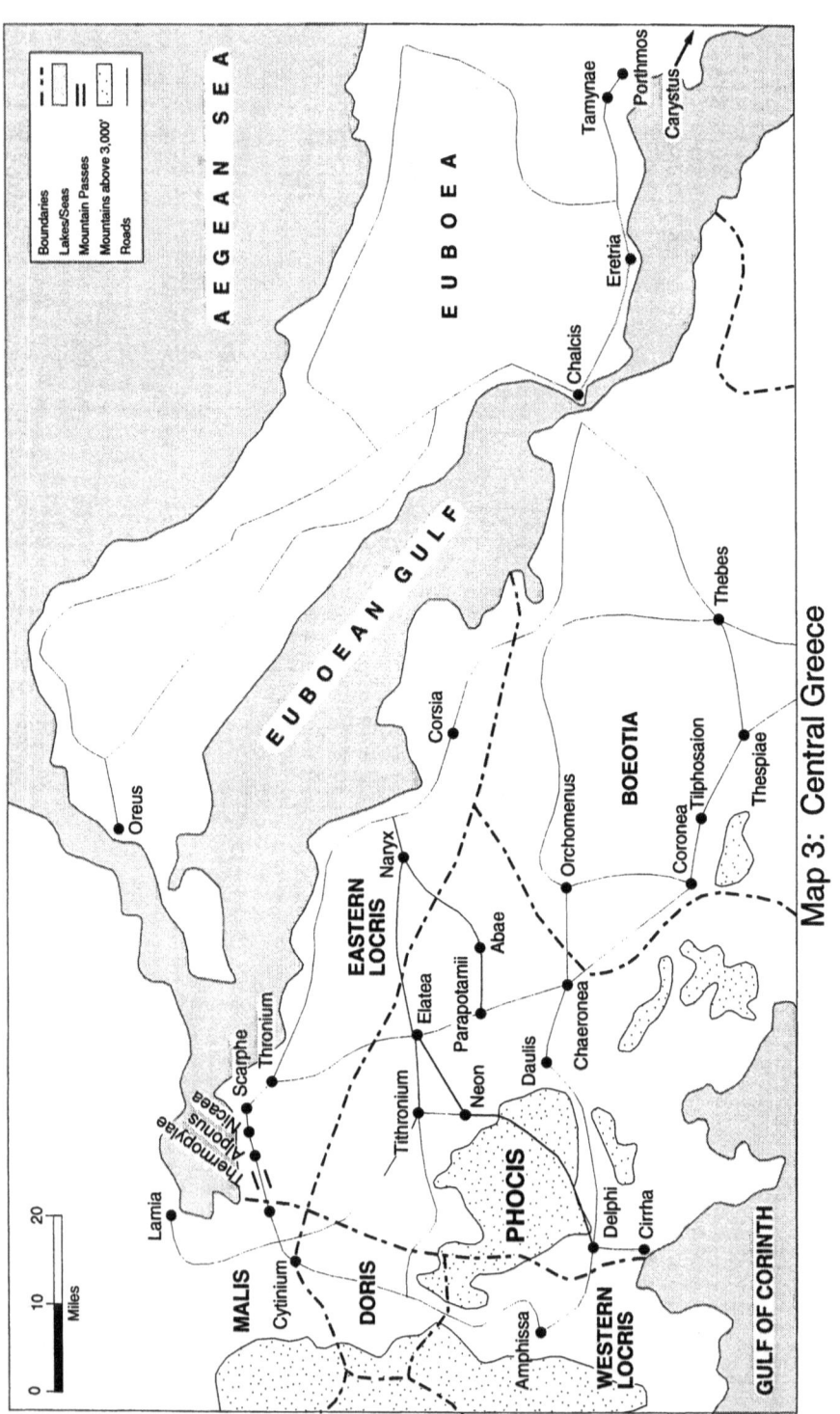

Map 3: Central Greece

His first action was to attempt to enlist the support of Sparta, as it was under a similar indictment.⁹ Philomelus promised the Spartan king Archidamus that if he supported him in seizing Delphi, the Amphictyonic decrees against Sparta from the Leuctrian War would be annulled. Although Archidamus was in sympathy with Philomelus' predicament, he declined to provide him with any troops but did give him 15 talents, to which Philomelus was able to add another 15 talents.¹⁰ Philomelus then used these funds to hire a force of mercenaries, who along with 1,000 Phocian peltasts seized Delphi in the summer of 355 B.C.¹¹ A group of Delphians named the Thracidae who were guarding the oracle were killed, and their possessions were confiscated.¹² This provided Philomelus with the necessary funds to pay his mercenaries for several additional months. When the Locrians heard of the Phocian seizure of the shrine, they immediately marched their army to Delphi. A battle was fought above the Phaedriades (the great cliffs dominating Delphi), and the Locrian army was badly defeated. Some of its soldiers were forced to jump from the cliffs, and a large number of others surrendered as prisoners.¹³

Although Philomelus had signed a formal alliance with Athens and Sparta, he had yet to obtain any troops from them. Thebes convened the Amphictyonic Council in the autumn of 355 B.C. in an attempt to enlist support for prosecuting the war. Thebes was clearly disappointed with the result because the Thessalian League remained preoccupied in its continuing struggle against the Pheraen tyrant house while the other members preferred to await the outcome of events before committing themselves. The Council, however, did manage to pass a declaration of a sacred war against Phocis. In support of the Council's action, the Boeotians and their allies began to mobilize their army. Philomelus saw that Phocis' survival depended solely upon it being able to field a large force of mercenaries. This, of course, took money and a great deal of it because mercenaries were expensive (the wages of a force of 1,000 mercenaries totaled about five talents a month). To quickly raise a large force of mercenaries, Philomelus offered one-and-a-half times the normal wage.¹⁴ The proceeds for this generosity were obtained from extortions of the wealthy inhabitants of Delphi. A sizable force of 5,000 mercenaries was raised by such means. They were, however, stigmatized by most Greeks as the scum of the earth.

When his army was fully mobilized in the autumn of 355 B.C., Philomelus marched into eastern Locris.¹⁵ The area was strategically important because it lay upon the most likely route for the Thessalians and Boeotians to join forces. After skirmishing inconclusively with the Locrian army, Philomelus overran the open country. Gathering up large quantities of plunder for his mercenaries, he then returned to Delphi for the winter. Although the Boeotians had taken no steps to oppose Philomelus' march, it was clear that they were in the process of raising their full force against him. Philomelus attempted to enlist the support of Athens and Sparta, but both again refused to commit any troops, the Athenians being hesitant to involve themselves in sacrilege and the Spartans being afraid to have their actions during the Leuctrian War brought up again. In the meantime, the Aenianians, Boeotians, Dolopians, Dorians, Locrians, Magnesians, Perrhaebians and Thessalians reaffirmed their determination to continue the war against Phocis. The only effective military option remaining to Philomelus was to begin appropriating temple funds to raise a still larger mercenary force.

Philomelus again invaded eastern Locris in the spring of 354 B.C., this time with an army numbering 10,000.[16] He began his campaign by winning a battle against the combined cavalry forces of the Boeotians and Locrians. Philomelus then cut off and defeated a 6,000-strong force the Thessalian League had sent to join Boeotia and Locris near Argolas Ridge.[17] This action drove the Thessalians into civil war. The Thessalian League of the inland plain sought the support of Philip of Macedonia, while Lycophron allied the coastal area of Thessaly with Athens. Once again the Boeotians marched in support of Locris, this time with an army of 13,000. The Phocians were reinforced by 1,500 Achaeans from the Peloponnese.[18] Although the two armies camped nearby each other for some time, they did not engage in combat. The Boeotians then announced that all mercenaries captured who had enlisted in the army of the Phocians would be treated as temple robbers and would be liable to immediate execution. They then proceeded to execute all the mercenaries recently caught foraging. This, of course, enraged the mercenaries, who then persuaded Philomelus to execute prisoners from the Boeotian army. After camping in close proximity of each other for some time, both armies marched off in different directions.

In the autumn of 354 B.C., a Boeotian army and a considerably smaller Phocian army stumbled into each other in some heavy woods near Neon, on the north side of Mt. Parnassus, near the Phaedriades cliffs. The heavily outnumbered Phocians were defeated and suffered heavy casualties in their retreat through almost impenetrable country. Philomelus was wounded in the battle and driven to the top of some cliffs. Fearing torture if captured, he chose instead to leap to his death. The Boeotians, believing that their victory was decisive and that the Phocians would now submit to a peace, returned to their own country. Onomarchus, one of Philomelus' commanders, led the survivors of the Phocian army back to Delphi.

Onomarchus

Upon their army's return to Delphi, the Phocians proceeded to discuss their future strategy. Onomarchus, who represented the war party, successfully argued against any peace policies being considered. He had a strong self-interest in the Phocians continuing the war because the Amphictyonic Council had levied an almost ruinous fine against him. Appointed commanding general of the Phocian army, Onomarchus began recruiting a new mercenary army to replace the heavy losses sustained at Neon. Liberal use was now made of the temple funds not only to pay the high wages needed to recruit another large mercenary force but to bribe many Greek political leaders to support Phocis or stay neutral. The two factions of the now divided Thessaly, which were more intent on squaring off against each other, were easily bribed by Phocis to forego active participation in the war.[19] Any Phocians openly disagreeing with Onomarchus' policies were either imprisoned or executed and their estates were confiscated.

5: CAMPAIGNS OF PHILIP II

After the Boeotian victory at Neon, the Thebans, being in extreme financial straits and convinced that the war was now virtually over, hired out an army of 5,000 of their troops under Pammenes to assist Artabazus, the satrap of Hellespontine Phrygia, in his revolt against the Persian king.[20] Taking advantage of the situation, Onomarchus invaded eastern Locris with a large army early in 353 B.C. He captured Thronium, one of three cities controlling the pass through Thermopylae, and Amphissa, which dominated the mountain route into central Greece west of Thermopylae. Turning south to devastate Doris, Onomarchus then marched west into Boeotia. When the Boeotian army declined to take to the field, he captured Orchomenus. After he laid siege to Chaeronea, however, the Boeotians marched to its relief. Although only sustaining a small defeat by their army, Onomarchus returned to Phocis at the end of August 353 B.C.

Philip invaded Eastern Thessaly at the request of the Thessalian League. Being allied with Phocis, Lycophron requested its assistance. In response, Phayllus, Onomarchus' brother, was sent into Thessaly with a 7,000-man army.[21] Upon entering the country, however, he was defeated by a combined force of Boeotians, Macedonians and Thessalians and was forced back into Phocis. Hearing of the defeat, Onomarchus broke off his Boeotian campaign in the autumn of 353 B.C. and marched north with the entire Phocian army, which numbered 500 cavalry and 20,000 infantry. He then fought an indecisive battle against Philip's army of 3,000 cavalry and 20,000 infantry but was able to defeat him in a second battle, which was an ambush.[22] In that battle, Onomarchus had deployed along a ridge with his line formed in the shape of a crescent. Stone-throwing catapults were concealed on each flank. Luring the Macedonians into the plain opposite the ridge by a feigned withdrawal, Onomarchus was able to bring them under the heavy fire of his catapults.[23] This bombardment, in conjunction with rocks rolled down from the heights, broke the ranks of the phalanx. At that point, Onomarchus counterattacked, and the Theban and Thessalian troops took such heavy losses that they began to break up. Philip had little choice but to retire north during the winter to rebuild his army. He reassured his allies, however, that he would come back in the spring like a ram to butt all the harder.[24]

In the spring of 352 B.C., Onomarchus attacked Boeotia in an attempt to drive it out of the war. Any captured cities there would also give him valuable bargaining chips in the negotiations he mistakenly thought that a now desperate Philip would soon be pursuing. Onomarchus succeeded in defeating the Boeotian army and capturing the Boeotian cities of Coronea, Corsiae and Tilphosaion.[25] He was then notified that Philip had reappeared in Thessaly. To Onomarchus it now seemed possible for Phocis to end the Third Sacred War victoriously. If he could unite with Lycophron in Thessaly, he was convinced the combined force could again defeat Philip and then force Boeotia out of the war. Onomarchus marched north in high hopes. Philip, meanwhile, had marched south in an attempt to interpose his army between Lycophron and Onomarchus. The opposing armies met on the plains of Crocus Field.

Battle of Crocus Field Lycophron called on Phocis for assistance, but by the time Onomarchus was able to arrive, Philip had occupied Pagasae and had already passed on to Crocus Field. There the plain allowed him the proper room to deploy fully his cavalry. Chares arrived with a fleet from Athens sometime after Pagasae had fallen, but as the port was now held by Philip, he was unable to land any force along the coast to assist Lycophron. Onomarchus, however, was able to join Lycophron, and their combined force totaled 500 cavalry and 20,000 infantry.[26] Philip and the Thessalians were able to field a joint army of 3,000 cavalry and 20,000 infantry.[27]

Although little is known about this battle, it appears that Philip's cavalry again played the primary role in his victory. The defeated Phocians fled to the beaches and attempted to swim to the offshore ships of Chares. Being weighed down by their armor, however, many were drowned. Onomarchus was either killed outright in the battle or he drowned while trying to escape to the Athenian ships. A total of 6,000 Phocians and allied mercenaries were killed in the battle and 3,000 were taken prisoner.[28]

If Philip had marched against the Phocians immediately after the battle of Crocus Field, he would probably have been able to force their surrender and end the Third Sacred War. Many of Philip's allies expected him to do just that, but he instead moved against Pherae, undoubtedly believing it necessary to first secure his line of communications by thoroughly pacifying eastern Thessaly.[29] With the capture of Pagasae, the only usable port on Thessaly's coast, Philip prevented the Athenians from landing any troops in support of Lycophron. Philip also acquired the Thessalian naval force based at the port, which allowed him to begin raiding Athenian shipping. Philip then lay siege to Pherae. As Lycophron was surrounded by a hostile population, he was soon forced to negotiate terms. In return for surrendering the city, he was allowed to depart peacefully into the Peloponnese with the 2,000 mercenaries in his employ.[30] He subsequently joined forces with the Phocian army, now under Phayllus. Pherae's rule in Thessaly had finally come to an end.

By the time Philip had concluded his operations in Thessaly and moved south, the Phocians had been able to request and receive troops from Achaea, Athens and Sparta. The Athenians occupied Thermopylae with a force of 400 cavalry and 5,000 infantry under command of Nausicles.[31] Concluding that the position was too strongly held for him to carry, Philip withdrew back into Thessaly.

Phayllus

Shortly after the death of Onomarchus at the battle of Crocus Field, his brother Phayllus succeeded to the command of the Phocian army. To rebuild the army's ranks that had been depleted by the 9,000 casualties it sustained at the battle, Phayllus began to appropriate massive amounts of Delphi temple funds. Offering double the normal pay, he recruited another large force of mercenaries.[32] He also received numerous troops from his allies: the Achaeans provided 2,000 infantry; Athens, 400 cavalry and 5,000 infantry; Sparta, 1,000 infantry; and Lycophron, the former tyrant of Pherae, 2,000 mercenaries.[33] Athens now feared an invasion of Attica, while Sparta and Achaea thought that if Philip entered the Peloponnese many of the city-states there would quickly join him. In July 352 B.C., Philip marched on Thermopylae. Upon receiving intelligence of the presence of Phayllus there, however, Philip again reversed his march and retired to the north. Any attempt by his army to force the pass when it was defended in such strength would have resulted in unacceptably high casualties. Philip was also unable to remain in the area because it was largely denuded of provisions, while Athenian naval supremacy precluded any dependable source of supplies being delivered by sea. Then too, Philip had only Thessaly as an ally, the Boeotian League being reluctant to risk an attack on Phocis as long as Phayllus held Coronea, Corsiae, Orchomenus and Tilphosaion. Because Philip had been prevented from entering central Greece through Thermopylae Pass, the Phocians had been given the time to recruit another large force of mercenaries. In the autumn of 352 B.C., Phayllus marched into Boeotia but was defeated at Orchomenus, sustaining heavy losses. Beaten again in another battle near the Cephissus River, he suffered 400 prisoners and 500 killed.[34] A few days later Phayllus lost yet another battle with the Boeotians near Coronea, this time sustaining a loss of 130 prisoners and 50 killed.[35]

Phayllus now decided to invade eastern Locris, and he captured all the cities there except Naryx. Although a small Phocian force had entered that city by treachery at night, it had been driven out the next day at a cost of 200 casualties.[36] While Phayllus was encamped near Abae, the Boeotians attacked at night and heavily defeated him. The Boeotians then invaded Phocis, capturing a large quantity of booty. On their way back home, the Boeotians decided to assist Narycara, then being besieged by a Phocian force. As the Boeotians were deploying, Phayllus unexpectedly appeared. After attacking and putting the Boeotian army to flight, Phayllus stormed, sacked, and razed Narycara. During the winter, Phayllus died of a wasting disease.

Phalaecus

Phalaecus, a son of Onomarchus, was now appointed to command the Phocian army. Because he was an adolescent, General Mnaseas was designated as his adviser. Not long after he was appointed, however, General Mnaseas was killed in a night attack by the Boeotians. In the spring of 351 B.C., Phalaecus lost a cavalry battle against the Boeotians near Chaeronea.[37] The Boeotians then proceeded to devastate Phocian territory around Hya. Encountering Phalaecus near Coronea, the Boeotians were defeated with heavy losses. When the Phocians occupied several Boeotian cities, the Boeotian army again took to the field, invaded Phocis, and destroyed its grain. Upon the Boeotians' return home, however, they were defeated by Phalaecus.

In 350 B.C., there was only desultory fighting because the Thebans were virtually bankrupt. They sent an emissary to the Persian king, Artaxerxes, and received 300 talents for their effort.[38] Nevertheless, they could do little more than conduct skirmishes. The Phocians, faced with Athenian unwillingness to finance the war, turned to Sparta and Corinth for support. Sparta, however, having sent an army under its king, Archidamus, to campaign in Italy for some badly needed revenue, was unable to provide any troops.[39] The Sacred War had reached a stalemate.

The Boeotians again invaded Phocis in 349 B.C., devastated the state, and won a victory against its army at Hyampolis, but they were then defeated by the Phocians near Coronea. The Phocian army pillaged Boeotia in the early summer of 348, using the three fortified Boeotian cites that it held there — Coronea, Corsiae and Orchomenus — as its base of operations. The Boeotians, being short of both manpower and money, were forced to call on Philip II of Macedonia for assistance. Initially, he only sent a small number of troops to assist them both because he wanted to humble their pride and because he did not want to appear to be indifferent over the looting of the sacred treasury at Delphi.

A Phocian force attempted to fortify Abae, a holy shrine to Apollo. Upon the arrival of the Boeotian army, the Phocians dispersed, some to nearby cities and others to the temple, where they thought they would be safe under the protection of the gods. Scattered around and inside the temple were large quantities of combustible material. A fire ignited by one of the nearby campfires spread rapidly, burning alive the 500 Phocians sheltering inside the structure.[40]

In the spring or summer of 347 B.C., the moderate Phocians opposing Phalaecus managed to remove him from command of the Phocian army under allegations of appropriating Delphi temple treasure for his personal use. Phalaecus did, however, continue to command the support of a large force of mercenaries camped nearby Thermopylae. While the investigation was being conducted, the generals Callias, Deinocrates and Sophanes were appointed to command of the Phocian troops. Philon, who had responsibility for the temple funds, identified under torture those participating in the theft.[41] The perpetrators were forced to return whatever remained of the temple funds, after which they were hanged as temple robbers. The investigation concluded that over 10,000 talents had been removed from the temple treasury.[42]

In the autumn of 347 B.C., representatives from the Phocian government received intelligence that Philip was about to march on Thermopylae. In response, they asked Sparta to provide a force of 1,000 troops to defend the pass and informed Athens that they would turn over to it the three cities controlling the pass — Alponus, Nicaea and Thronium — if Athens would send a force to occupy them.

Because the Athenian fleet denied Philip access to central Greece by sea, he desperately needed Thermopylae, the only viable overland route into central Greece.[43] Because a large force occupied the pass, however, Philip knew that it would be extremely difficult, if not impossible, to carry it by assault. His first step was to get Phalaecus reinstated to the command of the Phocian army. This he was able to do easily, no doubt by bribing a number of influential Phocian politicians and providing Phalaecus some funds he could use to pay the wages of his army, which had slipped into arrears. When Athens sent Proxenus to take possession of the cities promised it by the Phocian representatives, Phalaecus, in fear that Athens or Sparta might support his political opponents, repudiated the agreement. Upon

Proxenus' return to Athens, the expedition to occupy the cities was canceled. The Spartan leaders, having arrived with 1,000 troops to occupy Thermopylae, were rudely told to return to the Peloponnese, which they promptly did.[44] Philip then opened negotiations with Phalaecus for possession of Thermopylae. Undoubtedly, this was agreeable to Phalaecus, and as a gesture of good faith to Philip he must have moved the Phocians out of their positions at Thermopylae and in their place substituted his mercenaries.

Although Phocis still held the Boeotian towns of Alponus, Coroneia, Corsiae, Nicaea, Orchomenus and Thronium, Phalaecus was well aware that without funds from the Delphi treasury Phocis would be unable to meet the continuing wage expense of the mercenaries, who were already beginning to grow disorderly from the irregularity of their pay.[45] If their wages were not soon forthcoming, the mercenaries in Phocian employ were likely to disband. As the Phocians had all but exhausted the temple funds, they were now reduced in desperation to digging beneath the temple for some buried treasure mentioned in the *Iliad*.[46] While in negotiations with Philip, Phalaecus sent an embassy to Athens to determine what support he could expect from the city.

When Phalaecus repudiated the Phocian offer to turn over the cities controlling the pass at Thermopylae, the Athenians became convinced that Phocis would lose the war. In response, the city immediately sent a delegation to query Philip on his terms for ending it. Philip was agreeable to a negotiated end to the war because he did not want to be associated with any massacre of the Phocians that might result from their defeat in any renewal of the fighting. He also was reluctant to break Phocian military power, as it was the only check on Theban expansion in central Greece. All the major participants in the war, including Euboea, Phocis, Sparta and Thebes, sent representatives north to Pella in April. Philip met with each delegation separately, encouraging everyone to believe that a settlement would be in their own best interest. He requested all to stand down from war preparations, indicating that he was personally convinced that peace was imminent. Philip, of course, refused to return Amphipolis to Athens but said he would suspend further military operations in the Chersonese while negotiations were in progress. He promised many unspecified benefits to Athens if it would only ally with him.

The returning Athenian embassy deliberately magnified the hopelessness of Athens' ability to carry on the war and Philip's sincere desire to end it. The assembly was led to believe that Philip secretly wished to protect Phocis and to punish Thebes for starting the war. On that basis, it approved a proposed peace treaty and sent a second embassy to Philip to secure his ratification. A Phocian delegation sent by Phalaecus arrived in Athens just as the second Athenian embassy was reporting back to the assembly on the treaty it had just signed with Philip.

When the Athenian Assembly heard that Philip had not only excluded Phocis and Halus from the treaty but had authorized the Amphictyonic Council to determine the nature of the settlement, its members became highly dissatisfied with the treaty. They were now not only convinced that Phocis, their long-standing ally, was likely to be harshly treated but they also feared that Athens might be implicated as an accomplice in the Delphi sacrilege. The Athenians now turned full circle and voted to send a force to march on Thermopylae in support of the Phocians. Cooler heads apparently soon prevailed, however, and the army's marching orders were indefinitely postponed.

Philip had delayed the oath swearing for the peace with the excuse that all of his allies were not yet present for the treaty ratification. He did, however, mobilize his army, ostensibly for use against Halus on the Gulf of Pagasae. The city had broken away from Pharsalus, and the Macedonians had been besieging it on Pharsalus' behalf since spring.[47] Parmenio, Philip's best general, had been rather indifferently conducting the siege, largely to enable Philip to continue a ruse he had planned. Instead of augmenting the besieging force at Halus as he had indicated was his intention, Philip bypassed the city, marched through Lamia, made camp outside of Thermopylae, and proceeded to open negotiations with Phalaecus. He also requested that Athens, as his newfound ally, should join him at Thermopylae with its army. If the Athenians had complied, not only would he have had the Athenian army in his power but its presence with him would have undoubtedly intimidated the Phocians. Philip's unexpected arrival at the pass and the exclusion of Athens' ally, Phocis, from the peace treaty had soured the Athenians against him. They were too ready to believe Demosthenes' warning that once the Athenian army was within Philip's reach he would to hold it hostage to intimidate Athens. As a result, the Athenians refused to allow any force to be sent to Philip.

Upon their return the Phocian ambassadors told Phalaecus that Athens desired peace, even at the expense of Phocis, but this was not the worst. Athens had indicated that if the Phocians did not immediately surrender Delphi, it would march against them and compel them to do so by force of arms. Although it might have been possible to hold Thermopylae against Philip, it was clearly impossible to hold the pass against Athens as well. Also, once the Amphictyonic Council again took possession of Delphi the investigation it was sure to initiate would quickly implicate Phalaecus in sacrilege. Phalaecus therefore decided to accept Philip's offer while he still had some leverage to do so because it was clear that the Macedonians were completing preparations to assault the pass. In one of the most contemptible actions of the war, Phalaecus turned over control of the pass to Philip in return for being allowed to depart peacefully with his 8,000 mercenaries into the Peloponnese, although without weapons and horses.[48] With the desertion of the mercenaries, Phocian military strength became inadequate to carry on the war against Philip, especially in light of the fact that he had now gained access to the interior of their state. The Phocians saw no option but to surrender unconditionally all 22 of their towns to him. For details on the negotiations and terms of the peace, see Appendix A, Peace of Philocrates.

Philip had sided with Thebes in the Third Sacred War largely because the Thessalians were its ally and the enemy of the Phocians. He could not afford any unrest along his line of communications through Thessaly. He also desperately needed the Thessalian heavy cavalry for his anticipated campaign against the Persian

Empire, whose army was largely comprised of heavy cavalry. Philip had, in fact, been appointed archon of Thessaly largely to campaign on its behalf against the Phocians. As the Phocians were universally condemned for their sacrilege against the temple treasury at Delphi, had Philip allied with them he too would almost certainly have been cursed by the Greeks.

Philip prevented any severe penalties being imposed on the Athenians and made the treaty with them in an attempt to obtain their naval support for his projected war against Persia. Sparta, too, was let off lightly in the hope that it might also eventually become an active ally in his campaign. This, however, proved to be only wishful thinking. The Spartans chose to remain aloof from any participation in both his attempt to unify Greece and his projected Persian campaign. The smaller states of Greece, however, were led to believe that they had at last found someone to support them against the larger imperialistic states, especially Athens and Sparta. Philip kept his promise and retired north immediately after the peace was made. It was to be seven years before it would be necessary for the Macedonian army to move south again into central Greece. This time it would be led by Alexander against a Theban revolt.

Generalship

Philip's victory in the Sacred War was won as much by duplicity and bribery as by battle. His successful bribing of Phalaecus to turn the Athenian and Spartan armies back from Thermopylae and his ruse over Halus effectively ended the war in a victory for himself. While these tactics were contemptible morally, they were effective techniques he would continue to make good use of in the future. Philip's victory over Phayllus was followed by two defeats Onomarchus inflicted on him. This forced his withdrawal back into Macedonia to regroup. In his second defeat, Philip had apparently been badly surprised in a disadvantageous tactical position and had seen his army begin to break up. This would indicate that some elements were not fully trained, making it necessary for him to spend the winter in rectifying this deficiency. It is clear that Onomarchus' retention of the initiative had maneuvered Philip into a disadvantageous tactical situation and he had suffered significant military defeats, but these reverses did not weaken Philip's resolve or Macedonia's military power.

During the next campaigning season, Philip was much better prepared. Preventing the Athenians from reaching the battlefield of Crocus Field by the capture of Pagasae, Philip was at last able to select ground on which he could maneuver his cavalry. He subsequently decisively defeated the Phocians when they engaged him in battle. In his second campaign, Philip clearly held the initiative from beginning to end and was able to exploit his strategic and tactical military abilities as well as his obvious skills at bribery to good advantage. Thermopylae was taken, and the Phocian army was so weakened by the subsequent withdrawal of its mercenaries that without Athenian assistance it was unable to continue to resist Philip effectively. The Phocians were forced to surrender unconditionally to Philip, finally bringing the Third Sacred War to a close.

The Macedonian Coast

Siege of Methone

Methone's position on the coast allowed it to maintain successfully its independence from Macedonia throughout the fifth century. Methone lay between Pydna and the Haliacmon River and adjacent to the road south to Tempe and Thessaly. The only way around it was an arduous trail through the mountains.[49] Although Methone was a constant strategic threat to Philip, he was too preoccupied initially with the problems of his succession to deal with it. When his throne was finally secured, however, he was able to turn his full attention to the city, which was quickly becoming an important base for the Athenian navy.

Philip deployed his army nearby Methone for some time prior to the beginning of siege operations in the hope that the city might be coerced to surrender. When this did not happen, he put the city under siege during the winter of 355 B.C. The city threw back at least one Macedonian assault in which Philip lost his eye to an arrow. Being on the edge of famine, however, the city was soon forced to surrender. The citizens were forced to leave the city, each being allowed to take only a single garment. Upon their departure, Philip razed Methone and distributed its land to Macedonians.[50] The capture of the city removed the last Athenian base along the Macedonian coast and eliminated the possibility of any Athenian raids being conducted into the interior of Macedonia.

Siege of Pydna

Pydna lay along the coast, five miles south from Methone.[51] The city was besieged by Philip in late 357 B.C., just after the fall of Amphipolis, and it fell through treachery. Although the anti–Macedonian element in the city was enslaved, Pydna was not destroyed, nor were its walls dismantled. Instead, the city was incorporated into Macedonia. Pydna apparently became an administrative center for both the territory around Methone and for Philip's interaction with the League of Corinth.[52]

Chalcidice

The Thracian kings had no particular strategic or political interest in the Chalcidice, deriving only a small annual income of 30 talents in land tax from the area and 200 talents in harbor duties.[53] Athens, however, saw the peninsula as a key strategic position along Macedonia's line of communications in any eastward expansion through Thrace. Philip also saw that he must control the Chalcidice before he could contemplate any campaign against Persia. The Chalcidian League in the 380s B.C. had been able to overrun the coastal plain of Macedonia as far inland as Pella, which it captured. In 360 B.C., the League was able to field a combined army of 1,000 cavalry and 10,000 peltasts.[54] This was dangerous enough, but if the

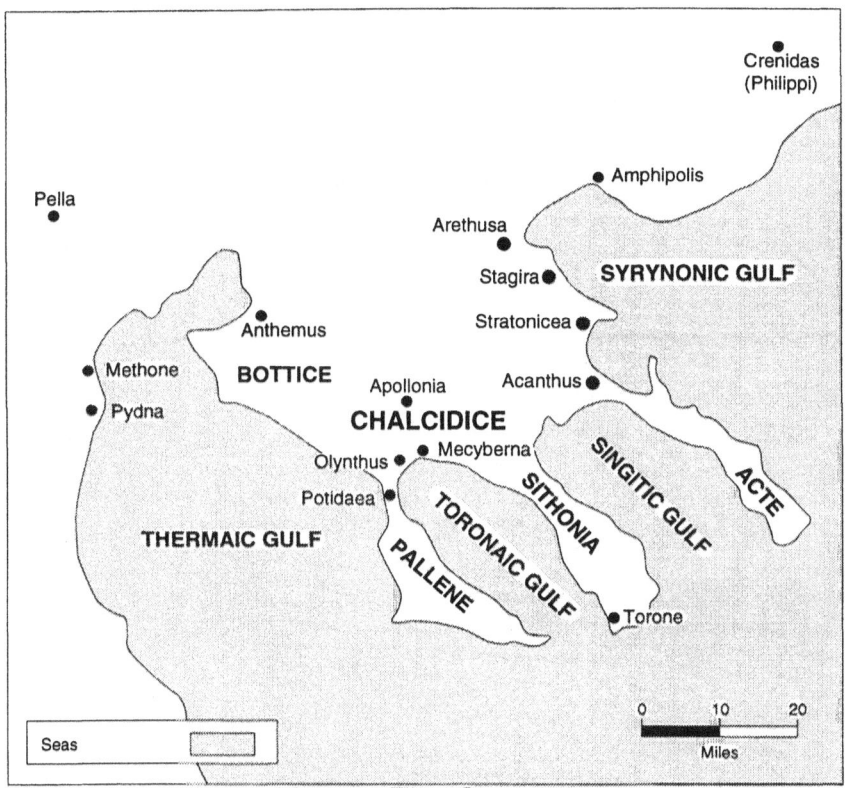

Map 4: The Chalcidice

Chalcidians combined forces with the Athenian bases at Potidaea and Torone, they might be tempted to repeat their earlier invasion of Macedonia in an attempt to deprive Philip of his power base. This had to be prevented at all costs, and for Philip the only viable solution was to eject the Athenians from the Chalcidice, disband the Chalcidian League, and incorporate the Chalcidice peninsula into Macedonia.

Potidaea

Potidaea itself did not have a harbor and was therefore vulnerable to overland isolation. The city was a commercial rival of Olynthus, and a large portion of its population was comprised of Athenians. In July 356 B.C., Philip and his Olynthian and Chalcidian allies put Potidaea under siege, and the city soon fell. The Athenians had voted to send a relief force to the city, but the Etesian Winds and Athenian indecisiveness in actually sending out the expedition ensured that the force arrived too late to serve any useful purpose, as was to be all too often the case.

When Potidaea fell, Philip turned the city over to the Olynthians as he had promised. He also released all the Athenians he had captured there without ransom, having no desire at the time to antagonize Athens unnecessarily. Philip claimed that the attack of Potidaea was not made with any hostility towards Athens but was merely in support of his ally, Olynthus. Because Philip believed that the Potidaeans had willingly admitted the Athenians into their city, they were sold into slavery and their land given to the Chalcidian League.

Stagira

Occupying a strategic position alongside the road between Macedonia and Amphipolis, Stagira was among the first Chalcidice cities to be attacked. It was captured and razed by Philip in the autumn of 349 B.C.

Eastern Chalcidice

Nearby towns in eastern Chalcidice, including Acanthus, Apollonia, Arethusa and Statonice, submitted to Philip without resistance. No single town was able to oppose Philip for long in the field by itself, instead of being forced to undergo siege. Being so heavily outnumbered by the Macedonians, however, especially in heavy cavalry, the League's generals refused to commit their combined army to a risky field battle against a vastly superior Macedonian army. Philip was thus able to secure the area quickly and prevent any east-west movement along the Strymonic Gulf coastline to Olynthus.[55] He then turned his attention to Olynthus.

Olynthus

Olynthus was located along a river, about one and a half miles inland from the Toronaic Gulf, and had a population of 10,000 males.[56] Its economy was based on the export of corn and shipbuilding timber, which brought in large revenues. Olynthus had been founded by Chalcis, a city in Euboea, which, in turn, had been founded by Athens. In 432 B.C., several of the Chalcidian cities, having withdrawn from the Athenian Empire, formed the Chalcidian League, which eventually grew to 32 cities by 349 B.C.[57] Olynthus was established as the League's capital. The city probably accounted for half the Chalcidian League's military force, being able itself to field some 500 cavalry and 5,000 hoplites.[58]

Although Olynthus was a member of the Second Athenian Confederacy, when Athens commenced operations against Amphipolis, Olynthus and other cities of the Chalcidice peninsula sent assistance to the city. Before attacking Amphipolis, the Athenians captured Potidaea, a city located a mile or so from Olynthus. The Athenian cleruchs settled in the city greatly restricted Chalcidian intervention against any Athenian operations on the peninsula.

With the rise of an aggressive Macedonia under Philip, the Olynthians recognized a much more serious threat than Athens to their freedom. When Philip besieged Amphipolis in 357 B.C., Olynthus opened negotiations with Athens in the hope of enlisting its support for the defense of the Chalcidice. The Athenians, however, ignored the Olynthian proposals, as they were mistakenly convinced that Philip was conducting the siege of Amphipolis on her behalf. Having no other option, the Olynthians approached Philip and concluded a peace with him. One of the stipulations in the subsequent treaty prohibited the Olynthians from conducting negotiations with Athens in the future. This allowed Philip to reduce the other cities of the Chalcidice League without interference from either Olynthus or Athens.

In the summer of 349 B.C., Olynthus, concerned that Macedonia was continuing expansion in the Chalcidice, again approached Athens with an offer of an alliance. Philip, looking for an excuse to take action against the city, demanded that his stepbrothers, Arrhidaeus and Menelaus, who had been granted refuge there, be immediately turned over to him. Their continued presence so close clearly belied Olynthus' hostile intentions towards his throne. When Olynthus refused to consider his demand, Philip had his justification, if he needed one, for moving against the city. Olynthus had also violated the treaty of alliance that it had signed with Philip by conducting negotiations with Athens. Philip doubtless suspected that it would be only a matter of time before Olynthus obtained Athenian assistance against him.

The Athenians soon dispatched a force of 30 ships and 2,000 peltasts in support of Olynthus.[59] Nothing, however, is known of the activities of this force, and it may be presumed to have accomplished little, if anything. Moving down the west side of the peninsula through Bottice and Pallene, Philip began conquering the Chalcidice League cities, one by one. By the spring of 348 B.C., the western part of the peninsula had been overrun. The scattered cities, being too weak to take the field separately against the Macedonian army, were forced at the appearance of Philip to withdraw into their cities to undergo siege and eventual capitulation.

Olynthus was not yet under attack when an Athenian force under Charidemus consisting of 18 triremes, 150 cavalry, and 4,000 peltast mercenaries arrived from the Hellespont between March and May.[60] Charidemus conducted raids in Philip's rear and was able to occupy the Pallene and devastate Bottice. Instead of continuing his successful campaign, however, Charidemus turned his attentions to indulging in debaucheries, and it ground to a halt. In the late spring or early summer of 348 B.C., Mecyberna, the port of Olynthus and Torone, fell to Philip by treachery.[61] This cut Olynthus off from the Toronaic Gulf. Philip now told the Olynthians that either they would have to leave Olynthus or he would have to renounce the Macedonian crown.

When Charidemus' attack subsided, Philip was able to continue his advance on Olynthus. When he attempted to cross the Sardon River, however, the Olynthians put up such fierce resistance that the Macedonians failed to gain the far bank.[62] In the summer of 348 B.C., the Olynthian army was defeated in two field battles and forced to fall back into its city to undergo siege.[63] Olynthus sent Athens a last desperate appeal for assistance, requesting a relief force of Athenian citizens in place of the usual expendable mercenaries. In response, the Athenians voted for an expeditionary force of 17 triremes, 300 cavalry, and 2,000 Athenian hoplites under command of Chares.[64] The Etesian Winds, however, delayed the force, and

Olynthus fell before its arrival. The Athenians, being fearful of Olynthian treachery, may well have slowed the mobilization of the force until the beginning of the Etesian Winds gave them a convenient excuse for inaction. Sending expendable mercenaries on a faraway campaign was one thing, exposing the lives of Athenian citizens was quite another. Olynthus had been under siege for two months and had apparently thrown back several assaults with heavy losses to the Macedonians. Although 500 nobles of the Olynthian cavalry under the command of Lasthenes defected to Philip, the city continued to hold out in the hope that Athenian reinforcements would soon arrive. In August/September 348 B.C., one year after being besieged, the city fell in a hard-fought storming.

The citizens of Olynthus were enslaved, and their city was razed. The land holdings of the city were distributed to the Companion cavalry, and the considerable income from their sale, along with the booty that was taken, provided Philip with sufficient funds with which to continue his campaign in the Chalcidice. Philip's two stepbrothers, Arrhidaeus and Menelaus, who had taken refuge in Olynthus, were put to death. The Chalcidice peninsula now became, in effect, a Macedonian province. Athens somewhat belatedly offered citizenship to any Olynthians who had escaped. Philip released all Athenians captured at Olynthus without ransom. In reaction to Philip's stated desire to make peace with them, the Athenians attempted to form a Greek coalition against Macedonia during the winter of 348–47 B.C.[65]

Thessaly

After the assassination of the Tagus Jason in Thessaly, the lack of any strong central leadership there and the inability of the leading noble families to cooperate with one another resulted in almost continual political instability. During the seventh and sixth centuries, when Thessaly had been united, its power had rivaled that of Sparta. In the fifth century, however, the growth of powerful cities had resulted in a breakdown of central authority and the leading noble families were able to reassert control and prevent the reestablishment of central authority. By the fourth century, Thessaly had divided into two hostile factions, the western area organizing itself into the Thessalian League and the eastern area falling under the domination of the tyrants of Pherae.

Alexander, the tyrant of Pherae who succeeded Jason, was assassinated by his wife, Thebe, and her brothers Lycophron and Tisiphonus.[66] Tisiphonus assumed the office of tyrant and began a period of constitutional rule in Thessaly. As a result, an uneasy peace prevailed between the Thessalian League and Pherae. Upon Tisiphonus' death, however, his brother Lycophron assumed the position of tyrant. Initially posing as a democrat, Lycophron soon revealed himself to be nothing more than a despot. Employing a large force of mercenaries, he was able to impose his rule on Thessaly by force. Lycophron was now opposed by the Thessalian League and its two major cities: Larisa, under the control of the Aleuadae, and

5: CAMPAIGNS OF PHILIP II

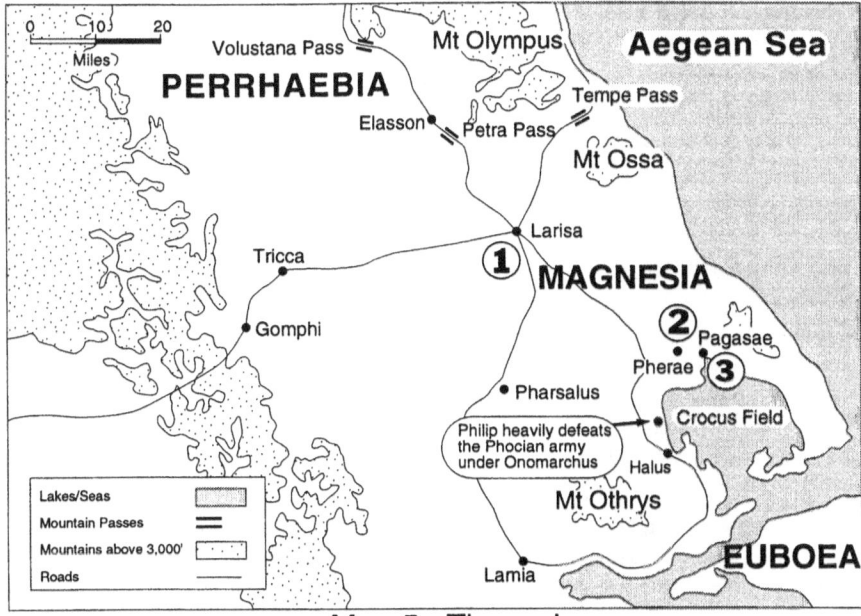

Map 5: Thessaly

1. The seat of power of the Thessalian League. 2. The seat of power of Lycophron. 3. Thessaly's only harbor.

Pharsalus, under control of the Daochidai. Finding itself, however, too weak to oppose Lycophron effectively, the League sought help from Boeotia. Unfortunately, with the outbreak of the Third Sacred War during the spring of 356 B.C., the Boeotians were heavily involved in mobilizing against the Phocians and were unable to provide the League any assistance.

As a member of the Amphictyonic Council, the Thessalian League, despite its internal troubles with Pherae, felt compelled by its sacred duty to Delphi to respond to the declaration of war against Phocis issued by the Amphictyonic Council. After leaving behind a sufficient force to hold Lycophron in check, the League sent a 6,000-strong army to join the Boeotians in the spring of 354 B.C.. Before the force could effect a junction, however, it was heavily defeated by Philomelus at Argolas Ridge. In the aftermath of the Phocian defeat at Neon sometime later that year, it appeared to the Thessalian League that the Third Sacred War was over. As this had been the only unifying factor in Thessaly, civil war now broke out between the Thessalian League and Lycophron. Steadily losing ground against the tyrant, the Thessalian League was forced to call upon Philip of Macedonia for assistance.

Philip was eager to control Thessaly. The military potential of the country was considerable because it was able to field a combined force of 3,000 heavy cavalry and 20,000 peltast infantry.[67] The state was famous for its horse breeding and its cavalry that was the equal of the Macedonian Companions in both training and combat effectiveness. The Thessalian plain was also one of the few places in Greece where large bodies of cavalry could be provisioned, trained, and maneuvered.

In late 354 B.C., Philip entered the district of Perrhaebia, in Thessaly, which had recently broken away from Larisa.[68] He annexed the northern area of the district, giving him control over the two vital passes into Macedonia — Petra and Volustana. Gomphi and several other towns were garrisoned with Macedonian troops to prevent the hill tribes from conducting raids out of the Pindus Mountains. The remainder of Perrhaebia was allowed to administer its internal affairs undisturbed. The Thessalian League generally approved of these actions because they contributed to its general peace and prosperity and safeguarded the line of communications with Philip.[69]

In the spring of 353 B.C., Lycophron again began to gain the upper hand over the Thessalian League, and the League was forced to issue another call to Philip for assistance.[70] The Thessalian League appears to have been in serious disarray: Larissa, Pelinna, Pharcadon and Tricca having defected from it as a result of continued Phocian victories in the Third Sacred War. Philip, however, apparently campaigned so successfully in Thessaly that Lycophron was forced to appeal to Phocis for assistance. In response, Onomarchus sent his brother Phayllus with an army of 7,000 men into Thessaly, but he was soon defeated by Philip and driven out of the country.[71] Onomarchus then appeared in Thessaly with the entire Phocian army, which included 400 Athenian cavalry, 5,000 Athenian infantry, and 2,000 mercenaries. He took position in highly defensive terrain, lured Philip into a trap, and defeated him in two battles. Although Philip was forced to withdraw into Macedonia to reorganize his army, upon leaving he was heard to have said that he would return like a ram to butt all the harder the next time.

True to his word, in 352 B.C., Philip again returned to Thessaly with a Macedonian army to assist the Thessalian League against Lycophron. Now convinced that it needed a unified command to combat Lycophron and Phocia, and the unconditional military assistance of Macedonia, the League appointed Philip as archon. This office gave him military and economic control over all of Thessaly lying within the territory of the Thessalian League.[72] Another reason for Philip's appointment was the League's concern that he might open negotiations with Athens to end the Sacred War to their detriment. In his new capacity, Philip promptly put Pagasae under siege, thereby cutting off Pherae from any hope of reinforcement from the sea.[73] This action prompted Pherae to appeal for assistance from Phocis, and in response, Onomarchus again marched north with the entire strength of the Phocian army. Although Pagasae managed to hold out several weeks, Onomarchus arrived too late to prevent its fall to Philip. He was able, however, to engage Philip's army on the Crocus plain but was severely defeated in the battle, losing his life in the process.

Instead of immediately marching on Phocis and ending the Third Sacred War, Philip lay siege to Pherae. Isolated from any hope of Athenian reinforcements by sea now that Pagasae had fallen and faced by a hostile population in Pherae,

Lycophron concluded negotiations with Philip that allowed him to evacuate Pherae under an armistice. Marching 84 miles to Thermopylae Pass with his 2,000 mercenaries, Lycophron joined the Phocian army under Phayllus. The whole of Magnesia — eastern coastal Thessaly — now fell to Philip. In August, Philip marched on Thermopylae but found it strongly held by the force of Achaeans, Athenians, Phocians, and Lycophron's mercenaries. Unable to force the pass without incurring crippling casualties, Philip returned to Macedonia and then marched off to Thrace in March 346 B.C. Just prior to Philip's march on Thermopylae, Halus had revolted from Pharsalus in an attempt to regain its independence. Philip supported Pharsalus in attempting to regain Halus, sending Parmenio in command of a force to besiege the city.[74]

The Thessalian League had expected that with the end of the Sacred War and the expulsion of Lycophron, Philip would resign his archonship and evacuate Magnesia, Pagasae and Perrhaebia.[75] When he refused to withdraw from territories he considered his by right of conquest, mounting civil unrest in Thessaly in 345 B.C. forced him to occupy Larisa, Pherae, and several strategic locations in Magnesia formerly held by Lycophron. In the territory of the Thessalian League, Pharcadon and Tricca were both stormed and destroyed. The tyrants were expelled from the cities captured, and Macedonian garrisons were installed in their place. Polemarchs, who had been elected for a one-year term to govern the four tetrarchies into which Thessaly had been divided, were replaced by tetrarchs appointed by Philip. The polemarchs had protected the rights of the cities against the tagos of the central government, but the tetrarchs were likely to place Macedonia's interests above those of Thessaly's.

Late in 344 B.C., the nobles saw the success of the tetrarchs as a threat to their position and they began to suppress the more openly pro–Macedonian elements. This led to the Thessalian League again calling upon Philip for assistance. Entering Thessaly during the spring of 343 B.C., Philip drove out the Aleuadae from Larissa and Pherae and installed Macedonian garrisons in both cities.[76] Other cities that revolted were dealt with in a similar manner. As justification for his action, Philip declared that he was acting as the champion of Thessalian freedom. To prevent any further revolts Philip established decadarchies, or boards of ten, in all cities of doubtful loyalty. Thessalian cities loyal to Philip retained their autonomy, with the exception that their foreign policy was directed by him. All public revenues of Thessaly were paid to Philip, and the Thessalian troops were incorporated into his army. Philip's temporary appointment as archon of the state was made permanent for life, and Thessaly became virtually a Macedonian province.

Thrace

Thrace consisted of a number of independent tribes residing between the Danube and the Aegean, the kingdom extending from west to east from the Chersonese to Byzantium. Several cities along its coast — Maronea, Perinthus and

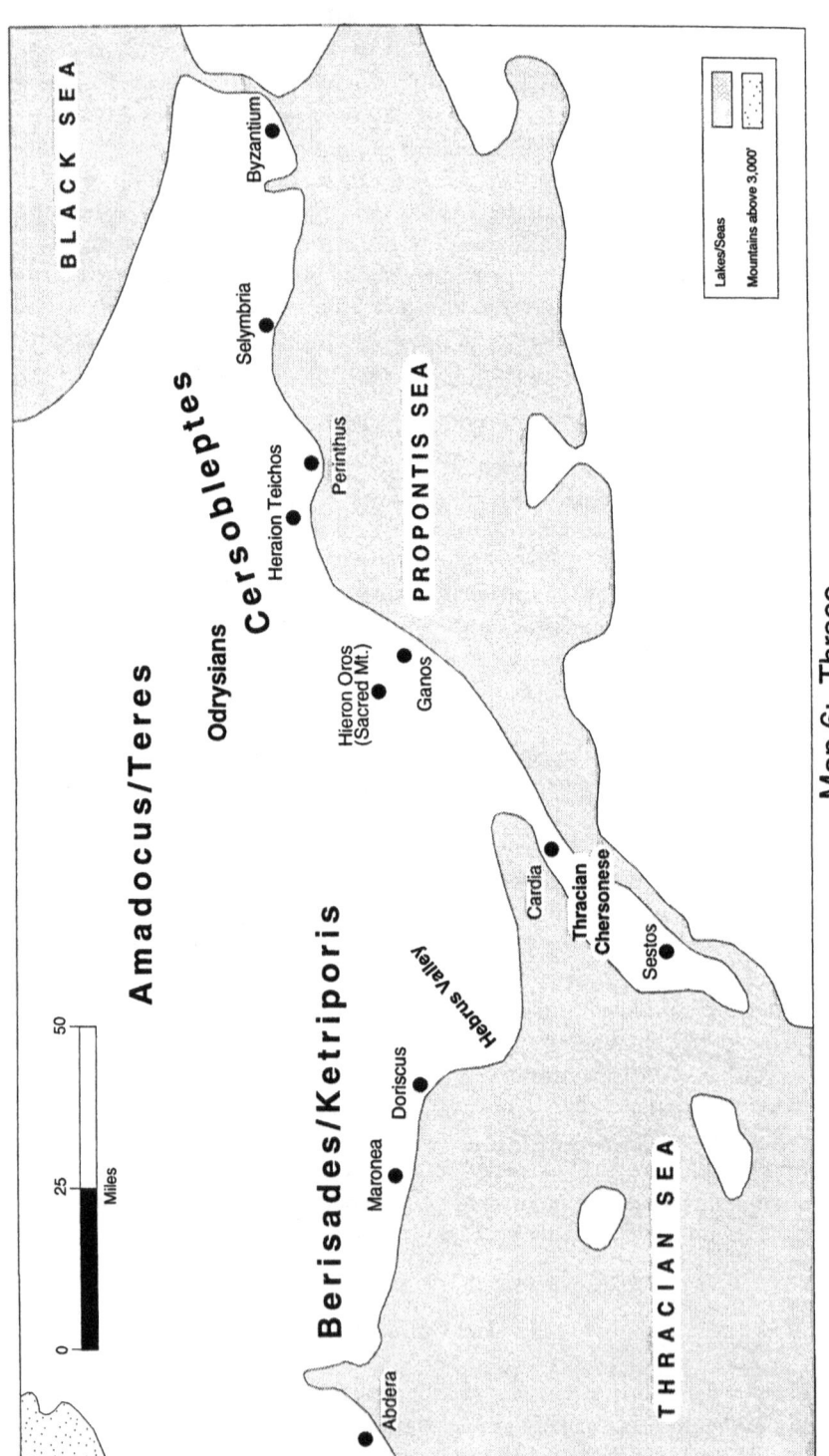

Map 6: Thrace

Byzantium — had been colonized by Greeks and remained relatively independent of Thracian rule. If united under a single king, the Thracians had the potential to be a formidable power because of their large population and a strong economy. Cotys, who ruled the southern-most of the Thracian tribes known as the Odrysians, was successful in beginning to unify the various tribes of Thrace, but he was murdered in 360 B.C. before he could achieve his ambition. His kingdom was divided among his three sons: Cersobleptes ruling the eastern area, from the Hebrus River to Byzantium; Berisades, the western, from the Strymon River at Amphipolis to Maronea; and Amadocus, the inland area. All three Thracian kings upon assuming their thrones signed a treaty of alliance with Athens.

Siege of Amphipolis

Amphipolis was a commercial city on the Strymon River between Thrace and Macedonia, with access to the gold and silver mining area near Mt. Pangaeus.[77] The city had been founded by Athens in 437 B.C. but had revolted from them in 424 B.C. The Athenians spent considerable time and effort to recover the city, in the belief that it was legitimately their colony. This was substantiated a number of times by the Greeks. Before its revolt from Athens, Amphipolis had carried out the duties of a colony, and Amyntas, Philip's father, had recognized the Athenian claim to the city at a congress held in Athens during the winter of 370–69 B.C.[78] In 368 B.C., after the battle of Leuctra, another Greek congress confirmed the Athenian claim to Amphipolis, while two years later another Greek congress concurred.[79] Philip himself had renounced all claim to the city when he withdrew the Macedonian garrison from it in 359 B.C.[80] Now, however, Amphipolis had no desire to return to Athenian control.

For Philip, Amphipolis had great strategic importance because it controlled the only viable crossing point of the southern Strymon River. Lake Cercinitis, which extended a considerable distance to the north of the city, blocked any east-west movement.[81] As Amphipolis was also the only viable defensive position in the area, its possession by Athens would effectively block any Macedonian move towards Byzantium. If Philip's projected campaign against the Persian Empire were to begin, he had to hold Byzantium. To gain access to Byzantium, however, he had to first control Amphipolis.

Some time after Philip had assumed the Macedonian throne, he put Amphipolis under siege, believing the city to be disposed against him. By a series of continual attacks, he was able to breach the city's walls and carry it by assault. Philip soon became involved, however, in a struggle to secure his throne against several claimants. In order to ensure that Athens would not actively support any of them, Philip withdrew his garrison from Amphipolis, denounced all claims to the city, promised Athens that he would assist it in recovering Amphipolis, and strongly urged an alliance between Macedonia and Athens. Athens eagerly fell for Philip's ruse, wishing to believe, no doubt, that Amphipolis would easily be restored to it with Philip's help and at no effort or cost to itself.

By 357 B.C., when Philip had secured his position in Macedonia, the citizens of Amphipolis had become convinced their independence would soon be coming to an end. Philip's withdrawal of the Macedonian garrison in 359 B.C. and his peace feelers to Athens indicated that if he gained control of their city he would either cede it to Athens or incorporate it into Macedonia. Amphipolis therefore refused to be again occupied by a Macedonian garrison and instead continued negotiations with Athens. As a result, Philip's patience became exhausted and he laid siege to the city in the spring of 357 B.C.

Although Amphipolis had been hostile to Athens for nearly 70 years, its citizens offered to again become a colony of Athens in exchange for military assistance against Macedonia. The Athenians declined to assist the city, however, even though they were in a strong position to do so. The Euboean revolt had ended and Chares had just arrived at the Hellespont with a large force of mercenaries. The Athenians were unable to offer assistance because Philip cleverly began the siege of the city during the height of the Etesian Winds, which began blowing from the north in the middle of July. Frequently reaching gale force, the winds made it almost impossible for any sailing to occur in the northern Aegean until mid-October. In any event, it is unlikely that the meager Athenian resources in men and money would have altered the result. Under the circumstances, the Athenians probably had no option but to go along with Philip's assurances that he was prosecuting the siege of Amphipolis on their behalf and would turn the city over to them when it fell.

In the latter part of 357 B.C., the walls of Amphipolis were breached and the city was stormed and captured.[82] Its annexation into Macedonia in 356 B.C. was immediately followed by an Athenian declaration of war against Macedonia. Philip, however, largely ignored this declaration because Athens was in no position to prosecute military operations effectively against Macedonia at the time. In exchange for Amphipolis, Athens had previously agreed to turn over Pydna to Philip, although Athens knew that the city would never agree to this. Philip used this insincerity as a justification for his attack on Amphipolis. Under increasing pressure to subdue the Illyrian tribes, Philip then attempted to make peace with Athens. As a show of good faith, he sent back the Athenian citizens he had captured at Amphipolis without any ransom demands. Philip also acknowledged the Athenian claim to the city. Athens again had little choice but to trust in Philip because the Macedonians had occupied the city and Athens was now diverted by a war against its former allies in the Social War. As a result, Philip's retention of Amphipolis could not be militarily challenged at the time and his control of the city became permanent.

When Philip attacked Amphipolis in 357 B.C., the cities of the Chalcidian League became extremely concerned over his eventual aims on their peninsula. He cleverly offered to besiege Potidaea on their behalf and to cede Anthemus to the them. Potidaea had not only disassociated itself from the League but had encouraged the immigration of Athenian cleruchs in 361 B.C. Anthemus was a Macedonian possession that gave the League access to an agriculturally rich inland valley. The League thus broke off the negotiations it had been conducting with Grabos, king of the Grabaioi, in order to align itself closer to Macedonia. The subsequent treaty the League made with Philip stipulated that neither party would make a separate peace with Athens.

Although the Chalcidian League cities on the peninsula was at first hostile to Athenian overtures of alliance, Philip's growth of power and his eastward expansion convinced its members that it was only a matter of time before he moved against them. As a result of Philip's two defeats in Thessaly by Onomarchus, the Chalcidian cities, under the leadership of Olynthus, decided that it was an opportune time to break with Philip and establish an alliance with Athens.

Crenidas Mining Settlements

In May 356 B.C., Cersobleptes decided to violate his treaty with Amadocus, Athens, and Berisades, and invade the Crenidas mining settlements 39 miles east of Amphipolis, in the territory of Cetriporis, the son of the recently deceased Berisades. His objective was either to reunify the Thracian kingdom his father had ruled or to block any further Macedonian expansion eastward from Amphipolis. Cetriporis, finding himself both weak and isolated, appealed to Philip for assistance. The settlements there were located in a commanding position in the Angites Valley, widely known to be rich in silver and gold mining, although its full potential had not yet been developed. Philip, who was currently besieging Potidaea, divided his army and moved against Crenidas with 5,000 troops, arriving there three days after setting out.[83] Cersobleptes, who was probably not expecting such a strong reaction, doubtless withdrew at Philip's approach. Philip then consolidated the several small communities there into one settlement that he named Philippi. It was heavily fortified and settled with a large number of Macedonian colonists who quickly displaced the native Thasians.

During the summer of 356 B.C., Cetriporis and his brothers made an alliance with Lyppeius, the Paeonian successor to Agis, and Grabos, the ruler of an Illyrian tribe to the northwest, the Grabaioi. They hoped to defeat Philip with their combined strength, although each had been separately defeated by him in the past. Athens joined the alliance in July, although she was unable to honor any new commitments at the time and play any role in the upcoming struggle. Receiving intelligence of the alliance, Philip moved against each tribe separately. Both the Paeonians and the Grabaioi were defeated by Parmenio and were forced to ally with Philip. Simultaneously with Parmenio's victories, Potidaea fell to Philip.

Abdera/Maronea

To facilitate the march of Pammenes and his Theban army to Asia Minor, Philip requested safe conduct for them through Thrace. Cersobleptes agreed to the request, but Amadocus, who was an Athenian ally at the time, refused to do so. As Abdera and Maronea were allies of Amadocus, Philip may have invaded them during the summer to punish Amadocus for his refusal or because they lay along his projected line of communications to Persia. Both towns possessed considerable wealth through their trade with the interior of Thrace. Because the cities stood on a bluff along the coast that was surrounded by marsh, they were inaccessible to a land approach. Philip was therefore forced to move troops against them by sea. Despite Athenian naval supremacy, Philip was able to elude their ships, land his troops, and capture both towns. Unable to proceed any further against Amadocus because of his tenuous line of communications across the Athenian-dominated sea and the small and poorly developed harbors of the two towns, Philip reembarked his army on his small fleet and sailed for home.

Thracian Coastal Forts

In the late spring or early summer of 353 B.C., Chares sailed to the Chersonese, where he captured Sestos. All the males there were killed and the remaining population enslaved. A number of Athenian cleruchs were then sent out to the city. The key to Athenian control of the Chersonese peninsula was Cersobleptes, whose territory bordered it. In spite of the agreement with Athens, however, Cersobleptes had continually worked against its interests. Receiving little, if any, aid from Philip against Amadocus and being suspicious of Philip's future intentions towards him and strongly influenced by Philip's recent defeats by Onomarchus, Cersobleptes decided to accept the Athenian terms offered him. These called for assisting Athens to recapture Amphipolis and renouncing any claim over the cities in the Thracian Chersonese, except Cardia. In return, the Athenians would assist Cersobleptes in establishing a number of fortified locations along the Thracian coast, which included Doriscus, just west of the Hebrus Valley; Ergiske; and Serrion, near Doriscus.[84] The agreement induced Cetriporis and Amadocus to discard their alliance with Athens for one with Philip. Athens, however, expressed little concern over events in mainland Thrace, being primarily focused on recovering towns on the Thracian Chersonese peninsula, which would allow it to control the Hellespont. For this campaign, Athens only needed the friendship and cooperation of Cersobleptes, in whose territory the peninsula was located.

Cersobleptes again returned to his old policy of attempting to restore his father's kingdom with Athenian support. In the autumn of 352 B.C., when he attacked Amadocus over a territorial dispute, Byzantium and Perinthus came to Amadocus' support. Philip now lent his support by besieging a fort at Hieron Teichos. This unexpected response forced Cersobleptes from the disputed territory and ended the war. Cersobleptes was forced to surrender his son to Philip as a hostage, while Amadocus was deposed and replaced by his son Teres. When first hearing of Philip's intervention, the Athenians had assembled a fleet of 40 triremes manned by Athenian citizens.[85] They soon, however, thought better of their action and rescinded the decision they had made in the heat of the moment. The forces arrayed against them were too overwhelming.

Hieron Oros

In April 346 B.C., Philip marched eastward to the Black Sea and defeated Cersobleptes at Hieron Oros. He then subdued the bases Cersobleptes had established along the Thracian coast with the assistance of Athens.

Cardia

Athens had sent a large number of cleruchs to the Thracian Chersonese. They soon came into conflict with Cardia, a city allied with Philip since 346.[86] The cleruchs had established two settlements nearby and to the north of Cardia to cut the city off from any access to the interior. Diopeithes, the local Athenian commander, was ordered to support the colonists. However, having neither adequate supplies or revenues from Athens, he was forced to plunder ships in the north Aegean and levy forced contributions from the coastal towns in the vicinity to pay the wages of his mercenaries. Cardia naturally appealed to Philip for assistance and was sent a garrison by him. During the winter, Diopeithes kidnapped a Macedonian herald from Macedonian territory and took him to Athens, where the dispatches in his possession were read out loud before the Assembly. The herald was then imprisoned for 10 months. Diopeithes later captured two towns in Thrace, namely Crobyle and Tiristasis, carrying off their inhabitants as slaves.[87] Amphilochus, the ambassador Philip sent in 341 B.C. to negotiate for the release of the remaining inhabitants, was tortured and was only released after a ransom of nine talents was paid. When Philip threatened to invade the Thracian Chersonese in support of his ally Caria, the Athenian Assembly was initially inclined to recall and punish Diopeithes. Demosthenes so vigorously defended Diopeithes' actions as being in the best interest of Athens, however, that the Assembly decided to take no action against him. Philip then requested that Athens submit the matter to arbitration, but it declined to do so.

Final Reduction of Thrace

In 343 B.C., Cersobleptes began reducing Greek cities in the Hellespont bordering on his kingdom. Philip thereupon invaded eastern Thrace, using as his justification the continuing attacks upon the free Greek coastal cities by Cersobleptes. Philip formed an alliance with Kothelas, king of the Getae, ratifying it by his marriage with Kothelas' daughter Media. In 342 B.C., Philip concentrated on isolating the Thracians with a series of alliances to preclude them from obtaining any outside support in the future. Because Philip had become ill during the last 10 months of the year, he had to terminate his campaign in Thrace prematurely and return to Macedonia to recover.

Upon his recovery, Philip was reinforced by fresh troops and initiated a series of final attacks on Teres and Cersobleptes. He was finally able to defeat them decisively in the winter of 341 B.C. Both kings were removed from their thrones and replaced by Macedonian generals, who then governed their territories in the interest of Macedonia. Macedonians were now settled in the Hebrus Valley to ensure Philip's hold over Thrace. The state was required to pay taxes directly to Macedonia and was forced to open up its territory to Macedonian trade and mining exploration. A tribute of one-tenth the land's produce was assessed on central and eastern Thrace.[88] Thracian peltasts and heavy cavalry units were incorporated into the Macedonia army's reserves.

Generalship

Philip's final campaign against the Thracians had lasted about two years. Neither weather, terrain, or sickness had stopped his progress. He divided and conquered the kingdoms of Thrace, being careful to pay particular attention to the pacification of the coast. He wanted to take no chances on revolts breaking out along his projected line of communications through the area when he marched east to Asia Minor. The Thracians in the interior would remain independent only as long as they did not act against him. For all practical purposes, the Thracian coast had become a tributary province to Macedonia.

Siege of Perinthus

Philip attacked Perinthus in July 340 B.C., we are told, because he believed that the city was friendly towards the Athenians. A far more likely reason was Perinthus' failure to assist him in his campaign against Cersobleptes, the king of eastern Thrace. Although not as strategically important as Byzantium, the city did lie on the strategic Hellespont, was allied with Athens, and could potentially threaten Philip's line of communications into Asia Minor.

Perinthus was located on a 182-foot-high hill on a peninsula joined to the mainland by a strongly fortified 200-foot-wide land bridge.[89] Because of the steep cliffs along the shore, the city could not be assaulted from the sea. The tall houses encircling the hill on which the city was built had the defensive capability of several walls. Also, being a port city, Perinthus could be resupplied with both men and provisions from Athens, its Greek allies, or the Persians unless Philip was able to control the sea in the vicinity. This, however, was unlikely, considering the relatively small fleet at his disposal and its inability to base itself near the city.[90]

Philip built siege towers overlooking the Perinthian walls that enabled him to quickly suppress the small number of the city's catapults. However, since he did not have command of the sea, the city could not be isolated and almost immediately began to receive outside help. For the Macedonian fleet to operate effectively against Perinthus, Philip would have had to hold friendly anchorages where he could base his fleet. Virtually the entire coastline was, however, firmly in control of Athenian cleruchs in the Thracian Chersonese, unfriendly Thracian tribes, or hostile Greek cities.

The Macedonian army of 30,000 was divided into shifts to enable the siege against Perinthus to be continued both day and night.[91] The constant barrage of the siege engines caused heavy casualties to the defenders manning the city's walls, and after several weeks Perinthus requested Byzantium's assistance. Although the Byzantines had initially believed that the attack on Perinthus was merely a diversion by Philip to precede his eventual main attack on their city, they nevertheless sent Perinthus large numbers of men and flexon catapults. As a result, Perinthus was able to attack the Macedonian artillery with more effective fire, thereby diluting its ability to deliver a concentrated and sustained barrage. The Persian satraps along the coast of Asia Minor also responded by sending provisions, weapons, and a large force of mercenaries to Perinthus. The Athenians chose, however, not to assist the city because they believed the Byzantines fully capable of defending themselves. Although a section of the city's wall finally collapsed, the Perinthians were able to seal it off by falling back to the next row of houses and filling in the alleyways to form, in effect, another wall. This process could be continued up the hill, making it all but impossible for Philip to achieve a decisive breakthrough, as each wall of houses would be smaller and easier for the Perinthians to man. The siege had continued for about three months, from July to September 340 B.C., when Philip took the main body of his army and marched on Byzantium. Being also unsuccessful in prosecuting that siege for many of the same reasons he failed at Perinthus, Philip withdrew his army, broke off the three sieges he was conducting, and escorted his fleet back to Macedonia, after which he embarked on a campaign against the Scythians.

Generalship In besieging Perinthus, Philip had clearly attempted to do more than he was capable of at the time. In effect, he had put the cart before the horse. The key to the prosecution of a successful siege against the city was actually the occupation of the Thracian Chersonese and the Thracian coast, as he later recognized. Its retention by unfriendly Athenian cleruchs and hostile Thracians prevented him from using his small fleet to blockade Perinthus because there was nowhere nearby where he could establish a safe base. Also, an Athenian fleet superior in numbers and quality to his was always able to base itself near the city in order to break any sea blockade Philip might attempt. This meant that Perinthus was able to receive considerable reinforcements of men, armaments, catapults, and provisions from both Byzantium and Persia, none of which Philip could interdict.

Added to these problems was the inherent strength of the city. Even when Philip breached its walls, the concentric rows of houses running up the hill presented him, in effect, with a series of walls, each higher and more difficult to assault than the previous row. Any penetration made would have been confined to a narrow frontage and have incurred casualties disproportionate to what could have been achieved. It is problematical if Philip would have ever been able to conclude the siege successfully under such disadvantageous circumstances. In response to a difficult situation, Philip took the militarily correct approach by breaking off the siege. As Alexander was also later to discover at Halicarnassus and Tyre, a successful siege could not be conducted against a port city without local naval superiority.

Siege of Selymbria

Philip had apparently placed Selymbria under siege en route to Byzantium. This would have been necessary in order to safeguard his line of communications between Perinthus and Byzantium. As justification for his seizure of the Athenian corn fleet, Philip accused Athens of planning to use it to reprovision Selymbria. Outside this one reference, however, nothing more is known of the siege, although it is quite certain that Philip broke it off when he was forced to abandon the sieges he was conducting against Perinthus and Byzantium.

Siege of Byzantium

Philip needed control of Byzantium in order to secure his line of communications into Asia. Once an Athenian ally, the city could have provided Athens with a base of operations for interdicting the Hellespont in order to cut Philip off from his Macedonian and Greek reinforcements. Because of Athens' predominance in the Pontic, or Black Sea, corn trade, however, any move against Byzantium would almost certainly result in a declaration of war from the city. As the justification for his attack on the city, Philip claimed that the Byzantines were participating in pirate raids on Thracian cities allied with him in support of Diopeithes, which was probably the case.[92]

Philip took a large portion of his army away from the siege of Perinthus to besiege Byzantium in September 340 B.C. He knew that the Byzantine army had neither sufficient numbers nor the combat effectiveness to meet even a portion of his army in a field battle. Philip hoped that the Byzantines had so weakened their defenses in assisting Perinthus that they might quickly fall to a surprise attack. In this, however, he was to be disappointed.

Philip had brought his small fleet up through the Hellespont in the company of his army. In mid-September, the corn ships from the Black Sea usually gathered in the Bosporus to await convoy escort to Athens. As their usual anchorage was denied them by Philip's siege of Byzantium, the 230 corn ships anchored at the small port of Hieron on the Asiatic shoreline, near the mouth of the Bosporus.[93] Although the Athenian general Chares was supposed to be on duty in the Hellespont with a fleet of 40 ships, he was absent at the time, attending a conference with Persian naval commanders to discuss the level of support that should be given Perinthus. Philip saw his opportunity, ferried his soldiers across the strait on his small number of ships, and boarded the corn ships.

Of the ships captured, Philip released the 50 owned by neutrals but kept 180 of Athenian registry.[94] These he then broke apart, using their wood to construct siege engines for use against Byzantium. The sale from the cargoes of the Athenian merchant ships brought 700 talents in badly needed revenues that would pay the wages of his army for almost six months.[95] Although the loss of the corn fleet was serious for Athens, it was not fatal. The ships were only a portion of its Black Sea fleet, and Athens had other sources of food. Philip sent off a dispatch to Athens accusing its corn fleet of actually being bound for Selymbria in an attempt to undermine the siege that he was conducting against that city. This, he claimed, gave aid to Macedonia's enemies and was clearly an act of war against him. The Athenians, of course, were enraged at Philip's high-handed actions and immediately declared war against him.

The city of Byzantium occupied the high ground at the most eastern part of the Golden Horn. Its massive walls were comparable to those at Rhodes, having been designed to protect the city against Thracian land assaults.[96] The shoreline of the city was largely unwalled, however, because the strength of its naval forces was relied upon for protection there. Artaxerxes "Ochus," the king of Persia, declined an outright declaration of war against Macedonia, rightly deducing that the loss of its corn fleet would provoke Athens to take this action. He did, however, order his Asia Minor satraps to provide Byzantium with armaments and funds for its defense.

Byzantium soon received troops from Chios, Cos, Persia and Rhodes.[97] Athens ordered Chares to take his 40 ships, land a mercenary force at Byzantium, and commence active operations against Philip. Chares was successful in forcing Philip's fleet into the Bosporus and then, with the assistance of the Byzantine navy, into the Black Sea. At the entrance to the Bosporus, Chares established a base from which he was able to control naval movement through the strait. He seems to have accomplished little else, however. The Byzantines now became suspicious of him, both because he had failed to protect the Athenian corn fleet and because he had campaigned against them during the Social War. The extent of their feeling was so strong that they refused to admit him into their city, fearing that if given the chance he might commit some act of treachery against them. Consequently, Athens sent another force under Phocion to the support of Byzantium. With the arrival of that force just before winter, Chares was relieved of his duties. Phocion was warmly welcomed by the Byzantines. He was very highly regarded by Leon, the Byzantine general commanding the defenses of the city at that time. The two had been good friends when they had studied together with Plato at the Academy in Athens.

Philip was able to undermine and breach a section of Byzantium's wall in the early spring of 339 B.C. He then planned a night assault against the city. However, as his assault troops approached the walls, barking dogs alerted the city to their approach and the attack had to be called off. The Byzantines were able to repair the walls quickly during the night, apparently making another such assault attempt impracticable.

The siege of Byzantium continued throughout the winter of 340–39 B.C. In the spring, Philip decided to abandon the operation because there was little possibility of successfully concluding it any time in the near future and there appeared little likelihood of any internal treachery that might deliver the city to him. Parmenio and Antipater were detached to suppress some Thracian tribes that had revolted in Philip's rear. The Maidoi in the upper Strymon Valley, in the Balkans, had also revolted and allied themselves with the Danthaletae. Philip's son, the future Alexander the Great, had managed, however, to defeat them and end the revolt, even though he was only 16 years old .

Philip now contrived to issue a false message indicating that he was immediately marching to Thrace to quell a revolt that had broken out there and isolated several Macedonian detachments. After ensuring that the dispatch fell into the hands of Phocion, Philip lifted the siege of Byzantium and marched off to the west. Phocion fell for the ruse and immediately set sail for Thrace. With his departure, the Macedonian fleet was at last able to escape from the Black Sea. Philip met his fleet in the Hellespont and marched his army in support of it along the hostile Thracian coast and then back to Macedonia. The Athenian fleet was unable to engage the Macedonian fleet successfully because of both the treacherous sailing conditions along the Thracian coast and the close proximity of the Macedonian army.

Generalship At Byzantium, Philip had clearly overreached himself. His arrow-shooting catapults apparently had little effect upon the massive walls of the city, and any breach made was likely to be small and containable by the Byzantines. His undermining of the wall could not have been very extensive because the Byzantines were able to repair it in only a single night. He then tried to surprise the city by a night attack but this too failed when barking dogs alerted the Byzantines to the operation. Since another surprise attack was not attempted, it seems that no further opportunity existed for such an operation to be repeated. Therefore the city was not now likely to fall by assault, nor was it likely to fall by siege. The Athenians not only maintained naval superiority over the small Macedonian fleet, but the generally hostile shoreline along the Thracian Chersonese and the coast of Thrace also greatly hampered Philip's naval operations. There were no friendly ports or beaches available for his fleet to take shelter during adverse weather, to perform routine maintenance, or to make needed repairs. The fighting effectiveness of his small fleet had therefore steadily eroded. The result was that it was not in his power to capture the city. Once Philip recognized this, he did not spend any more time in futile attacks on the massive stone walls but quickly concluded the operation. Although it can be said of Philip that he did make mistakes, he never made the same one twice.

Epirus

In 352 B.C., fighting broke out between Arybbas of Epirus and Philip, undoubtedly because of the reverses Philip had suffered at the hands of Onomarchus in Thessaly the previous year. Arybbas no doubt believing that Philip had been severely weakened by those defeats, thought that events were favorable for him to declare his independence from Macedonian rule. At the conclusion of hostilities, about which nothing is known, Arybbas was evidently defeated and Alexander of Molossus, for whom Arybbas was regent, was taken to Macedonian to be raised and educated by Philip. This action was taken, no doubt, to ensure that he would not be killed by Arybbas upon coming of age to assume the throne of Epirus. Arybbas was allowed to continue to rule in Epirus in the expectation he might remain as coregent when Alexander of Molossus assumed the throne.

Late in 350 B.C., just before winter snow would isolate Epirus from Macedonia, Philip marched up the Haliacmon Valley and crossed the Pindus range into the southern plain of Dodona. This campaign was probably made necessary by Arybbas' attempt to reassert his sovereignty. The need to safeguard Macedonia's southwest flank and to maintain control over the road that ran from Epirus to the

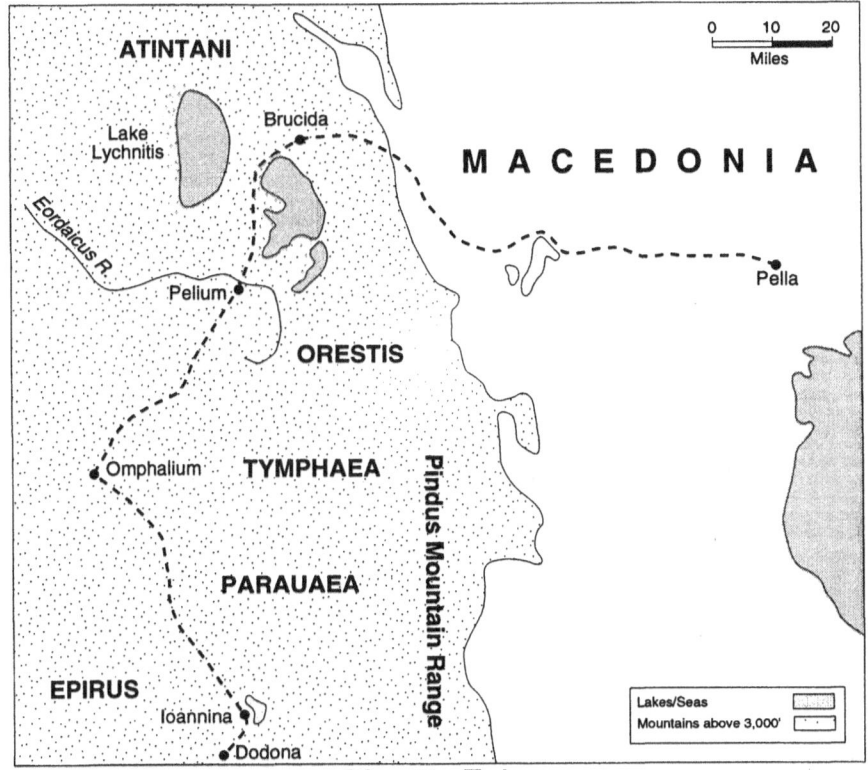

Map 7: Epirus

northwest Peloponnese may also have played a significant role in Philip's invasion decision. In return for Philip's promise of a safe departure into exile, Arybbas did not oppose the entry of the Macedonian army into Epirus. Arybbas left for Athens, where citizenship had been extended to him. Although the Athenians promised to support him in recovering his kingdom, nothing ever came of it. Shortly after Arybbas' departure, Philip made Alexander of Molossus king of Epirus.

Euboea

The island of Euboea was of considerable strategic importance to Athens. There were only two ways that Philip could invade Attica: overland through the pass at Thermopylae or by sea from the island of Euboea. At Thermopylae, the Boeotians could be relied upon to defend the pass against Philip. In Euboea, however, Philip was likely to be warmly welcomed as an ally of Thebes during the Third Sacred War. The two key cities on Euboea were Carystus and Chalcis. Carystus lay along the route of the Athenian corn fleet; Chalcis controlled the bridge across the strait into Attica.[98]

In February 348 B.C., Euboea was seeking a way to withdraw from the Second Athenian Confederacy. In its place, an independent Euboean League was likely to be established that would almost certainly be resistant to Athenian control. The present state of political turmoil on the island and the Macedonian presence along the northern Pagasaean Gulf gave Philip a considerable opportunity to stir up trouble there, and Athens began to fear that he might be invited to occupy the key cities on the island.

Eretria

Early in 348 B.C., Plutarchus, ruler of Eretria and an ally of Athens, requested her support. He had recently overthrown Menestratus but was now himself threatened by a rising under Cleitarchus.[99] Interestingly enough, although Euboea was considered vitally important to Athens, Demosthenes persuaded the Assembly against supporting a Euboean expedition, as he was pressing at the time for a large force to be sent to the Chersonese. Nevertheless, a small force under Phocion was sent out in February 348 B.C., in the hope that it would be significantly augmented by Euboean forces.[100] Callias, the ruler of Chalcis, mobilized a Euboean force against Phocion and also directed his brother to hire a force of mercenaries from Phocis. Being outnumbered by Callias' force, Phocis made camp on a ridge alongside a ravine lying across from the plain of Tamynae. This was a dangerous position because the Athenian force was cut off from any hope of reinforcement by either land or sea and if confronted by an enemy could only extricate itself by fighting and winning a battle. Although Plutarchus accompanied Phocion with a force of mercenaries, the expected Euboean reinforcements failed to appear.

An Euboean army, which included troops from Callias, the tyrant of Chalcis; Plutarchus, the tyrant of Eretria; and a group of Phocion mercenaries, arrived and made preparations to attack Phocion. It had been the Athenians' plan to stay on the defensive behind a prepared position, but Plutarchus, disregarding his orders, precipitated the battle by a rash attack from the camp and was defeated. His subsequent flight disordered the Athenian cavalry troops, who also fled from the battlefield. Despite this, Phocion was able to defeat the Euboean army after a hard fight. Considering Plutarchus' conduct at the battle as treachery against Athens, Phocion expelled him from Eretria. At the same time, Callias left the island and took refuge with Philip.

Phocion shortly departed Euboea, leaving behind Molossus in command of the remaining Athenian force there. Things, however, went badly for Molossus; his force was defeated and captured in the summer of 348 B.C. Athens was forced to pay a ransom of 50 talents for the release of Molossus and the troops under his command.[101] In the subsequent peace treaty, the Athenians were forced to acknowledge the independence of all Euboean towns except Carystus.[102]

After Plutarchus and his mercenaries were forced to leave Eretria, the citizens debated between enlisting the support of Athens or Macedonia. In 343 B.C., the pro–Macedonian faction in Eretria under Cleitarchus, Hipparchus and Automedon succeeded in persuading the city's demos to imprison or exile their pro–Athenian opponents. When Chalcis called upon Philip's aid, he readily responded, being eager to distract Athens from interfering in his Chalcidian campaign that had just begun. In 342 B.C., Philip landed a large force of mercenaries in northern Euboea, where they conducted operations for the next three months. In May 341 B.C., Philip sent three groups of mercenaries to Euboea in support of Eretria. A 1,000-strong force was sent in with Hipponicus and an unknown number of troops with Eurylochus and Parmenio.[103] Hipponicus destroyed the walls of Porthmos, which served as the harbor of Eretria. Not only had large numbers of exiled Eretrian democrats taken refuge there, but it was also where the Athenians had landed troops in Eretrian territory in 348 B.C. Hipponicus then marched back to Eretria to suppress mounting public dissatisfaction there.

Oreus

Although Euphraeus had once lived in Athens, he had returned to Oreus in order to establish a democracy there. In an attempt to achieve this, he indicted Philistines, one of Philip's agents in the city, as a traitor. In response, Philip directed a band of thugs to arrest Euphraeus on a charge that he was inciting the city to riot. The citizens reacted indifferently to the situation, thereby encouraging Philip to send troops into the city on the pretext of quelling the unrest that he himself had precipitated. Once Philip securely held the city, he exiled or murdered those whose passivity had facilitated his control of it. Unfortunately, Philip's overly aggressive actions on Euboea largely canceled out the goodwill in Greek opinion he had tried so hard to cultivate. Thebes, especially, now became extremely suspicious of Philip's motives regarding the island. When the Macedonian mercenary force had reestablished Philistides in power, Philip's generals and mercenaries left the island.

Athenian Reconquest of Euboea

In the summer of 341 B.C., envoys from Chalcis came to Athens indicating the desire of their city to form an alliance. Athens, anxious to regain a secure base on Euboea, agreed to the offer and a former subject became an independent ally. An Athenian force subsequently landed on the island. During the attack on Oreus by both land and sea, Philistines was killed. The following month an Athenian force under Phocion crossed over into Euboea, forced Cleitarchus from Eretria and Philistines from Oreus, and restored democracies at both cities. An independent Euboean confederacy was then formed that allied with Athens, no doubt under the coercion of a strong Athenian presence on the island.

Generalship

Although Philip's plan for threatening Athens through Euboea was an excellent one, it does not appear to have amounted to much. After his forces defeated the Athenian force under Molossus, Philip seemed to get bogged down on the island, despite the fact that his best generals were assigned to conduct operations there. It may well be that Philip's enthusiasm for the campaign steadily waned in proportion to the increase in bad press that began to build up in Greece against what was widely seen as his blatant aggression. Or it could be that Philip's operations on Euboea were intended to distract Athenian attention away from his campaign in the Chalcidice and when he had achieved his purpose there was no longer any need to remain there. Either reason may well explain why he so readily and quickly abandoned his supporters on the island. Athens, or course, willingly stepped back into the vacuum left by Philip's departure and immediately began to reassert its former control there.

Scythia

Philip was determined to preserve the Danube River as an advanced outpost protecting northern Macedonia. The Scythian king, Ateas, however, had crossed the Danube with his people and settled in the vicinity of Dobrudja, between Mt. Haemus and the Danube. When the Scythians went to war against the Histriani tribe, Philip had responded to Ateas' request for aid by sending some Macedonian troops to assist him. Upon their arrival, however, they were promptly dismissed, the death of the Histriani king having ended the threat of war to Scythia. Ateas then rather insultingly replied to Philip that the Scythians did not fear war, nor did they require Macedonian protection.

While Philip was besieging Byzantium, he began to run low on supplies for his troops. He solicited foodstuffs from Ateas, no doubt thinking it would be provided in appreciation for the troops he had previously sent to his assistance. Ateas, however, indicated that he could provide Philip nothing because the harsh climate and poor soil conditions not only precluded any food surplus but supply frequently was insufficient to satisfy even Scythian needs. It must now have been painfully clear to Philip that the Scythians could not be counted among Macedonia's friends. Yet because of their strategic location, they were in a position to pose a significant threat to his projected line of communications to Asia Minor. At this point, Philip had undoubtedly determined to deal with the problem militarily. In 339 B.C., he demanded the right to dedicate a statue of Heracles at the mouth of the Danube River, fully expecting that the anticipated Scythian refusal would provide him with the justification he needed for a war against them. Ateas told Philip that if he sent him the statue he would see to it that it was placed where indicated and would prevent it from being disturbed. He would not, however, allow Philip to cross the Scythian border. Ateas indicated that if Philip attempted to do so, the Scythians would melt the statue down and make arrowheads out of it for use against him.

Philip fought and won a decisive battle with the Scythian army on the plain of the Dobrudja, in southeast Rumania. Ateas, who was nearly 90, was killed in the fighting. During the battle Philip was wounded by a spear that passed through his leg with enough force to kill his horse.[104] The harsh terms of the peace settlement called for the Scythians to turn over to Philip 20,000 of the Scythian women and children and 20,000 mares.[105] It is significant to note that no male slaves or stallion horses were taken. It is quite clear that Philip's objective was to increase the future population of his border settlements and his horse herd. Captured Scythian lands were given to Philip's allies, the Getae and the Histriani.[106]

Fourth Sacred War

The Locrians of Amphissa bordered Cirrha. A large number of pilgrims usually landed at the port of Cirrha and then traveled through to the nearby Oracle of Delphi. When Cirrha began taxing the pilgrims, however, the Delphians enlisted the assistance of the Amphictyonic Council. The First Sacred War was subsequently fought, resulting in the destruction of Cirrha. The plain surrounding Cirrha was then dedicated to Delphi and cultivation of the land was forever forbidden. The Locrians now began to cultivate some of the nearby sacred land. They had not been called to account earlier for their sacrilege partly because of the services they provided to the visitors of the temple and partly because of the hardships they endured supporting the Amphictyonic Council during the Third Sacred War, while other members held back. At the conclusion of the conflict, however, the Locrians began a massive cultivation of the sacred lands, in order to compensate it for the losses they had endured from the ravages of the late war. The Amphictyonic Council convened in February or March 339 B.C. at Delphi. The Locrians, to extract revenge against Athens for allying with the Phocions during the Third Sacred War, lodged a complaint against the city for an inscription appearing in a temple recently rebuilt there "From the Medes and the Thebans, when they fought against the Greeks,"[107] referring to the Theban alliance with Persia during the second Persian invasion of Greece. The Locrians had proposed that a fine of 50 talents be levied against Athens. Believing that the Locrians were acting on behalf of Thebes in the matter, Aeschines, an Athenian politician, denounced Locris for cultivating the sacred lands on the plains of Cirrha in such an emotional and inflammatory manner that the members of the Amphictyonic Council were moved to uncontrollable fury. Their anger overrode all rational judgment and instead of merely voting sanctions against the Locrians, as normally would have been the case, they decided to exact immediate retribution the following day.

At dawn, the entire adult population of Delphi appeared at the temple, where they were subjected to an emotional tirade of the Locrian sacrilege. Anyone refusing the summons was to be cursed. The crazed mob then rushed down to the port of Cirrha, demolished the harbor installations, set fire to some houses in the town, and proceeded to loot the now deserted buildings there. Upon hearing the approach of the howling mob, the terrified residents of the port fled to Amphissa, eight miles west of Delphi. In response, the Locrians immediately sent out an armed force, but by the time they arrived at Cirrha, the sobering reality of what they had done dawned on the mob, and they ran off.

The next morning a full session of the Amphictyonic Council was convened. Western Locris was bitterly condemned and judged guilty of sacrilege against the gods and threatening actions taken against the Amphictyonic representatives. The members of the Council were instructed to return to their various cities and meet again at Thermopylae to discuss the issue further.

Demosthenes saw that the discord Aeschines had sown between Athens and Thebes could be disastrous because Philip could be defeated only if the two states acted in concert. He persuaded the assembly by his argument, and they agreed not to send any representatives to Thermopylae. Thebes likewise refused to send any representatives, because it could not in good conscience ally itself against the Locrians, who had been steadfast allies of Thebes during the Third Sacred War.

In the spring or early summer, the Amphictyonic Council reconvened at Thermopylae. There it was decided that the Locrians should be coerced by military force. This was done, and the Amphictyonic army was able to compel the Locrians to agree to pay a fine in installments to Delphi, exile all those who had cultivated the sacred lands, and recall any who had been exiled for opposing the sacrilege.[108] Upon the Council's army departure, however, the Locrians reneged on the terms. In response, the Council again attempted to mobilize an army to enforce Locrian compliance with the decree but this time the members were indifferent to the appeal. Cottyphus, who had been elected as the head of the Council, now called upon Philip of Macedonia to enforce the Amphictyonic will and conduct a holy war on its behalf against the Locrians of Amphissa.

This, of course, gave Philip another opportunity to enter central Greece. In November 339 B.C., Philip marched south into Thessaly, where Amphictyonic contingents from the Aenianians, Aetolians, Dolopians, Phthiotians and Thessalians joined him.[109] At that point, the Thebans drove the Macedonian garrison out of Nicaea, which controlled Thermopylae, and occupied it themselves. Despite the fact that Philip was their ally, the Thebans were determined to deny him entry into central Greece. Upon reaching Lamia, Philip sent a detachment to occupy Thermopylae while he marched to Cytinium with his main force.[110] Dropping off a garrison at Cytinium, he continued on to Elatea, once the principal Phocion town. Philip then halted and sent a delegation to Thebes requesting that his army be allowed to pass through Boeotia en route to Attica. The subsequent delay gave Chares, commanding a force of 10,000 mercenaries, time to occupy Gravia Pass, a few miles north of Amphissa, effectively blocking Philip's further progress.[111]

In the summer of 338 B.C., Philip decided to force Chares' position at Gravia Pass. He had seen to it that a forged letter from Antipater fell into Chares' hands requesting the Macedonian king's return to Thrace to suppress a revolt there. To substantiate the ruse, Philip withdrew his troops from Chares' front. With the threat of an enemy no longer immediately before him, Chares' force soon became careless in its military discipline and vigilance, neglecting to guard the pass properly. Philip, anticipating this kind of slackness from Chares' hodgepodge force of mercenaries and troops from small city-states, sent a force under Parmenio to force-march on the pass at night. Catching Chares' force by surprise, Parmenio virtually annihilated it. Amphissa was occupied, its walls pulled down, and its politicians banished. With the capture of Amphissa, the Fourth Sacred War had been concluded. Philip's actions had indicated, however, that this military operation was only a preliminary to an all-out military confrontation for domination of central Greece.

Phocis

Philip's halt at Elatea, a strategic location on the main road into western Boeotia, produced considerable consternation throughout Greece. If, as Philip said, he was simply carrying out his Amphictyonic obligations against the Locrians, he should have marched southwest on Amphissa from Cytinium. Instead, however, he had marched southeast on Elatea, both fortifying and garrisoning it. The suspicion of the skeptics was soon confirmed when Philip sent a delegation to Thebes. They stated that Philip had come to attack the Athenians and requested Theban assistance. He would allow the Thebans to either march with him against Athens or allow the Macedonians to march through their territory. If they cooperated, the Thebans could enrich themselves with Athenian plunder; if they did not they would be plundered themselves by the Macedonians. The Thebans were caught between their old enemy Athens and their new one, Macedonia.

When the Athenians learned of Philip's arrival at Elatea, they became unnerved. He was only three day's march from the borders of Attica, no preparations had yet been made for the defense of their territory, and neither the population nor its moveable goods had yet been transported to the safety of Athens. In the past, when the Phocions could have been relied upon to hold the passes west of Thermopylae, Athens had no fear of an advance from that area. With the disarmament of Phocis at the end of the Third Sacred War, however, the unoccupied pass at Parapotamii could now be crossed by Philip whenever he chose.

Although the Athenian Assembly was convened in a high state of excitement, when the herald twice asked if anyone wished to speak, no one dared to respond. After a considerable period of time had passed, Demosthenes finally stood up. He told the members of the Assembly not to despair, for although Philip was at Elatea and Thebes was hostile to Athens, he did not believe that Thebes was yet Philip's ally. In time, however, Philip would obviously force Thebes to support him, unless, that is, the Athenians took immediate and decisive action. Demosthenes urged that the Athenians keep in mind that their own best interest would be served by the preservation of Thebes as a counter-weight to Macedonian expansion. If Thebes capitulated, Athens would be forced to undergo siege. Their long-standing enemy Thebes should be offered full Athenian military support with nothing being requested in exchange. He proposed that a delegation be sent to Thebes, immediately followed by the Athenian army. It was so voted by the Assembly, and Demosthenes was commissioned to lead the delegation. Athens was then able to recruit support among its allies, which included Acarnania, Achaea, Corcyra,

Euboea, Leucas and Megara.[112] These allies were said to have provided Athens with a combined force of 2,000 cavalry and 15,000 infantry.[113] Arcadia, Elis, Messenia, and Sparta chose to remain neutral in the upcoming confrontation. Philip was only supported by the Thessalians and some of the smaller Amphictyonic members.[114]

Demosthenes arrived at Thebes just as the Macedonian envoys had finished speaking. The difficulties that he had to overcome were truly monumental. Not only did Thebes consider Athens a rival and a long-standing enemy, but Philip was an ally of the Thebans who was now only requesting them to reciprocate for the support he provided them during the Third Sacred War. Demosthenes, however, was up to the task, effectively appealing to the Thebans on two levels. On one hand, he stressed Thebes' heroic past; on the other he emphasized its own best self-interest. He promised Athens would support Theban supremacy over Boeotia and acknowledge Thebes as supreme commander on land in the upcoming struggle, Athens being supreme commander at sea. He also offered to pay two-thirds the cost of the war.[115] The Thebans, after carefully considering his proposals, decided that an Athenian alliance would allow them to extend their power while one with Macedonia would almost certainly subordinate them to Philip. Philip must have been greatly disappointed at the result, for not only had he failed to persuade his old ally to support him but his new ally Athens had joined Thebes against him.

The Theban army held the pass between Mt. Parnassus and Hedylium at Parapotamii, a pass that controlled entry from Phocis into the Boeotian plain.[116] Chares, commanding a force of 10,000 mercenaries, occupied Gravia Pass, a few miles north of Amphissa.[117] The Greek allied occupation of the passes not only protected Boeotia and Attica against an overland attack from the north but also cut Philip off from access to the Gulf of Corinth and his Peloponnesian allies there. He was also unable to remain indefinitely at Elatea because a shortage of local provisions in the area would eventually force him to fall back into Thessaly. If he chose to attack the allies in the passes, however, not only would he almost certainly suffer heavy casualties but he would be unlikely to achieve any decisive result. Even if he was able to carry one of the passes, the Greek allies could always fall back to the strong position at Chaeronea. During the winter, Philip attempted to maneuver the Greeks out of their position but being unsuccessful he then settled down to wait for better weather and additional reinforcements from Macedonia and Thessaly.

In the summer, Chares' vigilance was relaxed by a ruse used by Philip, and his force was surprised and virtually eliminated by a night attack. After Amphissa was occupied, Parmenio was ordered to take a force and push on to Naupactus on the Gulf or Corinth, two days' march away. Capturing the city, Parmenio turned it over to the Aetolians to fulfill the promise Philip had earlier made to them. He then rejoined Philip at Elatea. Because Philip was now able to move round the passes through Amphissa and cut the Greek army's line of communications to Thebes and Athens, the Greeks withdrew to Chaeronea.

The Battle of Chaeronea

Philip was reluctant to fight the Greeks at Chaeronea. This was not that he thought he would be defeated by the hodgepodge allied Greek army but that a crushing victory over the proud Greeks would only unite them more fiercely against himself. If he were to defeat them too heavily, the only policy left to use against them would be coercion. This would create a simmering hatred against what they would consider to be enslavement by a foreign power and would make a future revolt against him all but inevitable.

With Thermopylae firmly held by the Thebans and Chaeronea occupied by the Greek allies, Philip's only other route into central Greece lay through Thisbe and Thespiae. It would be extremely difficult and dangerous for him to obtain supplies along this route, however, because it was a rough road that was susceptible to ambush anywhere along its length. Also, the Greek army, being on an interior line and having good roads at its disposal, could readily intervene anywhere it chose against his line of march while he was strung out in column.

The allies had chosen a strong defensive battlefield. Their left flank was anchored by mountain foothills and the Chaeronea acropolis, while the Cephissus River, a swamp, and Mt. Akontion precluded any turning move on the right. The allies' position completely blocked any Macedonian movement down the valley and imposed a frontal attack on Philip along a battlefield only one and a half miles wide. Kerata Pass in the rear of the allied line provided a secure line of communications and a protected line of retreat from any pursuit by the Macedonian cavalry. The level battlefield would facilitate cavalry operations, however, and this would be of considerable advantage to Philip, as the battle would clearly demonstrate.[118]

The Greek allied army fielded a force of 1,400 cavalry and 35,000 infantry. A force of 10,000 Boeotians was deployed along the allied right wing, with the 300-strong Theban Sacred Band occupying the far right position. This was an elite unit whose members swore to die rather than retreat. The left wing contained 10,000 Athenian hoplites commanded by Statocles, Lysicles and Chares. The center was held by 6,000 allied hoplites, 2,000 each from Achaea, Corinth and Megara, and was stiffened to the rear by 2,000 Greek mercenaries in the employ of Athens. The 1,400 allied Greek light cavalry, being unable to stand up to the Macedonian heavy cavalry, were echeloned back from the right flank in support of the Sacred Band. A total of 5,000 light infantry from Boeotia, Locris and Phocis anchored the allied Greek left flank in the rough ground there.

The Macedonian army fielded a total of 2,000 cavalry and 30,000 infantry.[119] Philip commanded the right wing, consisting of 3,000 hypaspists in the plain and 5,000 light infantry stationed in the foothills, near the acropolis. The 12,000-strong phalanx was deployed in the center. Philip's 18-year-old son, Alexander, commanded the 2,000 Companion cavalry on the left flank.[120]

Philip knew that the Theban Sacred Band was the most effective unit in the Greek allied army. In both training and combat effectiveness, its soldiers were the equals of the Macedonians. It was also a certainty that they would fight with desperation because they knew their fate if they fell into Philip's hands after the

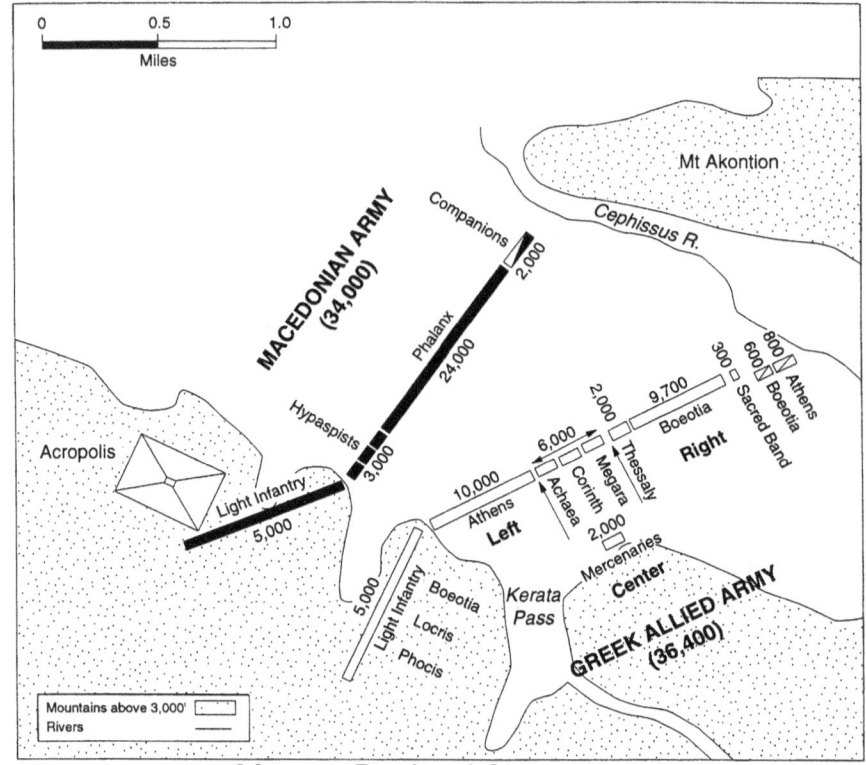

Map 8: Battle of Chaeronea

treachery of their city. On the other hand, the Athenians opposite Philip were the weakest element in the Greek allied army. They were citizen volunteers with little combat experience or discipline. Philip planned to use these vulnerabilities against the Athenians to lure them away from the allied line so that he could defeat them separately.

The battle took place at dawn on September 1, 338 B.C. Philip echeloned his line back from the left flank and advanced to engage the Athenians with the hypaspists on his right flank. As he had expected, Statocles moved the Athenians out in front of the allied line to meet the advancing hypaspists. Philip now abruptly reversed direction with his right flank, however, and marched to the rear, falling back before the advancing Athenians.[121] At the same time, Alexander advanced the left flank. This swung the Macedonian line like a gate, pivoting on the phalanx in the center. Statocles, being well below the level of mediocrity, completely misunderstood Philip's planned withdrawal and eagerly led the now disorganized Athenians forward against what he perceived was a beaten enemy in full retreat. Philip continued withdrawing up the valley for perhaps half an hour, falling back about 160 yards.[122] As the Athenians rushed forward, they uncovered their own right flank as well as the Boeotian left. In an attempt to close that gap, the Boeotians inclined to their left, thereby creating a number of small gaps in their formation. Alexander saw that these openings would allow access to his cavalry, and he immediately charged into them. He was thus able to collapse the Boeotian right flank and isolate the Sacred Band from the main line. Working his way round the left flank of the Sacred Band, Alexander was able to gain its rear. Philip, meanwhile, halted his retreat, turned round, and countercharged. The Athenian line was broken, with 1,000 being killed, 2,000 being taken prisoner, and the survivors fleeing back through Kerata Pass.[123] Although the Greek allied army was swept from the field, the members of the Sacred Band emulated the Spartan stand at Thermopylae by fighting and dying where they stood. Of the 300 Thebans of the Sacred Band, only 46 were said to have survived. Although victorious, Philip did not order a general pursuit. This was, no doubt, because his army was exhausted and he would have found it difficult to force his way through the narrow Kerata Pass.

Results Chaeronea was one of the decisive battles in ancient history and established Macedonia as the predominant power in Greece. The Greek states, with the exception of Sparta, were eventually forced to ally themselves to Macedonia in a common political and military league. Athenians reacted to the disaster at Chaeronea initially, however, with a heroism not seen since their disaster at

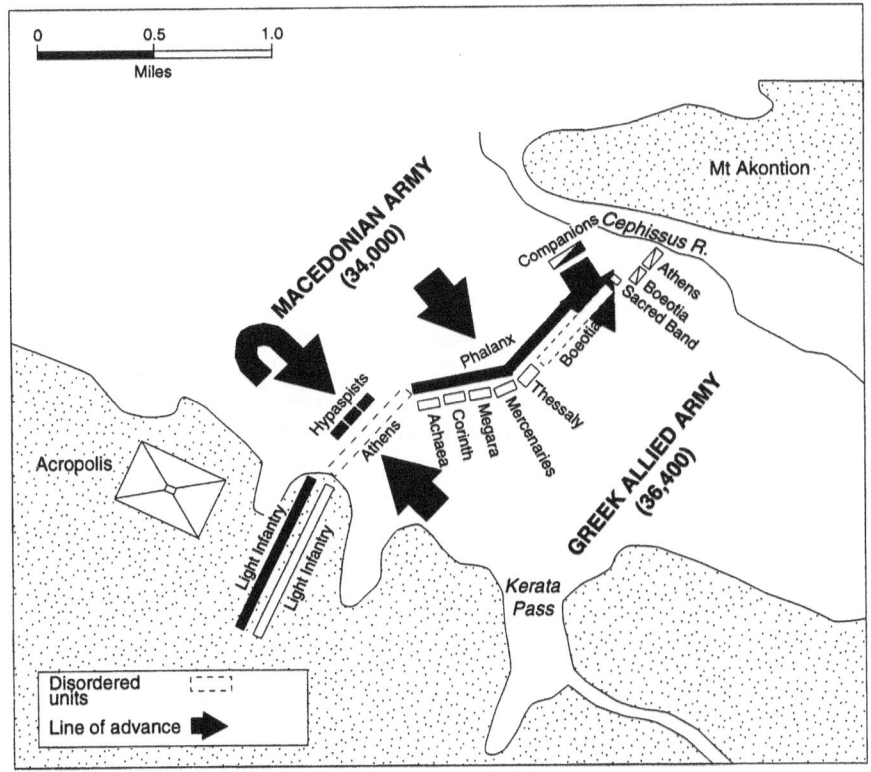

Map 9: Battle of Chaeronea

Aegospotami during the Peloponnesian War. They made ready to arm and free any of their 150,000 slaves who would fight in their behalf.[124] The temples were stripped of arms to equip the slaves, and large contributions were made by wealthy citizens to purchase additional weapons. The city walls were strengthened by trees felled near the city and stones taken from Athenian graves. Considering the 14-mile length of the walls between Athens and Piraeus, the low military capabilities of the slaves, and the difficulty of properly arming even a fraction of them, the successful defense of the city would have been problematical at best, however.[125] Also, it seems that the Athenian walls did not contain towers nor room for catapult emplacements, both necessary for neutralization of an attacker's catapult fire.[126] This would have given Philip a decided advantage in any assault that he made against the city.

Philip, being eager to avoid alienating Athens, now went out of his way to placate the city. Athenian acknowledgment of his supremacy would keep many of the potentially dissident cities in line. It also wasn't a sure thing that he would be able to storm Athens successfully. He had been unable to succeed in similar circumstances at Perinthus and Byzantium. Protected by its massive walls and large fleet, Athens would have time on its side. The more time that passed, the greater the possibility that Greece would rekindle its patriotism to assist Athens or the Persians would interfere. Also, Philip would be deep in unfriendly territory at the end of an extremely tenuous supply line that could easily be cut.

The 2,000 Athenian prisoners Philip had captured at Chaeronea were returned without ransom. Athens had not, like Thebes, betrayed an alliance with him, nor had Athens been actively involved in soliciting Persian support, as Thebes had. Also, Athens was the center of Greek culture and only she would be able to provide the means of Hellenizing both Macedonia and Philip's anticipated conquests in Persia. With these considerations in mind, Philip sent Alexander and two of Philip's greatest generals, Antipater and Alcimachus, to escort the remains of the Athenians who had died on the battlefield back to their city. Athens was informed that it would not be garrisoned by Macedonian troops, nor would Macedonian ships be stationed in Piraeus. Although Athens was allowed to keep its Aegean islands, which included Delos, Imbros, Lemnos, Samos and Scyros, it was forced to relinquish all other territorial claims, dissolve the Athenian Maritime League, and become Macedonia's ally.[127] Athens readily accepted what it considered extremely lenient terms.

The loss of the battle ended Theban control of Boeotia. Philip dissolved the Boeotian League, which in fact was only a subterfuge for a Theban Empire, and gave the individual Boeotian cities their freedom. Thebes was forced to recall all political exiles, the anti–Macedonian faction there was banished, and an oligarchy of 300 people friendly to Philip was set up to govern the city. A Macedonian garrison was also installed in the Cadmea. Unlike the Athenian prisoners, the Thebans were sold into slavery, and an exorbitant price had to be paid by relatives to bury their dead. Those Theban politicians who supported the war were exiled or executed and had their property confiscated.

Other Greek states moved to conclude treaties of alliance with Macedonia. Byzantium, Selymbria and Perinthus all capitulated to Philip. In return, they were given a limited degree of independence. The Spartans stood alone in refusing to submit to the Macedonians. The primary reasons for their intransigence were the recognition of the independence of Messenia by the League of Corinth and Sparta's injured pride in having to assume a subordinate position in Greek affairs. Because of Sparta's resistance, it was invaded and its border territory was ceded to unfriendly neighbors. The Greek states, with the single exception of Sparta, were now allied in a common political and military league. The congress of the League met at Corinth in late 338 B.C. This was an offensive and defensive alliance, each Greek ally being required to provide military forces to the League proportional to its military strength. For additional details on the League of Corinth, see the Glossary.

The battle of Chaeronea marked the effective end of the hoplite era.[128] Although the hoplites would continue to be used for another century, it was clear that they had become an archaic heavy infantry formation. The weaponry and formation of the Macedonian phalanx was clearly superior to that of the hoplites while the inability of the hoplites, to fight over broken ground or to engage in sustained hand-to-hand combat doomed them against the Roman legionaries.

Generalship   Lack of command control was clearly a predominate cause of the allied Greek defeat. There was no overall general designated to coordinate and control the allied army. No one had the authority to council or restrain Statocles from his fatal decision to rush madly upon Philip's withdrawing right wing. At lease two of the Athenian generals on the field, Statocles and Chares, were clearly incompetent. Lysicles was later condemned to death by Athens, Chares appears not to have returned to the city, and Statocles quickly disappeared. The allied leadership was clearly significantly inferior to that of Macedonia and was unable to analyze effectively Philip's tactics or to properly react.

The Greek allies had chosen their defensive position well. The site negated any turning movement by Philip on either flank, forcing him to attack frontally along a narrow battlefield. The Athenian citizen-levied army was, however, clearly not the equal of Philip's professionals, and this was the glaring weak spot in the allied line. The euphoria of battle all too quickly went to the heads of the Athenians, and they overreacted to the situation, promptly losing their cohesion in the process. Once Philip began to withdraw his right flank, the Athenian generals probably lost all control over their troops as they surged excitedly forward after the allegedly retreating Macedonians. The subsequent disorder turned the formation into little more than an undisciplined mob. Not only were the Athenian hoplites less effective as a fighting force than the Macedonians, their morale was fairly unstable and susceptible to sudden change. Any unexpected setback was likely to have a disproportionate adverse effect on their resolve. This brittleness mandated against any Athenian staying power in a protracted engagement.

The hoplite formation of the allies placed them at a distinct disadvantage against the Macedonian phalanx. The hoplites could only fight at parity with the phalanx if they were deployed defensively behind an obstacle.[129] Otherwise, the phalanx had an almost overwhelming combat advantage: its soldiers had 21-foot sarissas, while the hoplites had spears. Thus all the weapons of the first five ranks of the phalanx could be used in combat against the first two ranks of the hoplite formation. The sarissas would not only engage the hoplites long before they were able to respond, but the phalanx formation would target 10 weapons against each of the frontline hoplites.

It is easy to see from whom Alexander inherited his outstanding tactical ability; he had only to observe closely his father. Philip had a difficult dilemma to solve in this battle. The allies had both flanks solidly anchored and were deployed on a narrow front with an army superior in numbers to his own. Many lesser commanders would have hesitated to engage in so unequal a struggle, but not Philip; he would create an advantage for himself where none apparently existed. Philip correctly gauged that the weakest component of the allies was the Athenians and developed a brilliant strategy to defeat them. He took advantage of the superb discipline of his own elite troops to simulate a retreat in the expectation that the undisciplined Athenians would leave their position in the allied line to pursue his troops recklessly. In doing so, they would expose not only their own right flank but would force a prolongation of the Boeotian and allied Greek line as it edged to the left in attempt to close up the steadily receding Athenian right flank. This would give Alexander the opportunity to drive his cavalry into the numerous small gaps subsequently created and collapse the Theban Sacred Band, while Philip, in turn, reversed his withdrawal and fell upon the already disorganized Athenians. It was an excellent plan and went exactly according to script, resulting in a victory that was in the same league as any Alexander would later have in Asia. This battle clearly indicated that had Philip, instead of Alexander, commanded the invasion of Persia, both strategically and tactically his successes would not have been in the least way inferior to any that his illustrious son was later to achieve.

Peloponnesus

Athenian Panhellenic Congress

Demosthenes attempted to organize an alliance against Philip in 340 B.C. Although the Achaeans, Corinth and Megara promised men and funds, most other cities refused to break their alliance with Macedonia. Athens was successful, however, in recruiting Aetolia, Ambracia, Corcyra and Leucas. Early that year Athens convened a congress to conclude the alliance. Although war was not declared against Philip at that time, several towns allied to him were captured, while Athenian privateers preyed on Macedonian ships from the Peloponnese. Any Macedonian crews captured were sold into slavery.[130]

Sparta Invades Arcadia

During the Third Sacred War, the Spartans, under their king Archidamus, recalled their troops from Phocis to deploy them against Megalopolis, the capture of which would allow Sparta to subdue Messenia and reassert its former dominance in the Peloponnese. Phayllus sent the Spartans 3,000 Phocion mercenaries in support, and Lycophron of Pherae sent 150 cavalry.[131] Archidamus marched the Spartan army to Mantineia in Arcadia, cutting the Argives off from Megalopolis. He then attacked Orneae in Argos and defeated the Argives. A Theban army of 500 cavalry and 4,000 infantry in command of Cephision now arrived, joining the Argives and Arcadians.[132] Although their combined force was far superior to that of the Spartans, it was poorly disciplined, and in the subsequent battle, the Spartans were able to achieve a marginal victory against them. This defeat induced the Argives and Arcadians to return home.[133] After devastating an area of Arcadia, the Spartans stormed Helissus and then returned to Sparta. The Thebans fought three battles against the Spartans, beating them in the first two but being defeated by them in the last one.[134] When the war dragged on inconclusively, however, Sparta made peace with Megalopolis. All the allies on both sides then returned home.

Philip Invades Laconia

During the fall of 338 B.C., Philip marched on the Peloponnese. At the battle of Chaeronea, Arcadia, Argos, Elis, Massena and Sparta all had remained neutral in the conflict while the Achaean League and the towns on the Akte peninsula had fought against him. Although Corinth and Megara had initially prepared to defend their cities, they soon thought better of it and upon Philip's approach both surrendered to him. From Corinth, Philip went to Argos, now firmly in control of his supporters. There, all the states in the Peloponnese came to submit to him, with the single exception of Sparta, whose historic tradition prevented her submission. This forced Philip to issue an ultimatum demanding that all territory Sparta had seized from its neighbors be returned to them. Upon Sparta's refusal to do so, Philip invaded Laconia. He met little resistance because his army was too large for Sparta to engage in the field with any hope of victory. Although Philip proceeded to lay waste to Laconia, he refrained from attacking the city of Sparta. Philip then withdrew northward. The areas along Sparta's border were now given to adjacent city-states Sparta had been almost continually at war with: Argos received Thyreatis and eastern Cynuria, Tegea received Sciritis and Caryae, Megalopolis received Belbinatis, and Massena received Denthaliatis and southwest Messenia on the Gulf of Kalamata.[135] Sparta was now surrounded by states that had received and held its territory solely through Philip's support. A congress of all the Greeks states then confirmed the territorial adjustments made in the Peloponnese. Philip had no desire, however, to eliminate Sparta, leaving her small army intact. This would give Sparta hope that she could somehow revenge herself on those neighbors who had wronged her. This would greatly work to Philip's

Map 10: The Peloponnese

1. Major mercenary recruitment base.

advantage in the Peloponnese because not only would the states surrounding Sparta be focusing their attentions on an almost certain Spartan attempt to regain her lost land but would increase their dependency on Macedonian leadership and military support to keep the Spartans in check.

Asia Minor

In 336 B.C., a 10,000-strong force of Macedonians and mercenaries was ferried across the Hellespont to Abydos.[136] Parmenio appears to have been the commander in chief of the force, while Attalus and Amyntas were his subcommanders.

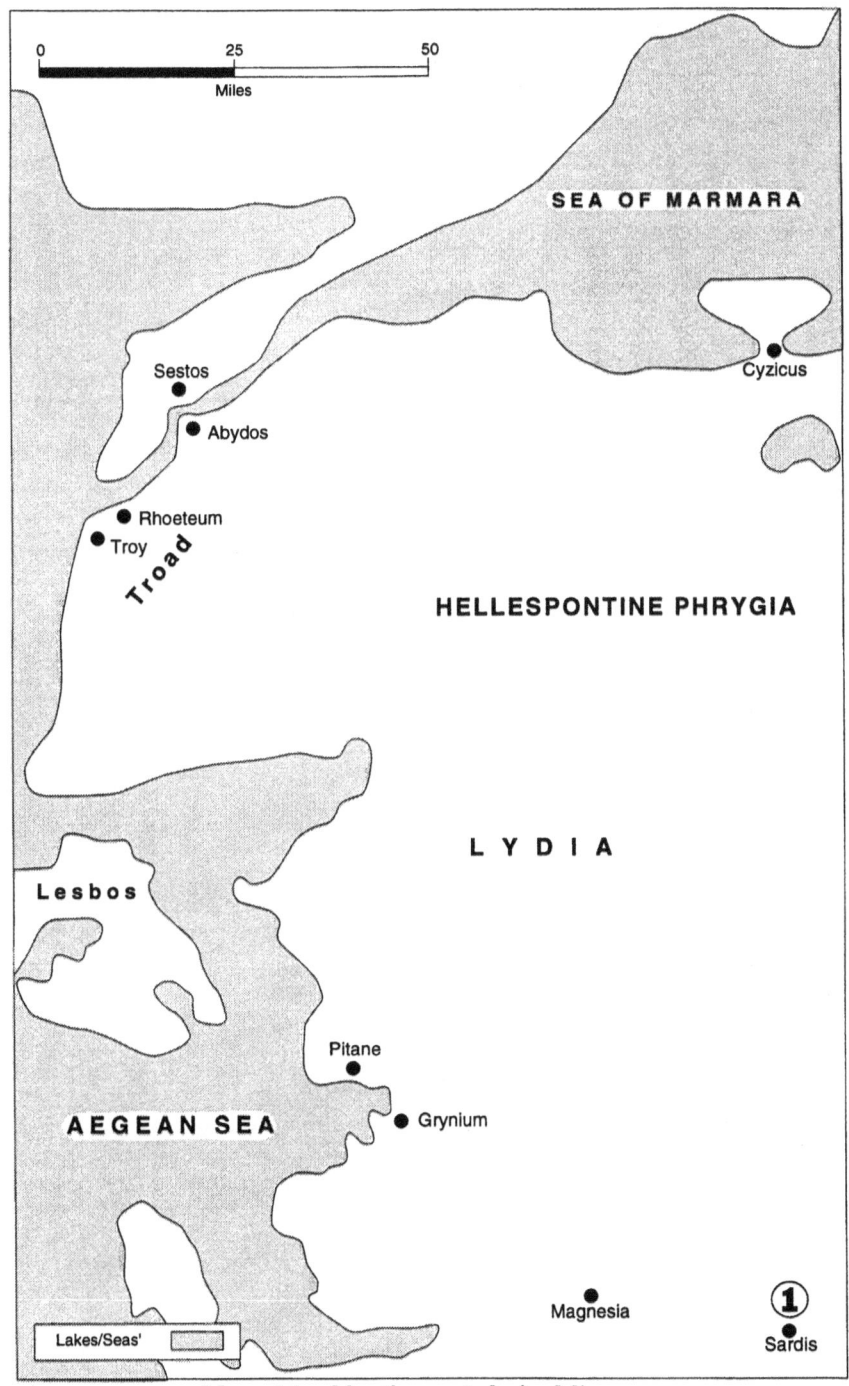

Map 11: Northwest Asia Minor

1. *Capital of Lydia.*

Attalus led the Macedonian infantry and Amyntas the Greek allies and Greek mercenaries.[137] The force had invaded in late autumn, the adverse weather at that time of year virtually prohibiting the Persian fleet from sailing against them. This would make it possible to move down the coast of Caria and capture all the anchorages there without any interference from the Persian fleet. As the Macedonians moved along the coast of Asia Minor, the democrats in the Greek cities rose in revolt against the Persians as far south as Ephesus. Several of the Aegean islands also revolted, including Tenedos, Lesbos and Chios.

By the end of 336 B.C., a Macedonian force under the command of Calas, who had replaced the murdered Attalus, had pushed out just past Magnesia. Memnon of Rhodes, who commanded a force of 4,000 mercenaries in Persian employ, was entrenched about five miles distant from the city.[138] Although heavily outnumbered, Memnon attacked Calas and forced him back into Magnesia. Parmenio, who was besieging Pitane at the time, immediately raised the siege and marched off to join Calas. Believing himself to be overextended, Parmenio began withdrawing to the north. As he did so, all the Persian-supported oligarchs resumed control of the cities abandoned by the Macedonians, virtually all of them willingly opening their gates to the advancing Persian army.

In the second half of 335 B.C., Memnon, now in command of 5,000 mercenaries, crossed Mt. Ida undetected and attempted to capture Cyzicus, an island city connected to the northern coast of Asia Minor by a bridge.[139] The city was an important Greek supply base in the Propontis Sea. Although failing to capture it, Memnon's bold strategy caused Parmenio to be again concerned over the length of his line of communications and he began to withdraw towards the Troad. Being continually outmaneuvered by Memnon's smaller force, Parmenio was eventually forced back to the west coast of the Troad, in the vicinity of Rhoeteum.

Generalship   Parmenio seems to have waged a very conservative campaign in Asia Minor, allowing himself to be outmaneuvered continually by Memnon's considerably smaller force. He did not display a particularly high level of generalship, and his achievements there could hardly have lived up to expectations. When Alexander would cross over into Asia Minor, Parmenio would hold little more than the shoreline of the Hellespont. Although this would guarantee Alexander a safe crossing, it would give him little else.

In contrast, Memnon seems to have conducted his campaign against Parmenio with great skill. Although being outnumbered at least two to one by the Macedonians, he was able to force them steadily back to the Troad by constantly threatening their line of communications. There do not seem to have been any stand-up field battles fought during the campaign, the focus apparently being more on maneuvering for position. Memnon obviously did well in this campaign and seems to have held the initiative and completely dominated the cautious Macedonian leadership.

Part III

Campaigns of Alexander the Great

6. Greece

With the death of Philip II, Alexander was faced with the resurgence of several Balkan tribes and increased dissatisfaction in Greece with Macedonian rule. He thus embarked on an immediate campaign to safeguard the northern frontiers of Macedonia against attack and occupation, by subduing the free Thracians, Triballians, Getae, Dardanians, Taulantians, and Autaratians. While at Pelium in northwest Macedonian, Alexander was informed of the Theban revolt. Fearing that if left unchecked it would spread to other areas of Greece — particularly Argos, Athens, or Sparta — he immediately marched south to deal with it. Instead of meeting an allied Greek army as his father Philip II did at Chaeronea, Alexander had to contend only with the Thebans. The other city-states of Greece preferred to hang back and await events, evidently thinking that the Thebans had acted too hastily and were thus likely to be defeated. After a hard fight, Alexander defeated the Theban army in a field battle, pursued the disorganized survivors into Thebes, and entirely destroyed them. Deciding to make an example of Thebes, he razed the city and sold its citizens into slavery. For these acts he was hated and despised throughout Greece, Thebes being one of the oldest and most renowned cities there. Alexander was also feared for his action, however, because it was a clear example of the price which might have to be paid for any revolt against him. Although Greece, except for Sparta, dared not revolt against Alexander while he lived, its citizens only awaited the day when they could throw off his hated rule. They merely bided their time, refusing to extend to Alexander any more than a grudging minimal assistance to his campaign against the Persian Empire. Ironically, in the war's opening stages, many more of Greece's citizens were serving in Persian employ than in Alexander's army.

Thessaly

Alexander marched south from Pella, though Methone and Pydna. In the valley of the Tempe River, between Mt. Olympus and Mt. Ossa, the Thessalian League's army occupied a five-mile-long pass that was virtually impregnable to frontal assault.[1] It was said to be only wide enough for a single mule to pass through at a time.[2] At Alexander's approach, the Thessalians ordered him to halt his march while they discussed what action to take. Alexander complied with their demand but then ordered his engineers to cut steps known as "Alexander's ladders" up the

Map 12: Greece

side of Mt. Ossa that lay along the coast. His army then climbed the steps over the mountain and deployed on the plain behind the Thessalians, taking them completely by surprise. Rather then fight in such a disadvantageous position, the Thessalians opened negotiations. Alexander's subsequent intimidation, persuasion, and flattery convinced them to confirm him as archon of the Thessalian League for life, investing him with Philip's former control over both their army and national revenues. The Thessalian heavy cavalry was incorporated into Alexander's army, while their peltast infantry was dismissed from service and allowed to return home unhindered.

The Balkans

Alexander's objective in conducting the Balkans campaign was to secure the northern frontier of Macedonia from attack before he moved east against Persia.

This was not to be the kind of punitive expedition Philip II had conducted several years earlier but a campaign of conquest and subjugation. The growing threat that had built up in the area since Philip's campaign had convinced Alexander that a preemptive strike would only delay, not remove, the danger. For Alexander's campaign to be effective, he would have to crush the resistance of the resurgent Balkan tribes in the 100 miles of territory between Macedonia and the Danube. That broad river could then serve as a solid defensive boundary protecting northern Macedonia from any further Balkan raids. The option of a diplomatic solution to the Balkans problem was not readily available to Alexander. The tribes there had fought each other for centuries, usually to obtain both loot and slaves. As a result, they had little desire to cooperate with neighbors with whom they preferred to be at war.

In addition to securing the lives and property of northern Macedonia, a successful Balkans campaign would result in several other important benefits. Antipater, who was Alexander's regent in Macedonia, would be able to concentrate solely on the unrest expected in southern Greece instead of having to divide his forces to also watch the northern Macedonian frontier. After the expected defeat of the Balkans, their manpower levies would be available for service with Alexander's army. They would, in fact, comprise about 20 percent, or 7,000, of the infantry with which Alexander would invade Persia and would constitute the majority of his skirmishing troops. Then, too, Balkan troops serving with his army would effectively act as hostages for the continued good behavior of their homeland tribes, who would be unlikely to revolt in Alexander's absence with so much of their manpower serving in his army.

The military tactics that the Balkan tribes adapted to their environment revolved around hit-and-run raids and ambushes in rough terrain and heavy woods. In these circumstances, fighting effectiveness depended more on individual prowess and mobility than on the discipline of organized formations. Should the Balkan tribes ever have to fight either the Companions or the phalanx in a field battle on open ground, however, they would find themselves to be completely outclassed, being lightly armed and armored. The Macedonian army that invaded the Balkans contained the phalanx taxies of upper Macedonia; cavalry squadrons from Amphipolis, Boeotia, and upper Macedonia; slingers; and archers. Although the army only numbered about 15,000, it was almost exclusively Macedonian in composition and was far more effective than any Balkan force it would encounter.[3] The superior morale, discipline, and weaponry of the Macedonians would make them all but invincible in any stand-up battle with the impulsive, undisciplined, and lightly armed tribes of the north.

Free Thracians

With the melting of the snows in the mountain passes in the spring of 335 B.C., Alexander began his Balkans campaign. He marched east from Pella, then northeast from Amphipolis. Crossing the Nestos River, he turned north to Philip II's outpost at Philippopolis. From there he crossed into the territory of the free

168   III: CAMPAIGNS OF ALEXANDER THE GREAT

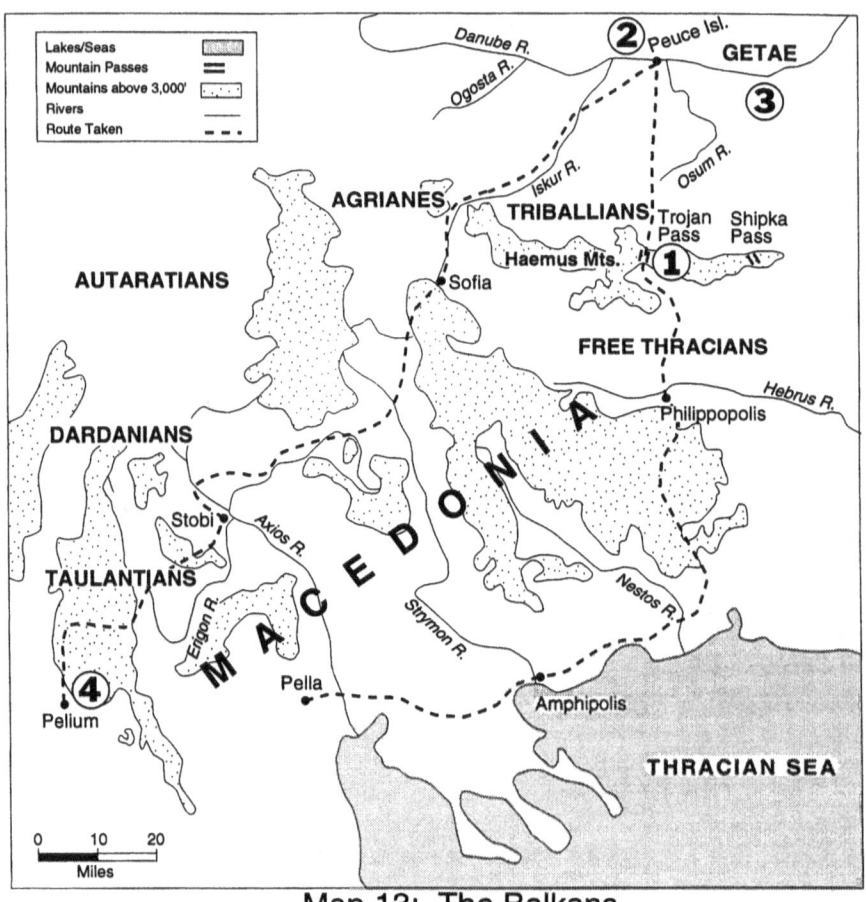

Map 13: The Balkans

1. Alexander is victorious against the free Thracian mountain cart defense. 2. Alexander is unable to capture Peuce Island. 3. Alexander defeats the Getae. 4. The Dardanians, under Cleitus, capture Pelium.

Thracians who had remained outside of Philip's earlier acquisition of Thrace. Ten days later Alexander arrived at Trojan Pass, a narrow canyon through the Haemus Mountains.[4] On high ground at the head of the pass, the Thracians drew up their light mountain carts in a defensive stockade, in apparent anticipation that Alexander would march uphill along a narrow front and attack their entrenched position.

Alexander, however, guessed that the impetuous nature of the poorly disciplined Thracians would not allow them to await passively an attack by the Macedonians. He correctly foresaw that they would probably roll their carts downhill into the phalanx in an attempt to disorder their ranks and inflict heavy casualties upon them. Then, before the Macedonians could reform their ranks and recover their morale, the Thracians would charge down the hill and overwhelm the phalanx.

With the Macedonian lines broken and their long sarissas next to useless in hand-to-hand combat, they would be almost helpless to defend themselves against the Thracian broadsword attack.

Alexander informed his men of the nature of the expected Thracian tactics and instructed them that where the ground permitted, they should break formation, open their ranks, and let the carts pass through. Where there was no room to maneuver, the Macedonians should lie down, lock shields closely together, and let the carts bounce over them. Alexander formed the phalanx in the center and the archers on his right flank. The Agrianians and hypaspists were deployed under his personal command on the left flank.[5] The Macedonians dressed their ranks and then advanced up the hill. As Alexander had expected, the Thracians carts came careening down. The disciplined Macedonians reacted as they had been carefully instructed, and although no one was killed, there must have been quite a few broken arms and legs and many bruised bodies from the impact of the bouncing carts, which probably had been filled with rocks. The Macedonians, however, quickly reformed their lines and continued their advance. Alexander brought his archers from the right wing to the front of the phalanx, where they broke up a Thracian charge by missile fire.[6] The phalanx then moved to close quarters against the confused mob of Thracians, who broke before Alexander could bring his left wing into contact. The Thracians flung down their broadswords and fled down the mountainside, leaving over 1,500 dead behind them.[7] Because of their lack of armor and their familiarity with the area, most who fled managed to escape. The Thracian women, children, and baggage, however, were all captured and immediately sent to the coast under guard of Lysanias and Philotas for transport to Macedonia.[8] Alexander was not going to repeat Philip II's mistake of compromising his army's safety by the need to protect its booty. The way was now open for a continuation of the move north to the Danube.

Triballians

Alexander then crossed the Trojan Pass and entered the land of the Triballians. Advancing to the Lyginus River, he made camp about three day's march from the Danube.[9] Under their king Syrmus, a large force of Triballian warriors, along with their women, children, and a number of free Thracians, evacuated to Peuce (Pine Tree) Island, which lay in the middle of the Danube River.[10] A much larger Triballian force slipped in behind Alexander to cut his line of communications with Macedonia.

Turning back to deal with the blocking force, Alexander surprised the Triballians, who were engaged in making camp. They quickly took shelter in a wooded glen near a river. Because it would be costly to attack the Triballians there, where their light weapons and open-order combat formation would give them a significant combat advantage, Alexander determined to draw them out in the open, where his Companion cavalry and phalanx could effectively deal with them. He knew that although the Triballians were skilled at ambushes, their lack of discipline made them vulnerable themselves to an ambush. All that was necessary was to provide an irresistible lure and their well-known impetuosity would probably override sound military judgment.

Alexander ordered his archers and slingers to advance without the support of heavier troops and to direct a heavy missile fire into the woods to provoke a Triballian attack while the remainder of the army remained concealed. As expected, after enduring casualties from the missile fire and observing that the light troops were apparently unsupported, the Triballians sallied out in a wild charge. Philotas, with the cavalry from upper Macedonia, then moved out against their right flank, while Heracleides, with the Boeotian cavalry, and Sopolis, with the Amphipolan cavalry, charged their left flank.[11] The phalanx, preceded by the remainder of the cavalry, advanced on the Triballian center.[12] The Triballians stood their ground, while the Macedonians were at missile range but when hand-to-hand combat was eminent, their lines broke and they were cut to pieces. The Triballians sustained 3,000 casualties, mostly in fatalities.[13] Few prisoners were taken because the dense woods along the river and the approaching darkness facilitated the escape of those who attempted to flee. Fatalities among Alexander's men were a mere 11 cavalry and 40 infantry.[14]

Alexander resumed his march and three days later arrived at the Danube River, where he met the squadron of warships he had earlier ordered to sail through the Black Sea.[15] Manning the small number of ships with a portion of his phalanx and archers, Alexander then attempted an amphibious assault against Peuce Island. He was unable to gain a foothold there, however, because steep banks along the shoreline were heavily defended by the Triballians, the narrow waterway surrounding the island had a swift current, and his fleet was too small. As it was now the harvest season, Alexander decided to bring the Triballians to terms by overrunning and devastating their country. Leaving a force behind to accomplish this, Alexander marched off with the bulk of his army towards the Getae, who had gathered in large numbers just north of the Danube. The Triballians, who were facing starvation as a result of Alexander's systematic destruction of their crops, decided to surrender to him when they learned of his victory over the Getae.

Getae

The Getae lived on both banks of the lower Danube in the area the Roman Empire would later call Dacia. They had mobilized an army of 4,000 cavalry and 10,000 infantry north of the Danube in an attempt to prevent the Macedonians from crossing.[16] Ironically, the very presence of this large force induced Alexander to consider the Getae a potential threat, and on that basis he decided to attack them. Appropriating all the native dugouts he could lay his hands on, filling sewn-up tent-covers with hay to serve as floats, and using the small fleet that had sailed up the Danube, Alexander managed to ferry 1,500 cavalry and 4,000 infantry across the Danube during the night.[17] The force then concealed itself in a tall cornfield.[18]

At dawn the next day, Nicanor led the phalanx out of the cornfield, followed by Alexander with the cavalry. Alexander moved off to the right, while Nicanor formed the infantry up into a square.[19] The sleeping Getae were taken completely by surprise in the subsequent attack, never imagining that Alexander could cross the Danube without a bridge, let alone at night. Alexander's cavalry charge scattered the Getae before contact was ever made, and they fled in confusion back to a weakly fortified settlement four miles away.[20] When the phalanx advanced on the site, the Getae took their women, children, and horses and scattered into the nearby desert. Alexander declined the futility of a pursuit, contenting himself instead with looting and burning the abandoned settlement. Meleager and Philip were detailed to escort the resulting plunder back to camp.[21] Without incurring a single casualty, Alexander then retired back across the Danube.

Alexander marched south from the Danube back towards the Trojan Pass. Instead of crossing there and continuing on to Macedonia, however, he turned southwest to Agriania, near the modern-day city of Sofia, for a visit with his old friend King Langaros. While he was there, reports came in that three Illyrian tribes were mobilizing to attack western Macedonia: the Dardanians under Cleitus, from Yugoslavia; the Taulantians under Glaucias, from Albania; and the Autaratians, from Serbia.[22] The Dardanians, whose forces were first into the field, captured the Macedonian border fortress of Pelium that dominated a key road junction between Illyria, Macedonia, and central Greece. Unless the city was recovered, northwest Macedonia would again be subjected to destructive Illyrian raids. The Autaratians were reportedly intending to attack Alexander while he was strung out in column marching to the relief of Pelium. Langaros offered to deal with that tribe himself with newly mobilized troops, thereby enabling Alexander to concentrate on preventing the Taulantians from linking up with the Dardanians. Alexander's entire army, which numbered 5,000 cavalry and 25,000 infantry, accompanied him on the campaign.[23]

Dardanians

By a forced march down the Axios and Erigon valleys, Alexander was able to arrive at Pelium just in advance of the Taulantians. The city was surrounded by high ground and heavy woods on three sides, the only approach to it being through a narrow wooded canyon along the Eordaicus River known as Wolf's Pass. The pass was only wide enough for four men abreast to march through.[24] Beyond it lay a small plain. The Dardanians occupied the high ground just outside Pelium. As Glaucias had not yet arrived, however, Cleitus feigned an attack on Alexander's right wing but then withdrew into the city at his approach. The Macedonian army moved up to the walls of the city and made camp. Cleitus' Dardanians were to remain pinned inside the city until Alexander's withdrawal back through Wolf's Pass.

Taulantians

Instead of immediately assaulting Pelium, which was actually only lightly held at the time, Alexander decided to encircle the small city with a wall. It is quite possible that the difficulty of the approach to the city precluded the siege train from being brought up. It appears Alexander thought that without it the casualties for the assaulting force would be unacceptably heavy. The next day, however, Glaucias arrived with his Taulantians and occupied the mountain pass in Alexander's rear, directly across his line of communications back to Macedonia.

When the baggage animals, which needed to graze, were sent out to a nearby plain escorted by Philotas and a portion of his cavalry, Glaucias anticipated the move by occupying the heights surrounding the grazing plain in strength. When this was reported to Alexander, he took the hypaspists, Agrianians, archers, and 400 cavalry and went in support of Philotas.[25] At Alexander's approach, Glaucias quickly abandoned the heights, and the baggage animals were safely escorted back to camp.

Alexander could not assault Pelium without exposing his rear to an attack by the Taulantians, nor could he afford to play a waiting game. His supplies on hand were nearly exhausted, and he was cut off from receiving any additional provisions by the Taulantians' occupation of the approaches to Wolf's Pass. Unable to fight his way out with any reasonable prospect of success because of the entrenched positions of the Taulantians in the foothills, Alexander desperately needed to draw them off the high ground they occupied for a fight in the plain, where the superior discipline, armament, and fighting effectiveness of his troops could decide the issue. To achieve this end, he devised a clever plan. The next morning he drew up his phalanx 120 ranks deep and stationed a squadron of 200 cavalry on each flank.[26] The formation then proceeded to execute a drill in absolute silence. The evolution of the sarissas in perfect formation, all without a word being spoken was too much for the undisciplined Taulantians to resist. Their curiosity got the better of them and they slowly came out onto the plain for a closer look. When most of them had come down from the foothills, Alexander formed the cavalry on the left wing and charged, while the phalanx advanced to the attack. The sudden Macedonian deployment to the attack and the accompanying cacophony of noise broke the Taulantians' morale, and they fled in wild confusion, abandoning their positions on the heights.

Alexander's line of retreat was again open, and he now decided to withdraw from the dangerous position he occupied. A group of Taulantians still occupied, however, a small hill covering the ford across the Apsus River that Alexander's troops would have to cross in their retreat. Alexander ordered the Companions and hypaspists to deploy against the position and told them that if the Taulantians should continue to hold their ground, half the cavalry was to dismount to support more effectively those who remained mounted.[27] At the approach of Alexander's force, however, the Taulantians abandoned the hill and fled into the mountains. Alexander proceeded to occupy the position without opposition. He then ordered a 2,000-strong advance force consisting of Agrianians and archers to cross the river and hold a position on the far bank until the hypaspists and the phalanx were able to cross.[28] They were then to move to the left to support the flank of the phalanx there. The Taulantians now rallied, however, came down from the high ground, and prepared to attack the hypaspists as they withdrew towards the crossing. The cavalry and the phalanx charged and broke the Taulantian line while the Agrianians and archers moved up to the river at a run.[29]

Then Alexander proceeded to withdraw across the river and retreat through Wolf's Pass. The Macedonian withdrawal from the city released the Dardanians, who now joined the Taulantians in the pursuit. As the rear guard, which included the Agrianians and archers, fell back to the river, they were hard pressed by the two Balkan tribes. Alexander deployed the catapults on the far bank of the river, and all troops with missile weapons were ordered to advance to the river and fire their weapons at long range. The archers were told to fire their bows from midstream.

The subsequent heavy missile fire, along with the stones of the catapults, kept the Balkan tribes back and allowed the withdrawal to be completed safely. Almost unbelievably, not a man of Alexander's force was lost in the retreat. This action had the distinction of being only the second recorded instance in history where light catapults were used tactically in a field battle.

Alexander now withdrew a few miles from the pass, camped, and sent out reconnaissance parties. Three days later they reported back that the Dardanians and Taulantians were continuing to celebrate their apparent victory with heavy drinking, had dangerously extended their lines, and had neglected to entrench their camp. Even more interesting was the fact that they had not posted sentries, so convinced were they that Alexander was only concerned with fleeing their territory. Alexander immediately marched back to Pelium that night with the hypaspists, Agrianians, archers, and the taxies of the phalanx of Perdiccas and Coenus.[30]

This advance force was followed by the remainder of the army. When Alexander arrived back at the pass, he thought the situation so favorable that he ordered an immediate assault in column with his lead units, which were the Agrianians and archers.[31] Completely surprising the Dardanians and Taulantians, the advance force massacred large numbers of them as they slept off their drunken stupors, while the survivors fled in sheer panic. Alexander's cavalry pursued the fugitives right up to the mountains, and none escaped who did not first discard their heavy broadswords. Cleitus, now finding Pelium deserted, burned the city and fled with Glaucias to the vicinity of present-day Durazzo. After a short time, he surrendered to Alexander.

Autaratians

The Autaratians were the least warlike of the three Illyrian tribes that Alexander faced. They were located in the present Herzegovina. Langaros, king of the Agrianians, had agreed to march west against them with forces he had specifically levied for the purpose. Unfortunately, outside of the fact that Langaros invaded Autaratian territory, the details of his campaign are not known to us. It is apparent, however, that he was completely successful in diverting the Autaratians' attention away from Alexander because they were unable to intervene against him.

Generalship

By any standard, Alexander's Balkan campaign was immensely successful, Macedonia's northern border remaining trouble-free throughout his reign. The peace treaties imposed on the defeated Balkan tribes specified that they were to provide troops upon demand to Alexander. Balkan manpower levies would account for a significant number of the Macedonian army's light infantry troops used in the campaigns in Greece, the Persian Empire, and western India. They were also disproportionately used on secondary missions and as garrison troops throughout the Persian Empire and India, thus allowing the more combat effective Macedonians to remain concentrated in the field army. The cost of the campaign was negligible in terms of Macedonian losses and invaluable in developing the army's ability to operate in difficult terrain and adapt to unexpected conditions.

Alexander clearly demonstrated some exceptional abilities in this conduct of the campaign. His anticipation of the Thracian cart tactic and the effective countermeasures he devised against it completely frustrated the Thracian plan of attack. A more tradition-bound general would have simply assumed the logical Thracian reaction of a passive defense behind their carts in order to force the Macedonians to attack uphill at a disadvantage. His tempting of the Triballians out into the open where he could deal them a certain defeat was cleverly done, as was his crossing of the Danube opposite the completely surprised Getae. He brilliantly organized his withdrawal from the Taulantians' trap at Pelium and then patiently waited in the vicinity of the city with the well-founded hope of a successful return. His crowning achievement, however, must surely be the "silent drill" that extricated him from the dangerous trap of the Taulantians. Alexander used his opponents' own uncontrollable curiosity and lack of discipline against them in a simply devastating attack.

Alexander's generalship, however, was not flawless. This was his first strategic campaign, and he did make a number of mistakes. His attempted landing against the Triballian force on Peuce Island was clearly in error. There were too many disadvantages to the operation, but he stubbornly insisted on pursuing it. He did, however, eventually realize his mistake and took the appropriate steps to resolve the situation. Alexander also erred in attempting to besiege Pelium when time was of the essence. Although he might not have had his siege train available, he should have at least attempted to assault the city. The situation called for decisive action on Alexander's part, and he clearly opted for a conservative approach. In similar circumstances later in Persia and India, he would have no such qualms against attempting unsupported city assaults. Alexander's most glaring oversight, however, was letting himself get boxed onto the plain in front of Pelium by the Taulantians. The situation might easily have ended with the cream of the Macedonian army taking heavy casualties in an attempt to cut their way out of the trap. For the remainder of his reign, however, Alexander rarely made serious strategic or tactical mistakes, with the exception of being outmaneuvered by Darius at Issus and his crossing of the Makran Desert. It was in the Balkans that Alexander's obvious tactical and strategic skills were honed to a fine edge.

The Macedonian army was, of course, superb, being far and away the most formidable combat force in the central or eastern Mediterranean at that time. It had been combat trained under Philip II, and its effectiveness, discipline, and moral could not be equaled. The army was extremely well officered and its weaponry, both offensive and defensive, gave it a significant advantage over its lightly armed and mostly nonarmored Balkan opponents. The various Balkan tribes Alexander fought were, admittedly, little more than lightly armed mobs of warriors who tended to fight as individuals, much in the Greek Homeric tradition. They were impetuous and easily set up for deception, qualities that Alexander capitalized on during most of the encounters that he had with them. Since they were not very disciplined, the Balkan tribes tended to have relatively little staying power; at the first setback they usually fell apart and fled in wild confusion. After a defeat, it was almost impossible to rally them. Nevertheless, that type of warrior could be deadly in the right circumstances, as the Romans later learned at Teutoburger Wald. Those conditions did exist in the area Alexander campaigned in: rough terrain, heavy forests, and a mobile and impetuous enemy. The Macedonians had Alexander, however, and he managed to stay one step ahead of events. None of the tribes was really ever able to spring one of their traps in the face of his vigilance and luck, although they set several.

Central Greece

A faction of Thebans who wanted to overthrow the Macedonian occupation of their city recalled a number of exiles. After murdering two senior officers of the Macedonian garrison stationed at the citadel on the Cadmea, the rebels went before the assembly of Thebes and in a passionate speech convinced them to throw off Macedonian domination. They supported their action by the elation of the populace at recovering their freedom, the promise of Athenian assistance, and assurances that Alexander had died in Illyria.[32] When the news of the Theban revolt reached Athens, Demosthenes convinced the Assembly to provide military assistance immediately. The Athenians soon thought better of the idea, however, and withheld any active support for Thebes until events should clarify its ability to resist effectively the Macedonian army that would soon be sent against it. Thebes then sent ambassadors to Arcadia, Argos, and Elis to request military support. A revolution in Elis deposed and exiled Macedonian sympathizers. The Arcadians sent a force as far as the Isthmus, and although its generals ignored threats from Antipater, they refused to march any closer to Thebes.[33] Other cities in Greece, although sympathizing with Thebes, refused to support her because they thought that she had acted too hastily and was likely to be punished by the full strength of the Macedonian army.

When Alexander was informed of the revolt, he was at Pelium, 300 miles northwest of Thebes.[34] Although his troops needed rest, he immediately set out on a force-march. Unless the revolt was quickly suppressed, he feared that Aetolia,

Athens, or Sparta might be persuaded to support it. On the seventh day after leaving Pelium, Alexander reached Pelinna in Thessaly.[35] On the thirteenth day, he arrived in Boeotia. He had taken the inland route through Doris instead of the usual coastal route through Thermopylae, which might have easily been held against him.[36] At Pelinna, Corinthian League contingents from Boeotia, Phocis, and Plataea joined him. Alexander reached Onchestus, seven miles northwest of Thebes, before his presence was reported there.[37] Even so, the Thebans believed that the Macedonian forces were under the command of either Antipater or Alexander (son of Aeropus). It was only the next day when the Macedonian army encamped outside the city that the Thebans realized that Alexander himself was present. Alexander's army of 3,000 cavalry and 30,000 infantry considerably outnumbered the Thebans, who were only able to field a Boeotian army of about 1,100 cavalry and 11,000 hoplites when fully mobilized.[38]

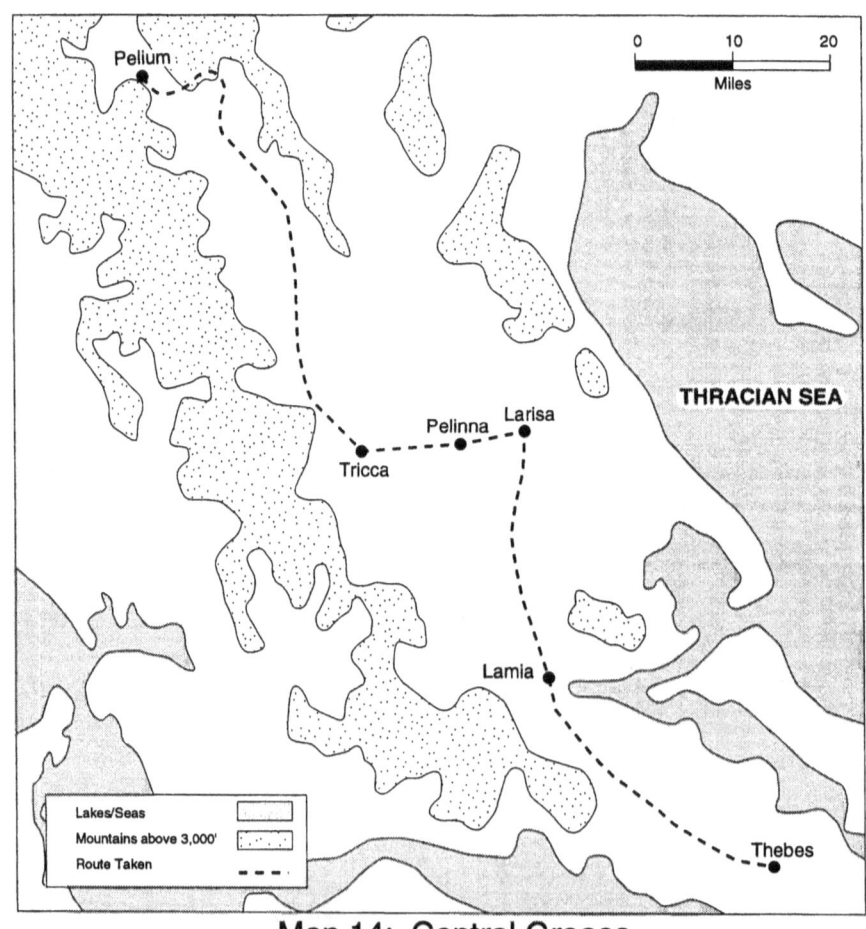

Map 14: Central Greece

Alexander was willing to forgive the Thebans, providing that they submitted to him. If he had indeed been dead, as they had alleged, the League treaty with Macedonia would have clearly been voided, Alexander having left no heir. As this was obviously not the case, however, Alexander now merely wanted the situation restored to that existing before the revolt. He only required confirmation of his office as hegemon of the League, acceptance of a Macedonian garrison on the Cadmea, and the surrender of the instigators of the revolt. The Thebans who had led the revolt and those exiles who had returned argued against Alexander's terms, believing their acceptance meant death for them. They stressed the exhilaration of their restored freedom and their distrust of Alexander. They also pointed out that the city was well prepared for a siege, the walls were in good repair, the Theban cavalry and hoplites were the best in Greece, and the Macedonian garrison on the Cadmea was effectively isolated by a double stockade built round it. The rebels won over the city's assembly, and it promptly voted to reject Alexander's terms. The Thebans sallied out with some cavalry and light troops, engaged the Macedonian outposts of the camp in long-range missile fire, and then advanced on the camp itself.[39] In response, Alexander sent out some light troops and archers, who easily drove the sortie force back. Alexander then brought his army round south of the city opposite the Eleutherae Gate and across the road to Athens. Here he was not only within supporting distance of his garrison on the Cadmea but was in a position to prevent any Athenian force coming to the assistance of Thebes. Alexander made no additional offensive move and continued to delay in the hopes that the Theban Assembly would realize how generously their treachery was being dealt with. An answer to Alexander's patience was not long in coming. A Theban herald loudly proclaimed that negotiations could commence whenever Antipater and Philotas were delivered up to the Thebans. The herald then issued an invitation to any freedom-loving Greeks to join the Thebans and the Great King of Persia in arms against the Macedonian tyrant. This action obviously was designed to enrage Alexander, which it did, with fatal consequences for Thebes.

Battle of Thebes

The Thebans made the decision to fight outside their walls and trust their luck to a field battle. They deployed most of their 7,000 hoplites on a narrow front opposite the Cadmea behind two stockades or fortified lines.[40] The Theban cavalry manned the first stockade, the Theban hoplites the second, and 12,000 freed slaves, refugees, and resident aliens garrisoned the city's walls.[41] Alexander divided his army into three separate forces: one to attack the stockade that was manned by dismounted cavalry; a second to attack the stockade that was manned by the Theban hoplites; and a third to be held in reserve.

Perdiccas, who was in command of the camp guard, upon receiving a signal from the garrison on the Cadmea or seeing some weakness in the Theban deployment, advanced to the attack with his taxies of the phalanx before Alexander's signal was given. Amyntas (son of Andromenes), seeing Perdiccas break into the first

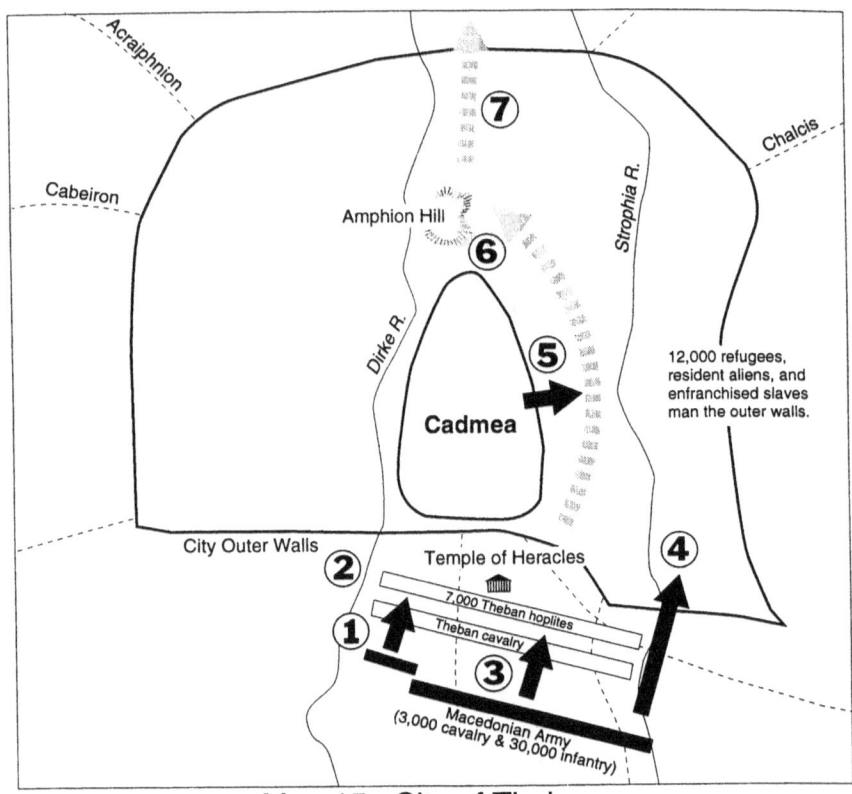

Map 15: City of Thebes

1. Perdiccas attacks prematurely. 2. Perdiccas is wounded. 3. Alexander's phalanx engages the Theban hoplites. 4. Entry through deserted postern gate. 5. Macedonian attack on stockade wall. 6. Theban retreat. 7. Escape route used by some Theban cavalry.

stockade, moved his taxies forward in support. Alexander then advanced the archers and Agrianians to reinforce the attack. After breaking through the first stockade, Perdiccas assaulted the second, but in the fighting he was wounded and carried back to camp.[42] Alexander ordered his remaining phalanx to engage the Theban hoplite line. The Thebans, however, were able to fight the phalanx to a standstill, their superior body strength apparently offsetting the Macedonian advantages of formation and weaponry.[43] Even when Alexander threw in his fresh reserves, he was unable to break the Theban battle line, so desperately did they fight.

Spotting a deserted postern gate beyond the right of the Theban line, Alexander sent a force there that was able to pass into the city without opposition. Once the Theban hoplites saw that the Macedonians had gained their city behind them, they attempted to withdraw back through the gate to their rear. The Theban cavalry then panicked, mounted up, and galloped into the city through the withdrawing hoplites, riding a number of them down and generally throwing the rest into confusion. As the Theban hoplites were not able to disengage completely from the Macedonians, the gates of the outer and inner walls could not be closed against them and the Macedonians were able to enter the city along with the withdrawing Thebans. Other Macedonian troops were able to scale the now virtually deserted walls because most of the Theban defenders there had been called away to augment their field force. The soldiers of the Macedonian garrison on the Cadmea, seeing Alexander's forces overrunning the walls, sallied out against the now weakly held stockade wall opposite them and carried it. The pressure of the three-pronged Macedonian attack soon fragmented the withdrawing Thebans and destroyed any hope for a coordinated defense.

The surviving Thebans fell back to Amphion Hill. There they turned on the pursuing Macedonians and counterattacked with the desperation of fear, driving them back. The commander of the archers, Euryotas, was killed in the Theban counterattack, and the archers, having lost 70 in dead alone, were forced to fall back behind the hypaspists.[44] Being no longer able to maintain a continuous defensive line, however, the Thebans broke apart into small groups, fighting and dying where they stood, neither asking for nor giving quarter. With the end in sight, some of the Theban cavalry managed to escape through the northern gate and ride off across the plain. Once inside the city, the Boeotians, Phocians, and Plataeans, all with long-standing grudges against the Thebans, began indiscriminately killing soldiers and civilians alike, granting mercy to none they encountered.[45] Neither age or sex was spared, and even those sheltering in the temples were massacred. The Macedonians and other regular troops, having no particular hostility towards the Thebans, appear not to have participated in the slaughter.[46] Although the Macedonians suffered 500 killed in the assault, they had inflicted some 6,000 casualties on the Thebans.[47]

Alexander left it up to the allies who fought with him in the battle to determine the fate of Thebes. He well knew that their enmity towards the city, as was clearly reflected in their brutal massacre of its helpless population, would be merciless.[48] This, however, apparently fell in with his overall plan to terrorize the other Greek states into submission. The League of Corinth, which Alexander claimed was represented by his allies on the field, decreed that Thebes should be razed except for the Cadmea and its surviving population be sold into slavery. The only exceptions to enslavement were to be the priests and priestesses; supporters of Alexander; the poet Pindar, whom Alexander admired; and Pindar's relatives. The 30,000 Thebans who were enslaved and eventually sold brought Alexander 440 talents in badly needed revenue.[49] Alexander appropriated another 100 talents that the Thessalians owed the Thebans.[50] Any Thebans who escaped capture were exiled from Greece. Theban lands were given to surrounding Boeotian cities, and the allies declared their intention to rebuild Orchomenus and Plataea, which had been destroyed during the Peloponnesian War.

Although Alexander's harsh treatment of Thebes doomed any future cooperation from Greece, he probably would not have received it in any case. As soon as he was beyond the range of interference, Athens, Sparta, or Thebes, or perhaps all three, would have quickly revolted. As it was, the terror of what had happened to Thebes was a constant reminder to all cities of the price that might have to be paid for any uprising against Macedonian rule. Alexander was hated and despised for destroying one of the most ancient and distinguished cities in Greece, but he was also feared for it. As a result, all the Greek states, except Sparta, rushed to make amends with Alexander, either for their hesitation in failing to support him or to acknowledge their mistake in opposing him. The Arcadians condemned to death their anti–Macedonian leaders who had persuaded them to ally with Thebes, while the Eleans recalled their pro–Macedonian leaders. The Aetolians sent Alexander their regrets for having allied themselves with Thebes, indicating that they had only done so because they had been falsely told that Alexander had died in Illyria. Somewhat cynically, Athens congratulated Alexander on his victory and gave its grudging support to the judgment imposed on Thebes. Alexander took no punitive action against any of those who had refused to support him; his point had clearly been made. He did, however, demand that Athens surrender to him those whom he considered hostile to Macedonia: Chares, Charidemus, Diotimus, Ephialtes, Hypereides, Lycurgus, Moerocles, and Polyeuctas.[51] Upon the refusal of Athens to comply with the demand, Alexander then only ordered that Charidemus be exiled, whereupon he promptly fled to the court of Darius. Strategically, the destruction of Thebes removed one of the three most powerful states in Greece, only Athens and Sparta now remaining as major powers. They were separated by the narrow Isthmus of Corinth, however, so cooperation between the two states could be readily inhibited by the stationing of a Macedonian garrison at either Corinth or Megara. His campaign against the Thebans being successfully concluded, Alexander then returned to Macedonia.

Generalship   Alexander conducted the Theban campaign with his usual effectiveness. His 300-mile forced march caught the Thebans completely by surprise. When negotiations failed, Alexander moved his army to a position that isolated the city from Athenian assistance. Tactically, the battle moved out of Alexander's control with Perdiccas' premature attack. Although the first stockade held by the Theban cavalry was easily taken, the Theban hoplites rather unexpectedly managed to fight the phalanx to a standstill. Even the commitment of the Macedonian reserves could not break them. As the Thebans had chosen to engage Alexander in a field battle just outside the city, they took the chance that if defeated they would be unable to disengage from the Macedonians and reenter the city without also admitting the Macedonians. Ever alert to any opportunity during a battle, Alexander had spotted an unguarded gate off his fight flank. The Theban hoplites who, up until this time, had held their own, began to retreat once they became aware that the Macedonians were entering their city behind them. At this point, the battle was all but won.

It is interesting to note, however, what a hard fight the Thebans gave the Macedonians. The phalanx was apparently unable to overcome the Theban hoplites in a frontal attack when the hoplites were positioned behind an obstacle. The actual details of the battle that reflected unfavorably on the Macedonians were largely excluded, however, from the historical record. It would be impolitic to either impugn the fighting effectiveness of the Macedonian phalanx or downplay Alexander's own involvement in this battle.

The Peloponnese

In 336 B.C., shortly after Philip's death, Alexander marched down to the Peloponnese to compel the states there to acknowledge his leadership in the war against Persia. All there did so, except for the Spartans, who indicated that their customs did not permit them to follow the leadership of others.[52] Although Philip ceded a portion of Laconia to its unfriendly neighbors and looted the suburbs of Sparta itself, he otherwise left the Spartans alone. He wanted to leave them as a continuing threat to their neighbors. This would tend to focus the attentions of these neighbors on Sparta and facilitate their greater reliance on him to keep in check an aggressive state that would exact revenge at the first opportunity.

In 330 B.C., with Antipater engaged in suppressing a revolt in Thrace and Greece simmering in discontent from Alexander's Exile's Decree, King Agis of Sparta decided that the time was right to attempt again to capture Megalopolis, as a first step to reestablishing Spartan domination in the Peloponnese. Thus, he marched the Spartan army to Megalopolis and lay siege to the city. Antipater, being informed of the Spartan mobilization, immediately ended his campaign in Thrace and marched south. He passed through the Isthmus of Corinth without opposition. Notified of the approach of the Macedonian army, Agis raised the siege of Megalopolis, which he had been unable to either storm or starve out, and withdrew to more suitable ground to fight the expected field battle.

Battle of Megalopolis

Megalopolis was a city in the Peloponnese organized by the Thebans as a northwest barrier against a Spartan move in that direction in the aftermath of the Spartan defeat at the battle of Leuctra. The various surrounding Arcadian villages were incorporated into the city, which was then fortified with a double wall. Megalopolis was located in a flat plain southwest of Sparta through which the Eurotas River ran.[53] Because of the lack of roads in the Peloponnese, rivers and riverbeds were the major transportation arteries there. This automatically made any city like Megalopolis a key strategic objective.

The Spartan army for the battle was about 22,000 strong, which included 2,000 cavalry, 10,000 hoplites mustered from virtually every city in the Peloponnese, and 10,000 Greek mercenaries.[54] Antipater's army numbered about 40,000, with large numbers of Balkan and Greek allied troops, primarily Thessalians, allies from central Greece, and allies from Peloponnesian states hostile to Sparta.[55]

Agis, the Spartan king, fell back to the hilly terrain in the south to cover the road leading to Laconia. The plain where the battle took place limited the forces engaged to the smaller size of the Spartan army. It was hoped that this would offset the larger numbers of Antipater's army. The Spartans initially managed to fight Antipater's phalanx units to a standstill in a frontal battle. The Macedonians were able to keep feeding in fresh troops, however, while the smaller number of Spartans were forced to fight without respite. After a long, drawn-out fight, the Spartans finally became exhausted and were forced to retreat. Agis, who had been wounded early in the battle, was being carried from the field when his party was overtaken. He immediately rearmed himself and fought on until he was killed by a thrown javelin.

Antipater lost 3,500 killed in the battle, while the Spartans and their allies sustained 5,300 killed, with virtually everyone else being wounded.[56] Such heavy losses forced Sparta to sue immediately for peace. The subsequent terms imposed on it probably required that the remaining mercenaries in its employ be sent to join Alexander in Asia.[57] A total of 50 of Sparta's most illustrious nobles were demanded for surrender as hostages to ensure the city-state's continued good behavior. Sparta's allies, the Achaeans and Eleans, were forced to pay an indemnity of 120 talents to Megalopolis for the damage done to the city by the siege.[58] It was recognized that the Tegeans had entered the war under extreme pressure from Sparta, and they were consequently pardoned for their involvement. Only the faction responsible for persuading that city to revolt was punished.

Alexander had let Sparta off relatively lightly. He undoubtedly realized that the crushing number of casualties it had sustained in the battle had probably all but destroyed its military potential to destabilize the Peloponnese any further. If left alone, Sparta would undoubtedly be forced to adjust to its new status as a second-class power. Agis' successor, his younger brother Eudamidas, was indeed content to limit any further risk to Sparta's now severely reduced military manpower.

Generalship Antipater chose to engage the Spartans in a stand-up fight in terrain disadvantageous to his own larger army. This allowed the Spartans to fight him to a standstill initially, and it was only his continual pouring in of fresh reinforcements that finally exhausted the Spartans and drove them from the field. Alexander is alleged to have called it a battle of mice not men, referring either with contempt to the battle or to the tendency of a cornered rat to fight viciously to the death.

Although Antipater won the battle, it cannot be said from what little is known of it that he displayed a particularly high level of generalship. He appears to have merely conducted a battle of attrition against the Spartans, and it is only by weight of numbers that he achieved victory. His one big advantage was the superiority of the phalanx, but even this was not decisive until the Spartan army was virtually exhausted. This would indicate that the phalanx at his disposal was not of the highest caliber and would clearly demonstrate the damaging effect of Alexander's constant conscription of the best of the Macedonian army to fight in Asia.

Agis badly overestimated the dissatisfaction and willingness of the Greek states to join in Sparta's revolt against Alexander. Sparta was not particularly well liked in Greece. Its subsequent revolt was seen not as a fight for Greek freedom but as an attempt to reestablish the former domination of the Peloponnese it had earlier been deprived of by Thebes. Also, the larger states of Greece, notably Athens and Aetolia, were not yet ready to challenge Alexander when so many of their citizens were still held hostage in both his army and navy. The smaller Peloponnesian states were too fearful of Spartan aggression to commit themselves. Moreover, Alexander had demonstrated an unbroken series of victories in Persia that had opened up that empire to exploitation by the Greeks, the most ambitious of whom stood to make great fortunes. As a result, Sparta's probability of obtaining any significant Greek allies was almost nonexistent. Sparta was, however, able to acquire the services of most of the Greek mercenaries who had managed to escape from the battlefield of Issus, and these reinforcements at least allowed Agis to engage Antipater with some hope of success.

Agis had underestimated Antipater's ability to react quickly to Sparta's revolt and had overestimated Sparta's ability to conduct a successful siege against Megalopolis. When Antipater made his appearance, Agis was able to select a tactical battlefield that at least initially negated the superior numbers of the Macedonian army. In the extended fight which ensued, however, the Spartan army was gradually worn down by Antipater's constant influx of reinforcements and was eventually defeated. Even on a restricted battlefield, Agis was to discover to his dismay that numbers still counted heavily in determining victory. Overall, Agis' strategic abilities were definitely average at best, although tactically he seems to have done somewhat better than Antipater. Personally, however, Agis' conduct was nothing less than heroic, and the glorious manner of his death rivaled that of Leonidas at Thermopylae.

7. The Western Persian Empire

Alexander's campaigns in the western Persian Empire began with his crossing of the Hellespont into Asia Minor and concluded with the occupation of Ecbatana, the capital of Media. The area contained virtually all the large cities of the empire, all four of its capitals (Babylon, Ecbatana, Persepolis, and Susa), and most of its wealth. It was also the commercial focus of all the major trade routes from the south, east, and west, where goods were exchanged for transshipment. When Alexander reached Ecbatana, Darius had only days to live. Upon his murder, Alexander became the Great King's heir by right of conquest.

Militarily, the shores of Asia Minor and Phoenicia sustained the mighty Persian fleet, the largest in antiquity, consisting of just over 1,200 triremes during Xerxes' invasion of Greece. Although the Persians appeared to have been only able to mobilize about 400 triremes against Alexander, this was still over twice the size of any fleet that the Macedonian king was able to field against them. The fighting efficiency of the Persian fleet, crewed largely by highly skilled Phoenician crews, was far superior to Alexander's, which was largely comprised of non-seafaring personnel, a fact he readily acknowledged by his demobilization of the fleet in Asia Minor. It was only when Alexander was able to raise a fleet in Phoenicia that he was able to achieve naval supremacy in the western Mediterranean.

The Persian empire had no effective heavy infantry and was therefore forced to recruit Greek mercenaries in an attempt to offset the Macedonian phalanx. The western Persian empire had ready access to Greek mercenaries because of its naval domination of the eastern Mediterranean and the availability of huge gold and silver reserves with which to pay them. When Alexander, however, occupied Asia Minor and the Phoenician coast, the Persians were cut off from Greece and the ability to recruit any additional mercenaries. This meant that they were unable to oppose the Macedonian phalanx on open ground.

The main native arm of the Persian army, its heavy cavalry, was largely recruited in Asia Minor and in the central and eastern Persian empire. The performance of the arm on the battlefield was dismal, to say the least, and it really never achieved anything of consequence, being notable only for its large numbers. After Alexander's third defeat of the Persian army at Gaugamela, the Persian heavy cavalry was not used in a field battle again. The cavalry actions were henceforth confined to raids and ambushes by light cavalry.

Asia Minor

Asia Minor was for Alexander only a land passage between Europe and Asia.[1] It held relatively little strategic importance for him, and he neither completely conquered it nor attempted any large-scale Greek settlement there. No continuous road ran along the coast of Asia Minor; to travel eastward across the country one had to move inland through Ancyra, cross the Taurus Mountains through the Cilician Gates, and then proceed along the Cilician coast. The upland area, known as the Anatolian or Cappadocian Plateau, was a treeless plain. It was fertile for cereal crops and fodder and could easily meet the supply requirements of any large force moving through it.[2] Its wide plain also made it ideal cavalry country.

In the spring of 336 B.C., an army of 10,000 Macedonians and Greek mercenaries under command of Parmenio was ferried over the Hellespont to Abydos. Philip's orders to the force were to liberate the Greek states along the Persian shore and take possession of the northern grain-growing areas of Asia Minor. As the Persian Empire had been in turmoil for about two years after the murder of the Persian king, Artaxerxes Ochus, in 338 B.C., the force Philip sent to Asia Minor was able to expand the area under its control as far south as Ephesus without encountering any serious resistance. Thereafter, however, Memnon of Rhodes was able to conduct a successful campaign against them, steadily driving Parmenio back to the north and then to the west. By the time of Alexander's crossing, the territory controlled by the Macedonian advance force appears to have been confined to the Troad. While this did not provide Alexander with jump-off positions for his campaign, it at least ensured him a secure bridgehead for his crossing into Asia.

Sestos

In the spring of 334 B.C., Alexander set out from Pella with his army and marched to the Hellespont. The force under his command consisted of 5,100 cavalry, 32,000 infantry, and 7,500 servants, for a total of about 45,000.[3] The cavalry was comprised of 1,800 Companions, 1,800 Thessalians, 600 Allied Greeks, and 900 Thracians/Paeonian Lancers.[4] The infantry included 9,000 Macedonian phalanx troops, 3,000 Macedonian hypaspists, 500 Macedonian archers, 500 Agrianians, 7,000 Greek allies, 5,000 Greek mercenaries, and 7,000 Balkan troops (3,000 Thracians, 3,000 Illyrians, and 1,000 Triballians).[5] A total of 5,100 servants accompanied the cavalry (one for every trooper) and 2,400 accompanied the infantry (one for every 10 Macedonian phalangites, hypaspists, Greek allied/mercenary hoplites). The advance Greek force of 10,000 mercenaries under Parmenio was probably detached for garrison duty along Alexander's route of march through Asia Minor.

It took Alexander 20 days to cover the 300 miles to Sestos.[6] He crossed the Dardanelles at the Narrows, the same place Xerxes had crossed when he invaded Greece.[7] Since the advance force Philip had sent out under Parmenio securely held the Asian bank at the crossing site opposite Abydos, Alexander was able to ferry

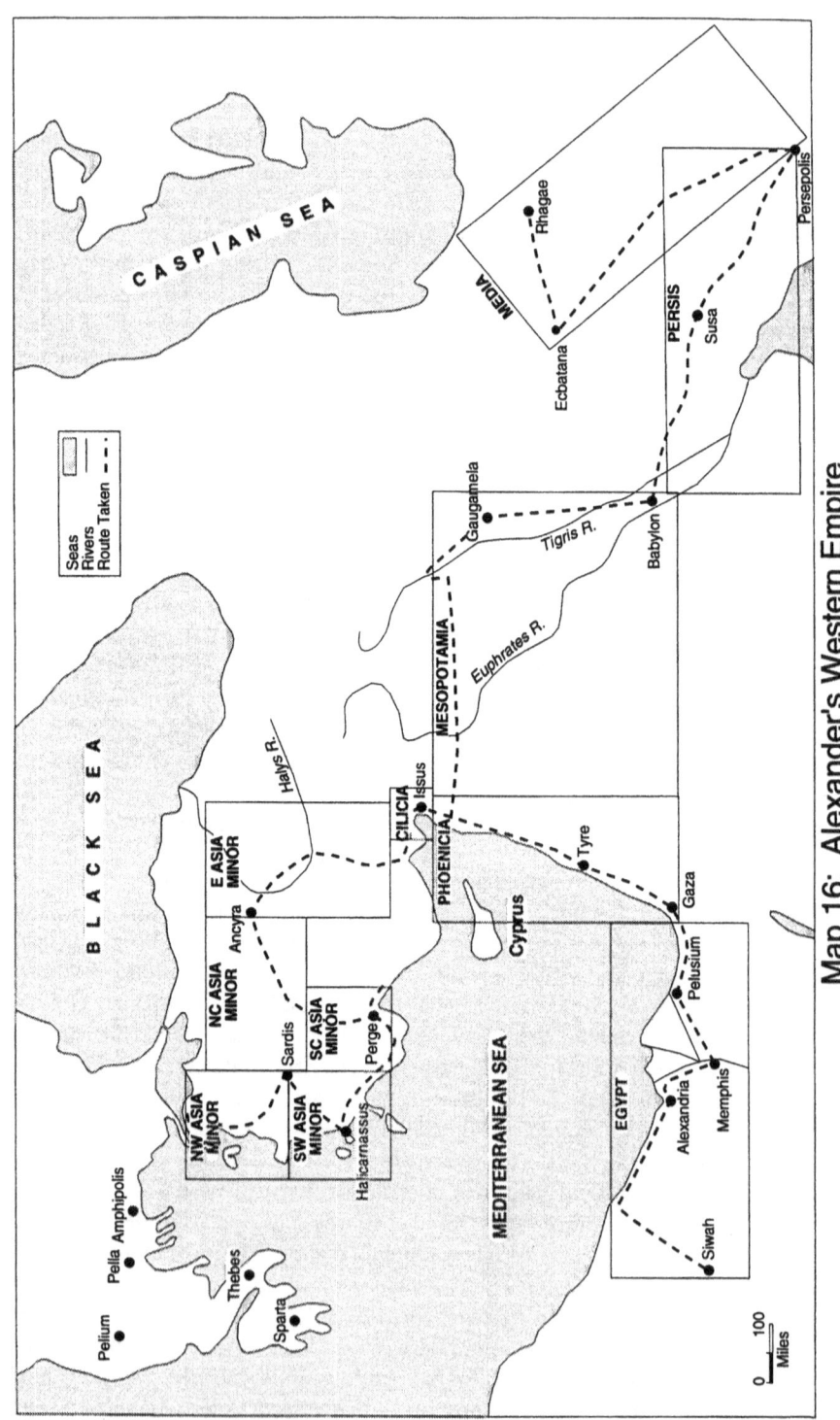

Map 16: Alexander's Western Empire

his army over on the 160 triremes of his navy without any Persian interference.[8] Had the Persian fleet been able to obstruct the crossing, the results might have been disastrous, isolating a major portion of the Macedonian army in Asia. The Persian fleet was double the size of Alexander's and ship for ship was much more combat effective than his relatively green and heterogeneous force. The Phoenician and Cyprian contingents were unavailable for duty with the Persian fleet, however, quite likely being in refit after their service in Darius' Egyptian campaign.[9] It would take them several months to mobilize.

Troy

Leaving Parmenio in command of his army's crossing of the Hellespont, Alexander detached a force of 60 smaller ships and 6,000 men for a visit to the legendary city of Troy.[10] He was the first of his party to step ashore, throwing a spear into the ground and proclaiming that Asia would be won by the spear and granted by the gods. Alexander was crowned with a golden wreath by Menoetius, his navigator, and Chares, an Athenian general.[11] Then he and Hephaestion paced garlands on the tombs of Achilles and Patroclus.[12] Alexander dedicated his armor to Athena, goddess of Troy, exchanging it for a sacred shield in the shrine believed to have been from the Trojan war. Eight years later in India this shield would save his life. When Alexander was asked by the townspeople if he was interested in seeing the lyre of the Trojan prince Paris, the son of Priam, king of Troy, he replied that he had no interest in seeing an instrument used to seduce women but did express a desire in seeing the lyre of Achilles, which was used to glorify brave deeds. From Troy, Alexander rejoined his army at Abydos. The next day he marched northeast to Percote, bypassed Lampsacus, and made camp by the Practius River.[13] At Hermotus, Alexander sent out scouts ahead of his army led by Amyntas (son of Arrabaeus).

Battle of Granicus River

When Alexander crossed the Hellespont into Asia, his weakness in logistics largely determined the initial strategy there. Having one month's supply of provisions and only 60 talents in his treasury (enough to pay his army for two weeks), Alexander desperately needed to win an early field battle against the Persian army.[14] Any lengthy delay might result in his army being forced to disperse to forage for provisions and plunder. This eventuality, together with the sullen and unstable temper of the large contingent of allied Greek, Balkans, and mercenary troops might well precipitate the dissolution of his army and a disastrous end to his Asian campaign. Alexander, however, was fortunate in that the Persians, for reasons of their own, were willing to accommodate him for an immediate battle.

Darius was largely contemptuous of the young Alexander. He thought him an envious and greedy boy who was oblivious to the danger awaiting him when he invaded the Persian Empire. Macedonia was considered unable to field an army large enough to campaign in the vast expanses of the east. The Great King mistakenly thought that his satraps in Asia Minor, with the assistance of a portion of

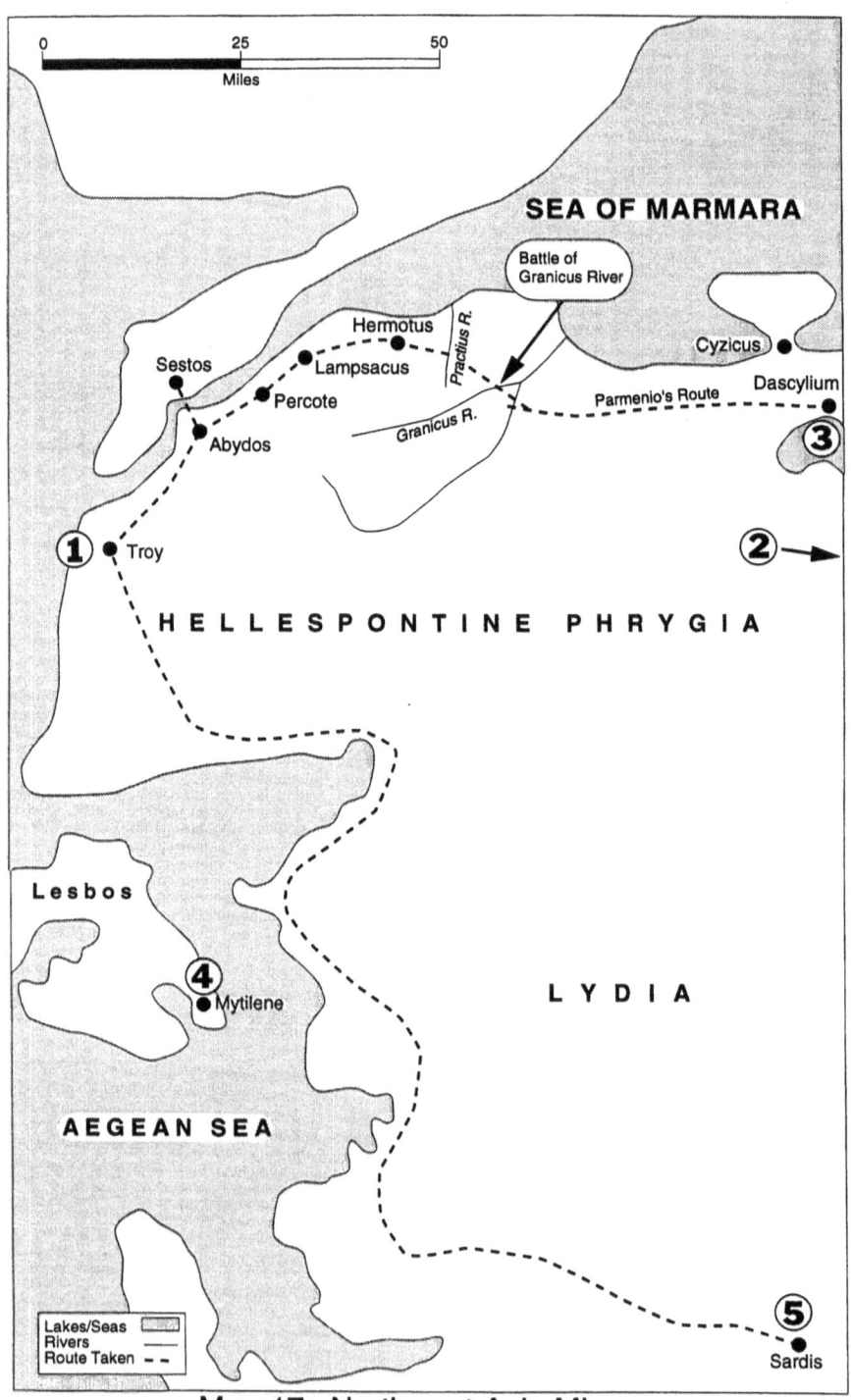

Map 17: Northwest Asia Minor

7: THE WESTERN PERSIAN EMPIRE

Memnon's Greek mercenaries, would be able to deal easily with any attempted Macedonian invasion. He left it to their judgment to determine just where and when to fight Alexander. Darius' only noteworthy instructions to his satraps in Asia Minor were related to the disposition of Alexander and his invading army after their expected defeat. Alexander was to be dressed in a purple robe and brought before the Great King in chains. The Greek ships and their crews were to be sunk at sea, while Alexander's soldiers were to be transported to the furthest shore of the Red Sea.[15]

When Alexander crossed over into Asia, he invaded Arsites' satrapy of Hellespontine Phrygia. In response to Arsites' request for assistance, Arsames, satrap of CIlicia; Spithridates, satrap of Lydia and Ionia; his brother, Rheomithres; and Mithridates, governor of Cappadocia, marched to join him with the troops at their disposal. The Asia Minor satraps were also joined by Memnon of Rhodes, commander of the Greek mercenaries; Arbupales, Darius' son-in-law; and Pharnaces, a brother of Darius' wife. The Persian forces established a base camp at Zeleia, just east of the Granicus River. They then convened a meeting to discuss the joint strategy to be pursued against Alexander.[16] Memnon began by recommending that the Persians not engage Alexander in battle. Instead, he urged that they should immediately retreat and attempt to deny the Macedonians any provisions or plunder by burning all crops and fodder and evacuating all moveable property in his line of march. Memnon pointed out that it was widely known that Alexander had little money and few provisions and was counting heavily on obtaining both in Asia Minor. Memnon believed that if Alexander were forced into a prolonged campaign and was unable to either pay or supply his army, he would soon have no choice but to withdraw back along the way he had advanced or see his army disbanded to pillage for both food and money.

In an attempt to mitigate the distaste of such a purely defensive strategy for the Persians, Memnon suggested that they could assemble their fleet and take the war directly to Macedonia. As Alexander had obviously taken his best troops with him to Asia, the Persians were only likely to find an inferior army stationed in Macedonia, largely made up of young boys, partially trained troops, and old men. Also, considering the simmering hatred in Greece against Alexander, the Persians would likely obtain considerable support from a large number of dissatisfied Greek cities in any campaign they conducted there. On the other hand, Memnon warned the Persians that if they should attempt to engage Alexander's army in a field battle, they would almost certainly be defeated. The battle, as Memnon saw it, would revolve around a typical Greek heavy infantry fight. In such a situation, the inferior Persian levy infantry, being low in morale, largely untrained, and poorly armed would be unable hold their own against the highly disciplined and combat-effective Macedonian phalanx. His conclusion was largely based on the defeats the Persians

1. Alexander visits the tombs of Achilles and Patroclus in Troy. 2. The Persian satraps meet in this area prior to the battle at Granicus River. 3. The capital of Phrygia. 4. Memnon of Rhodes dies in Mytilene. 5. The capital of Lydia.

had sustained at the hands of the Greeks in the heavy infantry battles of Onomarchus (352 B.C.) and Marathon (338 B.C.). Memnon was not able to foresee at the time, however, that Alexander's arm of decision in the upcoming battles in Asia would not be the heavy infantry but the Companion cavalry. In retrospect, it would make little difference, as either the Companions or the phalanx were able to defeat the Persians with equal ease.

Instead of giving Memnon's advice serious consideration, Arsites replied emotionally, refusing to condone the deliberate destruction of even a single house in his satrapy. In this, he was fully supported by his neighboring satraps. The Persians were clearly insulted by Memnon's remarks questioning the martial abilities of their army. They also distrusted the motives behind his advice. In their eyes, being merely a mercenary for hire, it was to Memnon's advantage to prolong any conflict as long as possible not only for the personal financial gain to himself and his men but for the continued retention of the high office Darius had conferred on him. It had also not escaped their attention that Alexander had left Memnon's estate near Abydos untouched. This obviously left the Persians with the suspicion of some sort of collusion between Alexander and Memnon, and they believed that Memnon's advice was designed in some way to assist Alexander. The Persian leaders therefore decided to give battle to Alexander as soon as possible in order to bring his invasion to a quick end.

If, as Memnon had so forcefully indicated, Alexander desperately needed an early victory, the Persians were convinced that he would seek them out and attack without delay. This meant that they would not only be able to choose their battlefield but also benefit from the advantages of standing on the defensive. The main question then became where should they make their stand. If they attempted to block Alexander from marching south along the coast, they would have potentially hostile Carian and Ionian Greek cities across their line of communications and the threat of a Macedonian seaborne landing behind them. The Persians therefore decided to choose a position inland, preferably one with an obstacle across their front that would disorder Alexander's phalanx, which they considered the most effective arm of the Macedonian army. The Granicus River to them seemed best suited to these requirements. Not only would the river and its steep banks protect their front, but both flanks would be securely anchored by natural obstacles: a swamp to the north and rough ground to the south.[17] The choice was made solely by tactical considerations of terrain and was probably the best advanced position the Persians could have chosen for an infantry defense. As the Persians had a large cavalry force and only a small effective infantry contingent, however, the strength of their position was greatly compromised by their inability to man it with the proper force.

Alexander received reports that the Persians were concentrating a large force of cavalry and Greek mercenaries near Zeleia. He immediately marched off with his frontline troops to engage them,. He left behind the Greek allied units because he doubted their loyalty, the Greek mercenaries because he suspected they might be reluctant to fight against their fellow mercenaries in Persian employ, and the

Balkan infantry, except the Agrianians, because of their lack of discipline. The third day after landing in Asia Minor, Alexander reached the plain of Adrasteia. It was within sight of the Granicus River and just west of it.

In his advance to the Granicus, Alexander deployed his army as if he expected an attack by a superior Persian cavalry force at any moment. His lancer cavalry and 500 light infantry, led by Hegelochus, screened his advancing phalanx which was deployed in a depth of 16 ranks.[18] A gap was left between the eighth and ninth ranks to allow the rear ranks to reverse direction and face an expected Persian cavalry envelopment from behind. The Macedonian army was closing on the Granicus when returning scouts reported the Persian deployment on the east bank of the river. It was past noon sometime in late May or early June. The first great battle for possession of the Persian Empire was about to commence.

The Persians assumed a strong defensive position behind the Granicus River that securely anchored both their flanks and protected their front by its steep and muddy riverbanks.[19] Although the river was fast-flowing with the spring runoff, it was confined to a relatively narrow channel only three feet deep and 130 feet wide and was easily fordable in several places.[20] On the Persian side of the river, the level ground along the riverbank abruptly rose up in muddy nine- to 13-feet bluffs, thus ensuring that any close-order force would be disordered in attempting to climb them.[21] From the top of the bluffs, an open rolling plain continued for about a mile and then terminated in a low ridge.

As the Macedonian army closed up on the Granicus River, Parmenio attempted to convince Alexander to encamp and delay his attack until the following morning. He pointed out that the Persians occupied a strong position and were obviously hoping to be attacked at a disadvantage. The Macedonians would have to ford the Granicus River in a narrow column that would inevitably become disordered when the soldiers began climbing the steep and muddy eastern bank. Emerging out onto the plain in small and isolated groups, their infantry would then be vulnerable to being ridden down by the large numbers of Persian cavalry. Besides, it was already late in the afternoon and even if Alexander did manage to win the battle, darkness would facilitate a Persian retreat and largely preclude any decisive result. Parmenio believed that the Persians, if left alone, would undoubtedly withdraw a safe distance from the river line during the night, as was their usual practice.[22] The Macedonians, Parmenio pointed out, could then cross the Granicus under the cover of darkness and be fully deployed at dawn, ready to meet the advancing Persians when they attempted to reoccupy the river line. Parmenio's advice was obviously sound from a tactical point of view but less so from what Alexander perceived the strategic situation to be. If the Persians had seen his army deployed on their side of the river, they might simply have decided to withdraw from the battlefield, which their superiority in cavalry would have allowed them to do easily without interference. In that case, Alexander would have had to contend with a strategic disaster of an indefinitely delayed field battle. Considering the Persian temperament, however, the probability of them withdrawing was remote because their code of conduct mandated that a battle be fought when within the vicinity of the enemy. The Persians considered any withdrawal under such circumstances to be an unacceptable disgrace.

Alexander needed an immediate victory against the Persian field army for three strategic reasons: it would probably convince many cities along his line of march in Asia Minor to surrender to him on terms rather than force him to conduct costly and lengthy sieges against them, it would prevent the Persian army from withdrawing intact and forcing Alexander to deploy for battle at virtually every bottleneck throughout the mountainous terrain of Asia Minor that the Persians chose to obstruct, and it would preclude the rapid reinforcement of an already existing Persian army in the field.[23] Time was on the Persian side, and Alexander knew it. With both money and provisions running lower every day, Alexander needed an immediate battle to ease both his logistical and political problems. He also obviously felt, more from inexperienced nervousness than a realistic analysis of the situation, that he could not chance the possibility of a Persian withdrawal from the Granicus River. In this regard, Alexander was largely reacting nervously to imagined fears. Seeking to cover the embarrassment that he probably felt over this, Alexander almost insultingly replied to Parmenio that having crossed the wide Hellespont so easily he would be ashamed to be held up by the insignificant Granicus River. Therefore, despite the lateness of the hour, orders were issued for an immediate attack.

The main striking arm of any Persian army was its heavy cavalry, which in this battle numbered about 20,000.[24] Of the 20,000 elite Greek mercenaries in Darius' employ, only about 5,000 were made available for deployment under Omares in support of the satrapal army in Asia Minor. The remainder continued to serve aboard the Persian fleet as marines. A force of 15,000 Persian levy-infantry had also been raised by the satraps in Asia Minor and brought to the battlefield. These troops were of little military value, however, being largely undisciplined, of low morale, and poorly trained and armed. In total then, the effective Persian army at the battle of Granicus River numbered about 25,000. Since the Greek mercenaries were deliberately deployed almost a mile back from the river, however, the Persians' frontline strength was limited to their heavy cavalry.

Although Alexander's total infantry strength stood at 32,000, which was over six times the effective strength of the Greek mercenaries in Persian employ, the frontline infantry he deployed at the Granicus was only about 13,000. The remaining infantry were either Greek allies, Balkan troops, or Greek mercenaries. Alexander was not inclined to use these troops in his battle line because of their uneven effectiveness and his fear that they might either refuse to fight against their fellow countrymen or desert outright to the Persians.[25] Even so, Alexander's Greek forces still outnumbered the Greek mercenaries in Persian employ by almost three to one. The arm of decision in this and the next two great field battles, however, was to be not the infantry but the heavy cavalry. Here Alexander's 3,600 heavy cavalry was only about one-fifth the strength of that of his Persian counterpart. Standard military doctrine indicates that, all other things being equal, odds of three to one or greater are usually required for a decisive military result. Alexander was

7: THE WESTERN PERSIAN EMPIRE

to prove conclusively in this battle and every other one that he fought in Asia, however, that disparity in numbers had little meaning when one of the great armies of history faced an opponent of such uneven military effectiveness as the Persians.

The Persian frontline along the bluffs behind the Granicus River consisted solely of their 20,000 cavalry. The Cilician cavalry of Arsames, satrap of Cilicia, and the Greek mercenary cavalry of Memnon of Rhodes occupied the Persian left. In the center Arsites, the satrap of Hellespontine Phrygia, was stationed next to the left wing with the Paphlagonian cavalry. Alongside him, on the right, the Hyrcanian cavalry was deployed under the command of Spithridates, the satrap of Lydia and Ionia, who was accompanied by his brother Rhosaces. Somewhere in the center, possibly to the right of Spithridates, were deployed Arbupales, Niphates, and Petines with their troops.[26] On the right wing, Rheomithres commanded 6,000 cavalry, which included 2,000 Bactrians and 2,000 Medes.[27] The Persian levies were stationed well behind the cavalry, while the Greek mercenaries occupied a ridge about a mile in the rear of the Persian front line.[28]

The Persian tactical battlefield deployment has generated much controversy throughout history. Militarily, it seemed to make little, if any, sense. The effectiveness of cavalry is greatest in the delivery of a charge over distance, that of infantry, in holding a fixed position. The Persians, however, reversed the roles of these two arms in this battle. Instead of having the Greek mercenaries hold the bluffs, which dominated the crossings of the Granicus, the Persians designated their cavalry to do it and placed the mercenaries, in effect, off the battlefield. One might well question the military rationale for such an incredible deployment. The explanation was that it was based more on emotion than military logic.

When Memnon belittled the fighting capabilities of the Persian army at the military conference at Zeleia just before the battle, he had humiliated the pride of the Persian aristocracy, which constituted the cavalry arm. Based on their easy victories over the relatively ineffective mobs they usually fought against in their own empire, the Persians had rather naively imagined themselves to be great warriors, much superior to the Greeks. One would have thought that their conspicuous failures in the invasion of Greece under both Darius I and Xerxes, and the March of the Greek Ten Thousand through the western portion of their empire would have humbled their arrogance, but they apparently chose to close their eyes to the reality of the situation and embrace their more agreeable fantasies. In order to demonstrate this supposed superiority, especially to Memnon, the Persian leaders undoubtedly insisted on their cavalry taking its place in the front line to enable them alone to engage the Macedonians. The honor of single-handedly defeating Alexander would then fall solely to the Persian cavalry, the Greek mercenaries merely looking on as admiring spectators. It is probably more for this ridiculous reason than for any other that the cavalry formed the front line of the Persian deployment.

The Macedonian army was divided into two wings, a left under Parmenio and a right, nominally at least, under Philotas (son of Parmenio).[29] The role of the left

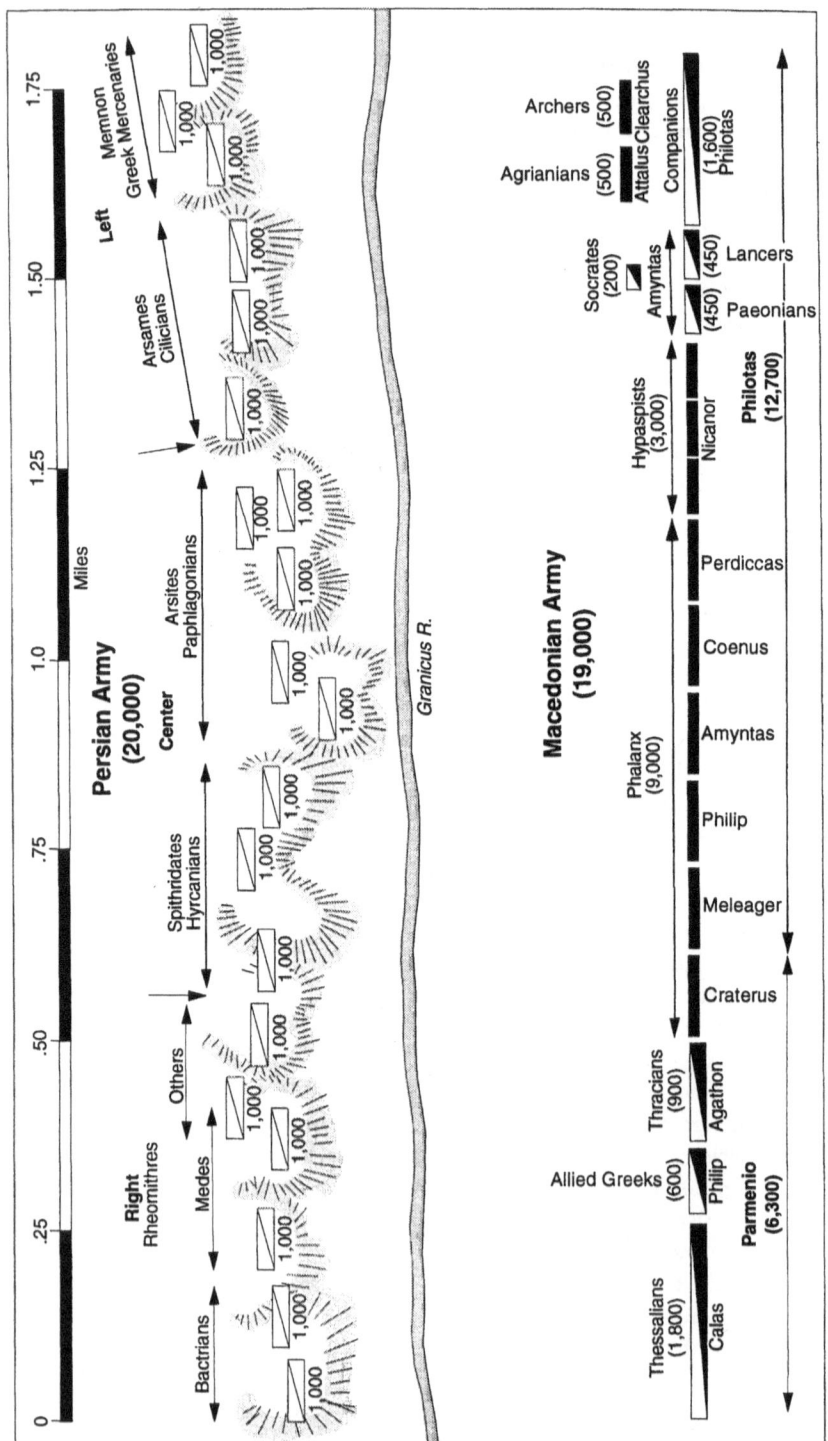

Map 18: Granicus River

7: THE WESTERN PERSIAN EMPIRE

wing was defensive, in that it was to hold the line of the Granicus River against any attempt by the Persian cavalry to force it. Parmenio had under his command the Thessalian, allied Greek, and Thracian cavalry and two taxies of the phalanx, under Craterus and Meleager, for a total of 3,300 cavalry and 3,000 infantry. Philotas had under his immediate command all the elite units of the army—the hypaspists, Companion cavalry, and Agrianians. In addition, his wing included the Paeonian and Lancer cavalry, four taxies of the phalanx—under Perdiccas, Coenus, Amyntas, and Philip—and the archers. The right wing totaled 2,700 cavalry and 10,000 infantry.

Alexander deployed about 19,000 troops across the Persian front. Although he did not outnumber the Persians, he had at his disposal a well-balanced, combined-arms force of heavy and light cavalry and heavy and light infantry. This would give him great flexibility in conducting the battle, as he could respond more effectively to a wide variety of situations. On the other hand, the Persians, having only cavalry deployed in their front line, were much more limited in their tactical options. Not only were cavalry troops at this time unable to engage close-order heavy infantry, but they were quickly thrown into disorder if attacked in a stationary position.

The anchored flanks of the Persian line appeared to work more to the Macedonians' advantage than to theirs. In all Alexander's battles, he never once sought to encircle a Persian flank. His cavalry attacks were always delivered along the Persian front line. Although the large cavalry component of the Persian army lent itself to encircling tactics, for some strange reason in this battle as well as the next, the Persians selected battlefields that largely denied them the use of this option. By anchoring their flanks, the Persian limited their tactic to a straight-up, frontal fight. As their troops were generally far less effective than their Macedonian counterparts, a fight with equal frontage would always place them at a decided disadvantage. In this case, however, their disadvantage would be somewhat offset by the fact that Alexander's attacking force would be disordered by having to cross the Granicus River and climb its steep and muddy banks.

Macedonian Right Flank Amyntas and his three cavalry units moved forward from Alexander's wing on an oblique right angle against Memnon's cavalry on the Persian far left flank. Socrates' squadron of the Companions led the advance. No sooner had Amyntas advanced into the river than he received a heavy volume of javelin missile fire from the Persian cavalry at the top of the bluffs. As Amyntas attempted to leave the river, Memnon's cavalry came down from the heights and engaged him. Although Amyntas subsequently took heavy casualties, his line did not break, but he was not able to make any headway against the bluffs. After an unequal struggle on the insecure footing of the riverbed, Amyntas was slowly forced back. Alexander then advanced his Companion cavalry through Amyntas' withdrawing force and broke Memnon's cavalry, which had been disordered by its fight with Amyntas. Alexander was then engaged by Arsames' fresh cavalry that came down from the bluffs. After a hard fight, the greater combat effectiveness, superior weaponry, and higher morale of the Companions also defeated Arsames'

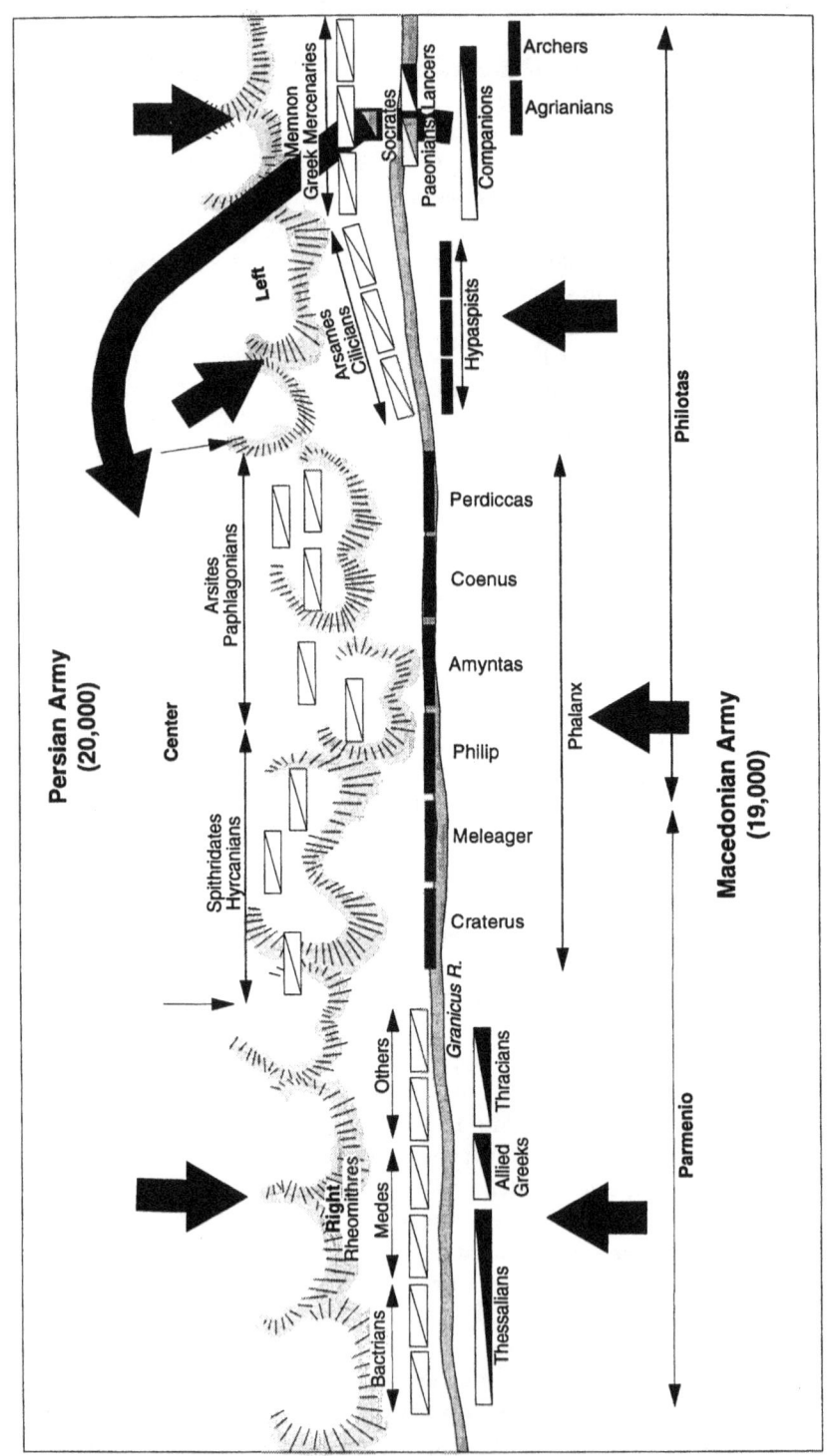

force. The Companions were able to gain the top of the bluffs, but in noticeable disorder.

Observing this Companion advance, Mithridates, Darius' son-in-law, put himself at the head of a large cavalry force, which included 40 high-ranking Persian nobles, formed them into a wedge, and charged the Companions.[30] Alexander, having broken his spear in the fight climbing up the bluffs, called on Aretes, one of his aides, for another. Unfortunately, he too had broken his in the same action. Demaratus the Corinthian, a bodyguard, gave Alexander his spear. The Macedonian king put himself at the head of the Companions and led them into a counterattack against the oncoming Mithridates. Although the Persian threw his javelin at Alexander with enough force to penetrate his shield and cuirass, it wounded him only slightly. Alexander, however, was able to thrust his spear into Mithridates' face, instantly killing him. Rhoesaces then rode up and cracked Alexander's helmet with his sword, temporarily stunning him with the force of the blow. Alexander quickly recovered and was able to kill him with a spear thrust that penetrated his cuirass. Spithridates, Rhoesaces' brother, now came up behind Alexander and was about to strike him a fatal blow when "Cleitus the Black" severed his right arm at the shoulder.

The Agrianians and archers soon came up on the right of the Companions, spreading confusion in the ranks of the stationary Persian cavalry.[31] Disordered and fighting at a disadvantage against the longer spears of the Macedonians, the Persian left flank cavalry finally broke. Moving up behind the Companion cavalry, the hypaspists were able to climb the bluffs without interference. Deploying into formation on the level ground at the top of the bluffs, they soon went into action against the Persian cavalry in the center, which was already being steadily pushed back by the phalanx. The entire Persian line now broke under the additional pressure.

Macedonian Center The phalanx advanced across the Granicus River and began climbing the bluffs. The steep and muddy banks quickly disordered its formation and delayed its attack until just before Alexander had broken the Persian left flank. When the phalanx finally closed with the Persian center, Alexander's Companions were collapsing the left flank of the Persian center; the Persian line wavered and broke from the pressure and then routed off the battlefield.

Macedonian Left Flank On the Persian right, Rheomithres had crossed the Granicus and engaged the cavalry holding Parmenio's left flank. The heavily weighted-down Persian cavalry must have been considerably disordered, both by the ride down the steep muddy embankment and by their crossing of the Granicus.[32] When they emerged out into the open, they were doubtless hit hard by a charge from the Thessalians. In the subsequent hand-to-hand combat, Rheomithres' force was steadily forced back across the Granicus and up the bluffs. Now in noticeable disorder, the Persian right flank, upon hearing of the defeat on the left, fled as Parmenio's cavalry gained the bluffs.

Greek Mercenaries in Persian Employ When the Persian line collapsed, Alexander declined to pursue the retreating Persian cavalry on the flanks, instead ordering his cavalry to surround the Greek mercenaries on the ridge in the rear of the battlefield. When the mercenaries saw the Persian cavalry ride off, they held their position rather than attempt a retreat, believing no doubt that they would be unable to withdraw successfully without support in the face of Alexander's approaching cavalry. Anyway, they had high hopes of being able to negotiate with the Macedonian king for their services. Unfortunately for them, however, Alexander was so enraged at their presence on the battlefield in the support of the Persians that he refused to extend any terms to them. Instead, he led the phalanx against the Greek mercenaries frontally while his cavalry enveloped both their flanks. The result was a massacre, the shorter spears of the mercenaries being relatively ineffective against the sarissas of the Macedonian phalanx and Companions. After sustaining almost 3,000 casualties, the remaining 2,000 Greek mercenaries unconditionally surrendered.[33] They were put in chains and taken back to Macedonia to hard labor.[34] Alexander had sustained his heaviest casualties of the battle in the fight against them.

Losses The Macedonian dead were said to have numbered only 25 Companions, 60 other cavalry, and 30 infantry.[35] Persian cavalry losses were 1,000, about 5 percent of the number engaged.[36] Of the Greek mercenaries, 60 percent were killed and the remaining 2,000 taken prisoner.[37] The soldiers of the Persian levy infantry, caught unsupported out in the open, were virtually defenseless and appear to have suffered upward of 50 percent casualties, or fully 7,500 in killed or wounded.[38] Heavy losses were also sustained by the senior Persian leaders. A total of eight are known to have died on the battlefield: the cavalry commanders, Niphates, Petines, and Rhoesaces; Spithridates, satrap of Lydia and Ionia; Mithobuzanes, satrap of Cappadocia; Mithridates, Darius' son-in-law; Arbupales, eldest son of Artaxerxes II; and Pharnaces, brother of one of Darius' earlier wives. Arsites, satrap of Hellespontine-Phrygia, survived the battle only a short time. Holding himself to blame for the defeat, he subsequently committed suicide.[39]

Results Although much of the remaining Persian cavalry escaped when Alexander diverted his army to eliminating the Greek mercenaries, the death of many of the high-level Persian leaders and the loss of their only effective infantry, the Greek mercenaries, meant they were unable to field an army that could prevent Alexander from overrunning Asia Minor. The only bright spot in the Persian failure was that much of the surviving cavalry was able to escape and would again see service with Darius in the next battle.

Generalship Although the Persians did do a few things right, they did most things wrong and paid the price for it. The satraps were civilian amateurs who obviously had little, if any, experience at conducting military operations against an opponent as formidable as Alexander. They greatly overrated their own military effectiveness and seriously underrated that of the Macedonians. There was no evidence of any coherent tactical battle plan. The Persian satraps had selected a highly defensible position, but their most effective defensive force for manning it, the Greek mercenaries, were virtually deployed off the battlefield. Although the Persian battle plan was clearly defensive in nature, their right flank crossed the

Granicus and actually assumed the offensive against Parmenio. The Persian left flank went half that far by leaving its position on the bluffs and fighting alongside the river. Most of the supposed advantages of position were rather quickly forsaken, it seems, at the whim of the local commanders. There appears to have been no command control exercised on the battlefield by any central Persian high command. Instead, the Persians gave way to impulse, false bravado, and civilian politics and, as a result, were heavily defeated.

The Persians erred in fighting Alexander at all because they had much more to lose than he by a precipitous battle. If Alexander were defeated, he could always withdraw back across the Hellespont under cover of his navy. Although he might suffer some political repercussions for the withdrawal, his military force would remain intact. If the Persians were defeated, however, they were likely to lose all of Asia Minor. It took a long time to raise Persian armies, and if the one that the satraps had in Asia Minor was lost, it could take a year or more to mobilize another. The Persians would have been much better off using their army merely as a powerful presence. A scorched-earth policy might well have crippled Alexander at a time when he had very little logistical staying power because he lacked both money and provisions.[40] Without an early victory in a major field battle, many cities which willingly surrendered to Alexander might have been inclined to resist him, sustained by the knowledge that a Persian army was nearby in the field. To take virtually every city by siege or storm would have been a time-consuming operation, imposing in all likelihood a severe strain on Alexander's logistics and undoubtedly resulting in an unacceptably high level of casualties. Postponement of the battle would have also allowed the Persians an intact field army that could dispute every pass and bottleneck across the rugged and highly defendable terrain of Asia Minor. Any shaky start for Alexander's Asian campaign might well have produced widespread revolts in central and southern Greece that the Persians could have both supported and extended. The Persians' strategic decision to fight Alexander as soon as possible was clearly a bad one and was more a matter of politics and emotion than military logic. Part of the decision arose from the typical political inclination to be overly sensitive to civilian dislocation and a reluctance to face the unpleasant impact of harsh military decisions. Then too, there was the injured pride of the Persian aristocracy that mandated they stand and fight rather than endure the supposed disgrace of a withdrawal. Memnon's insulting analysis of their inferior military capabilities had apparently hit all too close to home. The Persians were eager to erase this slur, even if it meant jeopardizing their empire.

The Persian battlefield deployment appeared to violate all military logic and has continued to confuse and mystify both historians and military analysts The placement of their cavalry in a static role defending the fords of the Granicus River was a terrible misuse of the arm. The greatest effectiveness of ancient cavalry, as Alexander was so convincingly to demonstrate, was one of shock impact or momentum collision. This takes both running room and level ground for the cavalry to work up the necessary charge speed. When fighting from a stationary position, cavalry was far less effective against enemy cavalry and was highly susceptible to being thrown into disorder by any infantry. To make matters even worse, the Persians on the left flank appear to have completely lost their heads in the heat of battle and rode down to the bluffs to engage Amyntas at the river line. True, the Macedonians experienced a certain amount of disorganization crossing the river under the subsequent heavy Persian missile fire, but by their precipitous action the Persians gave the Macedonians a present of one less obstacle to cross, while assuming that burden and the resulting disorganization themselves. Tactically, they also placed themselves in an extremely dangerous position. If the Macedonians were defeated, they could easily make their escape back across the shallow river and reform behind the shelter of their phalanx, which the Persian cavalry would be unable to close with. A Persian defeat along the river line, however, would probably be disastrous because they would have to conduct a fighting withdrawal up nine- to thirteen-feet muddy bluffs while closely engaged by an aggressive enemy. If, on the other hand, the battle had been fought at the top of the bluff and the Persians had been defeated, they could simply have maneuvered back across the plain and reformed behind the Greek mercenaries on the ridge, a mile to the rear. In the event of a Macedonian defeat at the top of the bluffs, however, the precipitous slope at their back would make any withdrawal very costly in casualties. As a result, the attack by the Persian left wing threw away many of the Persians' military advantages of position for the chance to prove their mettle in battle.

The Persian attack on the Macedonian left flank was another significant error in judgment. Instead of occupying a constricted front behind two obstacles, the Granicus River and the bluffs, in the hope of engaging a Macedonian force whose ranks would be disorganized by his force, Rheomithres chose to cross those obstacles to engage Parmenio's cavalry. An outright defeat suffered by the Persians might well have resulted in their annihilation because their retreat over the same obstacles they had crossed unmolested could be fatally dangerous when they were engaged by a mobile enemy in close pursuit. On the other hand, any Persian success would be difficult, if not impossible, to exploit because reinforcements would be impeded by having to cross those obstacles themselves. Also, the Macedonian phalanx could stop the Persian cavalry attack dead in its tracks by merely forming a front against it.[41]

The Persians were probably incapable of military defeating the Macedonian army at the Granicus under any circumstances with the forces under their disposal and the position that they had taken, but they just might have been able to force a draw on the Macedonians.[42] The Persians' best move would have been to occupy the bluffs with infantry and hold their cavalry in reserve on the plain to seal off any breakthrough by immediate charges. Unfortunately, they did not have enough frontline infantry for this option. The 5,000 Greek mercenaries could have occupied less than 2,000 feet, or less than one-fourth the frontage across the bluffs. The remainder of their line would have had to have been filled in by either the worthless Persian levies or the heavy cavalry. The inclusion of the mercenaries in the front line, however, would clearly have considerably strengthened whatever position they were stationed in. Had they been deployed on the Persian left, they

7: THE WESTERN PERSIAN EMPIRE

might well have stopped Alexander's attack dead in its tracks. If Alexander had experienced a major reversal, it is likely that the amount of daylight would have been insufficient to him to reorganize his troops for another attack that day. Had the Persians then slipped off during the night, Alexander would have been faced with an initial defeat, an intact Persian army in Asia Minor, and an indefinitely postponed battle, the very things he feared the most.

Another option would have been to deploy the Persian cavalry on the plain to hit the Macedonians with a shock charge as they began deploying onto the bluffs. The Macedonians would have been disordered and available only in small numbers at first. A well-timed charge, which was well within the capacity and temperament of the Persian commanders, would have probably pinned the Macedonians against the edge of the bluffs and greatly restricted their ability to expand their frontage. In the best-case situation, the impetus of the cavalry attack might have forced the Macedonians back into their own troops struggling up the muddy slopes, causing mass confusion in their ranks. This would have produced heavy casualties and undoubtedly would have forced Alexander to call off the attack and withdraw back over the river.

Another interesting scenario would have been the release of the entire 20,000 Greek mercenaries serving with the Persian navy to the satraps of Asia Minor. With a force of that size, the mercenaries would have been able to man fully the entire front line along the Granicus River. Against these battle-hardened veterans, Alexander's tactical tricks would have been useless, and he would have been forced to conduct a straight-up, frontal infantry fight with all the combat advantages on the side of the Greek mercenaries. In such a situation, victory could go to either side. This scenario would have undoubtedly offered the Persians their highest probability for success against Alexander. Of course, this tactic would have been predicated on foreseeing that the Persians would fight by a defensive battle. Although the preponderance of cavalry in the Persian army might lead one to assume logically that they would undertake a tactical offensive, Darius' own inclinations were heavily defensive, as he would demonstrate in the next two battles, so it is somewhat surprising that he did not provide his satraps in Asia Minor the entire force of Greek mercenaries. That he did not was probably a result of his underestimation of the threat posed by the Macedonian army and his overestimation of the ability of his satraps and army to handle the situation with the forces they brought with them to the battle. Darius also had high hopes that the remainder of the mercenaries, if left with the fleet, would be able to operate successfully against Alexander's line of communications. This was to prove another bitter disappointment because his fleet accomplished little in the way of anything effective against Alexander.

Alexander clearly won the battle of the Granicus River, half with luck, half with brilliance. From a strictly military combat point of view, excluding all logistical and political considerations, Parmenio gave Alexander sound advice to delay the battle. Had Alexander followed it, he would, in all likelihood, have gained the bluffs the next morning with no opposition from the Persians. They would have almost certainly withdrawn back from the river during the night, as was their normal practice. True, the next morning they then might have attempted to retreat rather than engage in battle, but it is also more than likely, judging by the temperament of their commanders, that they would have gone ahead and fought anyhow. In this case, Alexander, suffering none of the disadvantages of position or deployment, would have quite likely badly beaten the Persians in the resulting field battle and having the better part of the day for pursuit might well have completely destroyed their army instead of only crippling it.[43]

After an initial setback with Amyntas' attack, Alexander achieved his victory by a frontal attack and hard fighting, despite the disadvantages of terrain. The difficulty of his task cannot be underestimated. He was attacking a strongly posted enemy with secure flanks late in the day. There was only time for one assault before dark. His opponent outnumbered him, and he had to cross two obstacles to even reach him and undergo heavy missile fire in the advance to contact. That he was successful with his attack is obviously a tribute to the superb fighting qualities of his Companion cavalry. Of course, it did not hurt that Amyntas' attack had brought the Persians opposite the point of Alexander's main attack down to the riverbed, disordering their ranks. This made the initial battle a straight-up fight, the Companions being equally disadvantaged. They were not only deprived of the benefits of the charge in their crossing of the river but also had their formation disordered by it.

Alexander's conduct of the battle was not, however, flawless. He did make one rather glaring mistake. Instead of pursuing the Persian cavalry on the wings, he chose to surround the mercenaries with his cavalry. This was not a sound strategy and was probably chosen more out of emotion than sound military logic. If Alexander had pursued the Persian cavalry, not only would he have inflicted far heavier losses on them but he would also have been active in the rear of the Greek mercenaries, thereby greatly restricting their ability to withdraw successfully from the battlfield.

In other words, the mercenaries were as good as bagged when the Persian cavalry routed off the field; it was unnecessary to focus specifically against them. Alexander's mobile hypaspists, archers, and Agrianians could have conducted an effective pursuit against the slower-moving mercenaries, pinning them in place by harassing missile fire until the phalanx was able to come up and deal with them.

Ironically, the Greek mercenaries had no intention of withdrawing. They were eager to negotiate with Alexander for their services. These 5,000 troops were excellently trained and would have been a valuable addition to Alexander's army at the time, although he might have had some difficulty in paying their wages of 25 talents a month.[44] It has never been satisfactorily explained why Alexander was so intransigent towards the mercenaries. Perhaps it was one of those emotional rages that in later years so frequently took possession of him. It is possible that he really was offended by what he considered their treachery in serving the Persian king. In the future, however, Alexander would discontinue this disadvantageous policy and always seek to come to terms with any mercenaries who opposed him.

Dascylium

After the battle of Granicus River, Parmenio was sent to capture Dascylium, the capital of Hellespontine Phrygia.[45] It was occupied without incident, the city's Persian garrison fleeing upon his approach.[46]

Sardis

While Parmenio proceeded to Dascylium, Alexander marched south to Sardis. When he was about nine miles from the city, Mithrines, commander of the acropolis guard, surrendered both the city and its treasury to him.[47] Amyntas (son of Andromenes) was sent on ahead to secure the citadel. Alexander then appointed Pausanias (a territorial officer) to command the citadel and Nicias to oversee tax collections. The Argives were left behind to garrison the citadel. Asandrus (son of Philotas) was appointed governor of Lydia and the remainder of Spithridates' district.[48] Calas (son of Harpalus) and Alexander (son of Aeropus) were sent back to the Troad with the Peloponnesian troops and most of the Greek allies.[49]

Ephesus

From Sardis, it took Alexander four days to march the 70 miles to Ephesus.[50] The city was an important communications center on his line of march. At his approach, Amyntas (son of Antiochus) and the mercenary garrison of the city fled on two triremes.[51] Alexander immediately recalled the exiles and restored democratic government to the city. The exiles, however, proceeded to exact revenge on all those who had either brought the Persians into the city, ransacked the Temple of Artemis, or had desecrated any of the local statues and tombs. Syrphax, the ruling oligarch, his son, and the children of his brother were forcibly removed from the temple and stoned to death.[52] A general massacre then ensued that Alexander soon put an end to, as citizens were now being put to death solely for reasons of hatred and plunder. The exiles, however, had achieved their objective of ridding the city of their oligarch enemies and were extremely grateful to Alexander.

Magnesia/Tralles

Shortly after the occupation of Ephesus, representatives of Magnesia and Tralles arrived to offer the submission of their cities to Alexander. Parmenio was dispatched there in command of a force of 200 cavalry, 2,500 Macedonian infantry, and 2,500 allied infantry.[53] He occupied the cities without incident.

Ionia

Alcimachus (son of Agathocles) was sent with a force of 300 infantry, 2,500 Macedonian infantry, and 2,500 allied infantry to occupy any Ionian cities still held by Persian troops.[54]

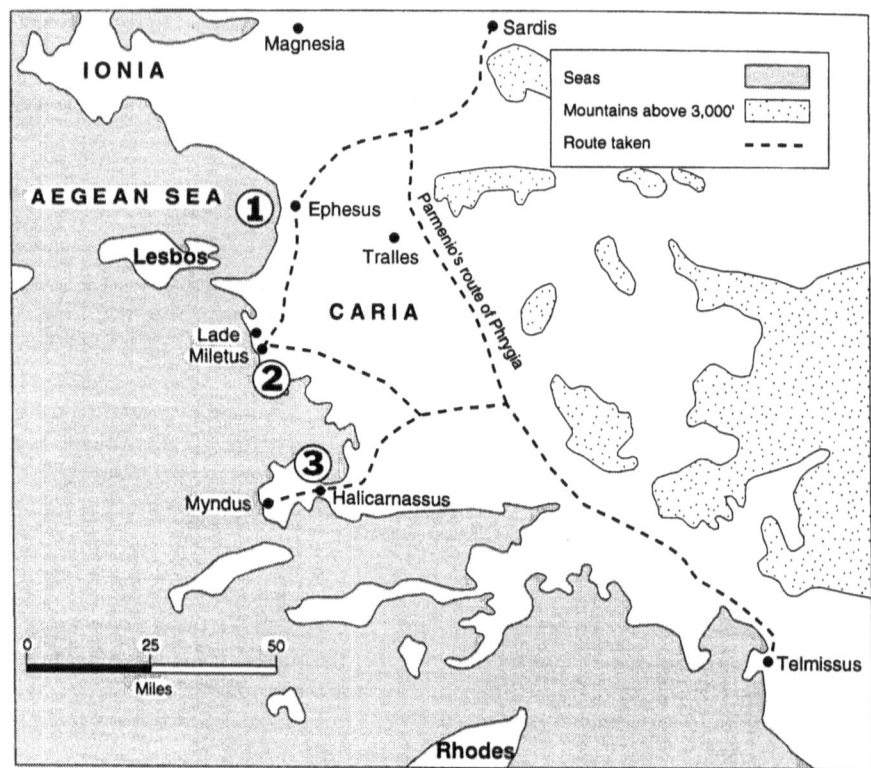

Map 20: Southwest Asia Minor

1. Greek mercenaries flee by sea at Alexander's approach. 2. Alexander disbands his Greek allied fleet. 3. Halicarnassus is captured after a seven-month siege.

Miletus

After leaving Ephesus, Alexander marched south on Miletus with the archers, Agrianians, Thracian cavalry, the Agema of the Companion Cavalry, and three other Companion ilea.[55] The city was located on a peninsula in the Lamian Gulf. Hegesistratus, who had been appointed by Darius to command the city's garrison, withdrew into the inner defenses upon Alexander's approach, abandoning the outer walls without a fight. He had initially thought his position hopeless and offered to surrender the city to Alexander. When the Persian fleet was sighted off Caria sailing for Miletus, however, his hopes revived and he decided to resist.

Nicanor now arrived off Lade, an island just of Miletus, three days in advance of the Persian fleet.[56] He had with him 160 triremes of the Greek allied navy.[57] Lade was immediately fortified and garrisoned with a strong force that included the Thracians and about 4,000 Greek mercenaries.[58] Upon their arrival, the 400 ships of the Persian navy were forced to anchor in an exposed position under Mt. Mycale, nine miles distant from Miletus.[59] The Persians used Mycale as a base to interdict Miletus. Every morning they attempted to provoke a battle with the Macedonians by lying off Miletus, but Alexander refused to be baited. At midday, the Persians were compelled to return to Mycale to make camp and purchase, cook, and eat their meals. They then rowed back to Miletus during the early afternoon to resume their blockading station until late afternoon, when they were forced to return to Mycale.

Parmenio had suggested to Alexander that even though his fleet was outnumbered, it should attempt to fight the Persian fleet in a sea battle because a victory would bring it great prestige. As to a possible defeat, he indicated that it would make no difference, for no matter what the result the Persians would still retain naval supremacy. Alexander rejected Parmenio's advice, indicating that his partially trained and heavily outnumbered fleet would almost certainly be defeated. Alexander's greatest fear was that his unsteady crews might desert in battle and their defeat might trigger a general revolt against him in Greece.

Glaucippus, the oligarch of Miletus, met with Alexander to deliver a proposal from the citizens of the city and the foreign mercenaries who formed their garrison. He indicated that if Alexander would raise the siege, Miletus would in return offer unobstructed use of its harbor and entry into the city to both Persians and Macedonians. Alexander refused the terms because he had no desire to provide the Persian navy with a protected anchorage. He then informed Glaucippus that he would assault the city the next morning. At dawn the following day, Alexander's siege engines were wheeled up. After the battlements were cleared of defenders, the walls were bombarded at close range. The rams were then brought up and several breaches were made. An assault was launched, and Miletus was carried. Most of the city's mercenaries died fighting on the walls.

In conjunction with Alexander's attack, Nicanor's fleet set out from Lade for Miletus. He deployed his ships close alongside each other across the entrance to Miletus' harbor to prevent the Persian fleet from assisting in the defense of the city. Each ship was packed with troops. With the fall of the city, about 300 of the Greek mercenary garrison escaped by paddling out on their shields to the small island of Acronnesus, just outside the harbor.[60] As the island had a steep shoreline, Alexander attached scaling ladders to the bows of his ships and made preparations for a landing there. The mercenaries on the island refused to ask for terms and prepared to fight to the death. Alexander was so moved by their courage that he offered to spare their lives if they took service with him, which they agreed to do. The surviving citizens of Miletus were given their freedom, but all foreigners captured there were sold into slavery.

Alexander sent Philotas with the cavalry and three columns of infantry to Mycale.[61] This cut the Persians off from their only source of water at the mouth of the Maeander River, forcing their withdrawal from the site. The Persians then established a new base of operations at Samos, where the Athenian cleruchs allowed them supply and harbor rights.

Alexander now decided to disband his navy because he thought it more a liability than an asset at the moment. It was not only expensive to maintain, but its effectiveness in battle was suspect. Having captured key agricultural areas in Asia Minor, he no longer required his navy to maintain a seaborne line of supply for his army. Later, however, Alexander would find a navy to be indispensable for operations against strongly defended coastal cities. At Tyre, he would learn the hard lesson that Philip had at Perinthus and Byzantium: a land siege against a strongly defended coastal city having a navy was usually unsuccessful unless the besieger had naval supremacy.

Siege of Halicarnassus

Being informed that a considerable force of Persians and Greek mercenaries that had withdrawn from the battlefield at Granicus River had concentrated at Halicarnassus, Alexander now marched there. Halicarnassus was the capital of Caria, the largest city in the satrapy and the primary Persian naval base in the southern Aegean. It was located on a small peninsula and had an exceptionally strong defense, the walls facing the mainland being 45 feet high and six feet thick. Instead of the usual single citadel, Halicarnassus had three: the original acropolis in the northwest; a fortress in the southwest, along the sea; and Salmacis, at the harbor entrance. The city was surrounded by a moat 45 feet wide and 22 feet deep.[62] The garrison included 2,000 Greeks commanded by Ephialtes, an Athenian, and a large Persian force under Orontobates, the satrap of Caria. The Persian king had appointed Memnon of Rhodes overall commander of the city's land and naval forces. The Persian fleet was anchored in the harbor to sortie out against any nearby Macedonian ships or to provide its crews as a reserve to assist the city's garrison in an emergency. Halicarnassus was well provisioned to withstand a long siege, having abundant supplies of military equipment and food. Large numbers of siege engines were also in storage. Because Alexander had recently disbanded his fleet, the city could be easily resupplied with men, armaments, and food at the Persian fleet's choosing. When Alexander moved against Halicarnassus shortly after the fall of Miletus, in the autumn of 334 B.C., he expected a long siege.

From Lasus, Alexander took the coast road through Bargylia to Halicarnassus. He encamped about a half mile southeast of the city, opposite the Mylasa Gate.[63] A reconnaissance provoked a sortie by the soldiers of the garrison who, after engaging in long-range missile fire, withdrew back into the city. Alexander knew that to conduct a successful siege of Halicarnassus he needed the siege artillery he had left behind at Tyre. He had initially hoped to sail past the patrolling Persian navy undetected and land it at Myndus, a small port about 10 miles west of Halicarnassus. A group of traitorous citizens inside the city had previously established contact with him, and arrangements had been made for the city gates to be opened at midnight on a certain night. Alexander brought the hypaspists; Companion cavalry; the taxies of the phalanx of Perdiccas, Amyntas, and Meleager; the Agrianians; and the archers up on the designated night in anticipation of entering the city.[64] For some unexplained reason, however, the traitors backed out of the plot, and the city gates remained shut to him. Although he did not have any siege equipment with him, Alexander was nevertheless able to collapse a section of the wall and a tower. Reinforcements by sea to the city convinced him, however, that Myndus could not be taken at that time, and he returned to Halicarnassus.

Alexander made several unsuccessful attempts to take Halicarnassus by assault, but only when he able to land the siege artillery at a nearby deserted cove along the coast was he finally able to prosecute the siege effectively. Filling in the moat along the northern section of Halicarnassus, Alexander brought up his siege engines and began to pound the wall there. Two towers and the wall between them collapsed, and a third tower was heavily damaged. A taxies of the phalanx repeatedly assaulted through the rubble but was driven back by Memnon's Greek mercenaries and the covering missile fire they received from the nearby walls. The garrison of the city made a night sortie to burn the siege towers Alexander had moved up for the assault the next day but was driven back by the hypaspists before they could carry out their mission. The city garrison lost 170 men, the Macedonians 16 killed and over 300 wounded.[65]

While the city defenders were frantically attempting to build an inner crescent wall to seal off the breach made on the high ground overlooking Mylasa Way, two drunken soldiers of Perdiccas' taxies of the phalanx set out for that area to prove who was the braver. They were promptly killed by some of the city garrison troops, who then begin firing missile weapons at other Macedonians standing in the distance, confident that both their numbers and position on the high ground protected them. Perdiccas sent reinforcements to the scene, as did Memnon. The garrison got the worst of the subsequent fight and was driven back through the city gates. If Alexander had attacked the crescent wall then, he might well have carried the city. The wall itself was still incomplete and lightly manned because most of the troops on station there had been drawn off to the fight in front of the crescent wall and were only slowly reentering the city through the gates.

Sometime later Alexander planned an attack on the newly completed crescent wall. As the siege towers were pushed forward, the city garrison sallied out in another attempt to burn them. One of the towers was set on fire, but troops under the command of Philotas and Hellanicus were able to save the other. When Alexander led some troops in a counterattack, the city garrison troops threw down their torches and weapons and fled back into the city.

After the second attempt to burn Alexander's siege towers had failed, Memnon entrusted Ephialtes with the responsibility of leading an assault against the Macedonians with the Greek mercenaries in a last attempt to save the city.[66] Two forces of 1,000 Greek mercenaries each would sally out at daylight.[67] The mission of the first force was to burn all Alexander's catapults and siege towers and to engage any Macedonian fire fighters and their support troops. The second force, under the command of Ephialtes, would exit from the "triple gate" and fall on the flank and rear of the Macedonians who counterattacked the first force. Ephialtes would be supported by a 150-foot tower behind the crescent wall that Memnon had packed with javelin men, archers, and catapults. This would provide a highly effective overhead covering fire for the troops fighting below.[68]

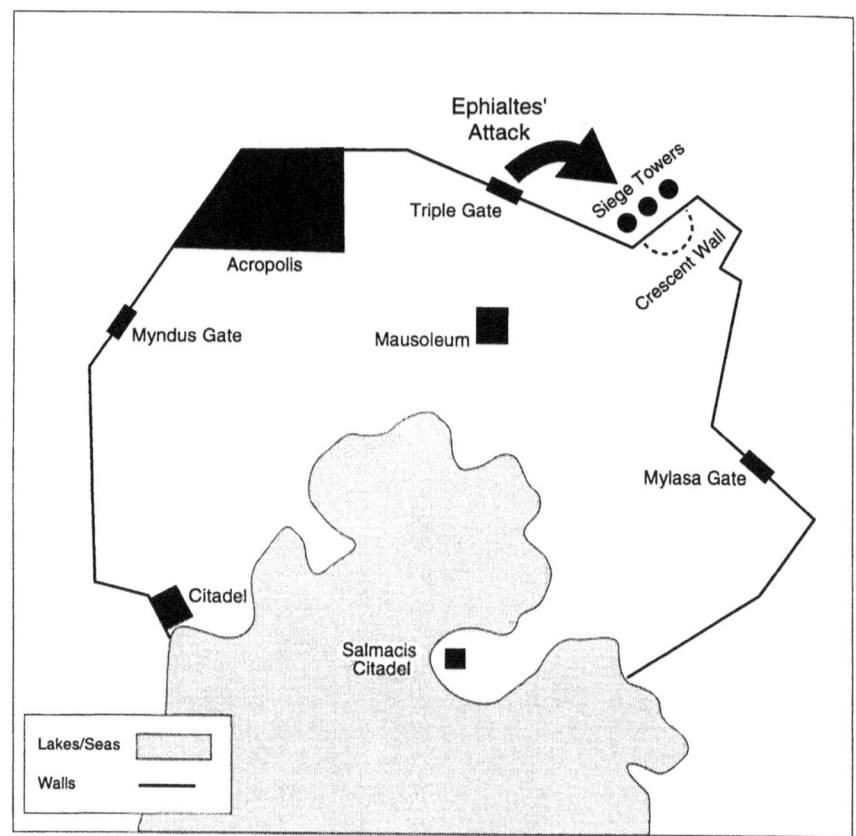

Map 21: Siege of Halicarnassus

A few days later Alexander brought up his siege engines to assault the crescent wall. The first group of attackers promptly rushed out of the city to set fire to them. The Macedonians reacted exactly as Ephialtes had anticipated, and his second attack column caught their counterattacking force completely by surprise and at a serious disadvantage. Alexander had deployed his Macedonian troops in the front line and a force of hand-picked veterans in reserve. Hemmed in on three sides, however, they were fighting in a highly disadvantageous situation.

Memnon now rushed up in support of Ephialtes with reinforcements, and Alexander found himself unable to make any headway in the fight. The older Macedonians, who were exempt from combat duty because of their age but who had fought and won many battles under Philip in their youth, formed up, overlapped their shields, and entered the battle. They smashed into Ephialtes' assault group from the city, greatly surprising them because they believed they had already won the battle. The unexpectedness and ferocity of the Macedonian counterattack and Ephialtes' death early in the battle threw the sortie troops into panic and they fled back to the city. They found the gates closed against them, however, for fear that the Macedonians might enter along with the returning garrison. The sortie force outside the city jammed onto the narrow bridge over the moat in such numbers that it collapsed under their weight, throwing many down 20 feet into the moat below. There they were either trampled by those struggling to climb out or were killed by Macedonian missile fire from above. It the Macedonians had followed up their success with an immediate attack on the city, it would have, in all likelihood, fallen, so lightly were its walls now manned. Alexander, however, sounded the recall. He did so, it was said, because he still had hopes of the city surrendering, especially in light of the 1,000 casualties he had just inflicted on its garrison during its recent sortie.[69] Alexander had reputedly only taken 40 casualties in the counterattack, although these must have only been his killed, his wounded likely being from 10 to 20 times that number.[70] Among the Macedonian officers known to have been killed were Ptolemy, the captain of the Royal Guards; Clearchus, commander of the archers; and Addaeus, an infantry commander.[71]

Immediately after Ephialtes' unsuccessful sortie, a military conference was held in Halicarnassus. Because of the failure of the latest attack, the breach in the wall, and the shortage of troops available for manning the walls, Orontobates, the satrap of Caria, agreed with Memnon's recommendation to evacuate the city and concentrate as many of their best surviving troops as possible inside the two citadels along the seashore. The remaining force and everything that could be evacuated would sail to the island of Cos. Those military stores inside the city that could not be removed were set afire about midnight, along with the 150-foot wooden tower used in support of the recent night sortie. The houses near the wall were also torched, undoubtedly to keep Alexander from entering the city and interfering with the evacuation. The wind, however, spread the flames throughout the city, with the result that a large portion of it burned to the ground.

Alexander decided against attempting to assault the two citadels held by the remaining Persian/Greek mercenary garrison. Not only were they strongly built and garrisoned but being alongside the shoreline they could be supplied by the Persian fleet at will with men, armaments, and provisions. Instead, he occupied that portion of the city surviving the fire, surrounded the enemy-held citadels with a wall and trench, and left 200 cavalry and 3,000 Greek mercenary infantry behind under Ptolemy (son of Lagus) to contain the Persians.[72] Alexander then marched eastward to Pamphylia.

When Alexander had occupied the city of Halicarnassus, he had effectively neutralized the port. Although the two seaside citadels continued to hold out for several months, the Persians were unable to use the harbor as a base of operations for their navy. The citadels could be easily maintained, but they were now of little actual military use to the Persians. About 12 months after Alexander marched off from the city, Orontobates engaged Ptolemy and Asandrus in a field battle and was heavily defeated, losing 50 cavalry and 700 infantry killed and 1,000 prisoners[73]. As a result, both seaside forts surrendered, and the siege of Halicarnassus was finally brought to a close.

Generalship During the siege of Halicarnassus, Memnon demonstrated a high order of military capability. He conducted a superb defense of the city and frustrated several attempts by Alexander to take advantage of the breaches he had made in the city's walls. Memnon had so effectively sealed the critical breach with a crescent wall that had Alexander returned to the assault there he would have been met by an overwhelming volume of missile fire delivered from both the wall and the 150-foot wooden tower on the front, flank, and rear of his attacking force. Ephialtes' night attack was well planned and executed, coming very close to success. When it failed, however, Memnon knew that it was time to withdraw and did so in a manner that preserved his forces for use in a more favorable situation in the future. All in all, Memnon proved a worthy opponent for Alexander, and Halicarnassus was the only known instance in which the legendary Macedonian king was unable to emerge completely victorious.

Although it is true that Alexander achieved his strategic mission of denying the Persian navy the use of Halicarnassus as a port, he had only contained the position, not fully captured it. There is an interesting lack of initiative and innovation in Alexander's siege of Halicarnassus. We see none of the cleverness and dedication that so characterized his later sieges at Tyre and the Rocks of Sogdiana, Chorienes, and Aornos. Alexander seems to have largely reacted to Memnon's sorties here, appearing perfectly content to pursue a long, traditional siege. Instead of smashing his opponent, he was repeatedly checked and narrowly escaped defeat in the night attack. Then Alexander just marched off, leaving the city to be starved out. Diodorus provides some fascinating details on the difficulties of the siege, as does Arrian. This appears to be one of those rare instances when reality replaces the usual Macedonian propaganda extolling a triumphant Alexander. This operation was definitely not one of Alexander's best, and it may well have been one of his worst, notable chiefly for the lethargic and unimaginative manner in which he prosecuted the siege.

Hellespontine Phrygia

Alexander gave Parmenio command of a cavalry ilea, the Thessalian cavalry, and the Greek allies and ordered him to conduct a winter campaign to subdue Hellespont Phrygia.[74] Unfortunately, nothing is known of Parmenio's campaign there.

Tralles

Alexander redeployed his siege engines against Tralles. After capturing the city, he razed it, leaving behind a garrison on the site.

Hypani

Taking the remainder of the army along the coast into Lycia and Pamphylia, Alexander's objective was to deny the Persians any base of operations along the coast of south central Asia Minor. Upon his approach, all the cities there surrendered without resistance, with the single exception of Hypani. There, however, the mercenaries were also soon convinced to surrender on terms.

7: THE WESTERN PERSIAN EMPIRE

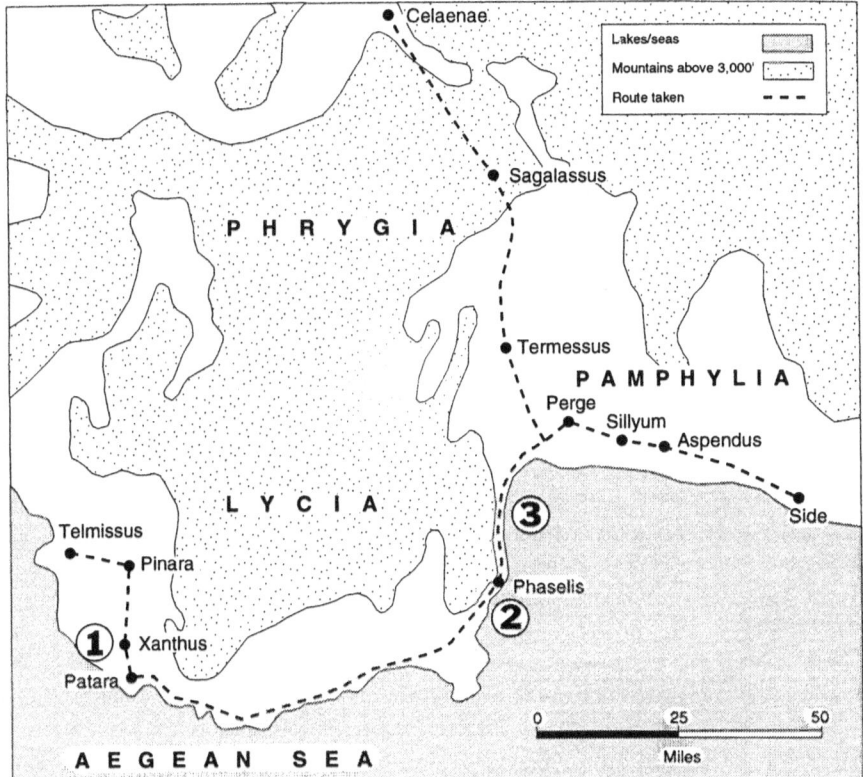

Map 22: South Central Asia Minor

1. A bronze tablet predicting Alexander's victory in Asia is spewn up by a geyser. 2. Alexander learns of plot by Alexander (son of Aeropus) to assassinate him. 3. Alexander crosses submerged pass alongside Mt. Climax.

Lycia

In Lycia, the cities of Pinara, Xanthus, and Patara quickly submitted to Alexander, as well as 30 other strongholds.[75]

Xanthus

Alexander stopped at Xanthus. Legend has it that at a local spring there a bronze tablet was spewn out of the water by the eruption of a geyser. It was inscribed with some ancient writing which, interestingly enough, was translated to read that the Persian Empire would be destroyed by a Greek.[76] This event was obviously well received by Alexander and his entourage, the consensus being that his campaign against the Persians was favored by the gods.

Phaselis

Although envoys from Phaselis met Alexander and presented him with a gold crown, they were forced to hand over their city to him. While there, Alexander was informed of Alexander of Aeropus' assassination plot against him. (For additional details on the plot, see Appendix B.) Leaving a garrison in the city's citadel, Alexander marched off to Pamphylia.

Mt. Climax

Between Phaselis and Perge, a narrow and steep pass had to be crossed alongside the 7,000-foot-high Mt. Climax in Lycia.[77] The only alternative route lay along a long, narrow, and difficult mountain road. Alexander had the Thracians cut steps and widen the gorge through the pass. He then sent the bulk of his force along the mountain road, while he and a small party rode along the shore, skirting the base of Mt. Climax. His route emerged onto the Pamphylian plain south of Beldibi but was only negotiable when a strong north wind was blowing. At this time, however, a galelike wind from the south had submerged the crossing in water. When the wind shifted and blew from the north, the water receded from the coastal route and Alexander and his party were able to cross without further incident.

Aspendus

A delegation from Aspendus offered to surrender the city to Alexander on the condition that a garrison not be stationed there. Alexander agreed, providing that the city paid 50 talents in tribute and surrendered the horses it bred for Darius.[78] The terms were agreed to by the delegation, and Alexander marched east to Side. The citizens of Aspendus, however, rejected the terms as being confiscatory and refused to honor the agreement. Because the city was located on a very steep hill overlooking the Eurymedon River and because Alexander was currently engaged in besieging Syllium, the citizens there hoped that he would be either unwilling or unable to detach sufficient force to coerce them into compliance. Alexander, however, needed both their money and horses, and returned back to Aspendus with his army. At his approach, the citizens withdrew from the outer wall to the center of the strongly fortified hill on which their city stood. The base of the hill was encircled by a low wall on flat ground that the citizens had determined could not be held. Seeing Alexander's army occupy the lower area of their city and hearing of his presence with them, the citizens of Aspendus lost their nerve and requested that they be allowed to surrender on the terms previously agreed to. Observing the strong position of the hill and not wanting to be delayed by a long siege, Alexander allowed them to surrender, but on harsher terms than he had originally offered them. He doubled the amount of their payment to 100 talents, required them to pay an annual tribute, appointed a satrap to rule over them, took all the leading citizens hostage, and required the return of all lands they had wrongly appropriated from their neighbors.[79] Aspendus had no real option but to comply with the new and much harsher terms.

Side

Upon Alexander's approach, the city of Side surrendered. Alexander left a garrison in the citadel and backtracked west to Syllium.

Syllium

Alexander had been informed that Syllium was fortified and garrisoned by a mixed force of natives and Greek mercenaries. Not being able to take the city without extensive siege operations, he marched back to Aspendus. After that city's submission, Alexander marched on Telmissus.

Telmissus

The city of Telmissus was located on a steep 3,000-foot cliff under which the road passed. As the opposite side of the road was also dominated by a steep cliff, it was relatively easy for a small force deployed on the heights on either side of the road to resist a much larger attacking force. With the defender having both flanks secured, any attack would have to be channeled on a narrow front alongside the road and would receive simultaneous missile fire from the front, both flanks, and the rear. When warned of Alexander's approach, the citizens of Telmissus marched every available man out of their city to man the position at the pass. Alexander, however, did not attempt an assault upon his arrival but went into camp at the base of the pass. He reasoned that at dusk most of the citizen-militia would return to the comfort of their nearby city, leaving behind only a small force to guard the heights. When this happened as he had predicted, Alexander took the archers, javelin men, and other light infantry and immediately marched on the pass.[80] The small garrison remaining there broke after the first volley of missile fire, fleeing before contact was ever made. Alexander then marched through the pass with his army and made camp near the city. While at Telmissus, he was visited by envoys from the Selgians, who immediately submitted to him. They told him of a route through central Asia Minor far less difficult than the one he had intended to take along the coast. Concluding that a siege of Telmissus would be too time consuming, Alexander moved on to Sagalassus, which was held by the Pisidians.

Sagalassus

The Pisidians occupied a hill in front of Sagalassus almost as strong as the city walls. Just before Alexander's arrival, they were joined by a force from Telmissus that had come to fight on their behalf. Alexander came up and deployed the hypaspists on his right wing and the phalanx on the left.[81] In advance of the hypaspists, he posted the archers and Agrianians while he screened the phalanx with the Thracian javelin men. Because of the narrowness of the front, the cavalry were of little use and were subsequently deployed in the rear.[82] Alexander took command of the right wing, assigning the left to Amyntas (son of Arrabaeus).

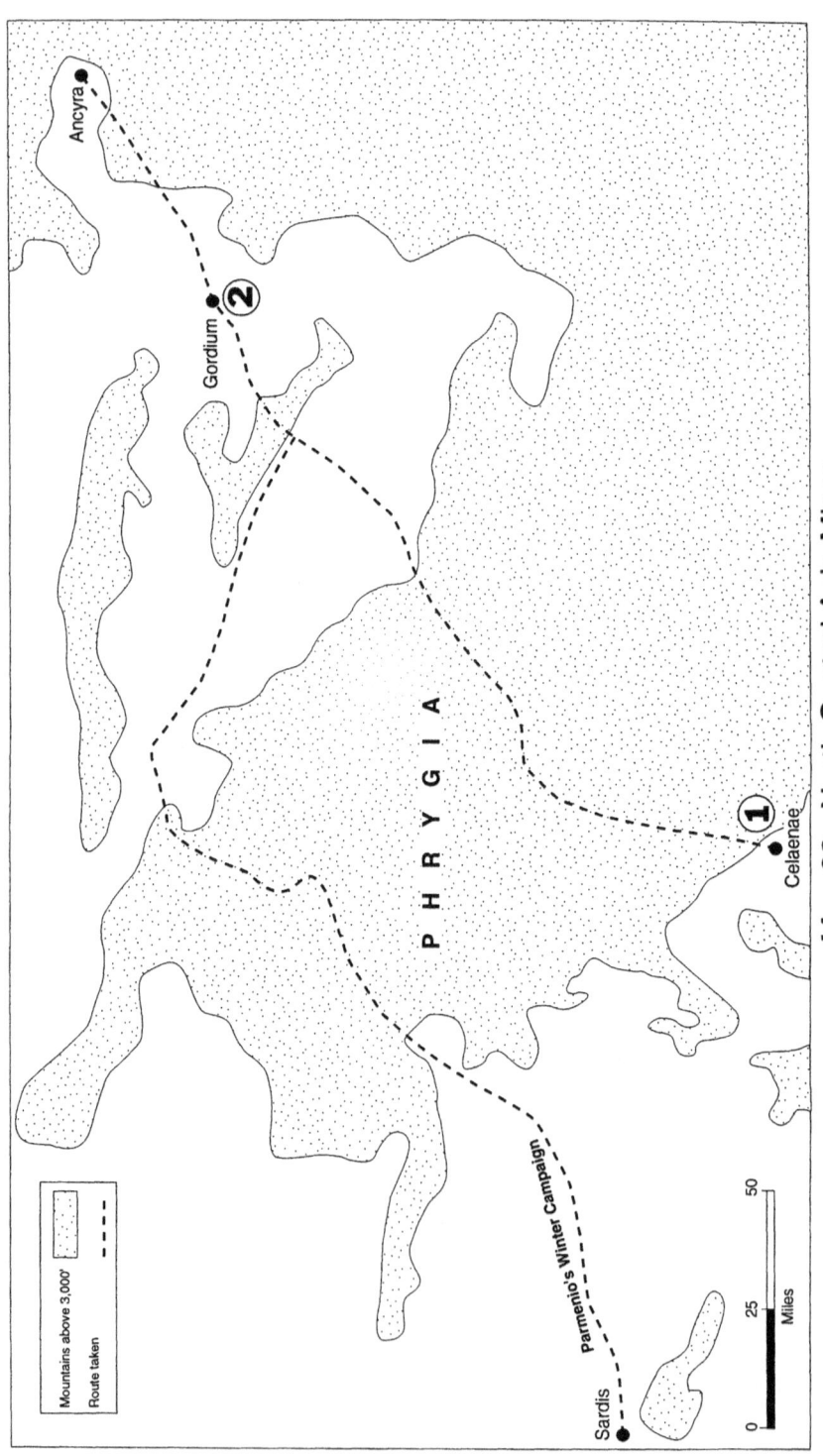

Map 23: North Central Asia Minor

Alexander's screening force began climbing up towards the Pisidians. While the Macedonians were struggling uphill, the Pisidians attacked, driving back the archers and killing their commander, Cleandrus. The Agrianians, however, managed to hold their position. Alexander then led the phalanx up the hill and engaged the Pisidians, who soon broke, leaving 500 dead behind them.[83] Being lightly armed and familiar with the area, many of the Pisidians were able to flee back to Sagalassus. Alexander closely pursued them, carrying the city on the first assault. After capturing a number of the Pisidians' remaining fortified positions, Alexander forced their complete surrender. Macedonian losses in the initial attack totaled 20 killed.[84]

Celeanae

From Sagalassus Alexander marched on Celeanae, the capital of Phrygia, reaching the city in five days [85]. It was situated at the head of two rivers, the Maeander and the Marsyas, and occupied a strategic position on a key communications junction with roads leading south to Pamphylia, west to Hermus, and north to Gordium. Before Alexander moved on, it was necessary to secure the narrow corridor Celeanae dominated. Failure to do so would allow the unsubdued tribes to the north and south to interdict his line of communications at will.

The outer city had been abandoned, its inhabitants having taken shelter in the strongly fortified acropolis. The garrison consisted of 1,000 Carians and 100 Greek mercenaries under command of the satrap of Phrygia.[86] Alexander surrounded the city and waited. Fifteen days later the satrap notified Alexander that if reinforcements did not arrive from Darius within two months, he would surrender to him.[87] Leaving behind 1,500 troops under command of Antigonus (son of Philip) to invest the city, Alexander marched off to the north on the Royal Road to Gordium.[88] When reinforcements did not arrive from Darius at the end of the stated time period, the garrison of Celeanae promptly surrendered.

Gordium

Gordium was the capital of Hellespontine Phrygia. Alexander selected the city as his army's winter quarters both because it stood alongside of the Sangarius River and because of the extensive meadows nearby, which could provide fodder for his cavalry. Parmenio had been ordered to meet Alexander there with the force he campaigned with in Phrygia. After Alexander untied the Gordian knot, he marched on Paphlagonia. (For details on the Gordian knot, see the Glossary.)

Paphlagonia

While Alexander was marching towards Ancyra, a delegation from Paphlagonia met him. Its members offered their submission and pleaded with him not to

1. The city surrenders in two months after hoped-for Persian reinforcements fail to arrive. 2. Alexander undoes the Gordian knot; Alexander refuses to release the Athenians he captured at the battle of Granicus River.

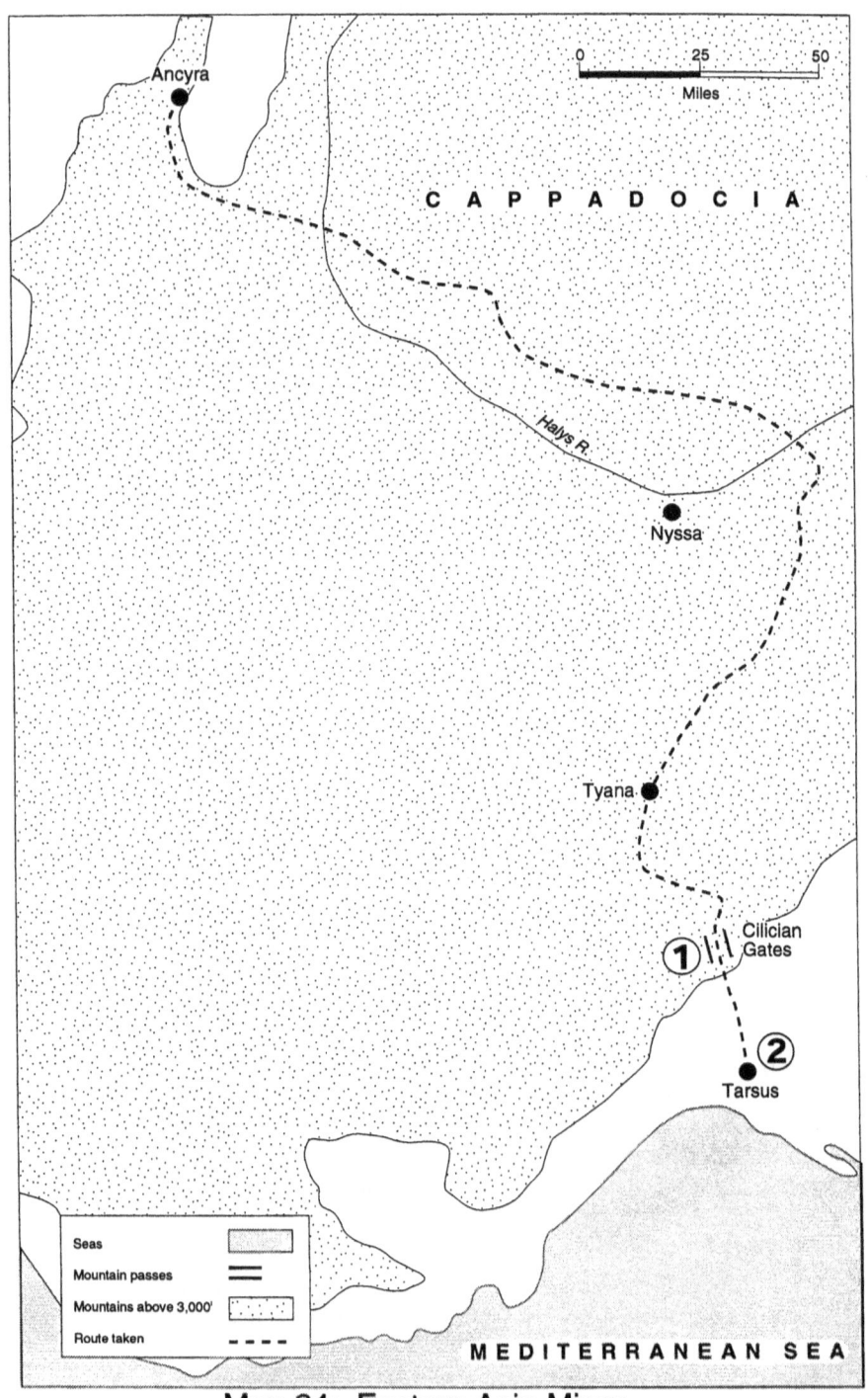

Map 24: Eastern Asia Minor

enter their territory with his army. Alexander agreed with their request, appointing Calas (son of Harpalus) as satrap over them. Alexander then continued his march on Cappadocia.

Cappadocia

Alexander received the surrender of all the territory south of the Halys River, Sabaces being appointed as satrap there.[89] It was a considerable period of time before the area could be subdued because Alexander had passed through too quickly to pacify it properly. Northern Cappadocia was left in control of the Persians.[90] Alexander then continued on to the Cilician Gates.

Antigonus was appointed satrap of Phrygia and entrusted with the responsibility of keeping open the narrow pass between Cappadocia and the Isaurians. This was vital because Alexander's line of communications ran through there. In the aftermath of Darius' defeat at Issus, a portion of the Persian army withdrew into Cappadocia, combined with the natives there, and attempted to occupy the pass. This force was, however, unsuccessful in its attack, being defeated by Antigonus after a hard fight. Although unable to seek out and destroy either the Cappadocians and Isaurians because of the inadequate force at his disposal, Antigonus was able to keep the pass open throughout Alexander's reign. Shortly after Alexander's death, Perdiccas ensured the safety of the pass by conquering both the Cappadocians and Isaurians.[91]

Cilician Gates

There was only one usable mountain pass through the Taurus Mountains separating Asia Minor from Syria and Mesopotamia, that being the Cilician Gates. It was a deep and twisting canyon at an elevation of 3,600 feet that was surrounded by high walls barely wide enough for two loaded camels or four men abreast to march through at its narrowest point.[92] A small force of archers could easily hold the pass against an army, and rocks rolled down into the canyon would completely block any section of it.

Arsames, who governed Cilicia, had been present at the battle of the Granicus River and had been greatly impressed with Memnon's "scorched-earth" advice. As a result, instead of deploying all his troops in the gates, which he almost certainly would have been able to hold against Alexander, he left only a small observation force there and used the remainder of his force to burn or destroy everything on the Cilician Plain in the rear of the gates.[93] The soldiers of the small force left behind in the pass understandably thought that they were being sacrificed in an untenable position, and only reluctantly maintained their position. Observing that the pass was held, Alexander made camp. Leaving Parmenio in command there with the heavily armed troops, Alexander took the archers, Agrianians, hypaspists, and Thracians on a night march on the position.[94] Although his

1. Alexander carries the gates against a token Persian defending force. 2. Alexander is incapacitated for a month after diving into the ice-cold Cydnus River.

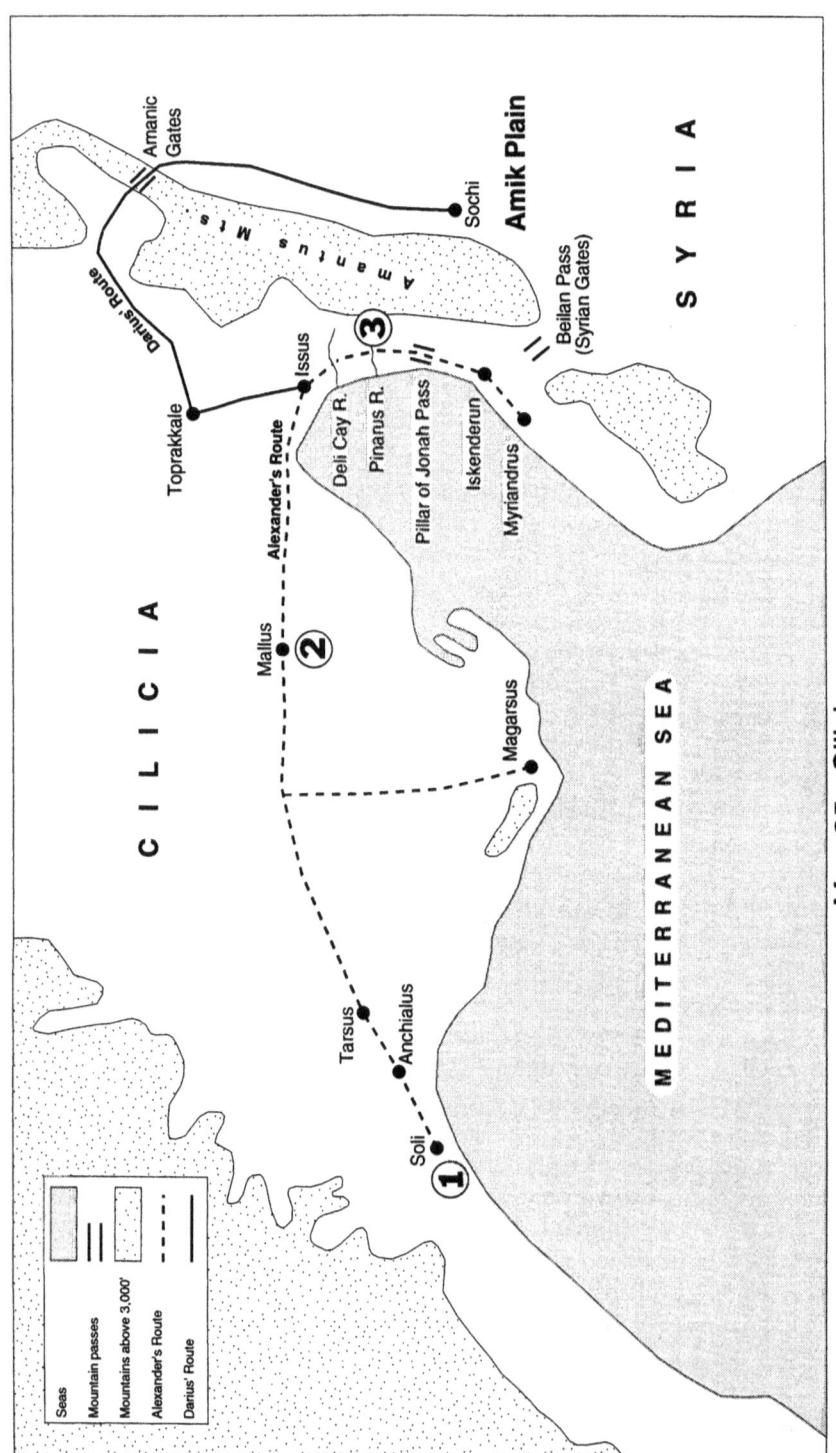

Map 25: Cilicia

approach was observed by the Persians, the report that Alexander was leading the assault collapsed their already low morale, and the defending force fled before contact was ever made. At dawn, Alexander marched his army through the pass and descended into Cilicia. He later said that he considered the ease with which he captured the Cilician Gates to be one of the luckiest events in his career.[95]

Cilicia

Cilicia encircles the Gulf of Issus at the northeast tip of the Mediterranean, being bordered by the Tarus Mountains on the north and west, the Amanus Mountains on the east, and Syria, the Gulf of Issus, and the Mediterranean Sea on the south. The only usable mountain pass through the Tarus Mountains was the one at the Cilician Gates leading to Tarus. There were three passes through the Amanus Mountains: the Pillar of Jonah Pass along the coast; the Beilan Pass (Syrian Gates), southwest of Alexandretta, leading to the Amik plain; and the Amanic Gates to the north, leading to Issus.

Tarsus

When Arsames learned that Alexander had forced the Cilician Gates, he began making plans to withdraw from Tarsus. The citizens there, fearing that Arsames would plunder and burn their city upon his departure, urged Alexander to occupy it without delay. Alexander immediately started out on a forced-march on Tarsus with his cavalry and light infantry. At his approach, Arsames fled the city in such haste that he was unable to loot or destroy it. Arriving at Tarsus, Alexander immediately plunged into the Cydnus River to relieve the discomfort of the day's heat. The resulting shock from the ice-cold river threw him into convulsions, and he quickly developed a violent fever that incapacitated him for almost a month.

Anchialus

When Alexander recovered his health, he marched southwest from Tarus to Anchialus, reaching the city in a single day. It submitted to him without incident, and he then continued marching west to Soli.

Soli

Alexander levied a fine of 200 talents on Soli for being friendly to Persia, took hostages, and installed a garrison in its citadel.[96] Then, taking a force of three taxies of the phalanx, the archers, and Agrianians, he attacked a force of Cilicians who had deployed on some nearby high ground.[97] After defeating them in a campaign lasting a week, he returned to Soli.[98] There, upon hearing of the fall of the citadels at Halicarnassus and the surrender of Cos, Alexander held a review of the army and then took the Agema and some infantry and marched off to Magarsus.[99]

1. Alexander is informed that the two citadels at Halicarnassus have fallen. 2. Alexander learns that Darius is encamped at Sochi. 3. Alexander defeats Darius at the battle of Issus.

After winning the battle of Issus sometime later, Alexander remitted the 50 talents he had levied against the Soli and returned all their hostages to them.[100]

Magarsus

Upon Alexander's approach, Magarsus submitted without incident. Alexander then marched on to Mallus.

Mallus

At Mallus, Alexander's first task was to end the civil unrest there. Because the city had been a colony of Argos, from which he himself claimed descent, Alexander exempted it from any tribute. While there, he received reports in November that Darius had encamped his army on the plain at Sochi, two marching days away.[101] This gave Alexander three options: wait for Darius to come to him, ignore Darius and proceed south along the coast into Syria, or march against Darius to engage him in battle on the Syrian plain. Parmenio urged Alexander to deploy his smaller army on a narrow battlefield to await Darius' expected arrival. Unless the Persians were encountered before they reached the coast, however, they might attempt to link up with their fleet in the vicinity of Issus. This would allow them not only to receive seaborne supplies for their army but to land troops by sea anywhere along Alexander's line of communications running back through Tarsus. To march south into Syria would allow Darius to cut Alexander's overland line of communications with Greece. As Persian naval superiority and the lack of a Greek fleet, which had been demobilized by Alexander at Miletus, would preclude a line of communications being established by sea, this option would likely isolate him. Alexander was not, however, temperamentally content to remain passively on the defensive to await the initiative of his opponent. As a result, he chose the third option and immediately marched south from Issus with every intention of engaging Darius in battle on the Syrian plain.[102]

Sochi

Alexander sent Parmenio on ahead with a 14,000-strong holding force consisting of the Thessalian cavalry, the Thracians, the Greek allies, and the Greek mercenaries.[103] His orders were to hold the passes of southern Cilicia in advance of the army's arrival there. Parmenio established a base at Issus, marched south along the coast, and occupied both the Syrian Gates and the Beilan Pass. Alexander left his siege train and his sick and wounded at Issus and continued south along the coastal road with the remainder of the army.

By the spring of 333 B.C., Darius had assembled an army from the infantry levies of Persis and Media and had augmented the cavalry units that had escaped from the battle of the Granicus River. Although the cavalry of the northeast frontier had not yet arrived, the Great King had decided to march without them. His army already considerably outnumbered the Macedonians, and he was eager to engage Alexander before he entered Syria. Thus in the early summer the Persian army marched out of Babylon. Its rate of march was slow because it was greatly impeded by the enormous baggage train that accompanied it.[104] Among other things, the baggage train contained 30,000 camp followers, a portion of the royal treasure, Darius' family, the noble ladies of the court, the Great King's 365 concubines, and several weeks' supplies for the large Persian army. Over 7,000 animals and a large number of wagons, each supplying 30 soldiers, were required to transport this vast paraphernalia. The lumbering Persian army spent five days crossing the Euphrates River at Thapsacus, and then marched to Sochi on the Amik plain, just east of the Amanus Mountains. The Persians had taken almost three months to complete the march from Babylon. That portion of the baggage train containing Darius' court entourage was sent to Damascus, 200 miles to the south, where it arrived some three weeks later.[105] The remainder of the baggage train moved with Darius to Sochi.

The Persian army had been at Sochi for about two weeks. Darius was hoping to attack Alexander as he exited the Syrian Gates onto the Syrian plain. His intention was to overwhelm Alexander's emerging force, which would probably be not only still in column of march but exhausted from the arduous mountain crossing. When Alexander showed no sign of moving south, however, Darius became impatient with his sit-tight strategy. His entourage encouraged him to attribute Alexander's failure to advance to his fear of the huge Persian army. Unknown to the Great King, however, the reason for Alexander's delay was not fear but illness.

The continued presence of Darius' large army in the Syrian plain for any extended period of time would eventually deplete the area's food supplies and probably trigger local unrest.[106] When this occurred, the strain on Darius' logistics net would quickly become critical. Alexander, on the other hand, could be easily supplied by sea almost indefinitely as long as he was not interfered with by the Persian navy.[107] Darius, now convinced that Parmenio's occupation of the passes through the Amanus Mountains was defensive in nature, indicating that Alexander's current offensive was confined to only to Cilicia, decided to move from Sochi. This was against the advice of Amyntas (son of Antiochus), his Macedonian-born adviser, who indicated that if Darius had a little more patience, Alexander would seek him out. Darius, however, preferring to believe his courtiers' picture of a fearful Alexander, decided to assume the offensive. His plan was probably intended to isolate Alexander, believed to be at Mallus, from Parmenio at the Pillar of Jonah Pass and destroy each force in detail.[108] Darius began his march on the Amanic Gates, about 93 miles to the northwest.[109] Passing through the gates without any opposition, he continued on to the coast. Being informed that Alexander had already moved south along the coastal road two days earlier to join Parmenio, Darius marched on Issus. Although missing the chance to attack Alexander's army in detail, Darius was now sitting squarely across the Macedonian army's line of communications. As the Great King doubtless saw it, Alexander would have to either turn round and fight his way back through the Persians or see his army starve in northern Syria. After butchering the Macedonian sick he had captured at Issus, Darius continued south along the coast to look for a suitable battlefield. He found one to his satisfaction at the Pinarus River and took up a defensive position along its steep north bank to await Alexander's expected arrival. To win a victory all Darius had to do is hold his position; a drawn battle would be equivalent to a defeat for Alexander.

Myriandrus

While Alexander was marching south to Myriandrus along the coast, Darius had unknowingly passed him marching north on the eastern side of the Amanus Mountains. Both armies were completely unaware that their opponent was in motion in the opposite direction. When Alexander arrived at Myriandrus several days later, he was surprised to hear that Issus, now 30 miles in his rear, was occupied by the Persian army.[110] At first he did not believe the reports and sent some of his personal staff by ship to verify the rumor. When the presence of the Persian army at Issus was confirmed, Alexander reversed his line of march and put his army in motion at sunset for the Pillar of Jonah Pass, nine miles to the north.[111] The Macedonian army reached the pass about midnight, encamping on the surrounding rocky ground. From this summit, the campfires of Darius' army could be clearly seen on the plain below.

Battle of Issus

At dawn the following day, the Macedonian army began to descend in column from the pass, the infantry deployed in front, followed by the cavalry. About three miles from the pass, the plain began to open up gradually. This allowed the cavalry room to deploy on the right flank. About 1,000 yards from the Pinarus River, the frontage widened out to about three miles, allowing the infantry to deploy from column into line. Alexander now advanced very slowly and halted frequently, ready at all times to receive a charge from the Persian cavalry. As Alexander had expected, the Persian cavalry, supported by light infantry, began to advance on him. Darius, however, was only using this show of strength as a screen to cover the final deployment of his infantry. When the Persian infantry and Greek mercenaries were in position, the Persian cavalry screen withdrew back over the river. It was now late afternoon. Alexander again ordered his army forward, and it continued to advance until it was just outside Persian missile range. His right flank occupied the so-called "dead ground," a low ridge that precluded Persian observation of any force deployed behind it. Here Alexander could make the final troop dispositions of his offensive wing unobserved. The time it took for Alexander to organize his forces for the assault allowed him to deal with the Persian light infantry in the foothills behind his right flank. This being done, Alexander was ready to advance to the attack.

The dominant geographical feature of the Issus battlefield was the Pinarus River. Although the water level was only three feet deep, its rocky bed and steep banks precluded infantry and cavalry from crossing various portions of it. There were four distinct sections of the river on the battlefield, each characterized by different terrain features that restricted crossings. The first ran from the mouth of the Pinarus to 500 yards inland; the second, another 1,750 yards inland; the third, another 1,500 yards inland; and the fourth, the remaining distance to the foothills of the mountains.[112] The first section of the Pinarus had a stony riverbed with three- to six-foot banks. Cavalry could cross here, but only with difficulty. Although the riverbed in the second section only ranged between 15 and 50 feet wide, its banks were steep. Infantry could cross here, but cavalry could not except at two small fords from 25 to 55 yards wide.[113] The riverbed in the third section alternated between wide and narrow, but its steep six- to 13-foot bank effectively prohibited both infantry and cavalry from crossing. The riverbed of the fourth section was 50 to 130 feet wide and had almost vertical banks, rising up a minimum of 10 feet high and in some places up to 60 feet high. This section was completely impassable for cavalry and could only be crossed by infantry using scaling ladders. The battle would be fought across the first two sections of the river, the Persian cavalry for the most part being deployed along the first section and their infantry along the second.[114]

The ground itself contained no vegetation except for some scrub. North of the river, on the Persian side, the ground was broken next to the mountains, then level, and finally gently sloping as it neared the sea. South of the river, on the Macedonian side, a low ridge ran down from the mountains, behind which was a low flat space, the so-called "dead area." From there to the sea, the ground was generally level.

Darius had originally planned to concentrate his cavalry on his left flank. He had determined, however, that not only was the ground too rough there, but the two small crossings of the Pinarus and high riverbank did not accommodate massed cavalry operations. He consequently transferred all his cavalry to his right flank along the seashore, where the ground was level, the riverbanks lower, and the fords more numerous. Darius' tactical plan was to remain on the defensive with the left wing of his army behind the steep banks of the Pinarus River and attack with the massed cavalry of his right wing along the seashore. The Great King posted his Greek mercenaries in the center to contain Alexander's phalanx, which he still believed to be the most effective force in the Macedonian army. Darius was confident that they would be able to deal easily with a phalanx disordered by crossing the river and climbing up the steep bluffs. On the right flank, alongside the coast, Darius deployed his cavalry. They would cross the river, crush Alexander's weakly held left flank by weight of numbers, and then roll up a phalanx pinned against the stationary Persian center and left flank.

Alexander's tactical plan was almost identical to Darius'. He planned to hold Parmenio's left wing along the coast on the defensive, pin the Persian infantry against his phalanx in the center, and break through the Persian left with his Companions. A vital part of the plan was to remove the Persian cavalry opposite the Macedonian right flank. He would do this by initially stationing only a weak 600-man Greek cavalry unit on his left flank as a lure to tempt Darius into concentrating all his cavalry against it. As it turned out, Alexander's ploy happened to fit right in with Darius' intention for an offensive from his right flank, and he willingly overcommitted all 24,000 of his cavalry opposite the Macedonian left.

Although many of the ancient historians numbered the Persian army at Issus at 600,000 or more, the reality is that it probably totaled no more than 80,000.[115] Having access to the central and eastern empire, Darius' cavalry would have definitely exceeded the 20,000 present at the battle of the Granicus River, and a

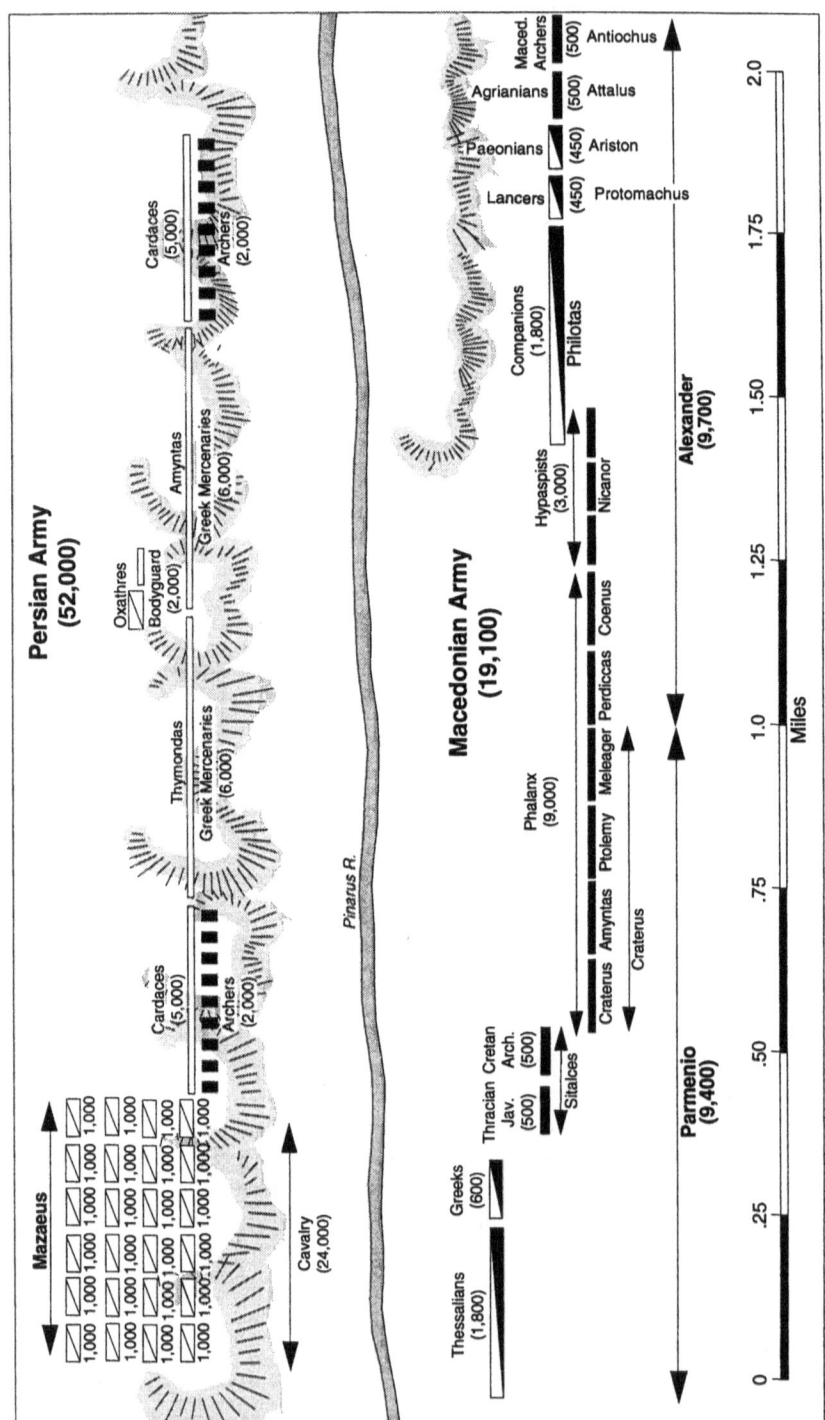

Map 26: Issus

total of 24,000 is a reasonable figure. The Greek mercenaries, still the best part of the Persian army, now fielded a strength of about 12,000. The Cardaces numbered about 10,000, while the Persian levies massed in the second line accounted for another 20,000. A total of 4,000 archers were also present to screen the Cardaces. The two units of Darius' Royal Bodyguards totaled 2,000. In the hills off Alexander's right flank, another 8,000 Persian light infantry might have been deployed.[116]

The frontline strength of the Macedonian army at Issus was fairly close to that it had fielded at the Granicus River. Two new units did, however, join the front line to augment Alexander's missile fire: the Thessalian javelin men and the Cretan archers. The Thracian cavalry and the Greek mercenaries, both of which had been present at Granicus River, appear to have been left behind to hold the Syrian passes. Alexander fielded a total frontline strength at Issus of about 5,100 cavalry and 14,000 infantry.

The left wing of the Persian army consisted of two lines of infantry. Darius took up position with his Royal Bodyguards directly behind the center of the 12,000 Greek mercenaries, who were divided into two units, Thymondas commanding the one on the right and Amyntas the one on the left. The Cardaces were deployed on both outer flanks of the mercenaries. These two 5,000-strong units were comprised of young Persians who had just completed their training. Although they are sometimes referred to as heavy infantry and thought to be an attempt to develop a Persian counterpart to the Greek hoplites, they were probably only peltasts who were unarmored, except for a shield. Darius, in effect, acknowledged the deficiencies of these units by screening them with all his archers in an attempt to break up any attack on them by a concentrated missile fire.

The right wing of the Persian line was comprised of 24,000 heavy cavalry crammed into a deep formation opposite the Macedonian left. In such a constricted frontage, the Persian cavalry must have extended at least 40 ranks deep. Its formation was like a giant battering ram to be used to smash through Parmenio's small cavalry force by sheer weight of numbers. The second line of the Persian army was made up of the almost worthless mass of Asiatic levies. In the foothills behind Alexander's right flank, a large detachment of several thousand light infantry troops were deployed. Their mission, apparently, was to attack the Macedonian army only if its flank or rear were exposed to them in the advance or if their army was retiring in obvious disorder. Overall, the Persian army was packed into a narrow battlefield far too small for its large numbers. This would severely impair the troops' fighting effectiveness and all but prohibit their ability to move laterally.

Alexander's deployment at Issus was almost identical to that at Granicus River. He divided the army into two wings, the left commanded by Parmenio and the right under his personal command. On Parmenio's far left flank, along the sea, the Greek allied cavalry was deployed in advance of the phalanx line. Behind and to the right of them were the Thracian javelin men and Cretan archers, both under Sitalces. Recessed off the right flank of the Cretan archers were Parmenio's taxies of the phalanx commanded by Craterus, Amyntas, Ptolemy, and Meleager. As soon

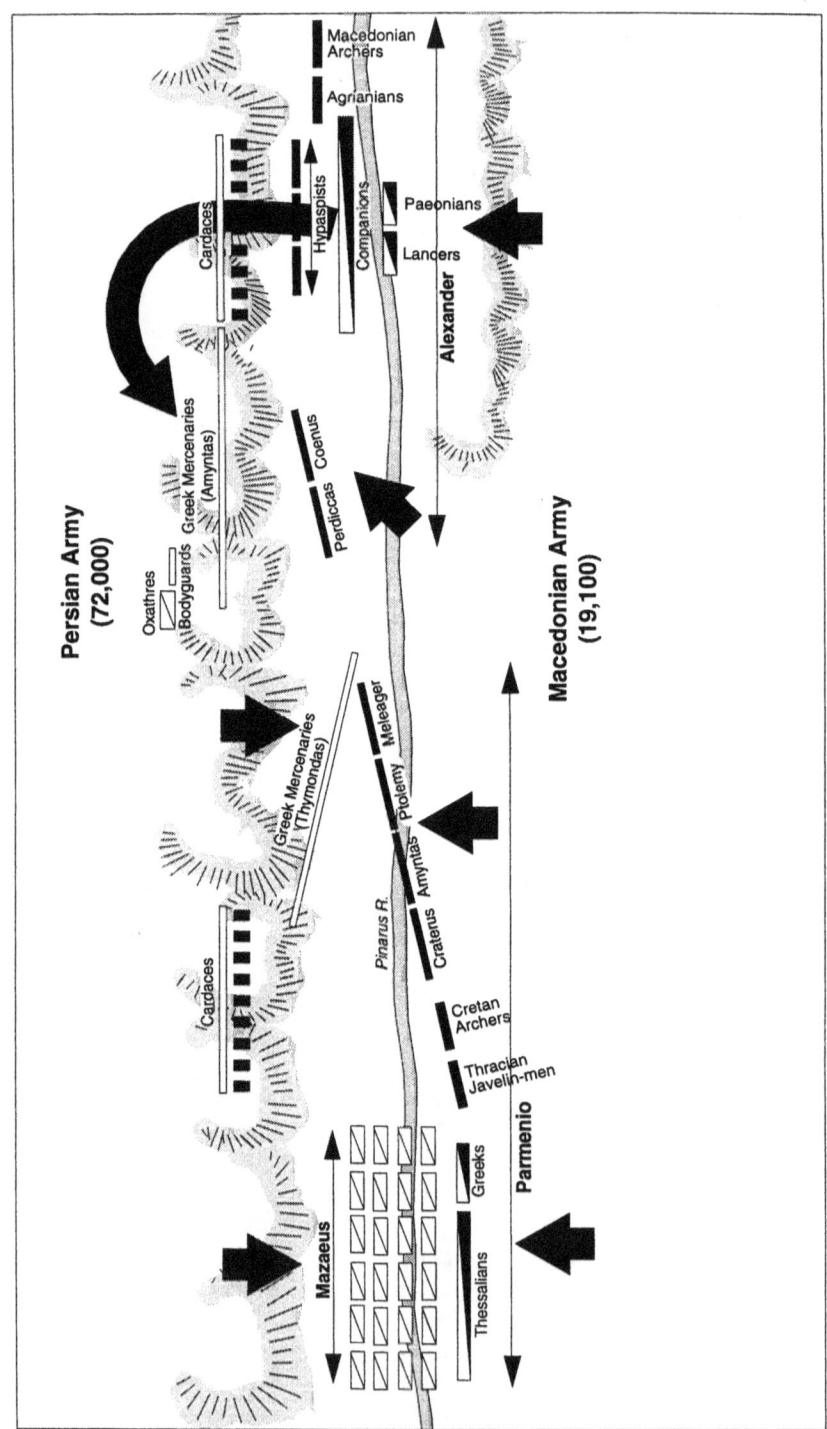

Map 27: Issus

as Alexander observed that the Persians had committed all their cavalry opposite Parmenio's wing, he moved the Thessalian cavalry up on the left flank of the Greek allied cavalry. With the conclusion of this move, Parmenio had 2,400 cavalry and 7,000 infantry at his disposal. On Alexander's right, in advance of his line, were deployed the Macedonian archers, Agrianians, Paeonians, Lancers, and Companion cavalry. Recessed and to the left of the Companions were the hypaspists and the taxies of the phalanx commanded by Coenus and Perdiccas. Alexander's wing totaled 2,700 cavalry and 7,000 infantry.

When reports were received about a Persian force occupying the mountain foothills off his right flank, Alexander detached some Greek mercenaries, Agrianians, archers, and some cavalry to attack them.[117] Upon the force's advance, however, the Persian light infantry withdrew to the crest of the hills. Deducing the unaggressive nature of the Persian force, Alexander reincorporated the majority of troops allocated to the operation back into his battle line, leaving behind a force of only 300 light cavalry to guard the bottom of the foothills.[118] As Alexander had correctly foreseen, the Persians on the hill were content to stay passively in place throughout the battle.

Macedonian Right Flank Alexander led the hypaspists across the Pinarus, surprised the Persian archers opposite him by the speed of his advance, and drove them back on the Cardaces.[119] During the confusion created by the Cardaces attempting to open their tightly packed ranks to allow the archers to pass through, Alexander was able to break quickly through the center of their line. The Companions followed close behind the hypaspists to exploit their breakthrough. The hypaspists passed through the disordered right flank of the shattered Cardaces, while the archers, Lancers, and Paeonians climbed up the bluffs on their right. In effect, Alexander had won the battle within the first few minutes of combat.

Having shattered the flank of the Persian left wing, Alexander deployed his two taxies of the phalanx against Amyntas' front while the hypaspists advanced against his rear. Although fighting in highly disadvantageous circumstances, Amyntas was, nevertheless, able to disengage from the unequal battle and withdraw his mercenaries intact. The Companions, screened on their right flank by the Lancers and Paeonians, moved across the rear of the Greek mercenaries in search of Darius. Oxathres, the Great King's brother, counterattacked Alexander with the Royal Household Cavalry, and a desperate fight ensued, from which Alexander received a slight wound in the thigh. The horses of Darius' heavy chariot became unmanageable, and he transferred to a lighter chariot that had been quickly brought up. Seeing that Alexander's advance on him could not be stopped, Darius fled the battlefield.

Macedonian Center Because Alexander's taxies of the phalanx had advanced so quickly to the oblique right in support of his attack on the Cardaces, a gap had developed between them and Parmenio's slower-moving line. Thymondas, who commanded the Greek mercenaries on the Persian right flank, observed this, saw his opportunity, and charged into it.[120] As a result, in the subsequent heavy fighting, the taxies of Meleager and Ptolemy (son of Seleucus) were slowly driven back down the mud bank and into the river. There Ptolemy (son of Seleucus) fell, along with 120 of his soldiers.[121] The push-back and heavy losses of the two taxies caused them to waver and brought them to the brink of breaking up. In desperation, Parmenio called on Alexander for help.

Macedonian Left Flank The Persian cavalry on the right flank under Mazaeus came down from the bluffs, crossed the Pinarus, and advanced on Parmenio's wing.[122] Although Parmenio's cavalry on the far left was heavily outnumbered by the Persians, the combat advantage actually lay with the Macedonians. The narrow frontage of the wing precluded the Persians from making use of their vast numerical superiority.[123] Although the Persians were able to deploy more cavalry across the front than Parmenio, because of their much denser formation, their massive depth proved to be of no advantage to them. If fact, it was more of a liability because it compressed their troops to such an extent that they were unable to maneuver or use their weapons effectively. The Thessalians, on the other hand, could both freely maneuver to the front and rear and had the skill and room to use their weapons to best advantage. As a result, they were able to inflict heavy casualties on the densely packed and almost helpless Persian cavalry. Although the fighting was fierce and the pressure on them unrelenting, Parmenio's cavalry held its position and conducted what must have been one of the greatest one-sided cavalry fights in history, being outnumbered overall by at least ten to one.

When it came to the attention of the Persian cavalry on the right that their left and left-center had collapsed and Darius had quit the field, they withdrew to avoid encirclement. Once again, however, their heavy armor became a fatal disadvantage because it so slowed their speed that the lighter armed Greek and Thessalian cavalry were easily able to overtake them. Consequently, the fleeing Persian cavalry sustained heavy casualties along the narrow and crowded roads leading to the rear. The mob of the Persian infantry levies of the second line, upon seeing their frontline troops routed, fled for their lives towards the mountains. Many, however, were ridden down by their own cavalry in their panicky flight to the rear. Those surviving the overrun were easily disposed of by the Greek cavalry.

Although Parmenio's taxies of the phalanx rallied after the Greek mercenaries under Thymondas withdrew back up the bluffs, they were too disordered to conduct a pursuit. Instead, they concentrated their efforts on looting Darius' camp. The Greek mercenaries under Thymondas were in a desperate situation. Although they had won their battle against Parmenio's taxies of the phalanx, the Cardaces and Greek mercenaries under Amyntas on their left had been routed, while the Persian cavalry on their right had abandoned them and rode off the battlefield. It was seven miles across a flat plain to the mountain pass with no strong points to rally behind and numerous deep streams to be crossed, each of which were likely to disorder a close-order formation such as theirs. Fortunately for the Persians, because of the rough handling Parmenio's taxies of the phalanx had received at their hands and their great difficulty in climbing the river banks, Thymondas was able to disengage from his front and begin his withdrawal without interference. Alexander had gone after Darius with his Companions while the Thessalians had pursued the Persian cavalry. The Persian archers, screening the Cardaces on their right, accompanied Thymondas' mercenaries and were probably effective in keeping any Greek cavalry troops encountered at a distance with their missile fire. The Greek mercenaries closed ranks and maintained a close-order formation throughout their withdrawal. They did suffer casualties, of course, but most of the unit was able to reach the pass and then make its escape. Darkness soon ended any effective pursuit of the Persian army.

Pursuit of Darius By the time Alexander began his pursuit of Darius, the sun was already setting. Not only did Darius have a head start of over half a mile, but he had unexpectedly taken the mountain path to Dortyol, which was jammed with retreating Persians. The Great King soon abandoned his chariot to proceed on horseback. Although under such circumstances Alexander's prospects of catching him were minimal, he nevertheless continued the pursuit until darkness forced him to return to his army. All he had to show for his effort was the capture of Darius' chariot, bow, and shield. Alexander had covered 25 miles in a chase that ran from the battlefield to Toprakkale, beyond which Darius had turned east into the hills.[124] The Great King rode on all through the night to ensure his escape. The next morning he was joined by the Bactrian cavalry, the remaining Royal Guard, and 2,000 of Thymondas' Greek mercenaries. The force continued eastward to Babylon.

Battle Losses Although Issus was a great victory for Alexander, it undoubtedly fell short of his personal expectations. Darius had, after all, escaped and would doubtless raise yet another army against him from the eastern provinces. This must have been a bitter disappointment for Alexander, especially as he had again personally come so close to capturing the Great King. Also, although the losses of the Persian army were heavy, it had not been eliminated as an effective force. The battle was fought late in the afternoon, and because of the onset of darkness a large portion of the Persian cavalry and Greek mercenaries were able to escape from the battlefield. Aside from this, Alexander's victory at Issus was nothing short of overwhelming. The Persian leaders known to have died in the battle were Rheomithres, who commanded the Persian right at Granicus River; Atizues, satrap of Phrygia; and Sabaces, satrap of Egypt.[125] Macedonian losses in the battle were extremely light, being only 150 cavalry and 300 infantry killed, which included 130 from the phalanx.[126] Another 2,000–4,000 might have been wounded.[127]

Alexander may not have eliminated the Persian army, but he had obviously crippled it as an effective fighting force. Persian casualties were unknown but obviously heavy, totaling no less than 15,000. The levy infantry suffered the greatest number of casualties, most of them occurring during their rout from the battlefield.[128] Although the pursuit was not directed against the Greek mercenaries, they were nonetheless to largely disappear from the Persian army's order of battle. Only 2,000 of Thymondas' Greek mercenaries withdrew to Thapsacus to join up with Darius after the battle. The remainder of his force marched to Cappadocia, where they conducted effective guerrilla raids against Alexander's line of communications for some time. The main group of mercenaries under Amyntas, who were stationed opposite Alexander's wing, withdrew into the hills and then marched to Tripolis in Phoenicia, where they were probably joined by the remaining mercenaries in Persian employ, in addition to a few thousand more who might have been raised and sent there. The total force of 12,000 or so mercenaries then boarded 60 of the 100 ships they had earlier beached, burning the remainder to prevent their use in any pursuit.[129] The force divided: a small group sailed for Cyprus; another force of 8,000 sailed for Crete, where they were employed to assist the Spartans in conquering the island; and a third force of 4,000 under Amyntas sailed to Egypt.[130] There Amyntas attempted to pass himself off as Darius' successor to the satrap of Egypt, who had been killed at the battle of the Granicus River. Taking control of Pelusium on the strength of his assertion, he then marched on Memphis. Having no particular inclination to be ruled by Amyntas, the Egyptians came out of Memphis in force against him but were defeated and driven back into the city. When the Greeks dispersed to loot, however, the Egyptians under Mazaces attacked, defeated, and massacred the mercenaries. Amyntas was killed in the fighting. The mercenaries who had gone to Crete assisted the Spartans in securing the island and then joined them to besiege Megalopolis in the Peloponnese. In the subsequent battle near the city, they were heavily defeated by Antipater. As a condition of their surrender, the Greek mercenaries surviving the battle were required to take service with Alexander.

Results Strategically, Alexander's victory at Issus resulted in the loss to Darius of the western half of his empire. It also opened the way to the coastal cities of Phoenicia which, when conquered, would effectively eliminate the Persian navy as an effective force in the eastern Mediterranean. The Persian fleet received the news of Darius' defeat while at anchor at the island of Siphnos. Although they immediately set sail for Phoenicia in an attempt to suppress the expected rebellions there, they arrived too late to prevent or control them. In 332 B.C., when Alexander began to move south through Phoenicia, all the major allied naval contingents there deserted the Persians to return to their recently freed cities. Shortly after their arrival back home, most of them took service with Alexander.

Even though Darius had sent most of his baggage train to Babylon, the remaining portion captured by the Macedonians on the battlefield amazed them. No less than 3,000 talents in gold was with the train.[131] This was an incredible fortune to Alexander, especially considering that he had begun his Asian campaign with a measly 60 talents in his treasury.[132] Basins and pitchers of gold and silver abounded and there was even a solid gold bathtub. Alexander is reputed to have said, "This, it seems is royalty," which was in obvious contrast to his Spartan standard of living at the time.[133] The noble Persian ladies of the court who had accompanied Darius on his campaign were deprived of all their jewelry and were roughly handled, some being stripped and beaten to the amusement of the Macedonian soldiers. Darius' tent, however, was put under guard, it being considered Alexander's personal property. It contained Darius' mother, Sisygambis; Darius' wife and sister, Stateira; his infant son; and two of his daughters.[134] Alexander treated Darius' family with all the respect due their royal status and realized their value as important political assets he might make effective use of in legitimizing his rule over the Persian Empire.

Generalship   The quality of generalship Darius displayed both strategically and tactically is best described as incompetent. His strategic decisions seem to have been guided largely by impulse and impatience, while tactically he greatly hampered the performance of his army by his poor battlefield selection, an almost complete lack of initiative on the battlefield, and faulty troop deployment.

Darius had decided to depart Babylon before the cavalry from his northwest satrapies arrived. There was no particular reason to leave exactly when he did. Granted, he might lose much of northern Phoenicia to Alexander, but those cities that did stay loyal to Persia, such as Gaza and Tyre, could be expected to delay the Macedonian army almost indefinitely. Up to that time, history had demonstrated that Greek sieges were seldom successful. Recent examples were provided by Philip II's failure to take Perinthus and Byzantium and Alexander's inability to fully capture Halicarnassus. The Macedonian army would, therefore, probably be pinned in place by a long siege with a powerful Persian army in the final stages of mobilization against him. It would have made far more sense for Darius to muster his entire strength for what he knew must be the decisive battle for the western portion of his empire. As events transpired, however, Darius had too much cavalry for the battle at Issus and not enough at Gaugamela. Had Darius, however, chosen to fight his battle at Sochi, as he had initially planned, instead of Issus, he might have found the additional cavalry to have been decisive.

It is puzzling why Darius did not exercise some initiative once he reached Issus and send his missile troops ahead to occupy the Pillars of Jonah Pass in Alexander's rear. In light of the fact that Alexander camped in the pass at night, Darius could have inflicted heavy casualties on him. There was no other way back to Issus for Alexander, and he would have had no option but to fight his way through the pass to restore his line of communications, regardless of the cost. Instead of acting decisively and sending a harassing force to the pass, Darius, true to form, merely passively waited for Alexander to make his appearance at the Pinarus River.

The decision to take along the Persian infantry levies does not appear to have been well thought out by Darius. At Granicus River the levies had achieved absolutely nothing. Asiatic infantry was composed of poor military material; the troops were virtually untrained, with inferior arms, no protective armor, little fighting efficiency, and low morale. Their staying power was nil, and at the first setback they usually broke, threw down their arms, and fled as fast as their feet could carry them. They were absolutely worthless on any battlefield with the Greeks and only provided clutter and additional mouths to feed. It is unlikely that militarily they were worth the food that they consumed, and they only appear to have placed an unnecessary burden on the Persian logistics. It was never clear exactly what role Darius expected them to play because they were always placed well back from the front line. It is possible that he envisioned them as being useful in the pursuit of an already defeated and demoralized Macedonian army, although his cavalry would have been a far more effective force for that type of mission.

Leaving the Sochi plain and seeking Alexander was one of Darius' biggest mistakes. He was repeatedly warned to remain there by Amyntas, his Macedonian-born adviser, who told him that Alexander would seek the him out and fight him no matter where he was. This was sound advice, and Darius would have done well to follow it. The open plains at Sochi were exactly suited for the kind of army that he had — a large cavalry force. The position would have given him the room to envelop Alexander's much smaller force. It would have allowed his cavalry the distance and level terrain over which to conduct proper charges to exploit their shock value. True, over time Sochi would become a logistically difficult position for Darius, but there is no indication that this was an immediate issue and it would have been much less of one had he left his hordes of worthless infantry levies behind. If Darius had just stayed put a few days longer, Alexander would have undoubtedly fought him at Sochi. In fact, as Darius moved north from there along the east side of the Amanus Mountains, Alexander was also in motion south, but along the coast to Beilan Pass. It is interesting to note how quickly Darius abandoned his advance on Alexander. Once Issus was reached, he all too readily slipped back into a defensive posture, which was much more agreeable to his preference.

One may wonder why Darius chose Issus for a battle. True, the battlefield did have significant defensive advantages. Its flanks were anchored by the sea and mountains and could not be turned. Since Darius had the larger army with a huge cavalry component, however, one would have expected that he would have been more concerned with turning Alexander's flanks than with protecting his own against such an attack by a smaller Macedonian force. Although the Pinarus River was not a significant obstacle in itself, its steep eastern banks were. These advantages of terrain, however, were more than offset by three major disadvantages. First, although Issus had good natural defensive advantages, Darius did not have enough effective infantry to man the position properly. He was forced to use the shaky Cardaces to prolong the line of the Greek mercenaries. This was to have fatal consequences when the Cardaces opposite Alexander were unable to pass the archers through their ranks without themselves becoming disordered. Second, the narrowness of the battlefield precluded a full deployment of Darius' more numerous troops and therefore actually favored the Macedonians who, man-for-man, were much more combat effective than the Persians in a straight-up fight. The dense formations of the Persians largely precluded the effective use of their weaponry and denied them any lateral movement. Third, the anchored flanks of the Persians prevented them from conducting any encircling operations. This was of tremendous benefit to Alexander because he did not have to detach any cavalry on secondary operations to guard his flanks. It would have proved much more effective for Darius' army if he had chosen a position on the Deli Cayi River, about seven miles north of the Pinarus. That location provided twice the frontage of the Pinarus and would have allowed him to deploy his army fully in line. It would also have provided his cavalry with the proper room both to maneuver and to use their weapons effectively.[135] Darius' rejection of the Deli Cayi was probably based on the fact that the banks of that river were less of an obstacle than those of the Pinarus.

7: THE WESTERN PERSIAN EMPIRE

Despite the fact that Darius' plan was a good one, in fact a reversed mirror image of Alexander's, it did not suit his army on this battlefield. He hoped to defend the Pinarus River with his infantry on his left flank and center and use the cavalry on his right flank to break through Alexander's line. Pinned in place by the Greek mercenaries and Cardaces, the phalanx would then be rolled up from left to right by the Persian cavalry. Fine in theory, but in practice the Persian cavalry troops were fatally handicapped by their tactical deployment. They were squeezed into an extremely narrow front along the sea and forced to deploy in great depth, all but prohibiting the very tactical maneuvering necessary to execute their plan. They could only ride straight ahead and would be unable to maneuver against Alexander's left flank. If this wasn't bad enough, they had to cross a stream with a stony riverbed and low but steep banks. After coming out on dry land, likely disordered, they would undoubtedly be hit by a charge from the Greek allied and Thessalian cavalry. The Persian cavalry entered combat under just about every imaginable handicap that could be devised, and it is not really surprising that the heavily outnumbered Greeks and Thessalians were able to fight them to a standstill.

Although it might be true that Alexander's final deployment on the right flank was screened from Darius by a ridge, there were two clues that should have alerted the Great King to what was occurring. First, at the Granicus, Alexander's main attack had been on the right flank and had been delivered by the Companion cavalry. Second, neither the Companion cavalry nor Alexander were in evidence on the left flank or in the center. A simple deduction would have been that they were both probably deployed in the "dead ground" for an attack on Darius' left flank.[136] With the large number of excess cavalry on his right flank, there was no reason why Darius could not have taken a sufficient force from there to have at least offset Alexander's 2,700 cavalry opposite his left flank. Alexander's Agrianians and hypaspists crossed the river at the run on a wide front in advance of the Companions who were restricted to using the two small fords there. If this advance infantry had been met by a heavily armed and determined cavalry charge, the Macedonians might have had a hard, if not impossible, time expanding their bridgehead atop the bluffs. Any failure of the hypaspists to advance would have bunched up and disordered the Companions coming up behind them. Interestingly enough, Darius appears to have initially had his cavalry deployed on his left flank but later thought that the two small fords and rough ground there would preclude large-scale cavalry operations. He thus redeployed them on his right flank, next to the sea. One must conclude that the decision to redeploy all his cavalry was a major error made by Darius, who was evidently obsessed to a dangerous degree with overwhelming the Macedonian left flank.

Darius' placement of the Cardaces in the front line also turned out to be a fatal error. They were a significant liability there, providing a point of weakness Alexander could always exploit. The mercenaries would have given Alexander a stiff fight at the riverbank, and considering the difficulty the phalanx had in climbing the bluffs opposite the Persian center, the Cardaces might have put in a better showing there, as the usual tactical tricks Alexander used out in the less obstructed ground on the Persian left flank would have not been possible there. The deployment of the Cardaces must have been made under the erroneous assumption that they would be able to hold their own against the Macedonian cavalry, it generally being virtually impossible to induce horses to charge well-ordered, close-order infantry. Darius, however, may later have had second thoughts on their ability to sustain the impact of a charge when he stationed his archers to screen them. It was obviously hoped that they would break up any enemy attack against the Cardaces by heavy missile fire. Also, the Cardaces were peltasts who actually traditionally fought in an open-order formation. At Issus, however, they were, like the cavalry, crammed into a narrow frontage that would greatly hinder them in the effective use of their weapons.

Although Darius managed to surprise Alexander strategically by unexpectedly showing up across his line of communications, he threw away all the advantages of this surprise by his subsequent poor choice of a battlefield, by the numerous tactical errors in judgment he made in the deployment of his troops, and in the execution of the battle. Failure to deduce Alexander's attack on his left flank, the overcommitment of cavalry on his right flank, a complete absence of cavalry on his left flank, and the placement of the Cardaces on the outer flanks of the Greek mercenaries were all significant deployment errors. Having his cavalry execute a crossing of the Pinarus was also not well thought out because they were disordered and subjected to a counterattack by the Thessalians while virtually stationary. It appears that Darius had little, if any, tactical ability and chose to ignore whatever sound military advice he might have received. An inferior army with incompetent leadership is a certain prescription for disaster, and it is no surprise that the Persians were frequently their own worst enemy on the battlefield against Alexander.

Alexander, of course, was his usual brilliant self, despite his rather rocky start. Losing track of the Persian army initially was a major mistake that could have proved disastrous. It forced him to fight a life and death battle for his line of communications; had he lost this battle, his army might well have been reduced to starvation. Except for this mistake and his mishandling of the Greek mercenaries, Alexander cannot be faulted, however, for how he then conducted this battle.

Once Alexander was aware of the presence of the Persian army at Issus he quickly retraced his steps, being careful not to tire his men out with a forced-march. Even so, his arrival of the Pinarus River battlefield caught the Persians by surprise and in the midst of deploying. Alexander then prepared two clever traps, one on each flank. On his left he deployed only a weak cavalry force to draw off the Persian cavalry there.[137] It was deceptive in apparent strength only, as Alexander was able to move up his Thessalian cavalry quickly in support. Although the Persians could still commit twice the frontline strength against Parmenio's cavalry, the dense Persian deployment would both restrict their maneuverability and compromise the effective use of their weapons. Alexander was clearly taking a gamble, but not as big a one as it appeared, considering the disparity in fighting effectiveness between his cavalry on that flank and the Persians'. Alexander's second trap was his secret deployment of his main assault force on his right flank. In the "dead ground," outside the observation of the Persians, he carefully adjusted his deployment to fit the situation across the river that his officers were able to report accurately to him from their positions of observation atop the ridge in front. When Alexander emerged into the open with the force he had deployed there, it was too late for the Persians to redeploy against it, even had they been inclined to do so.

The plan Alexander devised against the Cardaces on the Persian left flank was bold. It was an axiom in ancient warfare that cavalry could not break well-ordered, defending heavy infantry. How then was he to prevail against the Cardaces and at the same time contend with the disorder caused by his crossing of the river and climb up the riverbank? His solution was to force the Persian screening archers themselves to disorder the closely packed ranks of the Cardaces and then hit them with an attack before they could reform. In place of the cavalry, who could only slowly cross the Pinarus at two small fords, Alexander would use his peltasts — hypaspists — to cross the stream quickly on a wide front. The plan worked exactly as anticipated. The hypaspists surprised the Persian archers by the rapidity of their crossing of the Pinarus, forcing them to disorder the ranks of the close-packed Cardaces as they attempted to pass through them. In the midst of this confusion, the Companions crossed the stream, moved through the hypaspists in front of them, and rode into the disordered Cardaces, breaking their ranks. Alexander then quickly organized an attack by his Companions on the left flank and rear of Amyntas' Greek mercenaries and broke them. His degree of control over his Companion cavalry in the midst of battle has probably never been equaled by any other cavalry commander, ancient or modern. He could literally reorganize and reorient them at a moment's notice to take advantage of any unexpected tactical situation. This was a powerful advantage that would win more than one battle for him.

Although Alexander's personal attack on Darius and his relentless pursuit of him off the battlefield may seem somewhat reckless, it must be realized that with Darius' death or capture the Persian empire would be Alexander's not only by right of conquest but by right of succession as well. Alexander obviously thought that this legitimization would bring the fighting in Asia to an end. In point of fact, the bonds that held the Persian Empire together were not as strong as Alexander assumed, and most of the satraps would probably have been forced to swear allegiance to Alexander by military coercion, regardless of Darius' status.

After his defeat at Issus, Darius fled east to Babylon. Instead of pursuing him, however, Alexander marched south to Phoenicia.

Phoenicia

Aradus/Marathus

En route to Aradus, Alexander was met by Straton (son of Gerostratus), his father (the king) being away in service with the Persian fleet. He presented Alexander with a golden crown and surrendered to him both Aradus, which was an island,

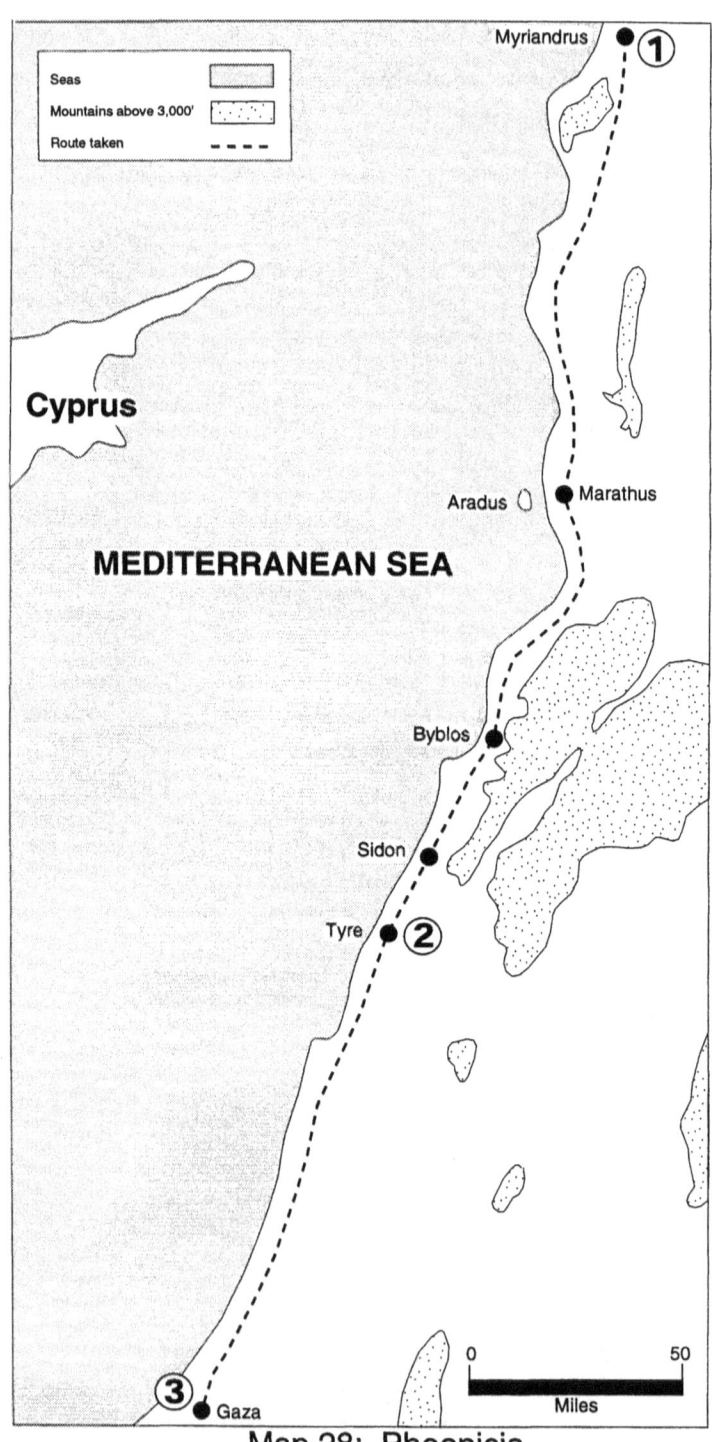

Map 28: Phoenicia

and Marathus, on the mainland. While at Marathus, Alexander received Darius' first peace proposal, offering an alliance with him.[138] Alexander, of course, refused it. Learning that Darius had placed Cophen (son of Cophen) in charge of his field army treasure and had sent it to Damascus, Alexander detached Parmenio there with a force to take possession of it while he marched off with the remaining army to Byblos.[139]

Byblos

Byblos submitted to Alexander upon his approach. Alexander then marched on to Sidon.

Sidon

The citizens of Sidon enthusiastically welcomed Alexander, their prime motivation being their hatred of the Persians. They had been in revolt against Persia only 10 years earlier and more recently had endured the forced billeting of Persian troops and the heavy financial burden of providing supplies to the Persian army. Alexander subsequently removed Sidon's king, also called Straton, from his throne because he had only submitted at the request of his people rather than from his own inclination. Hephaestion was requested to choose a new ruler for the city. At the time he was the guest of two young Sidonians distinguished above all their countrymen. Asking for their opinion on the matter, Hephaestion was told that they both endorsed Ballonymus as the new ruler for the city.[140] Although Ballonymus had a distant connection with the Sidonians' royal family, he humbly tended a garden in the suburbs. Alexander interviewed the prospective king and was clearly impressed with the stoic manner with which he endured his privation. Ballonymus was subsequently confirmed as king of Sidon. Alexander then marched on Tyre.

Siege of Tyre

Alexander's strategy in his campaign along the Phoenician coast was to deprive the Persian fleet of its naval bases. Without dockyards new ships could not be built and existing ships could not be properly maintained in a serviceable condition. The Persians also would be unable to recruit experienced crews in any numbers, and existing Phoenician crews would probably desert as soon as their home cities fell to Alexander. It would therefore be only a matter of time before the Persian navy would cease to exist as an effective force.

At the beginning of Alexander's Asian campaign, the Persian fleet held naval superiority in the Aegean. It was commanded by Memnon of Rhodes, a Greek mercenary of wide experience and considerable military ability. The sailors of the Persian navy were clearly superior to most Greeks in seamanship, the Phoenician crews

---

1. Alexander receives Darius' first peace proposal. 2. Alexander captures Tyre after a siege of seven months. Alexander receives Darius' second peace proposal. 3. Alexander captures Gaza after a siege of two months.

having no equal for their naval expertise except for the Athenians. In comparison, the Greeks serving with Alexander's navy came primarily from land powers and had few, if any, nautical skills. In any naval ship-to-ship action, the Persian fleet would clearly have a significant advantage over the Greeks. The transport capacity of the 400 ships of the fully mobilized Persian navy was considerable, and it was clearly within their ability to threaten several strategic areas in the Aegean that were critically important to Alexander.[141] The Persians might sail to mainland Greece to incite either Sparta or Athens to lead the city-states there in an open revolt against Macedonian rule. The crossing at the Hellespont might be interdicted, breaking Alexander's communications with Macedonia and cutting him off from access to Greek and Macedonian reinforcements. Landings might also be made on islands throughout the Aegean in an attempt to destabilize cities currently friendly or neutral to Alexander. Over all, Alexander would run a considerable risk if he left the Persian fleet free to stir up trouble whenever and wherever it chose. As Alexander had little chance of defeating the Persian fleet in open battle, however, a fact which he clearly recognized when he disbanded his allied Greek fleet of 160 triremes at Mytilene, he would have to rely on his army to deprive the Persians of all their port cities along the Phoenician coast.[142]

To allow any Phoenician coastal city to remain independent of his direct control, that is, unoccupied by a Macedonian garrison, would be to leave a constant threat behind that might either imperil a move south into Egypt or east in pursuit of Darius. If Alexander met with some reverse or if at some later time a port city should choose to cooperate willingly with the Persians, it could provide a useful base of operations for the Persian fleet to cut his vital line of communications to Macedonia or reassert Persian control over those areas that the Macedonians had conquered. This was especially true of Tyre, the most important Persian naval base in the eastern Mediterranean after Halicarnassus. For this reason, Alexander refused to compromise with the city; either it would consent to a peaceful occupation by his troops or it would be taken by assault. He would allow them no middle ground.

When Alexander arrived before the city, the reigning king of Tyre, Azemilk, was away leading a major portion of the city's navy in service with the Persian fleet. Ruling the city in his absence, his son, the crown prince, immediately opened negotiations with Alexander. Although Alexander was given a gold crown and offered the allegiance of the city, he knew that Tyre had in mind neutrality rather than submission. In order to draw out what he believed to be the true intentions of the Tyrians, Alexander expressed a desire to sacrifice in the city's temple dedicated to their god Melkart, widely identified with his ancestor Heracles.[143] It so happened that the main festival of Melkart was then in progress, but that only the king of Tyre was allowed to make the kind of sacrifice that Alexander requested. If Tyre had acceded to his request, it would have been tantamount to acknowledging Alexander formally as their king. As a compromise, the Tyrians declared the neutrality of their city to both Macedonians and Persians, suggesting that Alexander offer his sacrifice at the temple dedicated to Heracles at old Tyre on the mainland. At this suggestion, Alexander angrily dismissed the city's ambassadors, issuing strong threats for them to change their minds on the issue. The Tyrians were obviously trying to play both sides at the same time until it became clear whether the Macedonians or Persians would prevail.

Alexander almost certainly realized the dilemma in which he placed Tyre, for in all likelihood he had devised this strategy in cooperation with his new-found allies the Sidonians, the bitter trade rivals of Tyre. Tyre's reply would either enable Alexander to obtain his desired sovereignty over the city or it would publicly insult him and give him a legitimate excuse for war with Tyre. Angered over Alexander's threats, Tyre, contrary to all civilized protocol at the time, seized Alexander's heralds and threw them down from the city's walls to their deaths in full view of the Macedonian army.[144] This foolish act not only confirmed Alexander's mistrust of the Tyrians' motives but incited his army to exact retribution at their first opportunity.

To anyone but Alexander, Tyre would have seemed impregnable. The city stood on a walled island separated from the mainland by half a mile of open sea.[145] The shallow mud near the mainland dropped to a depth of three fathoms, or 18 feet, near the city.[146] Strong southwest winds frequently produced high and choppy waves that were likely to swamp any amphibious assault attempt. Having disbanded his navy at Mytilene, Alexander was unable to prevent the Persian fleet from resupplying Tyre with soldiers, armaments, and provisions by sea at will. Although a large portion of Tyre's navy was serving with the Persian fleet, the naval squadron stationed at the city consisted of 80 triremes.[147] In addition, there was every reason to expect additional naval assistance from Carthage, which was a colony of Tyre.[148]

A three-mile wall surrounded Tyre. It rose up directly from the water to a height of 70 feet on the eastern side of the city facing the mainland.[149] The city's population of 40,000 would provide an adequate force of soldiers to man its walls. Because space in the city was in short supply, the houses were built closely together and were often several stories tall. Should the need arise, the structures would provide a ready source of construction material for any repairs to the walls or additional fortifications that might be needed. The city contained two major harbors: Sidon facing north and Egypt facing south.

Tyre was at this time the greatest commercial trading city in the world. Its policy was to keep on good terms with everyone to facilitate the continued development of its extensive commercial trading network. From its trading profits, the city grew both wealthy and powerful. Tyre's food, all of which had to be imported, was obtained largely from Egypt, Judea, and Phoenicia and was usually transported to the city on its own fleet of ships.

For 13 years in the sixth century B.C., Tyre had successfully withstood a siege by Nebuchadnezzar, the king of Babylon.[150] As Alexander had no fleet with which to assault Tyre amphibiously and his siege artillery was ineffective at the half-mile distance the city lay from the mainland, there seemed to be no way that he could effectively blockade, bombard, or assault the city. The case for Alexander being able to capture Tyre was not convincing by historical precedent. The Greeks in their various wars were rarely able to take a walled city except by starvation or treachery. The Macedonians themselves would have all too clearly remembered Philip II's unsuccessful attempts to besiege Perinthus and Byzantium under more favorable circumstances than existed at Tyre. Both those cities had been accessible by land, and Philip had a small navy at hand, two advantages Alexander did not possess. Even then, however, Philip had been unable to capture either city.

Alexander opened the siege by ordering the construction of one of the most famous moles in ancient history.[151] The mole was nothing more than a causeway running from the mainland to the walls of New Tyre. It was mistakenly thought at the time that only from the end of the mole would it be possible for the Macedonians to breach the walls and assault the city. An adequate supply of nearby stone and rubble for the construction of the mole was available at Old Tyre on the mainland, while timber could be obtained from the forests of the Beqaa Valley in Lebanon. The construction process called for stones to be dropped into the water so that they would sink to the mud on the bottom. Wooden pylons were then pushed into the mud alongside the stones to anchor them in place. As the level of stones rose above the surface of the water, a layer of earth was added to provide a level causeway. To prevent the structure from being washed away by the continuous eroding action of the waves, additional wooden piles were driven into the mud along the outer sides of the mole. Thousands of men in the surrounding towns and villages were pressed into work details to assist the Macedonians in the construction.

At first the Tyrians were inclined to treat the mole as a joke. But in the shallow water near the mainland construction proceeded rapidly and the threat began to be taken much more seriously. When the mole approached Tyre, however, the sea deepened and progress slowed down to a crawl. Ton after ton of rock was dumped into the sea only to disappear from sight without any noticeable effect. Timber supplies also slowed down because of constant attacks on the work details by Arabs.

Although the mole might enable Alexander's army to approach the walls of Tyre, the Macedonians would sustain prohibitive casualties from enemy missile fire if their assaults were launched out in the open. To provide the necessary support to the attack, two of the ancient world's largest siege towers up to that time were built, each 70 feet tall. Their wooden frames were covered in lime, and animal hides were hung on them to absorb the impact of the missiles and stones fired by the enemy siege-engines and as protection against combustion. The various levels of the towers were crammed full of archers, and catapults were mounted within and atop them. The towers were wheeled up to the point of assault and made ready to clear the walls of enemy defenders by heavy missile fire. Once that was done or the enemy missile fire was diverted exclusively to the towers, the covered rams and bores could move up and begin battering the walls. If the defenders were forced back from the wall, a drawbridge might be lowered from the tower to allow a storming party to assault it from the top. Otherwise, the drawbridge would be lowered over the breach.

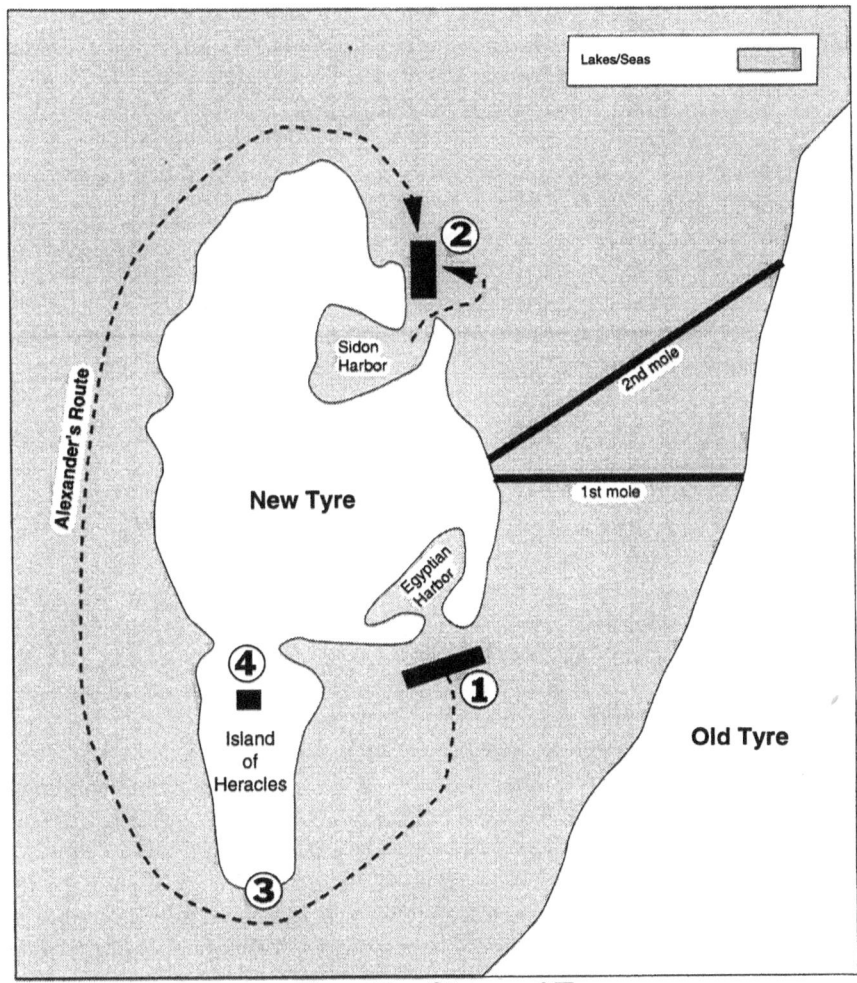

Map 29: Siege of Tyre

1. The Phoenician fleet blockades the harbor. 2. The Tyrians sortie against the Cyprian fleet. 3. Alexander breaches the wall and enters the city. 4. The king of Tyre and the Carthaginian ambassadors take refuge in the Temple of Heracles.

The first action the Tyrians took against the mole was to attempt to clear the workmen off it. They loaded up eight triremes with archers, slingers, and light catapults, concentrating a heavy missile fire into the thousands of unprotected workers on the mole and inflicting heavy casualties upon them. In response, Alexander immediately had a tall palisade constructed along the sides of the mole and set up his two huge wooden towers at its end to provide some effective missile fire down on the enemy ships.

The Tyrians now decided to launch a fire ship against the mole in an attempt to burn both it and the wooden towers, which were now seriously interfering with their ability to bring the mole under missile fire. An old horse transport was crammed full of dry firewood, its sails and ropes were doused with tar and pitch, and jars of highly flammable naphtha were hung from its yardarms. The ship was ballasted at the stern so that its prow would ride up over the edge of the mole on impact and push up against the base of the towers. The idea was to create a fire so fierce that it would be impossible to extinguish.

When a strong onshore wind was blowing against the mole, a partial crew was put on board the fire ship and two triremes hooked up tow ropes to it. The triremes rowed up to their maximum speed, cast off the tow ropes, and veered off to port and starboard. The crew on the fire ship quickly ignited its contents, jumped overboard, and swam back to the safety of the nearby triremes. The now blazing transport crashed into the mole near the wooden towers, edged up over its side, and became engulfed in flames, quickly setting on fire both the towers and mole. Two triremes filled with Tyrians then came up alongside the mole and began firing on any workers attempting to extinguish the flames and anyone attempting to escape from the burning towers. Once the towers were burning, a large number of Tyrian citizens rowed over to the mole in any available small craft. One group began tearing down the palisade built alongside the mole and then set fire to any catapults undamaged by the fire. The other group attacked the unarmed workers who had been carrying rocks from the mainland. Having achieved their objective, the Tyrians quickly withdrew. The entire length of the mole was on fire and hundreds of workers lay dying or dead.

Immediately after the fire burned itself out, a fierce storm raged over the mole. Great sections of it were torn away by the violence of the waves and many of the largest stones tumbled into the surrounding sea. Within the space of a few hours, several months of backbreaking work had been largely obliterated. As depressing as the devastation must have been, it did not deter Alexander. He immediately gave orders for the construction of a new mole, this time facing directly into the wind instead of perpendicular to it.[152] He expanded the mole's width to 200 feet to accommodate two additional siege towers at its end and strengthened its foundation by jamming entire trees into the rocks, branches and all. Work also began on the construction of four new siege towers.

It now became clear to Alexander that he would be unable to defend the mole without a navy. As long as the Tyrians had command of the sea, it was just too easy for them to continue to launch such highly devastating attacks at will. Leaving Perdiccas and Craterus in command of the mole, Alexander returned to Sidon with the Agrianians and hypaspists in an attempt to raise a navy. Luck was with him, for the breakup of the Persian fleet provided him with exactly the force that he needed. Upon hearing that their cities were in Macedonian hands, Enylus, king of Byblos, and Gerostratus, king of Aradus, deserted the Persian fleet with their naval contingents, returned to their home cities, and promptly placed their ships at Alexander's disposal. Alexander now had a naval force of 80 warships.[153] Shortly thereafter, 10 triremes arrived from Rhodes, 10 from Soli and Lycia, and one from

Macedonia.[154] A day or so later, the king of Cyprus, convinced that Alexander's victory at Issus signaled Darius' eventual defeat, arrived with 120 ships.[155] Within the short space of two weeks, Alexander had gained naval supremacy in the eastern Mediterranean, despite the return to Tyre of Azemilk with the Tyrian ships formerly in service with the Persian navy.[156]

Alexander embarked his hypaspists aboard his new navy ships, weighed anchor, and headed for Tyre in close-order formation. He commanded the right wing of the fleet, while Pnytagoras, the king of Cyprus, and Craterus jointly commanded the left. Upon hearing of his approach, the Tyrian navy sailed to intercept and do battle with what they assumed would be only the Sidonian fleet. Upon seeing Alexander's unexpectedly large naval force, however, they turned round and began to head back to Tyre. Observing that the Tyrian ships were heavily loaded with troops, Alexander thought that if he could beat them back to their harbors and prevent them from reentering, the city might quickly fall to him.[157] A desperate race now began. Three Tyrian ships, although they sunk one after the other, managed to hold off the leading elements of Alexander's fleet just long enough for the Tyrian navy to reach the safety of its harbors. At both the Sidon and Egyptian harbors, the Tyrians aligned their ships across the narrow harbor entrance, bows facing outward and crammed full of soldiers. Alexander saw that nothing more could be accomplished there and sailed to the mole, where he anchored his fleet. The next day his navy began the blockade of Tyre. The Cyprian fleet under Andromachus took station opposite Sidon Harbor in the north, while the Phoenicians blockaded Egyptian Harbor in the south.[158] The Macedonian and Rhodian ships stayed back to cover the mole.

Relieved from constant Tyrian naval interference, work on the mole proceeded much more quickly. The fire damage was repaired, the width doubled, and the mole now began to move steadily closer to Tyre. When a violent gale blew up from the northwest, Alexander's foresight in floating a number of giant untrimmed Lebanon cedars on the windward side of the mole before the full fury of the storm hit resulted in only minor damage to it. That which occurred was quickly repaired, and the construction had soon progressed to the extent that the mole was at last within missile range of Tyre.

The Tyrians had observed that the Cyprian fleet withdrew every day at noon from their blockade of Sidon Harbor to purchase, cook, and eat their meal ashore.[159] Only a single picket squadron remained on station to sound the alarm and engage any attackers. At about this same time, Alexander, who was usually present with the Phoenician fleet blockading Egyptian Harbor, would go ashore during the noontime heat to take a nap. To the Tyrians this seemed an ideal opportunity for a sortie against the Cyprians. Their hope was to duplicate Lysander's success over the Athenian fleet at the battle of Aegospotami in 405 B.C. When the Athenians had beached their ships on shore in search of food, Lysander, a Spartan general commanding the allied Greek fleet, made a surprise attack and quickly overpowered the picket squadron, capturing virtually the entire Athenian fleet of 160 triremes, along with most of their crews. If the Tyrians were able to inflict a defeat of this magnitude on the Cypriots, they might not only break the blockade but again be able to resume naval operations against the mole.

The Tyrians concealed their preparations inside Sidon Harbor behind the opened sails of their fleet. Unobserved, they assembled 13 of their best ships — 3 quinqueremes, 3 quadriremes, and 7 triremes — manned by their most experienced naval crews and an elite marine force specially chosen for their shipboard fighting skills.[160] The sortie force slipped silently out of the harbor in single file. Upon sighting the Cyprian picket ships, they raised a cheer, increased their rowing speed, and attacked. Three Cyprian quinquereme picket ships were immediately sunk, while the remainder of the squadron was driven up on the beach and disabled.[161] The onshore confusion was enormous as half-crewed ships pushed off to engage the attacking Tyrian naval force. Both crews and soldiers fought off an attack of the Tyrian marines along the shore who were attempting to burn the beached Cypriot ships.

Although Alexander had gone ashore as usual that day, he had, for some unknown reason, quickly returned to the Phoenician fleet on station off Egyptian Harbor. A signal from the mole alerted him of the situation at Sidon Harbor. Taking with him a number of quinqueremes that were fully manned and five triremes, he sailed round the southern tip of Tyre and along its west coast to assist the Cypriot fleet.[162] The Tyrians manning the walls saw Alexander's movement and frantically attempted to signal their sortie force, but in the confusion and noise of battle they were neither seen nor heard. Although it took Alexander the better part of an hour to arrive, when he made his appearance the Tyrians were still closely engaged with the Cypriot fleet. A few Tyrian ships spotted Alexander's approach and managed to escape back to the safety of Sidon Harbor, but most of the ships of the sortie force were unable to disengage and were helplessly rammed by Alexander's force from either stern or broadside and were sunk. Of those Tyrian ships able to flee, a quinquereme and a quadrireme were captured right in front of the entrance to the harbor. Although most of the ships of the sortie force were either sunk or captured, the loss in life of crew and marines was small, most being able to swim back to the city through the harbor.

The completion of the mole enabled Alexander to begin bombarding Tyre. Catapults of various sizes were brought forward for the bombardment, while archers from the towers proceeded to clear the defenders from the walls. Ships stationed round the island were also equipped with catapults. At the signal, Tyre was brought under fire from both the mole and the surrounding sea. Under cover of the bombardment by the catapults, the seaborne rams moved up. These were waterlogged or otherwise unserviceable ships tied together in groups of two. A large platform was suspended atop them on which the ram was placed. The ram was housed in a structure covered by hides as protection against missile fire and combustion. The ram-ships were run directly under the walls and anchored on all four sides to ensure the maximum stability of the platform. On the mole the rams were wheeled up to the walls. Troop assault ships stood by. Like the ram-ships, they were also tied together in pairs, but on the overhead platform suspended between the ships, the assaulting troops were deployed in place of the ram. Scaling ladders were attached to the ships, and some even had towers.[163]

The Tyrians did everything possible to frustrate the bombardment. They tried to break the impact of the stones against the walls by hanging down hides sewn together and stuffed with seaweed. Wooden towers were built on the walls to gain a height advantage against both the towers on the ships and those on the mole. It was hoped that they would suppress Alexander's heavy missile fire. At every point where the masonry weakened, the Tyrians quickly rushed to repair it. Although the bombardment continued throughout the day, not a single breach was made anywhere along the walls. Despite this lack of success, Alexander had decided to attempt a night attack on the city. As the assault was being prepared, however, a thick fog rolled in, followed by a gale. Several of the relatively unstable floating rams and assault ships were subsequently battered to pieces by the storm. The attack had to be canceled, and although only a few of the ram and assault ships had been destroyed, most of the fleet suffered heavy damage.

The water directly beneath the city's walls was relatively shallow. The Tyrians dismantled several houses and dropped large stones over the walls in an attempt to obstruct the floating rams from closing up to them. In response, Alexander brought in transport vessels with derricks and began clearing the stones away. These vessels were relatively unstable unless firmly anchored. The Tyrians sent specially constructed armored triremes to cut the rope cables to their anchors, thereby setting the salvage ships adrift. Alexander also armored a number of triremes and stationed them around the salvage vessels. The Tyrians then used divers to cut the anchor ropes. Alexander countered by replacing the ropes with chains. The laborious work of lifting the stone blocks out of the shallow water then proceeded unhindered by attacks from the Tyrians. Before long, the stones were completely cleared away, and once again Alexander's ships were able to anchor directly beneath the walls of the city.

Alexander's siege towers were wheeled into position opposite the walls. The floating rams took station around the city, and the mobile rams on the mole stood by. Troops and assault ships moved into final position. The long-awaited attempt to storm Tyre was finally about to begin. In these last moments before the assault, Tyre had been informed that it would face the ordeal alone. Both Carthage and the Persians had declined to provide any aid. The Persian navy was concentrating its efforts on conducting an offensive against the northern Aegean islands, while Carthage decided not to back what it considered to be a lost cause. Upon their return to Carthage, its ambassadors painted a dismal picture of the situation at Tyre and indicated that any attempt to save the city would involve the Carthaginians in a long and costly war. A delegation of 30 Carthaginian ambassadors returned to Tyre.[164] They told the city that Carthage was currently engaged in a life-and-death struggle with Rome, which at that time actually had an army encamped outside of Carthage's walls. The ambassadors regretfully informed the Tyrians that it was not possible for Carthage to assume the burden of any other large commitments at the time. This, of course, was a major disappointment to Tyre, all the more so because Carthage was its colony. But the Tyrians remained undaunted and continued their preparations for the soon-expected assault. The Carthaginian delegation did, however, offer to take Tyre's women and children under protection at Carthage to ease the burden on the city of having to feed those who could not contribute to its defense.[165]

The Tyrians carefully prepared for the final attack. A number of huge metal bowls were filled with sand and heated until white-hot. Poured down from the parapets, the burning sand would trickle between breastplates and shirts to inflict an agonizing pain on the victim as it burned into the flesh. Additional wooden towers were built on the walls overlooking the sea and more animal hides filled with padding were hung over the wall to absorb the impact of the catapult stones. Drop-beams were made ready for use in disabling the rams. Grappling irons, hooks, and barbed tridents were distributed to assist in pulling down drawbridges and bridging ladders. Fishing nets were even provided for entangling the attackers. As a final precaution, the Tyrians had the foresight to build an inner wall 15 feet thick and within seven and a half feet of their outer wall opposite the mole.[166] They then filled the space between the two walls with earth and stones. Everything possible had been done. There was now nothing left to do but wait. One of the greatest siege assaults in history was going to be met by a determined and skillful defense.

Sometime in July 332 B.C., Alexander ordered the assault to begin. The attack from the mole quickly proved almost totally ineffectual. The massive bombardment there making absolutely no impression against the outer wall, now buttressed by a strong inner wall. The floating rams were only able to make a small breach at the southern tip of Tyre, but a determined Tyrian counterattack threw back the Macedonian assault, forcing its reembarcation and withdrawal. At nightfall, Alexander reluctantly broke off his unsuccessful attack and so disappointing had been the result, he was said to have considered abandoning the siege and marching off to Egypt.[167] Upon closer reflection, however, he concluded that his reputation would be impaired if Tyre was successful in resisting him and he decided to continue the siege, despite the support of only one of his close friends, Amyntas, in that decision. The Tyrians, meanwhile, immediately rebuilt the portion of their wall Alexander had breached.

The seas now became rough, and Alexander waited for three days before he began a second assault on the city. The floating rams were again ordered into action. In the south, a significant breach was made near the first one. The floating rams were then withdrawn, and the troop assault ships were ordered up. One of assault ships contained a battalion of 1,000 hypaspists under Admetus, which Alexander accompanied, while the other held a 1,500-strength taxies of the phalanx commanded by Coenus.[168] The assault ships grounded themselves under the wall and lowered their drawbridges, and their infantry stormed into the breach. A fierce hand-to-hand battle ensued, and the hypaspists succeeded in capturing a portion of the wall. Admetus was killed by a spear thrust, but Alexander took command of the second attacking wave and drove the Tyrians back, advancing along the now abandoned wall all the way to the royal palace. The Phoenician fleet, meanwhile, had attacked the boom across Egyptian Harbor and broke through. As they moved into the city, the Tyrians manning the walls on Melkart Island opposite Alexander's breach, in fear of being cut off, withdrew north into the center of the city, barricading the narrow streets behind them. Although Sidon Harbor did not have a boom, it was occupied by the remnants of the Tyrian fleet. It appears, however, that the crews of the ships had been used to reinforce the defenders on the walls to the south, and in consequence, the Cyprian fleet was able to easily force the harbor entrance. Meeting with little opposition, the Cyprian soldiers were able to overrun quickly the northern part of the city. Many of the Tyrians, demoralized by Alexander's success in the south, withdrew into the city to better protect any remaining family and friends.

When Alexander's troops entered the city, all the pent-up frustrations of the siege were released against the Tyrians. The soldiers abandoned all self-restraint and became uncontrollable butchers, sparing neither women, children, or the elderly. Everyone they met was cut down without mercy, and no prisoners were taken. Heavy as the losses were, the slaughter would have been even greater had it not been for the intervention of Tyre's bitter commercial rival, Sidon. Horrified by the savagery of the Macedonians, the Sidonians placed 15,000 helpless Tyrian citizens under their protection and smuggled them safely out of the city.[169] The surviving Tyrian infantry had withdrawn to the Agenorium at the north end of the city to make a last stand. There they fought and died where they stood, neither giving quarter nor being offered any by the hypaspists. Azemilk, the king of Tyre, some leading citizens, and the envoys from Carthage took refuge in the temple of Melkart. Alexander, in respect for his alleged ancestor Heracles, spared the lives of all within his temple. Finally, exhausted by their killing frenzy, the Macedonian soldiers once more came under the control of their officers. One of the great sieges in ancient history had been brought to a close.

After a siege of seven months, lasting from February to August 332 B.C., Alexander had conquered Tyre by assault.[170] A total of 8,000 Tyrians had died in the final attack and sack of the city.[171] After Tyre's fall, an additional 2,000 of the city's men of military age were crucified along the seashore, while the city's remaining 13,000 citizens were sold into slavery.[172] Throughout the siege, Alexander's losses totaled 400 killed and possibly as many as 4,000 more wounded.[173] With Alexander's occupation of the last port city on the Phoenician coast, the Persian fleet went into a rapid decline. To the south, the Egyptians only awaited Alexander's arrival to submit and proclaim him pharaoh. Between Tyre and Egypt, only Gaza barred the way.

Alexander's successful siege of Tyre is widely considered one of his greatest military accomplishments. Few successful sieges had been conducted by the Greeks up to that time, and those that were had been won either by starvation or by treachery from within the city. Alexander had conducted his siege by bombardment and assault. He was faced by an opponent worthy of his best talents. The Tyrians were as skilled in seamanship as in land combat. They were about as innovative in their defense as Alexander was in his assault, and their resolution equaled

Alexander's own. The Tyrians were bold, brave, resourceful, and effective, a combination Alexander was seldom to face again. And although in the end the Tyrians were finally overcome, they had clearly given Alexander one of the most difficult fights of his career. It was a hard-won victory that Alexander could justly be proud of.

Generalship Alexander was both innovative and persistent in the his conduct of the siege. It was clear that he had progressed far from the siege of Halicarnassus. Located a half-mile off shore, Tyre was widely believed to be impregnable from a land attack. Alexander therefore brought the land to the walls of the city by building his mole. This, undoubtedly, was one of the great engineering feats of his day, and despite the problems involved in its construction and all the difficulties imposed by nature and the Tyrians, it was successfully completed. However, in point of fact, the city did not fall because of the mole. Tyre's double wall opposite the mole proved too strong to be assaulted successfully. Consequently, the critical breach was not made there but at the southern part of the city and by the navy. On the one hand, the tremendous effort that went into the construction of the mole can be seen as a complete waste. On the other, its very magnitude and the persistence with which the construction was pushed were probably successful in focusing much of the Tyrians' attention away from other areas of their defenses, undoubtedly facilitating Alexander's main assault in the south.

The successful implementation of Alexander's strategic land campaign along the Phoenician coast delivered the Phoenician navy to him at a time he most needed it. When the Cyprian navy was surprised by a Tyrian attack, Alexander displayed his martial abilities on the sea by rushing to their support and virtually destroying the sortie force himself. His use of the floating rams proved to be the tool that eventually cracked Tyre's defenses. The huge mobile siege towers that he built to operate on the mole were among the largest constructed up to that time. And although they were not especially successful in this siege, their basic design remained largely unchanged for the next thousand years, and few successful siege assaults were conducted without their use. The attention Alexander gave to suppressing enemy fire was also innovative. Catapults were lined up on the mole hub-to-hub to conduct a saturation bombardment which, although virtually unknown in ancient times, became the basis of modern attack preparation doctrine.

In his conduct of this epic siege, Alexander displayed many of the characteristics that made him stand out as the greatest combat commander of his age. No matter what problem he was faced with he met it head on and overcame it. When the ingenuity of the Tyrians placed obstacle after obstacle in his path, he took them in stride and always came up with another innovation to trump theirs. One might think that a flexible mind like Alexander's would be inconsistent with patience, but this was far from the case. He combined the two like few other generals of history, then or now. His inventiveness was complimented by a dogged determination to pursue whatever he undertook to the end, no matter how difficult or long the path.

While Alexander was still at Tyre, Darius sent him a second peace proposal. This time, he offered Alexander 10,000 talents for the return of his family, all the territory west of the Euphrates, marriage to his daughter, and an alliance.[174] Alexander refused the offer, indicating that he had no need for the money, had already taken the territory Darius had offered, and would marry the Great King's daughter whenever he chose to. Upon drafting his reply to Darius' offer, Alexander marched off to Gaza.

Siege of Gaza

After the fall of Tyre, Alexander marched south along the eastern Mediterranean coast towards Egypt. Some 150 miles away stood the fortress city of Gaza, 2.5 miles inland from the sea and just on the northern edge of the Egyptian desert.[175] The city itself was a rich commercial center under the command of a Persian governor named Batis. Gaza was located at the head of an old caravan route and was a major clearinghouse for the eastern spice trade.[176] Although not a port on the Mediterranean, the city nevertheless controlled the land approach to Egypt from Phoenicia. When the fall of Tyre became widely known, all the cities south of Tyre, except for Gaza, submitted to Alexander. When Batis was ordered to surrender, he refused, being convinced that Gaza was impregnable because of its location on a high hill surrounded by deep sand. Well stocked to withstand a lengthy siege, Gaza was also strongly garrisoned by a large force of veteran Arab mercenaries.

Although the Macedonian engineers indicated that the mound upon which Gaza sat raised the city up too high to be bombarded by siege artillery or carried by assault, Alexander was determined to prosecute the siege. His plan was to throw up a 55-foot-high mound on the south side of the city that would allow him to deploy his siege artillery level to the base of the city walls.[177] Local villagers were impressed as workers for the construction of the mound. As Alexander was directing the siege operations, he was hit on the head by a stone dropped by a bird.[178] This was taken as a bad omen by Aristander, the king's soothsayer. Thus, Alexander ordered his assault postponed, and his troops began to withdraw from their jumping-off positions. Batis mistook this for a retreat and sortied out in an attempt to set fire to the siege engines. When the defending Macedonians were pushed back over the mound, Alexander counterattacked with the hypaspists and forced Batis to withdraw back into the city.

With the completion of the mound and the arrival of the siege engines by sea from Tyre, the bombardment of Gaza's walls began. A breach was soon made, and the Macedonians cleared the towers adjacent to it with missile fire, inflicting heavy casualties on the Arab defenders. The siege towers, however, became stuck in the soft sand and were only moved with exhausting effort. Lacking their concentrated missile fire support, the first three assaults were thrown back from the breach. In the course of the fighting, Alexander was wounded in the shoulder by an arrow and was carried from the field.[179] Believing him to be dead, Batis held a victory celebration inside the city.[180]

Alexander soon recovered sufficiently, however, to order the resumption of siege operations. A section of the wall weakened by the constant battering of the siege

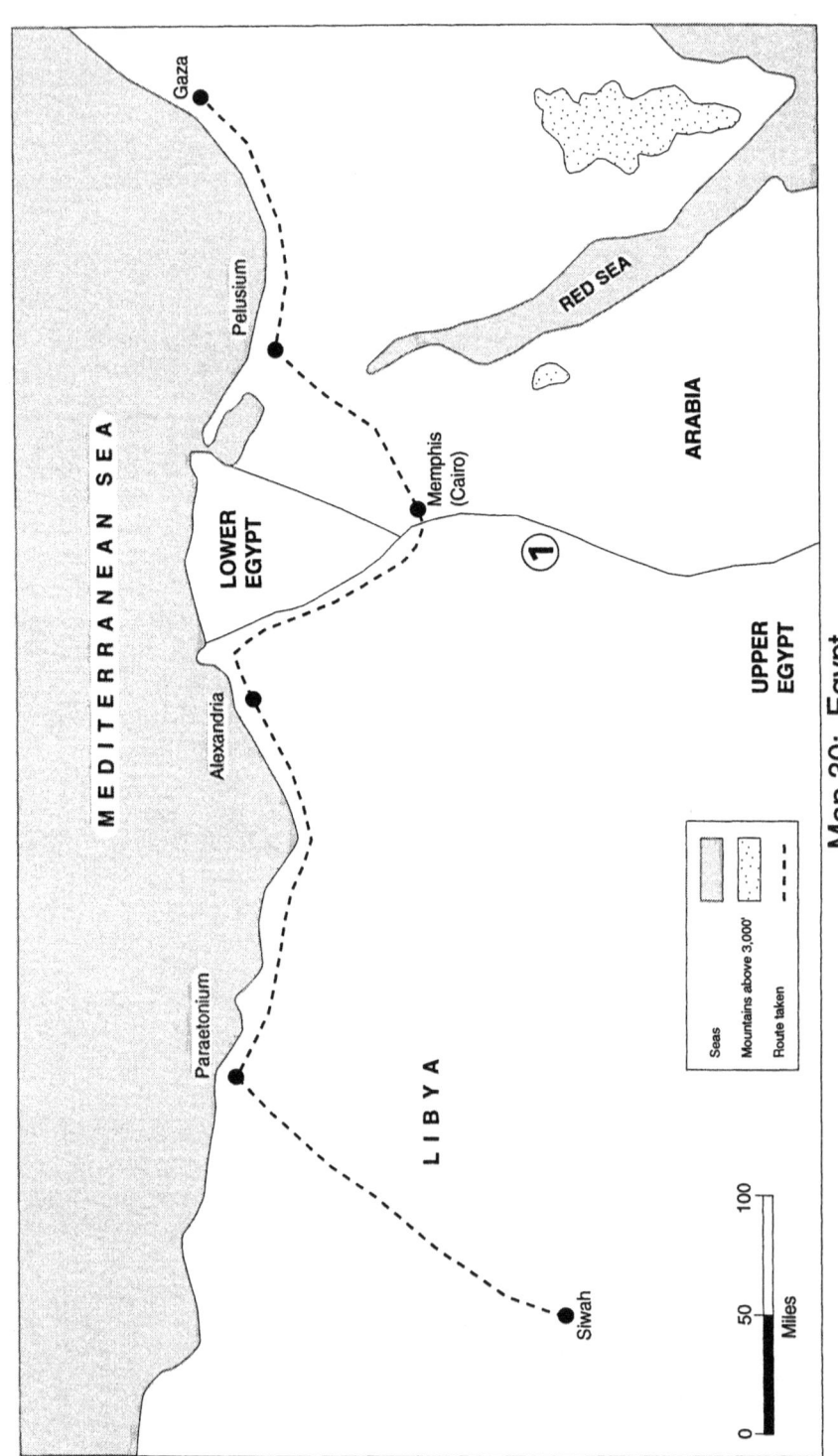

Map 30: Egypt

engines was mined and collapsed. In a fourth assault delivered through the new breach, Alexander was wounded in the leg with a stone while leading a taxies of the phalanx.[181] The attack this time was successful, and the taxies fought its way into the city, opened the gate from the inside, and admitted the rest of the army. Although the city had already fallen, the Arab garrison refused to surrender and fought on to the last man. The Macedonians, maddened by the length and difficulty of the siege and the discomfort they had endured from both the desert sun and shortage of water, butchered the city's remaining garrison without mercy. It had taken Alexander two months to bring the siege to a successful conclusion.[182] Of the estimated 10,000 defenders in Gaza, most were slaughtered in the final assault, with the surviving women and children being sold into slavery.[183] Alexander repopulated Gaza with natives from the interior of the countryside and established a strong Macedonian garrison in the city's citadel. He then marched his army south along the coast in the company of his fleet to Pelusium, in Egypt.

Generalship The main objective at Gaza for Alexander was to raise a mound up alongside the city to facilitate the use of siege artillery. The soft sand, however, proved an almost insurmountable deterrent to moving the siege towers, and the first three assaults were made without them. All failed because in the absence of the towers it was not possible to clear the defenders from the walls. A subsequent mining operation, however, created a breach that was soon carried, and the city fell after hard fighting. The siege was a fairly straight-forward operation, relying mostly on the fighting effectiveness of the Macedonian troops.

Egypt

Pelusium

Water is scarce along the route between Gaza and Pelusium, and the area around Lake Serbonis was surrounded by quicksand. It took six days for Alexander's army to cover the distance between the two cities.[184] Lying at the mouth of the Nile, Pelusium had been Egypt's first line of defense against invaders since the time of the early pharaohs. In the fourth century, the city's fortifications withstood several Persian siege attempts, falling only as a result of internal treachery. Now, however, Pelusium willingly surrendered to Alexander, and the Egyptians came out enmass to welcome his arrival. Alexander garrisoned the city's citadel and ordered his fleet to sail up the Nile to Memphis. He marched overland to the city with his army.

Memphis

Mazaces, who had been appointed satrap of Egypt by Darius, had not been left there with a Persian garrison. The residents of the city, being hostile to the Persians in resentment of their arrogance and avarice, could be expected to give a

1. Hector (son of Parmenio) accidentally drowns.

warm welcome to Alexander, whom they regarded as a liberator. Reflecting upon Darius' loss of the battle of Issus, his flight from the battlefield, the defection of Syria, the fall of Tyre and Gaza by siege, and the enthusiastic welcoming of Alexander by the Egyptians at Pelusium, Mazaces promptly went out to meet Alexander upon his approach to Memphis, surrendering to him both Egypt and the 800 talents in its treasury.[185] The Egyptians came out from Memphis to greet Alexander, believing him to be delivering them from the oppressive Persian rule. Alexander stayed in Memphis long enough to be crowned Pharaoh of Egypt. Then, in the company of his hypaspists, archers, Agrianians, and Agema of the Companions, he sailed back up the Nile to the delta.[186]

Alexandria

In exploring the delta, Alexander came across the settlement of Rhacotis, inhabited by herdsmen who reputedly guarded the entrance to the Nile for the pharaohs. He recognized the location as an excellent spot for a great trading city to replace Tyre as the focus for commerce in the eastern Mediterranean. Along an old coastal road on a narrow strip of land between the Mediterranean and Lake Mareotis, Alexander marked out a city that was about four miles long.[187] He named it Alexandria, after himself.[188] It was protected against the sea by the three-mile-long island of Pharos, the name being derived from the word *pharaoh*.[189] The city's harbor was three-quarters of a mile wide and deep enough to accommodate large merchant ships of 250 tons or more. Because the city was located on the west side of the delta, it would not be affected by the silting brought down the Nile. Both the land and sea approaches to Alexandria were easily defensible. Cool westerly winds gave the city a pleasant climate, even during the summer heat.

Siwah

Alexander now became obsessed with visiting the oracle of Siwah in the interior of the Libyan desert. The temple had stood high in the esteem of the Greek world since the fifth century B.C., being widely recognized as one of the great Greek oracles, second only to Delphi in importance. The god of Siwah was said to be infallible in its predictions.[190] Alexander had been interested in a trip to Siwah for several reasons. The question of his divinity had become increasingly important to him in recent months, and he wanted confirmation of his mother's belief that he was the son of Zeus. He was also at a stage in his campaigning in which he would soon be leaving the Mediterranean coast for the interior of the Persian Empire, and he wanted to know if the gods favored his campaign there. Then too, there were the mystical reasons for the trip that were to Alexander probably no less compelling than the practical ones. According to legend his Argead ancestors Heracles and Perseus had both made the difficult journey to visit the oracle, as had the Persian king Cambyses, who reputedly lost an army of 50,000 men en route there.[191] To equal or surpass the deeds of those mortals who had done noteworthy things was always an incentive to Alexander, and in this case the lure to do so was probably irresistible.

7: THE WESTERN PERSIAN EMPIRE

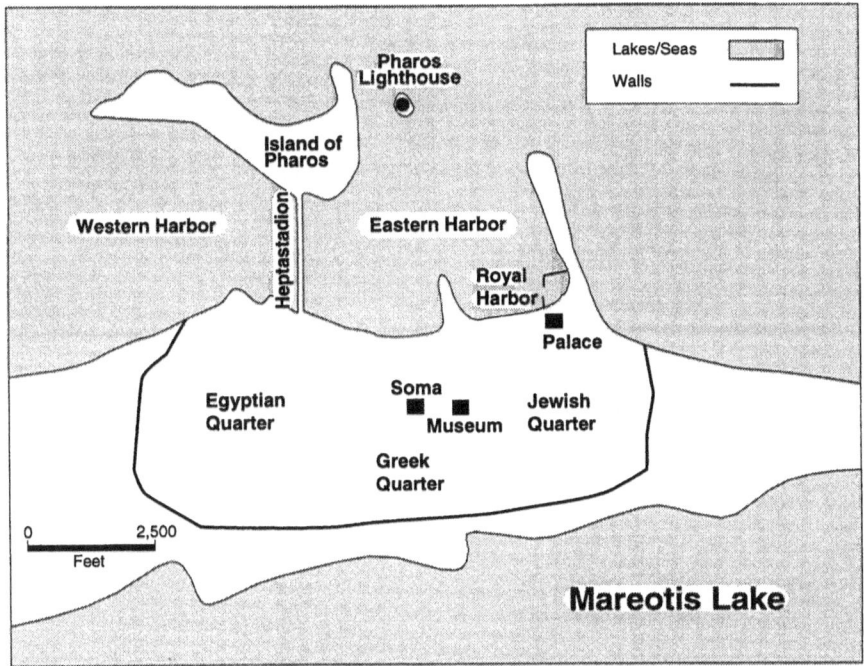

Map 31: Alexandria

In late January, Alexander began his journey to Siwah. Mounting camels, he traveled 200 miles west from Egypt to the village of Paraetonium, on the border with Libya. From there, he and his party headed southwest through the desert along an old caravan trail. Neglecting to take enough water along with them, they ran out four days from Paraetonium.[192] Fortunately, an unusual desert rainstorm saved them from disaster; Alexander and his party, of course, attributed this to divine assistance. Later a desert sandstorm, or Khamsin, blew up from the south, burying all recognizable landmarks and causing Alexander's guides to lose their bearings completely. Luckily, a flock of migrating birds heading for oasis guided them the remaining way, and they reached Siwah in late February, three weeks after setting out from Egypt.

The Siwah oasis occupied about 10 square miles and only existed because of the presence of five springs there.[193] The area was heavily planted with fruit trees, olives, and date palms. The temple sat on an isolated hill. It was rectangular in shape, encompassing an area of 150 feet by 144 feet. The inner shrine, at the far end of the temple, was a narrow 10 feet by 18 feet.[194] A golden boat containing the stone of the god sat on an altar inside the temple.

The priests at the temple of Siwah had undoubtedly heard of the belief of Alexander's mother that he was divine and of his crowning in Egypt as the pharaoh Ammon-Re. Believing that flattery might elicit some generous donations, the priests greeted Alexander as the son of Zeus. Alexander and his companions took this salutation to be a confirmation of his divine status. Only Alexander was allowed to enter the temple with the clothing he was wearing. The others in his party had to change theirs and wait outside. Once inside, Alexander was required to adhere to the same procedure as everyone else who consulted the oracle. The questions would be written on a tablet and submitted to a priest, who would then leave for the inner chamber of the temple. The boat containing the stone of the god was placed in a litter suspended by long poles along the shoulders of 80 priests.[195] When a question was asked, the bearers of the god's boat would move, sway, or bow, all supposedly at the god's direction. The officiating priest would carefully observe the movements of the bearers and then interpret the god's will. The god's power to speak through the priests bearing the litter was taken in the ancient world as an accepted fact.

None of Alexander's followers had been allowed to accompany him into the inner temple. As a result, no one but he and the officiating priest knew the questions asked and the replies received from the gods of Ammon. Alexander never confided to anyone what occurred in the temple. All he would say was that he had been told what his heart had desired. Alexander had written his mother Olympias that upon his return to Macedonia he would reveal to her the secrets given him at the temple. With his death in Babylon, however, he carried to the grave what had been told to him by the oracle.

It is clear that the visit to Siwah made a deep and lasting impression on Alexander. His subsequent actions and statements gave some indication as to what he believed had been told him. When Alexander returned to Memphis, he began to refer to himself in all orders and decrees as Alexander, king and son of Zeus-Ammon. At the commencement of the battle of Gaugamela, he called upon Ammon for victory. Four years later in India, Alexander would sacrifice in the Indian Ocean to the gods revealed to him by Ammon. It was obvious that in doing so he was obeying a prophecy given him at Siwah. By these actions, it was clear that Alexander believed that he had been confirmed in his divine parentage and that the gods had shown favor toward his desire to conquer Asia.

Memphis

After a short visit at Siwah, Alexander returned to Memphis along the same route that he had taken.[196] He then appointed two Egyptians, Doloaspis and Petisis, as governors of Egypt. When Petisis, however, declined the governorship, the responsibility was assumed solely by Doloaspis. Pantaleon of Pydna was appointed garrison commander of Memphis, and Polemon (son of Megacles) was appointed garrison commander of Pelusium. Lycidas, an Aetolian, was given command of the mercenaries. Apollonus (son of Charinus) was made governor of Libya, and Cleomenes, from Naucratis, became governor of Arabia, the area lying east of the Nile River, as well as tax collector of Egypt. Peucestas (son of Macartatus) and Balacrus (son of Amyntas) were appointed as commanders of the army left behind in Egypt, while Polemon (son of Theramenes) was made admiral of the fleet. In the vicinity of Heroopolis, Alexander divided the government of Egypt among several administrators and soldiers. The vast economic potential of the country had convinced him that it was unsafe to entrust it to any single man.[197]

In mid–April 331 B.C., Alexander left Egypt for Phoenicia. A bridge was constructed at Memphis to enable his army to cross the Nile. A garrison of 4,000 troops was left behind under Aeschylus, the Rhodian, and Peucestas, the Macedonian, to secure Egypt, and Polemon was given command of a fleet of 30 triremes for the defense of the delta.[198]

Mesopotamia

Although Darius had mobilized his army in Babylonia, he had no intention of waiting for Alexander there. He would soon be forced to leave the area because food supplies for his huge army were undoubtedly being depleted from his prolonged occupation. Darius had originally planned to fight his decisive battle against Alexander on the plain of Cunaxa, the battlefield where Artaxerxes had earlier defeated his brother Cyrus the younger. The site was located 60 miles northwest of Babylon and directly across the line of march of any force approaching the city from the north. The large plain there would give Darius' huge cavalry force the proper room it needed to deploy and maneuver. The Great King opened his campaign by sending an advance party of 3,000 Persian cavalry under Mazaeus, satrap of Babylonia, to Thapsacus to obstruct Alexander's expected crossing of the Euphrates River there.[199]

Receiving reports that the Persian army that had been mobilizing in Babylon was finally marching against him, Alexander moved to engage them in what he undoubtedly hoped would be the decisive battle of the war. In the spring of 331 B.C., Alexander is said to have marched his army west from Tyre to Damascus, then north to Aleppo. He more likely marched north along the coast to Antioch, however, then west to Aleppo. This would have facilitated his logistics because supplies could have more easily been delivered to his army by ship than overland. Alexander arrived at Thapsacus, on the Euphrates River, where he had ordered two bridges to be constructed by an advance party. Although Mazaeus had been able to delay the construction of the bridges, when Alexander came up with the main body of the army he was forced to withdraw and they were soon completed. Alexander's army then crossed over the Euphrates without further incident. Once over the river, Alexander surprised Darius by turning north instead of south to Babylon. The area south of Thapsacus was hot and arid and would have been completely stripped of all provisions by Mazaeus. Although the route to the north was equally hot, provisions were apparently more readily available because it was not expected that he would move north. The unexpected route would also allow the crossing of the Tigris to be made without Persian interference.[200] As Alexander's march to the Tigris would be occurring in September, the river was expected to be low and could be crossed at a ford, although the strong current was still likely to make the operation hazardous.[201]

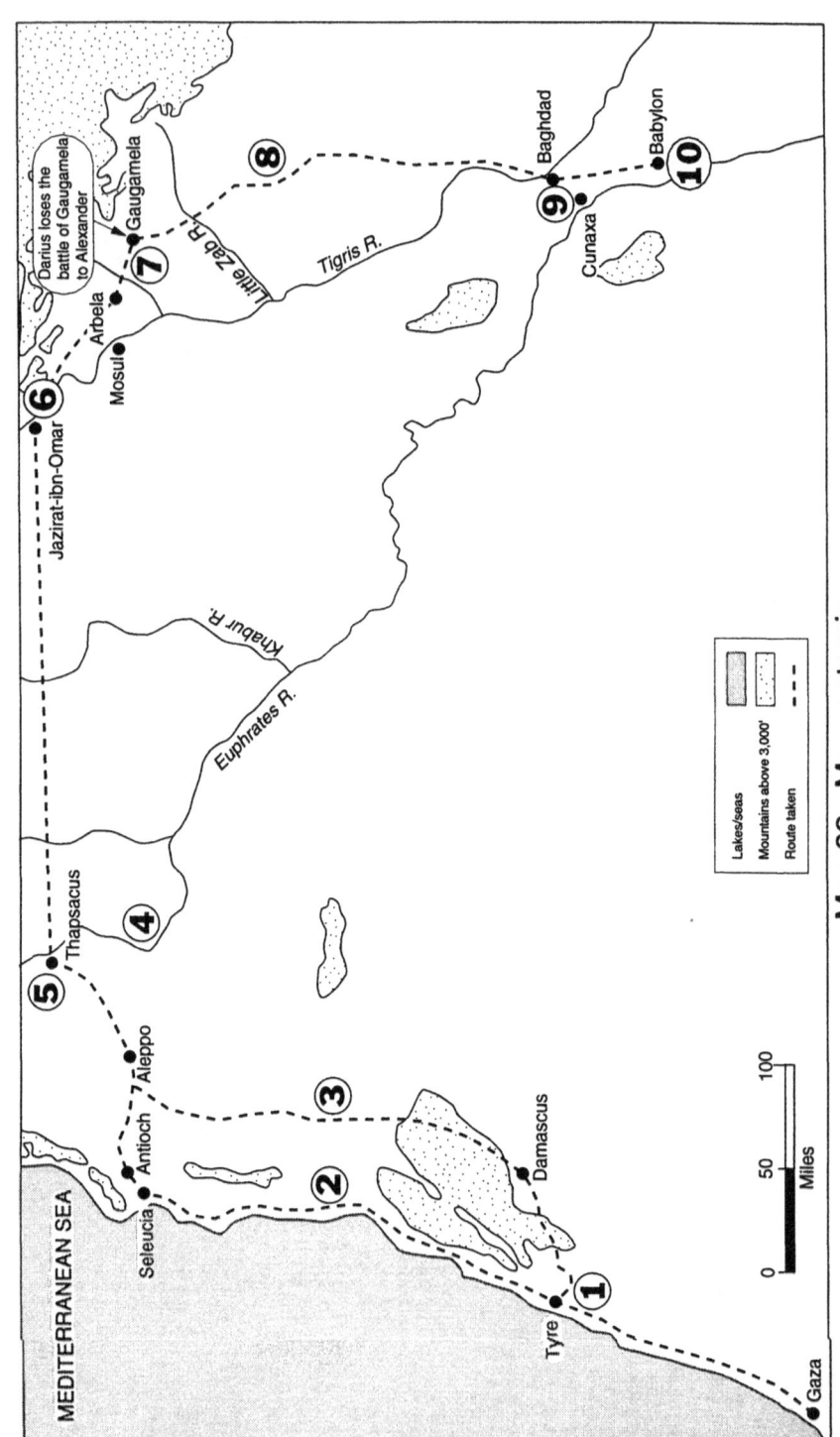

Map 32: Mesopotomia

Battle of Gaugamela

Darius now was forced to discard his strategic plan of fighting Alexander at Cunaxa and instead moved north in an attempt to block him at one of the crossings over the Tigris. There were four possible fords Alexander could use, but the only one that Darius might beat him to was at Mosul, 356 miles away and the closest to Babylon.[202] Darius' line of march would be north from Babylon along the Royal Road to Arbela, then due west to the ford at Mosul.[203] Marching northeast to Carrhae, Alexander turned east towards the Tigris River. But instead of crossing at Mosul, as Darius had expected, he crossed some 40 miles to the north, at Jabal Maqlub. Although the Tigris was fordable this time of year, fighting the strong current exhausted his troops, and Alexander was compelled to rest his army for two full days afterwards.[204]

While Darius was en route to Mosul, he received reports that Alexander had already crossed the Tigris further to the north. Again he had to recast his strategic plan because Alexander was now on the same side of the Tigris as the Persian army and only 50 miles away to the northwest. Darius had to locate quickly a wide and level plain that would allow him the room to deploy his cavalry and chariots effectively. His scouts found one at Gaugamela, about 75 miles west of Arbela.[205] Fortunately, the site was just off the road to Mosul.

After his army had sufficiently rested from the crossing of the Tigris, Alexander took an advanced force consisting of the Agema, one ilae of cavalry, and the Paeonians and moved on ahead. The main body of his army continued the march southeast, with the Gordyaean (Kurdish) Mountains on its left and the Tigris River on its right.[206] Four days after the crossing, Alexander's advance force sighted Persian cavalry.[207] From prisoners captured, Alexander learned that the main Persian army was encamped about seven-and-a-half-miles away at Gaugamela, which was hidden from view by the Jabal Maqlub massif.[208] When his scouts reported that the Persians were engaged in carefully leveling the ground along his front, Alexander knew that Darius had determined to stay and fight. Making an entrenched camp behind the massif for his baggage train, noncombatants, camp followers, and prisoners, Alexander rested his army for the next four days.[209]

On the night of the fourth day, a few hours before midnight, Alexander set out with his army for Gaugamela with the intention of deploying on the battlefield at daybreak. Descending to the plain below, Alexander arranged his army into battle formation in the darkness and then bivouacked under arms. Alexander's key officers were then called to a conference to discuss whether to make a surprise

---

1. Alexander refuses a request from the Athenians to release their citizens captured at the battle of Granicus River. 2. Alexander's probable route. 3. Alexander's possible route. 4. Darius expects Alexander to march south along the Euphrates. 5. Mazaeus obstructs Alexander's bridge construction at Thapsacus. 6. Alexander receives Darius' third and final peace proposal. 7. Darius' wife dies of travel fatigue just prior to the battle of Gaugamela. 8. The Persian Royal Road. 9. Darius expects that Alexander will fight the decisive battle of his invasion here. 10. Mazaeus surrenders the city and 40,000 talents to Alexander.

night attack on the Persians or wait until daylight. Although Parmenio spoke up for the night attack, Alexander was convinced that he could win a victory in open daylight and did not want it disparaged by the innuendo of a sneak attack delivered under the cover of darkness. The army would rest until dawn and would then move out to the attack.

Darius had chosen a wide plain for his battlefield where he would have adequate room to deploy his large cavalry and chariot force. To improve the site still further, he had his troops clear away all trees, rocks, and slopes from designated pathways to give the chariots an absolutely level field for their charges. One glaring error in the battlefield selection, however, was the presence of rough ground just off of Darius' left flank.

It had taken Darius a year and half after Issus to organize another army to take to the field. Except for northern Cappadocia, Syria, and Armenia, the western satrapies were under Alexander's control and unavailable for recruiting. As a result, Darius' new army was largely composed of troops from the eastern and northern areas of his empire. His cavalry was drawn from the northwest areas of Bactria, Sogdiana, and northwestern India and from the Saca tribes of the steppe, as well as from the central satrapies of Areia, Arachosia, and Parthyaea. The Great King had learned at least one lesson from Issus and began to replace the inferior javelins of his cavalry units with the longer and more effective spears with which the Macedonian cavalry were armed. By the battle of Gaugamela, however, only a few elite units had received them. The Greek mercenaries survived as a small remnant of 2,000, divided into two units under the command of Patron and Glaucous. The Persian infantry levies, as usual, were notable only for their numbers. In an attempt to offset Alexander's phalanx, 200 scythed chariots had been mobilized. Because the Greek mercenaries were no longer available in sufficient numbers to oppose the phalanx, it was hoped that the chariots would be able to disorder its formation sufficiently to enable the Persian cavalry to penetrate its ranks.[210] A total of 15 Indian war elephants were initially deployed in the center of the Persian line opposite the Indian cavalry but were later moved to the rear, where they were captured with the baggage train, possibly because only the Indian cavalry was trained to operate with them.[211]

Classical historians ridiculously overestimated the Persian army strength, placing it in excess of one million. Realistically, although the Persian army considerably outnumbered the Macedonian army, it was unlikely to have much exceeded 90,000 in total strength.[212] Their cavalry might have numbered as high as 34,000; effective infantry, up to 8,000; and the infantry levies, possibly as many as 50,000.[213]

The Persian army was divided into two lines, with the front line being further subdivided into three commands: a right wing under Mazaeus, formerly satrap of Syria; a center under Darius himself; and a left wing under Bessus, satrap of Bactria. The Persian front line was almost exclusively comprised of cavalry, screened by additional cavalry and the scythed chariots. It was a strictly offensive force whose full combat effectiveness was only achieved in the momentum of a charge. As a result, it was necessary for Darius to assume the initiative against the Macedonians. The

7: THE WESTERN PERSIAN EMPIRE

left wing battle line consisted of 13,000 cavalry, with units from Bactria, Scythia, Arachosia, Persia, Susiana, and Cadusia. Screening the line were 100 scythed chariots, 1,000 Bactrian cavalry, and 1,000 Saca (Massagetae) cavalry. The right wing battle line comprised 13,000 cavalry, with units from lowland Syria, Mesopotamia, Media, Parthyaea, Scythia, Tapuria, Hyrcania, Albania, and Sacesinia. They were screened by 50 scythed chariots, 1,000 Armenian cavalry, and 1,000 Cappadocian cavalry. The center contained cavalry from Caria and India; the Mardian (Carian) archers; the Greek mercenaries, stationed opposite the Macedonian phalanx; the Persian Foot Guards, known as the "Apple-bearers"; and the Kinsmen, the blood relatives of the Great King. The fighting strength of the Persian center totaled perhaps 7,000, and it was screened by 50 scythed chariots. The rear line, which was well back from the front, might have numbered as many as 50,000 levy infantry from Unian, Babylonia, the Red Sea area, and Sitacenia.

Alexander's frontline strength was estimated at 7,350 cavalry and 15,500 infantry. For this battle he divided his army into five separate forces: a left wing under Parmenio; a right wing under his personal command; a right and left flank guard, each echeloned back from the line; and a rear line. Alexander chose this deployment because he could easily form his army into a square to counter the expected Persian attempt to surround him with their vastly superior numbers of cavalry. Parmenio's force consisted of the taxies of the phalanx of Craterus and Simmias; the allied Greek cavalry under Erigyius, which consisted of units from Achaea, Locris, Phthiotis, and Phocis; and the Thessalian cavalry under Philip, for a total of 2,750 cavalry and 3,000 infantry. The right wing under Alexander consisted of the taxies of the phalanx commanded by Polysperchon, Meleager, Perdiccas, and Coenus; the hypaspists under Nicanor; the Companion cavalry under Philotas; the Agema, in advance of and to the right flank of the Companions; and next to them, half the Agrianians. The Companion cavalry was screened by the remaining half of the Agrianians under Attalus, the Greek mercenary archers, and the Balkan javelin men under Balacrus. The frontline strength of Alexander's wing totaled 2,000 cavalry and 10,500 infantry. The left flank guard consisted of an advanced line of the Greek mercenary cavalry under Andromachus, behind which were deployed, in echelon back from the left flank of the Thessalian cavalry, the Thracian cavalry under Sitalces, the allied Greek cavalry under Coeranus, and the Odrysian cavalry under Agathon, for a total of 1,550 cavalry. The first unit of the stronger right flank guard consisted of half the remaining Agrianians, off the Agema's right flank. Echeloned off the Agema's right flank were the Macedonian archers under Brison and on his right the Greek mercenary infantry under Cleander. Screening the Agrianians were the Lancers under Aretes and the Paeonian cavalry under Ariston. Deployed in front of them was the Greek mercenary cavalry under Menidas. This force totaled 1,050 cavalry and 2,000 infantry. The second line consisted of a mixed force of 12,000 allied Greeks, Greek mercenaries, and Balkan levies. They were instructed to either wheel to the rear to meet a possible Persian attack from that direction or to extend the line of the phalanx, should that prove necessary. The Thracian infantry was left behind at the massif to guard the army's fortified camp.

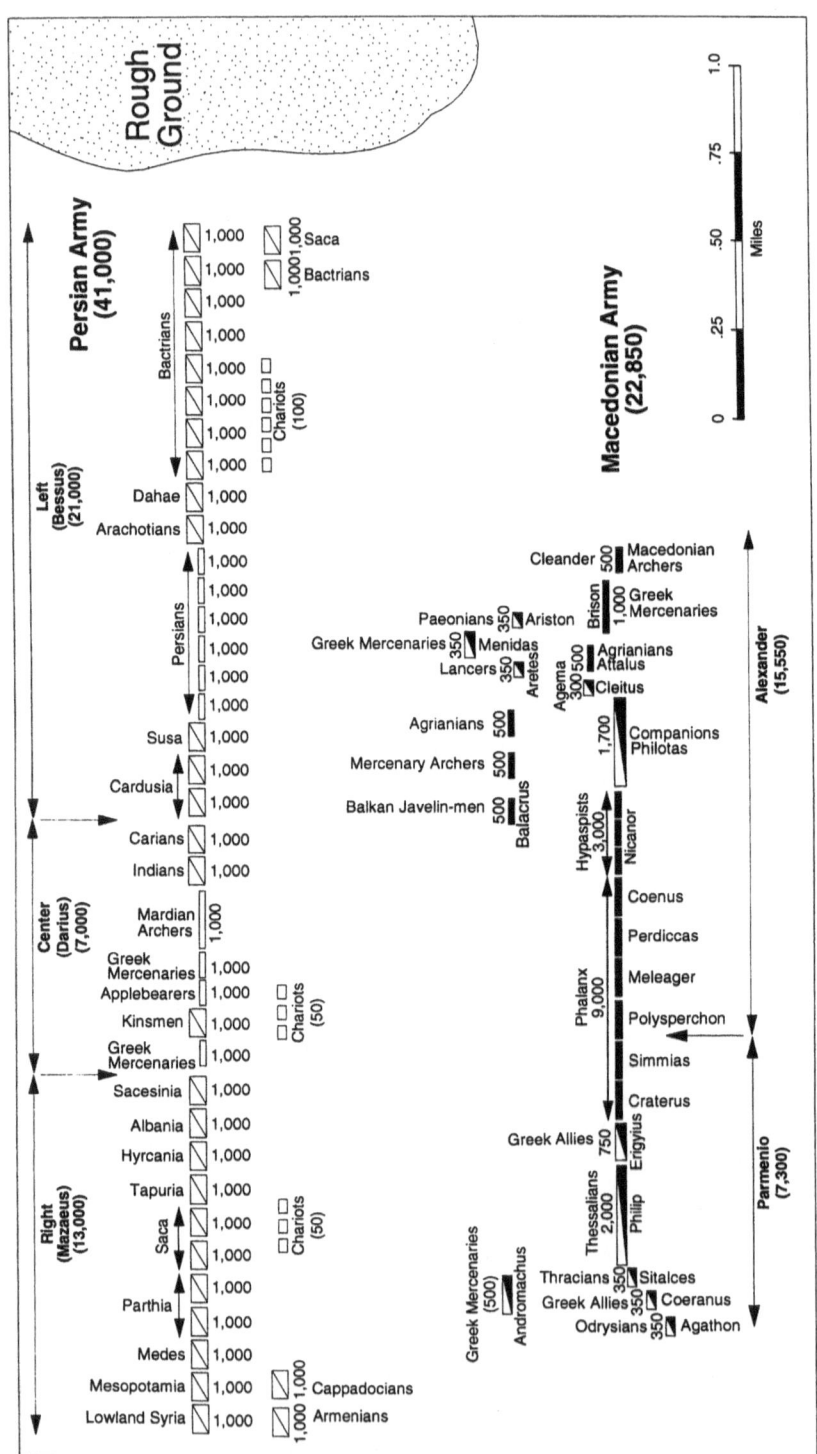

Although most of the senior Macedonian commanders wanted to attack the Persians at dawn, Parmenio recommended that the battlefield be properly reconnoitered first because the Persians had occupied it for several days and had been observed making careful site preparations. He was rightly concerned about blundering into some cleverly concealed Persian trap. This time Alexander fully agreed with him and at daylight rode out in front of the army accompanied by some Companion cavalry and light infantry.[214] He proceeded to reconnoiter carefully both the battlefield terrain and the Persian dispositions. Alexander made special note of the leveled paths in front of the chariots and the uneven ground on their left flank.[215] After making his observations, Alexander returned to his lines and prepared his final plan of attack. His reconnaissance had not been interfered with in any way by the Persians.

Darius had been extremely worried that Alexander might launch a surprise night attack. Not having the protection of an entrenched camp or enough reliable infantry to guard his cavalry properly, the Great King had had his army stand under arms in battle formation all night.[216] This, no doubt, had exhausted the troops and adversely lowered both their alertness and endurance for the battle the following day.

Alexander would once again concentrate his elite units on his right flank. His objective was to hold the Persian right in check with Parmenio and break through the Persian left with his Companions. This had to be done in the face of a substantial Persian superiority in numbers of cavalry, which would not only give them the initiative but also the ability to envelop both his flanks. Alexander, however, planned to negate this by his deployment and approach to battle. He first adjusted his formation to accommodate an effective defense against an expected Persian encirclement of both flanks. Two flank guards were created and echeloned back from his main line. These could either extend the front line or form a front perpendicular to the flanks. In the rear, Alexander stationed the allied Greeks and Greek mercenaries. Closing up the flank guards, the rear line would only have to turn 180 degrees about to provide the fourth side of a box that would completely enclose the Macedonian army in a square for all-round defense.

Alexander then echeloned his entire line back by the left.[217] This would advance his elite spearhead on the right and correspondingly recess Parmenio's defensive flank on the left. By increasing the distance that Mazaeus would have to traverse to engage the left flank, Parmenio was afforded some additional defensive protection. As Alexander's phalanx was opposite the Persian center, he moved obliquely to the right in an attempt to anchor his right on the rough ground off the Persian left flank. This would preclude any attempt by Bessus to envelop his flank because maneuvering over that ground would disorder the Persian cavalry formations and prevent them from building up adequate charge speed. Thus the only options that Bessus would have would be to hit Alexander's right flank head-on along the width of his front there or to disorder his own force by moving over the rough ground. In a stand-up fight, the superior training, discipline, armament, and maneuverability of Alexander's cavalry would give them a signifi-

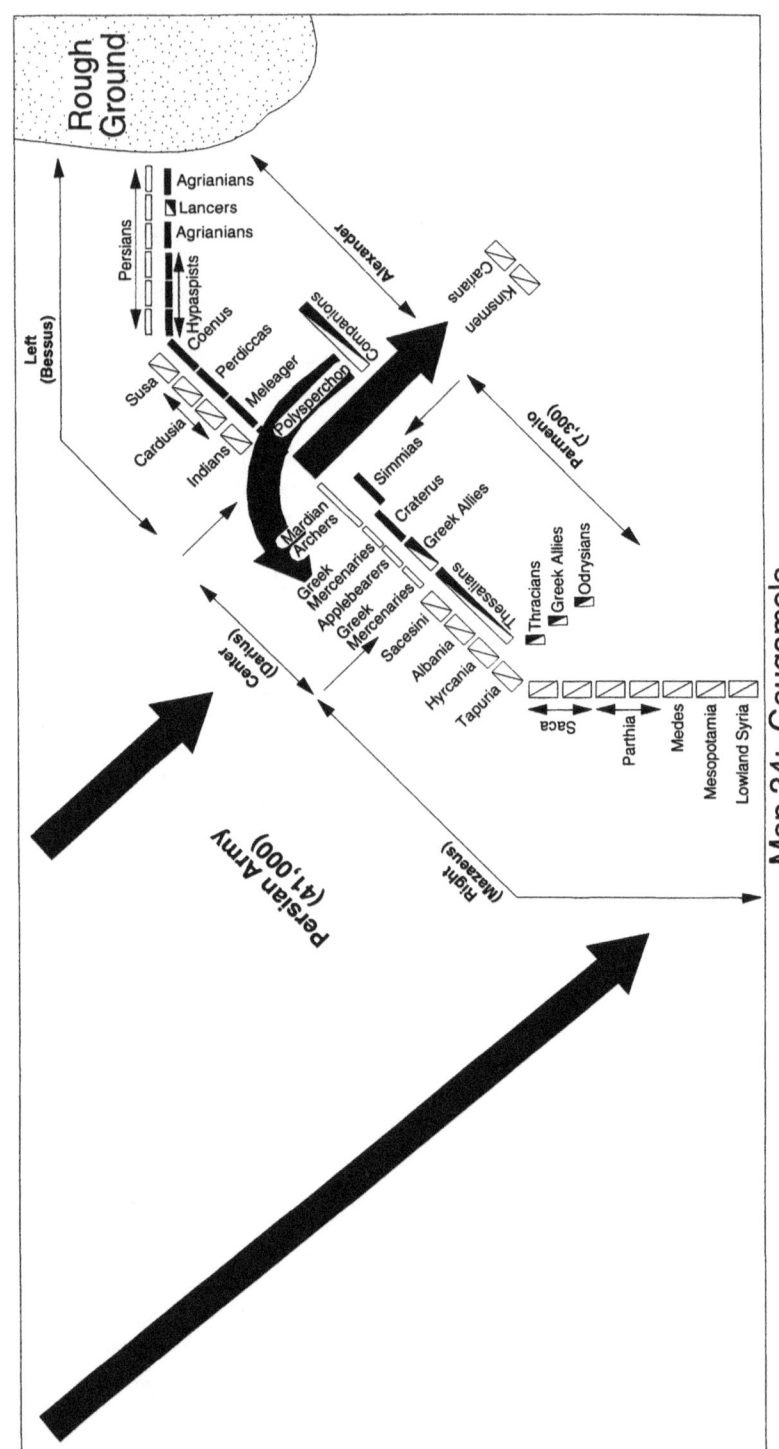

Map 34: Gaugamela

cant advantage over that of the Persians. If Bessus attempted to turn Alexander's right flank, the Persian cavalry would emerge disordered and virtually stationary, making them extremely vulnerable to a charge delivered by Alexander's cavalry there.

The overall Persian plan was for a double envelopment of both Macedonian wings by the cavalry: Bessus destroying the Companions on Alexander's right flank, Mazaeus doing likewise to the Thessalians on his left flank. The chariots would be used to break through and disorder the Macedonian phalanx, preparing the way for a successful cavalry attack against it. Darius obviously envisioned a complete collapse of the Macedonian army.

It was near noon when the Macedonian army was ready to advance. As Alexander moved forward, he echeloned his line back on the left and began to advance at an oblique angle to the right. Bessus sent the screening line of Bactrian and Saca cavalry out against Alexander to stop his lateral movement across his front, while the remainder of his densely packed line unsuccessfully attempted to shift to the left to support the attack. The chariots were forced to remain stationary until Alexander marched across the lanes prepared for their charge. Darius soon saw that if Alexander were allowed to continue his slide to his right, the Macedonian flank would soon be on ground too rough for the Persian chariots to operate on. To fix Alexander in place, Darius ordered Bessus' wing to launch an all-out attack.

Macedonian Right Flank When Darius had ordered Bessus to an all-out effort against Alexander's right flank, he also issued orders for the 100 scythed chariots screening the left flank to charge the Companions. The Agrianians, archers, and javelin men screening their front, however, overwhelmed the chariots with heavy volleys of missile fire on their approach. Only a few of the vehicles made it to the main line, where the Companions and hypaspists simply opened ranks to let them pass harmlessly through. The chariots were then easily dealt with in the rear area by the light infantry and grooms, who simply dragged many of the heavily armored drivers off their vehicles from behind. The dreaded scythed chariot attack on Alexander's right flank proved to be totally ineffective and caused few Macedonian casualties, although it did completely eliminate the chariot force.

When Alexander saw Bessus' 2,000 Bactrian and Scythian cavalry advancing on his flanking force, he ordered Menidas' flank guard cavalry to charge them. Menidas did so but was driven back by weight of numbers. Alexander now threw in Ariston's Paeonians and Cleander's Greek mercenary infantry. They charged against the Persian force, causing them to waver. In reaction, Bessus advanced the remainder of his Bactrian cavalry, which restored the situation, inflicted heavy casualties on Alexander's cavalry, and began to work his way round Alexander's flank. Alexander now committed the last cavalry of his flank guard. Aretes' Lancers charged the Arachosian and Dahae cavalry, who were clearly afraid of their long lances, and drove them back in confusion. Alexander had fought Bessus to a standstill and without committing his last cavalry unit on that flank, the Companions. In shifting to the left to engage Alexander, Bessus had created a gap between his wing and the Persian center. Now that the danger to his flank had been contained,

Alexander immediately formed his Companions into a wedge and charged into the gap, moved across the rear of Bessus right flank, and headed straight towards Darius.

Macedonian Center Alexander had marched so rapidly in his shift to the right that a gap had opened between his and Parmenio's taxies of the phalanx. Also, because of the pressure that Mazaeus was exerting on both Parmenio's flanks, Simmias and Craterus widened the gap by halting their taxies to provide some support to Parmenio's right flank.[218] The Persian and Indian cavalry in the center of Darius' line were ordered to charge into the widening gap in the center of the phalanx. The long sarissa was a clumsy and impractical weapon for a close-in fight, and the taxies of the phalanx that the Indian and Persian cavalry rode through were unable to defend themselves effectively. Instead of capitalizing upon their golden opportunity for rolling up the now almost helpless flanks on either side of their penetration, however, they foolishly rode right through the formation, making for Alexander's firstline transports, where they thought that they would find the captive Persian royal family. Quickly overpowering the surprised and largely unarmed attendants, they began a desperate search for Darius' family. Unable to locate them, the cavalry began looting the transports. Alexander's second line — consisting of the Greek allies, the Greek mercenaries, and the Balkan peltasts — quickly came up and began slaughtering large numbers of the disordered Persians and Indians, who were crowded together in no particular military order. After taking heavy casualties, the remaining Persian and Indian cavalry quickly rode off with all the loot they could carry.

Darius now advanced his center and right wing against the Macedonians.[219] As Alexander fought his way towards him, however, the Great King's fears of capture or death overcame him, and he once again fled the battlefield. At his departure, the center of the Persian line began to break up. With its collapse Bessus, fearing that Alexander would now wheel his Companion cavalry around and attack him in the rear, began to withdraw in good order from the battlefield.

Macedonia Left Flank The 50 scythed chariots in the Persian center had been ordered against Parmenio's taxies of the phalanx, while the last group of 50 chariots on the Persian right moved out against the Thessalians. In lieu of any defending missile fire, the Macedonians on Parmenio's left flank shouted, banged on their shields, blew their trumpets, and otherwise made all the noise they could. The din they raised was successful in frightening many of the horses sufficiently to turn them back into their own lines. Those chariots that did reach the Macedonian front line rode harmlessly through the lanes opened for them, taking heavy casualties from sarissas and spears jabbed into the sides of both horse and drivers as they passed by.

The Cappadocian cavalry followed in the wake of the chariot attack and overwhelmed the Greek mercenary cavalry by weight of numbers, driving deep into the front and left flank of the Thessalian cavalry. With his left being forced back and his taxies of the phalanx fully engaged in an attempt to stabilize his right, Parmenio was in danger of being both surrounded and overwhelmed. In desperation, he sent Alexander an urgent message for help. It is unclear whether Alexander saw what was happening on Parmenio's flank, planned all the time to assist him after the anticipated breakthrough on the right, or actually received Parmenio's message. Whatever the case, Alexander wheeled his Companions around and charged the retreating Parthian and Persian Horse Guard cavalry in an attempt to reach Parmenio. After a hard fight in which 60 Companions were killed and Coenus, Hephaestion, and Menidas were all wounded, Alexander was able to break through the Persian cavalry.[220] As the Persian cavalry of the center continued their retreat off the battlefield, Alexander rode on toward Parmenio.

Alexander's Pursuit of Darius Upon seeing that Parmenio no longer needed his assistance, Alexander rode off in pursuit of Darius, riding until nightfall. After a rest of a few hours, he pushed on, reaching Arbela the next day. By then, Darius was making good his escape over the mountains. Recognizing the futility of pursuing him any further, Alexander returned to his victorious army. When Mazaeus, who commanded the Persian left, learned of the collapse of the center, he also withdrew from the battlefield, though closely pursued by the Thessalians. The remainder of Parmenio's force captured the Persian camp, which included the baggage train, elephants, and camels.[221]

In his flight from Gaugamela, Darius rode straight for Arbela, 75 miles away.[222] There he was joined by Bessus, the largely intact Bactrian cavalry, the 2,000 Greek mercenaries, and the royal guards units.[223] Correctly anticipating that Alexander would march straight for Babylon and Susa, Darius instead took a road over the mountains into Media, a route that was impractical for use by a large force. His intention was to raise yet another army, this time from the eastern provinces.

Results Alexander' victory at Gaugamela had uncovered the central Persian Empire. The major cities and administrative centers of Babylonia, Mesopotamia, and Susiana, along with the enormous gold and silver reserves stored there, would fall to him without further effort. Darius was now little more than a fugitive. He had clearly lost the respect and allegiance of his satraps and would soon forfeit his life as a consequence. He was to die abandoned by his countrymen with just the company of an ordinary Greek soldier during his final minutes. Only Alexander and Darius' immediate family would mourn the passing of the Great King.

Alexander's dead numbered about 100.[224] The Macedonian army lost over 1,000 horses; half of these losses occurred in the pursuit of Darius.[225] Coenus, Hephaestion, Menidas, and Perdiccas were all wounded in the battle.[226] Persian losses were inaccurately stated by the ancient writers in the hundreds of thousands, many times the possible actual strength of their army. The reality was, however, that much of Darius' cavalry was able to withdraw successfully from the battlefield, not being impeded this time by any narrow mountain passes. The majority of Greek mercenaries also managed to get away relatively intact. The Persian levies, on the other hand, probably sustained heavy casualties because they were easily ridden down on the open plain. The 15 Indian war elephants were taken alive, and all of Darius' chariots were either captured or destroyed. The Persian baggage camp again fell into the hands of the Macedonians, who found there 4,000 talents of silver.[227] Although Darius' army was heavily defeated, the best part of it, the heavy cavalry and the Greek mercenaries, had successfully gotten away. Neither would fight Alexander again, however, Gaugamela had sealed the fate of both Darius and the Persian Empire.

Generalship At Gaugamela, Darius had selected a battlefield that allowed him to deploy fully his large cavalry and chariot forces. He also had enough time to prepare the site carefully in an attempt to facilitate the charge of his chariots. Unfortunately, this meticulous preparation would tie Darius to a fixed position and allow him to make use of his leveled pathways only if Alexander cooperated by properly aligning himself with them. Instead of dominating the engagement by using the superior numbers of his huge cavalry force offensively, Darius passively surrendered the initiative and was content merely to sit in place and let Alexander proceed against him as he liked. Darius' intention to remain on the defensive was so strong that he did not even take action to prevent Alexander from closely scouting out his position. This gave Alexander a tremendous advantage in determining the extent of Darius' site preparations, examining the Persian deployment, and then devising the most effective countertactics.

When Alexander advanced, he was allowed to maneuver freely across the Persian front without any hindrance whatsoever. Only when he began moving towards the rough ground beyond the Persian left did Darius react, but by then it was too late, as Alexander had already managed to anchor his right flank there. This made it extremely difficult for Bessus to work around behind his right flank and confined the Persians to conducting a head-on attack, emphasizing fighting ability rather than overwhelming numbers, exactly the reverse of what would have proved advantageous to the Persians. Darius' fixation on the scythed chariots had surrendered the initiative to Alexander, with the result that Bessus was precluded from delivering what might have been an overwhelming attack against Alexander's right flank.

In paralleling Alexander's move beyond his left, Bessus opened a gap between his wing and Darius' center. The Persians, as was typical of most ancient armies of the time, did not hold back reserves to meet such a contingency. Instead, in an attempt to squeeze all their forces into their constructed frontage, Darius had packed the Persians in so densely that they were all but incapable of moving laterally. As a result, when Bessus charged Alexander's right flank group in an oblique left direction, he inevitably created a gap in his wing that could not be closed, there being no forces in the rear to move up into it. If that gap had not been available for Alexander to exploit and his right had not been anchored against the rough ground, he might have been forced to use his Companions piecemeal to counter a turning move around his flank rather than having them available to exploit the gap that had been created in the Persian line. In that case, the Persians might just have been able to fight Alexander to a draw.

Historically, the chariots had always opened the attack of the Persian army. At Gaugamela, however, they could only do so when and if the Macedonians aligned themselves properly with the paths so carefully prepared for the chariots' run. If the scythed chariots were truly formidable weapons, there may have been some justification for Darius surrendering the initiative to Alexander to optimize their effectiveness. Unfortunately, this was not the case. Although it had some success in smashing into undisciplined mobs of Asiatic levies, the chariot was an archaic weapon that was extremely vulnerable to heavy missile fire and was relatively ineffective against disciplined troops who had the presence of mind to open their ranks. Drawn by either two or four horses, the chariots had little, if any, lateral maneuverability when working up speed for a charge. In effect, all they could do was bound straight ahead. While the chariots were still in their deployment area, their opponents could easily predict both their path and intended point of impact, enabling missile troops to target them with a high degree of hit probability. If the driver or one of the horses was wounded, the chariot would probably become uncontrolled and could frequently be turned back upon its own lines. Loud noises could also sufficiently frighten the horses to cause the driver to lose control of them. If the chariot survived the charge and was able to penetrate the enemy line, it became extremely vulnerable to enemy light troops. As the chariot slowed its speed to allow the winded horses to catch their breath or to turn around, the driver and attending warriors could either be easily pulled off the vehicle from behind or successfully engaged in combat by opposing light infantry.

If a scythed chariot attack was delivered as the spearhead of a cavalry attack, however, it could be devastating, provided, of course, that it was not overwhelmed by enemy missile fire. The scythed chariots themselves were not likely to cause appreciable casualties against well-disciplined infantry that opened lanes for them, but if any closely following cavalry could penetrate the line before the gaps were reclosed, they would seriously disorder the enemy formation in the resulting hand-to-hand combat. This tactic, however, was not contemplated by Darius, as he appears to have launched all three of his chariot attacks completely unsupported by cavalry. When the chariots succeeded in passing through Parmenio's lines, for instance, his dislocated ranks quickly closed up again before they were hit by the cavalry. Consequently, it seems that even had the chariots achieved some success, it could not have been expanded because of Darius' failure to integrate them properly with the cavalry in a combined-arms attack.

The charge of the Indian and Persian cavalry from the Persian center is one of the most perplexing aspects of the battle. Of any Persian force that day, it was in their hands to inflict a truly catastrophic defeat on Alexander. But instead of rolling back Alexander's phalanx from the center towards both flanks, the force simply rode away, apparently to loot the Macedonian first-line transports. Darius had foolishly ordered these units to attempt a rescue of his family, apparently being unaware that they were being held at Alexander's base camp hidden behind the Jabal Maqlub massif, seven miles off the battlefield. When the Persian cavalry ran into the Macedonian frontline transports, it quickly dispatched the guards and probably proceeded to disperse in a futile search for the royal family. Unable to locate them, the cavalry troops determined to make the best of the situation by grabbing whatever loot they could lay their hands on. When Alexander's rear line came up, the disorganized Persian cavalry was quickly driven off. Its charge had been a misguided waste of effort, having little practical effect on the battle except perhaps pushing Parmenio over the brink in requesting assistance from Alexander. Had Darius' orders to this force been of a military nature, instead of a personal objective, he just might have collapsed the phalanx and forced Alexander to use his Companion cavalry to stabilize his center rather than having them available to exploit the gap that developed in Bessus' line.

This was Alexander's third great field battle and clearly his most difficult to date. Everything appeared to be in the Persians' favor. They had an army comprised of their most effective shock arm, their heavy cavalry, and they also had a great superiority in numbers, a wide plain on which to deploy their forces effectively, and enough time to prepare the site carefully to their best advantage. In all likelihood, when Alexander advanced, he would be enveloped on both flanks and possibly attacked from the rear, as well. These disadvantages would have easily convinced most commanders to postpone the battle for another time and place, when circumstances might be less disadvantageous. But that is probably why they are not remembered as "The Great." Indeed, nowhere does Alexander better justify that suffix to his name than at Gaugamela. Rather than hesitating over the perils of the situation and assuming the defensive or even retreating, he carefully prepared a brilliant offensive plan. He organized his army so that it could be easily formed into a hollow square to defend itself against any attempt by Darius' cavalry to surround it. Cavalry units were detailed as flank guards and echeloned back behind each wing. A second line was organized and ordered to face to the rear to counter any enemy troops appearing from that direction. In the worst case, even if surrounded, Alexander had prepared an adequate plan to mitigate the effects of the expected Persian envelopment attacks.

When Alexander advanced, he did so only after careful reconnaissance. He marched across the Persian front to anchor his right up against rough ground, thereby precluding the Persian cavalry from attempting any rapid envelopment around the flank of his offensive wing. Alexander's echeloned formation inclined Parmenio's more vulnerable left flank back, making it more difficult for the Persians to envelop him. Although Alexander had the smaller army, his approach allowed him to project only his elite forces forward for maximum combat effectiveness against the Persian line. He managed to retain the initiative throughout the battle and to force the Persians to react to his moves instead of what should have logically been the other way around. Alexander's preparations and advance to the attack were flawlessly executed.

The rough ground to Alexander's right forced Bessus to assault Alexander's line head-on rather than attempting to use his superior numbers to envelop Alexander's flank. Although greatly outnumbered by Bessus' cavalry, Alexander was just able to check him with his Greek allied and mercenary cavalry. This allowed him to keep his Companions intact and relatively unengaged in the continuing fight. As a result, when Bessus' move to his left created a noticeable gap between his wing and the Persian center, the Companions were in a position to take immediate advantage of it.

Alexander's preparations against the chariots were extremely well thought-out, though he had never fought them before. He deduced their weakness to missile fire and concentrated a heavy volume of it to break up the chariot attacks while they were still approaching his line. Along his center and left flank, which was without missile fire support, Alexander relied on the clamor of noise to confuse the horses and turn them back upon their own start line. There too, few chariots actually penetrated the Macedonian line, and those that did caused little damage, being quickly attacked and overcome.

Alexander did make a rather large mistake, however, that could well have cost him the battle. In his rapid advance to make contact with the Persian line, he created a gap between his wing and Parmenio's slower-moving line. Darius evidently saw this and ordered a charge of the Indian and Persian cavalry into it. Fortunately for Alexander, the attacking cavalry quickly passed through the phalanx to another inconsequential objective. As a result, Parmenio was able to hang on just long enough for Alexander to turn the tide on his wing. This occurred when a gap appeared in Bessus' line that Alexander could exploit. Prior to this, Alexander, for all the tactical skill he displayed, did not yet have the upper hand in the battle; he was only effectively checking the Persians. Given enough time, the superior numbers of the Persians might well have forced him to dissipate his Companions to stabilize some part of his weakened line. In that case, the Persians might have been able to fight the battle to a draw. Luck was with Alexander, however, and instead of a stalemate he was able to win what is probably one of the greatest field battle victories of the ancient world.

Babylon

With Darius' defeat at Gaugamela, Alexander continued southwest to Babylon, which was about 50 miles south-southwest of Baghdad. Large numbers of Babylonians lined the walls of their city in their eagerness to welcome him; others went out to meet him as he approached. Bagophanes, the commander of the city's citadel and treasury, had flowers strewn over the entire length of the road leading to the city and placed altars on both sides of it piled high with frankincense and perfumes. Mazaeus, the city's satrap, came out to meet Alexander and surrender the city. In doing so, he ensured his reappointment to his office.

Alexander had the citizens who had come out to meet him fall in behind his army. Entering the city in a chariot, he went directly to the palace where the 50,000 talents of silver in the city's treasury were turned over to him.[228] A small portion of the funds he had captured were allocated to the priesthood for the rebuilding of the temples that Xerxes had destroyed. In grateful appreciation, the priests conferred upon him the ancient title of King of the Lands. Alexander had wisely represented himself as a benefactor of the city, delivering it from Persian oppression and avarice. Consequently, both officers and men were billeted in luxurious private houses, never lacking for wine, women, or food. Alexander spent five weeks

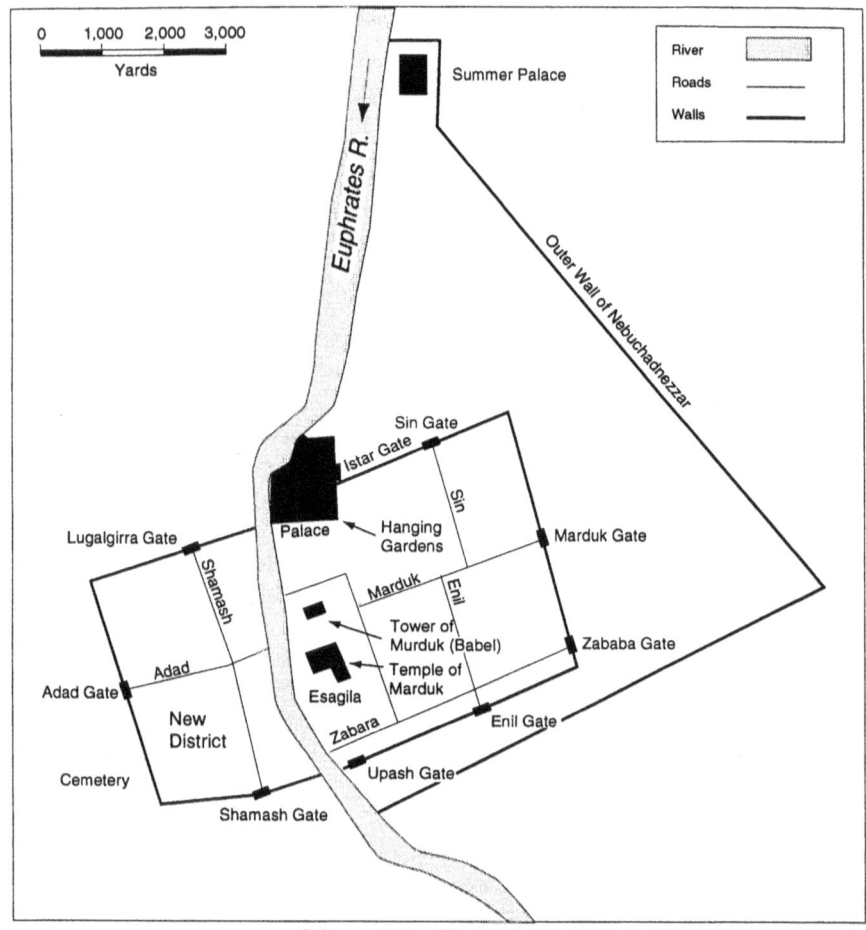

Map 35: Babylon

in Babylon resting his army. Before leaving, he designated the city as the new administrative capital of his empire, it being much more centrally located for that purpose than the Macedonian capital of Pella. Abulites was appointed satrap of Susa; Mazaeus, a Companion, commander of the garrison; and Archelaus (son of Theodorus), the area's general. Agathon was placed in command of Babylon's citadel with a garrison of 200 Macedonians and 300 mercenaries.

Susiana

Susa

Immediately after the battle of Gaugamela, Alexander sent Philoxenus, one of his officers, on ahead to obtain the surrender of Susa and take possession of its treasury. Abulites, the satrap of Susiana, surrendered the city without resistance and turned over the treasure stored there to Philoxenus. In mid-November, Alexander set out from Babylon for Susa. He covered the 375 miles between the two cities in 20 days.[229] Alexander was met by Abulites just west of Susa at the Choaspes River, known to the Greeks as the source of the Great King's drinking water, and was escorted into the city with much pomp and ceremony. Proceeding immediately to the palace, Alexander inspected Darius' treasury, which contained 50,000 talents of silver.[230] All the spoils taken from Greece by Xerxes were also stored there, and many statues and golden artifacts were returned to the Greek temples from which they had been stolen.

Alexander appointed Abulites, a Persian, satrap of Susiana; Xenophilus, one of the Companions, garrison commander of Susa, in command of 1,000 Macedonians; and Archelaus (son of Theodorus), general of Susiana, in command of 3,000 troops.[231] Before leaving the city, Alexander allowed Darius' mother, his daughters, and his son to take up residence there. He then marched off to Persis.

Persis

Four days after leaving Susa, Alexander crossed the Pasitigris River and entered the territory of the Uxians, lying within Persis just over the Susiana border.[232] It was a mountainous country with sheer cliffs and deep gorges in the north, gradually giving way to open plains in the south. The rugged highlands were occupied by the mountain Uxians, who had managed to remain fiercely independent. The Uxians of the plains had long ago submitted to Persian rule. Medates, a cousin of Darius, was the satrap of the plains Uxians.

Mountain Uxians

The mountain Uxians gathered in a pass and demanded from Alexander the same tribute for passage through their territory that they had always received from the Persian king. After assuring them that he would be delivering the expected tribute, Alexander formed a fast-moving task force numbering about 12,000 troops — including 3,000 hypaspists, 1,000 Agrianians, 1,000 archers, 1,000 Thracians, and 4 taxies of the phalanx — and set off on a forced night march along an unguarded side road.[233] The next day he attacked the Uxian villages in his line of march, killing many of their inhabitants and driving the rest into the hills. Marching on the pass held by the mountain Uxians, Alexander sent Craterus off to occupy the high ground across their expected line of retreat. Alexander then moved so quickly on the pass that the surprised and undisciplined Uxians fled before contact was even made. Although the Uxians took some losses from Alexander's advance and their subsequent disorderly retreat along the narrow and precipitous road that led to their rear, their heaviest casualties, by far, were incurred when they reached what they believed to be the safety of their mountains only to run unexpectedly into Craterus' force.

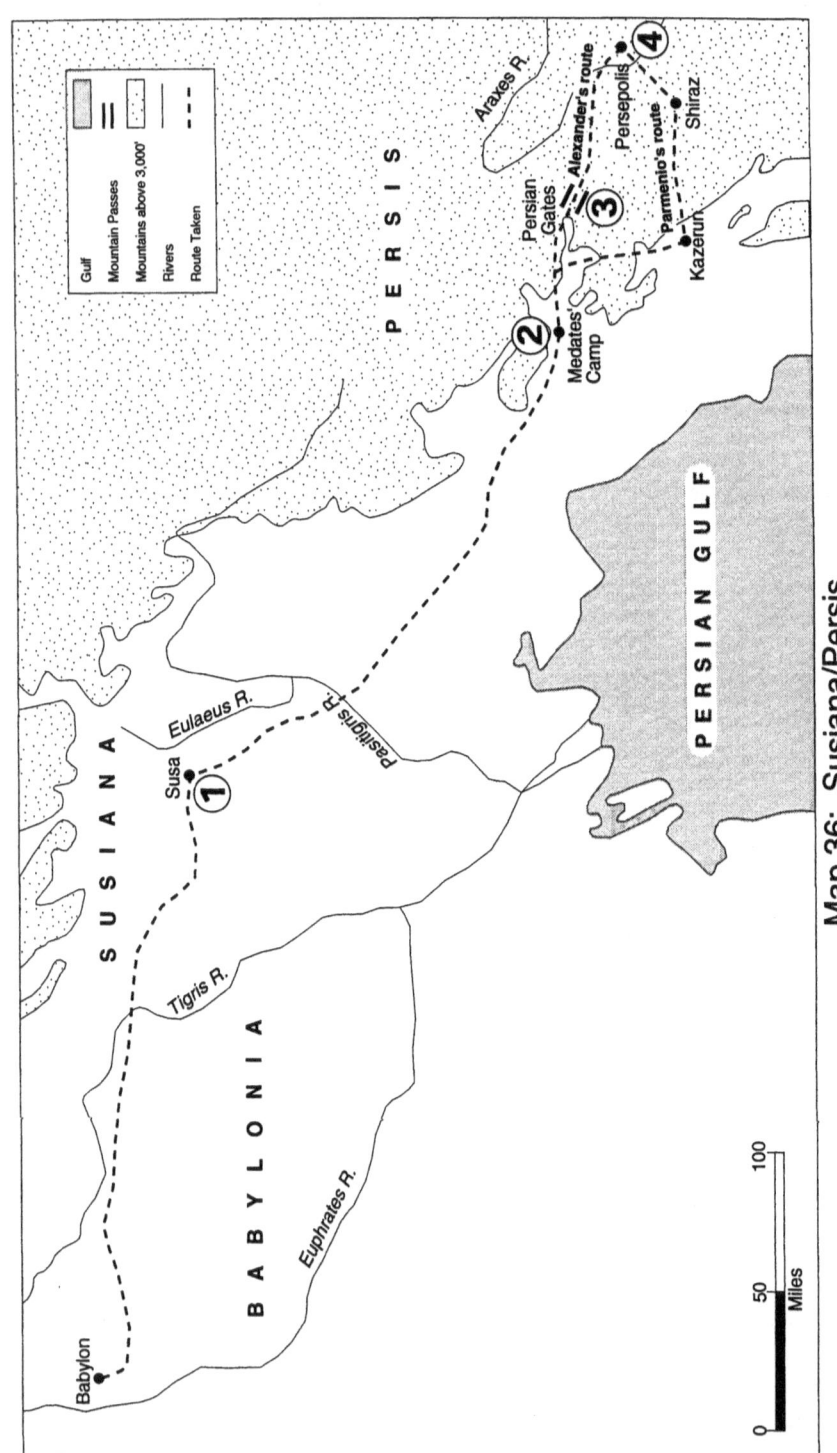

Map 36: Susiana/Persis

Plains Uxians

At Kotai-i Sangar, Medates waited for Alexander with Persian troops and the Uxians of the plains. The position was a strategic junction, one road leading directly to the Persian Gates and another through Shiraz and then northeast to Persepolis. Medates had fortified a narrow position in the gate between two sheer cliffs and occupied it with a force of 300 cavalry and 25,000 infantry.[234] Alexander attempted a frontal assault but because of rocks being rolled down from the heights and heavy defensive missile fire, it was thrown back with heavy losses. He then withdrew a short distance from the pass and made camp. Here Alexander questioned his prisoners to determine if anyone knew of another way around Medates' position. Being informed of a position overlooking Medates' line from the rear, Alexander sent 1,500 mercenaries and 1,000 Agrianians under command of Tauron to make a night march along the path disclosed to him.[235] At daylight, in order to pin down Medates, Alexander began a series of frontal attacks on his position. They were all thrown back with heavy losses, in large part because of the difficulties of the terrain. When his army refused to attack again, Alexander joined the front rank and ridiculed them for hesitating in front of such an "insignificant" obstacle. Alexander could not be prevailed upon to withdraw from his exposed position, and when the Persians began concentrating on him with long-range missile fire, the Macedonians reluctantly came up in close-order formation to protect him.

At last, Tauron began his attack from the high ground behind Medates' line. As the Persians began to waver and give way, Alexander attacked again and this time carried the position. Medates then withdrew into the citadel he had prepared in the rear and asked for terms, but Alexander refused to extend him any. In desperation, Medates sent a secret messenger to Susa, begging Sisygambis, Darius' mother, to intercede with Alexander on his behalf. He made this request on the strength of his marriage to the daughter of the dowager queen's sister. Sisygambis at first refused to intervene because she did not want to take advantage of the kindness that Alexander had shown her. She was eventually persuaded to ask Alexander to pardon Medates, however, both because he was her kinsman and he was approaching Alexander as a suppliant. Alexander reluctantly agreed to her request. Although he left the Uxians their freedom, Alexander incorporated them into the satrapy of Susiana and levied an annual tribute against them of 100 cavalry horses.[236] They were ordered to turn over immediately 500 draft animals and 30,000 sheep.[237] The nature of this tribute resulted from the fact that the Uxians were primarily herdsmen; they engaged in neither agriculture or trade and thus had no money. This proved to be a forerunner of how tribute was to be paid by the eastern provinces of the Persian Empire whose economies were also based on barter.

1. The Persian winter capital. Alexander captures 50,000 talents in the city's treasury. Alexander allows Darius' family to settle in the city. 2. Alexander defeats Medates. 3. Alexander defeats Ariobarzanes. 4. Alexander captures 120,000 talents in Persepolis' treasury.

Generalship   Although Alexander had overcome a mountain tribe that had successfully resisted the Persians for decades, it was only after a lot more fighting than he cared to admit. His frontal assaults on Medates were largely ineffectual and produced heavy casualties. Their lack of success was undoubtedly the basis of his reluctance to extend any surrender terms to Medates. In his fight with the mountain Uxians, Alexander's rapid marches and unexpected arrival quickly broke their unsteady morale and he won the position they attempted to defend without a battle. Against Medates, however, it was only Alexander's encircling force under Tauron that decided the issue. The costly and ineffectual assaults against the main position of the Persian line had clearly broken the morale of the attacking Macedonians, and Alexander was attempting to rally them when Tauron's surprise attack from behind the Persians turned the tide of battle. Had Tauron not been successful in his attack, it is doubtful if Alexander could have carried the position by frontal assault. He did prevail, however, and the way was now open to an advance on the Persian Gates.

Persepolis

Alexander's objective was not only to capture Persepolis but to prevent the huge treasure stored there from being removed. Denying Darius this treasure would greatly hamper his ability to raise a new field army. Alexander sent Parmenio with the Thessalian cavalry, the Greek allies, the Greek mercenaries, the phalanx, and the baggage train down the main road to Shiraz while he took a force consisting of the Companion cavalry, the mounted scouts, the Agrianians, and the archers along a secondary road running through the Persian Gates.[238] Alexander initially thought that he could fight his way through the pass. Ariobarzanes, however, occupied the Gates with 300 cavalry and 25,000 infantry.[239] He had built a wall across the pass and remained concealed until Alexander had marched about halfway through the canyon, the narrowness of which could only accommodate three men marching abreast.[240] Then from the surrounding cliffs on both sides of the road, Ariobarzanes' troops began rolling huge boulders down upon the closely packed Macedonian ranks. These often triggered landslides that buried entire units of Alexander's soldiers. Artillery and heavy missile fire from above also took a heavy toll. The Macedonians were unable to reply to the Persian missile fire and could not climb up the steep canyon walls or assault the wall blocking the pass with any hope of success. Neither could they stay where they were, unprotected against the boulders being rolled down on them. Alexander therefore was forced to order a withdrawal to a point three miles from the pass, where he built a fortified camp.

Alexander was now in an extremely dangerous situation, Ariobarzanes being in a central position between himself and Parmenio. Ariobarzanes could conceivably leave a small holding force manning the Persian Gates against Alexander and attack Parmenio with the bulk of his army, all well before Alexander could possibly march back along a rough mountain road to reinforce him. In desperation, Alexander had the prisoners he had captured questioned for any way around

Ariobarzanes' position. A Lycian, who had tended goats in the area for several years, told him that although there was no way through the mountains, there was a hidden path through the forest that led to the rear of the Persian position.[241] Despite the difficulty of the route, especially for armed men, Alexander had no alternative but to attempt it. The soldiers selected for the mission were ordered to arm themselves lightly and draw three days' rations.

Craterus was ordered to remain in camp with his and Meleager's taxies of the phalanx, some 1,000 mounted archers, and 500 cavalry.[242] He was to keep additional campfires burning throughout the night to make it appear as if the entire Macedonian army was still in camp. At daybreak, Craterus was to conduct a feint attack to distract the attention of the Persians. Alexander, meanwhile, made his way along the path in the woods with two groups: a lead one under himself, which included Perdiccas' taxies of the phalanx, the archers, Agrianians, Agema, and a double squadron of cavalry; and a following one under Amyntas, with the remainder of the army.[243] When Alexander emerged from the woods and was ready to attack, he would sound a trumpet. This was to be Craterus' signal to launch a full-scale assault against the wall.

Alexander began a 12.5-mile march through the woods that took three days.[244] The narrow path, steep hill faces, deep and drifting snow, and strong winds made footing insecure and progress both slow and exhausting. Then too, they faced the constant doubt as to the trustworthiness of their guide, who, for all that was known, might well be leading them into a Persian trap. When Alexander at last reached the summit of the mountain, he sent the group under Amyntas, which included his taxies of the phalanx commanded by Coenus, Philotas, and Polysperchon, down the direct path to Ariobarzanes' position, along a route easier to traverse and with adequate fodder for the horses.[245] Alexander took his group along a steeper and more roundabout route, exiting out beyond the Persian position. Although Alexander allowed his fatigued troops to rest at midday, at dusk he ordered them to continue their march.

At dawn the next day, Alexander's force sighted the Persian outposts, deployed for attack, and quickly defeated them. Instead of alerting Ariobarzanes to the presence of Alexander's force, the Persians fled into the hills. Alexander then gave command of 3,000 troops to Ptolemy, who was to assume a blocking position from a third direction.[246] As Alexander attacked the surprised Persian camp, he sounded the signal for Craterus to attack also. When the Persians manning the walls heard the commotion in their rear, they assumed their position to be turned. As they withdrew, they ran into the troops from the camp who were being driven towards them by Alexander. Craterus, meanwhile, had crossed the wall unopposed. With Ptolemy on their flank, Craterus advancing on their front, and Alexander coming up on their rear, the Persians were boxed in on three sides. Although the Persians put up a hard fight, they were quickly overwhelmed, many of them being forced off the steep cliffs to their deaths. Ariobarzanes, at the head of a force of 40 cavalry and 5,000 infantry, broke through the Macedonian lines and headed for Persepolis.[247] He was, however, refused admittance into the city by Tiridates, its garrison commander, and died fighting outside the walls against the Macedonians who pursued him.

Because the road was intersected in many places by steep ravines, Alexander's advance towards Persepolis was slowed. When he received a letter from Tiridates, however, stating that the city would be betrayed to him and urging his arrival before the treasury was looted, Alexander went on ahead with his cavalry, riding all through the night. At daybreak, he reached the Araxes River, the last major obstacle before Persepolis. Timber and stones were taken from nearby villages, and a bridge was quickly thrown across the river. Alexander entered Persepolis on January 31, 330 B.C., taking possession of a treasury containing 120,000 talents in silver.[248] At nearby Pasargadae, another 6,000 talents in treasure was seized.[249] Not wishing to leave behind any of his newfound wealth in either of the cities, Alexander assembled a large number of mules and 3,000 camels to transport it to Ecbatana.[250] Phrasaortes (son of Rheomithres) was appointed satrap of Persepolis, and Nicarchides was placed in command of its citadel with a garrison of 3,000 Macedonians.[251]

Curiously, although Parmenio advanced down the main road to Persepolis, ancient writers neglected to mention anything that happened to him. It is inconceivable that the Persians did not deploy a strong force to cover the main route to Persepolis, and Parmenio would clearly have had to do some heavy fighting along the way. We can only conclude that these writers deliberately ignored Parmenio's campaign as it might have detracted from Alexander's success in forcing the Persian Gates.

At a drunken party some months later, Thais, an Athenian prostitute, allegedly talked Alexander into burning down Persepolis. Parmenio advised Alexander against destroying his own property, but his council, as usual, was apparently ignored. Parmenio apparently did not understand that Alexander had determined all along to burn down the city that represented the seat of Persian power. He intended it as a signal to the Persians that one reign was ending and another beginning. To the Greeks the incident was portrayed as revenge for the Persian sacrilege committed against the temples of their homeland.

Generalship

The fight at the Persian Gates was not without difficulty, and Alexander was forced to place himself twice in potentially serious strategic jeopardy, once when he sent Parmenio along the road to Shiraz and again when he led a flanking column around Ariobarzanes through the woods. In both cases, he deliberately allowed the two wings of his army to be isolated from each other, with the Persian force in a central position between them. A competent Persian general would have held Alexander in place with a small force and fallen upon Parmenio with the bulk of his army. Parmenio had an unbalanced force consisting for the most part of less reliable and less combat-effective Greek mercenaries and allied Greeks, with few cavalry or missile troops. The Persians might well have been able to inflict an outright defeat on a general as cautious as him. On the other hand, if the Persians

7: THE WESTERN PERSIAN EMPIRE

had attacked Alexander along his route through the woods, they would probably have been able to block both his further advance and his withdrawal with a small number of light missile infantry. In all likelihood, this would have trapped his forces along a narrow path and made it impossible for them to deploy into any organized formation or to defend themselves properly. In such a situation, even if Alexander had managed to escape the trap, the cost in casualties he would have incurred would have been prohibitive.

Alexander's luck, however, held, and both his gambles paid off. Tactically, Alexander handled his flanking operation against Ariobarzanes superbly, boxing him in from three directions. And although the Persians apparently gave him a hard fight, the issue was never really in doubt after his attack began. Strategically, Alexander achieved the main objective of capturing the Persian gold and silver in Persepolis. He had done so by taking big chances and had more than his share of luck, but that is the nature of great generalship. His casualties were unknown but were apparently not disproportionately high in light of the situation he faced. It was a difficult campaign successfully concluded and within an acceptable level of losses.

Ariobarzanes had an opportunity few commanders who fought Alexander were ever presented with, a chance to defeat him in detail. When Alexander divided his army for his advance on Persepolis, he was several days' march away from Parmenio. This was a classic military situation offering a bold commander the possibility of maneuvering mobile units against an isolated and slow-moving force. Alexander would have obviously taken immediate action if their roles had been reversed. Ariobarzanes, however, decided to ignore the opportunity, if he ever saw it, and passively remain in what he believed to be an impregnable position. This was just about the worst thing he could do against a commander of Alexander's abilities. To hand Alexander the initiative was to allow him to assume the offensive, an event which invariably resulted in the defeat of his opponent. Ariobarzanes also failed to take even basic precautions against a potential flank attack on his position at the Persian Gates. Being familiar with the area by his continued occupation of it, it should have been an easy matter to surmise that Alexander might seek to make use of some unknown path to turn his position. Ariobarzanes could obviously have done what Alexander did and queried the locals to determine if Persian gold could discover the existence of such a path. If he had located one, it undoubtedly could have been effectively blocked by a relatively small force. Even if only a reconnoitering force was sent to the path, this would have been of critical importance to Ariobarzanes in alerting him that his flank was being turned.

Ariobarzanes was obviously a rather mediocre commander by any measure. He had little, if any, initiative and seems to have been perfectly content to sit passively behind his position at the Gates. He foolishly thought, no doubt, that Alexander would persistently attack in a desperate attempt to force the position frontally, regardless of the cost. He not only seriously underestimated Alexander's abilities as a general but was rather inept in even taking routine precautions against surprise.

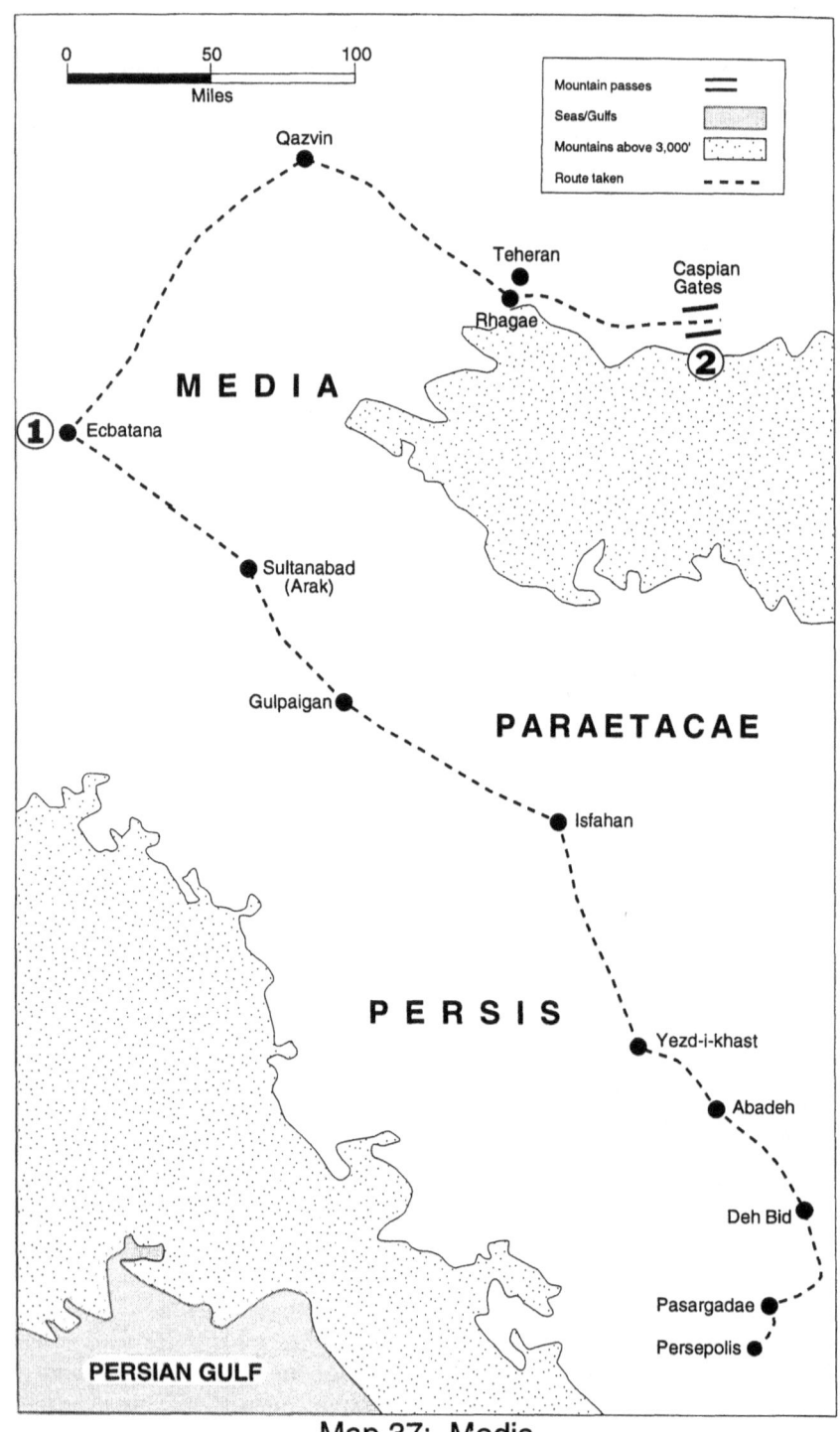

Map 37: Media

Media

Paraetacae

En route to Ecbatana, Alexander defeated the Paraetacae, a tribe living adjacent to the Uxians. No details are available about the campaign, but it appears that they were quickly subdued. Oxathres (son of Abulites) was appointed as satrap over the area. Forces under Craters and Amyntas were left behind as a military garrison, in addition to 600 cavalry and 600 archers.[252]

Caspian Gates

After his defeat at Gaugamela, Darius withdrew to Ecbatana, the capital of Media. If Alexander remained in Susa, it was Darius' intention to recruit yet another army from the areas of Bactria and the Caspian Sea. If Alexander should march directly against him, however, Darius proposed to delay his advance with a scorched-earth campaign as he withdrew through the Caspian Gates into Bactria. The eastern satraps of the Persian Empire did not rate highly Darius' chances of being able to hold Media and declined to commit much more than token forces to the effort. Darius was thus only able to raise an army of 3,000 cavalry and 18,000 infantry at Ecbatana.[253] Bessus had supplied most of the cavalry, while the infantry consisted of what was left of the Persian Guard and Greek mercenaries from Gaugamela, augmented by a small force of Persian levies raised from the nearby satrapies. Additional cavalry units from the Scythians and Cadusians were expected to arrive soon. With such a small force at his immediate disposal, however, Darius was unable to meet Alexander in the field. Consequently, when Alexander advanced against him, the Great King was forced to withdraw to the east through the Caspian Gates. As he did so, many of his troops began to desert him, either dispersing to their homes or surrendering to Alexander.

Upon receiving reports of Darius' plan to raise another army in an attempt to hold Media, Alexander immediately left Persepolis and marched northward for 12 days.[254] Learning that Darius had only been able to raise a small force but had nevertheless decided to fight, Alexander accelerated his march. Three days' march from Ecbatana, Alexander met Bistanes, a Persian noble who was allegedly a son of Artaxerxes III (Ochus).[255] He told Alexander that Darius had left the city five days earlier with a force of 3,000 cavalry, 6,000 infantry, and 7,000 talents of the Median treasury.[256] Alexander now organized a fast-moving pursuit force of 20,000 men, including his Companions, some taxies of the phalanx, the Agrianians, and the archers, and made a forced-march to Rhagae, which he reached 11 days later.[257]

---

1. The capital of Media and the summer capital of the Persian kings. Alexander has Parmenio murdered here. Alexander dismisses the Thessalians and the remaining Greek allies. 2. Alexander learns that Bessus has taken Darius prisoner.

Ecbatana

A force 6,000-strong in the command of Parmenio, which included four taxies of the phalanx, the Greek allies, the Greek mercenaries, and the Thracian cavalry, escorted Alexander's treasury to Ecbatana.[258] Over 7,000 tons of gold and silver was transported by 20,000 mules and 5,000 camels.[259] Upon his arrival there, Parmenio secured the city, which occupied a key position along the Macedonian line of communications. However, upon being implicated in his son Philotas' alleged assassination attempt against Alexander in the spring, Parmenio was sentenced to death. Polydamas, one of Alexander's Companions, was sent to Ecbatana with a warrant for Parmenio's execution, which was carried out by Cleander, Sitalces and Menidas, who were stationed there with Parmenio at the time. Alexander then ordered the mustering out of the Thessalian cavalry and the remaining Greek allies, although they were allowed the opportunity to reenlist with the army as mercenaries and many did so.[260]

Caspian Gates

Informed at Rhagae that Darius had already passed through the Caspian Gates, Alexander rested his troops for five days.[261] A force of cavalry and a few light infantry in command of Coenus were then sent out to forage because Alexander had been informed that the land beyond the Gates was a desert. After appointing Oxodates, a Persian, satrap of Media, Alexander marched on through the Caspian Gates.

Damghan

On learning from Bagistanes and Antibelus that Darius had been arrested by Bessus, Alexander pursued them with a force consisting of the Companions, the mounted scouts, and the strongest of the light infantry.[262] In such haste was Alexander that he did not wait for Coenus to return from his foraging mission but set out immediately. Craterus was placed in command of that portion of the army left behind and ordered to join Alexander as soon as possible, although he was instructed not to tire out his men unnecessarily by a forced-march.

Alexander's pursuit force traveled all night and the following morning, finally making camp at noon to rest during what was left of the day. Darius' arrest was confirmed, and the locals told Alexander that the Great King was now being transported in a wagon. At dusk, Alexander continued his pursuit, marching throughout the entire night. Reaching the deserted Persian camp at dawn, Alexander learned that Bessus had assumed Darius' sovereignty over the Persian Empire. Although his force was close to exhaustion, Alexander pushed them on all through the day and night until the following noon, when he arrived at the Persian campsite of the previous day. Being informed that Bessus had intended to march all night, Alexander made local inquiries to determine if anyone knew of a short-cut to intercept him. He was told that although one existed, it was desolate, with no water to be found along it. Because in these circumstances the infantry would no longer be able to accompany the pursuit force, Alexander dismounted 500 of his most exhausted cavalry and mounted infantry in their place.²⁶³ The pursuit was continued throughout the night, 50 miles being covered.²⁶⁴ At dawn, Alexander came upon a number of unarmed Persians, whom he routed. He was now just behind Bessus, who had been slowed down by his need to transport Darius in a wagon. Seeing that they would soon be overtaken, Bessus, Nabarzanes, and Barsaentes attempted to convince Darius to mount a horse. When he refused, they killed him near Damghan to prevent his capture and use by Alexander in legitimizing his rule.²⁶⁵

8. The Eastern Persian Empire

The eastern Persian empire differed radically from that of the west. Much of the area there was mountainous terrain, desert, or steppes. Moving past Persepolis, there were no large cities in the region, except for Taxila. The area's population tended to be nomadic or relatively isolated mountain tribes living in numerous small villages. Because of the difficulties of terrain and lack of cities, the tribes of the eastern Persian empire remained isolated and generated little trade and commerce. As their primitive economies were based on the barter system, they had little money and usually sent their tribute to the Persian king in foodstuffs or animal herds.

The infantry of the eastern Persian Empire consisted primarily of levies of rather undisciplined mountain and nomadic tribes who were usually untrained and lightly armed. They, of course, had little chance against the heavily armed and well-disciplined formations of the Macedonians and Greeks. Since virtually all the nomadic and steppe tribes had ridden horses from youth, the areas of Areia, Bactria, and Sogdiana were able to field a huge force of heavy and light cavalry, as were the Scythian tribes on the northern frontier. Although the Persian heavy cavalry was not very effective militarily, the Persian light cavalry was exceptionally proficient. In fact, so impressed was Alexander with their skill that he replaced the light Greek cavalry serving in his army with them.

Alexander's conquest of the eastern Persian Empire differed significantly from that of the west. He would fight no great field battles there. Instead, his military operations would consist of subduing mountain tribes, waging guerrilla war against mobile nomadic cavalry, and overrunning the light infantry of desert tribes. This called for far more flexible generalship than the stand-up fighting that characterized the western campaigns. Alexander, however, would rise to the occasion and subdue tribes that had remained independent of Persian rule for generations in a matter of weeks.

Hyrcania

After the murder of Darius, Bessus returned to Bactria, while Nabarzanes, accompanied by the Greek mercenaries, fled to Hyrcania.[1] The land approach to

Hyrcania lay through high and wooded mountains, behind which a level plain extended up to the shores of the Caspian Sea. After a march of three days, Alexander reached Hecatompylus, which lay just outside the mountain pass leading into Hyrcania. There he divided his army into three forces. Alexander led the mobile force, consisting of the hypaspists, the archers, Agrianians, some of the lightly armed phalanx, the Companion cavalry, and the mounted javelin men; Craterus commanded his own and Amyntas' taxies of the phalanx, some of the archers, and a small number of cavalry; and Erigyius had charge of the baggage train, the mercenaries, and the remainder of the cavalry.[2]

Tapuria

Alexander moved into Hyrcania through the Shamshirbun Pass, which neither the Tapurians nor the Greek mercenaries made an effort to defend. Upon reaching the first range of hills, Alexander left behind some troops to hold the roads against any enemy attempt to cut his line of communications and then marched ahead along a rough road with the hypaspists, some of the lighter-armed phalanx, and a number of the archers.[3] After moving through the pass, Alexander camped in a plain near a small river and waited four days to collect any stragglers. The Agrianians, who were acting as the rear guard, were attacked by long-range missile fire but drove the attacking troops off with little difficulty.[4] Then, while Alexander moved across the plain, Craterus veered off to the south against the Tapuria to screen Alexander's left flank and to attempt to locate the Greek mercenaries.

When Alexander halted at the Neka River, Nabarzanes, Darius' chilarch, surrendered to him. A short time later, Phrataphernes, satrap of Parthyaea and Hyrcania, also gave himself up. Alexander's three columns met at Zadracarta, the capital of Hyrcania. Alexander had secured the plain, while Craterus had successfully subdued the Tapuria in the foothills of the Elbruz Mountains, although he had been unable to locate the mercenaries. At the surrender of Autophradates, the satrap of the Tapuria, along with Artabazus and his three sons—Ariobarzanes, Arsames, and Cophen—submitted to Alexander. At this point, the Tapuria lay down their arms. The 1,500 Greek mercenaries then sent an envoy to Alexander to discuss terms of surrender, but he would offer none to them, ostensibly because they had fought with the Persians against the Greeks.[5] Having little choice but to trust in Alexander's mercy, the mercenaries surrendered unconditionally to him. Although the eastern Elbruz had been overrun without substantial resistance, the Mardi in the western mountains of the satrapy still remained unconquered.

Mardi

The Mardi lived in the dense forests and rugged mountain country of western Hyrcania. They were a warlike people accustomed to leading a life of brigandage. As they had refused to send any envoys to acknowledge Alexander's sovereignty, he had decided to subdue them forcefully. Although the Mardi had convinced themselves that Alexander would not invade a difficult, remote, and

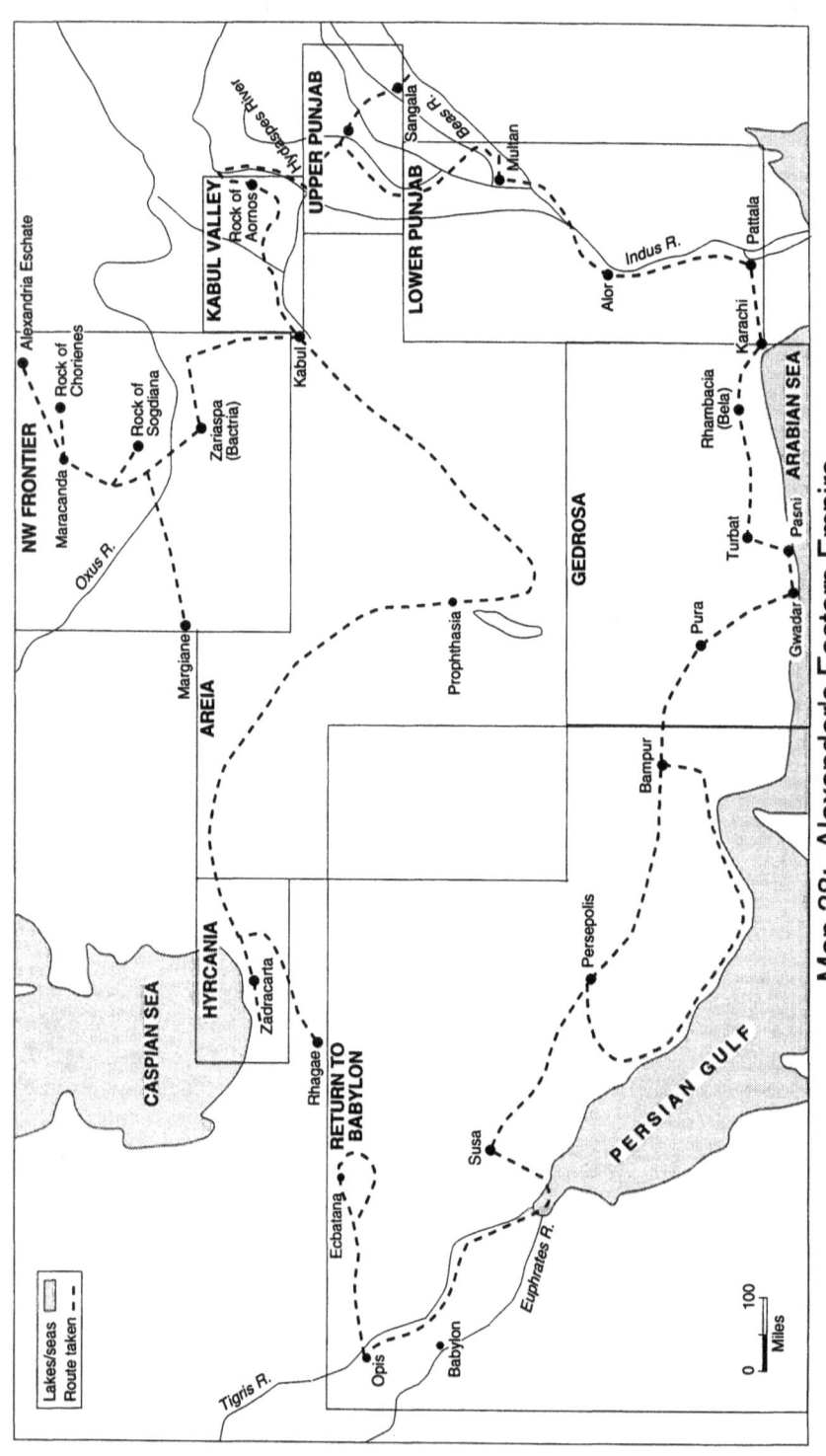

Map 38: Alexander's Eastern Empire

poverty stricken country such as theirs, they took the precaution of mobilizing a force 8,000-strong in a strategic mountain pass in their territory.[6] For his campaign against them, Alexander took the hypaspists, archers, Agrianians, Coenus' and Amyntas' taxies of the phalanx, half the Companion cavalry, and the mounted javelin men.[7] Marching all night, Alexander was in position to attack the Mardi at dawn. Completely taken by surprise, the Mardi broke as Alexander was advancing to the attack and quickly dispersed into the hills. Alexander attempted to pursue them but soon gave up the attempt as hopeless. The tangled and primeval nature of the forest forced the Macedonians literally to hack their way through it to advance. The Mardi soon sent envoys to Alexander to surrender their tribe. Their territory was incorporated into Autophradates' satrapy. Returning to Zadracarta, Alexander spent the next 15 days there and then marched off to Areia.[8]

Areia

First Revolt

When Alexander left for Bactria, Satibarzanes, satrap of Areia, armed the Areians and then persuaded them to rise up in revolt. Massacring Anaxippus and his small Greek garrison of 40 mounted javelin men, Satibarzanes then marched on Artacoana, Areia's capital.[9] From there, he had planned to join Bessus in Bactria for a joint campaign against Alexander. Upon hearing of Satibarzanes' revolt, Alexander discontinued his march to Bactria. Organizing his Companion Cavalry, mounted javelin men, archers, Agrianians, and Amyntas' and Coenus' taxies of the phalanx into a mobile strike force, he quickly marched off in an attempt to engage Satibarzanes. Craterus was left in command of the reminder of the army.[10] Alexander's arrival at Artacoana, 75 miles away, two days later took Satibarzanes completely by surprise.[11] His subsequent flight demoralized the Bactrians, and they deserted in such numbers that when Satibarzanes reached Bessus only 2,000 remained with him.[12]

Those of Satibarzanes' supporters who stayed behind in Areia took refuge in a strong position on a steep and high rock. Although Alexander initially laid siege to the site, he left Craterus behind to invest it while he continued the pursuit of Satibarzanes. Because Satibarzanes had a long head start, however, Alexander was soon forced to end the pursuit. After appointing Arsames satrap of Areia, Alexander returned to the siege Craterus had been maintaining. The rock was very steep on its western side but sloped gently down on the east, dense trees covering all sides of it. The site was four miles in circumference, topped with a grass-covered plain reputedly occupied by 13,000 armed men.[13] As the vegetation at that time of year was extremely dry, the Macedonians were able to start a fire on the eastern base of the hill. Driven by a strong wind, the flames engulfed the hill and burned to death virtually everyone who had taken refuge there.

Alexander now joined Craterus, who had been sent on ahead to besiege Artacoana. As the siege towers were moved up the walls of the city, its inhabitants

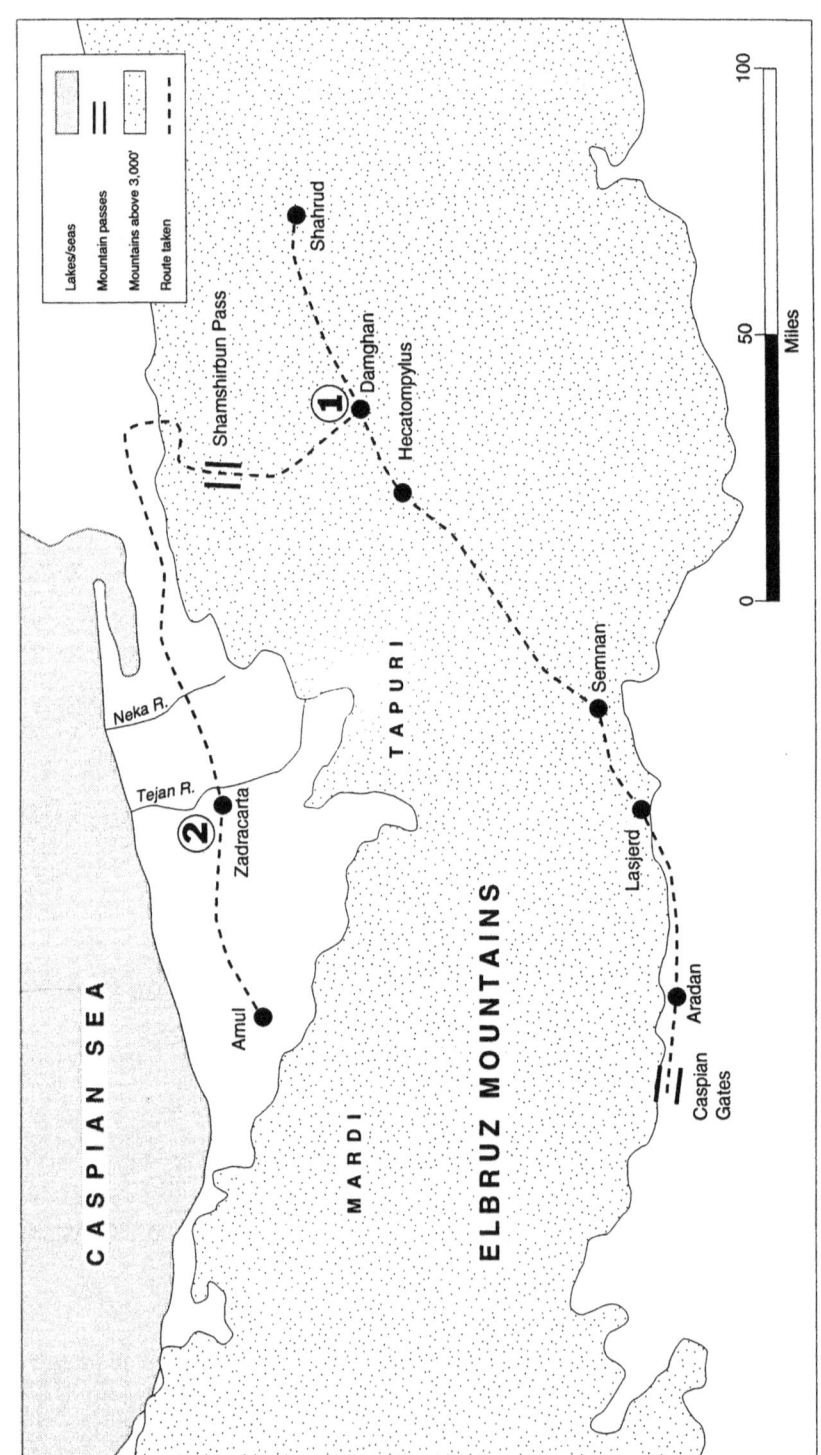

Map 39: Hyrcania

promptly surrendered. Alexander pardoned them and spent the next 30 days subduing the satrapy of any remaining dissident elements.[14] Leaving behind a strong occupation force under Craterus, Alexander appointed Arsames, a Persian, as satrap and marched south to Drangiana, where he rested his army.

Second Revolt

While Alexander was conducting a difficult winter campaign against Arachosia, he received reports that Satibarzanes had entered Areia with a force of 2,000 cavalry obtained from Bessus and had again persuaded the satrapy to revolt.[15] He sent Craterus; Artabazus, a Persian; and two Companions, Erigyius and Caranus, against him with a force of 600 cavalry and 6,000 Greek infantry.[16] Phrataphernes, the satrap of Parthyaea, was also ordered to provide assistance. Erigyius and Caranus were able to corner Satibarzanes and a fierce battle ensued. The Persians broke and fled only when Satibarzanes was killed in single combat by Erigyius. His death effectively ended Areia's revolt. Satibarzanes' force lost a total of 700, of which 300 were taken prisoner.[17] Macedonian losses were 80 killed and 350 wounded.[18]

Drangiana

From Areia, Alexander marched on Drangiana, as Barsaentes, the Persian satrap there, had been one of the murderers of Darius. At Alexander's approach, Barsaentes fled to India. Alexander then occupied Prophthasia, the capital of Drangiana. It was there that Philotas was tried and executed for an alleged conspiracy against him. Alexander then moved south into the area of the fresh-water lakes, one of the major agricultural areas in Persia. While wintering his army there, Alexander was informed of Satibarzanes' second revolt in Areia.

Arimaspians (Benefactors)

Alexander appointed Arsames the satrap of Drangiana and then marched into the nearby territory of the Arimaspians. Cyrus had named this tribe the Benefactors because they had brought him 30,000 wagons of provisions when he had run out of supplies while on a nearby desert campaign.[19] The Arimaspi welcomed Alexander and willingly submitted to his rule. Alexander stayed in their territory for 60 days.[20] In recognition of their loyalty to Cyrus, he gave the tribe a large sum of money and exempted them from all taxation.

Opposite: 1. Darius is murdered. 2. The capital of Hyrcania. The queen of the Amazons visits Alexander.

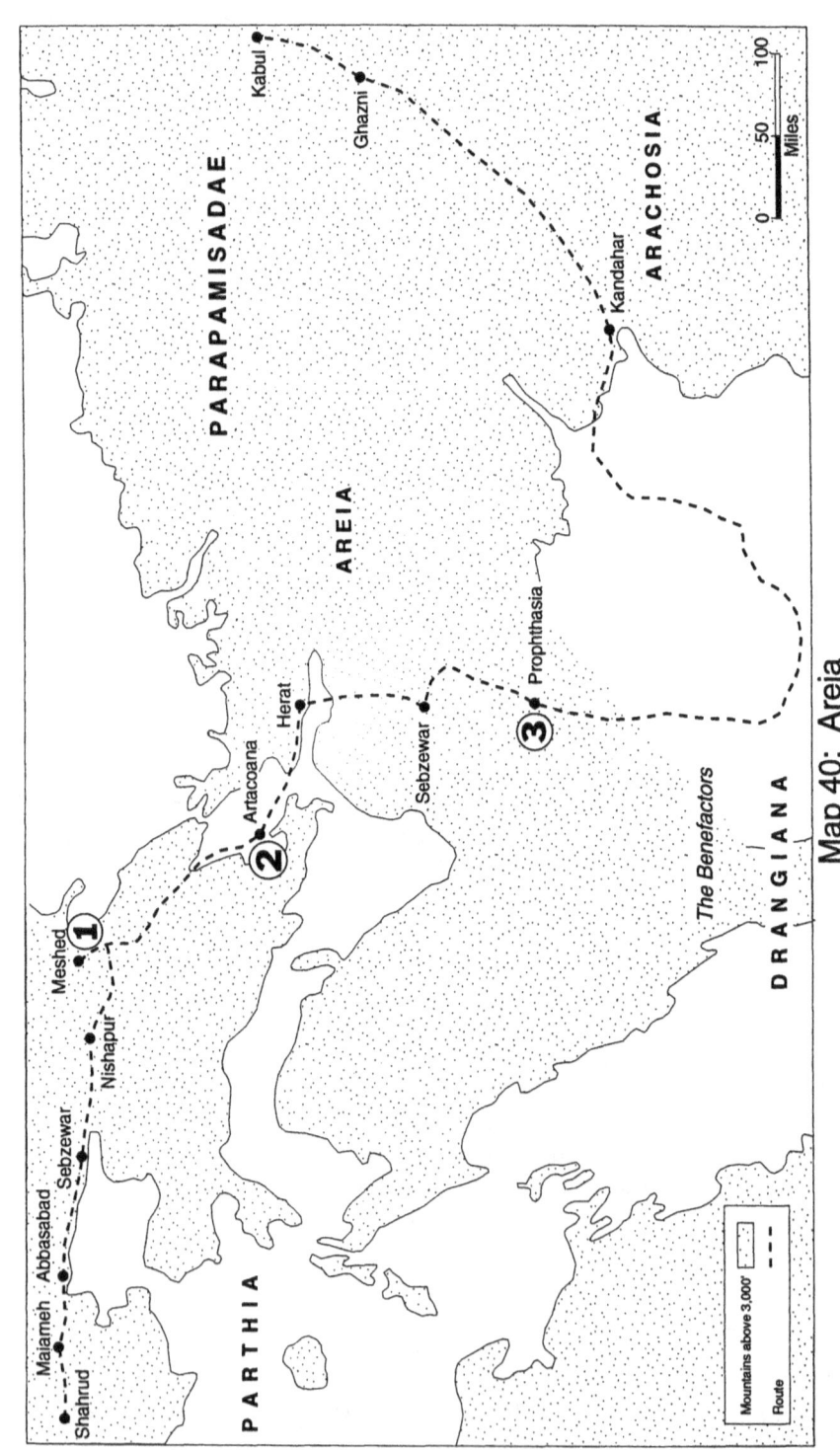

Map 40: Areia

Arachosia

While Erigyius and Stasanor marched against Satibarzanes, Alexander subdued Arachosia in a campaign lasting only a few days.[21] Menon was appointed satrap of the area and given a garrison of 600 cavalry and 4,000 infantry.[22] Alexander then marched against the Parapamisadae.

Parapamisadae

The Parapamisadae was located in a treeless, snow-covered northern plain. The extreme cold of the region had isolated the natives there from neighboring tribes, and they were considered uncivilized even by the barbarians. The climate was too cold for agriculture, and it was said that the constant snow and ice of the area prevented birds from landing there and animals from passing through the territory.

Alexander's army suffered greatly from exhaustion throughout the campaign, largely because of the harsh winter weather. Snow blindness was widespread, and many soldiers temporarily lost their eyesight because of it. Because of the glare of the sun on the snow, nothing could be clearly seen at a distance. It was only the smoke from the houses that enabled the Macedonians to locate the villages, and then only when they were almost on top of them. The inhabitants were so surprised and terrified to see armed strangers among them that they usually did whatever was demanded of them, only asking that their lives be spared. With the occupation of the villages, the hardships of the campaign were somewhat alleviated by the warm shelters and fairly abundant provisions usually stored within.

Hindu Kush

Alexander crossed Mt. Caucasus into the Hindu Kush in 17 days.[23] He appointed Proexes as satrap of the area and Neiloxenes (son of Satyrus) in command of the garrison left behind there.[24] He then marched to Bactria.

Bactria

The campaign in Bactria would pose difficulties for Alexander unlike any he had previously encountered in western Asia. Except for Zariaspa, also known as Bactria, which was the satrapy's capital and the last great city of the Persian empire not under Macedonian rule, there were no cities of any consequence to capture. The population there lived in small villages or was nomadic. The military poten-

---

1. Nicanor dies. 2. Satibarzanes massacres Anaxippus' guard. 3. The capital of Drangiana. Philotas (son of Parmenio) is convicted of plotting against Alexander's life and executed.

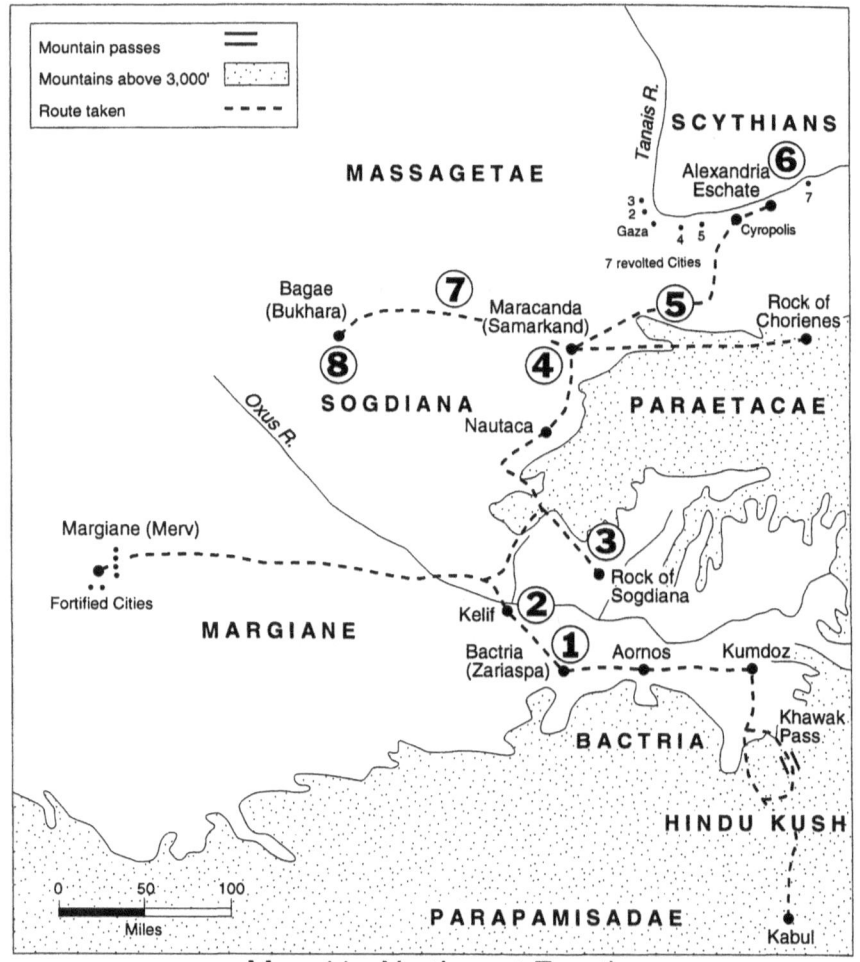

Map 41: Northwest Frontier

1. Alexander attempts to introduce Proskynesis to the Macedonians. Hermolaus, one of Alexander's pages, is convicted here of plotting against his life and executed. 2. As a result of a mutiny, Alexander is forced to muster out the unfit Macedonians and the Thessalians. 3. Roxane is captured. 4. The capital of Sogdiana, where a drunken Alexander murders Cleitus the Black. 5. Pharnuches' forces are virtually eliminated by Spitamenes. 6. Alexander defeats the Scythians. 7. Craterus defeats Spitamenes. 8. Spitamenes recruits 3,000 Scythians for a raid on Sogdiana. Coenus defeats Spitamenes.

tial of the country was, however, enormous, it being capable of fielding as many as 30,000 cavalry.[25] Occupying the area between the Hindu Kush mountains and the Oxus River, which was mostly rugged mountains and foothills, Bactria was ideal for guerrilla tactics. Being mostly comprised of cavalry, the Bactrian army's mobility would allow it always to select the battlefield of its choice and withdraw across the vast nearby steppes whenever necessary. There would be no great field battles here as had been fought against Darius; the lack of effective Bactrian infantry would largely preclude that. Instead, numerous skirmishes and hit-and-run raids would be the usual strategy pursued by the Bactrians. This type of warfare would call for a far different generalship than that required for the great field battles. Alexander, however, would rise to the occasion and conduct what many military historians would consider to be not only his most difficult but most successful campaign.

When Bessus had proclaimed himself as king of Asia, it was clear that it would only be a matter of time before Alexander would seek him out to settle the issue of Darius' succession. For the expected confrontation with the Macedonians, Bessus had gathered together a force of about 7,000 cavalry, consisting of Bactrians, Sogdians, some Persians, and a large number of Scythians from the Jaxartes River area.[26] Since Bessus had no trained infantry, he was unable to fight a stand-up field battle in the open terrain north of the Hindu Kush. He therefore decided to implement a scorched-earth policy to deny Alexander the possibility of obtaining any provisions there. Bessus was confident that the deep snows in the mountain passes and lack of any food in the area of Alexander's advance would force him to suspend military operations until at least mid-summer. Alexander, however, never being one to do the expected, chose to cross in the early spring and not at one of the lower passes but at the more distant Khawak Pass. This was the western-most of the seven possible passes, about 60 miles from Kabul. It was both the highest, at 11,600', and the longest, at 47 miles, of all the passes.[27] The narrowest part of the pass was only wide enough to accommodate three infantrymen abreast. The hardships in the crossing were evident by the fact that it took 16–17 days to cross instead of the usual four days.[28]

Because of the season of the year, the Macedonian soldiers suffered extensively from frostbite, snow blindness, and fatigue. Also, in the long barren stretch of the Hindu Kush Mountains, provisions ran out. Many of the horses died from starvation and overwork, and the troops were reduced to eating herbs, fish caught in the streams along the line of march, and finally the baggage animals. Since wood was unavailable for fires, the meat had to be eaten raw after all the carts had been burned. Although the crossing of the largely snowbound pass was difficult, Alexander was finally able to exit out into the plain about 80 miles east of Bessus' position. Stunned at finding himself outflanked, Bessus quickly withdrew his force across the Oxus River and into Sogdiana. As he did so, most of his Bactrian cavalry deserted him. The leaders who continued to accompany him now began to have serious doubts about his generalship.

Margiane Fort Line

Alexander advanced and occupied Zariaspa, the capital of Bactria, without opposition and appointed Artabazus, the Persian, satrap there. He then marched west to Margiane, establishing six forts on high hills round the city, each within supporting distance of the other, four facing east and two south.[29] A strong mercenary force of 3,000 cavalry and 10,000 infantry was left behind as a garrison in command of Amyntas.[30] Alexander founded two new cities in the satrapy that he settled with 3,000 camp followers of the Macedonian army and 7,000 Bactrians. They secured the pass leading to Media via Ecbatana, thereby shortening Alexander's line of communications by two-thirds. Alexander then marched into Sogdiana, leaving behind the phalanx taxies of Attalus, Gorgias, Meleager, and Polysperchon to watch over the area.[31]

Spitamenes' Raids

Believing that the Sogdianans had willingly collaborated with Spitamenes, Alexander divided up his army into five mobile columns under Hephaestion; Ptolemy (son of Lagus); Perdiccas; Coenus, who was accompanied by Artabazus; and himself and proceeded to execute a scorched-earth operation across the Zeravshan valley.[32] This thoroughly devastated the richest and most populous area of Sogdiana. He then marched on Maracanda and proceeded to reduce systematically the rebel strongholds still holding out there.

Spitamenes had fled into Massagetae and was able to recruit a force of 600 Scythians.[33] Returning to Bactria, he ambushed a force of 300 cavalry sent against him by Attinas, the governor of the region.[34] Concealing his forces in the woods, Spitamenes had a few men drive a herd of cattle into the nearby plain in the hope that the Greek force might break formation in pursuit of the booty. When this happened and the Greeks passed by the woods, they were unexpectedly attacked by Spitamenes and killed to the last man. A few days later Spitamenes raided the suburbs of Zariaspa. As his Scythians were withdrawing with their captured livestock, a hastily assembled force of 80 Macedonians and some mercenary cavalry, who had been left behind to recover from various illnesses, attacked him.[35] They inflicted heavy casualties on the Scythians and recovered all the stolen cattle. As the Greek force straggled back to Zariaspa, however, they themselves were surprised in a Scythian ambush. Leaderless at the time, in disorder, and attempting to guard the slow-moving cattle, the Greeks were badly defeated, losing seven Companions and 60 mercenary cavalry.[36]

As soon as intelligence was received that Spitamenes was raiding Bactria, Alexander assembled two taxies of his phalanx and a large force of mixed cavalry and immediately marched out in pursuit of him. Coenus was left in Bactria in command of his and Meleager's taxies of the phalanx, 400 Companion cavalry, and the mounted javelin men. Upon Alexander's appearance, Spitamenes immediately fled towards the desert. Before he could enter it, however, Craterus, whose force included over 1,000 Massagetae, was able to overtake him and force a battle.[37] Spitamenes was subsequently defeated, his force sustaining 1,000 casualties.[38] When Spitamenes fled into the desert, Craterus declined the futility of a pursuit.

Alexander now allowed Artabazus, satrap of Bactria, to resign his post because of old age. In his place, Amyntas (son of Nicolaus) was appointed as garrison commander with a force which included the phalanx taxies of Amyntas, Coenus, and Meleager; 400 Companion cavalry; all the mounted javelin men; and a number of the Bactrians and Sogdians.[39] They were allowed to go into winter quarters but were instructed to engage Spitamenes, should he raid there.

Spitamenes, now finding himself hemmed in by Alexander's network of forts, decided to attempt a raid where Coenus was stationed, the open terrain there being more suitable for cavalry operations. He had raised a force of 3,000 Massagetae for a sortie at Bagae, a stronghold in Sogdiana near the Scythian border.[40] In the ensuing battle, Spitamenes' undisciplined cavalry was badly beaten, sustaining over 800 casualties.[41] Coenus' losses were a mere 25 cavalry and 12 infantry.[42] During his retreat Spitamenes was deserted by both the Bactrians and Sogdianans. The Massagetae plundered the abandoned baggage trains of those troops and then followed Spitamenes into the desert. When the Massagetae heard that Alexander was pursuing them, however, they decided to cut their losses and sent Spitamenes' head to the Macedonian king as a peace offering. With Spitamenes' death all organized resistance on the northeast frontier collapsed. Nevertheless, when Alexander left for India some time later, he left Amyntas behind with a strong garrison of 3,500 cavalry and 10,000 infantry.[43]

Generalship

Alexander conducted a well planned and highly effective campaign against Bessus in Bactria. By selecting the most difficult and most distant pass to enter the satrapy, he ensured that his crossing of the Hindu Kush mountains would be unopposed. Alexander's strategic position on Bessus' flank forced him to withdraw from the satrapy rather than fight at a significant disadvantage. By his skillful strategy, Alexander had maneuvered Bessus' forces out of Bactria without fighting a battle.

Spitamenes proved to be one of Alexander's toughest opponents. On numerous occasions the Persian clearly demonstrated his expertise in conducting mobile warfare. After a few futile pursuits and one disaster, however, Alexander quickly devised effective countermeasures against him. By dividing up his army into multiple mobile columns and building an interlocking network of strong points, not only did Alexander deny Spitamenes the ability to recruit and reprovision within Bactria, he also prevented him from remaining long in any one area. If he did, he took the chance that his force might be pinned against Alexander's fort line and forced to fight one of his strong mobile columns, each of which was capable of defeating him.

Bessus' scorched-earth policy north of the Hindu Kush considerably complicated Alexander's provisioning of his army. Bessus failed miserably, however, in keeping track of Alexander's movements and totally underestimated Alexander's strategic options. Just because it was easiest to cross at one of the lower passes of the Hindu Kush in mid-summer did not necessarily mean that Alexander would do so. Lulled into a false sense of security, Bessus neither properly scouted the movement of Alexander's army on the south side of the Hindu Kush nor occupied any of the distant passes with either reconnaissance or blocking forces. The area abounded with men at home in the mountains, and if they had been used effectively they could have greatly impeded Alexander's already slow progress through the pass long enough to have caused a critical logistics problem for him. Any additional delay in crossing the mountains could easily have placed Alexander's army in an immediate state of starvation, so tenuous were his supplies. As it was, Bessus' complacency not only lost him the excellent defensive potential of the rugged mountains and foothills of Bactria but the support of the numerous and well-trained cavalry there, who promptly deserted him upon his abandonment of their homeland without a fight. Far more importantly, however, Bessus lost the respect of his fellow conspirators, who were shortly to betray him treacherously to Alexander.

Sogdiana

Oxus River

When Bessus crossed the Oxus River, he left behind the mountains of Bactria and entered the plains and deserts of Sogdiana. This was an ideal country for cavalry raids that could attack a marching column from any direction and then quickly ride off across the steppes to escape pursuit. Although Bessus had obviously suffered a major setback when Alexander had crossed the Hindu Kush Mountains, he attempted to convince his fellow satraps that the Macedonian army would be unable to cross the Oxus River anytime soon. That river was exceptionally broad, being about three-quarters of a mile wide at the Kelif crossing and deep with a fast-flowing current resulting from the melting snow runoff of the central Asian mountains.[44] Bessus had destroyed all the boats on the river, and trees were virtually nonexistent in the area. Even if the time-consuming effort of laboriously bringing up timber from distant areas to bridge the river was made, the sandy riverbed would preclude a solid foundation for the piles and the fast-flowing current was likely to carry them away quickly. Upon crossing the Oxus, Bessus continued towards Nautaca, where he made camp.

Alexander was not any more deterred by the Oxus River than he was by the Danube. He immediately collected the hides his troops used for tent covers, ordered them to be filled with chaff for buoyancy, and then had them stitched together for waterproofing. He then transported his army across the Oxus on the floats during the next five days.[45] As it was June, the army then had to cross 45 miles of desert during the dry season. They endured heatstroke during the day and frostbite at night. Dehydration and excessive overdrinking caused as many casualties as if the army had fought a major battle. As a result of this ordeal, the Thessalians and most of Philip's older veterans mutinied and demanded to be released from further service. They had marched almost 12,000 miles and now only wanted to return home. Alexander had no choice but to muster them out, albeit with generous bonuses.

When reports reached Bessus that Alexander had crossed the Oxus River, his credibility for military competence dropped to zero. As a result, Spitamenes and the Sogdiana barons decided to turn him over to Alexander in the hopes that this would end his campaign against them. Messengers were sent to Alexander to say that if a Macedonian officer would be sent with a small escort to a designated place, Bessus would be surrendered to them. Ptolemy (son of Lagus) was given command of the mission. Alexander, however, fearing treachery from Spitamenes, gave Ptolemy a strong force of 1,600 cavalry and 4,000 infantry.[46] It consisted of the Companion cavalry, the mounted javelin men, a hypaspist chilarchy, a taxies of the phalanx, the Agrianians, and half the archers.[47] By forced march, Ptolemy covered the distance to the rendezvous point in four days instead of the usual ten.[48] His early arrival took the conspirators by surprise, and they quickly rode off, leaving him to take Bessus into custody without incident. Bessus was later mutilated and sent west for eventual execution by Darius' kin.

Xenippa

In the vicinity of Xenippa, which borders on Scythia, a force of 2,500 Bactrian exiles had gathered.[49] Upon Alexander's approach, however, the natives there drove them off. The Bactrians then attacked Amyntas and were defeated by him, sustaining casualties of 700 killed and 300 taken prisoner.[50] Amyntas' losses were 80 dead and 350 wounded.[51] Despite their attack, Alexander pardoned the Bactrians and then marched off to Nautaca.[52]

Nautaca

Sisimithres, who ruled at Nautaca, blocked the pass giving Alexander access into his territory. Although the pass was strongly garrisoned, Alexander nevertheless assaulted and carried it and then pursued the retreating Sisimithres to a crevice, beyond which lay a steep hill. When Alexander began bridging the crevice, the morale of Sisimithres' troops collapsed and they abandoned their defenses and moved up to the top of the hill. Alexander sent Oxyartes to negotiate the surrender of Sisimithres. Although Oxyartes stressed that Alexander's victorious army was eager to press on to India, Sisimithres declined to submit. Soon regretting, however, a decision apparently made under the influence of his wife, Sisimithres recalled Oxyartes and immediately surrendered. Alexander subsequently restored Nautaca to Sisimithres before marching on to the Jaxartes River.

Jaxartes River

Upon his arrival at the Jaxartes River, Alexander sent out some foragers, a number of whom were killed by the local natives. A force of 20,000 natives took refuge on a steep mountain.[53] Alexander's first assaults against them were driven back by heavy missile fire. Despite the large number of casualties his force sustained, Alexander made several more attacks and finally carried the position. As many of the natives leapt to their deaths from the cliffs rather than submit, only 8,000 survived out of the original force.[54] During the fighting Alexander was struck in the ankle by an arrow that broke one of his bones.

Maracanda

Alexander then marched on Maracanda, reaching the city four days later. Accepting the city's surrender, he left a garrison of 1,000 men in its citadel and proceeded to devastate the surrounding area.[55]

Northern Fortified Line

En route to Maracanda, Alexander requested the presence of the leading nobles of Sogdiana for a meeting at Zariaspa. Suspecting that Alexander had discovered their plan to revolt, they told their people that he had summoned their cavalry because he wanted to kill them all. With the full support of the population, the nobles were able to raise a force of 7,000 cavalry and launch a full-scale revolt.[56] They proceeded first to wipe out the mercenary garrisons in the seven fortified settlements Alexander had established as a northern defense line against Scythian raids. The sites were located close to the Jaxartes River nearby Alexandria Eschate, and their fall removed the only obstacle preventing the Scythians from joining Spitamenes. If the two forces had combined, a long and exhausting campaign against the highly mobile Scythian horse-archers would have ensued. This had to be prevented at all costs; the line of frontier fortified cities had to be recaptured and quickly.

Craterus was ordered to lay siege to Cyropolis, where most of the refugees had fled. As Alexander marched on Gaza, he sent out his cavalry to surround the second and third most distant outposts to prevent the rebel garrisons there from escaping. Alexander quickly cleared Gaza's walls of defenders by a concentrated barrage of catapult and missile fire from his archers and javelin men, enabling his army to scale the low earth walls with little difficulty or interference. All males taken were massacred and the women and children were sold into slavery.

The next two cities Alexander quickly assaulted and carried. A few survivors and the rising smoke in the distance from the nearby burning cities convinced the rebels of the fourth and fifth cities to make an attempt to escape across the plain to the north. The Macedonian cavalry that had been stationed near those cities for just such a contingency caught the fugitives out in the open and massacred them. Then the virtually undefended cities were easily taken. Alexander's mobile campaign had recaptured two of the seven cities during the first day of the revolt and three more on the second day.

Alexander now marched on Cyropolis, the sixth fortified city. It had earlier been put under siege by Craterus, who had both dug a ditch and built a stockade around it. The city was surrounded by a high wall and strongly garrisoned. Alexander had originally intended to breach the walls with his siege engines and then conduct a traditional storming assault. He had noticed, however, that the river flowing through the city was almost dry and there now was enough space between it and the wall for soldiers to pass through. Under the cover of a diversionary assault against the walls, the hypaspists, Agrianians, and archers entered the city through the river channel.[57] Once inside, they fought their way to the gates, opened them from the inside, and admitted the rest of the army. The defenders, seeing that their city was about to fall, turned against Alexander's assault force in an attempt to eliminate it before reinforcements could arrive. Alexander was struck on the head and neck with a stone, while Craterus was wounded with an arrow.[58] Nevertheless, Alexander's force was able to clear the marketplace of the enemy and when reinforced by additional infantry entering through the gate, soon gained the upper hand in the fighting. A total of 8,000 Sogdianans were killed in the attack.[59] The next day the remaining 15,000 defenders of the city who had taken refuge in the citadel were forced to surrender because they had run out of water.[60] Although Alexander had initially determined to spare the city because it was founded by Cyrus, the obstinacy of its defense angered him and he instead razed it.[61] The seventh and last city, upon hearing the fate of Cyropolis, promptly surrendered, but Alexander ordered that all its inhabitants be killed.

Pharnuches' Massacre

At the same time Alexander was occupied in reducing the seven revolting settlements of his northern defense line, the Scythians assembled on the Jaxartes River, crossed over to its south bank, and assisted Spitamenes in besieging Maracanda. The city had nine miles of walls and a fortified citadel garrisoned by 1,000 men.[62] Alexander was now cut off from his troops at Ecbatana, and no further reinforcements could reach him until he broke the siege. He immediately sent out a relief force of 60 Companion cavalry, 800 mercenary cavalry, and 1,500 mercenary infantry, all under the command of Pharnuches.[63] Because he was a diplomatic officer by profession, with little, if any, actual military expertise, Pharnuches was accompanied by three military commanders—Menedemus, in command of the Companion cavalry; Caranus, in command of the mercenary cavalry; and Andromachus, in command of the mercenary infantry.[64]

Spitamenes' assault on the citadel of Maracanda had just been thrown back by its Macedonian garrison when it was reported to him that Pharnuches' relieving force was approaching. Immediately lifting the siege, Spitamenes withdrew to the north with Pharnuches in close pursuit. Pharnuches had force-marched 185 miles in three days to reach the city, and both his horses and troops were exhausted even before they began the pursuit. During his withdrawal, Spitamenes, who was reinforced by some 600 mounted Scythians, decided to go on the offensive.[65] Instead of closing in a hand-to-hand fight, however, Spitamenes' Scythians rode round and round the Greek force, firing arrows into their ranks at will. They were unopposed as Pharnuches had no missile troops with him. Whenever Pharnuches' infantry tried to charge, the Scythians simply rode out of their reach. Pharnuches' cavalry was unable to close with the Scythians, their horses being fatigued by the long march they had just undertaken and weakened by short rations over the past several days. The Greek force also appears to have had a crisis of command during the Scythian attack. Pharnuches, realizing that he did not have the necessary military ability, apparently tried to persuade one of the Macedonian military leaders to assume command of the force. They all, however, refused to do so, being afraid of being held accountable for any resulting defeat.

Pharnuches at first tried to stand his ground but when that did not prove possible, he attempted to withdraw under fire. Although his forces had suffered heavy casualties from the Scythian missile fire, Pharnuches was somehow able to form them up into a square and move them towards the Polytimetus River. There some nearby woods would offer protection against the Scythian missile fire. Caranus, in either fear or incompetence, crossed the river with his cavalry in such panic that he gave the infantry the impression they were being abandoned. As a result, they broke formation and stampeded towards the river so as not be left behind. The Scythians then rushed in among the fleeing mob and began butchering them as they desperately tried to climb the steep riverbank. A surviving group of Greeks managed to reform on a small island in the river but were quickly surrounded by the Scythians and eliminated by a sustained missile fire. The few prisoners taken were killed. Out of Pharnuches' original force of 2,300, only about 340 were able to escape.[66] Spitamenes then returned to Maracanda to resume its siege.

When the survivors of Pharnuches' force reported to Alexander, he ordered them to keep silent of what had occurred under penalty of death. Alexander immediately led a force consisting of half the Companion cavalry, the archers, Agrianians, and part of the phalanx and set off in pursuit of Spitamenes.[67] He force-marched 187 miles along the Jaxartes River, reaching Maracanda at dawn on the fourth day after starting out.[68] At Alexander's appearance, Spitamenes again broke off the siege of the city and rode off into the desert. Alexander attempted to follow but soon was forced to abandon the pursuit as hopeless when he reached the location of Pharnuches' massacre. After burying the Macedonian dead there, Alexander sent the taxies of the phalanx commanded by Attalus, Gorgias, Meleager, and Polysperchon to subdue Bactria while he returned to its capital with the remainder of the army. A force of 3,000 infantry under Peucolaus was left as a garrison in Sogdiana.[69]

Generalship

Spitamenes was clearly one of the most capable generals that Alexander ever fought, perhaps the most capable. He thoroughly understood how to wage effective mobile warfare and would have easily defeated any less of an opponent than Alexander. Against a second-string force like Pharnuches', Spitamenes demonstrated exactly how lethal he could be. However, when Alexander established his network of forts and divided his army up into a number of mobile columns, he severely limited Spitamenes' strategic options and ensured that any loss he was likely to sustain would be disproportionate to what he could achieve. When this happened, Spitamenes' unstable Scythian troops proved unable to cope with the subsequent heavy casualties, and they treacherously turned against him. Had Darius used a general of Spitamenes' ability on the Macedonian army's rear lines with an adequate force early in the war, Alexander might have had to spend a disproportionate share of his time and effort in securing his ever-lengthening line of communications into Asia. It is regrettable that Darius did not better utilize Spitamenes' obvious talents.

Alexander had definitely gotten off to a shaky start in the Sogdiana campaign and made some major mistakes along the way. Guerrilla warfare, however, was relatively new to him, and it took some time to master. The first mistake Alexander made was in seriously underestimating the general dissatisfaction with Macedonian rule in Sogdiana. The leadership there would never accept foreign domination and was only waiting for his absence to act treacherously against him. When that occurred, the rebels quickly reoccupied key strategic areas of their satrapy and eliminated the inadequate garrison left behind there with little difficulty. Once Alexander became aware of events he reacted with his characteristic speed. He proceeded to recapture the fortified cities quickly and then set about to terrorize the area into submission.

The second mistake Alexander made was related to the relief force under Pharnuches he sent to Maracanda. Virtually every error in the book was made here: the assignment of an overall commander without any military experience, the lack of flexibility in the orders issued to military subcommanders of the force, the inadequate military commanders assigned, and the faulty composition of the forces. It is most unusual for Alexander to make even a single mistake, yet in this case he made at least four. The only explanation can be that he truly believed that the mission on which he was sending the force out on would be diplomatic, not military, in nature. He had obviously seriously underestimated both Spitamenes' temperament and capabilities, thinking he would flee upon the mere appearance of Pharnuches' force. In that case, it was logical to have a diplomat in a strong position of authority who could repair the political damage done by the revolt. This conviction undoubtedly led to an overall carelessness in organizing the force for what was, after all, basically a military mission.

It was bad enough to have a diplomat in charge of a military force, but to compound the mistake, it appears that none of Pharnuches' subcommanders was designated to act as a second-in-command. This was a major oversight in the event of a military confrontation that made it almost certain that there would be a command vacuum when the force attempted to determine who its military commander should be. The worst thing a military force can do under attack is to surrender the initiative passively to a more mobile force, but this is exactly the disadvantage Alexander had imposed on the relieving force. Whatever orders Alexander had written for the mission obviously failed to provide any guidance for the unexpected situation in which the force found itself. The orders apparently only dealt with diplomatic matters, and when the military commanders studied them in the midst of their crisis, they were unable to derive anything from them that could be of assistance.

The three military commanders Alexander appointed to the force also needs to be examined. They obviously were not frontline commanders, as evidenced by the way they reacted to the crisis that confronted them. None of them displayed the least bit of initiative. When asked to provide military leadership, all refused, apparently being more concerned about a potential blot on their mediocre military records than the safety of the force under their joint command. There appears to have been no cooperation between them, and neither Caranus, who commanded the mercenary cavalry, nor Andromachus, who commanded the mercenary infantry, seems to have been able to exercise effective command control over even their own men. The choice of the three military commanders for the expedition was poorly made. They were obviously selected for what was anticipated to be an uneventful mission demanding little, if anything, in the way of ability or effort from them.

The composition of the force itself was also faulty. It was disproportionately weighted in heavy infantry and heavy cavalry and was deficient in missile troops and light cavalry, being largely comprised of mercenaries, with a small unit of Companion cavalry. Events were all too clearly to demonstrate that the discipline and morale of the mercenaries were unstable, and at the critical juncture they all too quickly dissolved into panic. By contrast, Spitamenes' light cavalry force was extremely mobile and capable of delivering high volumes of missile fire. This would not only give him the initiative against Pharnuches but would allow him to engage in a missile fire attack that could not be answered.

The seriousness with which Alexander reacted to the defeat of Pharnuches is evident in his death penalty threat to the survivors of the massacre if they discussed the incident. He recognized that he had treated the matter far too carelessly and, as a consequence, had suffered a humiliating defeat. Politically, it could have been disastrous. The image of invincibility that Alexander had built up was highly advantageous to his military operations because enemy leaders and cities frequently surrendered to him largely on the basis of his reputation as an unbeatable military commander. If that belief were shaken and it was thought that he could be defeated, resistance might increase to a degree that would exceed his ability to cope with it effectively. If every city defended itself like a fortress instead of falling almost effortlessly into his hands, Alexander could be tied up for years having to besiege them one at a time. In the process of reducing them, he was also likely to suffer a level of casualties which over time might be detrimental to the discipline and effectiveness of his army. As a result, Alexander now awoke from his lethargy and became his old self. He conducted the remainder of the campaign in Sogdiana with his usual brilliance and made no additional mistakes.

Alexander immediately split his army into five mobile forces and implemented a scorched-earth policy throughout the most populated and fertile part of Sogdiana to deny Spitamenes a source for both troops and supplies. He then built a series of mutually supporting forts along the northern border areas of the satrapy, not only making it difficult for Spitamenes to penetrate for a raid but making it impossible for him to linger in the area. Once inside Alexander's defensive network, Spitamenes could be surrounded or run to ground by any of Alexander's mobile forces. Although Alexander got off to a bumpy start, he completed the campaign in Sogdiana with his usual effectiveness. The satrapy was now permanently subdued and caused no further problems during Alexander's reign.

Siege of the Rock of Sogdiana

In the spring of 327 B.C., Alexander marched on the Rock of Sogdiana, where Oxyartes had concentrated a large force. Although Oxyartes himself was not present at the position, he believed it to be so impregnable that he had sent his wife and daughters there. The rock was 19,800 feet high, and its summit was almost 19 miles in circumference.[70] The site had sheer rock faces on all four sides, with deep snow making any advance on it virtually impossible. A total of 30,000 people were reported to have taken refuge there.[71] The position was well stocked to withstand a siege, having a two-year supply of food and much deep snow that could easily be converted to drinking water.[72] The Sogdians considered the rock impregnable and told Alexander in reply to his summons for them to surrender that they would do so if he could field winged soldiers against them, believing nothing else to be effective.

Alexander asked for volunteers from his army with mountaineering experience, and 300 stepped forward.[73] As the Sogdians only guarded the frontal approach to the rock, Alexander deployed the mountain climbers to scale the opposite face. Once atop the position, they were to announce their presence to him by waving signal flags. Alexander offered a huge monetary incentives to the first 12 men to reach the top: the first up was to receive 12 talents; the second, 11 talents; and so on down to the twelfth, who would receive one talent.[74] Each talent was the equivalent of about 16 years' wages for the climbers.[75] The volunteers took spears, swords, and rations for two days.[76] The hazardous climb was begun at night, and by dawn the survivors were on top of the rock. Thirty of the climbers, or 10 percent of the total force, fell to their deaths in the snowdrifts below.[77]

When Alexander saw the white flags fluttering atop the Rock of Sogdiana at sunrise, he called to the Sogdians to witness his winged troops and surrender. Although the Sogdians heavily outnumbered the relatively few mountaineers, so stunned were they by the totally unexpected event that they immediately complied with Alexander's demand. Perhaps they mistakenly thought that the climbers were an advance force of a much larger one. Oxyartes' daughter Roxane was one of the prisoners who fell into Alexander's hands when he captured the site. It was said that except only for Darius' wife she was the most beautiful woman in Asia.[78] Nevertheless, Alexander later married her probably less for her alleged beauty than for political expediency; their marriage effectively ended the revolt in Sogdiana.

Generalship The siege of the Rock of Sogdiana was won by a ruse that was both clever and extremely dangerous to the participating troops. Alexander proved once again that he was able to analyze a desperate situation correctly. There is no indication that he had determined upon a plan to carry the Rock of Sogdiana by either siege or assault. Heavy snow on the ground, the high and steep cliffs surrounding the rock, the large garrison, and its ability to undergo a lengthy siege mandated that even if a successful operation could be conducted against the position, it would be time consuming and difficult to supply. Such a protracted siege would have proved a stiff challenge, even for Alexander. The trick that Alexander came up with was very risky. Just the climb up the sheer rock face resulted in a loss rate to the assault force that was far higher than in any of Alexander's great field battles. Once the handful of some 270 mountain climbers did get to the top, they were exposed to virtual annihilation. Being outnumbered 100 to one, unable to retreat, isolated from any reinforcement by the main army, and having no missile weapons, shields, or armor, the Macedonian climbers would have been massacred if the Sogdians had attacked. Alexander's luck held, however. The Sogdians were so stupefied by the daring of an event almost beyond their comprehension that they surrendered more because of befuddlement than the dictates of military logic.

Paraetacae

Rock of Chorienes

Although military activity in Sogdiana had ended with the capture of the Rock of Sogdiana and Alexander's marriage to Roxane, the Sogdiana noble Chorienes still occupied the Rock of Chorienes, in the neighboring Paraetacae. The fortress was located over 13,000 feet above sea level, was seven and a half miles in circumference at its summit, and had a sheer drop-off on all sides.[79] The only way up to it was along a narrow, single-file road. The position was surrounded by a deep ravine that prohibited any traditional assault from being attempted.

Crude ladders made from pine trees were used to descend to the bottom of the ravine. Then stakes were driven into both walls from bottom to top. Upon the upper stakes, a bridge was laid and covered with earth to form a platform. The construction progressed only 30 feet a day during daylight and considerably less at night, despite the fact that the entire army was employed round the clock in the effort.[80]

In the early stages of construction, the Sogdians treated the project with contempt and thought it quite hopeless. The slow but steady progress of the effort and the ineffectiveness of the Sogdiana missile fire against the Macedonians working behind the protection of their defensive mantlets unnerved Chorienes, however, and he requested Alexander to send Oxyartes to confer with him. Oxyartes attempted to persuade him to surrender, stating that no position was impregnable to Alexander. He told Chorienes that the Macedonian king was widely respected as a man of honor and justice, indicating that his own treatment was proof of his words. Chorienes was assured that he could expect fair treatment from Alexander if he surrendered. After thinking it over, Chorienes decided to surrender unconditionally. As his reward, he was restored to his former position. Chorienes reciprocated by giving Alexander a two-month supply of food for his army from the stores he had accumulated for the siege.[81]

Generalship At the Rock of Chorienes, Alexander had an adequate plan to carry the position. Instead of attempting to do the virtually impossible and fill in the ravine completely, he suspended a bridge over it to be used as a platform for the attack. Although an assault was not actually launched against the Rock of Chorienes, so formidable was the preparation for an attack that Chorienes chose to surrender rather than risk the consequences of its probable success. Once again Alexander's innovativeness and careful preparations had mastered an extremely difficult situation.

Catane/Austane

While Alexander marched toward Bactria, he sent Craterus with 600 cavalry, his own taxies of the phalanx, and those of Alcetas, Attalus, and Polysperchon on a campaign in the Paraetacae against the Austane and Catane.[82] They were the only tribes still in rebellion in that area. Craterus fought and won a hard-fought battle against them, eliminating the Catanes on the battlefield and making prisoners of the Austanes. Craterus losses were 120 allied cavalry and 1,500 allied infantry.[83] Shortly after the battle, Craterus rejoined Alexander in Bactria with his captives.

Scythia

As Alexander was building the walls around his new outpost city of Alexandria Eschate (the Farthest), a large force of Scythian cavalry gathered opposite him on the northern side of the Jaxartes River.[84] They were led by Carthasis, brother to the Scythian king, whose instructions were to drive Alexander from the borders of the Scythian territory. The Scythians made known their intention of supporting any local uprisings against Alexander and dared him to cross the river. Alexander, unable to endure the Scythian insults any longer, was deterred from crossing the river by unfavorable sacrificial omens. Alexander called for another sacrifice but again the omens proved to be against him. Aristander, Alexander's seer, warned the king that to go against the will of the gods would put his life in peril. Alexander replied, however, that he was prepared to face any danger to end the ridicule of the Scythians.

Alexander ordered 12,000 floats to be prepared for the river crossing.[85] These were made from canvas tent coverings stuffed with straw for buoyancy and sewn shut to waterproof them. Although the Jaxartes River was narrower at Alexandria Eschate than elsewhere along its length, the banks were still far enough apart as to be beyond missile range. Although this would facilitate a safe embarkation, once the floats reached the center of the river they would undoubtedly come under a heavy Scythian missile fire to which neither the missile troops on the far shore nor those on the floats would be able to reply. Because the floats could not be steered but merely twisted and turned uncontrollably with the current, the resulting insecure foothold made it impossible for missile weapons to be fired from them with any accuracy. Alexander therefore lined his catapults up hub-to-hub along the river bank and opened a concentrated barrage against the Scythians on the far bank. They were greatly surprised by the attack that killed a number of them.

Unable to reply to the fire of the longer-ranged catapults and being demoralized by the death of their champion in the barrage, many of the Scythians withdrew in confusion from the riverbank. Alexander then gave the signal for his amphibious invasion of the far bank to begin.

The troops in front of the floats knelt down behind their shields to give those in the rear some protection from the expected Scythian missile fire. The horses were held by their reins and swam behind the floats. Despite the Scythian disorganization and withdrawal from the riverbank, virtually every Macedonian shield on the floats was filled with their arrows. The highly effective catapult fire the Macedonians were able to deliver from the far bank of the river, however, had disordered the Scythian cavalry formations sufficiently to allow the establishment of a beachhead. The archers landed first, followed by the phalanx and then the cavalry.[86] When the entire force had disembarked, Alexander ordered a regiment of mercenaries and four squadrons of spearmen, about 1,000 men in all, out in front of his force in an attempt to draw out a Scythian attack.[87] The undisciplined Scythians could not resist the bait and promptly circled round the small force, shooting their bows all the while. Alexander now ordered a mixed force of cavalry, archers, Agrianians, and light troops under Balacrus to break the Scythian formation circling across the front of his advance force.[88] Another force, consisting of three squadrons of the Companions and all the mounted javelin men would support Balacrus by expanding the shoulders of the penetration he was expected to make.[89] Alexander took personal command of the remaining cavalry, which was deployed in column and held in reserve.

When Balacrus' attack broke into the Scythian circle, its formation was thrown into disorder. Alexander then committed his support force to widen Balacrus' penetration and reinforce his attack. Pinned in a stationary position in an unequal fight with the light troops, the Scythian cavalry troops soon broke and were driven from the field. After a pursuit of about 10 miles, Alexander drank some tainted water and was carried back to camp with a severe attack of dysentery.[90] His condition, no doubt, confirmed the accuracy of Aristander's unfavorable sacrifice. Alexander's incapacitation caused the Macedonian pursuit to falter, allowing most of the Scythians to escape.

As a result of the battle, 1,000 Scythians were killed, 150 taken prisoner, and 1,800 horses were captured.[91] Macedonian losses were 60 cavalry and 100 infantry killed and 1,000 wounded.[92] Shortly after the Scythian defeat the king of Scythia sent an envoy to Alexander to assure him that the Macedonians had been attacked by lawless brigands who were in no way condoned by either him or his people. The Scythian king put himself at Alexander's disposal and promised to obey any orders he might care to issue to him. Alexander, however, was not inclined to conclude his campaign against the Scythians upon such suspicious circumstances. As he was drafting his reply, another envoy from Scythia arrived. He announced that the king of Scythia had just died and had been succeeded by his brother who was hoping to conclude an alliance with Alexander. He hoped to seal it by the marriage of his daughter to the Macedonian king. If Alexander was not inclined to marriage, noble Scythian brides would instead be provided to his generals. The Scythian king also offered to visit Alexander in person, if requested to do so. Alexander, of course, politely refused the proposed marriages but nevertheless signed a treaty with the Scythians, thereby bringing the war with them to a close. In Asia, the Scythians were widely believed to be invincible, and Alexander's victory over them convinced many that it was impossible for any single nation to defeat him.[93] Having secured the northeastern frontier of his newfound empire with the subjugation of Bactria and Sogdiana, Alexander was now ready to extend his eastern border into India.

9. India

Alexander's main objective in conquering India was to complete his conquest of Asia. The justification he gave to his troops for the campaign was that western India had at one time been part of the Persian Empire and as heir to Darius' crown he was obligated to restore it. It was uncertain, however, exactly how far Persian control in India reached. Cyrus had extended the eastern boundary of the Persian Empire to the Indus River.[1] Darius I might have gone slightly beyond that river, but it is doubtful whether he actually ruled more than the Sind and eastern Punjab as Persian satrapies. By the time of Darius III, however, Persian rule extended only as far east as the Kabul valley, which bordered the satrapies of Bajaur and Swat on the south.

Alexander's real reason for his campaign in India, however, probably lay more in his mystical motivation to complete the conquest of Asia. His overwhelming desire was to stand on the shore of the Eastern Ocean that Aristotle believed was actually visible from the summit of the Hindu Kush Mountains. To occupy this area would establish him as the greatest conqueror of all time, exceeding even the accomplishments of Cyrus the Great. Semiramis, the legendary Assyrian queen, had made plans to invade India but had allegedly died before she was able to carry them out. Dionysus was reputed to have campaigned in India, evidence of his presence there being the growth of ivy near the city of Nysa. Heracles' daughter was said to have become a queen in Indian, in command of an army of 500 elephants, 4,000 cavalry, and 130,000 infantry under her command.[2] A deed of such magnitude as the conquest of all Asia would clearly be worthy of divine recognition. This attainment of divinity was an extremely powerful motivation for Alexander all his life and goes far to explain his fixation for conquering India. An equally strong motivation would have been Alexander's love of conquest. Put simply, Alexander loved fighting for the sake of fighting.

Originally, Alexander believed India to occupy an area of no great size. However, as a result of discussions with Ambhi, Porus, and other Indians, he soon discovered that no Indian had actually ever seen the Eastern Ocean, thought to be India's eastern boundary. Instead, they told him of huge deserts, wide rivers, and numerous tribes of fanatical warriors. Alexander deliberately hid these facts from his army, preferring, instead, to deceive them with lies. He knew that if his men, who were clearly demoralized by their exhausting marches thus far, ever found out that the distance to the Eastern Ocean was unknown, they would probably refuse to continue marching eastward. This proved to be the case, for at the Beas River,

Alexander's deception was finally exposed. There were no more mountains, and all they could see was an endless plain. At that point, the troops mutinied and refused to march any further east. This revolt must have been shattering for Alexander because it ended forever his dream of conquering Asia and fulfilling his destiny, as he saw it.

Alexander had intended that India become a permanent part of his empire. The sad fact was, however, that despite the two years Alexander had campaigned there, within two years of his death India was again largely independent of Macedonian control. The Greeks Alexander had left in the country simply abandoned the cities they garrisoned and marched westward in columns numbering in the thousands, eventually to enlist in the armies of his successors. Alexander had only conquered and passed through India, conducting a murderous war of extermination as he did so. This resulted in a fanatical resentment on the part of the natives there, who only lived in hope for the day they could free themselves from his subjugation. The weakened Indian tribes left behind in Alexander's campaign in western India had no sooner thrown off Greek rule than they were quickly conquered by Chandragupta and integrated into his Mauryan Empire. In southwestern India, Greek kings managed to rule the Punjab until the second century B.C., after which nothing more is heard of them.

Despite the brief Macedonian occupation, however, western India was forever changed by Alexander's presence. The cities and ports that Alexander established were a focus for urbanization and undoubtedly stimulated trade. This encouraged even greater urbanization and trade in a continuously repeating cycle. The country was thus given the impetus to begin moving from a largely agrarian economy to one based on trade and commerce. Alexander had also significantly weakened the military power of the provincial kings by the war of extermination he waged against them. India was thus able to be centralized under a strong ruler much earlier than would have been the case had the local kings been able to offer more effective military resistance. Although India clearly benefited from this situation, it can hardly be said that a strong, hostile, and united state lying off Alexander's eastern border would have been advantageous to the safety of his newly won empire.

The campaigning in India was brutal to the extreme and consisted, for the most part, of the storming of cities and citadels and the massacre and enslavement of their populations. Alexander had clearly made a radical departure in the way he conducted his war in India. In the Persian Empire, he had made a consciousness effort to placate both the satraps and the people who submitted to him. The satraps were frequently restored to their offices, while the citizenry was left relatively undisturbed. The Persian aristocracy sat in places of honor at his table and were given high and prestigious commands in his army. In India, however, Alexander had evidently made the decision that it was futile to elicit the cooperation of the Indians and instead decided to rule them with a mailed fist. Terror and brutality became the order of the day, and Alexander waged a virtual war of extermination against them. This, no doubt, was done largely in reaction to the fanatical resistance of

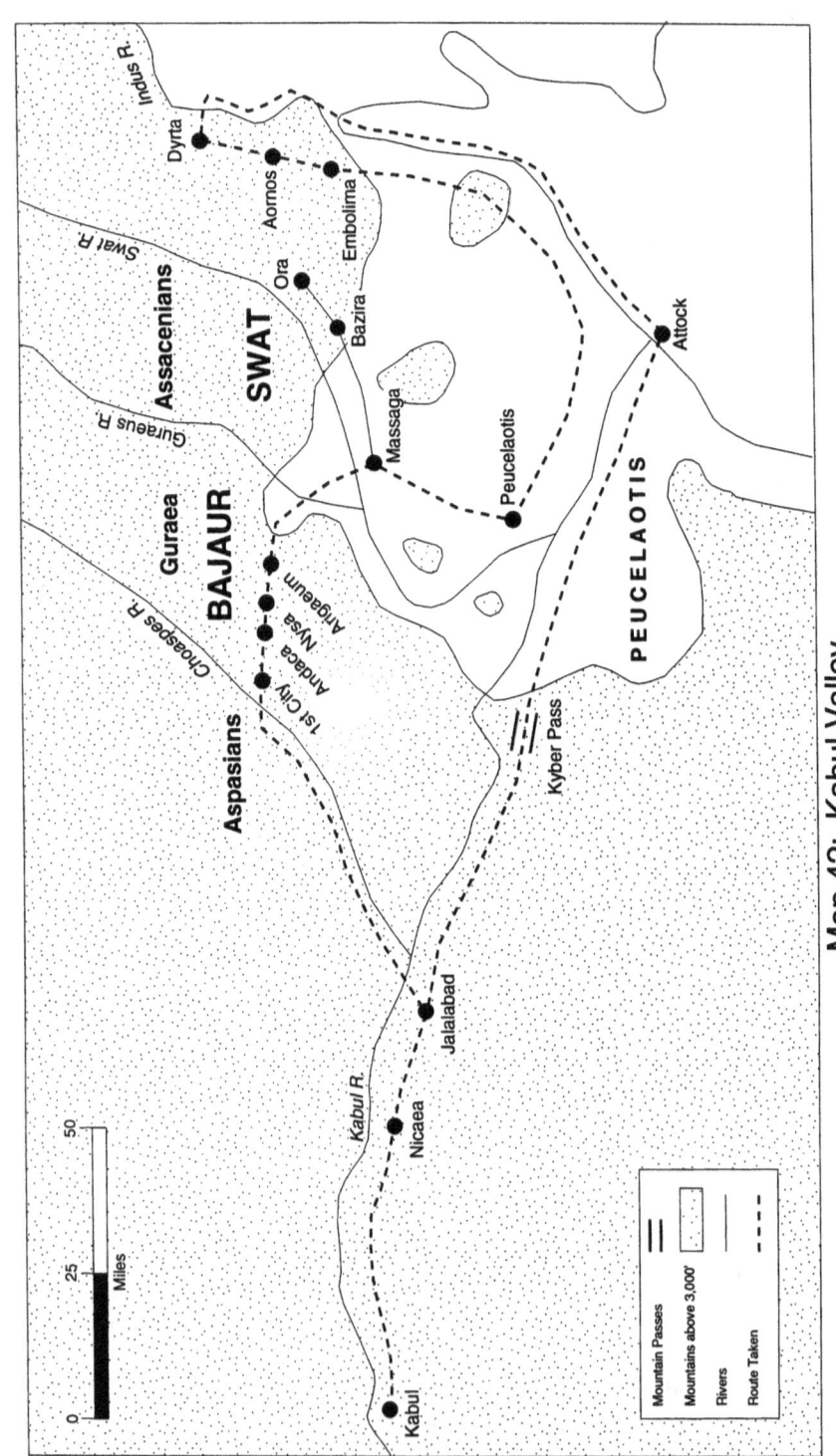

Map 42: Kabul Valley

the Indians against Alexander. The Indians had no desire to be ruled by Alexander or anyone else and clearly preferred death to subjugation.

In the mountainous northwest frontier, the Indian tribes defended their cities against Alexander with the tenacity of both fear and despair. Few cities willingly submitted to Alexander, and those that effortlessly fell into his hands usually had been abandoned by their inhabitants. Once Alexander emerged out into the Punjab he had to contend with the fanatical Brahmans, who not only fought desperately for every city but would frequently stir up revolts in his rear. As the soldiers in the Macedonian army had been badly frightened by the elephants at the battle of Hydaspes River and their morale had been broken by the unending number of sieges and stormings that they had to conduct, they frequently abandoned all self restraint and fought like savages against the Indians, with no holds barred and no quarter being given. Even had Alexander been inclined to restrain them, which he clearly was not, it probably would have been extremely difficult under the circumstances. The short-range result of this brutal policy was that Alexander was successful in terrorizing the Indians into submission, at least those within his reach. In the long run, however, this policy proved disastrous. Almost as soon as Alexander marched on, the Indians began to contemplate revolt.

Bajaur

Alexander had learned in Bactria that it was not wise to trust rulers in mountainous country who readily submitted. Confident in the protection that their mountainous terrain gave them, such tribes only waited for a suitable opportunity to revolt. Because Alexander planned to run his line of communications along the Kabul River, bordering southern Bajaur and Swat, he saw little choice but to militarily defeat the mountain tribes there. Dividing his army at Jalalabad, Alexander sent Hephaestion and Perdiccas with the taxies of the phalanx of Cleitus, Gorgias, and Meleager; half the Companion cavalry; and the mercenary cavalry on a campaign south of the Kabul River.[3] They were ordered to subdue all the tribes of Peucelaotis. Upon reaching the Indus River, the force was to construct a boat bridge across it and then await Alexander's arrival there at the conclusion of his campaign. He, meanwhile, would take the hypaspists, the remaining Companion cavalry, the remaining phalanx, the archers, the Agrianians, and the mounted javelin men on a campaign against the mountain tribes of Bajaur and Swat.[4]

Aspasians

Alexander marched along the west bank of the Choes River, crossing it with considerable difficulty. Learning that the Aspasians were fleeing to their stronger cities and into the hills, he mounted 800 infantry and combined them with his cavalry to form a fast-moving pursuit column.[5] Leaving his foot infantry behind, he rode to the first city on his line of march. The Aspasians retired into their city, and in the ensuing missile fire exchange Alexander was wounded in the shoulder by an arrow.[6] The city was surrounded by a double wall. At dawn the day after their arrival, the Macedonians easily carried the first wall, which had been haphazardly constructed. When the second wall was assaulted, the Aspasians quickly abandoned their positions, evacuated the city through the rear gate, and fled into the nearby hills. The Macedonian soldiers, being angered over Alexander's wounding, killed everyone still left inside the city and then razed it. Alexander left Craterus behind with a force to subdue other cities in the vicinity while he proceeded on to the city of Andaca, which quickly surrendered.

Alexander marched off with the hypaspists, archers, Agrianians, the guard cavalry, a portion of the Companions, half the mounted archers, and the taxies of the phalanx under Attalus and Coenus.[7] Two days later he arrived at the residence of the leader of the Aspasians. The inhabitants fled at his approach and were pursued and massacred all the way to the foothills. Ptolemy, with a small force, gave chase to the Indian leader, who was accompanied by a large group of his followers. When the foothills made the going too difficult for horses, Ptolemy continued the chase on foot. Although the Indian leader managed to wound Ptolemy in the ensuing fighting, he himself was killed by Ptolemy. At the Indian leader's death, his followers promptly fled. As the Macedonians were carrying off his body, however, the Aspasians came down from the mountains to fight for it. Alexander now arrived, dismounted his cavalry, and entered the fight alongside Ptolemy. Together they were able to beat back the attack, but only with considerable difficulty.

After crossing the mountains, Alexander moved on to the city of Argaeum. Upon his arrival there, the inhabitants set fire to the city and fled. Craterus then rejoined Alexander with the remainder of the army. As the city had been located in a strategic position, Alexander fortified and repopulated it with Aspasian volunteers and Greeks no longer able to serve with the field army. Receiving reports that the Aspasians were gathering in large numbers ahead of him, Alexander sent Ptolemy out to reconnoiter. When he returned to report that the numerous enemy camp fires seemed to indicate that the Aspasians heavily outnumbered the Macedonians, Alexander refused to believe him, mistakenly thinking, instead, that the Indians were merely maintaining a large number of fires in an attempt to magnify their forces. Alexander divided his army into three forces: one under Leonnatus, with the taxies of the phalanx under Attalus and Balacrus, the Agrianians, and the Balkan javelin men; another under Ptolemy, with one-third of the hypaspists, two taxies of the phalanx under Philip and Philotas, two battalions of archers, the Agrianians, and half the cavalry; and the last one under himself, with the remaining troops.[8] The Aspasians, seeing how heavily they outnumbered the Macedonians, came down from the hills in force and charged Alexander's force on the plain but were defeated with heavy losses. Ptolemy then attacked the Aspasii remaining on the hill and after a hard fight broke them. Leonnatus' attack against the Aspasii was also successful. Over 40,000 Indians were said to have been killed or captured during the campaign.[9]

Peucelaotis

Hephaestion and Perdiccas, meanwhile, campaigned through the territory of Peucelaotis. Cities along the way were either surrendered or taken by storm. Reaching the Indus River, they built a boat bridge across it as Alexander had instructed. Astes, the ruler of Peucelaotis, now revolted, however, forcing Hephaestion to return and besiege him at Charsadda, his capital. After a siege of 30 days, the city fell and Astes was put to death.[10]

Generalship

Alexander was clearly correct in his strategic assessment of the undependability of mountain tribes. The only way to ensure that they were subdued was to defeat them in open battle and occupy strategic locations within their territory. He waged a mobile campaign in Bajaur, always keeping the Aspasians off balance with his unexpected appearances. Although Alexander was unable to prevent the Aspasians from concentrating, once they did he had little trouble in defeating them in battle. Bajaur was subdued relatively quickly, considering that it consisted largely of difficult mountainous terrain and hard-fighting tribesmen.

Swat

Guraeans

Alexander took command of the Companions, mounted javelin men, the Agrianians, the taxies of the phalanx of Coenus and Polysperchon, and the archers and resumed his march to the east.[11] He crossed the Guraeus River with some difficulty because of its depth, rapid current, and slippery riverbed.[12] The Guraeans, upon learning of his crossing, feared to make a stand against him. At his approach, they broke up and withdrew to their cities of origin.

Assacenians

The Swat highland was a rich and prosperous area inhabited by the Assacenians, a warlike Indian mountain tribe. They were said to be able to field an army of 30 elephants, 2,000 cavalry, and 30,000 infantry.[13] Alexander could not simply bypass them because they would remain a continuing threat on his line of communications into the Punjab. After Craterus rejoined the army with the remainder of the phalanx and the siege train, Alexander marched on ahead with the Companions cavalry, the mounted javelin men, Coenus' and Polysperchon's taxies of the phalanx, the Agrianians, and the archers.[14]

Although they had intended to engage Alexander in a field battle, the Assacenians, perhaps because of their lack of discipline, instead retired into Massaga. This was their largest fortified city, being garrisoned by 31,000 infantry and reinforced by a large Indian mercenary force of 7,000 that had arrived just prior to Alexander.[15] To the east, Massaga was bordered by a fast-flowing river with steep banks; on the west and south, by steep cliffs. The city was surrounded by a wall almost four and a half miles long.[16]

While reconnoitering the city, Alexander was shot in the calf of his leg by an arrow.[17] Having heard reports of the erratic behavior of the Assacenians, he determined to use their weakness to his advantage. To induce them away from their fortifications, Alexander feinted a withdrawal towards a hill about a mile away from his camp.[18] As he had anticipated, the Assacenians assumed that he was falling back in fear of them and rushed out en masse to reap the benefits of a victory they believed they had already won. As they closed in on what they believed to be an army in rout, the phalanx suddenly turned around and rapidly closed to engage. The phalanx was closely supported by the mounted javelin men, the Agrianians, and the archers.[19] The Assacenians broke up at this unexpected turn of events and fled back to Massaga, leaving 200 dead on the field.[20] Alexander then brought his phalanx up to the city's wall. While performing a reconnaissance there, he was wounded in the ankle by an arrow.[21]

On the day after he had routed the Assacenians, Alexander brought up his siege equipment, breached the city's walls, and attempted to carry Massaga by assault. The tenacious Assacenians' defense of the wall, however, threw back the assault. On the second day Alexander brought up a wooden tower filled with archers. Although they cleared the walls with a heavy missile fire, the Macedonians were again unable to force their way through the breach. Yet another attempt to force the breach was made on the third day. Alexander again brought up the wooden tower, but this time with a drawbridge attached to it. When the drawbridge was lowered over the breach, however, such a large number of hypaspists crowded onto it in their desire to be the first across that their weight collapsed it. The Assacenians, upon seeing their confusion, directed a heavy missile fire against the struggling hypaspists and then rushed out of the city to engage them in hand-to-hand combat. The hypaspists were unable to disengage from the disadvantageous fight until Alcetas' taxies of the phalanx moved up to their support. The third attempt to take Massaga by storm had resulted in another dismal failure.

The next day Alexander again brought up another tower, this time with a reinforced drawbridge attached. While the final preparations for the assault were being completed, however, the Assacenians indicated a desire to surrender. They had become completely demoralized both by the large number of wounded they had sustained during the siege and by the loss of their leader the day before to a catapult bolt. Alexander agreed to accept their surrender, provided the Indians would enlist as mercenaries with him. They agreed to this condition, marched out of Massaga, and camped on a nearby hill. Upon receiving intelligence that the mercenaries were going to desert that night because they did not care to fight against their fellow countrymen, Alexander quietly surrounded the hill they occupied after sunset and slaughtered them all. He then assaulted Massaga, which, weakened by the loss of its most effective defenders, quickly fell. The siege of the city had cost the Macedonian army only 25 killed.[22]

Coenus was sent to Bazira to accept its expected surrender. Alexander had assumed that when its citizens heard of Massaga's fall, fear would force their surrender. Meanwhile, Alcetas, Attalus, and Demetrius proceeded to Ora.[23] Bazira, however, refused to submit, while Ora's garrison attacked Attalus' force. Alexander had initially begun to march on Bazira, but upon hearing that Abisares, king of Kashmir, was marching to reinforce Ora, he decided to go there instead. Coenus was instructed to fortify a position for a holding garrison at Bazira and join Alexander with the remainder of his troops at Ora. Soon after Coenus' departure, the Indians in Bazira sallied out against the force he had left behind, but after sustaining casualties of 500 killed and 70 captured, they withdrew back inside the city.[24] When Bazira heard that Alexander had captured Ora on the first assault, its citizens became demoralized and evacuated the city that night. This was the signal for the Assaceni to begin abandoning all their cities and concentrating their forces at what they considered to be an impregnable position at the Rock of Aornos. When Alexander heard that even Heracles had allegedly been unable to capture the position there, he was overcome with a desire to surpass his illustrious ancestor by taking it himself. Appointing Nicanor, one of his Companions, as satrap of Swat, Alexander built a wall round Bazira, strongly garrisoned it, turned Ora and Massaga into advanced fortified outposts, moved south through the Malakand Pass, and then north against the Rock of Aornos.

The Siege of the Rock of Aornos

About 75 miles north of Attock, where the Indus River turns to the east, the Rock of Aornos rises up 5,000 feet to form the north end of a north-south ridge with a flat top, which angles up sharply to 7,900 feet in the south. The summit occupied a circumference of about 25 miles.[25] The eastern and western sides of the ridge were very steep and rocky, most places being sheer drop-offs. A single narrow trail carved out of the side of the rock led to its summit. With enough arable land to accommodate 1,000 farmers, a heavy volume of snow, large woodlands, and a plentiful supply of spring water, the position could sustain a large population almost indefinitely.[26] As an added precaution, provisions had been accumulated at the fortress to enable it to withstand a two-year siege. It was a position that could have easily been blockaded with a small force, but Alexander, upon hearing that his ancestor Heracles had been unable to capture it, was seized by a desire to out-do him.

In the foothills of Aornos lay the town of Embolima. Alexander intended to use the site as a base of operations to conduct what he expected to be a long siege against Aornos. He sent out a foraging force under Craterus to begin gathering food in the surrounding area while he moved on the Rock of Aornos with a force of archers, Agrianians, Coenus' phalanx taxies, some lightly armed phalanx troops, 200 Companions, and 100 horse-archers.[27] A poverty-stricken local thoroughly familiar with the area came to the Macedonian camp. Informing Alexander that for a price he would guide him to a point that would overlook Aornos, he was promised the incredible sum of 80 talents for his assistance.[28] Ptolemy was ordered to follow the man with a force consisting of Alexander's personal guard, the Agrianians, some select men from the hypaspists, and the remaining light troops.[29] His orders were to hold the position to which the Indian guided him. Upon his arrival

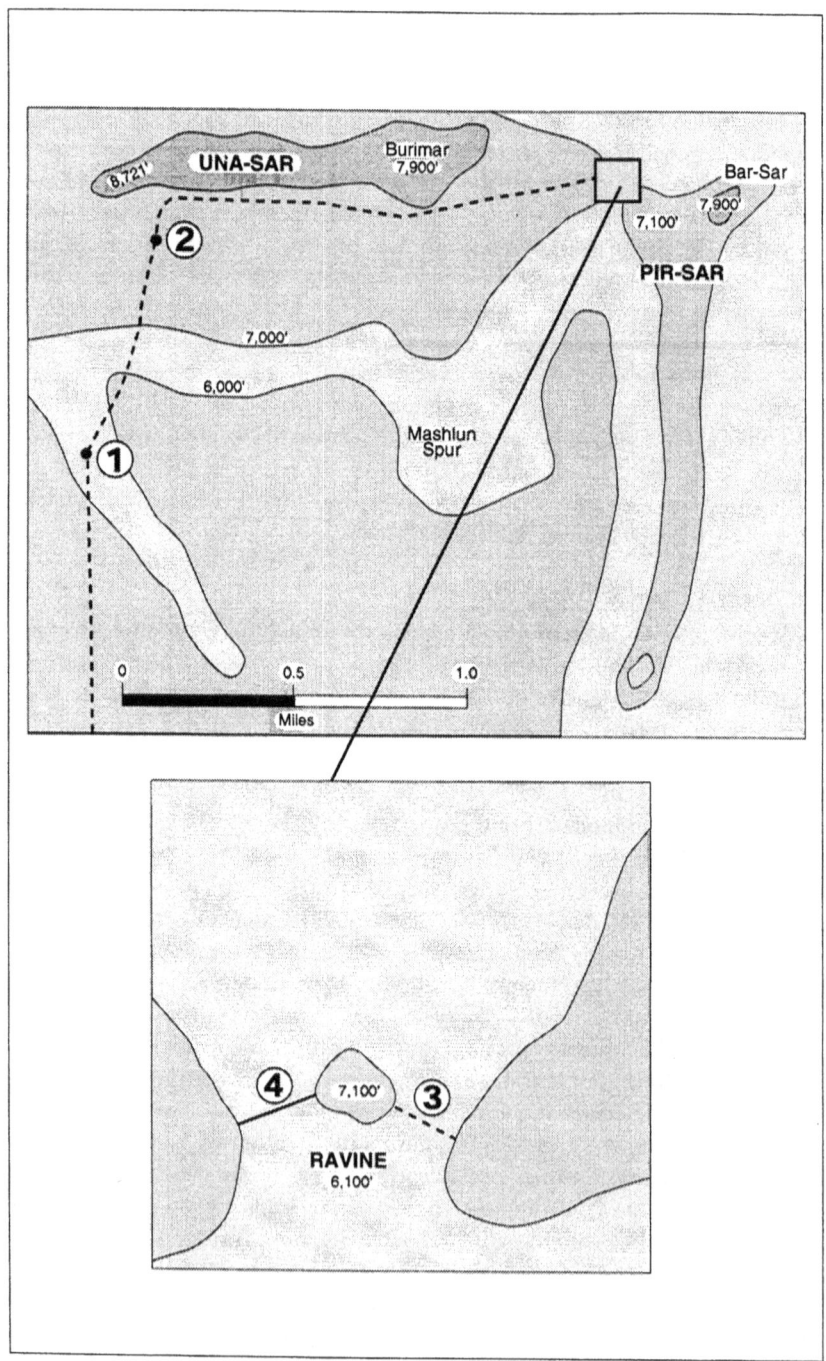

Map 43: Siege of the Rock of Aornos

there, Ptolemy was to signal Alexander, who would then advance to join him. Following the rough trail in the dark, Ptolemy reached his objective without interference from the Indians. After fortifying the position with a ditch and stockade, Ptolemy lit his signal. Upon seeing it, Alexander attacked but was unable to make any progress because of the difficult terrain and the strong resistance of the Indians. Observing Alexander's difficulty, the Indians left a small force to hold him in place and then advanced on Ptolemy in strength. Heavy missile fire and the strength of Ptolemy's defenses, however, drove the Indians back.

Alexander sent a message to Ptolemy that night to attack simultaneously with him the next day in an attempt to crush the Indians between them. At daybreak, Alexander began fighting his way along the same path Ptolemy had taken and was able to join forces with him. Together they tried to carry Aornos by assault but failed in the attempt. The next day Alexander ordered each man in his army to cut 100 stakes. These were to be used to anchor a bridge on the walls of the 800-foot-deep ravine between the Bar-sar ridge, which the Macedonians occupied, and the adjacent Pir-sar ridge, which the Indians occupied.[30] By the end of the third day, a bridge had been anchored on the upper tier of stakes and covered with earth. On the fourth day, Alexander captured a small nearby hill nearly level with Aornos. This enabled the assault against Pir-Sar to be conducted along a broader front.

The Indians on Aornos were badly demoralized by Alexander's capture of the small hill and immediately opened surrender negotiations. They intended to prolong the talks as a ruse until nightfall, when they hoped to slip through Alexander's lines and disperse back to their homes. Their plan came to Alexander's attention, however, and he prepared a trap for them. When night fell and the Indians had evacuated Aornos, Alexander scaled the walls with his personal guard and 700 hypaspists and took possession of the summit.[31] He then gave a signal, and the remainder of his army cut down the Indians as they attempted to escape. In their fear and confusion, many Indians met their death by falling over the edge of the surrounding cliffs. Alexander's capture of the Rock of Aornos, in effect, ended the Swat campaign.

Generalship At the Rock of Aornos, Alexander departed from sound military judgment in an egotistical campaign to carry a position he could have very easily isolated at little cost. Instead, he was ready to jeopardize the lives of his men needlessly in a direct assault on the fortress. Fortunately, subsequent events made the assault unnecessary, but if the Indians had withstood an assault, there is no doubt that Alexander was determined to make it.

Alexander's conduct of the siege was up to his usual high level of skill. Once again a supposedly impregnable position would have probably fallen to his final

Opposite: *1. Alexander's progress is blocked by attacking Indians. 2. Ptolemy's fortified camp. 3. Alexander's bridge across the 800-foot-deep ravine. 4. When Alexander occupies the hill, the Indians ask for a truce. 5. When Alexander finds out that the Indians plan to desert, he advances on a deserted sector of Pir-Sar with 700 hypaspists and successfully scales it.*

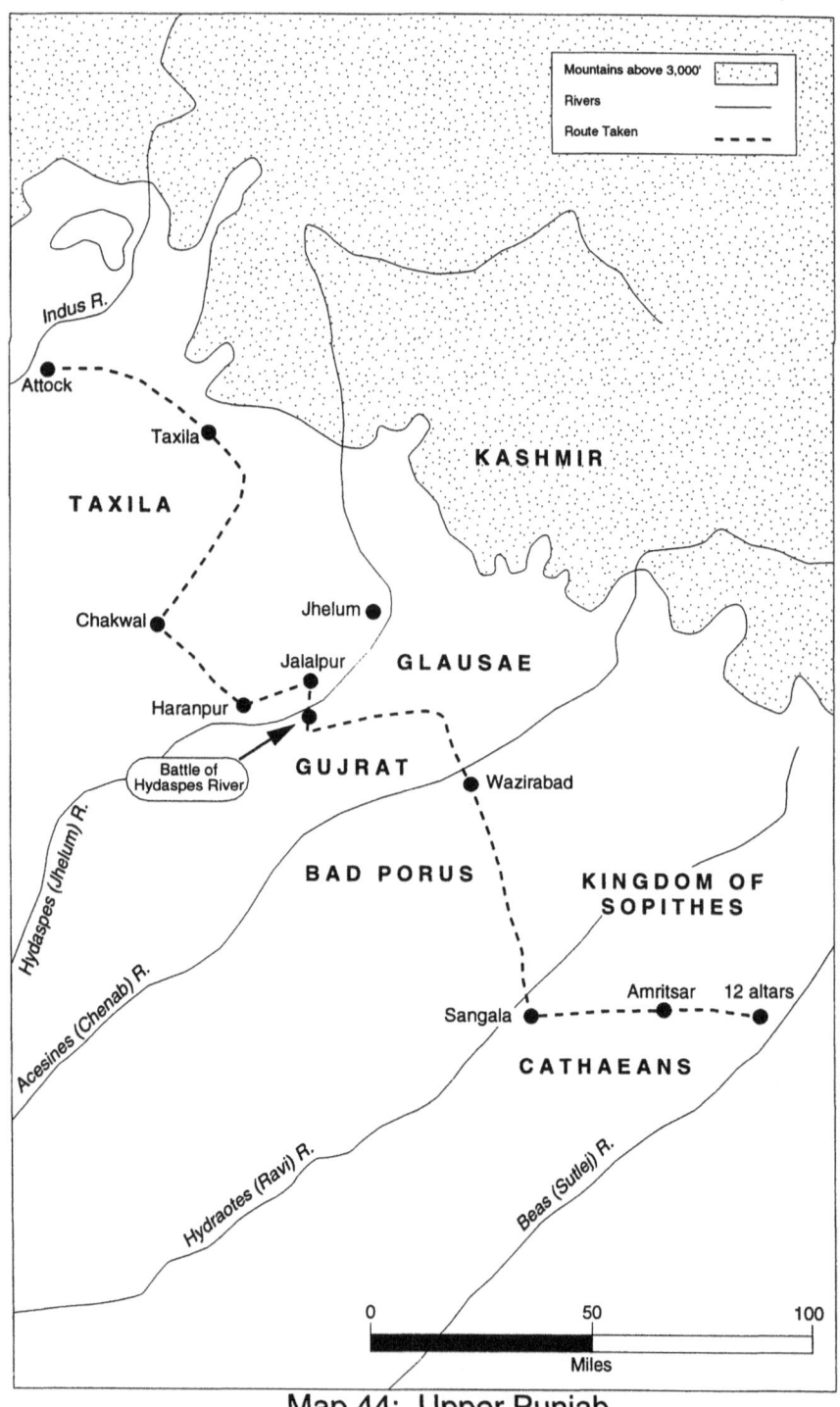

Map 44: Upper Punjab

assault, although casualties would no doubt have been heavy. Overall, Alexander's plans were well made, and he was equally well prepared to carry the position quickly by assault or to conduct a long, drawn-out siege against it.

Dyrta

While Alexander was at Aornos, he received a report that Oxyartes' brother Erices had taken refuge in the nearby hills with 15 elephants and an armed force of 20,000 tribesmen.[32] Arriving at the city of Dyrta, Alexander found both the city and surrounding territory deserted. He gave Nearchus command of the Agrianians and light troops and Antiochus command of his own taxies of the phalanx in addition to two others; he then ordered them to reconnoiter the area.[33] Alexander took the remainder of the army back to the Indus River. Along the way he rebuilt the roads, which in the isolated area had badly deteriorated, and rounded up numbers of stray elephants along the river. When Alexander reached the Indus, he built a number of ships of timber from the nearby woods and sailed down the river to the boat-bridge Hephaestion and Perdiccas had constructed across it. He then rested his army for the next 30 days.[34]

Generalship

Although having available only a portion of his army, albeit all the elite units, Alexander had conducted a highly effective campaign in Swat. He had subdued the central highlands there with relatively little effort except for Massaga, which took him four assaults to carry. Its fall, however, resulted in the evacuation of virtually the entire military population of Swat to the Rock of Aornos. Alexander conducted his campaign in Swat with a bloodthirsty ferocity. In two instances, both at Massaga and the Rock of Aornos, he deliberately massacred Indian troops whom he surely knew wanted nothing more than to return home. There was no military necessity which compelled this butchery, but for the fact that Alexander had apparently decided to rule the Swat highlands by terror. He most likely reasoned that he would never be able to enlist the cooperation of the fiercely independent mountain warriors. Whatever his rationale, Alexander's actions towards those tribes were irreconcilable with his lofty image of himself.

Upper Punjab

Taxila

At the Indus River, Taxiles, the king of Taxila, surrendered himself and his kingdom to Alexander, presenting him with 200 silver talents, 3,000 cattle, 10,000 sheep, 30 elephants, and the services of 700 cavalry.[35] In the company of Taxiles, Alexander crossed the Indus River on a boat bridge at Attock and marched to Taxila, the greatest city between the Indus and Hydaspes rivers. After appointing Philip satrap of the area and leaving behind a garrison of invalid soldiers, Alexander marched on to the Hydaspes River.

Battle of Hydaspes River

Alexander ordered Porus, the king of Gujrat, to meet him at the Hydaspes River with his tribute.[36] The Indian king replied that he would indeed be there, but with an army to fight for his kingdom. Alexander ordered Coenus (son of Polemocrates) back to the Indus River to bring up the boats used to construct the bridge there.[37] Because the beginning of the monsoon rains in early June would soon make the Hydaspes River unfordable, Alexander immediately marched to Haranpur, the closest crossing of the river. When he arrived, Alexander found Porus' army fully deployed on the eastern bank of the river opposite the crossing and fully prepared for battle.

Estimates of Porus' strength vary widely, but his army at the Hydaspes River probably numbered about 36,000, including 6,000 cavalry, 30,000 infantry, 300 chariots, and 85 elephants.[38] Alexander's overall strength was about 29,000, with 7,500 cavalry, 17,000 infantry, and 5,000 Indian allies. In preparation for his crossing of the Hydaspes, Alexander divided his army into three detachments: a crossing force under himself, which would cross the Hydaspes River somewhere upstream; a holding force under Craterus, to remain at the base camp to hold the attention of Porus; and a reserve force stationed midway between the other two to prevent any attempt by Porus to cross the river between them. Alexander's crossing force totaled 14,000 and was comprised of 5,000 cavalry and 9,000 infantry.[39] The cavalry contained the Agema; the Companion hipparchies of Coenus, Demetrius, Hephaestion, and Perdiccas; some Scythians; and the Dahae horse-archers.[40] The infantry included the hypaspists, two taxies of the phalanx, under Cleitus and Coenus; the Agrianians; and the archers.[41] It is not specifically identified who commanded the reserve force, which totaled 5,500, with 500 Greek mercenary cavalry and 5,000 infantry. The infantry consisted of three taxies of the phalanx under Attalus, Gorgias, and Meleager; and 500 Greek mercenary infantry.[42] Craterus would command the holding force, which totaled 10,000 and included 2,000 cavalry and 8,000 infantry. The cavalry comprised Craterus' own hipparchy and units from Arachosian and Parapamisadae.[43] The taxies of the phalanx under Alcetas and Polysperchon totaled another 3,000, while Taxiles' Indians had a strength of 5,000.[44]

Porus was determined to fight a strictly defensive battle for the moment. His hope was that the fast-flowing and quickly rising Hydaspes River, swollen to about a half-mile wide at the Haranpur crossing from the melting snows of the Himalayan Mountains, would delay Alexander long enough for an army led by Abisares, king of Kashmir, to reinforce him.[45] Porus thought that Alexander would lack sufficient waterborne transport and would thus be unable to land more than a small harassing force across the river that could be quickly and easily dealt with.

Alexander was aware that Abisares was marching to Porus' assistance with a large army and was eager to prevent a junction between the two. There was little chance, however, of successfully attacking Porus in his present position opposite Haranpur Ford. The Hydaspes was deep, wide, and fast flowing there. The few ships that Alexander had hauled overland in pieces could only transport a small number of troops. Also, Alexander's main striking arm, the cavalry, would be useless in any attack on the crossing because the horses would quickly become unmanageable in the presence of Porus' elephants on the opposite bank. Alexander would therefore have to cross the river somewhere well beyond interference from Porus' elephants. After conducting a thorough reconnaissance, his scouts located a suitable crossing point 19 miles upstream from his base camp, opposite the heavily wooded island of Admana.[46] It was located beyond a sharp bend in the Hydaspes River, providing an ideal screen for the operation.

If the crossing was to be unopposed, an effective diversion was necessary to keep both Porus' attention and his elephants at the ford. A serious attempt to cross the Hydaspes at the base camp would, therefore, have to appear to be made. Alexander's final orders to Craterus were, however, that his holding force at Haranpur was not to attempt a crossing until Porus moved out most of his troops to engage his crossing force and took all his elephants with him. If Porus left any of his elephants behind, Craterus was instructed not to attack.

Alexander needed to disguise the noise that the departure of his crossing force was sure to make as it left the base camp. By constantly shifting his troops noisily up and down along the river, he hoped to convince Porus to disregard these movements as meaningless. Then when he actually did move out for his upstream crossing, Porus would not consider the resulting noise to be of any consequence. Every night for weeks Alexander moved his cavalry up and down his side of the river, having it make as much noise as possible. At first, Porus reacted to each incident by bringing up his elephants and cavalry and paralleling Alexander's movements. But as this activity was repeated night after night to no apparent purpose, Porus began to ignore the noisy demonstrations and remain in camp. Alexander further lulled Porus into complacency by accumulating large quantities of supplies in plain sight at the base camp, making it appear as if he was settling in until the Hydaspes receded and was again fordable.

Alexander marched his crossing force out at night during a violent storm, accompanied by deafening thunder and heavy rain. It was the perfect cover to muffle the sounds of his movement. As an added precaution, his army marched through an inland route to further minimize the chance of detection. Allowing about six hours for the march during monsoon conditions, it was probably about 3:00 A.M. when Alexander reached his intended crossing site. Stuffing and sewing up the tenting and animal hides for floats, and embarking his hypaspists on his few ships probably took up the better part of perhaps another two hours.[47] Everything then being ready, Alexander led his troops across the river. The hypaspists boarded the triaconters of his small navy, while everyone else proceeded across on the floats. Although the rain had stopped, thick clouds blocked out the light so that in the extreme darkness a man's features were not discernible, even at a close distance. Voice commands could not be understood because of the loud and constant noise from the gusty winds.

Being unfamiliar with the area, Alexander had mistakenly landed his force on the island of Admana instead of on the mainland, as he had intended. The rain

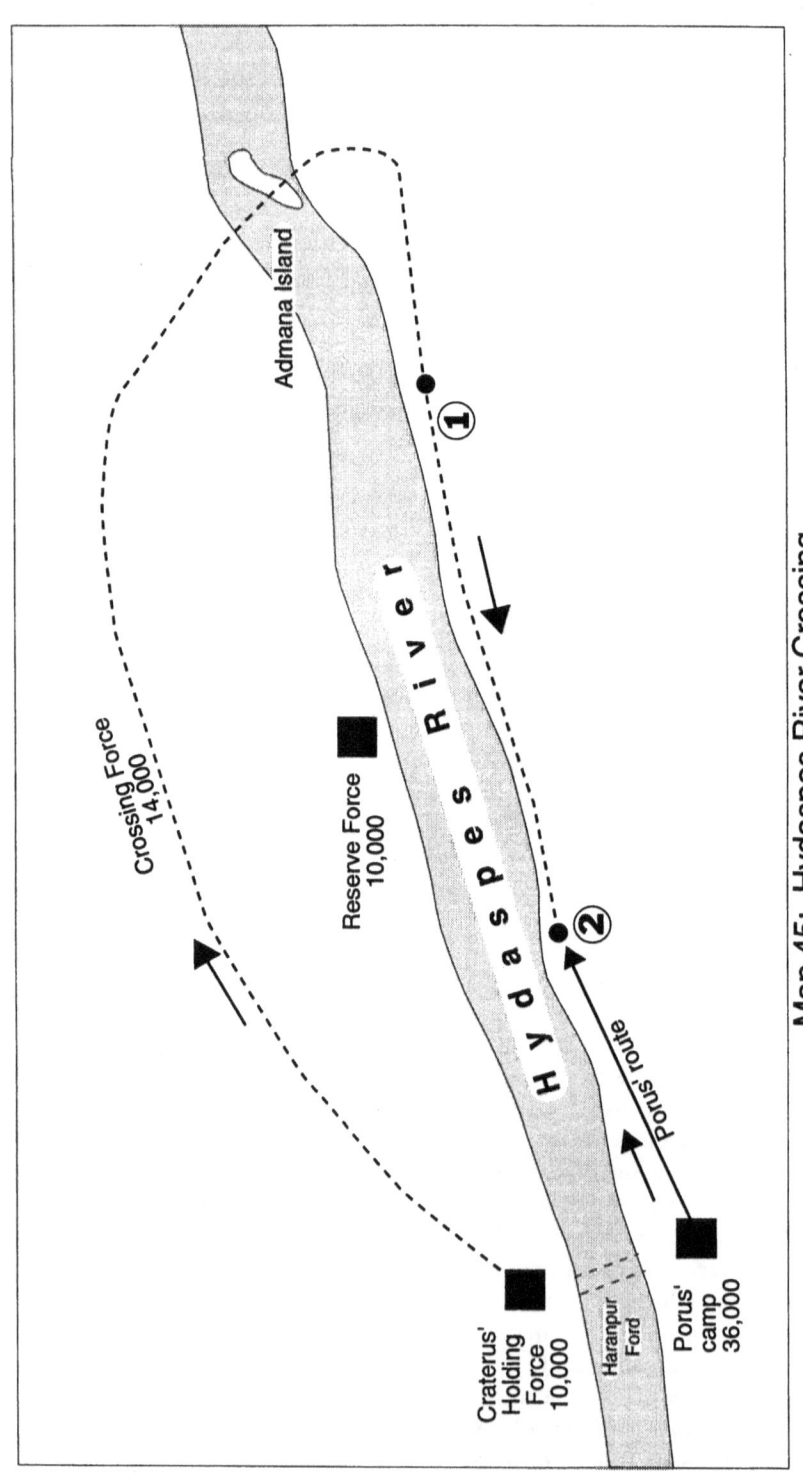

Map 45: Hydaspes River Crossing

had raised the water level so high that the normally fordable channel between the island and the mainland was now both wide and deep. It was with no little anxiety that a search was made for a crossable ford, there being no time to reembark the entire force for another landing before daylight. A usable ford was finally found, but it was deep, the water reaching up to a man's chest and a horse's neck. Nevertheless, Alexander's troops began to slowly cross over it. When they finally set foot on the mainland, the Companion hipparchies of Coenus, Demetrius, Hephaestion, and Perdiccas were formed up on Alexander's right flank, and the horse-archers were brought over to screen them.[48] Part of the phalanx was deployed on the left of the cavalry, next to them the hypaspists, and then the remainder of the phalanx.[49] On either side of the phalanx, the archers, Agrianians, and javelin men were stationed.[50] The foot-archers were then brought to the front of the infantry to enable them to engage any elephants at long range. While his infantry was still forming up, Alexander moved on ahead with his Companions and a flank guard of archers under Tauron. After advancing about two-and-a-half miles, Alexander saw Aristobulus closing on him in the distance.

Aristobulus When it was reported to Porus that the Macedonians had crossed the Hydaspes, he at first did not believe that they were more than a diversionary force. Porus thought that a strong mobile force would suffice to destroy the small bridgehead that Alexander was obviously attempting to establish upstream. He therefore put 2,000 cavalry and 120 chariots under the command of his son Aristobulus with orders to ride northeast and eliminate this force.[51] As Aristobulus advanced, he was surprised to see Alexander's flanking force approaching him fully deployed in battle order. Immediately swinging his forces into line, Aristobulus attacked with his chariots. Unfortunately, the ground was muddy from the previous night's heavy rain and quickly bogged down the heavy vehicles, forcing many of the crews to abandon them. Those that were still able to maneuver either had their crews thrown off when the potholes hidden in pools of water were hit or they were disabled by heavy missile fire from Alexander's horse-archers. Aristobulus' cavalry were then simply overwhelmed by Alexander's Companion cavalry. The advance Indian force soon broke and fled the battlefield, leaving behind 400 dead, all the chariots, and Aristobulus, who had been killed in the fighting.[52] Macedonian casualties were apparently light, but Bucephalas, Alexander's beloved horse, received a fatal wound from which he would soon die.

Porus When Porus learned of the defeat of the mobile force under Aristobulus, he was faced with a difficult decision, whether to merely delay Alexander and hold his main force in position at the site of the impending crossing or to only leave a holding force there and engage Alexander with his main force. The choice was made more difficult by the fact that Porus could see that Craterus was clearly in his final preparations for crossing the river. Porus unhesitatingly and correctly made the decision to attack Alexander with his main force. Leaving a small holding force of his most inferior infantry and a few elephants opposite Craterus, Porus

1. Alexander defeats Aristobulus. 2. Alexander defeats Porus at the battle of Hydaspes River.

marched towards Alexander through the mud. When he found an area firm enough for his cavalry, chariots, and elephants to maneuver on, he halted and deployed his army from column into line of battle.

Porus had on hand to fight Alexander about 4,000 cavalry, 30,000 infantry, 180 chariots, and 85 elephants.[53] His main line contained his elephants, which were deployed about 100 feet apart across the front.[54] The infantry of his rear line extended beyond the elephant line on both flanks.[55] The cavalry was stationed on both flanks of the infantry and was in turn screened by the chariots.[56] Porus took station on the far left of the elephant line atop a huge war elephant. His infantry battleline was two and three-fourths miles long, over four times the frontage of Alexander's infantry. Upon completing his deployment, Porus awaited Alexander's arrival.

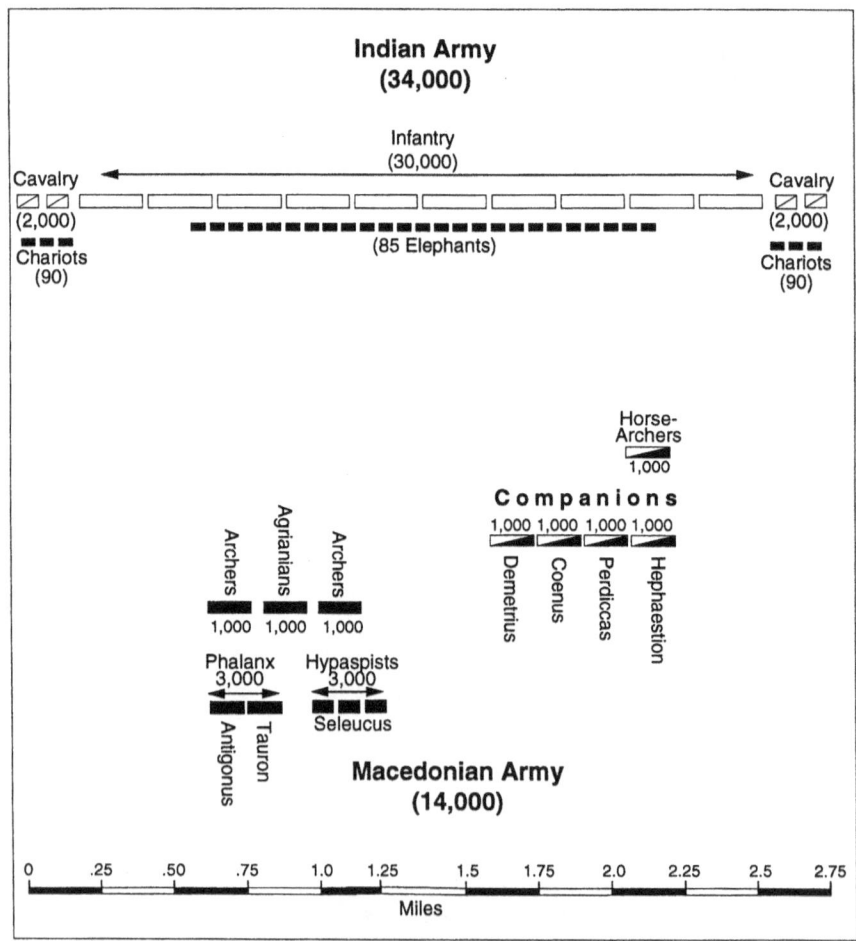

Map 46: Hydaspes River

9: INDIA

Alexander was riding with his cavalry about two miles ahead of his infantry when he sighted Porus' army. Ordering up his infantry, he carefully reconnoitered the Indian's position. Alexander then reassigned several of his senior officers, Coenus being ordered to command Demetrius' cavalry, Demetrius posted as second-in-command, and Tauron and Antigonus assigned commands on the left wing of the army. These changes were necessary because the command structure used for crossing the river was not suitable for a field battle. Antigonus' taxies of the phalanx occupied the far left of the battleline, Tauron's taxies closed up on his right, and the hypaspists, under Seleucus, were stationed on Tauron's right. The Agrianians and archers screened the phalanx and hypaspists. Alexander commanded the right wing, which consisted of the Companion hipparchies of Demetrius, Coenus, Perdiccas, and Hephaestion. The horse-archers screened the right flank of the Companions. Alexander's strength for the battle was about 14,000 with the infantry deployed on the left and the cavalry on the right.

Porus placed great reliance upon his elephants. He envisaged that the battle in the center of his line would largely be between Alexander's infantry and his elephants because the Macedonian cavalry would be rendered unmanageable by the elephant's unfamiliar smell.[57] If Alexander's infantry attempted to pass through the elephant line, they would be engaged by Porus' infantry in front and trampled by the elephants from the rear. On the other hand, if Alexander's infantry engaged the elephants directly, they would suffer heavy casualties and be disordered, giving Porus' lighter infantry the advantage they needed to sally out against them.

Alexander knew that in this battle the infantry would be the decisive arm because Porus' elephants would prohibit his cavalry from closing with the Indian battle line. His plan was to eliminate the Indian cavalry as an effective force so that it would be unable to interfere with his infantry's fight against the elephants. Once the Indian cavalry was successfully dealt with, Alexander did not anticipate that his phalanx would have much trouble in defeating the Indian infantry line, which was, after all, only composed of nonarmored archers armed with cumbersome two-handed broadswords.

Alexander determined to set a trap to draw the Indian cavalry out. He would induce Porus to concentrate all his cavalry opposite the Macedonian right wing. To effect this, Alexander would have Coenus ride towards the Macedonian left with his and Demetrius' hipparchies as if they were leaving to reinforce it. Alexander believed that when Porus saw that he now substantially outnumbered the remaining Companions opposite his left, he would attack at what he perceived to be an advantage. As Porus' cavalry became engaged frontally, Coenus would then circle back and fall on its exposed flank and rear. Only after the Indian cavalry was defeated would the phalanx be allowed to move out against the elephant line.

Macedonian Left Flank Porus reacted to Alexander's cavalry concentration as anticipated and began to redeploy the 2,000 cavalry from his right wing to his left.

As ancient authors failed to mention the actions of the chariots on Porus' right wing, it is quite likely that the Indian cavalry there maneuvered across their front

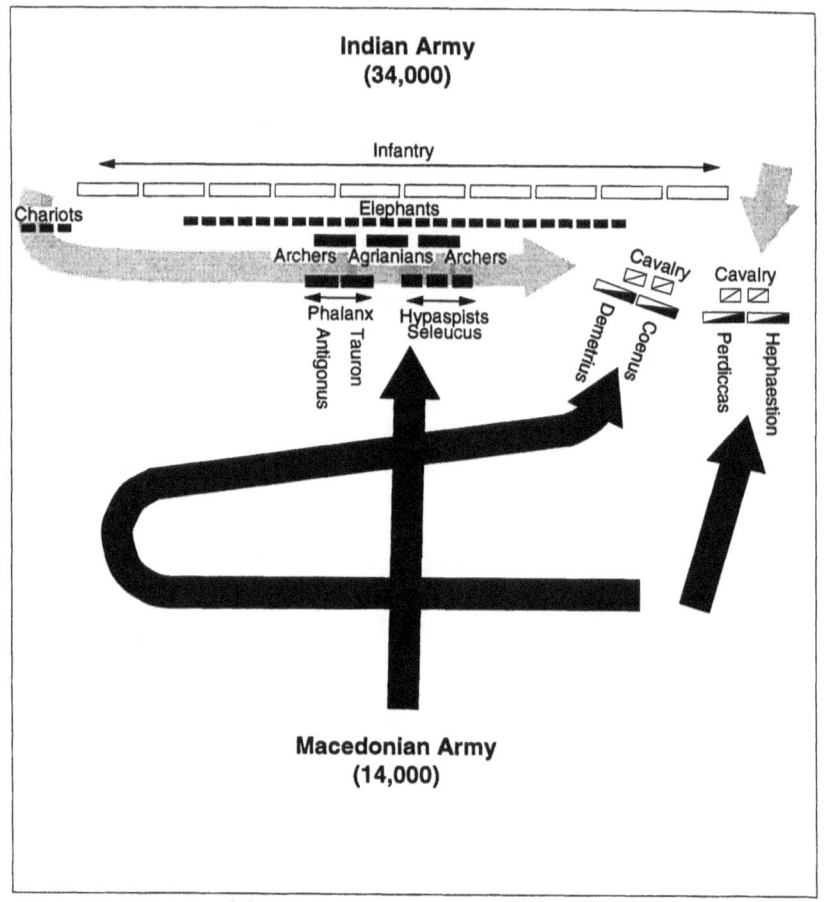

Map 47: Hydaspes River

in proceeding to the left flank, inhibiting their movement until Alexander had closed with the elephants. By then, it was too late for them to advance, as the Macedonian infantry was already joined in battle with the elephants.

Macedonian Right Flank Alexander opened the battle by advancing his mounted archers against the chariots screening Porus' cavalry on his left wing. They were all but helpless against the concentrated fire of the 1,000 horse-archers, who devastated the largely unprotected six-man chariot crews, either wounding or killing virtually every one of them.[58] The Indian cavalry deployed immediately behind the chariots were also disordered by the heavy missile fire. Before the Indian left wing cavalry could recover, Alexander advanced on them with the Companion hipparchies of Perdiccas and Hephaestion. Observing the reduced strength of Alexander's cavalry facing them and seeing their cavalry beginning to arrive from their right wing, the Indian cavalry of the left wing, although disordered, rode out to engage the Companions remaining on Alexander's right flank.

Porus' cavalry from his left wing continued to advance on Alexander, although hesitantly. Coenus now arrived and charged the flank of the Indian cavalry from the right wing that had been advancing in column. At the same time, Alexander charged the unsteady Indian left wing cavalry with the two hipparchies under his command. The Indian right-wing cavalry quickly broke under Coenus' attack, while their left wing cavalry was unable to stand and receive Alexander's charge. All the Indian cavalry withdrew into the shelter of the elephants in Porus' battle line, where they caused significant confusion. The Indian cavalry regrouped behind the elephants and then charged out against the Macedonian cavalry, who were again united. The Indian cavalry suffered another defeat and once more withdrew through the elephants, causing even greater confusion than before. The Indian cavalry took heavy casualties during their retreat because many of the elephants attacked either from fear or anger.

Macedonian Center With the defeat of his cavalry a second time, Porus began to maneuver his line to the left in an attempt to engage Alexander's cavalry with his elephants. The movement, however, was greatly hampered by the slow pace of the elephants.[59] As Porus' line began its shift, the Macedonian phalanx was ordered to advance to the attack. The light infantry screening the phalanx brought massed missile fire down on both the elephants and their mahouts. The Agrianians and hypaspists then attacked the elephants with two-sided axes and broadswords to hamstring them. When the phalanx closed, they used their sarissas effectively against both elephants and mahouts. All this was to have its effect in time but not against the initial elephant charge. Great gaps were knocked in the phalanx formation, and the elephants crushed and gored the infantrymen almost at will. Men were tossed through the air by the trunks of the elephants as if they were weightless. Casualties in the phalanx were heavy, and the only thing that prevented the troops from breaking was their superb discipline. Alexander is reputed to have said, "At last I behold a danger worthy of my spirit; I am dealing at the same time with beasts and with remarkable men."[60]

Despite the deteriorating situation, Porus decided to lead one last desperate charge with his elephants. It failed because the Macedonian light troops managed to keep just out of their reach, while at the same time continuing to wound the elephants. Finally, exhausted and weak with wounds, the elephants refused to advance any further and on their own inclination began to slowly back away from the Macedonians. The Indian infantry also had considerable difficulty stringing and firing their bows on the rain-soaked ground, and the high humidity made many bowstrings inoperable.[61] As a result, the Indians were unable to provide the elephants with effective support. The Indian cavalry was now tightly compressed round the elephants and was suffering progressively heavier casualties. Stationary horses attacked by anything were liable to be thrown into great confusion, and this is exactly what happened to the Indian cavalry. The Indians were now helpless and should have been offered terms, but the Macedonians in their fear at the nightmare battle they had just gone through with the elephants were not inclined to give quarter. Instead, Alexander surrounded the Indian army with his cavalry and had his phalanx lock shields and advance. What followed was a massacre, and the Indian army finally broke from the slaughter.

Despite the failure of his final counterattack with the elephants and his own wounds, Porus continued to fight atop his huge elephant.[62] When Alexander sent Taxiles to ask Porus to surrender, the Indian king turned his elephant around and attempted to run Taxiles through with a lance, considering him to be a traitor for allying himself with Alexander. Finally, an Indian named Meroes persuaded the weakened Porus to dismount and submit to Alexander. It was as if one brave king was acknowledging another after a valiant struggle. When Alexander asked him if he wished anything, Porus replied that he wished to be treated like a king and said that one phrase contained everything in his request. Porus' courage and that statement won Alexander's admiration, and they became good friends. Sometime after the battle Porus was restored to his kingdom, which was subsequently greatly enlarged by Alexander.

Craterus' Holding Force   It is not known exactly when Craterus crossed the river, but it was probably just after the Indian army routed. At that point, the Indian holding force at the Hydaspes would have probably received word of Porus' defeat, and not containing particularly good troops to start with, would probably have quickly dissolved. Craterus, although unable to participate in any part of the battle, was probably able to join in the pursuit of the Indians.

Losses   Casualties for the Indians were extremely heavy, being about 3,000 cavalry, 20,000 infantry, and all the chariots.[63] Only the surviving elephants and 9,000 Indians were alleged to have been taken alive.[64] Two of Porus' sons and many of the officers of his army fell in the battle.[65] Macedonians killed amounted to 80 phalanx infantry, 10 horse-archers, 20 Companions, and 200 other cavalry.[66] The overwhelming victory won by Alexander gave him complete control over Porus' kingdom. After the battle, Alexander rested his army for 30 days.[67]

Generalship   Initially, Alexander had cleverly deceived Porus into relaxing his vigilance to facilitate his march 19 miles upriver to a crossing opposite the island of Admana virtually undetected. Few generals in the ancient world were as bold as to cross a rising river in the aftermath of such a violent storm and with such a small force; Alexander's crossing force only numbered 14,000. Once across, Alexander quickly reorganized his forces behind a screen of horse-archers and marched on Porus. Aristobulus' attack was quickly and easily dispensed with, his chariots bogging down in the mud and his cavalry being overwhelmed by waves of attacking Companions.

Meeting Porus on a battlefield of the Indian's choosing, Alexander was confronted by one of the most difficult tactical situations that he had yet encountered. The presence of the elephants completely negated the use of his Companion cavalry, which had been the arm of decision in all the major field battles he had fought in Asia. Because his horses could not approach the elephants without becoming unmanageable, Alexander's infantry would have to decide this battle. It was necessary, however, to prevent the Indian cavalry from interfering with them after they had engaged the elephants. Consequently, Alexander developed a brilliant plan to defeat them. He lured the Indian cavalry out into the open, disordered the Indian left wing cavalry by missile fire, broke the approaching Indian right wing cavalry with an unexpected flank charge by Coenus, and then defeated the combined force when it again sallied out from the elephants.

Although initially hard-pressed, Alexander's frontline infantry began to slowly gain the upper hand over the elephants. The great broadswords and battle-axes of his peltasts hamstrung the elephants and severed their trunks, while the sarissa was effective in stabbing them, as well as their mahouts. The light infantry, meanwhile, continued a heavy missile fire against both elephant and drivers. Finally, the elephants, many of them wounded and in a state of exhaustion, began to back slowly away from the Macedonians. Alexander, seeing that he could now surround the Indians, ordered his phalanx to lock shields and advance on their front while he swung his cavalry round behind them. The resulting combat was a massacre, the Indians being compressed to such a degree they were denied adequate room to use their weapons effectively.

Of the four great field battles Alexander fought, that on the Hydaspes River was one of the most difficult but also clearly the most decisive. He not only completely smashed the opposing army but captured its commander, who was also that nation's king. With this one battle, Porus' Indian kingdom was totally defeated. It was about as decisive a result as could be achieved, and Alexander was almost flawless in both his strategic and tactical conduct of the battle. Although Alexander had little hand in the actual fight of his infantry against the elephants, he had prepared his soldiers well for their battle.

Strategically, Porus' strategy of holding the line of the Hydaspes River was a sound military decision. The rising river resulting from the beginning of the monsoons would make a crossing dangerous and could be expected to delay a major battle until the expected reinforcements from Kashmir arrived The defensive position Porus chose at Haranpur effectively controlled the only possible crossing of the Hydaspes in the immediate vicinity, and such was its natural strength that Alexander never seriously considered attacking it head-on as long as it was occupied in strength,. While it is true that Alexander did successfully cross the Hydaspes, it was at a distance of fully 19 miles from his base camp. In effect, there was little that Porus could do to oppose a crossing that far away from him. Alexander outnumbered him in cavalry as it was, and Porus could not afford to disperse his own cavalry for 20 miles on either side of the Hydaspes in an attempt to guard against what he perceived to be the unlikely possibility of any large-scale crossing at such remote points.

As to Porus relaxing his vigilance, while it is true that he no longer continually responded to Alexander's noisy forays in the neighborhood because they just deprived his army of sleep, Alexander did not take advantage of this to cross the Hydaspes anywhere in his immediate vicinity. On the night that he marched to the crossing, a violent thunderstorm and torrential rain in addition to the inland march would have largely screened his crossing force from discovery no matter how diligently Porus patrolled his front. Even if Alexander's absence had been discovered,

Porus stood no better chance of attacking Craterus across the Hydaspes than Craterus stood of attacking him and probably much less so because Porus had no way of getting his elephants across the river. As far as crossing the river to determine or interfere with Alexander's march, the reserve force that Alexander left along the river above his camp had been deployed to counter just such a contingency.

Once Alexander crossed the river, Porus acted with appropriate prudence. He made an almost immediate decision to send a fast-moving force to engage Alexander. Unfortunately, although his decision was strategically correct, almost no force he could have sent would have caught Alexander at a disadvantage; this is precisely why Alexander had crossed the river 19 miles away. But if Alexander had had more trouble in getting off Admana onto the mainland, he might have been caught by Aristobulus in the middle of debarkation and been roughly handled. Although the mud would undoubtedly still have crippled Aristobulus' chariot attack, his 2,000 cavalry might have created havoc for Alexander's slowly expanding bridgehead.

When Porus heard of Aristobulus' defeat, he again reacted correctly by immediately taking virtually everything he had to confront Alexander in a decisive field battle. With great economy of force, he left just enough of his castoffs at the base camp to deter Craterus from crossing. Under the circumstance, he selected probably the best battlefield available in which to meet Alexander. At least it was considerably drier than most of the other sites within immediate reach, although it was still wet enough to cause considerable difficulty for the Indian archers in stringing and operating their bows. Over all, it can definitely be said that Porus handled his strategic role with a high order of competence and boldness. Porus took a gamble with Aristobulus' force, but when his son suffered a defeat Porus quickly recast his plans and almost immediately moved out against Alexander. In contrast to Darius, who was caught by Alexander with his troops still out of position at Issus, Porus was fully deployed to meet him.

Tactically, Alexander clearly overshadows Porus. He drew out Porus' cavalry in a clever gambit and not only negated its ability to interfere in the infantry-elephant battle, but used the Indian cavalry's confusion to disorder Porus' elephant line. The chariots on Porus' left flank were shot to pieces by missile fire before they ever got a chance to accomplish anything. Even if the chariots had been able to initiate a charge, however, it is likely that the heavy missile fire the Macedonians would have been able to bring against them would have decimated the lumbering vehicles well before they ever reached the phalanx.[68] Then too, the wet condition of the ground would have probably bogged the vehicles down, as had happened with Aristobulus. In their use, Porus made the same mistake as Darius and significantly overestimated the effectiveness of the chariots against disciplined troops supported by heavy missile fire.

Although the elephants had decimated the Macedonians at the beginning of the battle, towards the end of it they had clearly been totally defeated. What, if anything, Porus could have done against the axes, broadswords, and sarissas that were used by the Macedonians so effectively against the elephants is difficult to say. Porus' infantry soldiers were essentially light infantry archers, and had he tried to use them to provide direct support to the elephants, the Agrianians and hypaspists would have easily overpowered them in a stand-up fight. Perhaps the elephants could have been covered in chain-mail, if they could have withstood the weight, but chain-mail would have had to be prepared well before the battle and would doubtless have slowed the already slow movement of the animals down to a crawl.

It is curious, however, that the vulnerability of the elephants had not been exposed in any of the battles the Indians had previously fought with them. It is entirely possible that because the Indians seemed to subscribe to some strict time-honored rules of chivalry whenever they fought, they considered it unthinkable to fight elephants in the barbarous manner that the Macedonians did. In any case, the effectiveness of the elephants tended to be highest during their initial impact and then dropped off relatively quickly.

When the battle was clearly going against the Indians, Porus himself led a last desperate elephant charge in the heroic style of Alexander. It was unsuccessful, of course, because both the elephants and the battle were too far gone by then. But this charge and Porus' valiant fight to the end marked him to be an unrelenting and courageous warrior who would not acknowledge defeat as long as a single unit of his army fought on; it is no wonder that Alexander admired him so. Overall, however, mistakes notwithstanding, Porus clearly gave Alexander the hardest fight of his career, and one can bet that when Alexander's veterans sat around the campfires with the new recruits, they were always asked to recount the horrors of the battle alongside the Hydaspes River. In fact, the Macedonians were so affected by their battle with the elephants there, that Alexander could never persuade them to even consider repeating the experience.

Glausae

After his victory at the battle of Hydaspes River, Alexander left Craterus behind at the river with a portion of the army with orders to build and fortify the two new cities he had founded near the battle site, which he named Nicaea and Bucephala.[69] He then took half the Companion cavalry, a detachment of the phalanx, the mounted archers, Agrianians, and foot-archers and invaded the territory of the Glausae, which bordered Porus' kingdom on the east.[70] During the spring campaign, over 37 cities surrendered without resistance, the smallest being over 5,000 in population and the largest well over 10,000.[71] The area was then given to Porus to rule. At this time, Taxiles was allowed to return to his own kingdom.

Assacenians

Alexander was informed that Sisicottus, satrap of the Assacenians, had been murdered by his subjects. In response, he sent Philip and Turiaspes with a force to subdue them.[72] Alexander then moved on to the Acesines River with the remainder of the army.

Bad Porus

Alexander crossed the Acesines River with considerable difficulty because it contained numerous sharp rocks, a swift current, and was apparently almost two miles wide.[73] Although the crossing of the river was safely done on the hide floats, several of the boats were wrecked on the rocks. Alexander left Coenus with his taxies of the phalanx at the Acesines to supervise the completion of the army's crossing while Porus was sent back to his own kingdom to recruit additional soldiers and elephants. Alexander then took the light troops in pursuit of another ruler named Porus, whom the ancients called the "bad Porus." Although the Indian had no particular animosity towards Alexander, he clearly hated Porus, king of Gujrat. Upon hearing that his enemy's territory had been enlarged and that Alexander was now marching on him, the "bad Porus" fled to Gandhara with a large number of his followers.

Alexander pursued the "bad Porus" to the Hydraotes (Ravi) River. Although that river was as wide as the Acesines, its mild current made for an uneventful crossing.[74] Hephaestion was given command of two taxies of the phalanx, his own and Demetrius' hipparchies of the Companion cavalry, and half the archers and ordered to subdue the territory of the "bad Porus."[75] When this was done, he was to hand over control of the area to Porus, the king of Gujrat.[76] Meanwhile, Alexander crossed the Hydraotes River without difficulty and accepted the voluntary surrender of most of the tribes along his line of march. Those who resisted him were quickly conquered.

Cathaeans

It was reported to Alexander that the Cathaeans were preparing to oppose him. The tribe was already under arms because of its recent battles against Porus and Abisares, and its soldiers were said to be both numerous and fierce. Alexander moved quickly against them. Two days after leaving the Hydraotes River he came to Sangala. Upon Alexander's arrival there, the Cathaeans concentrated their forces on a hill in front of the city, which was their capital, surrounding themselves with a triple line of carts. Their plan was to have Alexander disorder his infantry by attacking through the carts, whereupon they would defeat his confused forces in hand-to-hand combat. To cover his deployment, Alexander ordered his mounted archers to pin the Cathaeans in place with long-range missile fire.[77] On his right wing, Alexander deployed Cleitus' mounted regiment, the special cavalry squadron, the hypaspists, and the Agrianians.[78] His left consisted of Perdiccas' Companion hipparchy and the remainder of the Companions.[79] The archers were stationed on both wings.[80] As Alexander was completing his deployment, his rear guard arrived. He used the additional cavalry to strengthen his wings and additional infantry to augment the phalanx.

Observing that the carts on the Cathaean left flank were set farther apart than elsewhere and that the ground there was more level, Alexander led a cavalry attack against them. Unable to draw the Cathaeans out from their cart line, Alexander dismounted and joined the phalanx in an assault on them. Although the Cathaeans were driven from the first line of carts after a hard fight, they were able to rally at the second line. Because this line was shorter than the first, the Cathaeans were able to deploy in close-order. This placed the attacking Macedonians at a serious tactical disadvantage, their formation being disordered by the limited number of gaps between the carts that they were forced to pass through. Nevertheless, they were able to fight their way through the second line of carts. The Cathaeans now became demoralized and when the Macedonians advanced again, they made no attempt to defend the third line of carts but immediately withdrew into Sangala. Alexander tried to surround the city but lacked the troops to cover both its lengthy walls and the nearby shoreline along the adjacent shallow lake. He did, however, deploy patrols round the lake because he suspected that the Cathaeans had been sufficiently demoralized to attempt a nighttime retreat through it. As Alexander had predicted, at nightfall the Cathaeans began to slip out across the lake. When they were attacked by Alexander's cavalry patrols, however, they concluded that the shoreline of the lake was strongly held and quickly withdrew back into their city.

Alexander now surrounded Sangala by a double stockade, except along the lake, and brought up his siege engines. Some deserters from the city indicated that the Cathaeans would again attempt to escape across the lake that night. Ptolemy (son of Lagus) was ordered to deploy the hypaspists, the Agrianians, and one battalion of the archers around the lake.[81]

Gathering up the carts abandoned outside the city, Ptolemy scattered them over the Cathaeans' expected route. Late that night the Cathaeans opened the gates and made their way to the lake. Stumbling over the carts in the darkness, they were thrown into confusion. Emerging from the carts, the Cathaeans were then attacked by Ptolemy's waiting force and driven back into Sangala with the loss of 500 casualties.[82]

Porus now arrived with the rest of his elephants and 5,000 Indian reinforcements.[83] Alexander then began mining operations that collapsed a section of the wall. Attacking through the subsequent breach, the Macedonians were able to carry the city by storm.

The Cathaeans' sick and wounded were slaughtered without mercy. Shortly afterwards, Sangala was razed, rebuilt, and settled by natives in the vicinity who had submitted to Alexander. Porus was allowed to install his own garrison in the new city's citadel. Over 17,000 Cathaeans were killed during the siege and 70,000 taken prisoner.[84] The Macedonians are reported to have had 100 killed and over 1,200 wounded.[85]

Alexander sent Eumenes with 300 cavalry to two nearby rebel cities to announce the fall of Sangala and order the citizens there to await his arrival.[86] Upon hearing of the massacre at Sangala, however, the cities' inhabitants fled in terror. Although Alexander went in immediate pursuit, the head start of those who had fled enabled most to escape. The 500 who were caught, however, were put to death.[87] Porus was then sent back with his troops to garrison the cities that had recently been captured.

Sopithes

Alexander embarked the hypaspists, archers, Agrianians, and a squadron of cavalry on board the ships of Nearchus' fleet.[88] Craterus was to march a force of the cavalry and infantry along the west bank of the Indus River, while the remaining army and 200 elephants under Hephaestion would march along the east bank.[89] Philip's force was to start out three days later. All forces were to converge on Sopithes' capital. On the approach of Alexander's army, the capital at first seemed deserted because no one could be seen along the walls. Soon, however, a gaudily overdressed Sopithes came out and surrendered both himself and his kingdom to Alexander. He was subsequently restored to his office.

Phegeus

The kingdom of Phegeus was next to be invaded. Upon Alexander's approach, however, the king immediately submitted. When questioned about the lands to the east, the king told Alexander about a 200-mile-wide desert taking 12 days to cross.[90] This desert was bordered by the Ganges River, which was four miles wide and the deepest river in all India.[91] Lying beyond the Ganges was Ding Xandrames' kingdom; his field army was reputed to consist of 20,000 cavalry, 200,000 infantry, 2,000 chariots, and 3,000 elephants.[92] Doubting the accuracy of what Phegeus was telling him, Alexander turned to Porus for comment. He promptly confirmed everything said, disdainfully adding that Xandrames was of low parentage, being only a barber's son.

Beas River

Alexander marched east in July, shortly before the end of the monsoon. The Indian monsoons were a series of summer storms of torrential intensity, usually lasting several weeks. They were accompanied by high humidity, continuous rains, and heavy flooding. During the downpour, metal would rust within five to six hours of being polished, and a light green mold would quickly rot canvas, leather, and fabrics in a few weeks. The army suffered extensively from foot-rot and prickly heat. The ground was continually steamy, the air hot, humid, and filled with mosquitoes. When the rains began, the rivers overflowed and in a matter of days covered the land with water to a depth three times that of a standing man. Snakes were driven to high ground by the rain, and their sheer numbers and ferocity often forced the local villagers to abandon their houses, even though they were on 24-foot-tall pylons. Cobras hid in tents, clothing, cooking pots, under brush and rocks and people who were bitten died quickly and in great agony unless the services of an Indian snake charmer were immediately obtained. The only protection from the snakes at night were hammocks suspended between the trees.

Heavy rain fell continually for the next 70 days. Rumors of the terrors of what lay ahead wildly circulated among the men. It was believed that numerous tribes of increasingly fierce warriors numbering in the hundreds of thousands would soon be encountered. Elephant armies thousands strong would bar their way, the men feared. When the Beas River was reached, most of Alexander's army knew that it had marked the eastern border of the Persian Empire under Darius I. The mental and physical endurance of Alexander's army now collapsed and they mutinied, refusing to march any farther east. For additional details on the mutiny at the Beas River, see Appendix A.

Although Alexander tried bribery, inspiration, intimidation, and shame, he was unable to persuade the rank and file of the army to change their minds. He had no better luck with their officers, whose spokesman Craterus lectured him on knowing his limits. In a face-saving attempt, Alexander called for a sacrifice before crossing the Beas. It, of course, proved to be unfavorable to the enterprise, making it appear that Alexander was only acting in obedience to the will of the gods in discontinuing his march to the east. His men, of course, reacted with hysterical joy. Alexander then had constructed twelve 75-foot-high altars on the Beas River and laid out a camp and barracks at double the usual size, surrounding it with a ditch 50 feet wide and 40 feet deep, the dirt from which was used to construct an equally impressive wall.[93] He intended to leave behind the impression that a race of giants had passed by. Alexander then retraced his route back to the Hydaspes River to assist Craterus in completing the construction of the fortified cities of Nicaea and Bucephala.

Lower Punjab

Alexander received reports that the Malli and the Oxydracae were intending to join forces against him. They had recently been fighting against each other and were reported to have a combined army in the field of 700 chariots, 10,000 cavalry, and 80,000 infantry.[94] Upon hearing of Alexander's approach, they quickly made peace with each other. Being unable to agree, however, on who should command their combined army, they all dispersed back to their home cities. When Alexander's veterans realized that instead of the uneventful voyage they had anticipated, another exhausting campaign lay ahead that would require them to battle great numbers of fierce Indian warriors and elephants, they again threatened to mutiny. After telling them every lie he could think of to calm their fears — the ocean was so close that you could smell the sea breeze, the Malli fought like women — Alexander managed to persuade them to continue on. The army's morale, however, remained at rock bottom and if faced by a hard battle they were as likely to mutiny as to go berserk and fight like madmen. Alexander's army had now been pushed to the limit of its endurance and had become extremely brittle. It was barely on the edge of command control.

Five days after leaving the Haranpur crossing Alexander arrived at the junction of the Hydaspes and Acesines rivers. At this point, both rivers were very narrow, and the resulting swift current formed numerous and violent whirlpools. The ships attempted to cross the rapids by hard rowing but were smashed against each

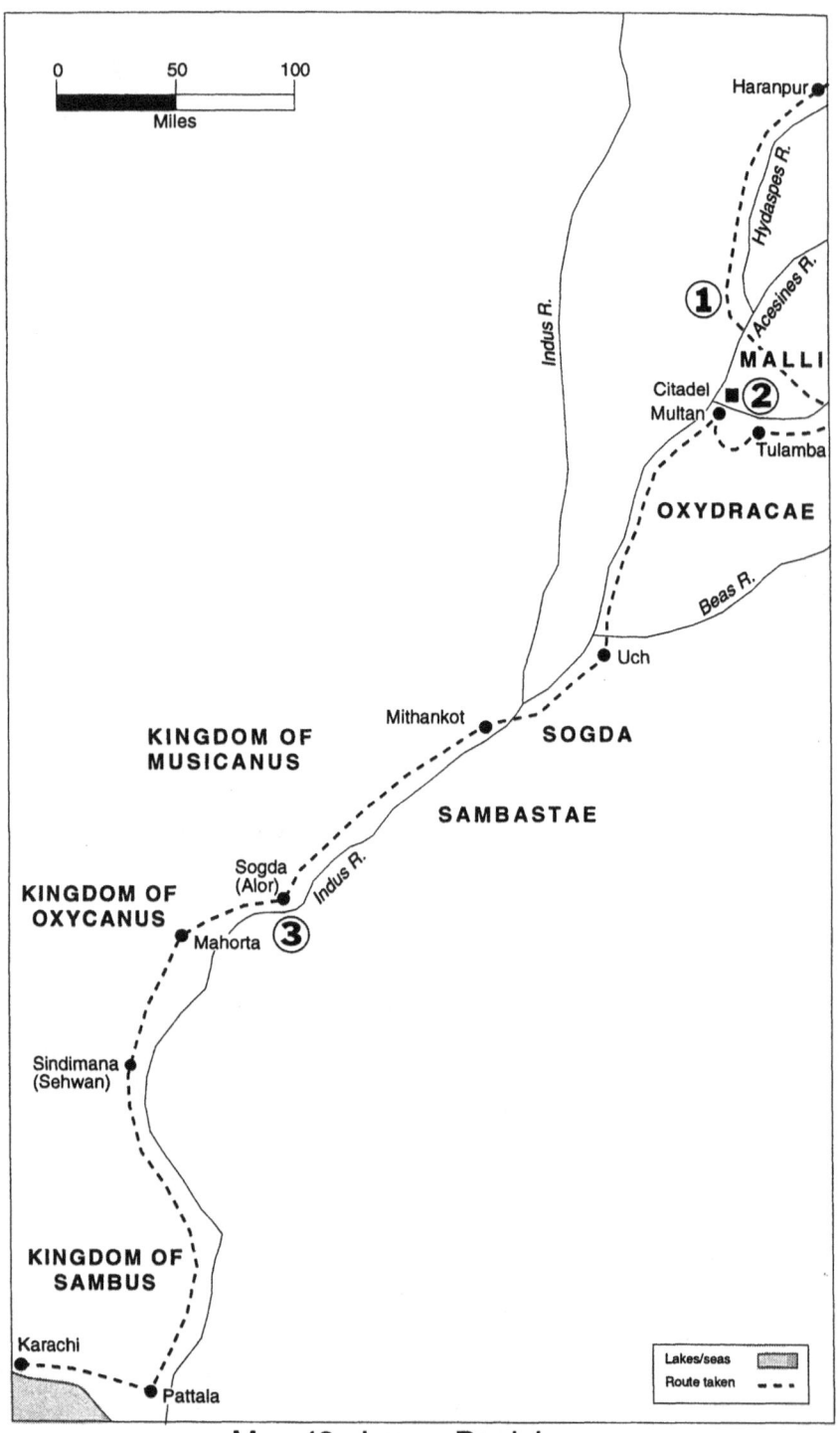

Map 48: Lower Punjab

other, with heavy loss in crews. Although the merchant ships and other wide boats whirled round uncontrollably, much to the terror of their crews, they made it through the rapids with little damage. When the river widened, Alexander ordered the fleet to put in on the right bank, which provided some shelter from the current. There the damaged ships were repaired. Nearchus then proceeded down river to the boundary of Malli territory. Here Craterus, Hephaestion, and Philip and rejoined Alexander with their troops.

Mali/Oxydracae

Alexander's plan was to defeat the Malli before they could be reinforced by the Oxydracae from the south. Nearchus was given command over the 2,000 ships of the navy, with orders to sail three days in advance of the army.[95] He was to establish a base camp at the junction of the Acesines and Hydraotes rivers, where all the forces would converge to await Alexander's arrival at the conclusion of his campaign.[96] The army was divided into four forces under the command of Craterus, Hephaestion, Ptolemy, and Alexander himself. Craterus was given command of the Indian troops of Philip (son of Machatas), Polysperchon's taxies of the phalanx, the mounted archers, and the elephants, with orders to lead his force down the west bank of the Acesines.[97] Hephaestion was to set out five days after Craterus' departure, but down the east bank of the river.[98] Ptolemy was to start out three days after Hephaestion.[99] Alexander would accompany Craterus' force. The strategic plan was that Craterus would defeat any forces he encountered, while Hephaestion and Ptolemy would engage any Indians evading or fleeing Craterus.

When all the forces had arrived at the junction of the Acesines and Hydraotes rivers, Alexander took a fast-moving mobile force consisting of half his Companion cavalry, Peitho's infantry Companions, the mounted archers, hypaspists, a mounted taxies of the phalanx, and the Agrianians and made an unexpected attack deep into the center of Malli territory from the north.[100] He hoped that this attack would drive the Malli away from the Oxydracae and back on Hephaestion and Ptolemy, but he was to be disappointed because despite his rapid approach, the two Indian tribes were able to unite.

On the first day Alexander marched about 13 miles, making camp at a small pond where his army resupplied itself with water.[101] The next day and night his soldiers marched 50 miles though the desert, and the hardships they endured nearly broke their morale.[102] At dawn on the third day, Alexander's cavalry surrounded the first Malli city. His attack out of the northern desert came as a complete surprise to the inhabitants there, and they were caught unawares, being largely unarmed and walking about outside the city. Although a large number of them were slaughtered, the survivors managed to reach the safety of the nearby city.

Alexander surrounded the city with his cavalry to prevent any warning getting out to nearby cities. When his infantry came up, he gave Perdiccas command

---

1. Coenus dies. 2. Alexander is seriously wounded by an arrow. 3. A key strategic city controlling the high road through the Bolan Pass, which led into the Iranian plateau.

of his and Cleitus' cavalry and the Agrianians, and he ordered Perdiccas to surround the next closest city while he himself conducted an assault on the one before him.[103] This same tactic was used on city after city along Alexander's line of march, each first being isolated by the cavalry and then being taken by storm when the infantry came up. Many of the Indian defenders in the city that Alexander was besieging were killed, only 2,000 survivors taking refuge in the citadel.[104] Although most of the Indians there were incapacitated by wounds, they were still able to mount a defense of their walls. In the final assault, however, all the Indians in the citadel were killed. Meanwhile, when Perdiccas arrived at the second city, he found it deserted and burning. He immediately pursued the fleeing inhabitants with his cavalry, ordering the light infantry to catch up as best they could. All those who were unable to escape into the marshes were killed.

Alexander force-marched throughout the entire night. He reached the Hydraotes River at daybreak, just as the Malli rear guard was crossing. After riding them down, he crossed the river with his cavalry and continued the pursuit, killing a great number of the scattered Malli along the way. The retreating Malli then attempted to make a stand at a strongly fortified position, but Alexander overran it with his infantry, Peitho's force, and two hipparchies of the Companions.[105] All the Malli captured there were enslaved.

Being informed that a number of the Malli had taken refuge in the city of the Brahmins, Alexander now marched there. He surrounded the city walls with the phalanx and began mining operations. The defending Indians, driven from the walls by heavy missile fire, withdrew into the citadel. A small force of Macedonians entered the citadel in the confusion of the Indian retreat but were quickly driven out, sustaining 25 casualties.[106] Alexander then undermined a tower of the citadel and led an assault through the breach. The Macedonians apparently lagged back, for Alexander was the only one to mount the wall. Feeling ashamed to see their king there alone, the Macedonians grudgingly came up alongside him in small groups. When the Indians saw that the Macedonians held the citadel, they set fire to their houses and resumed the battle. Over 5,000 Indians were said to have fallen in the fighting, with only a few being taken alive.[107]

Alexander rested his army for one day before resuming the pursuit.[108] Finding the cities now deserted because the inhabitants had fled into the desert, Alexander paused for an additional day. The next day he sent the Companion hipparchies under Demetrius and Peitho back to the Hydraotes River.[109] They were ordered to kill any Malli hiding in the woods along the river bank who refused to surrender. Large numbers of fugitives were found and killed. Alexander continued the pursuit with his cavalry, which rode on well ahead of the infantry. The Malli now took up a defensive position on the banks of the far side of the Hydraotes River. When Alexander reached midstream with his cavalry, the Malli withdrew from their position in good order. However, when the Malli saw that his cavalry had no infantry support, they massed their 50,000-strong force in close-order and advanced to the attack.[110] Alexander was able to hold them off by skillfully maneuvering his cavalry just outside the reach of their infantry. The Agrianians and archers then came up in support and partially stabilized his position. When the Malli saw Alexander's phalanx forming up in the distance, they broke and fled to a citadel across the river from Multan. Alexander closely pursued them and inflicted heavy casualties on them. He then surrounded the citadel with his cavalry to prevent any Malli from escaping and waited for the arrival of his infantry. When they finally came up, it was evident that their long forced-march and crossing of the Hydraotes River had exhausted them. As it was late in the day, Alexander decided to postpone his attack on the citadel until the following morning.

The citadel occupied a commanding position along the Hydraotes River. It was surrounded by two walls, an outer one along the river bank and an inner one.[111] Alexander divided his forces in front of the position between Perdiccas and himself.[112] The Malli now drew back from the outer wall, intending to hold only the citadel. Alexander's force tore down a small gate and passed through the outer wall, well in advance of Perdiccas' men, who had experienced considerable difficulty in scaling the walls. Assuming that the walls had already been carried and the gates opened, they had not bothered to bring any ladders with them and had to attempt several time-consuming improvisations to scale the wall.

Observing that his soldiers carrying the ladders were hanging back in fear, Alexander grabbed one away, carried it to the wall of the citadel, and climbed up it. He then fought and killed several Indians defending that portion of the wall. Rather than engage him in hand-to-hand combat, the Indians began firing arrows at him from the adjacent towers. The hypaspists frantically motioned Alexander to jump back down towards them. In their excitement over his safety, the hypaspists overloaded the few scaling ladders they had with them and the excess weight broke them to pieces. As Alexander stood there alone, he must have seen the scene as a page out of the *Iliad*: a Homeric hero standing between a choice of fame and glory on one hand and caution and safety on the other. He did not hesitate for a moment and, much to the consternation of his troops, leaped down alone inside the city.

Once on the ground Alexander put his back to the wall and took position beside a large tree that served to protect his unshielded right side. A group of Malli advanced on him, but Alexander quickly killed them. Other Malli now arrived but refused to engage him in hand-to-hand combat. Instead, they formed a semicircle around Alexander and threw or fired whatever missile weapons they had at hand. Alexander was quickly joined by Peucestas, his shield-bearer; Abreas, a highly decorated Guard's officer; and Leonnatus, an officer of his bodyguard. They were the only Macedonians able to cross the wall before the ladders had broken. Abreas was soon shot in the face and killed. Then a long arrow struck Alexander in the breast, apparently penetrating his lung.[113] Although bleeding profusely and dropping to one knee, Alexander still was able to run his sword through a Malian who rushed at him. Suffering a violent hemorrhage, he then lost consciousness. Peucestas and Leonnatus covered Alexander with their shields in an attempt to deflect the almost continuous missile fire the Indians directed at him. In the course of the volleys of javelins, Perdiccas was wounded three times by javelins and Leonnatus sustained a neck wound, at one point falling unconscious at Alexander's feet.[114]

When the Macedonian soldiers saw Alexander leap inside the city their reluctance turned to extreme anxiety. As the few ladders they had been able to find were too fragile to use, some men drove stakes into the clay wall and dragged themselves up, others climbed on shoulders to boost them up over it. When they reached the top of the wall, some of the soldiers jumped down to protect Alexander, while others went to open the gate. By this time, however, the engineers had been able to smash open a postern gate and were already pouring through. The Macedonians then rushed in and, overcome by their own anxiety over Alexander's condition, began massacring the Malli, sparing neither man, woman, or child, no matter how young or old. Alexander, meanwhile, was carried off on his shield to his tent outside the citadel. When word spread through the army that he was dying, his troops were dumfounded. They saw no one else capable of leading them but Alexander and believed that if he died they would be doomed to death.

Alexander soon recovered sufficiently to inform his troops in writing that he was not dead and would be rejoining them soon. The army, however, suspected that the letter had been forged by the king's senior officers in an attempt to conceal his death from them. When this was reported to Alexander, he knew that only his personal appearance before his men could restore their morale and prevent them from dissolving into anarchy. Although his wound was still not healed, and in fact never would be, he had himself carried by litter to the river. There he was put on a high platform constructed over two ships that had been bound together. He then sailed down the river to the army's base camp. When his troops saw him, they became hysterical and shouted themselves hoarse. Upon docking at the base camp, Alexander waved his litter away, mounted his horse, and slowly rode to camp. He was showered with flowers and repeatedly touched to confirm that he was actually alive. His heroic bravado had accomplished its purpose.

With the fall of their citadel, the Malli concluded that it would be hopeless to continue fighting Alexander and unconditionally surrendered. A 150-man delegation also came from the cities of the Oxydracae to discuss terms.[115] They asked Alexander for his pardon, agreed to accept any governor he cared to appoint over them, and to pay whatever tribute was levied against them. Alexander ordered that 1,000 of the most distinguished men of the tribes were to be enrolled in his army for the duration of his war against the Indians.[116] They would also serve as hostages for the tribe's continued good behavior. A force of 500 chariots was also said to be provided, although this was not requested.[117] Philip was appointed as satrap over the Malli and given a 10,000-strong garrison that included all the remaining Thracians. Alexander then dismissed the 1,000 Malli hostages but, interestingly enough, kept the chariots. A naval port was built at the citadel in the hope that nearby Multan would become a prosperous trading center.

Abastani

After he had recovered sufficiently to travel, Alexander embarked 1,700 Companions and 10,000 infantry aboard the fleet and sailed down the Acesines River to the Indus River.[118] There he awaited Perdiccas' arrival from his campaign against the Abastani.[119] The reunited force then sailed down the Indus to Sogda (Alor), where Alexander built a new city, complete with fortifications and dockyards.

Musicanus

It was now reported that the Indian prince Musicanus was preparing to oppose Alexander. Immediately embarking an assault force aboard ship, Alexander moved with such speed that the stunned Musicanus quickly surrendered to him. After acknowledging his error in attempting to resist Alexander, Musicanus was pardoned and restored to his throne. Craterus was ordered to fortify and garrison Musicanus' capital city.[120]

Oxycanus of Porticanus

At this point, Alexander was faced by a revolt led by the Brahman priests in the area south of Sogda ruled by Oxycanus of Porticanus. The followers of the Brahmans proved to be excellent soldiers, being both numerous and fanatical. The Brahmans, however, not only experienced great difficulty in coordinating their efforts with Oxycanus but were unable even to effectively combine their own huge forces.

Alexander took advantage of this confusion by quickly moving against Oxycanus with a river assault force consisting of the archers, Agrianians, and cavalry.[121] He successfully stormed two of Oxycanus' largest cities, capturing Oxycanus himself in the second one. Oxycanus was executed, and all the Brahman prisoners were sold into slavery. With Oxycanus' death the remaining cities in his kingdom quickly submitted to Alexander.

Sambus

With the defeat of the Brahmans, Alexander moved against Sambus, who had appointed himself the satrap of the Indian hill men. He reputedly commanded an army numbering 500 chariots, 6,000 cavalry, and 60,000 infantry.[122] The capital city of Sindimana (Sehwan) surrendered upon Alexander's appearance. The other cities held by the fanatical Brahmans had to be assaulted one after the other. The defenders of the last city were tricked into making a sortie against 500 Agrianians who simulated a retreat.[123] Their resulting losses were so heavy, with 600 being killed and 1,000 captured, that the remaining 1,400 Brahmans holding the city surrendered.[124] With the fall of Sindimana, Sambus fled to the east with 30 elephants. He apparently had not held any particular animosity against Alexander but was an enemy of Musicanus and had become apprehensive when Alexander had so quickly pardoned him. Throughout the campaign the Brahmans sustained very heavy losses, probably not as high as the 80,000 indicated by Curtius and Diodorus but clearly as heavy as those of the Malli.[125] Many of Alexander's wounded died as a result of poisoned arrows; even the slightest scratch usually proved to be fatal.

Musicanus Revolts

When Alexander left Musicanus' territory to campaign against the Sambus, Musicanus decided to revolt. Peithon (son of Agenor) was sent against the interior of Musicanus' territory, while Alexander reduced the outer cities. Those cities which resisted had their populations massacred, with any survivors being sold into slavery. The city was then usually looted and razed. If the city surrendered, however, the population was spared and the citadel was occupied by a Greek garrison. Musicanus was captured by Peithon and hanged by order of Alexander, along with many of the Brahmans who had instigated the revolt. This effectively brought an end to the insurrection. The way was now open for Alexander to advance to the Arabian Sea.

Alexander ordered Craterus to take the taxies of the phalanx under Antigonus, Attalus, and Meleager; some of the archers; most of the Companions; all of the Macedonians recently mustered out; and the elephants and march through Arachosia and Drangiana to subdue the tribes reported to be in revolt there.[126] Upon the completion of their mission, they were to meet Alexander in Carmania. He would accompany the remainder of the army, nominally under Hephaestion, on a campaign through Gedrosa.

Soeris

Soeris, the king of Pattala, came to Alexander and surrendered to him his territory, which extended from Pattala along the Indus River to the delta. Alexander sent him back to Pattala to make arrangements to receive the Macedonian army. When Soeris returned there, however, he took the greater part of the area's population with him and fled. Alexander pursued them with his light troops and persuaded those he was able to capture to return, telling them their imagined fears about him were groundless. After a time, most of the population of Pattala that had fled returned to their homes. Alexander ordered Hephaestion to fortify the city's citadel and build a harbor and dockyard on the site because the Indus River divided into two branches there. An enormous supply depot was established at the city to meet the requirements for the projected campaign of Alexander's army in support of his navy's exploration of the Gedrosian coast. A four-month supply of provisions was gathered there.[127]

Generalship

Although Alexander was successful in executing his strategic plan for conquering the Punjab, he did so only after exhausting fighting and bloodthirsty savagery. His entire campaign was characterized by sheer brutality in an attempt to instill fear in the local population. Apparently believing that the Indians would never consent to be ruled by him, he became determined to wipe out all resistance by the mailed fist. Many of the Indians were not even given the opportunity to submit to terms. This generated a bitter and lasting resentment of Alexander, and although he had conquered the area, he had by no means subdued it.

In the process of his campaigning, Alexander had finally pushed the army past its limits; it was barely obedient to his commands. Alexander's obsession with endless warfare had blinded him to the brittleness of his increasingly unstable army. His men were no longer youths to be motivated by glory, conquest, and riches. His original veterans were now middle-aged or past and exhausted. They now only wanted to enjoy whatever wealth they had been able to accumulate in Greece among their family and countrymen.

When Alexander was forced to concede to the demands of his soldiers at the Beas River, they had assumed that he concurred in their understanding that there was to be no more fighting. This was not to be the case, however, because Alexander had determined to secure the southeastern boundary of his empire. He marched into the Punjab and his army found themselves engaged in yet another exhausting campaign, against a number of fierce Indian armies. The men's morale dropped to zero, and their temperaments became extremely unstable. Admittedly, Alexander had conducted a successful campaign of extermination against the Indians of the Punjab but at the price of all but destroying the morale of one of the great armies of history.

10. The Southern Persian Empire

Gedrosa

Upon reaching Pattala on the Indus River, some 70 miles from the Arabian Sea, Alexander established a harbor, a dockyard, and an enormous depot in support of his campaign through Gedrosa. He was said to have made the decision to march through the Makran Desert there in order to conquer the forces of nature that had allegedly destroyed the armies of the Babylonian queen Semiramis, the mystical founder of the Persian Empire, and Cyrus the Great. Only 20 of Semiramis' army were said to have survived the ordeal and only seven of Cyrus'.[1] Although the desire to outdo these two great Persian conquerors was probably a factor in Alexander's decision to conduct the campaign, it was far more likely made on the basis of the need to secure the southern border of his empire by suppressing the tribes there that had refused to submit to him — the Arabitae, Gedrosians, and Oreitans. Perhaps even more importantly, Alexander wished to explore the feasibility of establishing a sea-borne route linking India to both the Euphrates delta and Egypt. He thought that the Gedrosian coast could be as prosperous a trading center as Phoenicia and was most eager to explore it for possible colonization. The seaborne link would also provide a more secure line of communications to India that would not be affected by any of the frequent disruptions of a long overland route.

Alexander planned to march along the coast of the Arabian Sea with the main body of the army. Between the rivers, the army would periodically dig wells to supply the fleet with drinking water and gather any food along the way. The fleet would carry a limited amount of food and water on board as a floating reserve for use by both the army and the navy during times of shortage. The army's ability to transport food was extremely limited; it was able to carry only a few days' supply on its pack animals. As long as the army and fleet stayed together, they could mutually support each other, but if they separated, as actually happened when Alexander was forced to march inland, one or both would suffer. In this case both suffered, although the army had by far the worst of the ordeal.

The Makran was not composed of solid ground but of constantly moving sand.[2] This sand was exhausting to walk through and would burn bare feet in sunlight. Daytime temperatures rose as high as 127°F, while at night the temperature did not generally drop below 95°F.[3] All reports Alexander received indicated that the Gedrosian coast was a virtual wilderness for several hundred miles.

Alexander set off on his march through the Makran from Pattala in mid-July, 325 B.C. It was timed to coincide with the beginning of the monsoon rains and crop growth cycle to maximize the availability of supplies of both food and water for his expedition. The beginning of the march was along the coast and through relatively fertile territory. It was not possible to obtain much in the way of food supplies from the natives because little was grown locally, but the army was adequately supplied from its depot at Pattala and was able to dig wells along the shore. Water was found, but only with difficulty. Thoas (son of Mandrodorus) was sent out in advance to reconnoiter the coast.[4] He returned to report that the route ahead to the west was largely barren and was blocked by the Taloi mountain range, which came right down to the sea. This prohibited the planned march along the coast. Alexander was now forced to cross the Harridan Pass and march inland. Up until this point, supplies had been barely adequate to sustain the needs of the army.

For his march through Gedrosa, Alexander took with him the hypaspists, Agrianians, some of the archers, three taxies of the phalanx, the Companion cavalry, and the horse-archers.[5] The fighting component of his army totaled 30,000 combat troops, of which 13,000 were Macedonians.[6] As many as 18,000 camp followers also accompanied the army, including servants, traders, women, and children. Craterus, with Polysperchon as his second-in-command, had taken the remaining three taxies of the phalanx commanded by Antigonus, Attalus, and Meleager; two-thirds of the hypaspists; the remaining archers; the elephants; and all Macedonian veterans whose length of service had expired, perhaps 9,000 in all, on a campaign to suppress rebellions in Areia and Drangiana.[7] Crossing over the Mulla (Bolan) Pass, they marched down into the Helmund Valley. After successfully completing his mission to subdue the area, Craterus rejoined Alexander in Carmania.

Arabitae

Alexander marched to the Arabis River and entered the territory of the Arabitae. Although they had failed to submit to him, he had not thought them worth attacking. At Alexander's approach, the Arabitae fled into the desert. Alexander ordered wells to be dug along the coast for the fleet and then divided his army between himself and Hephaestion. Further dividing his cavalry into three forces, Alexander crossed the narrow Arabis River and adjacent desert at night and systematically devastated the plains of Las Bela and Welpar, killing any Oreitans he encountered there.[8]

Upon reaching Sonmiani, Alexander had a difficult choice to make. He could not go back the way he had come because he had thoroughly devastated the area behind him. If he took the inland route through south Drangiana, as Leonnatus was later to do, his army would be sufficiently supplied with both food and water, but the navy would have to provide for itself. Considering the barrenness of the

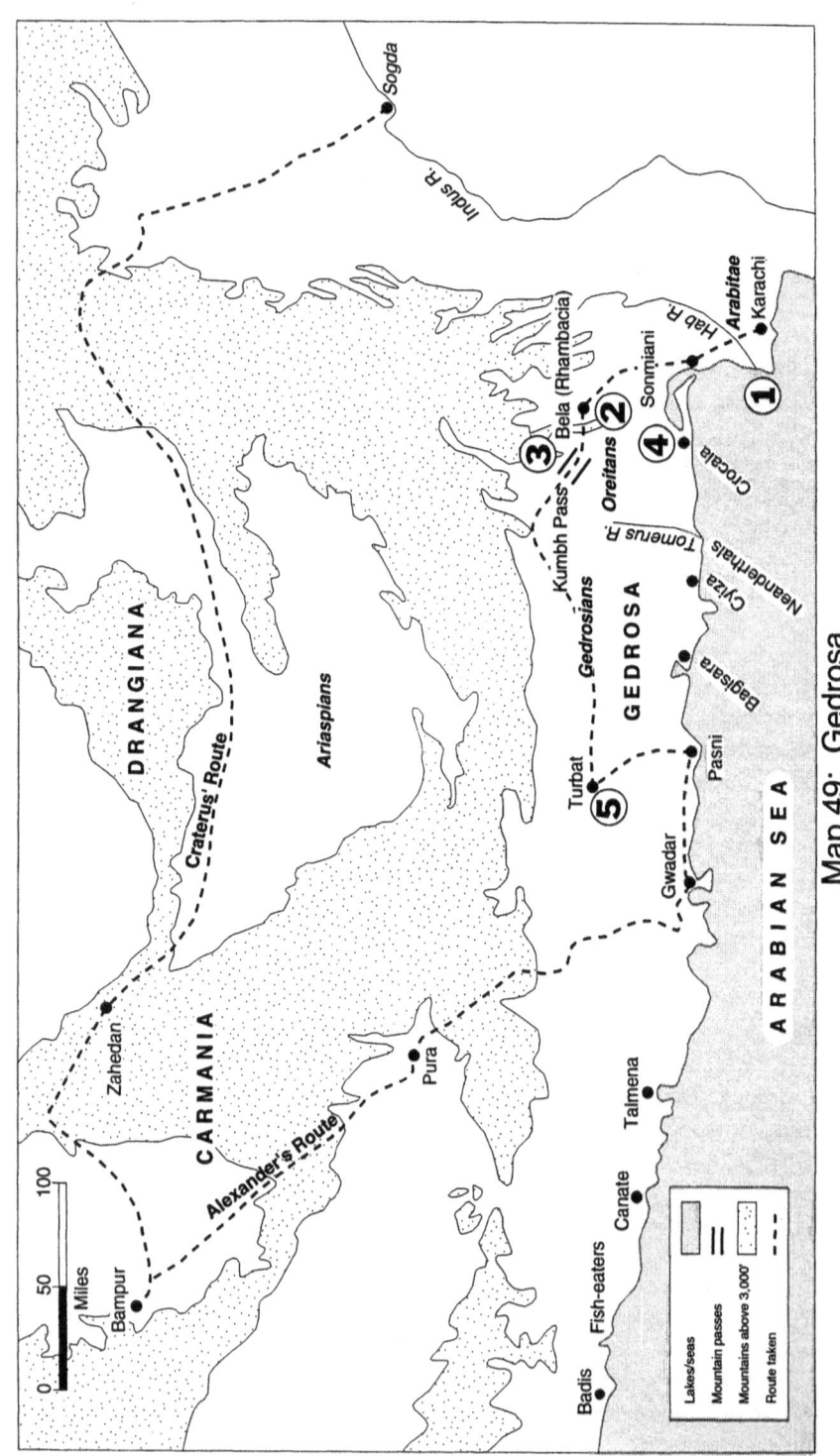

Map 49: Gedrosa

coastline that Thoas had reported, Alexander no doubt thought that this route would be virtually condemning the fleet to starvation. To go through the Makran desert, however, would definitely endanger his army because food and water were sure to be in short supply. But there, at least, he would have the possibility of communicating with the navy. Alexander's exaggerated fears for the safety of his navy persuaded him to select the desert route for his army.

Oreitans

Hephaestion rejoined Alexander with the remainder of the army, and together they marched on to Bela (Rhambacia), the largest village of the Oreitans. Recognizing the strategic importance of the site, which was located in the center of the most productive agricultural land in the area, Alexander left Hephaestion behind with orders to establish a city there. He then took half the hypaspists, the Agrianians, a squadron of the cavalry, and the mounted archers and continued his pursuit of the Oreitans.[9] They had withdrawn into the narrow Kumbh Pass, bordering Oreitan and Gedrosian territory, and had joined forces with the Gedrosians. At Alexander's approach, however, the Gedrosians promptly deserted, leaving the Oreitans isolated and with little choice but to surrender.

Apollophanes was appointed satrap over the Oreitans, and Leonnatus was appointed the military commander of a strong force consisting of the Agrianians, archers, cavalry, and most of the Greek mercenaries.[10] Leonnatus was ordered to reduce the area to submission, build a permanent citadel, gather supplies, and await the arrival of the fleet, which he then was to reprovision. Almost as soon as Alexander left the area with the main body of the Macedonian army to march against the Gedrosians, however, the Oreitae revolted. Not only had the Macedonian army thoroughly devastated the area's supplies, but Leonnatus' continuing requisitions threatened them with famine. Although the Oreitae were able to raise a force of 400 cavalry and 8,000 infantry, Leonnatus defeated them in a hard-fought battle in which they sustained over 6,000 casualties and lost virtually all their key leaders.[11] On the Macedonian side, Apollophanes, the satrap Alexander had appointed over the Oreitae, had been one of the casualties.[12] In his victory over the Oreitae, Leonnatus ensured the safety of the coast in his immediate vicinity, and when Nearchus arrived in November, he was able to reprovision his fleet with 10 days' supply of grain. A month or two later, Leonnatus marched his forces to Persepolis along the inland route through the agriculturally rich southern area of Drangiana. He encountered few difficulties or hardships along the way.

Gedrosians

The area between Bela and Jhau was still in the monsoon area, and water, food supplies, and fodder, although not abundant, did meet the minimum needs

---

1. The Arabitae flee into the desert at Alexander's approach. 2. The capital of the Oreitans. 3. When deserted by the Gedrosians, the Oreitans surrender to Alexander. 4. Leonnatus defeats an Oreitan revolt. 5. Alexander sends supplies on ahead to his fleet.

of that portion of the army with Alexander. The small population inhabiting the area had stored up three years' provisions to carry them through lean years. As Alexander's army moved through the area, it took everything, leaving the Gedrosians to starve. The supply trains came less and less frequently from Pattala the farther the army moved from Oreitan territory and finally stopped arriving altogether when the Oreitans rose in revolt.

Somewhere along Alexander's march, camp was made near a wide and virtually dry stream. The baggage train and noncombatants mistakenly made camp inside the stream bed. That night it rained heavily in the mountains, and without warning a wall of water roared down the stream bed. Many of the women and children were drowned in the resulting flash flood, and much of the equipment and remaining food supplies of the army were lost. The soldiers who were camped well back from the bank of the stream escaped drowning but lost everything except whatever clothing, armor, and weapons were in their immediate possession at the time.

As Alexander's army moved out of the monsoon area along the coast and away from populated centers of the interior, it began to undergo both thirst and famine. Water holes were frequently from 25 to 75 miles apart, precluding marches from being completed at night. This exposed the army to a march during the debilitating furnacelike heat of the day.[13] When water was reached, the thirst-crazed men frequently plunged into it, armor and all, and many drank such excessive amounts that they swelled up and died. The numerous deaths that usually occurred at the water holes frequently polluted them for everyone else and doubtless resulted in numerous cases of severe intestinal illness. As a result, Alexander was forced to make camp as much as three miles away from a water hole to enable his officers to maintain some degree of command control over his troops.[14]

The soldiers painfully climbed up and down the endless sand dunes. Wagons sank to the axles and men up to the calves of their legs, making each step a heavy burden. During daylight, the fine sand burned at the touch and reflected the light, increasing the debilitating effects of the already broiling sun. Poisonous snakes and scorpions lay hidden under rocks and in the sand. Animals who ate any of the many poisonous plants along the way died an agonizing death. The difficulties encountered with the wagons of the army became almost insurmountable; they either got stuck in the soft sand or were abandoned because there weren't enough animals to haul them. As a result, the wagons were frequently dismantled and the wood used to cook those animals that had just died. This, of course, spelled a death sentence for the wounded or ill being carried on the wagons. In most cases, they were simply laid alongside the line of march and left to die. After the wagons were gone, the animals which had died of exhaustion were eaten raw because the area that the army passed through contained no trees. When the hunger became extreme, even the living animals were killed for food. Once the desert was entered the only hope was to get through it as quickly as possible. To straggle was to be left behind, to be left behind was to die. It was literally the survival of the fittest. Everyone needed all their strength just to save themselves, and many were left on the side the road only to watch their kin and friends ignore their pleas for help and plod lifelessly onward.

Because of his unhealed wound from his battle with the Malli, Alexander had been riding on horseback. After the flash flood, however, when nearly everyone else in the army had lost either friends or relatives and virtually all their possessions, Alexander attempted to rally their low morale by himself dismounting and ordering all officers who still had horses to do the same. The thought behind this order was that the soldiers might bear their ordeal better if they could see that everyone, including their officers, was suffering equally. Alexander, of course, suffered considerably now that he was afoot. He was seen to be greatly affected by thirst and gasping for breath as a result of the exertion placed on his punctured lung. When some of his scouts found a tiny puddle containing some muddy water, they carried some of it in one of their helmets to Alexander. It was said that he thanked them for their kindness and then poured the water out into the sand. The story quickly spread to every man in the army and boosted morale like nothing else could have. It was said, somewhat extravagantly, that the gesture was worth a drink of water to everyone who heard of it. Alexander had valued his pride above life itself and was determined to live up to his image of the hero even if it killed him, and it probably came close to doing just that. Only his amazingly strong constitution pulled him through the ordeal.

Turbat was located in a densely populated area, at least for Gedrosa, which was extensively farmed. For the first time in 150 miles of marching, the army was supplied with sufficient quantities of both food and water.[15] Alexander, now having some excess food, made an attempt to send a supply train on ahead to the fleet. It was about 75 miles to Pasni, which lay on the Arabian Sea. In moving towards the desolation of the coast, however, the escort troops ran out of food and were forced to consume the supplies designated for the fleet. Considering their circumstances, Alexander was obliged to approve of their decision.

Although Alexander did not know it at the time, his order dismounting his officers probably saved the army from destruction. A violent dust storm blew up and obliterated all the known landmarks of the area. The guides were completely lost, and the supreme crisis was at hand. The army could not stop, nor could it afford to increase the distance it had to travel by veering away from the sea. Alexander took the last of the horses and led a scouting party forward in a desperate attempt to find the sea. In the noon heat, horses died along every mile of the ride. With only five horses remaining, Alexander finally reached the sea.[16] By the time the army came up, his scouting party had located and dug water holes.

Alexander marched west along the coast from Pasni. Seven days later he turned northeast at Gwadar and rejoined that portion of his army under Craterus.[17] Alexander then passed through the Dashatiari plain and into Bampur. There he allowed his soldiers a few days' rest from their nightmare march, which had begun 60 days earlier.[18] Normal supplies of food and water were finally available because Bampur obtained supplies from southern Drangiana, one of the major granaries of Persia. Alexander them pushed on to Bandar Abbas on the border of

Carmania. There he found additional supplies from Drangiana and other nearby satrapies.

It is widely recognized that the Alexander's march through the Makran Desert was the greatest disaster ever to befall him. He suffered heavy but largely unknown losses. While it is true that the majority of the losses fell on the camp followers, his combat arm nevertheless sustained casualties far exceeding those of any field battle Alexander had ever fought. Heavily armed soldiers weighed down with arms, equipment, and loot who had been on starvation rations for several weeks could not march day after day for two months through ovenlike temperatures without incurring a large number of casualties. Those who fell seriously ill along the way were as good as dead, no one having the strength to assist them. The progressive exhaustion Alexander's solders suffered on the extended march would have broken down all but the strongest constitutions. Then too, there was the disastrous effect on the army's morale that was to be all too clearly demonstrated at Opis. From Gedrosa onward, the Macedonians had become highly suspicious of Alexander's intentions. This would be evident at Susa, when he offered to settle the army's debts, and again at Opis, where the army broke out in open mutiny against his mustering out of the veterans. Never again would the army trust Alexander at his word; he had broken it to them once too often.

Generalship

Although Alexander apparently made careful preparations for his march across the Makran Desert, his underlying assumptions were based on risk factors over which he had no control. In previous campaigns Alexander had always, in some manner, been able to influence directly any risk he had assumed. In this campaign, however, he could not affect the outcome of events. The result was a disaster of the first magnitude that painfully demonstrated that fortune does not always favor the bold.

Alexander set out with his army for Gedrosa in mid-July, which coincided with the start of the southwest monsoon rains he had counted on to fill the coastal rivers with water and the beginning of the crop growth cycle. These factors were expected to generate adequate supplies of both food and water for his army and fleet as they moved along the coast. Unfortunately, that year the monsoon rains fell in the mountains but not along the coast. Ironically, had Alexander been able to march along the coast, the condition of the navy might have been far worse. The meager food supplies there had been barely adequate to sustain the minimal needs of the navy, and had the army marched through the region in advance, the navy might have been reduced to starvation instead of occasional hunger. Even if food supplies had been adequate for both forces, the adverse winds held the fleet in port an additional month after its planned departure date. This meant that the army, which could not stay in place to await the arrival of the fleet, would be marching in advance of, instead of in conjunction with, the fleet. Unless a strong guard was left with each supply depot along the way, the probability was that local natives would appropriate any supplies left behind. Nevertheless, Alexander left

10: THE SOUTHERN PERSIAN EMPIRE

Leonnatus in garrison along the Oreitan coast to await the arrival of the fleet that he was to reprovision. When Nearchus arrived in late October, he took on board 10 days' supply of grain. This was the first and last infusion of supplies that the fleet was to receive from Alexander.

The southwest monsoon created strong adverse onshore winds and rough seas for the navy. Although Nearchus was able to sail his fleet as far as Karachi, strong winds and rough seas kept him in harbor during the next month. This unexpected delay in the fleet's sailing destroyed any chance of Alexander being able to coordinate the movements between his army and fleet. When Alexander reached Sonmiani, he was informed that the Taloi mountains came right down to the sea so it would not be possible for his army to proceed along the coast as he had planned. He would be forced to go inland, severing all communications with the fleet. This was a serious issue for Alexander because his basic assumption had been that without the army to gather supplies, the fleet would be exposed to starvation. Alexander could not march along the coast, could not stay where he was for any length of time, and could not countermarch back over the way he had come, so thoroughly had he devastated the area behind him. The only thing he could do was to go forward through the desert if he was to have any possibility of contact with his fleet.

Three major factors predominated in Alexander's march through the Makran: water, food, and his noncombatants. Alexander must have known that water would be a severe problem without the usual monsoon rains. Water holes were frequently too far apart to conclude marches during darkness. The water holes also posed difficulties in supplying his army with adequate quantities of water. It was a much more time-consuming process for an army to derive water from a water hole than from a river. In a river a great number of men can drink at one time, whereas at a water hole only a few. This would not only considerably slow the drinking process but tend to string the army out, causing greater straggling and an increasing loss of command control. While it is true that several rivers crossed Alexander's route of march, most were dry from the lack of rain.

As to the procurement of food, Alexander was expecting it from three sources: the Oreitans, adjacent satraps, and Gedrosa itself. The supplies from Oreitae were, of course, terminated with the beginning of the revolt there. When it ended, Alexander was already out of effective range of land transport from that area. This meant that even had deliveries been resumed, the supply trains from Oreitae territory would not have done him much good because the meager quantities that would have been delivered at that extended range would not have justified the great effort to transport them. In any case, this supply source could not have been effective much beyond Bela. As the choice of the inland route had not been made by Alexander until he was already marching north from Sonmiani, the neighboring satraps were only notified of it somewhat after that time, when messengers hurriedly sent from Alexander reached them. They were therefore unable to do any advanced planning in either mobilizing the necessary pack animals or establishing advanced depots. This had not been part of Alexander's initial plan, and it was unreasonable to expect that the satraps could have reacted effectively to these radically changed conditions while Alexander was on the march. Alexander, however, unfairly held them strictly accountable for not providing supplies. This was completely unjustified by any reasonable standard, but many lives were forfeited in an attempt by Alexander to make it appear that the satraps were at fault for the disaster he had brought about. Although some supplies were gathered from the Gedrosa itself, even in the best of the times the small population of the area did not produce much in the way of agricultural crops. When Alexander moved through their country, his army confiscated everything it could find in the way of food, taking even the Gedrosian seed crop reserved for their next planting. Although this, in effect, signed the death warrant for many of the Gedrosians, that apparently was of little concern to Alexander, whose army was already on starvation rations. These were the only supplies Alexander was able to obtain between the Jhau and Turbat, and they were just barely enough to keep his army alive.

When Alexander reached Sonmiani, he had two other choices before him, whether to detach his camp followers along the northern route or to follow that route with the entire force under his command. Although Alexander's overriding concern for his fleet mandated that his army march through the desert, there appears to have been no logical reason why he did not allow the camp followers accompanying the army to take the northern route. Their presence was clearly an impediment to the rate of march of the army, their slow movement and inability to negotiate steep inclines often necessitating lengthy detours around the high sand dunes along the route of march. In addition, not having the discipline of combat troops, they tended to consume disproportionate quantities of scarce food and water. To carry them along was to subject the army to much unnecessary suffering. Alexander either seems not to have been aware of their detrimental effects or, for some unknown and unexplained reason, thought it necessary to take them along.

The Makran Desert march definitely portrays Alexander at his worst. He seems to have gambled that the forces of nature would accommodate him and was unprepared for the result when they did not. The planning he did seems adequate on the surface, but if one examines it in detail it was both shortsighted and unworkable.[19] In fact, much of the logistical plan seems to have been concocted after the fact in an attempt to shift the blame for the disaster away from himself, where it really belonged.

Thus far Alexander had had an extremely successful track record for invincibility. It is apparent that even he appeared to believe that he was indeed the favorite of the gods in this regard, and it may well be that Alexander's overconfidence clouded his usual good judgment. What subsequently happened is hard to explain otherwise. The march through Gedrosa, of course, destroyed the nonsense about being divinely favored and must have shaken Alexander greatly because it clearly demonstrated that he was not as infallible as he thought. More importantly to Alexander, however, was the fact that his humiliation was also there for everyone else to see.

Carmania

When Alexander reached Bampur, the first thing he did was to blame the tragedy of the Makran Desert march on the neighboring satraps. Apollophanes had escaped arrest by dying in the rebellion of the Oreitans, but the satraps from Carmania, Persis, and Media; Abulites, satrap of Susiana; his son Oxathres, satrap of Paraetacae; and Stasanor, satrap of Areia, were all executed. The charge was always either treason or misrule. Four senior army commanders were also executed, including Cleander and Sitalces, both of whom had been involved in Parmenio's murder.[20] They were convicted of misrule and of plundering the temples. The vacated satrapies were reassigned to Macedonians, Thoas receiving Carmania, Sibyrtius receiving Arachosia and Gedrosa, and Peucestas receiving Persis and Susiana.[21]

11. Return to Babylon

Persis

Pasargadae

While Hephaestion marched along the Arabian Sea with a portion of the army that included the baggage train and elephants, Alexander proceeded inland with the main body.[1] His first stop was at Pasargadae to view the tomb of the Persian conqueror Cyrus the Great, whom he greatly admired. He was both shocked and angered to find that the tomb had been broken into and looted. The only items still remaining inside the tomb were a golden sarcophagus too large to fit through the door and too massive to have been broken apart, the bones of Cyrus scattered along the floor, and a single couch.

Alexander had the damage to the sarcophagus repaired and restored the tomb to its condition at the time of Cyrus' burial. The door was then walled up and affixed with Alexander's royal seal. He had the Magi, who had the hereditary responsibility of guarding the tomb, tortured in the hope that they would either admit their own guilt or implicate the perpetrators. When they did neither, he released them. Bagoas, however, in revenge for the lack of respect shown him by Orxines, satrap of Persis, informed Alexander that he suspected the Persian of plundering the 3,000 gold talents allegedly buried with Cyrus.[2] Alexander subsequently found Orxines guilty of mismanagement of government and pillaging of the royal tombs and ordered him hanged.

Susiana

Susa Weddings

When Alexander reached Susa, he ordered a mass wedding between a number of Companions and noble Persian women according to Persian rites. Alexander himself married Darius' eldest daughter Stateira, otherwise known as Barsine, and Artaxerxes married Ochus' youngest daughter, Parysatis. Hephaestion married Drypetis, a daughter of Darius; Craterus married Amastrine, a daughter of Darius' brother Oxyartes; Perdiccas married a daughter of Atropates, the satrap of Media; Ptolemy married Artacoana, a daughter of Artabazus; Eumenes, his royal secretary, married Artonis, another daughter of Artabazus; Nearchus married the daughter of Alexander's former mistress, Barsine; and Seleucus married the daughter of Spitamenes.³ In all, 80 Companions were wed in a single ceremony. Following the weddings, Alexander presented several gold crowns for unusual bravery and distinguished service. Peucestas received a crown for saving Alexander's life in the campaign against the Mallians; Leonnatus, one for his victory over the Oreitans; Nearchus, one for his Indian Ocean voyage; and Onesicritus, one in recognition of the skillful performance of his nautical duties as helmsman of the royal ship in India.⁴ Hephaestion also received a crown but for no discernible reason other than that he was Alexander's "favorite."⁵ The remaining bodyguards also received crowns.⁶

The Tigris River

In leaving Susa, Alexander ordered Hephaestion march the bulk of the army alongside the Eulaeus River and down to the Persian Gulf. He embarked the hypaspists and a few Companions on Nearchus' ships and sailed down the river alongside him.⁷ When they reached a canal near the gulf, Hephaestion followed it to the Tigris River while Alexander sailed out into the gulf. As Alexander sailed up the Tigris, he dismantled the "weirs" Darius had constructed to prevent navigation of the river by enemy vessels.⁸ Alexander was, of course, more interested in opening up the river to trade with India than in protecting himself against an invasion along it by some unidentified enemy.

Opis

Meeting Hephaestion at his encampment alongside the Tigris, Alexander accompanied him up the river to Opis. There, when Alexander announced the mustering out of 10,000 Macedonians he deemed unfit for duty, his army's reaction was to mutiny and demand that all the Macedonians be released. (For more detail on the mutiny, see Appendix C.) After settling the mutiny, Alexander marched off to Ecbatana.

Media

Ecbatana

At Ecbatana, Alexander's closest friend, Hephaestion, died, either as a result of alcohol abuse or poisoning. On his march out of the city, Alexander divided his army. Perdiccas led a force to escort Hephaestion's body back to Babylon and make arrangements for his funeral (for details on Hephaestion's funeral, see Appendix D), while the remainder of the army accompanied Alexander on a winter campaign against the Cossaeans, a nomadic tribe living in the mountains north of Susa.

Cossaeans

The Cossaeans had refused to acknowledge both Persian and Macedonian rule. Their livelihood was derived by raiding the caravans in the lowlands and

354 III: CAMPAIGNS OF ALEXANDER THE GREAT

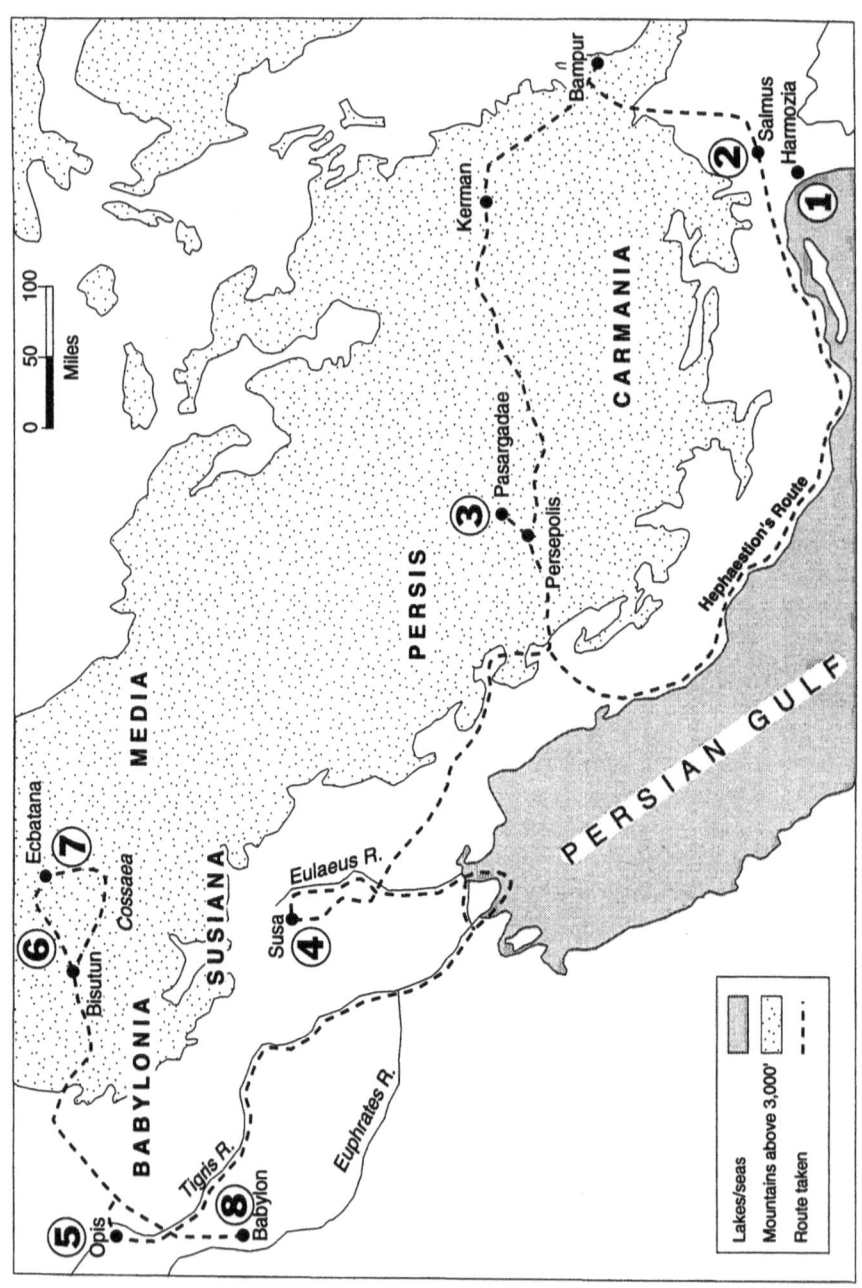

Map 50: Return to Babylon

when pursued, scattering into the mountains. There they would regroup preparatory to resuming their raids. Alexander was determined to break the tribe's resistance and end its continual brigandage. It is also quite possible that he held the tribesmen responsible for the massive theft of Darius' Nesaean horse herd, whose numbers had diminished from the 150,000 known to have existed during Darius' reign to only 50,000 during Alexander's.

Alexander spread the rumor that he was going to Babylon to preside at Hephaestion's funeral. He then made a forced-march at night with his cavalry and light infantry to occupy the strategic mountain passes leading into the Cossaeans' territory. Finding the passes unmanned, Alexander was able to enter the Cossaean valley without opposition. Alexander opened his winter campaign against the Cossaeans by devastating the area. Being able to easily track the Cossaeans' movements through the snow, he forced them to fight stand-up battles they could not win. After a campaign lasting 40 days, the Cossaeans were forced to submit to Alexander.[9] The terms of surrender were that they give up their nomadic way of life and settle in the cities Alexander had founded at strategic points within their territory. They were now to become farmers instead of brigands. This change, however, was not well received by the Cossaeans. Their dissatisfaction was still evident when Antigonus entered the area in 317 B.C. Even then, he found a bitterly discontented people who had clearly considered themselves forced to earn a meager livelihood in a manner repugnant to them.

Generalship

The Cossaean campaign, which was, incidentally, Alexander's last, demonstrated his ability to wage a successful operation against nomadic guerrillas. His use of deceit, rapid movement, and winter weather to track the Cossaeans were both innovative and effective. He not only brought about their surrender, which the Persians had been unable to do, but forcibly resettled them. Alexander's conduct of this campaign was clearly a model for an effective guerrilla campaign.

Babylonia

Babylon

From Ecbatana, Alexander marched to Babylon. As he approached the city, Chaldaean seers came out to meet him with a warning from their god Bel (also known as Marduk) that he would imperil his life if he entered the city from the

---

1. Nearchus' landing site. 2. The capital of Carmania, where Nearchus rejoins Alexander and Alexander begins his satrapal purges. 3. Alexander visits Cyrus' tomb. 4. The place where Alexander conducts his "Susa Weddings," awards his gold crowns and conducts Calanus' funeral. 5. The Macedonian army mutinies. 6. The Nesaean fields, where the royal horses were pastured. 7. Hephaestion dies of overindulgence of wine. 8. Alexander dies.

east. Because of the extensive swamps surrounding Babylon, however, it was not possible to enter it from any other direction. Although Alexander's friends ridiculed the warning of the Chaldaeans and relegated their religion to nonsense, the now highly superstitious Macedonian king reluctantly entered the city, seemingly only partially convinced that he wasn't doing so under a cloud of doom. Alexander then quickly left Babylon to inspect the irrigation system in the marshlands north of the city. Ironically, in seeking to escape an imaginary threat of death in Babylon, he may well have exposed himself to a real one in the swamps. It was later alleged that while in the stagnant waters of the irrigation reservoirs Alexander caught malaria, which, given his weakened condition from his unhealed punctured lung, caused his death a short time later. Another story indicates that he was poisoned by Antipater's family. Whatever the case, his death was disastrous for Babylon. Instead of being the center of an empire, the city languished during the period of the Hellenistic kingdoms which were ruled by Alexander's generals. By the first century B.C., Babylon had fallen into ruins.

12. Arabia

Alexander's next major campaign after India was to be against Arabia. He intended to conquer the Arabian peninsula, colonize its coast and then establish a coastal trade route linking India with both the Euphrates delta and Egypt. The numerous islands and safe anchorages along the Arabian coast would facilitate the development of many rich trading cities, and Alexander thought that the resulting prosperity there would rival that of Phoenicia. As Alexander knew little of Arabia or its size, from Ecbatana he ordered that a reconnaissance be made of its coast and any nearby offshore islands. A total of four separate explorations were to be made. Three of them originated from the Indian Ocean to explore the eastern side of Arabia, Archias sailing as far as the island of Tylus, or Bahrain; Androsthenes, farther down the Arabian peninsula; and Hieron of Soli, as far south as Ras Mussendam on the Egyptian side of the Arabian peninsula.[1] All three explorers reported most favorably on Arabia's prosperity. Timber supplies were available in the nearby mountains, while spice trees grew in abundance. When Androsthenes reported that he thought Arabia was comparable in size to India, Alexander, instead of being dismayed, was overcome with his natural desire to tackle the seemingly impossible The last voyage under Anaxicrates sailed west from the Gulf of Suez as far as Yemen before being forced to turn back because of insufficient water supplies.[2]

Babylon's harbor capacity was enlarged to accommodate the berthing of 1,000 ships that were to be used for the Arabian campaign.[3] Phoenician galleys were sawed into pieces, carried overland on carts, reassembled at Thapsacus, and sailed down the Euphrates River to Babylon. When Alexander arrived at Babylon, he found already assembled 50 Phoenician vessels, including 2 quinqueremes, 3 quadriremes, 12 triremes, and 30 triaconters.[4] Workers were ordered to cut down cypress trees near the city to build additional ships. If it had been completed, this fleet would have been the second largest in antiquity, only being exceeded by the 1,200 triremes of the Persian fleet during Xerxes' invasion of Greece. Nearchus was again appointed admiral of the fleet, and large numbers of crews were hired in Phoenicia.[5] Miccalus of Clazomenae was sent to Phoenicia and Syria with 500 talents to recruit crews.[6] As in India, neither the troops nor crews were to be told how long or dangerous the voyage was likely to be. An army was also assembled at Babylon. Peucestas supplied 20,000 archers from Persia, a force of Cossaeans, and Tapurians; Philoxenus supplied Carian troops; Meleager, Lydians; and Menidas, cavalry.[7]

The campaign was to begin in June, the army to march on June 4, and the fleet to sail on the following day. The fleet would accompany and supply the army as it marched down to the southern tip of the Arabian coast, which it expected to reach by October. At that time, the wind would then shift to blowing from the southeast, facilitating the fleet sailing back up the Arabian western coast to Egypt.

On May 23, 323 B.C., Alexander attended a banquet in honor of Nearchus' appointment as commander of the fleet. As he was about to retire, Medius, a Thessalian friend, invited him to another party in honor of the death of Heracles. Alexander attended but fell ill, it was said, after drinking an enormous goblet of wine all at once. During the next two weeks his health gradually deteriorated. Throughout that time he continued to meet with commanders of the Arabian expedition and issue orders concerning its organization and departure. Alexander's fever soon entered a critical stage, however, and he completely lost his voice. Four days later he lapsed into a coma and died. Upon his death the Arabian expedition was canceled by his successor generals, who would soon need to concentrate all their time and resources in the upcoming struggle to either hold what they were given or take what they could of Alexander's empire.

Appendices

Appendix A: Peace of Philocrates

First Athenian Peace Embassy (December 347)[1]

The first Athenian delegation was sent to Macedonia to negotiate the terms for ending the Sacred War. The Athenian Assembly would either accept or reject those terms. The envoys were selected by the Athenian assembly and included Aeschines, Aristodemus, Cimon, Ctesiphon, Demosthenes, Dercyllus, Iatrocles, Nausicles, Philocrates, and Phrynon.[2] The envoys left Athens by sea from Marathon, crossed over to Euboea, and traveled to Oreus at the northern tip of the island. They then crossed over to Halus, which although under siege by Parmenio, was not yet cut off from the sea. From there, the envoys passed through Pagasae and Larisa to Pella. The trip had taken them about a week.

Philip refused to discuss the independence of the Thracian coastal forts, the claim to Amphipolis, and Athenian naval assistance to Halus were nonnegotiable items for Philip.[3] He did, however, recognize the Athenian claim to the Chersonese, promised that his army would not enter the area while negotiations continued, and supported restoration of Athenian control over Euboea. The price Athens would have to pay would be alliance with Macedonia. The Athenian delegation knew that they must either accept Philip's peace terms or continue the war. Since it was apparent that Phocis would be unable to prevent Philip from marching through central Greece into Attica, the Athenian delegation believed they had to conclude a peace before the situation further deteriorated.

The delegation arrived back in Athens at the beginning of March.[4] One of them, Ctesiphon, told the Assembly that Philip had gone to war against Athens unwillingly and now only wanted to end the conflict. He praised Philip's kindness and generosity, and reading from a letter Philip had given him, he stressed his desire for peace and his willingness to grant Athens numerous but unspecified benefits in the future. The Athenians approved of Ctesiphon's report. Demosthenes rose in the Assembly to speak against the treaty and was shouted down by Philocrates, who warned the assembly members that if they did not ratify the treaty, Chios, Megara, Rhodes, and Thebes were likely to join Philip in a war against Athens.[5] The Athenians did not realize the danger of Philip's presence in central Greece, rather naively preferring to believe that he was intending to punish the Thebans and to protect the Phocians.[6] It was also believed that Philip intended to compensate Athens for the loss of Amphipolis and allow her to resume control of Euboea.

Second Athenian Embassy (Early April, 346)[7]

The objective of the second Athenian delegation was to swear oaths with Philip to the terms previously negotiated. The treaty was to become effective as of the date of Philip's oath swearing, and all parties were to retain any territories in their possession at that time. The second Athenian embassy was composed of the same members as the previous one. They went across Euboea, up to Oreus and then slowly to Pella, their trip taking a full three weeks. Once the delegation arrived in Macedonia, they had to wait another three weeks for Philip's return from Thrace, where he was conducting a war against Cersobleptes. Awaiting Philip were also envoys from Sparta, Thebes, and Thessaly. Philip met with the ambassadors separately, promising each what they most wanted to hear.

Philip delayed the oath swearing on the pretext that not all his allies were present. Meantime, he marched his army south, allegedly to besiege Halus. Although the Athenian ambassadors claimed that they had no choice but to accompany Philip's army, they may well have been bribed to do so in order to preclude the Athenian Assembly from hearing of Philip's move south in time to rush troops to Thermopylae by sea, as they had done before. The oath swearing finally took place at Pherae, in Thessaly, and the second delegation returned in early July, just prior to Philip reaching Thermopylae.[8]

The Athenian Assembly convened to hear the report of their delegation who had just signed the peace with Philip. Although news was received that Philip had reached Thermopylae, Aeschines stated that his intentions were to protect Phocis, restore freedom to the Boeotian cities, and punish Thebes for instigating the Sacred War. He further stated that it was his belief that the Boeotian League would be broken up and Thebes would be forced to compensate Delphi for the treasure that Phocis had appropriated. Some in the Assembly were clearly angered at having so little time for their deliberations on whether to oppose Philip or not, but the Assembly reluctantly made the best of a bad situation. Its members were deliberately misled by their own delegates, however, as to the fate of Phocis. When Demosthenes rose to warn the Assembly of the danger of Philip's unexpected appearance at Thermopylae, he was shouted down by others who were desperate to have the treaty. Philocrates then proposed a decree extending the peace treaty with Philip into perpetuity and another indicating that if the Phocians should refuse to evacuate Delphi, Athens should militarily force them to do so. Both decrees were enacted by the Assembly.

Although many in Athens considered the peace to be a bad one, it protected the city against the Amphictyonic Council, which would have liked to declare a Sacred War against Athens for supporting Phocis. Many Athenians also thought that the treaty could always be repudiated later. Other Athenians believed Philip's promises of future advantages to Athens. In support of their viewpoint were Philip's keeping of his promises not to enter the Chersonese with troops while peace talks were in progress and his return of Athenian prisoners after the oath swearing.[9]

Sometime after the treaty had been ratified by Athens but before the Macedonian army had occupied Thermopylae, Philip requested that Athens mobilize its army and join him to give the appearance of a united front against the Phocians. The mood of the Athenian Assembly had by this time definitely swung round against Philip, and Demosthenes now had no trouble convincing them that once their army was in Philip's reach he would undoubtedly use it to intimidate the Athenians into submission. The Assembly, thereupon, refused to comply with Philip's request and sent no troops to his support. Philip no doubt viewed this a sign of bad faith.

Third Athenian Embassy (July 346)

A third Athenian embassy was sent to Philip. Although its purpose was not entirely clear, its mission was probably to attempt to persuade him to determine the fate of the Phocians himself rather than leaving it to the Amphictyonic League to do so. Following the passage of Philocrates' decree in the Athenian Assembly, all the members of the first and second delegations were reappointed to the third delegation. Demosthenes, however, refused to accept the office, indicating that he did not want to leave Athens at that time. The other delegates were concerned that if Demosthenes were left behind he might convene a special assembly and rescind the decrees they had just been passed. Aeschines concocted an illness so that he could also remain behind to oppose anything that Demosthenes might attempt and to help mitigate the adverse effects of the expected news of the Phocian surrender. The third embassy departed Athens in July, again traveling to Macedonia by way of Euboea. Its members got as far as Chalcis, in Euboea, when they learned that the Phocians had unconditionally surrendered all their cities to Philip. Presuming their mission was at an end, they promptly returned to Athens.

Peace Conditions

The imposition of the following peace conditions ended the Sacred War.

Athens

- Renounced its claim to Amphipolis
- Concluded both a peace treaty and a defensive alliance with Macedonia
- Lost its right of precedence in consulting the oracle at Delphi

Phocis

- All cities excepting Abae, both because it was the site of a sacred temple and because its inhabitants had not participated in the looting of Delphi, were to be dismantled and the Phocians resettled in villages of no more than 50 houses located no closer together than 220 yards (Diodorus XVI:60).
- The 10,000 talents of sacred monies appropriated from Delphi were to be repaid at a rate of 60 talents per year (Diodorus XVI:60).
- Those responsible for the temple robbery were to be placed under a curse and were liable to seizure wherever found (Diodorus XVI:60).
- All Phocian weapons were to be surrendered and destroyed and all horses

confiscated and sold. The Phocians were prohibited from owning either until the entire amount that had been appropriated from temple funds was repaid (Diodorus XVI:60).

• All Phocian rights over the temple of Delphi were revoked (Diodorus XVI:60).

Boeotia

• The Boeotians, under the leadership of Thebes, had begun the Sacred War in the hope that they could reestablish their power in central Greece at the expense of Phocis. They failed, however, to make any new gains and only received back the three cities they had lost during the war — Coronea, Corsiae, and Orchomenus — whose walls were then torn down. The Boeotian League treated the now defenseless cities mercilessly, selling their citizens off as slaves (Diodorus XVI:60).

• Nicaea, which controlled the pass of Thermopylae, had been given to the Thessalians. This action would largely preclude the Boeotians from conducting any military operations into southern Thessaly (Diodorus XVI:60).

• Although the Boeotian League continued to exist, Theban domination of it was ended. The reestablishment of independent Boeotian cities allowed the League to function again as an autonomous federation. Also, the restoration of Orchomenus, Plataea, and Thespiae, all of which were hostile to Thebes, would considerably reduce whatever influence in Boeotia Thebes still retained.

Sparta

• As an ally of Phocis, Sparta was deprived of its two seats in the Amphictyonic Council.

Macedonia

• Philip was allowed to exercise the two votes in the Amphictyonic Council formally held by Phocis (Diodorus XVI:59).

Appendix B: Assassination Attempts Against Alexander

Alexander was the victim of several assassination plots, some only alleged, others discovered in the process of being carried out. In every case, he dealt ruthlessly with the alleged perpetrators and often used the incident to pursue revenge against those who had once either opposed him or in some manner insulted him. Alexander's Orientalization policies, his despotic demeanor, and his drunken lifestyle were the basis of many of the attempts against his life.

Alexander of Lyncestis (son of Aeropus) (333 B.C.)

The plot of Alexander of Lyncestis was revealed to Alexander at Phaselis, in Asia Minor, by Sisines, a Persian messenger from Darius captured by Parmenio.[10] Under questioning, the Persian disclosed that Alexander of Lyncestis had sent a written proposal to Darius offering to assassinate the Macedonian king in exchange for 1,000 talents in gold and the throne of Macedonia.[11] Alexander called a meeting of his closest Companions, allegedly to obtain their opinions as to what action should be taken. They told him that it had been a mistake to appoint someone so untrustworthy to lead one of the army's elite cavalry units — the Thessalian cavalry — and that Lyncestis should be removed from that command before he had the chance to foment rebellion among them. Alexander followed their advice and sent Amphoterus, Craterus' brother, to Parmenio, who was Alexander of Lyncestis' commander, with verbal instructions for his arrest. This was done on the eve of the battle of Issus.

Alexander of Lyncestis was kept under close confinement for three years, until late 330 B.C., when Philotas was tried and executed.[12] Although there was no hard evidence against Lyncestis, Atarrhias, a veteran commander, demanded that he be brought to trial. Unfortunately, Lyncestis, as a result of his lengthy confinement, was unable to conduct a coherent defense, while the prosecutor was able to make a convincing circumstantial case against him. Judged guilty of treason, Lyncestis was immediately executed by the assembled troops.

Hermolaus (328 B.C.)

One of the most disturbing assassination plots for Alexander was that of a group of his own pages. Hermolaus, who was a royal page, had been publicly whipped by Alexander and deprived of his horse for having usurped the king's prerogative of the first kill of a boar on a hunt. In revenge for what he considered to be an injustice, Hermolaus enlisted four other pages in a conspiracy to murder Alexander. The next day one of them, Eurylochus by name, disclosed the plot and the conspirators were apprehended.[13] Hermolaus, in his final remarks, attempted to justify his action on the basis of Alexander's arrogance, cruelty, alcoholism, increasing Orientalization, and dictatorial behavior. None of the other pages made any attempt to deny their guilt or defend their actions. The conspirators were all convicted by an assembly of the Macedonian army and stoned to death. Although Callisthenes, who was Alexander's historian, was not implicated in the plot, Alexander considered him a participant, both because of his position as instructor to the pages and his well-known remarks in support of assassinations. He was arrested several months after Hermolaus' execution and appears to have died in prison some three years later.

Philotas (330 B.C.)

While standing outside Alexander's tent near Zarangia, Philotas was approached by a youth named Cebalinus. The boy told him that his brother Nicomachus, who was the lover of Dymnus, a member of the king's bodyguard, had been invited by him to join in a plot against Alexander's life. This Nicomachus had refused to do. Philotas assured Cebalinus that he would bring the information to Alexander's attention. He knew that Philotas had seen Alexander several times during the past two days but had apparently told him nothing about the plot, which was to be carried out on the following day. Cebalinus told his story to Metron, one of the pages. While Alexander was taking his bath, Cebalinus was brought out to repeat his story. After ordering the arrest of Dymnus, Alexander questioned Cebalinus. When asked about the two-day delay in reporting the plot, Cebalinus told Alexander that Philotas had known of it immediately but, for some unknown reason, had failed to pass it on.

When Dymnus was informed of his arrest, he immediately killed himself with his sword. Alexander then summoned Philotas for questioning. Philotas told him that he initially did not believe the story, thinking it merely a lovers' spat. Upon hearing of Dymnus' suicide, however, he realized that a conspiracy indeed might have existed and apologized for having taken the information so lightly. Alexander extended his hand to Philotas and assured him that he believed his failure to act was from a mistake in judgment rather than complicity. However, Alexander appeared to believe that Philotas had passively condoned the plot. Convening a meeting of his closest friends and advisers, Alexander discussed the plot with them. Upon hearing the facts that he presented, they believed that Philotas was definitely implicated in the plot and demanded his trial. Alexander, pretending to be persuaded, ordered Philotas arrested that evening. Having obviously intentionally deceived Philotas as to his true beliefs, Alexander had cleverly manipulated the presentation to his friends to implicate him. The arresting officers found Philotas asleep. Unaware of his precarious predicament, he offered no resistance. After all,

Alexander had held him blameless in the matter. What Philotas did not see, however, was Alexander's hidden agenda against his family.

The next morning Alexander ordered several thousand troops of his army to present themselves before him. These included the taxies of Ptolemy, the Companion cavalry, and the hypaspists, elite troops completely loyal to Alexander. They would likely be unsympathetic to Philotas, whom they considered to be arrogant, pretentious, and disdainful of the high honors Alexander had bestowed on him. In addition, Philotas was widely disliked because of the way he used Alexander's protection to ridicule and insult with impunity those he chose to. When the body of Dymnus was brought in, the troops were thrown into a high state of excitement. Alexander then explained the details of the conspiracy and how Dymnus came to die, after which he dramatically announced that not only did he believe Philotas to be involved in the plot but was convinced that his father, Parmenio, had orchestrated it. Alexander then ordered Philotas to be brought in. He was dressed in the rough clothes of a peasant and had his hands tied behind him.

Speaking to the assembly in his defense, Philotas indicated that there was no evidence against him, only suspicions. He therefore requested that the charges against him be dropped. The assembled soldiers, now being in a position to take revenge against Philotas, denied his request. They were much more inclined to agree with the inflammatory speeches of Amyntas; Coenus, who was Philotas' own brother-in-law; and Bolon, a crude veteran officer. The assembly, now worked up to an emotional frenzy, was easily persuaded to demand the death penalty for Philotas. A decision was made to put Philotas to torture in the hopes that he would somehow incriminate himself, and his bitterest enemies were, of course, designated to conduct it.

Philotas endured the beginning of the torture stoically, much to the surprise and anger of his tormentors, who only renewed their efforts. Finally, however, the pain became unbearable, and he indicated that he would confess to whatever they wanted, provided he would be given a quick death. During the subsequent interrogation, Philotas implicated both himself and his father in the assassination plot against Alexander. After his confession, Philotas was immediately taken to the location of the conspirators named by Cebalinus and along with them was stoned to death. Alexander then ordered Parmenio's assassination.

Antipater (323 B.C.)

It was alleged that Antipater led a plot which resulted in the death of Alexander the Great. In 323 B.C., Alexander ordered Antipater to relinquish his regency in Macedonia to Craterus and accompany 10,000 reinforcements to Babylon. The order came just after Alexander's mass executions of satraps and military commanders, and Antipater believed he had good reason to fear his own execution. He was the last of the "old guard" Macedonians, and it was clear that he was not being summoned to Babylon to be honored. His regency in Greece had been severely criticized by Olympias, Alexander's mother, and many of the Greek cities resented his continued support of oligarchies there in preference to democracies.

To determine Alexander's attitude towards him, Antipater sent his son, Cassander, to Babylon on his behalf.

When Cassander laughed during a banquet at what he considered the ridiculous spectacle of proskynesis, Alexander repeatedly banged his head against a wall. It was now apparent that Antipater was in disgrace, and in his mind it had now come down to a case of either kill or be killed. Aristotle, whose nephew Callisthenes had been executed by Alexander, was said to have mixed the poison and Cassander to have carried it with him to Babylon. It was thought to have been administered to Alexander by his cup-bearer, Iollas, who was another of Antipater's sons. Medius, who invited Alexander to the fateful party, was Iollas' lover. Approximately two weeks after allegedly taking the poison, Alexander was dead.

Appendix C: Macedonian Army Mutinies

Oxus River

It was June 329 B.C. when Alexander began his march to the Oxus River. This meant that the Macedonian army would have to cross 45 miles of desert during the dry season, suffering from heatstroke during the day and frostbite at night. Dehydration and overdrinking were to cause as many casualties as if a major battle had been fought. As a result of their ordeal, the Thessalians and most of Philip's older veterans mutinied and demanded to be released from further service. They had marched over 9,000 miles in Asia and had had enough. Now all they wanted to do was to return home. Alexander had no choice but to accede to their demands, mustering them all out with generous bonuses.

Beas River

In 326 B.C., Alexander reached the Beas River. His army was physically and mentally exhausted. During the past eight years, they had marched through forest, plain, desert, and mountains in every imaginable kind of weather. Their arms were worn out from use, and the unrelenting monsoon rains of the past three months had literally rotted the clothes off their backs. The food was constantly mildewed, and weapons began to rust almost as soon as they were cleaned. The excitement of their youth had long ago worn off, and many of Alexander's troops now only longed to return to Greece. Morale dropped to an all-time low.

Alexander was aware of the mood of his soldiers but mistakenly thought that he could turn it around. He seemed to believe that his men were relatively unintelligent, being motivated only by fear, greed, or ambition, and if he temporarily satisfied one or more of these vices, they would again come under his control. He decided to let the men go off on a looting spree, and in their absence gave their wives and children free rations for a month. When his soldiers returned, they stood in silence to Alexander's speech about the glorious exploits awaiting them once they crossed the Beas River. Alexander had badly misjudged their mood, and becoming highly dissatisfied with their complete lack of enthusiasm for marching any farther east, angrily dismissed them.

The officers were now summoned. Alexander tried to convince them that the unknown they feared always seemed more terrifying in their mind than the reality of it. Rumors exaggerated the widths of the rivers before them and both the numbers and ferocity of any Indian tribes they were likely to meet. He told them that the elephants were not nearly so numerous as they had imagined and, anyway, they had defeated them once and could doubtless do so again. Very soon the Eastern Ocean would be reached, and they would then be conquerors of all Asia. Why turn back when they were so near to the logical conclusion of all their efforts? The Ganges River lay a mere 12 days' march away and the Ocean itself just beyond it. To not march to it would be to throw away all that they achieved thus far. The tribes in their rear that they had failed to subdue would be inclined to revolt once it was learned of their failure to march further east, and they might lose much of what they had gained.

When Alexander finished speaking, the officers remained silent. Finally, Coenus rose to reply. He told Alexander that the men were done in because they had been pushed beyond the limits of human endurance. They were broken in spirit and now only wanted one thing, to return home. Alexander could return to Greece and recruit younger men who would willingly follow him in his future conquests, but the men in his army now were worn out. Coenus told him that a successful man should know when to stop. As he sat back down, the officers applauded his remarks in unanimous agreement. Alexander, furious beyond words, angrily dismissed them.

The officers were called before Alexander again the following day. He told them that any who wanted to return home were free to do so because he would find men enough to follow him willingly. He considered, however, that they were deserting their king in the midst of his enemies. Alexander again dismissed the officers and retired to his tent, refusing to see anyone for the next two days, including his Companions. When the army stood firm, however, Alexander was forced to relent. In an attempt to save face, he announced on the third day of his sulk that he would offer sacrifice to determine the omens for a crossing of the Beas River. They were, of course, unfavorable, much to the joy of the soldiers who, hysterical with relief, surrounded Alexander's tent.

Although the Indian and Asian troops would have been willing to follow Alexander across the Beas River, he probably knew that they were not equal to the hard military campaigning that lay ahead in India. Only the Macedonians could guarantee him success; they held the trump card and knew it. The troops had presented their viewpoint in silence. There was no insubordination on their part, just a complete lack of confidence in Alexander's vision of future operations. Alexander was unsuccessful at convincing his men to advance farther east and instead of ordering them to do so regardless, instead let a sacrifice decide the issue. On the surface, of course, this appeared to be the case. Appearances here were clearly deceptive, however, for many animosities were simmering below the surface. Alexander most assuredly would have held a deep grudge against his men both for the humiliation he had endured at their hands and their part in denying him his destiny of the conquest of all Asia. The Macedonian soldiers, on the other hand, had good reason to consider this incident another of Alexander's lies to them which, undoubtedly, only served to reinforce their distrust of him.

With the flexibility of mind that had always characterized his actions, however, Alexander had come up with a face-saving way to restore the affections of his army. Then he promptly redirected them on a campaign in southwestern India. Being so relieved at not having to marching into the unknown east, his army raised no recorded objection at all to marching off into the unknown south.[14]

Punjab

From the Hydaspes River, Alexander advanced into the Punjab in 326 B.C. Porus told him that he had been trying for some time to subdue the Malli tribe there but had been unable to do so. Reports now came to Alexander that the Malli and the Oxydracae were mobilizing in force against him. Their combined army in the field was rumored to number 10,000 cavalry, 80,000 infantry, and 700 chariots.

When Alexander's army realized that instead of the uneventful voyage that was anticipated another arduous campaign confronted them, they again threatened to mutiny. After telling them every lie he could think of to calm their fears, for example, the ocean was so close that you could smell the sea breeze and the Malli fought like women, Alexander managed to talk them into pressing on. Their morale, however, was at rock bottom, which would be clearly evident in the fighting that lay ahead.

Opis

In the summer of 324 B.C., the Macedonian army had reached Opis, a city on the Tigris River, 125 miles northwest of Babylon. There Alexander announced that he was discharging all Macedonians unfit for service in the field. The older veterans who were to be discharged resented being treated like so much used-up excess baggage while the younger troops did not care to remain in an army that would soon be dominated by the "barbarian slaves"—Persians—they so despised. The two heretofore separate groups now joined together and demanded the discharge of all the Macedonians. They insultingly told Alexander to continue his campaigns with his father Ammon, a mocking reference to his divine pretensions. When Alexander attempted to respond, he was repeatedly interrupted by shouts and the army quickly became insubordinate.

This mutiny must have frightened Alexander because for the first time both his officers and men of all ages had combined against him. He jumped down from his platform and, accompanied by the hypaspists, pointed out 13 of the most obvious agitators who were taken into custody for immediate execution. He then accused the soldiers of ingratitude, reminding them of their former glorious conquests and how he had shared their dangers and his treasure with them. He told the mutineers they could leave if they liked because he would now turn to the people he had conquered for support. Alexander then angrily left the assembly and secluded himself in his tent for the next two days.

On the third day after the mutiny, Alexander offered the Persians command of units formerly led by Macedonians and selected Persian troops to fill their ranks.

Persian counterparts to the hypaspists, Companion cavalry, phalanx, and Agema were now organized. The Persian commanders were to be treated as the king's equals, being allowed to greet him as a kinsman with a kiss. This proved to be too much for the Macedonians, who had thus far managed to maintain their solidarity. The leaders of the mutiny were dead, the army's wages were in arrears, and they realized the truthfulness of all Alexander had told them. They surrounded his tent, threw down their arms and refused to leave until he had accepted them back. Now that his army had submitted, Alexander was able to relent, and he forgave them in a tearful scene on both sides.

Soon after the incident Alexander threw a large banquet attended by 9,000.[15] The Macedonians were specially honored by being seated between the Persians and Alexander, in return for which they were to reconcile themselves with the Persians. When the festivities were over, 10,000 Macedonian infantry and 1,500 cavalry were mustered out of Alexander's Asian army.[16] They were to receive full combat pay throughout their journey home and an additional talent as severance pay, the equivalent of about 16 years' normal pay for most of the soldiers.[17] Children whose fathers had died while serving with Alexander were to receive their fathers' pay.

The departing troops were placed under the command of Craterus and on their return journey to Macedonia, were accompanied by a number of officers, including Polysperchon and Cleitus the White. Interestingly enough, because of alleged tensions that would be created in Macedonia, the Oriental wives of the soldiers and their children were to stay behind. Alexander promised the fathers that he would see to it that their offspring were brought up as Macedonians, with particular emphasis being given to their military training. It was thought that by this action Alexander intended to raise a kind of Praetorian Guard of 10,000 whose loyalty to him would be absolute.

On the face of it, the objection of Alexander's army to the dismissal of the disabled troops seems ridiculous. Not only were a number physically impaired but many were in their 60s and 70s and should have been glad to enjoy their remaining years among family and friends. Alexander was, after all, only complying with his soldiers' demand to return home that they had stated so adamantly at the Beas River. Their discharge bonus was extremely generous, and most of them could live very comfortably for the rest of their lives without ever having to work again. What then was their issue? The primary grievance of the soldiers was the steady erosion of their influence and prestige resulting from the increasing Orientalization of the Macedonian army. It was more a question of hurt feelings and the thought that after all they had given they were being discarded like some broken-down animal that had outlived its purpose. It was purely an emotional reaction to pent-up frustrations and the realization that Alexander was now a Persian rather than a Macedonian king. His army, however, seems to have quickly accepted the reality of the situation. When Alexander implemented the discharge, there were no further incidents.

For Alexander's motivation, we must also look deeper. Why would he take such an action just before a major campaign in Arabia where those veterans could have been put to good use? Alexander probably saw that the old-guard Macedonians were the last impediment to the creation of his Asian army. Many of the men to be discharged ranged from middle-age to elderly. They represented the generation of old Macedonia that continued to stubbornly oppose the Orientalization of his army. They would never accept serving alongside the despised Persians and would always actively resist Alexander's concept of an Asian army. Any success in this regard had to be predicated on their departure. Alexander clearly saw this, and when the dust settled the old-guard Macedonians probably saw it as well. A new, young, and eager generation of Macedonians had arrived, their enthusiasm doubtlessly stimulated by the glorious conquests of Alexander in Asia and the riches to be made there. As their elders passed the young recruits on their way to the rear, they must have seen reflections of themselves as they were when they had begun their great adventure. It was probably apparent that with their departure one era was ending and another beginning. The so-called Hellenistic era would open up the riches of Asia to Greece and stimulate trade and commerce in Asia as never before. It was an age of rising expectations and the last glorious resurgence of ancient Greece.

Appendix D: Hephaestion's Funeral

In 324 B.C., Hephaestion apparently contracted a severe fever as a result of drinking to excess at an all-night party in honor of Dionysus. Instead of following his doctor's advice for a cure, he resumed his drinking and unexpectedly died. Alexander's grief was overwhelming, as Hephaestion was both his "favorite" and his best friend. He lay upon Hephaestion's body in tears for an entire day and night and then stayed in mourning for another two days, going without food during the entire period. After either beheading or crucifying Hephaestion's unfortunate doctor, Alexander cut his own hair in his friend's memory, as did his ancestor Achilles upon Patroclus' death, and ordered the tails of all the horses in camp to be also cut short. The sacred fires in temples throughout his empire were ordered extinguished, an honor usually only reserved for the death of a Persian king. Determined to honor Hephaestion above all others, Alexander made plans to give him one of the most spectacular funerals in history.

Alexander ordered his empire to undergo a period of mourning. He sent orders to all the nearby cities and kingdoms for contributions. Macedonian officers of the army, foreign envoys, and natives all made massive donations to win Alexander's favor or to ensure their safety by openly demonstrating that they were not secretly pleased at Hephaestion's death. In any case, the gold poured in, and it is well that it did, for Hephaestion's funeral was reputed to have cost no less than 10,000 talents.

The scope of Hephaestion's projected funeral pyre was truly megalomanical. To accommodate the structure that was to be built, a quarter mile of Babylon's wall would have had to have been torn down. The edifice was to be about an eighth of a mile on a side and six stories tall. Projecting from the first story were to be the prows of 240 quinqueremes; upon each were to be placed full-sized figures of two archers and one armed soldier. Red banners were to be hung between the ships. The second story was to be surrounded by 22-foot-high torches. The base of the torch was to contain a golden wreath of entwined snakes, while eagles with outspread wings were to be perched behind the top of the torch containing the flame. Wild animals pursued by hunters were to be the motif of the third story. The fourth story was to contain scenes of golden centaurs, and the fifth, golden bulls and lions. The sixth story was to be covered with Macedonian and Persian arms. The top of the structure was to be ringed with hollowed-out statues of Sirens, inside of which a choir would continually bemoan the untimely death of Hephaestion.[18]

Over 3,000 competitors were to engage in a gymnastic and music festival that would accompany Hephaestion's funeral, and 10,000 animals were to be sacrificed on his behalf.[19] It is thought that Alexander intended to build a permanent ziggurat in Babylonia as a lasting memorial to his beloved friend on an even grander scale than his funeral pyre. It is extremely doubtful, however, that Hephaestion's funeral monument was ever built. Not only did the time span between his friend's death and Alexander's return to Babylon all but preclude the construction of a gigantic structure, no trace of it has yet been found in the ruins of Babylon. Despite Diodorus' claim that the structure was actually built, it is likely that by the time of Alexander's death perhaps only a portion of the materials had been gathered at the site.[20]

Appendix E: Mileage of Alexander's Campaigns

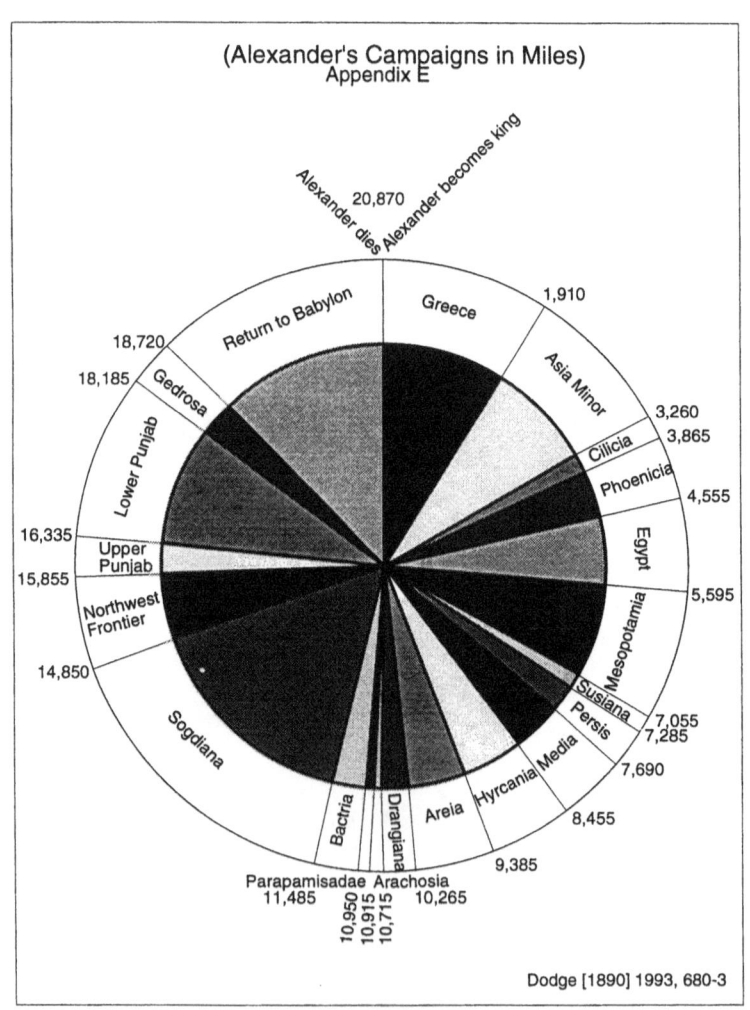

Appendix F: Alexander's Income and Expenses

Macedonian Income

The royal income from Macedonia proper was a mere 200 talents annually, derived almost totally from the land tax. Because of the heavy burden of military service imposed on the peasants, the tax rate could not be increased. The northern coastline of Macedonian was relatively unprotected from southwest gales or from the northern Etesian Winds, making shipping extremely hazardous. If this wasn't bad enough, sandbars off the mouths of the major rivers often caused heavy damage to any ships attempting to cross them. As a result, Macedonia's development of waterborne commerce was greatly restricted, and the country was only able to derive about 40 talents annually from import and export taxes.[21] From the conquered territories—the Chersonese, Thessaly, and Thrace—a tribute of one-tenth of the harvest was usually levied.[22] The Chalcidice included significant deposits of gold, silver, copper, iron ore, lead, and large stands of timber.[23]

When the Asyla mining district, just east of Crenidas in Thrace, was acquired by Philip, it eventually generated revenues of 1,000 talents annually.[24] This new income, however, was almost exclusively used to expand the Macedonian army, which grew so rapidly that the mining revenues covered less than one-third its annual wages.[25] Much of the remaining shortage of funds had to be made up from loot acquired on the various campaigns. When Philip died, he left Alexander a debt of over 500 talents and the pay of the army seriously in arrears.[26] To exacerbate the situation, Alexander upon becoming king abolished direct taxation in Macedonia.[27] This precipitated a financial crisis. It was clear that Alexander was faced with one of two choices, either reducing the size of his army or seeking out additional revenues from somewhere outside the state to pay for its continued maintenance. Alexander, of course, chose the latter option and looked to his campaign against the Persian Empire in Asia as a solution to his financial problems.

The sale of captives from Alexander's Balkan campaign largely eliminated the debt Philip had left behind him.[28] Alexander's council agreed that his invasion of Asia could not be postponed beyond the spring of 334 B.C.; otherwise he would be faced with bankruptcy and would then see his army dissolve when his soldiers' pay again slipped into arrears. Meantime, for the next six months, money had to be found to pay the troops. Only Athens could loan Alexander the money he needed, but considering its animosity towards Macedonia, this was clearly not going to be a viable option. The only other recourse left to Alexander was to borrow from his Companions and sign his crown lands over to them as collateral for the debt. He managed to raise 800 talents in this way.[29] When this had been done, Perdiccas asked him what he had left for himself. Alexander was said to have answered, "hopes."[30] Perdiccas then told him that was also good enough for him. Although Alexander had managed to pay off all his debts, when he sailed for Asia his treasury contained only a paltry 60 talents.[31] This would pay his troops for two weeks and purchase about a month's provisions for his army. Alexander's Asian campaign was starting out on a very shaky financial base.

Persian Income

Alexander captured much booty on his campaigns in the Persian Empire. The following list includes some duplicate entries to show how various ancient writers stated Alexander's income.

- At Egypt, Mazaces surrendered the Egyptian treasury of 800 talents (Curtius IV:7).
- At Issus, 3,000 talents were captured from Darius' baggage train (Arrian II:11).
- At Gaugamela, 2,600 talents in coined money and 500 pounds in wrought silver were captured from Darius' baggage train (Curtius III:13).
- At Gaugamela, 4,000 talents were captured from Darius' baggage train (Curtius V:1).
- At Susa, Alexander captured 50,000 talents in silver ingots from the Persian treasury there (Arrian III:16; Curtius V:2).
- At Susa, Alexander captured 40,000 talents in bullion and 9,000 talents in gold darics from the Persian treasury there (Diodorus XVII:66).
- At Susa, Alexander captured 40,000 talents from the Persian treasury there (Justin XI:14; Plutarch, 558).
- At Persepolis, Alexander captured 120,000 talents from the Persian treasury there (Curtius V:6; Diodorus XVII:71).
- At Pasargadae, Alexander captured 6,000 talents from the Persian treasury there (Curtius V:6).
- At Media, Alexander was said to have amassed 26,000 talents from recent booty (Curtius VI:2).
- At Hyrcania, mention was made of 21,000 talents obtained from plunder (Diodorus XVII:74).
- In the pursuit of Darius, Alexander was said to have come into possession of 8,000 talents (Diodorus XVII:74).
- Orsines presented Alexander with 3,000 talents in silver coin (Curtius III:13; X:24).
- The annual income derived from the Persian Empire about the time of its invasion of Greece, which excluded India, amounted to about 16,000 talents.[32] Alexander used what the Great King's subjects had customarily paid him as the basis

for determining the tribute he required of them, usually without any change (Arrian I:17).

Satrapy Number	Talents	Areas
1	400	Aeolians, Carians, Ionians, Lycians Magnesians, Milyans, and Pamphylians
2	500	Cabalians, Hygennians, Lasonians, Lydians, and Mysians
3	360	Asiatic Thracians, Hellespontians, Mariandynians, Paphlagonians, Phrygians, and Syrians
4	500	Cilicians
5	350	Country from Posideium to the borders of Egypt (includes Cyprus, Palestine, Phoenicia, and Syria)
6	700	Egypt and Libya
7	170	Aparytae, Dadicae, Gandarians, and Sattagydians
8	300	Susa and other parts of Cassia
9	9,540	Babylonia and the rest of Assyria (1,000 talents are reduced to the Euboic scale)
10	450	Agbatana and other parts of Media, together with the Orthocorybantes and Paricanians
11	200	Caspians, Daritae, Pausicae, and Pantimathi
12	360	Bactrian tribes
13	400	Armenia, Pactyica, and the countries reaching to the Euxine
14	600	The islands in the Erythraean Sea, Mycians, Sarangians, Sagartians, Thamanaeans, and Utians
15	250	Caspians and Sacans
16	300	Arians, Chorasmians, Parthians, and Sogdians
17	400	Ethiopians of Asia and Paricanians
18	200	Alarodians, Matienians, and Saspeires
19	300	Macrones, Mares, Moschi, Mosynoeci, and Tibareni
Total	16,280	

Indian Income

The Persians had collected about 4,680 talents annually from the western area of India under their control. In the campaign of virtual extermination that Alexander waged against the Indians, however, he was able to derive little, if anything, in the way of income from the area. As a result, soon after entering India, he was forced to request loans again from among his friends. This was mostly a logistics problem, however, because apparently none of Alexander's treasure at Ecbatana was being transported to India.

Spending

However great his income, Alexander's spending was also of monumental proportions. Again, the following listing has some duplicate entries to show the reader how various ancient and modern writers have stated Alexander's expenditures.

Gordium   500 talents given to Amphoterus, in command of a fleet at the Hellespont, and Hegelochus, in command of the land forces at the Hellespont, and 600 talents to Antipater, who was to raise ships to be sent to the Hellespont. (Curtius III:3).

Phoenicia   3,000 talents given to Menes, who was governor of Cilicia, Phoenicia, and Syria, to be sent to Antipater for his campaign against Sparta (Arrian III:16).

Memphis   1,000 talents given to Apollodorus, of Amphipolis, and Menes, of Pella, both military governors at Babylon, as well as to other satrapies as far away as Cilicia to enlist as many soldiers in their service as possible (Diodorus XVII:64).

Gaugamela   6 mina given to each cavalryman, 5 mina to each allied cavalryman, 2 mina to each phalanx soldier, and two months pay to each mercenary (Diodorus XVII:64).

Babylon   600 drachma given to each Macedonian cavalryman, 500 drachma to each mercenary cavalryman, 200 drachma to each Macedonian infantryman, and two months' pay to each mercenary (Curtius V:1).

3,000 talents given to Menes to be forwarded to Antipater for the war with Sparta (Arrian III:16).

1,000 talents given to Menes, satrap of Babylonia, and Apollodorus, satrap of Cilicia (Curtius V:1).

1,000 talents given to Apollodorus, of Amphipolis, and Menes, of Pella, both appointed military governors of Babylon, and other satraps as far away as Cilicia for use in raising troops (Diodorus XVII:64).

Hyrcania   12,000 talents distributed as a largess to the Macedonian army (Curtius VI:2).

12,000 talents were embezzled from Alexander (Curtius VI:2).

Persepolis   2,000 talents given to 4,000 Greek prisoners who had been tortured and disabled by the Persians (Curtius V:5).

3,000 drachma given to 800 elderly mutilated Greeks who had been carried off to Persepolis by the Persians when they had invaded Greece (Diodorus XVII:69)

Ecbatana   2,000 talents given to the Thessalian cavalry and the Greek allies as a severance bonus (Arrian III:19).

One talent given to each Greek cavalryman dismissed and 10 mina to each allied Greek infantryman dismissed. Three talents were given to any of those mustered out who chose to remain with the army as mercenaries (Diodorus XVII:74).

13,000 talents distributed to the soldiers. One talent was given to each cavalryman and 10 mina to each infantryman. A bonus of three talents was given to all troops mustered out who decided to remain with the army (Diodorus XVII:74).

Media   13,000 talents given to those who participated in the pursuit of Darius (Justin XIII:1).

12,000 talents given as a largess to Alexander's soldiers (Curtius VI:2).

Over 12,000 talents embezzled by those in charge of Alexander's treasury (Curtius VI:2).

Indus River 200 talents presented to Alexander by Taxiles (Arrian V:3).

Sogdiana Two talents given to each cavalryman and 3,000 drachma to each infantryman at the Oxus River (Curtius VII:24).

One talent given to each cavalryman and 1,000 drachma to each infantryman mustered out of the army (Curtius VI:2).

A one talent gratuity given to Macedonians unfit for service because of old age or wounds (Arrian VII:11).

Taxila 1,000 talents given to Taxiles (Curtius VIII:12).

80 talents in silver coin given to Alexander by Taxiles as a gift (Curtius VIII:12).

Susa 20,000 talents used to pay off the Macedonian army's personal debts. (Arrian VII:5; Justin XII:11).

10,000 talents used to pay off the army's personal debts (Diodorus XVII:109).

9,870 talents used to pay off the army's personal debts (Curtius X:2; Plutarch, 573).

An unknown dowry given to 80 noble Persian women and 10,000 women of the people (Bury, Cook, and Adcock [1927] 1978, 428; Fuller 1958, 274).

Golden crowns of an unknown value given to those who had distinguished themselves by bravery (Arrian VII:5).

Golden crowns valued at 15,000 talents awarded to Alexander's generals (Fuller 1958, 274).

Opis One talent given to each of the 10,000 infantry veterans discharged (Arrian VII:2; Curtius X:2).

Babylon 10,000 talents allocated to pay for Hephaestion's funeral (Arrian VII:14; Plutarch, 574).

12,000 talents collected to pay for Hephaestion's funeral (Curtius X:4; Justin XII:12).

5,000 talents stolen by Harpalus (Curtius X:1).

10,000 drachmas a day spent for Alexander's table (Plutarch 551).

20 talents a day or about 75,000 talents over Alexander's 11 years' campaigning in Asia spent as wages for his field army.

10,000 talents allocated for the restoration of Greek temples (Bury, Cook, and Adcock [1927] 1978, XIII:428).

800 talents given to Aristotle for research (Curtius I).

Six great temples were to be built at a cost of 1,500 talents each (Bosworth 1988, 164-65; Hammond and Walbank 1988, 20).

A tomb for Philip was to be built on the scale of the great pyramid at an unknown cost (Bosworth 1988, 164).

In less than a decade, Alexander had spent a large portion of the money that the Persians had taken several generations to accumulate. It is said that at the end of Alexander's reign his treasury had been reduced to 50,000 talents.[33] Alexander had obviously spent profligately, but he could afford to do so. This pace, however, could not have been continued indefinitely, and had Alexander lived longer and kept to these spending habits, he would have begun to run a deficit, probably within the next five years. Alexander's massive spending did fuel a prosperity that the Greeks and Persians had never known. Coinage circulated freely, and trade was stimulated both by the new cities Alexander founded and the new opportunities his empire offered. Asia had never experienced anything like it before, and in the process many economies were transformed from an agrarian base to one where trade and commerce flourished.

Appendix G: Alexander's Funeral Train

The funeral train that eventually conveyed Alexander's corpse to Egypt has never been surpassed for either its scale or magnificence. The coach itself took two years to build. The carriage platform was 12 feet wide and 18 feet long. A pavilion was supported by several Ionic columns. Each of the four panels on the sides of the carriage had a different raised motif: the first showed Alexander in a chariot attended by Macedonian and Persian bodyguards; the second, Indian war elephants; the third, cavalry in line of battle; and the fourth, a fleet of ships. The open spaces between the columns were draped with golden netting that protected the sarcophagus from sun and rain but allowed it to be clearly viewed. At the corners of the carriage, a golden victory held out a trophy. A pair of golden lions guarded the entrance of the inner chamber, in the rear of which sat an empty throne on which hung crowns representing all the nations that Alexander had conquered. At the foot of the throne lay a solid gold sarcophagus containing Alexander's preserved body. It is said that 300 years later when Alexander's face was viewed through the colored glass of his sarcophagus, it still retained its handsome features. Alexander's weapons were spread out over a cloth of gold-embroidered purple. A team of 64 mules pulled the train grouped in sets of four. The animals were specially selected for both their size and strength.

Virtually everything on the funeral train was overlaid with gold: the axles, the spokes of the wheels, the carriage, the columns, and even the mules. The axles of the wheels were capped in lion heads holding spears in their teeth. The top of the pavilion was surrounded by a golden cornice embossed with ibex heads. A garland ran though golden rings hung from the noses of the ibex on which bells were hung, ringing continuously with the motion of the coach. The collar and harness of each mule was covered with gold and precious stones, a gilded crown, and a golden bell.

Alexander's dying request was to be buried at the temple of Ammon in the oasis of Siwah. The distance from Babylon to Egypt was about 1,000 miles. Huge numbers of workmen repaired roads, strengthened bridges, and leveled any obstacles along the route of the funeral train. Huge crowds came out to see the funeral train, not wanting to miss such a grand and historic event. One eyewitness stated that the carriage was too magnificent to describe with words. The funeral train proceeded along the road, covering from five to fifteen miles a day, depending upon the difficulty of the terrain and the weather.

After a journey of about three months, the funeral train finally reached Egypt. It was met by Ptolemy, one of Alexander's generals now ruling the country. He immediately saw the political benefits of burying Alexander at Alexandria, his new capital. The funeral car was moved to Memphis (modern Cairo), where it lay for several years while Alexander's tomb (or Soma) was being built. Julius Caesar is said to have visited the tomb, as did Augustus. In 89 B.C., however, Ptolemy IX melted down the gold sarcophagus, turning it into coin to pay for an army of mercenaries used against his own rebellious Egyptian army. Alexander's body appears to have disappeared during the city riots that occurred in the latter half of the third century A.D. and was never seen again.

Appendix H: Kings and Satraps

Satrapy	King/Satrap	Reason Left Office	Ancient References
Arabia (east of the Nile R.)	•Cleomenes		Arrian III:5
	•Apollonius		Curtius IV:8
Arachosia	•Barsaentes	Revolted against Alexander	Arrian III:8,21; Curtius VIII:12
	•Menon	Fell ill and died	Arrian III:28; Curtius VII:3; IX:10
	•Sibyrtius		Arrian V:6; VI:27; Curtius IX:10
Areia	•Satibarzanes	Revolted and killed in battle by Erigyius	Arrian III:8,25,28; Curtius VI:6; VII:4; Diodorus XVII:78,83
	•Arsames	Removed for ill-will towards towards Alexander	Arrian III:25,29
	•Stasanor		Arrian III:29; IV:18; VI:27
Armenia	•Mithrines		Arrian III:16; Curtius II; V:1; Diodorus XVII:64
Babylonia	•Mazaeus	Died	Arrian III:16; IV:18; VII:18; Curtius IV:9; V:1; VIII:3; X:1
	•Harpalus		Curtius X:1
	•Stamenes		Arrian IV:18; Curtius VIII:3
Bactria	•Bessus	Revolted against Alexander, proclaiming himself Darius III's successor	Arrian III:8,21; Curtius V:6,8,9; Diodorus XVII:73-4
	•Artabazus	Retired due to old age	Arrian III:29; IV:15,17; Curtius VIII:1
	•Cleitus the Black	Murdered by Alexander in a drunken rage	Curtius VIII:1
	•Amyntas (son of Nicolaus)		Arrian IV:17; Curtius VIII:2
	•Oxyartes		Curtius IX:8
Cappadocia (north)	•Mithobuzanes	Killed at Granicus River	Arrian I:16; Curtius II; Diodorus XVII:21

APPENDIX H

Satrapy	King/Satrap	Reason Left Office	Ancient References
Cappadocia (south)	•Sabiktas		Arrian II:4
	•Sabistamenes		Curtius III:4
Caria	•Orontobates		Arrian I:23
	•Ada (daughter of Hecatomnus)		Arrian I:23; Curtius II; Diodorus XVII:24
Carmania	•Astaspes	Removed for suspicion of wanting to revolt while Alexander was in India	Curtius IX:10
	•Sibyrtius		Arrian VI:27
	•Tlepolemus (son of Phthophanes)		Arrian VI:27
Cilicia	•Arsames		Curtius III:4
	•Socrates		Curtius IV:5
	•Balacrus (son of Nicanor)	Killed in a skirmish with the Pisidians and Isaurians	Arrian II:12
Cilicia, Phoenicia, and Syria	•Menes (son of Dionysius)		Arrian III:16
Drangiana	•Barsaentes		Arrian III:21; Curtius VI:6
	•Arsames		Curtius VII:2; VIII:3
	•Stasanor		Arrian IV:18; Curtius VIII:3
	•Menon		Arrian III:28
Egypt	•Sabaces	Killed at Granicus River	Arrian II:11
	•Sabaces	Killed at Issus	Curtius III:11; IV:1
	•Amyntas	Killed in Egypt	Diodorus XVII:48
	•Aeschylus & Peucestas		Curtius IV:8
	•Tasiaces	Killed at Issus	Diodorus XVII:34,48
	•Mazaces		Arrian III:1
	•Doloaspis & Petisis		Arrian III:5
Gedrosa	•Tiridates		Diodorus XVII:81
	•Apollophanes	Killed in a revolt against Alexander	Arrian VIII:23; VI:27
	•Thoas	Fell ill and died	Arrian VI:27
	•Menon	Fell ill and died	Arrian III:28; Curtius IX:10
	•Sibyrtius		Arrian VI:27; Curtius IX:10
Hellespontine Phrygia	•Arsites	Committed suicide shortly after Granicus River	Arrian I:12
	•Calas (son of Harpalus)		Arrian I:17; Curtius II; III:1
Hindu Kush (Caucasus)	•Proexes		Arrian III:28

APPENDIX H

Satrapy	King/Satrap	Reason Left Office	Ancient References
Hyrcania	•Phradates	Removed from office for greed and tyranny	Curtius VIII:3
	•Phraphernes		Arrian III:22; V:20; VI:27; VII:6; Curtius VIII:3
	•Amminaspes	Removed from office	Arrian III:22; Curtius VI:4
Ionia	•Spithridates	Killed at Granicus River	Arrian I:12; Curtius II; Diodorus XVII:19,20
	•Asandrus (son of Philotas)		Arrian I:17
India			
West of the Indus	•Philip (son of Machatas)	Assassinated by mercenaries	Arrian V:8; VI:2,15,27; VIII:19; Curtius X:1
	•Nicanor		Arrian IV:28
	•Eudamus (Thracian general)		Arrian VI:27
Northern Punjab	•Porus		Arrian V:29; VI:2; Curtius VIII:14; Diodorus XVII:89,91
Southern Punjab	•Oxyartes/Peitho		Arrian VI:15
Hindu Kush	•Abisares	Died a natural death	Arrian V:29; Curtius X:1
Kashmir	•Proexes		Arrian III:28
Punjab	•Taxiles		Arrian V:8
Swat	•Taxiles/Eudamus		Arrian VI:27
Taxila	•Mophis/Taxiles		Diodorus XVII:86
	•Omphis (Taxiles)		Curtius VIII:12
Libya	•Apollonius (son of Charinus)		Arrian III:5; Curtius IV:8
Lycia	•Nearchus		Arrian III:6
Lydia	•Spithridates	Killed at Granicus River	Arrian I:12,16; Curtius II
	•Asandrus (son of Philotas)		Arrian I:17
	•Asander		Curtius II
	•Menon (son of Kerdimmas)		Arrian III:6
	•Antigonus		Curtius II; IV:1
Media	•Mazaeus	Died	Curtius VIII:3
	•Oxodates	Removed for ill will towards Alexander	Arrian III:20; IV:18: Curtius VI:2; VIII:3
	•Arsaces		Curtius VIII:3
	•Parmenio		Diodorus XVII:80
	•Atropates		Arrian IV:18; VI:29; VII:4,13; Curtius X:4
	•Baryaxes	A pretender who was executed	Arrian VI:29
Paphlagonia	•Calas (son of Harpalus)		Arrian II:4; Curtius III:1

APPENDIX H

Satrapy	King/Satrap	Reason Left Office	Ancient References
Paraetacae	•Chorienes		Arrian IV:21
	•Oxathres (son of Abulites)	Executed for abuse of his office	Arrian III:19; VII:4
Parapamisadae (Hindu Kush)	•Turiaspes (Tiryaspes)	Removed for conducting his office in a disorderly manner	Arrian IV:22; VI:15
	•Terioltes	Put to death for greed and corruption	Curtius IX:8
	•Oxyartes		Arrian VI:15; Curtius VIII:4
Parthyaea	•Phrataphernes		Arrian III:23,28; IV:7,18; V:20; VI:27; VII:6; Curtius IX:10
	•Barzanes	Executed	Arrian IV:7
	•Amminaspes	Removed for being unable to prevent Bessus from instigating a revolt in his province	Arrian III:22
Persis	•Ariobarzanes		Arrian III:18
	•Orxines	Hanged for robbing tombs and executing Persians without just cause	Arrian VI:29,30
	•Peucestas (son of Alexandros)		Arrian VI:28,30; VII:6
Phrygia	•Ariobarzanes		Diodorus XVII:17
	•Atizues		Arrian I:25
	•Antigonus (son of Philip)		Arrian I:29; Curtius II
	•Arsites		Curtius II
	•Atizues	Committed suicide, as he blamed himself for the Persian defeat at Granicus River	Curtius II
	•Calas (son of Harpalus)		Arrian II:4; Curtius II; III:1
Sogdiana	•Oxyartes		Curtius VIII:4
Susiana	•Abulites		Diodorus XVII: 65
	•Abulites	Executed for abuse of power	Arrian III:16; VII:4; Curtius V:2
Syria	•Mazaeus		Curtius V:13
	•Arimmas	Failed to adequately prepare for Alexander's march to the Euphrates River	Arrian III:6
	•Asclepiodorus (son of Eunicus)		Arrian III:6; IV:13
	•Andromachus	Burnt alive by the Samaritans	Curtius IV:8
	•Menon		Curtius IV:8

APPENDIX H

Satrapy	King/Satrap	Reason Left Office	Ancient References
Syria (Coele)	•Parmenio		Curtius IV:1,5
	•Andromachus	Burnt alive by the Samaritans	Curtius IV:5
	•Menon (son of Kerdimmas)		Curtius IV:8
Syria (lowland)	•Mazaeus		Curtius V:13
	•Memnon (son of Kerdimmas)		Arrian II:13
Agrianes	•Langaros		Arrian I:5

Tribes	King/Ruler	Reason Left Office	Ancient References
Amazons	•Thalestris/Minithya		Justin: XII:3
	•Thalestris		Diodorus XVII:77
Arimaspians (Benefactors)	•Tiridates		Diodorus XVII: 81
	•Amedines		Curtius VII:3
Assacenians	•Sisicottus	Assassinated by Assacenians	Arrian V:20
Chorasinians	•Pharasmanes		Arrian IV:15
	•Phrataphernes		Curtius VIII:1
Dardanians	•Bardylis		Arrian I:5
	•Cleitus		Arrian I:5
Gangaridae	•Aggrammes		Curtius IX:2
Malli	•Philip (Son of Machatas)		Arrian VI:14
Mardi	•Phradates	Removed from office for greed and tyranny	Curtius VIII:3
	•Autophradates		Arrian III:24; IV:18
	•Phrataphernes		Curtius VIII:3
Oreitae	•Apollophanes	Killed in a revolt. Removed for neglecting orders	Arrian VI:22,27
	•Thoas (son of Mandrodorus)	Died of an illness	Arrian VI:27
	•Sibyrtius		Arrian VI:27
Oxydracae	•Philip (son of Machatas)		Arrian VI:14
Paeonians	•Agis		Diodorus XVI:4
Pattala	•Soeris		Curtius IX:8
	•Aggrammes		Curtius IX:1

APPENDIX H

Tribes	King/Satrap	Reason Left Office	Ancient References
Tapuria	•Phradates	Removed from office for greed and tyranny	Curtius VI:4; VIII:3
	•Autophradates		Arrian III:23
	•Phratapherenes		Curtius VIII:3
	•Autophradates		Arrian III:24; IV:18
Taulantians	•Glaucias		Arrian I:5
Triballians	•Syrmus		Arrian I:2-4; Curtius I
Scythians	•Atheas		Justin IX:2
Uxians	•Medates		Curtius V:3

Cities	King/Ruler	Reason Left Office	Ancient References
Aradus	•Gerostratus		Arrian II:13,20
	•Straton (son of Gerostratus)		Arrian II:13
	•Straton		Curtius IV:1
Byblos	•Euylos		Arrian II:20
Ephesus	•Syrphax	Stoned to death by the city's democrats	Arrian I:17
Gaza	•Batis	Dragged to death behind Alexander's chariot	Arrian II:25; Curtius IV:6
Marathus	•Straton (son of Gerostratus)		Arrian II:13
Memphis	•Mazaces		Curtius IV:7
Methymna	•Aristonicus		Curtius IV:5
Miletus	•Hydarnes		Curtius IV:5
	•Hegesistratus		Arrian I:18
Nautaca	•Sisimithres		Curtius VIII:2
Nysa	•Acuphis		Arrian V:1
Pasargadae	•Gobares		Curtius V:6
Persepolis	•Phrasaortes (son of Rheomithres)		Arrian III:18
	•Tiridates		Diodorus XVII:69
Peucelaotis	•Astes	Killed in the siege of Peucelaotis	Arrian IV:22
	•Sangaeus		Arrian IV:22
Sardis	•Mithrines		Arrian I:17; Curtius II; V:1; Diodorus XVII:21,64

APPENDIX H 391

Cities	King/Ruler	Reason Left Office	Ancient References
Sidon	•Straton	Removed as he had submitted not by his own inclination but by that of his people	Curtius IV:1
	•Abdalonymus		Curtius IV:1; Justin XI
Susa	•Archelaus		Curtius V:2
Tyre	•Azemilcus		Arrian II:24
	•Straton	Deposed because of his friendship for Darius	Diodorus XVII:47
	•Philotas (son of Parmenio)		Curtius IV:5
	•Ballonymus		Diodorus XVII:46

Appendix I: Chronology of the Macedonian Empire

A number of dates, especially in Philip II's reign, are only approximate.

1193	•Agamemnon's siege of Troy begins
515	•Darius I expands the eastern border of the Persian Empire to the Indus River
513	•Darius I's campaign against the Scythians ends in his defeat
437	•Amphipolis is founded by Athens
432	•The Chalcidian League is formed
401	•Artaxerxes II defeats the revolt of his brother, Cyrus the Younger, at Cunaxa, 75 miles northwest of Babylon
	•Cyrus the Younger, the brother of Artaxerxes II, is killed at the battle at Cunaxa
397	•Dionysius I of Syracuse besieges and captures Motya, a Carthaginian-held city in Sicily
384	•Demosthenes is born
382	•Sparta seizes the Cadmea at Thebes
	•Philip II is born
	•The Chalcidians capture Pella
374	•Jason, tyrant of Pherae, proclaims himself Tagus of Thessaly
371	•Epaminondas of Thebes defeats Sparta at the battle of Leuctra, in southern Boeotia (Jul)
370	•A Theban army under Epaminondas invades the Peloponnese
	•Philip recognizes the claim of Athens to Amphipolis
	•Jason, Tagus of Thessaly, is assassinated
368	•The city of Megalopolis, in Arcadia, is founded
	•Alexander, tyrant of Pherae, succeeds Jason as Tagus of Thessaly.
	•Philip is taken to Thebes as a hostage, at the age of 15
366	•A Greek congress confirms the Athenian claim to Amphipolis
365	•Athens occupies Samos
362	•Epaminondas defeats Sparta at the battle of Mantineia, in Arcadia (summer)
	•Epaminondas is killed at the battle of Mantineia
	•Ariobarzanes, the Persian satrap of Dascylium, dies
361	•Athens sends cleruchs to Potidaea
360	•Cotys, king of the Odrysian Thracians, is assassinated
359	•Perdiccas III, king of Macedonia, is defeated by the Dardanians under Bardylis (early spring/summer)

APPENDIX I 393

- Perdiccas III, King of Macedonia and Philip's brother, is killed in battle with the Illyrians

Reign of Philip II

359
- Cersobleptes, king of eastern Thrace, invades western Thrace
- Philip escapes from Thebes and assumes the Macedonian throne (summer)
- Philip marries his daughter Cynna to Amyntas
- Philip withdraws Macedonian troops from Amphipolis
- Argaios marches on Aegae in an unsuccessful attempt to assume the Macedonian throne
- Philip defeats Argaeus, a pretender to his throne, near Methone
- Philip signs a treaty with Bardylis
- Philip marries Audata (daughter of Bardylis)
- Artabazus, satrap of Phrygia, revolts from the Persian Empire
- Alexander, Tagus of Thessaly, is murdered by his wife Thebe and her brothers Tisiphonus, Peitholaus, and Lycophron
- Agis, king of Paeonia, dies

358
- Philip campaigns against the Paeonians (spring)
- Philip marries Philinna of Larisa
- Artaxerxes III (Ochus) assumes the Persian throne
- Philip campaigns against the Dardanians (spring)
- Philip annexes upper Macedonia
- Philip defeats Bardylis' Illyrians in the battle of Erigon Valley
- The Thessalian League requests Philip's aid
- Philip enters Thessaly (autumn)
- Arrhidaeus, the future Philip IV, is born

357
- The Social War begins when Chios, Cos, and Rhodes revolt from Athens
- Philip allies himself with Epirus
- Berisades, king of western Thrace, dies
- Audata, Philip's wife, dies (spring)
- The Chalcidian League allies with Grabos of the Illyrians (summer)
- Neoptolemus, king of Molossia, dies
- Athens is defeated by its revolting allies at Chios (summer)
- Philip allies himself with the three Thracian kings
- Philip captures Crenidas, in Thrace, renaming it Philippi
- Upon the death of Neoptolemus, king of Molossia, Arybbas, his brother, becomes regent for the dead king's adolescent son, Alexander of Molossia
- Philip captures Amphipolis by assault (late summer)
- Philip marries Olympias, daughter of Neoptolemus, the king of Epirus (autumn)
- Athens captures Euboea from Thebes
- Athens rejects a Chalcidian request for an alliance
- Philip allies himself with the Chalcidian League
- Philip captures Potidaea
- Philip turns Potidaea and Anthemus over to the Chalcidice League
- Philip defeats Lycophron in Thessaly
- Philip captures Pydna by treachery (winter)

APPENDIX I

- Athens declares war on Philip for backing out of the commitment he made to her on Amphipolis (late)
- Athens drives the Thebans out of Euboea

356
- Philip captures Apollonia, Galepsus, and Oisyme
- Philip annexes Amphipolis
- The Amphictyonic Council passes a decree threatening a sacred war against Phocis if the fine previously levied against her is not immediately paid (spring)
- Cersobleptes, Lyppeius, and Grabos form a northern coalition against Philip (spring)
- Cersobleptes prepares to break his alliances with Athens (May)
- Berisades makes an alliance with Lyppeius, king of Paeonia, against Philip (summer)
- Alexander the Great is born (July)
- Philip defeats Paeonia
- Philip defeats the northern coalition
- Philip occupies Crenidas, in Thrace
- Chares, an Athenian general in command of a mercenary army, takes service with Artabazus in Asia Minor
- Athens joins the northern coalition against Philip (July)
- Parmenio defeats Grabos in Illyria (Aug/Sep)
- Crenidas appeals to Philip for assistance against Cersobleptes
- Philip annexes Thessaly
- Philip founds Philippopolis
- Philomelus allies Phocis with Athens and Sparta (late)
- Sestos revolts from Athens

355
- Chares wins a victory in behalf of Artabazus, satrap of Phrygia, against Artaxerxes III (early)
- The Social War ends when Athens grants her former allies their independence (summer)
- Cleopatra, Alexander's sister, is born
- Philomelus occupies Delphi (May)
- Larisa, in Thessaly, appeals to Philip for assistance
- Philomelus defeats the Locrians of Amphissa at Delphi
- Philomelus heavily defeats the Thessalians
- The Amphictyonic Council declares a sacred war on Phocis (autumn)
- Philomelus campaigns in eastern Locris (autumn)
- Philip begins the siege of Methone (winter)

354
- Philip captures Pagasae (spring)
- Philomelus successfully campaigns in eastern Locris, winning a battle against a Boeotian/Locrian army (spring)
- Philomelus defeats a 6,000-strong force sent by the Thessalian League at Argolas Ridge (spring)
- Philomelus, the Phocian army commander, is killed at Neon
- As a result of the Thessalian defeat at Argolas Ridge, the Thessalian League allies itself with Philip, while Lycophron allies himself with Athens (spring)
- Cersobleptes allies himself with Philip (summer/autumn)
- Xenophon, an Athenian general and historian, dies at Corinth
- Timotheus, an Athenian admiral, dies at Chalcis

APPENDIX I

- Philip captures Methone (summer)
- Philip loses an eye during the siege of Methone (summer)
- Philomelus is defeated by the Boeotians at Neon (summer)
- Philip captures Abdera and Maronea (late summer)
- Philip enters Thessaly and subdues Perrhaebia (autumn)
- Chares unsuccessfully attempts to ambush Philip's small fleet at Neapolis

353
- Onomarchus invades eastern Locris, capturing Thronium and Amphissa (early spring)
- Cersobleptes allies himself again with Athens (early spring)
- Mausolus, king of Caria, dies
- Pammenes leads a 5,000-strong Theban army into Asia Minor in support of the revolt of Artabazus, the Persian satrap of Phrygia (spring)
- Philip allies himself with the Boeotian League (spring)
- Onomarchus invades Doris
- Olynthus requests an alliance with Athens
- Onomarchus invades Boeotia, capturing Orchomenus but failing to take Chaeronea
- Athens sends cleruchs to the Chersonese
- Philip campaigns in Thessaly in support the Thessalian League (summer)
- Cersobleptes cedes the Chersonese to Athens
- Chares captures Sestos (summer)
- Onomarchus is defeated near Chaeronea (August)
- Lycophron requests Phocian assistance against Philip and in response an army of 7,000 is sent under Phayllus, Onomarchus' brother. It is, however, defeated by Philip and driven out of Thessaly.
- Onomarchus defeats Philip in two battles, forcing his withdrawal from Thessaly (autumn)
- Philip besieges Heraion Teichos, in Thrace (Nov)

352
- The tyrants surrender Pherae to Philip and are expelled from Thessaly (early spring)
- Onomarchus invades Boeotia and captures Coronea, Corsiae, and Thiphosaion
- The Boeotians are defeated by Onomarchus at Narycara
- Philip annexes western Thrace from Berisades
- Onomarchus sustains three defeats by the Boeotian army at Orchomenus, Cephissus River, and Coronea
- Byzantium, Macedonia, Perinthus, and Amadocus form an alliance against Cersobleptes (May)
- Onomarchus invades eastern Locris
- Artabazus and Memnon take refuge with Philip after their unsuccessful rebellion against the Persian king
- Philip marries Nicesipolis of Pherae (summer)
- The Boeotians invades Phocis
- Philip returns Heraion to Perinthus
- The Thracian kingdoms are forced to submit to Macedonia
- Philip is elected Archon of Thessaly
- Philip defeats Onomarchus at the battle of Crocus Field, in Thessaly (spring/early summer)

- Onomarchus, commander of the Phocian army, is killed at the battle of Crocus Fields
- Philip captures Pagasae (early summer)
- The Chalcidian League makes peace with Athens (summer)
- Philip advances on Thermopylae but finding it strongly occupied against him marches off to Thrace (Jul)
- Philip signs a peace treaty with Olynthus (autumn)
- Phayllus invades Boeotia and is defeated near Orchomenus, Cephissus, and Coronea (autumn)
- Philip annexes the Thessalian districts of Perhaebia and Magnesia
- Phayllus invades eastern Locris and captures all the towns there except Naryx
- Phayllus encamps near Abae and is defeated in a night attack by the Boeotians
- The Boeotians invade Phocis
- The Boeotians, returning from Phocis, attempt to relieve Naryx but are defeated by Phayllus who then storms, captures, and razes the city
- Philip campaigns against Arybbas, in Epirus
- Philip campaigns in Thrace against Cersobleptes (autumn)
- Cersobleptes attacks Amadocus who receives support from Byzantium and Perinthus
- The Spartans invade Megalopolis and camp near Mantineia
- Sparta captures Orneae
- Sparta defeats the Argives who comes to Orneae's assistance
- Philip besieges and captures Heraion Teichos, in Thrace (Nov)
- Philip is taken ill in Thrace (Nov)
- Cersobleptes surrenders his son as hostage to Philip (late)
- Phayllus, commander of the Phocian army, dies of a wasting disease

351
- Philip invades the Chalcidice (early)
- General Mnaseas, guardian of Phalaecus, is killed by the Boeotian army during a night attack (spring)
- Phalaecus captures Chaeronea but is later expelled from the city by a Boeotian army returning from the Peloponnese
- Artemisia, wife of Mausolus, the king of Caria, dies
- The Boeotian army invades Phocis
- Philip's wife Nicesipolis dies shortly after giving birth to Thessalonike
- Charidemus is sent to the Hellespont with 10 ships to secure the Athenian corn route
- Philip campaigns in Paeonia and Illyria (summer)
- Thebes requests funds from Artaxerxes III and receives 300 talents in exchange for a commitment to provide troops for his Egyptian campaign
- Philip campaigns in Epirus (summer)
- Philip appoints Arybbas, uncle of Alexander of Molossus, as regent of Epirus
- There is only desultory fighting in the Sacred War, as the Thebans are in severe financial straits
- Philip's half brothers, Arrhidaeus and Menelaus, take refuge at Olynthus (winter)
- Philip invades Epirus

APPENDIX I

349	• Philip captures and razes Stagira, in the Chalcidice (early)
	• Philip demands that Olynthus surrender his step-brothers (spring)
	• The Chalcidian League allies itself with Athens (summer)
	• Philip invades the Chalcidice (summer)
	• An Olynthian proposal for an alliance with Athens is rejected (summer)
	• The Thessalian tyrants return to Pherae but are soon expelled by Philip
	• The Boeotian army invades Phocis, winning a victory at Hyampolis but being defeated near Coronea
	• Athens receives the 1st Olynthian appeal for assistance (Jul)
	• The 1st contingent of Athenian reinforcements is sent to Olynthus (autumn)
348	• An Athenian force under Phocian defeats the Euboeans at Tamynae (Feb)
	• Philip begins his military intervention on Euboea (Feb)
	• Athens receives a 2nd Olynthian appeal for assistance
	• Aristotle leaves Athens
	• Molossus succeeds to Phocian's command on Euboea. His defeat and capture forces Athens to acknowledge the independence of all Euboean towns except Carystus
	• Upon the fall of Olynthus Philip captures and executes his two half-brothers, Arrhidaeus and Menelaus.
	• A 2nd contingent of Athenian reinforcements is sent to Olynthus (spring)
	• Philip expels Peitholaus from Pherae (spring)
	• Plutarchus, tyrant of Eretria, requests Athenian assistance against Cleitarchus (spring)
	• Philip overruns the districts of Boeotia and Pallene in the western Chalcidice peninsula (Mar)
	• Philip captures Mecyberna, the port of Olynthus and Torone (late spring)
	• The Boeotians destroy the Phocian corn crop (early summer)
	• Challis proposes an alliance with Athens as a free city (summer)
	• Athens makes peace with Euboea (summer)
	• Phalaecus invades Boeotia, with engagements occurring at Neon and Hedylium
	• Phocian expels Plutarchus from Eretria
	• An Athenian force under Molossus is captured by the Euboeans (summer)
	• Athens unsuccessfully attempts to form a Greek alliance against Philip (winter)
	• Philip defeats the Olynthians in two field battles, forcing them back into their city to undergo siege
	• Olynthus is betrayed to Philip (Aug/Sep)
347	• Philip campaigns in the Chalcidice (early)
	• Philip releases his Athenian prisoners
	• The philosopher Plato dies
	• Athenian peace embassy I arrives in Pella (Mar)
	• Phalaecus is re-appointed commander of the Phocian army (Jul)
	• Athens assists Cersobleptes in establishing Thracian coastal forts
	• Cersobleptes surrenders to Philip (Sep)
	• The Thebans request aid from Philip. He responds by only sending a few soldiers
	• The 1st Athenian Sacred War peace embassy leaves Pella (Dec)

APPENDIX I

346
- Phocian representatives offer to surrender the cities dominating Thermopylae pass to Athens. Their offer is later repudiated by Phalaecus (Jan)
- Halus, in Thessaly, revolts from Pharsalus
- Amadocus, king of central Thrace, dies
- The 1st Athenian Sacred War peace embassy arrives in Pella (Mar 12)
- Philip captures the Thracian coastal forts (April)
- The Athenian assembly approves Philocrates' peace treaty with Philip (April 18-19)
- The Thessalian League rises up against Philip
- The 2nd Athenian Sacred War peace embassy leaves Athens for Pella (April)
- Philip defeats Cersobleptes at Hieron Oros and subordinates him to Macedonia. (April)
- Philip arrives at Thermopylae (July)
- The 3rd Athenian Sacred War peace embassy leaves Athens for Pella (Jul)
- Phocis surrenders to Philip, ending the Sacred War (Jul)
- Chalcis proposes the creation of an Euboean League
- Teres succeeds Amadocus as king of central Thrace
- Philip returns to Macedonia (late)
- Philip begins the siege of Halus (winter)
- Cardia, in the Thracian Chersonese, allies itself with Philip

345
- The Peace of Philocrates is ratified (summer)
- Philip campaigns against the Ardiaioi
- Philip is seriously wounded in the leg during his campaign against the Ardiaioi
- A Persian army under Artaxerxes captures Sidon, in Phoenicia
- Philip campaigns against the Illyrians

344
- Philip enters Thessaly, expels the Aleuadae from Larisa, and captures Pherae (summer)
- Philip supports Argos and Massena in their war against Sparta (summer)
- A Persian embassy arrives at Argos, Athens, Sparta, and Thebes to obtain mercenaries for the Great King's forthcoming campaign against Egypt (late winter)
- Argos sends 3,000 troops and Thebes 1,000 hoplites in support of Artaxerxes' Egyptian campaign (late)

343
- Phocis begins repaying war reparations
- Philip is ill for 10 months
- Philip enters Thessaly and occupies Larisa and Pherae (spring)
- Philocrates flees Athens just in advance of his impeachment (summer)
- Philip sends mercenaries to Euboea who defeat Athenian supporters at Porthmos (summer)
- A pro-Macedonian faction seizes control of Elis (summer)
- In Eretria, the pro-Macedonian faction exiles Athenian opponents who take refuge at Porthmos
- At Oreus, the pro-Macedonian faction imprisons Euphraeus, the pro–Athenian leader
- Cersobleptes begins reducing Greek cities bordering his kingdom in the Hellespont
- Philip signs a non-aggression pact with Artaxerxes III

APPENDIX I

	• A pro–Macedonian faction seizes control of the Euboean cities of Eretria and Oreus
	• Artaxerxes III, king of Persia, reconquers Egypt (winter)
	• Argos, Megalopolis, and Massena ally themselves with Philip (late)
342	• Philip campaigns in Epirus (winter)
	• Athens allies with Chalcis of Euboea (early)
	• Philip removes Arybbas as king of Epirus and replaces him with his nephew Alexander
	• Hipponicus assists the tyrants at Eretria, on Euboea (spring)
	• Philip divides Thessaly into tetrarchies (spring)
	• Philip hires Aristotle as Alexander's tutor (summer)
	• Philip campaigns for much of the year in Thrace
	• Cersobleptes and Teres are defeated and removed from their thrones in Thrace (summer)
	• Athens attempts to isolate Cardia, an ally of Philip's in the Thracian Chersonese (autumn)
	• Eurylochus of Eretria, in Euboea, requests Athenian assistance to combat an uprising under Cleitarchus
	• Philip establishes military colonies in the Hebrus Valley, in Thrace (winter)
	• Philip captures the last of the Thracian coastal forts (late)
341	• Philip supports Cardia, in the Thracian Chersonese, with a garrison (early)
	• Chalcis, in Euboea, proposes an alliance with Athens (spring/early summer)
	• Philip marries Meda, the daughter of Kothelas, king of the Getae
	• Dropeithes attacks Thracian coastal towns
	• Philip sends three mercenary forces into Euboea (May)
	• The Athenians ally themselves with Chalcis, in Euboea (June)
	• Phocian captures Eretria and Oreus (summer)
	• Phocian crosses to Euboea and expels Chitarchus from Eretria, in Euboea (Jul)
	• Philip makes an alliance with Kothelas, king of the Getae (late)
	• Philip campaigns on the west coast of the Black Sea
340	• Philip besieges Selymbria
	• Athens unsuccessfully attempts to organize a Greek alliance against Philip
	• Antigonus loses an eye during the siege of Perinthus
	• At age 16, Alexander is appointed regent of Macedonian while Philip is away besieging Perinthus and Byzantium
	• Alexander defeats the Maidoi, a revolting Balkans tribe (summer)
	• Philip unsuccessfully besieges Perinthus (late Jul)
	• Phocian Sacred War reparations are reduced by half
	• Philip unsuccessfully besieges Byzantium (Sep)
	• Philip captures the Athenian corn-fleet (mid-Sep)
	• Athens declares war on Philip after his capture of her corn-fleet (Oct)
	• Phocian replaces Chares as the commander in the Hellespont (autumn/winter)
	• Chares blockades Philip's fleet in the Black Sea
	• Philip responds to a request from Scythia and sends troops to her aid
339	• Thebes occupies Nicaea, a city controlling the pass at Thermopylae (early summer)
	• Philip campaigns in Scythia (spring/summer)

- The Amphictyonic Council declares a sacred war against Amphissa (May/Jun)
- The Triballians steal the Scythian booty away from the Macedonian army as it marches through their territory (summer)
- While passing through the territory of the Triballians, Philip is seriously wounded in the thigh by a spear (summer)
- Thebes forms an alliance with Athens (Nov)
- The 4th Sacred War begins when Cottyphus, commander of the Amphictyonic forces, calls upon Philip for assistance to enforce the Council's decree against Amphissa
- Philip II is elected Hegemon of Thessaly (Oct)
- Philip II tricks Phocian and extricates his fleet from the Black Sea
- Philip II occupies Elatea and Kytinion in Euboea (Nov)

338
- Parmenio captures Gravia Pass, then the city of Amphissa, forcing the Greek allied army to retreat on Chaeronea (Aug)
- Philip defeats the Allied Greek army at the battle of Chaeronea (Sep)
- Artaxerxes III (Ochus) is assassinated by his vizier, the eunuch, Bagoas (winter)
- Philip campaigns in the Peloponnese

337
- Philip convenes the League of Corinth
- Alexander offers to marry the daughter of Pixodarus, satrap of Caria
- A Greek sacred war is declared against Persia
- Philip marries Cleopatra, Attalus' niece (spring/summer)
- Alexander and his mother Olympias go into exile
- Philip campaigns against Pleurias, in Illyria (autumn)
- Attalus marries Parmenio's daughter

336
- Philip sends an advance force of 10,000 mercenaries under Parmenio into Asia Minor (spring)
- Alexander of Epirus marries Olympias' daughter Cleopatra (spring)
- Philip is assassinated by Pausanias at Aegae (Oct)

Reign of Alexander the Great

- Alexander flanks the Thessalians out of the pass at Tempe River (late summer)
- Darius III becomes king of Persia (Jun)
- Cleopatra, wife of Philip II, is forced to commit suicide by Olympias
- Alexander campaigns in the Peloponnese
- Alexander is proclaimed king of Macedonia
- Parmenio captures Ephesus but is soon forced to withdraw towards the Hellespont by Memnon of Rhodes
- The League of Corinth confirms Alexander as Hegemon

335
- Antipater is appointed regent of Greece by Alexander
- Alexander campaigns in the Balkans
- Coenus marries Parmenio's daughter
- Alexander storms Thebes, later razing the city (Oct)
- Amyntas, son of Perdiccas III, is executed for conspiring against Alexander
- Alexander appoints Callisthenes as his historian

APPENDIX I

- Memnon of Rhodes, in command of a mercenary army in Persian employ, drives Parmenio's advance force back into the Troad
- Darius III reconquers Egypt (winter)

334
- Alexander campaigns in Asia Minor (spring)
- Alexander defeats the Persian satraps at the battle at the Granicus River (May)
- Ada, wife to a former king of Caria, adopts Alexander as her son
- Alexander captures Sardis
- Alexander besieges and captures Miletus (summer)
- Alexander disbands his fleet at Miletus
- Alexander besieges Halicarnassus and captures all but two citadels (autumn)
- Alexander campaigns in Lycia and Pamphylia

333
- Alexander crosses the Cilician Gates (summer)
- Miletus reverts back to Persian rule
- Barsine, daughter of Artabazus, is captured at Damascus and allegedly becomes Alexander's mistress
- Alexander campaigns in Cilicia
- Darius' family is captured by Alexander at Issus
- Memnon of Rhodes dies while besieging Mitylene (late summer)
- Alexander becomes ill at Tarsus (Aug)
- Alexander defeats Darius at the battle of Issus (Oct)
- Alexander is wounded in the thigh by a sword at the battle of Issus (Oct)
- Alexander (son of Aeropus) is executed by Alexander for participation in an alleged assassination plot against him
- Alexander campaigns in Phoenicia
- Charidemus, an Athenian advisor, is executed by Darius III for belittling the military competence of the Persian army

332
- Byblos and Sidon surrender to Alexander
- The Persian fleet breaks up (spring)
- Alexander receives Darius' first peace offer at Marathus (Jun)
- Alexander besieges and captures Tyre (Jan–Jul)
- Alexander besieges and captures Gaza (Sep – Oct)
- During the siege of Gaza Alexander is wounded in the shoulder by an arrow which penetrates his corselet (Sep/Oct)
- During the siege of Gaza Alexander is hit in the shoulder by a catapult bolt which penetrates his shield and corselet (Sep/Oct)
- During the siege of Gaza Alexander is wounded in the leg by a stone (Sep/Oct)
- The Spartan army invades and conquers Crete (summer)
- At the conclusion of the siege of Gaza Batis is allegedly dragged round the city behind Alexander's chariot
- The last two citadels of Halicarnassus surrender to Ptolemy
- Alexander enters Egypt and is crowned pharaoh at Memphis (Nov)

331
- Andromachus, the Macedonian military commander of Sumaria, is burnt alive by rebels there (early)
- Alexander founds the city of Alexandria, in Egypt (Apr)
- Alexander visits the oracle at Siwah, in Libya (early spring)
- Alexander returns to Tyre (spring)
- Alexander, king of Molossus, is assassinated, while campaigning in Italy

- Alexander receives Darius' second peace offer while he is besieging Tyre (summer)
- Alexander appoints Harpalus as his treasurer
- Alexander campaigns in Mesopotamia
- Stateira, Darius III's wife, dies from travel fatigue while with Alexander's army just prior to the battle of Gaugamela (Sep)
- Darius III sends Alexander his third and last peace offer just before the battle of Gaugamela
- Alexander defeats Darius at the battle of Gaugamela (Oct)
- Alexander is slightly wounded in the right thigh by a sword at the battle of Gaugamela (Oct)
- Coenus, Hephaestion, and Perdiccas are wounded at the battle of Gaugamela (Oct)
- Alexander enters Babylon (Oct)
- Alexander enters Susa (Dec)
- Alexander campaigns against the Uxians (Dec)
- Olympias retires to Epirus
- Alexander captures the Persian Gates (Dec)

330
- Alexander enters Persepolis (Jan)
- Alexander campaigns in the Parapanisadae (Mar)
- Alexander burns Persepolis (May)
- Alexander releases the Greek allies from service with his army at Ecbatana, in Media (May)
- Darius III is murdered by Bessus at Damghan (Jul)
- Alexander campaigns in Hyrcania (summer)
- Sparta is defeated by Antipater at the battle of Megalopolis (late summer)
- Agis, king of Sparta, is killed at the battle of Megalopolis (late summer)
- Philotas is executed for participation in an alleged assassination attempt against Alexander (Oct)
- Alexander orders Parmenio's assassination
- Alexander campaigns in Drangiana (late Aug)
- Alexander campaigns in Arachosia and the Parapamisadae
- A seventh taxies is added to Alexander's phalanx

329
- Alexander crosses the Hindu Kush at Khawak Pass (Mar)
- Alexander campaigns in the Kabul Valley (spring)
- When Alexander crosses the Oxus River, he musters out the unfit Macedonian veterans and Thessalian volunteers (May)
- Alexander campaigns in Bactria (May)
- Bactria and Sogdiana revolt against Alexander (autumn)
- During the Sogdianan revolt, Alexander recaptures the seven fortified settlements of his northern defense line (autumn)
- Alexander is hit on the head and neck with a stone at the siege of Gaza, one of the seven fortified settlements of his northern defense line against the Scythians
- Craterus is wounded by an arrow at the siege of Gaza
- Alexander captures Bessus (summer)
- Satibarzanes is killed in combat by Erigyius
- Bessus is betrayed to Alexander and is later executed by Darius III's surviving family

APPENDIX I

- Alexander campaigns against the Scythians (summer)
- In pursuing the Scythians, Alexander drinks tainted water and is carried back to camp suffering from diarrhea
- Spitamenes ambushes and virtually eliminates a force under Pharnuches, which was sent to the relief of Maracanda (autumn)
- Alexander campaigns against Spitamenes

328
- Alexander murders Cleitus the Black in a drunken rage at Maracanda, in Sogdiana (late autumn)

327
- Alexander besieges and captures the Rock of Sogdiana (late winter)
- Alexander besieges and captures the Rock of Chorienes
- Alexander marries Roxane (spring)
- Alexander executes Hermolaus for his participation in an assassination attempt (The Pages' Conspiracy) against him (spring)
- Callisthenes ruins Alexander's attempt to introduce proskynesis to the Macedonians in Bactria (late spring)
- While in Bactria, Alexander orders 30,000 Persian youths to be trained in Macedonian fighting methods
- Barsine, daughter of Artabazus, allegedly bears Alexander a child named Heracles
- Erigyius dies
- Alexander executes Callisthenes for his participation in Hermolaus' assassination attempt against him

326
- Alexander campaigns in the Northwest Frontier: in Bajaur and Swat (winter)
- While campaigning in Bajaur Alexander is wounded in the shoulder by an arrow that penetrates his breastplate
- While reconnoitering Massaga in Swat Alexander is wounded in the ankle by an arrow
- Ptolemy and Leonnatus are wounded while campaigning in Bajaur
- Alexander besieges and captures the Rock of Aornos
- Taxiles submits to Alexander (Apr)
- Alexander invades India (early spring)
- Alexander defeats Porus at the battle of Hydaspes River (May)
- At the conclusion of the battle of Hydaspes River, Bucephalas, Alexander's horse, dies
- Alexander's army mutinies against him at the Beas River, in India
- During an assault on Sangala Lysimachus is wounded
- Alexander campaigns in the upper Punjab (summer)
- During an attack on Massaga Alexander is wounded in the calf of his leg by an arrow
- Alexander campaigns in the lower Punjab (fall)
- In the realm of the Sambus, Ptolemy is wounded in the left shoulder
- While storming the citadel north of Multan, Alexander is seriously wounded in the lung by an arrow (Nov/Dec)
- Coenus dies of an illness

325
- Craterus campaigns in Arachosia and Drangiana (Jun)
- Artabazus, satrap of Bactria, dies of old age
- Alexander occupies Pattala (Jul)

- Harpalus, Alexander's treasurer, flees to Asia Minor
- Chares, an Athenian general, dies
- Alexander campaigns in Gedrosa (late Aug — mid Dec)
- Alexander defeats the Oreitans (Sep)
- The Indian monsoon rains begins (end Oct)
- Nearchus sails west along the Arabian Sea (Nov)
- After suppressing revolts in southern Drangiana, Craterus rejoins Alexander, in Carmania (Dec)
- Alexander begins his satrapal purges (Dec)

324
- Alexander re-enters Persepolis (Jan)
- Peucestas is appointed satrap of Persis by Alexander (early)
- Greece deifies Alexander at his request. Macedonia and Alexander's army in Asia, however, refuse to do so (Mar)
- Alexander re-enters Susa (spring)
- 30,000 Persian youths trained in Macedonian fighting techniques join Alexander at Susa
- Alexander conducts his Susa marriages
- Alexander visits Cyrus' tomb at Pasargadae
- Alexander's army mutinies against him at Opis, on the Tigris River (Jul)
- Harpalus flees from Asia Minor to Athens (Jul)
- Alexander issues his Exile's Decree (Jul/Aug)
- Alexander enters Ecbatana (autumn)
- Athens prepares to resist implementation of Alexander's Exile's Decree (autumn)
- Hephaestion dies at Ecbatana (Oct)
- Harpalus is murdered by Thibron in Crete (Oct)
- Alexander marries Stateira and Parysatis at Susa
- Alexander campaigns against the Cossaean (Dec)
- Craterus is appointed to succeed Antipater as Regent of Greece

323
- Alexander commissions an expedition to explore the Caspian Sea
- Demosthenes is found guilty of taking bribes from Harpalus (Mar)
- Alexander officiates over Hephaestion's funeral in Babylon (May)
- Alexander returns to Babylon (spring)
- Cassander is sent by Antipater to negotiate with Alexander
- Alexander plans the Arabian campaign
- Alexander dies (June 10)

Alexander's Successors

323
- The son of Alexander and Roxane is born and named Alexander IV
- Arrhidaeus and Alexander IV are declared joint regents of Alexander's empire (summer)
- Eurydice, daughter of Amyntas, marries Arrhidaeus
- The cynic philosopher Diogenes of Sinope dies

322
- Leonnatus is killed in battle
- The philosopher Aristotle dies on Euboea
- Demosthenes poisons himself to escape Macedonian capture (Oct)

APPENDIX I

321	•Cassander is appointed commander of the Macedonian cavalry
	•Alexander's body is taken to Egypt
	•Craterus is killed in battle in Asia Minor by Eumenes of Cardia
	•Ptolemy I assassinates Cleomenes
	•Perdiccas is assassinated in Egypt by his army officers
319	•Polysperchon is appointed Antipater's successor as supreme commander in Greece
	•Antipater dies of old age
317	•Arrhidaeus (Philip IV) is murdered by Olympias
	•Eurydice, wife of Arrhidaeus, is forced to commit suicide by Olympias
316	•Cassander imprisons Roxane and Alexander IV
	•Eumenes of Cardia is executed by Antigonus
	•Olympias is murdered by Cassander
315	•In India, Chandragupta replaces the Nanda dynasty with his Mauryan dynasty
312	•Seleucus establishes himself at Babylon
	•Roxane and her son Alexander IV are poisoned by Cassander
309	•Barsine, alleged mistress of Alexander the Great, dies
	•Heracles, the alleged son of Alexander, is murdered by Polysperchon
	•Cleopatra, daughter of Philip II and wife of Alexander of Epirus, is murdered by Antigonus
305	•Demetrius Poliorcetes lays siege to Rhodes
303	•Polysperchon dies
301	•The battle of Ipsus is fought
	•Antigonus is killed at the battle of Ipsus
300	•Clearchus, the historian, dies
298	•Cassander dies of a wasting disease
290	•Meander dies
283	•Ptolemy I dies of old age
281	•The battle of Corupedium is fought
	•Lysimachus is killed by Seleucus at the battle of Corupedium
	•Seleucus is assassinated by Ptolemy Ceraunus, Ptolemy I's eldest son

Glossary

Abae A Phocian city widely known for its temple and oracle of Apollo. Inhabitants of the city were thought to be of Thracian origin (Avery 1972, 1; Lempriere [1788] 1987, 1).

Acesines River An Indian river also known as the Chenab (Savill 1993, 117).

Achaemenid The Persian royal house founded by Achaemenes and ending with the murder of Darius III in 330 B.C. (Hammond and Scullard 1970, 4).

Achilles In mythology, Achilles was the only son of Pileus, king of Thessaly, and Thetis, the sea nymph. Although Achilles' prowess and courage on the battlefield was admired, he was considered a barbarian who was only able to resolve situations by violence. Frequently his anger and grief overrode any mercy or compassion, but at times he could be moved by tears. Achilles was unable to tolerate criticism and generally resented authority.

Thetis dipped the young Achilles in the River Styx to make him invulnerable. Because she had held him by his heel when he was being dipped, this was the only part of his body that was unprotected. During Achilles' adolescence, Thetis asked him whether he preferred a long uneventful life or a short glorious one. When he chose the short one, his death was foretold: he was to be slain by Paris, the son of Priam, the fabled king of Troy. In an attempt to avoid this fate for her son, Thetis sent him to the court of Lycomedes, king of Scyros, an island in the Aegean. She disguised Achilles as a woman, apparently putting a spell on him so that he would forget he was a man. When it became apparent to the Greeks that Troy could not be taken without Achilles' assistance, Ulysses was sent to Scyros to persuade him to join their cause. When Ulysses presented Achilles a choice of either jewels or weapons, he chose the latter, realized his sex, and prepared to go to Troy. Before he departed, Thetis persuaded Vulcan to make him a suit of armor invulnerable to all weapons.

Achilles arrived at Troy in command of the Myrmidons and 50 ships. He greatly distinguished himself in a number of engagements, capturing 23 towns. However, when Agamemnon forced him to give up his captive Briseis to him, Achilles not only refused to fight in the Greek army's behalf but begged his mother to enlist Zeus' support to punish Agamemnon for his injustice. After Agamemnon was heavily defeated in the next engagement with the Trojans, he offered to atone for his earlier slight against Achilles. Instead of accepting his apology, Achilles continued to sulk in his tent. During the next engagement, Patroclus, Achilles' best friend and lover, put himself at the head of the Myrmidons in Achilles' place in an attempt to prevent the Trojans from burning the Greek camp. When Achilles heard that Patroclus had been killed in the subsequent fighting, he resumed command of his followers, routed the Trojans, and killed Hector, the king of Troy's son. He then cruelly dragged Hector's body around Troy behind his chariot.

Achilles became infatuated with Polyxena, and in courting her at the temple of Minerva, lifted his vulnerable heel off the ground. As was foretold, Paris shot Achilles with an arrow in the exposed heel. Achilles died and was brought to Sigeum, where divine honors were paid to him for his accomplishments. Neoptolemus, the son of Achilles, chose Andromache, the widow of Hector, as his prize when Troy fell. Their offspring was Molossus, founder of the royal line of Epirus and ancestor of Olympias, the future mother of Alexander the Great. (Hammond and Scullard 1970, 5; Lempriere [1788] 1987, 5–6; O'Brien 1992, 22; Radice [1971] 1973, 47; Warrington [1961] 1978, 4).

Acropolis The general name for the citadel of a Greek city. Typically located on high ground, the acropolis was the most heavily fortified area of a city. It was designed to be held against attack even if the rest of the city fell. The main temples of the city were usually located on the acropolis. (Avery 1972, 6; Warrington [1961] 1978, 5).

Aegae The ancient Macedonian capital. It was replaced by Pella prior to Philip's reign. (Bury, Cook, and Adcock [1927] 1978, VI:204).

Agema The word means "that which leads" and refers to an elite Companion ilai that was Alexander's guard when he fought on horseback. The unit was frequently used on the battlefield as the spearhead of the army's main attack. (Warry 1993, 73).

Agrianians An elite body of Paeonian peltasts from the Mount Haemus region of the Balkans in the northeast corner of Paeonia. They were used extensively by Alexander on missions of special difficulty or on operations where a forced-march or extreme tactical mobility was required. (Bosworth 1980, 65)

Aleuadae The aristocratic family that ruled the city of Larisa in Thessaly. (Grote 1900, XI:202; Lempriere [1788] 1984, 30)

Alexandria When Alexander returned from Siwah in the winter of 332-31 B.C., he engaged the services of Deinocrates, a Rhodian architect who had redesigned Ephesus, to assist him in laying out a new city at the head of the Nile delta that he named Alexandria. Deinocrates persuaded the king to choose the axial-grid layout for the four-mile-long city. Alexandria had two 45-feet-wide, unpaved central boulevards, one running from east to west and the other from north to south. Most other streets were only wide enough for pack animals. All streets were unpaved, with closed drains running alongside them. Drinking water was supplied to the city from underground pipes beneath the streets from a channel of the Nile. The cisterns of Alexandria were said to be capable of holding a year's supply of water for the entire population of the city. The walls of Alexandria were 10 miles in circumference and extended along the coast as protection against both weather and pirates.

The cornerstone of Alexandria was laid on January 20, 331 B.C. The city was self-governing and subject only to the rule of Alexander himself. Alexandria was populated by natives from the surrounding area, a large number of Jews, mainland Greeks, Macedonians, and veterans from Alexander's Asian army. The various nationalities lived in their own sections: Egyptians in the southwest, Jews in the northeast, and Greeks between the two. The citizens were divided into three classes: the first consisting of Macedonians, Balkans, and Greek soldiers; the second, of all other free men; and the third, of slaves. It was only members of the first class who had the right to bear arms and govern the city.

Alexandria became one of the greatest cities of the ancient world. It rapidly grew to a population of 300,000 free persons. With the inclusion of slaves, the total population rose to about 1 million . The city also had the distinction of containing more Jews than any other city in the world. Within 100 years of its founding, Alexandria was larger than Carthage. The Egyptians dominated agriculture, while the Greeks monopolized industry and trade. As Alexander had foreseen, Alexandria became a focus for commerce in the eastern Mediterranean. Of the hundreds of descriptions of the city, virtually all indicated an awe of its wealth. Alexander was to receive no less than 6,000 talents annually from Egypt. Alexandria became the focus for drugs, grain, minerals, papyrus, perfumes, and spices, and the city was the terminus of caravan routes from Arabia, India, and even China. One of the primary objectives of Ptolemaic foreign policy became to maintain control over the trade routes radiating north, east, and south from the city.

Alexandria was also renowned for many other things in the ancient world. Ptolemy I transferred the capital of the Egyptian government from Memphis to Alexandria early in his reign, and the city became the royal residence of his line. Alexandria was the beneficiary of many magnificent public works and monuments because of its incredible wealth and the sponsorship of Ptolemy I, one of the very few truly scholarly kings of the ancient world. Alexandria also became the center of learning during the Hellenistic period, being the scientific counterpart to the concentration of humanistic studies at Athens.

Alexander the Great's body was interred

within the royal quarter of the city, bestowing an almost mythical political benefit Ptolemy was not slow to exploit. Numerous notable military and political figures throughout the following centuries made pilgrimages to Alexandria to gaze upon Alexander's body. In 30 B.C., Alexandria was annexed by Rome, becoming the second most important city in the empire. Along with Sicily, Egypt became one of the main granaries of Rome, exporting 300,000 tons of wheat annually to the city. With the capture of Alexandria by the Arabs under the Caliph Omar in A.D. 640, however, the city quickly slid into decline. During the tenth century, when Cairo was built, Alexandria became virtually a deserted city and its days of greatness were relegated to history. (Avery 1972, 20; Curtius IV:7; de Camp 1972, 286; 1974, 127; Diodorus XVII:52; Hamilton 1973, 55; Lempriere [1788] 1987, 33; Toynbee 1967, 112, 114, 116–7; Warrington [1961] 1978, 31)

Amazons A mythological tribe of female warriors living near the Caspian Sea. They were said to have founded an extensive empire in Asia Minor (modern Turkey). The Amazons were believed to have invaded Attica in 1256 B.C. to recapture their queen, Antiope, who had been carried off by Theseus. When they were defeated by the Greeks near Thermodon, however, the Amazons migrated east, crossed the Jaxartes River, and settled near the Caspian Sea. According to Homer the Amazon queen Themiscyra aided Troy during its war with Agamemnon. She was reputedly killed by Heracles, Alexander's ancestor, who made war on the Amazons to capture their queen's girdle. From that time the Amazons were said to have gone into decline.

The Amazons were a strictly female warrior society. In order to propagate their race, they visited men in adjacent territories for a few days to be impregnated. Only the female children were retained, any males reputedly being strangled.

The chief occupation of the Amazons was hunting and war. They were typically armed with the bow and an axe or spear, all of which they used on horseback. For protection, they had a crescent-shaped shield. The right breast of the Amazon was burnt off so that it not hinder her in either throwing the javelin or shooting the bow.

According to Arrian, while Alexander was in Maracanda, Pharasmanes, king of the Chorasinians, sought his assistance to invade the Amazons, who lived on his borders near the Euxine Sea. He offered to act as a guide for the campaign and to provide anything necessary for its maintenance.

Sometime later, Autopates, satrap of Media, presented Alexander with 100 women, claiming them to be Amazons. Their queen had come in the hope of receiving an offspring from the Macedonian king. (Arrian IV:15, VII:13)

According to Curtius, while Alexander was at Ecbatana, Atropates, satrap of Media, brought him 100 Amazons armed with axes and shields. [Curtius X:4)

In another chapter of his book, Curtius indicates that Thermodon was given permission to visit Alexander while he was in Hyrcania. She came attended by 300 women warriors. When asked if she had a request to make, she told Alexander that she had come to beget children by him, indicating that if the issue was a female she would keep her, if a male, Alexander could keep him. Thermodon stayed 13 days with Alexander and allegedly had her desire fulfilled. Asked if she wished to take service with his army, Thermodon replied that she must return home because she had left her kingdom without a guard. [Curtius VI:5)

Diodorus indicates that Thalestris, queen of the Amazons, met Alexander in Hyrcania. Leaving her army on the border of the satrapy, she proceeded to Alexander in the company of 300 female escorts in full armor. Stating that she had come to beget a child by him, her rationale was that since she had proven herself to be superior to all women and Alexander had proved himself superior to all men, the offspring would surpass all other mortals. Alexander granted her request, and 13 days later Thalestris left for her home country. [Diodorus XVII:77)

Justin indicates that Thalestris, or Minithya, traveled for 25 days from her home country to reach Alexander in Hyrcania. She came in the company of 300 women. Her object in making the visit was to obtain a child from Alexander. She left pregnant 13 days later. [Justin XII:3)

The historical references to the Amazons were thought to have been derived from the Scythians, who occupied the alleged home of the Amazons in ancient times. Their women, like the Amazons, were taught to ride from birth and fight in battle from horseback.(Bury 1913, 75; Hammond and Scullard 1970, 50; Lempriere [1788] 1987, 36; Radice [1971] 1973, 56; Tarn [1948] 1978, 327; Warrington [1961] 1978, 34)

Amphictyonic League A religious association responsible for administering the affairs of the temple of Apollo at Delphi. Its members included the Boeotians, Dolopians, Dorians, Ionians, Locrians, Magnetes, Malians, Oeteans, Perrhaebians, Phocians, Phthiotics, and Thessalians. Although each member had two votes, the League was largely dominated by Thebes. (Bradford 1992, 29; Cawkwell 1978, 63; Hammond and Scullard 1970, 54)

Amphissa A town in Phocis on the western slope of Mt. Parnassus. It was named for Apollo's beloved, Amphissa. In 340 B.C., the members of an enraged Amphictyonic League moved against the city from Delphi to avenge its cultivation of the sacred plain of Crissia. Unable to force Amphissa to pay the fine levied against it, the League called upon Philip of Macedonia for assistance. Philip subsequently captured and destroyed Amphissa. (Avery 1972, 24)

Amphora A nautical unit of volume equaling about 1/40 of a ton, or 50 pounds. (Torr 1964, 25)

Antalcidas, Peace of Antalcidas was a Spartan general who convinced Artaxerxes II that Persia had more in common with Sparta than with Athens. In 386 B.C., he negotiated a Spartan alliance with Persia that required the mainland Greeks to relinquish control of all Greek cities in Asia Minor to Sparta. Antalcidas forced the Athenians to accept the treaty by blockading the Hellespont with the Spartan fleet. (Hammond and Scullard 1970, 66; Warrington [1961] 1978, 42)

Aornos, Rock of A fortified mountain in Bajaur that even Heracles was said to have been unable to capture. Alexander prepared to besiege the position in 326 B.C., and so convincing were his preparations that the Indian garrison surrendered rather than suffer an almost certain defeat. (Arrian IV:28)

Apollo Apollo was the third son of Zeus and Latona and one of the 12 Greek gods. The Oracle of Delphi was dedicated to him, and he was alleged to inspire the predictions given there. Apollo was the god of eloquence, medicine, music, and poetry.

Upon being denied admittance to the oracle of Delphi because of his impurity, Heracles took the sacred tripod there and threatened to set up his own oracle. Apollo came from Olympus and fought with him; they were only parted by Zeus. It was said that this fight in 1,100 B.C. marked the beginning of the Dorian invasion of Greece. When his son was killed by Zeus with a thunderbolt for raising the dead, Apollo murdered the Cyclops who had made the thunderbolts. For this act, he was banished from Olympus. Upon earth, Apollo hired himself out for nine years as a shepherd to Admetus, the king of Thessaly. He then assisted Neptune in building the walls of Troy, but when Laomedon refused to honor the promise he made to him, Apollo destroyed the inhabitants of the city by a plague. (Avery 1972, 119; Lempriere [1788] 1987, 61; Radice [1971] 1975, 61)

Apple-Bearers The Persian royal foot guard of Darius III. They were named for the golden apple decorations on their spear butts.

Arabia The current country of Saudi Arabia. In ancient times, Arabia was widely known for frankincense and aromatic plants. (De Camp 1972, 108; Lempriere [1788] 1987, 64–65)

Aradus An island city 1¾ miles off the shore of Phoenicia. The site the city was located on was 800 yards long and 500 yards wide. (Fuller 1958, 207)

Archon A title conferred on the ruler of Thessaly.

Argeads Alexander's family line that was allegedly traced through Philip to Heracles and through Olympias to Achilles.

Argyraspids The word means "silver shield." Alexander allowed the hypaspists to carry silver shields in India, and after his death, the hypaspists fiercely insisted on bearing the exclusive title of Argyraspids to distinguish them from all other hypaspist units raised by the successors. (Justin XII:7)

Arimaspians A tribe in Drangiana also known as the "Benefactors." They were so named by Cyrus the Great for once providing him with 30,000 wagons of provisions when he had run out of food while campaigning nearby. (Diodorus XVII:81)

GLOSSARY

Artacoana The capital of Areia. (Greek 1991, 337; Lane Fox 1974, 280)

Artemis The temple dedicated to Diana at Ephesus, one of the seven wonders of the ancient world. According to Plutarch, the temple allegedly burnt down on the day of Alexander the Great's birth because Diana was said to have been too busy assisting in his delivery to save it. It appears, however, that the temple was actually burned down by a man named Gerostratus, who wanted to achieve immortality by the act.

When Alexander passed by the temple during his campaign in Asia Minor, he offered to pay the entire cost of its reconstruction if it would be dedicated in his name. His offer was politely refused on the basis that one god could not dedicate a temple to another. (Avery 1972, 38; Clayton and Price 1988, 83; Cottrell 1962, 79–86; Lempriere [1788] 1984, 83; Plutarch 1952, 541; Warrington [1961] 1978, 76)

Asia Minor Otherwise known as Anatolia. The area corresponds to modern-day Turkey.

Assault Ships Usually two merchant ships lashed together with a platform suspended over them on which the assault troops were deployed. The assault ships contained scaling ladders, and some also had towers. Once a breach was made in a city wall along the seashore by a ram ship, the assault ship would move up and debark troops through it. These ships were very unseaworthy and usually suffered extensive damage in heavy seas.

Assembly A political body in democratic states comprised of all adult male citizens who could meet the specified property ownership qualifications.

Astibus The capital of Paeonia. (Hammond and Walbank 1988, 40.)

Autarians One of the most powerful Illyrian tribes. Its territory was near the Nis and Morava rivers in the Balkans. (Bosworth 1980, 66)

Babylon The name Babylon was supposedly derived from an old Semitic name Bab-ili, meaning "the Gate of God." It was the largest city of its time, with a population of over one million. The city's prosperity was based on its location beside the area's major trade routes. Babylon was laid out in a square, about 15 miles on a side, enclosing an area of about 225 square miles. The city was surrounded by a moat 85 feet wide and 22.5 feet deep, behind which lay 60 miles of outer brick wall, reputedly 75 feet high. This wall was said to be 32 feet wide and it is said that two four-horse chariots could pass each other atop it. Towers, each 28 feet wide, stood 144 feet apart along the wall. An inner wall was later built, which, although not as wide as the outer wall, was no less inferior to it in strength. Eight gates gave access through the city's walls.

The city's citadel was surrounded by a wall 2.5 miles long and 80 feet high. The roof of the citadel contained the famous hanging gardens of Babylon, one of the seven wonders of the ancient world. The main street in the city was 65 feet wide and was bordered by 60 stone lions on each side. Houses within the city were mostly three and four stories tall.

The sacred ziggurat in the city's center was seven stories tall. It had been built by Nebuchadnezzar and was called the Tower of Babel by the Jewish Bible. Babylon had over 1,179 temples of worship. Almost as famous as the Hanging Gardens in ancient times was the 400-foot-long bridge in the city over the Euphrates River. For several centuries it was the only such structure in the world. It was a wooden drawbridge 380 feet long that rested on seven piers of baked brick and stone, each with a base of 28 feet by 65 feet. The piers were so massive that they occupied half the width of the river, significantly increasing the velocity of water flow in the vicinity.

Temperatures which routinely exceeded 100 degrees F. at Babylon made it too hot for fighting during the summer, the sticky mud made maneuvering next to impossible during the winter, and the need to plant crops in spring and harvest them in the fall required the farmers to be home then. The only practicable time for the city's military forces to conduct military operations was during short periods in early spring and late fall.

The Euphrates River ran through the center of the city, providing it with a virtually uninterruptable water supply. It was said that during a siege, food crops could be grown on the 150 square miles of agricultural land enclosed within the city walls. The area around Babylon was intersected by man-made irrigation canals. The 10-inch annual rainfall was inadequate for cultivation, and the flooding of the Euphrates and Tigris between April and June occurred too late to help the winter crops and too early to help the summer ones. Nevertheless, so agriculturally productive was the city that it annually provided a third of the food supply of the Great King's enormous court when he was in residence there during the winter months.

Alexander made Babylon the capital of his newly won empire. However, upon his death in 323 B.C., the city went into a progressive decline. Babylon was sacked in 311 B.C. by Demetrius Poliorcetes. Rather than attempt to rebuild the ruins, Seleucid built a new capital for his empire on the bank of the Tigris River, which he named Seleucia. The Parthians drove the Seleucids out of Babylonia. Later, the Abbasid caliphs made their capital at Baghdad. By A.D. 116, Babylon again lay in ruins. (Avery 1972, 52; Curtius V:1; de Camp 1972, 126, 137–8, 143, 152; 1974, 71; Dodge [1890] 1993, 389; Hammond and Scullard 1970, 157; Herodotus I:178, 180; Lane Fox 1974, 245, 250; Lempriere [1788] 1987, 99; Roux [1966] 1992, 259)

Babylonia The southernmost of the kingdoms of ancient Mesopotamia. (Hammond and Scullard 1970, 157)

Bactria A Persian satrapy comprising the modern portions of northern Afghanistan, southern Uzbekistan, and Tadjikistan. The satrapy derived its name from the Bactrus River, a branch of the Oxus River. The area was known to the Greeks as "the Jewel of Persia," for its agricultural productivity. (Hammond and Scullard 1970, 158)

The capital of Bactria, also known as Zariaspa (Curtius VII:4)

Beam The width of a ship. (Morrison and Coates 1986, 238)

Beas River An Indian river also known as the Hyphasis. (Fuller 1958, 129)

Beilan Pass A pass through the Tarus Mountains between Cilicia and Syria. It had been in use for almost 3,000 years by Alexander's time. Also known as the Syrian Gates. (Avery 1972, 82; Fuller 1958, 79)

Benefactors see **Arimaspians**

Bodyguards They were eight officers from the Companions appointed by Alexander to act as his personal bodyguard and his aides-de-camp. They were frequently appointed to command large detachments on independent missions. The following Companions held positions of bodyguards at one time or another:
- Aristonous (son of Pisaeus).
- Arrhybas. Died of a disease.
- Balacrus (son of Nicanor). Appointed satrap of Cilicia.
- Demetrius. Arrested for complicity in Philotas' conspiracy against Alexander.
- Hephaestion (son of Amyntor). Died of alcohol overindulgence.
- Leonnatus (son of Anteas).
- Lysimachus (son of Lysimachus).
- Menes (son of Dionysius).
- Nicanor (son of Parmenio). Died of an illness in Areia.
- Peitho (son of Crateuas).
- Peucestas (son of Orontes).
- Ptolemy (son of Lagos).

(Arrian I:24; II:12; III:5, 6, 25, 27; IV:8,15, 24; V:13, 24; VI: 9, 22, 28, 30; VII:4; Curtius IX:8; Diodorus XVII:61, 99)

Boeotia An area in central Greece bordered on the north by Locris; on the west by Phocis; on the south by Attica, the Corinthian Gulf, and Megara; and on the northeast by the strait of Euboea. According to legend, Cadmus was said to have been instructed by the oracle of Delphi to follow a cow until it stopped and then found a city on the site. Cadmus named the city Thebes and the surrounding area Boeotia. During the late fifth century, the population of Boeotia was estimated at 150,000, of which 135,000 were free citizens.

The inhabitants of Boeotia were considered to be crude and illiterate, preferring physical strength over intelligence. Despite this, however, the muses were said to have dwelt occasionally in the Boeotian mountains.

The 11 districts of the area (Thebes comprising four of them) organized themselves into a confederation called the Boeotian League under the leadership of Thebes, the largest and most important city in the state. Each district was required to provide 100 cavalry, 1,000 hoplites, and 1,000 light infantry to the League army. (Avery 1972, 59; Buck 1979, 158; Demand 1982, 117; Lempriere [1788] 1984, 108; Warrington [1961] 1978, 101)

Bosporus A strait in northwest Asia

Minor separating Asia from Europe. At its narrowest, it was only 1.5 miles wide. (Lempriere [1788] 1987, 109)

Breach A large opening made in a wall by a catapult or ram that allowed attacking troops to assault through the wall rather than over it.

Breaking Array An Indian army formation where elephants were deployed in the center, chariots on the flanks, and cavalry on the wings. The formation was intended to break the enemy center with an attack by the elephants supported by the chariots. (Head 1982, 53)

Bucephala A city founded by Alexander near the battle of Hydaspes River in memory of his horse Bucephalas, which had been mortally wounded during the battle there. (Arrian V:19; Bury, Cook, and Adcock [1927] 1978, VI:409)

Bucephalas In 347 B.C., Philonicus, a Thessalian horse-breeder, offered to sell Philip II, king of Macedonia, a pedigree stallion for the huge sum of 16 talents. The horse was in his prime, being seven years old; he was jet black and had a white blaze on his forehead. The animal was named Bucephalas, meaning ox-head, after the horse farm at which he was raised.

The stallion was quite unmanageable when he was shown to Philip. As none of his grooms were able to ride him, Philip ordered Philonicus to take the horse away. At this, the 12-year-old Alexander remarked aloud that a fine horse was being lost because no one had the skill to control him. When Philip asked his son if he thought that he knew more than his grooms about horses, Alexander replied that he could do better than they had. Philip wanted to know what Alexander would bet if he failed to ride the horse. Alexander's reply was that he would pay the price of the horse. Philip agreed to the wager.

Alexander noticed that Bucephalas shied when he saw his own shadow on the ground, so he turned him into the sun. He calmed the horse down by talking softly to him and stroking him. He then jumped up on his back. At first, he held the horse to a tight rein but soon let him run free and they quickly galloped out of sight. Philip, of course, was extremely anxious for Alexander's safety. His son soon returned, however, and demonstrated how he could make the horse run, walk, and come to a halt at his command. The crowd that had gathered cheered Alexander, and his proud father is reputed to have told him that he should find another kingdom to rule because Macedonia was going to be too small for him. Demaratus of Corinth then purchased Bucephalas and gave the animal to Alexander as a present.

For the rest of his life, Bucephalas never permitted anyone but Alexander to ride him. The horse carried him into almost every battle he fought. During a campaign against the Uxii, a raid by the tribesmen carried off Bucephalas while he was being led through the woods by the royal squires. Alexander was so enraged that he threatened to kill every man, women, and child of the tribe he caught unless Bucephalas were returned. The horse was promptly brought back, and Alexander was so happy to be reunited with him that he rewarded the thieves.

Bucephalas was fatally wounded at the battle at the Hydaspes River in 326 B.C. He was 30 years old and old age and exhaustion may also have contributed to his death. The horse was given a state funeral, with Alexander himself leading the procession. As a tribute to his faithful horse, Alexander gave the name to Bucephala, one of the two cities that he founded near the battlefield, in honor of the animal. (Arrian V:19; Bury, Cook, and Adcock [1927] 1978, 409; Curtius I; Diodorus XVII:76; Plutarch 1952, 543)

Byblos A major port in Phoenicia 26 miles north of Beirut. Byblos was one of the earliest Phoenician settlements, and third in commercial importance only to Sidon and Tyre. The city derived much of its revenues from the export of timber. The word *bible* was derived from the name of Byblos, which exported large quantities of papyrus. (Avery 1972, 63; Hammond and Scullard 1970, 185)

Cadmea The acropolis at Thebes, the name of which was derived from its mythical founder Cadmus. The Cadmea, which was 750 yards long from north to south and 380 yards wide from east to west, was located on a long, low range of hills 150 feet high in the south and 200 feet high in the north. When Thebes revolted from Macedonian rule in 335 B.C., Alexander defeated its army and razed the city. During the Roman Empire, only the Cadmea of the city continued to be occupied. For additional information, see **Cadmus** and **Thebes**. (Avery 1972, 64; Bosworth 1980, 78; Demand 1982, 8)

Cadmus Cadmus was the son of Agenor, king of Phoenicia, and Telephassa. He was the founder of Boeotia and Thebes and was said to have first introduced the Phoenician alphabet into Greece.

According to mythology, Cadmus was sent to find his sister Europa, whom Zeus had carried away, and he was told not to return without her. Unable to find Europa, Cadmus sought the advice of the Oracle of Delphi. The Pydna instructed him to drive a cow across Boeotia until it stopped to rest. At that point, Cadmus was to build the city. Following her advice, he constructed a small citadel where the cow stopped, naming it Cadmea after himself. For his achievement, Athena designated Cadmus the king of the new settlement, and Zeus gave to him in marriage Harmonia, the daughter of Ares by Aphrodite. (Lempriere [1788] 1987, 114–15; Radice [1971] 1973, 80; Warrington [1961] 1978, 110)

Caltrops A ball of wood or iron with several sharp spikes projecting out one inch to two inches in various directions. When these balls were scattered along the ground, at least one spike of each ball would always be facing upwards. Any animal stepping on a caltrop would be immediately disabled. (Abbott, 171; Warry 1991, 60)

Cappadocia The territory in Asia Minor between the Euxine Sea, the Tarus Mountains, and the Euphrates River. During Alexander's reign, Cappadocia was divided into two satrapies separated by the Halys River, the northern one being ruled by a Persian loyal to Darius and the southern one by Alexander's designee. (Avery 1972, 69)

Cardaces The name is derived from the Persian word *karda*, which means "manly." It was used to refer to Persian youth trained as cavalry and archers. They accompanied the king on the hunt and at other times assumed the duties of a police force. Darius' shortage of reliable infantry was such that he was forced to use the Cardaces in the field. They were armed as peltasts and were assigned to guard the flanks of the Greek mercenaries. At Issus, their defeat by Alexander cost Darius the battle. Shortly afterwards, they were dropped from the Persian army's order of battle and nothing further is heard of them. (Bosworth 1980, 208)

Caria An area of Asia Minor bordered on the north by Lydia and Ionia, on the east by Lycia and Phrygia, and on the south by the Aegean Sea. When Alexander conquered the area's most important city, Halicarnassus, by siege in 334 B.C., he restored Queen Ada's rule in Caria. (Warrington [1961] 1978, 125)

Casualties The ratio of wounded to killed during the Macedonian era was anywhere from 8:1 to 20:1. Most of the wounded, however, were able to return to duty eventually. This was because the weapons were not made of steel, and the wounds were usually stab wounds—sword thrusts and spear punctures—which were usually nonfatal and noncrippling. Slashing wounds, like those delivered by the Roman legionaries, would hack off limbs and inflict such severe wounds as to permanently disable the victim. (Delbruck 1990, 189; Dodge [1890] 1993, 129, 248; Hammond 1981, 154; Livy XXXI:34)

Catapult The term means "shield protector" and refers to ancient artillery used in sieges. The belly bow and shield piercer were catapults that fired heavy arrows against enemy defenders on a wall. The stone thrower was a catapult that fired stones at the wall to breach it. The belly bow was referred to as a flexion catapult because it derived its torque from the bending of wood. Belly bows were used by Philip early in his reign.

The shield piercer and stone thrower were both referred to as torsion catapults because they derived their much greater torque by the use of twisted hair. This enabled them to throw heavier weights farther distances than the inferior flexion catapult. The shield piercer's first recorded use was by Philip during the siege of Perinthus in 340 B.C. while the stone thrower was first used by Alexander the Great in his siege of Tyre in 332 B.C. (Ferrill 1976, 171)

Caulking The insertion of sealing material into the seams of a ship's hull planks to water-proof them against leaks. (Morrison and Coates 1986, 239)

Causia A broad-brimmed Macedonian hat. (Fuller [1958] 1960, 51)

Celeanae The capital of the satrapy of Phrygia. (Tarn [1948] 1979, 177)

Chalcidian League A confederation of 32 Greek towns on the Chalcidice Peninsula formed in 432 B.C. under the leadership of Olynthus. A common constitution was established throughout the league allowing joint citizenship, inter-marriage, and land acquisition in any member city's territory. The League was able to field a combined military force of 1,000 cavalry and 10,000 hoplites. (Cawkwell 1978, 82; Hammond 1994, 32)

Chalcidice A peninsula just southeast of Macedonia also known as the Chersonese. The cities there were organized as the Chalcidian League under Olynthus.

Charsadda The capital of Peucelaotis, a district in the northeast Persian Empire. (Bosworth 1988, 125)

Chenab River An Indian river also known as the Acesines. (Savill 1993, 117)

Chersonese A Greek word meaning "peninsula." The term was most widely used to designate the peninsula of the Chalcidice, just southeast of Macedonia. The northern half of the peninsula contained extensive woodlands and minerals while the southern portion had large areas of agricultural and grazing land. (Avery 1972, 80)

Chilarch The Greek name for the Persian Grand Vizier. This was the highest political office in the Persian court next to the king. Alexander conferred the title on Hephaestion to designate him as his successor.

The term was also used by the Greeks to designate a commander of a thousand soldiers. (Cook 1993, 143)

Chilarchy A Macedonian cavalry unit of 1,000 troopers. (Cook 1983, 143)

A Persian subdivision of a satrapy. (Bury, Cook, and Adcock [1927] 1978, VI: 370)

Choinix An ancient measurement of 1.92 pints or 1.5 pounds. (Engels 1978, 125)

Cilician Gates The only viable pass through the mountains of Syria and Mesopotamia. It was only wide enough for the passage of two loaded camels or four men marching abreast. Alexander was able to drive off the small force left behind to defend this pass because instead of occupying the position in strength, Arsames used his army to implement a scorched-earth policy behind the pass in an attempt to deny Alexander any supplies from the area. This proved to be a significant strategic error, and Alexander considered his almost effortless occupation of the pass to be one of the luckiest events in his career. (Arrian II:4; Curtius III:4)

Circumnavigation see **Periplous**

Cleruchy An Athenian colony founded on conquered territory. As the land of the cleruchy was considered to be Attic territory, the settlers there retained the citizenship of their home city. Cleruchs were liable to their home city for both military service and taxation. Athens founded numerous cleruchies on conquered territories, especially in the Chalcidice, along the Thracian coast, and on the Thracian Chersonese. (Hammond and Scullard 1970, 252; Warrington [1961] 1978, 151)

Close-Order A Greek heavy infantry formation with a file frontage, or lateral distance, of three feet.

Coele-Syria

The name meant "Hollow Syria" and initially designated modern-day northern Syria. Later it also included Palestine. (Bosworth 1980, 225; Polybius V:34; Warrington [1961] 1978, 154)

Coinage In ancient times, paper currency and letters of credit did not exist. Financial transactions were carried out either in coin or by barter. Greek coins were struck with dies instead of being cast by pouring molten metal into molds. The anvil was engraved with the image of the coin, then struck onto a small heated disk. During the Macedonian era, the die was made of steel and was capable of producing 16,000 coins before having to be discarded.

At the beginning of Alexander's reign, there were three basic coin standards in the Eastern Mediterranean. In Asia, the Persian decimal coinage predominated, one gold Persian daric equaling 20 silver sigloi. In Macedonia, Philip's duodecimal coinage was the standard, one gold stater equaling 24 silver drachmae. In Greece, most of the trade was carried on with Athenian coinage, one Attic Owl being equal to 20 silver drachma. Alexander adapted the Athenian standard of coinage and made the Macedonian Stater equivalent to 20 drachma or one Attic Owl. By making use of a trusted standard already in wide use, trade was greatly facilitated in all parts of his empire.

The minting of coin was always considered a royal function in ancient times. However, with Alexander being on continuous campaigns in the east between 330 and 324

B.C., Harpalus, his treasurer, was likely designated to supervise both the minting and distribution of coin. In the early part of Alexander's reign, the Macedonian mints at Amphipolis, Damastium, Pella, and Philippi provided his coinage. Damastium produced silver coinage until 325 B.C. and Philippi both gold and silver coins until 328 B.C. Amphipolis was by far the largest mint, producing over 13 million silver coins over an 18 year period. In 330 B.C., Alexander established one additional mint in Greece, at Sicyon, in the Peloponnese. In Asia, Alexander's most important mint was at Babylon, followed by one at Tarsus. During the 320s several secondary mints were established throughout the east: in western Asia Minor, at Lampsacus, Miletus, Sardis, and Sidea; in Cilicia, at Myriandrus and Tarsus; in Phoenicia, at Ake, Aradus, Byblos, and Sidon; in Cyprus, at Citium; in Egypt, at Alexandria; in Babylonia, at Babylon; and in Media, at Ecbatana. The huge amounts of bullion that the Persian kings had stored at Susa and Persepolis were turned into coin and circulated freely through the eastern Mediterranean. This resulted in a dramatic increase in trade and economic activity throughout the Persian Empire. (Bosworth 1988, 244–45; Bury, Cook, and Adcock [1927] 1978, VI:428; Hammond 1981, 156, 163; Hammond and Scullard 1970, 259; Tarn [1948] 1967, 130)

Common Peace see **League of Corinth**

Contravallation A classical Greek siege tactic that called for surrounding a besieged city with a wall to isolate it from receiving any supplies or outside assistance. The surrounding wall faced both inward and outward. The operation was passive in nature, as it did not call for an assault on the part of the attacker. It did, however, require a great deal of patience because it could be several months before the defender was either starved out or betrayed by a political faction within the city. The tactic was also very costly in terms of the wages that had to be paid to the besieging force over an extended period of time. This siege tactic was sometimes called circumvallation. (Dodge [1890] 1993. 172–73; Warrington [1961] 1978, 147)

Cophen River Known as the Kabul River in modern times. (Bosworth 1988, 119)

Corselet A breastplate made of either brass, iron, or layers of linen glued together.

Crenidas A rich mining district in Thrace, about 40 northeast from Amphipolis. Its gold and silver mines provided 1,000 talents in annual income to Macedonia. Philip consolidated the settlements there into a single town that he named Philippi after himself. (Hammond and Griffith 1979, 249, 348)

Cretan Archers Elite archers from Crete who were extremely proficient with the bow. They hired out as mercenaries with both Philip's and Alexander's army. The Cretans were in wide demand not only for their archery skill but because they were also armed with a shield and sword. Unlike Greek archers, the Cretans were prepared to defend themselves in hand-to-hand combat, if the situation required it. (Head 1982, 100)

Cubit An ancient linear measurement of approximately 18 inches in length.

Cunaxa The site of a battlefield near the Euphrates 75 miles northwest of Babylon. A battle was fought there in 401 B.C. between Artaxerxes II, the king of Persia, and his younger brother, Cyrus the younger. Cyrus stationed 1,000 cavalry on his right flank along the river and next to them the 10,000 Greek mercenaries under Clearchus. Ariaeus, in command of the Asiatic troops, was placed on the left flank, while Cyrus took station in the center with 600 cavalry of the 2,600 cavalry of his command. Artaxerxes' army consisted of 6,000 cavalry and 30,000 infantry. His left wing was commanded by Tissaphernes and consisted of horse-archers and Egyptian infantry screened by scythed chariots. The Persian king occupied the center with a strong force of cavalry.

Cyrus ordered Clearchus to move obliquely against Artaxerxes' center, but the Greeks refused to do so because it would have exposed Clearchus' flank to an attack from the Persian left wing. Instead, Clearchus charged straight ahead, drove the Persian chariots from the field, and routed the infantry stationed behind them. He then pursued the Persians off the battlefield. Cyrus, encouraged by Clearchus' success, charged Artaxerxes' 6,000 cavalry with the 600 cavalry accompanying him. Although Cyrus wounded Artaxerxes in the subsequent melee, he himself was struck in the head with a javelin and killed. Cyrus' Persian troops then fled the field.

Discontinuing his pursuit of the Persians

after about three miles, Clearchus returned to the battlefield and plundered the Persian baggage train. The following morning Clearchus learned of Cyrus' defeat and death. In a subsequent peace negotiation, the Persians treacherously murdered all the key Greek leaders who attended. The Greeks then elected Xenophon as their leader and began their famous "March of the Ten Thousand" westward out of the Persian Empire and safely back to Greece. (Avery 1972, 106; Bury 1913, 507; Ferrill [1985] 1988, 152–t3; Hammond and Scullard 1970, 301)

Cyzicus An island town in Asia Minor lying along the southern shore of the sea of Marmara. The town was joined to the mainland by a bridge that could be disconnected. The commercial importance of the city was derived from its two harbors that provided the only safe anchorage for merchantmen sailing in the Propontis along the otherwise hazardous northern coast of Asia Minor. Cyzicus was in direct competition with Byzantium for the trade flowing from the Black Sea passing through the Hellespont. The town was allegedly named after a man killed on the site by Jason, of Argonaut fame. (Curtius II; Hammond and Scullard 1970, 309; Lempriere [1788] 1987, 188–89)

Dahae A Scythian tribe (Fuller [1958] 1960, 166)

Daily Record
A compilation of the daily orders, correspondence, and promotions issued by the Macedonian kings. The records were the personal property of the king and were not intended to be published. Great attention was placed on their accuracy and completeness because the king's official orders were based on them.

At a Macedonian king's death, his daily record was stored either at Pella or Aegae. The records were maintained by the king's secretary, who for both Philip and Alexander was Eumenes of Cardia. Alexander's daily record accompanied his funeral train to Egypt and was used as the basis for the history Ptolemy wrote of Alexander's campaigns. That work was extensively used by Arrian in writing his account of Alexander's reign. (Hammond 1981, 1; Hammond and Walbank 1988, 18)

Daochidai The family that ruled the city of Pharsalus in Thessaly.

Damghan A city near the southern border of Hyrcania where Darius III was reputedly murdered by Bessus, satrap of Bactria. (Dodge [1890] 1993, 424)

Dardanians A warlike Illyrian tribe occupying modern southern Yugoslavia. During the Macedonian Empire, the tribe was ruled by Bardylis and then his son Cleitus. (Bosworth 1980, 65, 69; Hammond 1981, 56; Hammond and Scullard 1970, 313)

Daric A Persian gold monetary unit, 300 of which equaled a Greek talent and one of which equaled 20 silver Sigloi. (Arrian IV:18; Bury, Cook, and Adcock [1927] 1978, 427)

Dascylium The capital of the satrapy of Hellespontine Phrygia. (Bosworth 1988, 44)

Dead Ground A low, flat space behind a ridge in front of the Macedonian right flank at the battle of Issus. Alexander used it to hide the deployment of his attacking wing from Persian observation.

Delphi Oracle The most famous oracle in Greece was located within Phocis. The predictions given there were allegedly inspired by the god Apollo. The oracle stood on the southern slope of Mount Parnassus, some 2,000 feet above sea level. Two reflecting rocks, called the Phaedriades "shining one," rose up 800 feet above the temple. The site of the oracle was reputed to be at the center of the earth.

The complex, which included the temple, contained over 20 individual treasuries and a small theater. It originally provided a meeting place for the Greek city-states. The Delphi oracle proved to be a powerful unifying force in Greece, bringing the various states together in athletic, musical, and literary competitions. A body of Greeks known as the Amphictyonic Council was established to oversee the affairs of Delphi.

Those petitioning the oracle would inquire if they could ask a question. If the oracle was favorably disposed, a response would be given by the Pythia, who was originally a young virgin but in later years was an elderly woman. The drug-induced delirium of the Pythia was believed to be the god taking possession of her. The Pythia's answers were given in verse that was interpreted by a male prophet. The ambiguity of the replies was often used to justify actions the petitioners had already decided to take. All colonists from early Greece consulted the oracle before setting out, inquiring about both the site to be colonized and the choice of a god for the new city. Important political, educational, art, and literary decisions were also frequently based on answers from the oracle.

It was said that Heracles was denied admittance to the oracle because of his impurity. Enraged, he took the sacred tripod and threatened to establish his own oracle. Apollo arrived to protect his shrine, and the two fought, only to be separated by Zeus. Allegedly, the fight between the two in 1,100 B.C. signaled the beginning of the Dorian invasion of Greece.

During the invasion of Greece by Persia, the Delphians asked their oracle if they should bury or remove the treasure stored there. They were told to leave it where it was as the gods would protect it. Xerxes reputedly sent a cavalry force into Phocis to carry off the treasury at Delphi. As the Persians approached, a bolt of lightning broke off two large rocks from Mount Parnassus and buried most of the Persian force. In the resulting confusion, the Delphians attacked the surviving Persians and massacred them. Only a small remnant of the original Persian force was able to escape back to Boeotia.

Sometime prior to the Second Sacred War, Delphi came under the control of Crissia, in Phocis. As the Crissians subjected pilgrims journeying to the temple to numerous duties, the priests of Delphi lodged a complaint to the Amphictyonic Council, which was charged with the maintenance of the temple. During the resulting Second Sacred War, circa 600 B.C.–590 B.C., Crissia was destroyed and its territory, the Cirrha plain, was dedicated to Apollo. Any cultivation of the land was forbidden. The end of the Sacred War resulted in great prosperity for Delphi. The individual Greek city-states made large offerings to the oracle, setting up several small temples at the site as depositories for the offerings and storage of vessels used for religious ceremonies.

The Third Sacred War began when the Phocians occupied and fortified the Temple of Delphi in 357 B.C. During the 10-year war, the Phocians systematically looted the temple treasury to pay the wages of the large mercenary army in their employ. By the end of the war, over 10,000 talents had been removed from the treasury of Delphi. Little of it was ever repaid.

Although Delphi was destroyed by an earthquake in 373 B.C., it was rebuilt in 330 B.C. After 189 B.C., the temple came under control of the Romans. In 91 B.C., Delphi was burned by the Thracians, and in 86 B.C. it was pillaged by Sulla. The emperor Nero carried off 500 of Delphi's 3,500 statues, and the emperors Constantine and Theodosius took several hundred more. The temple was finally destroyed in a series of earthquakes early in the Christian era. (Avery 1972, 117, 119, 121–23; Diodorus XVI:26; Hammond 1970, 323; Hammond and Scullard 1970, 323; Lempriere [1788] 1987, 198; Warrington [1961] 1978, 186)

Diadem A Persian purple and white band worn around a tiara. It was adopted by Alexander and his successors as a symbol of royal power. (Hammond and Scullard 1970, 333)

Didrachms A unit of Greek money equivalent to two drachma. (Warrington [1961] 1978, 154)

Diekplous ("Breaking Through") An Athenian naval ramming technique in which a trireme pretended to ram a ship, then rowed between two enemy ships in an attempt to damage their oars or rudders. The ship then wheeled round to ram one of the enemy ships before either could maneuver to meet the attack. The maneuver could be largely negated by the opponent deploying his ships in two lines. (Casson 1994, 75; Hammond and Scullard 1970, 341)

Dilochites The commander of a pair of files in the Macedonian phalanx. (Connolly [1977] 1978, 58)

Displacement The volume of a ship immersed in water. (Morrison and Coates 1986, 239)

Divine Honors The granting of divine honors to a living man was a recognition that the services he had performed for his city were equivalent to those a god might render. This recognition did not acknowledge the person as a god, just his deeds as godlike. Although Alexander requested and received divine honors from the Greeks, Macedonia and his own army refused to grant him this recognition. (Bosworth 1988 278; Hamilton 1973, 140; Hammond 1981, 248, 253)

Drachma A Greek unit of money equal

to 6 obols. One talent was equal to 6,000 drachmas. (Morrison and Coates 1980, 244]

Draft The depth of the underside of a ship's keel below the waterline. (Morrison and Coates 1986, 239)

Drangiana A Persian satrapy corresponding roughly to modern-day southern Afghanistan. (Weigall 1933, 248)

Ecbatana The capital of the satrapy of Media and the summer capital of the Achaemenid kings of Persia. The city was located 6,000 feet above sea level and was reputedly surrounded by seven walls, each painted a different color. Ecbatana was captured by Alexander the Great in 330 B.C. Parmenio, Philip II's greatest general, was murdered there on the orders of Alexander. In 324 B.C., Hephaestion, Alexander's closest friend, fell ill and died in the city. (Bosworth 1988, 94; Curtius V:8; Dodge [1890] 1993, 414–15; Hammond 1981, 168; Hammond and Scullard 1970, 368; Lempriere [1788] 1987, 218; Warrington [1961] 1978, 207; Weigall 1933, 238)

Elephants The elephant was primarily a shock impact weapon used by the Indian army. Its sheer bulk could crash through and disorder any close-order infantry formation. Elephants would gore enemy soldiers with their tusks, kneel on them, crush them with their foreheads, and throw them through the air with their trunks. Although the one-inch thickness of the elephant's hide made it almost impervious to missile fire or regular edged weapons, its legs could be hamstrung by axes and broadswords, its trunk could be easily severed, and its unprotected mahout could be killed by almost any weapon. Upon the death of its mahout, the elephant could easily become confused and unmanageable and would frequently go berserk, trampling both enemy and friendly troops without distinction.

All but the most disciplined troops would be routed by an elephant charge. Against highly trained troops properly armed to engage them, the effectiveness of the elephants was greatest in the initial contact and quickly fell off thereafter. Although Alexander was able to deal effectively with the elephants at the battle of Hydaspes River, his soldiers could not be coerced into ever fighting them again, so frightening had their experience been with the elephants.

Enomotarch The quarter-file commander in a Macedonian phalanx file. (Connolly [1977] 1978, 58]

Ephesus A city in Ionia allegedly built by the Amazons. Ephesus was famous in the ancient world for the Temple of Diana, one of the seven wonders of the ancient world. The temple was allegedly burnt down on the day Alexander the Great was born. Alexander's later offer to rebuild the temple was politely refused by the citizens of Ephesus on the grounds that it was not proper for one god to raise a temple to another. Alexander did, however, order that the tribute the city had formerly paid to the Persians should go into the treasury of Artemis, a fund which was to be used to rebuild the temple. (Hammond and Scullard 1970, 387; Lempriere [1788] 1984, 387)

Epigoni A reference to Alexander's Persian "inheritors." These were 30,000 Persian youth from the northeast satrapies whom Alexander ordered to be trained in the Macedonian method of combat. They joined him at his return to Susa from India. Alexander intended to form a new phalanx formation around them in the hopes that they would add significant missile fire support to a slightly weaker shock unit. He thought that this kind of formation would be more useful to engage future enemies who were likely to rely more on missile fire than shock combat. Before the new formation could be implemented, however, Alexander died. His successors promptly rescinded the innovation, and nothing more was heard of it.

Etesian Winds These were northerly winds that blew south across the Aegean from mid–July to October. They frequently exceeded gale force and made sailing extremely hazardous, if not impossible. Etesian Winds severely damaged Xerxes' fleet in 480 B.C. and prevented the Athenians from interfering in Philip's military campaigns in both the Chalcidice Peninsula and against Amphipolis. (Cawkwell 1978, 74)

Euboea The largest island in the Aegean. It had a length of 90 miles and a width varying between 30 and 40 miles. Located along southern Thessaly, east of Boeotia, and northeast of Attica, Euboea was separated from the mainland by a strait whose narrowest point, called Euripus, was only wide enough to admit a single trireme at a time. (Warrington [1961] 1978, 222)

Eunuch A self-castrated Middle-Eastern man associated with the cult of the Anatolian mother-goddess. The castration supposedly decontaminated the man, enabling him to perform rites requiring the purity of a virgin or child. (Hammond and Scullard 1970, 416)

Euxine Sea The Greek name for the Black Sea. See **Pontus Sea** for additional information. (Hammond and Scullard 1970, 425)

Exile's Decree At the Olympic games of 324 B.C., Alexander announced his Exile's Decree. It called for cities to receive back all former exiles and provided for the restoration of confiscated property and compensation for any loss incurred by being deprived of it. Only those guilty of sacrilege or murder or those exiled by either Philip or Alexander were to be excluded from the terms of the decree.

Alexander had three different objectives in issuing the decree. First, it was a convenient way to resolve the large number of Greek exiles and mercenaries garrisoned in Asia and causing serious local unrest in many areas. They frequently grouped together and used their numbers to terrorize the outlying areas, stealing, raping, and killing with impunity. Asia would never know peace until this lawless element, which had everything to gain by the continuing instability, was removed. When these exiles returned to their cities, Alexander's second objective would be achieved. The arrival of these belligerent elements would significantly destabilize most city governments. The restoration of confiscated property would probably entail a period of extreme confusion as the expected lengthy litigation proceeded. The political instability arising from the proceedings would probably leave the cities little time for plotting revolution against Alexander. The third objective was to have the exiles to look upon Alexander as their sole patron. In every city Alexander would always have a loyal faction that could be relied upon to support his interests, as their mutual interdependence would not allow one party to thrive and prosper without the other.

Alexander was clearly breaching the terms of the Corinthian League's charter by issuing the Exile's Decree. It was not a result of discussion and debate with the members of the League but the unilateral decree of a tyrant. Any interference in the internal affairs of member states was a violation of the League of Corinth's most basic principle, which guaranteed the preservation of existing government. Both Aetolia and Athens could be expected to react to Alexander's decree with a declaration of war. Aetolia had exiled the Acarnanian citizens of Oeniadae and occupied it with its own citizens, while the Athenians had done the same to Samos in 365 B.C.

Fortunately for Greece, the terms of the Exile's Decree were never implemented. Ten months after Alexander's announcement of it, he died in Babylon. His successors immediately notified the Greek cities that they should disregard the Exile's Decree. Needless to say, the Greek cities were greatly relieved. (Bosworth 1988, 220–28; Griffith 1966, 174–75)

Fathom A nautical measurement indicating a depth of six feet.

Favorite A reference to a homosexual lover.

File A column of soldiers extending from front to back. Commonly used in reference to Greek hoplite formations that had files of either 8 or 16 ranks deep during the Macedonian era.

Float A raft Alexander's troops constructed out of tent hides that were filled with chaff for buoyancy and then sewn shut for waterproofing. The floats were used to carry Alexander's army across the Danube, Jaxartes, and Oxus rivers.

Freeboard The distance between the water line and the gunwale of a ship. (Morrison and Coates 1986, 239)

Frontage The area extending laterally across the front of a unit. This was sometimes expressed as a number of files.

Furlong An ancient linear measurement equivalent to an eighth of a mile or 220 yards.

Gaugamela A site in Mesopotamia that was the location of the last field battle fought between Alexander and Darius III in 331 B.C. Darius' loss of the battle cost him his empire.

The name *Gaugamela* translates into "camel's pasture" and was assigned by Darius in commemoration of his awarding the town as a prize for the best performance of a camel on his Scythian expedition. (Cook 1983, 142; Plutarch, 555)

GLOSSARY

Gaza An ancient city in southern Palestine, 2.5 miles inland and on the edge of the Egyptian desert along a major overland trade route from Egypt. Gaza was successfully stormed by Alexander after a two-month siege in 332 B.C. (Hammond and Scullard 1970, 459)

Getae A Thracian tribe living along the Danube River in the area the Romans would later call Dacia.

Gomphi A city in western Thessaly located along an important route to Ambracia. (Griffith 1935, 178; Hammond and Griffith 1979, 541)

Gordian Knot At a time when Gordium was experiencing serious unrest, an assembly of citizens consulted an oracle for advice on what to do. They were told that a cart would bring them a king who would end their strife. Just then, Gordius, his wife, and their son Midas (later to be a king renowned for his riches) drove up in a cart drawn by oxen. The assembly immediately made Gordius king. The cart in which he was riding, the yoke, and the ox-pole were then consecrated to Zeus and preserved on the acropolis as a relic by the city.

The cart was connected to the ox-pole by a complex knot of cornel bark commonly known to sailors as a Turk's-head. Its main characteristic was that the ends of the cords were tucked inside. Tradition had it that whoever was able to undo the so-called "Gordian knot" would rule Asia. When Alexander heard the story he, of course, had an irresistible urge to see the wagon. After he had unsuccessfully tried to undo the knot by untying it, Alexander is reputed to have said that it made no difference how it was loosened. Then he either cut the knot in two with his sword or drew out the dowel pin that went through the knot and detached it from the pole. This would have revealed the ends of the thongs and allowed him to undo the knot in the conventional way. The thunder and lightning occurring that night was widely interpreted among the Greeks as another divine endorsement for Alexander's Asian campaign. (Abbott, 106–7; Arrian II:3; Curtius III:1; Justin IX:7)

Gordium The capital of the satrapy of Phrygia. (Olmstead [1948] 1970, 502)

Guardian A Spartan soldier who was responsible for the conduct of a Spartan boy's military education. The guardians were also called "lovers" because of their frequent homosexual relations with their charges. (Mitchell [1952] 1964, 195)

Guards A reference to the hypaspists.

Gunwale The upper edge of a ship's side. (Morrison and Coates 1986, 240)

Gymnosophists The name means "naked philosophers." It was given by the Greeks to Hindu and Buddhist monks of India, who frequently went about naked year round. Alexander first came across the gymnosophists at Taxila and was amazed at the bodily pain they regularly endured in complete silence. The Brahmans were thought to be a sect of Gymnosophists. (Arrian VII:2; Lempriere [1788] 1987, 260)

Halus An island city off the coast of Thessaly that had once belonged to the Athenian confederacy. It had apparently been occupied by pirates sometime later. Philip II besieged and captured it during the Third Sacred War. (Bury 1913, 703)

Hanging Gardens of Babylon The legendary hanging gardens of atop the citadel in Babylon were one of the seven wonders of the ancient world. The gardens were built by Nebuchadnezzar for his Median bride Amytis, who missed the mountains of her homeland in Media. The king built a terraced mountain of stone for her on the roof of his citadel that was 400 feet on a side and rose up 75 feet. The roof was covered with stone beams upon which a series of terraces were laid, each having a layer of reeds, one of bitumen, two layers of brick bound together by cement, and a layer of lead as a seal against leaks. The earth was then placed to a depth that would cover the roots of the largest trees, some of which were reputed to be 12 feet thick and 50 feet high. As mud brick, the usual construction material of the area, would not provide the necessary structural strength to support the massive weight of the earth, water, and trees of the garden, large quantities of stone had to be quarried and transported from great distances for the construction because none was available locally.

Water for the garden, which came from the Euphrates River, was raised up by mechanical devices powered by oxen or human slaves. The royal staterooms located directly below the garden were kept cool, even during the hottest time of year, by the constant stream of water flowing over the vegetation hanging down over their windows. (Clayton and Price [1988] 1989, 43–44; Curtius V:1; de Camp 1974, 69)

Hegemon The commander of the military forces of the League of Corinth. This office was held by Philip II of Macedonia and after his assassination by his son, Alexander the Great.

Hellespont This was a strait that separated Thrace from Asia Minor, connecting the Propontis Sea (Sea of Marmara) with the Aegean Sea. It was named for Helle, the sister of Phrixus, who allegedly fell off the back of a flying golden-fleeced ram and into the strait. The Hellespont, known in modern times as the Dardanelles, is 45 miles long and averages between 3 and 4 miles wide. At Sestos, however, the strait narrows to a width of only 1.25 miles. (Avery 1972, 158)

Hemilochites The half-file commander in a Macedonian phalanx file. (Connolly [1977] 1978, 58)

Heptastadion (seven furlongs) A three-quarter-mile-long mole connecting the city of Alexandria, in Egypt, to the island of Pharos. The mole (a causeway) separated the western side of the Great Harbor from the Harbor of Eunostos. Two gaps on either end of the Heptastade allowed water to flow through. This not only prevented silting of the harbors but facilitated the passage of ships between them. (Warrington [1961] 1978, 32, 399)

Heracles Alexander the Great traced his ancestry to Heracles, who was alleged to be the son of Zeus and Alcmene, the wife of Amphitryon of Thebes, in Boeotia. Although at birth Zeus had intended Heracles to rule over the race of Perseus, Hera had somehow persuaded him to swear that the first born of Perseus should be their ruler. She then went to Argos and caused Sthenelus' wife (Sthenelus was Perseus' son) to give birth to Eurystheus. Although this deprived Heracles of his birthright, there was nothing that could be done because Zeus could not break his oath. Hera seems to have pursued Heracles with a vengeance, even sending serpents to attack him in his cradle. Although an infant, Heracles managed to strangle them.

When Iole — daughter of Eurytus, the king of Oechalia — rejected Heracles' advances, he went mad and murdered Iphitus, the only son of Eurytus. Ironically, he had been Heracles' only supporter in his courting of Iole. When Heracles recovered, the gods struck him with a disorder that required him to go to Delphi for a cure. The Pydna there ordered him to be sold as a slave and told him that if he remained in that status for three years he would recover from his illness. Heracles was sold to Omphale, queen of Lydia, who restored his liberty and then married him. Croesus, the king of Lydia, is alleged to have descended from their issue.

Zeus had made Heracles subservient to Eurystheus because he had been born after him, thanks to Hera. When Heracles disobeyed Eurystheus, Zeus' punishment was to drive him mad. As a result Heracles killed his wife Megara, his children by her, and his brother Iphicles' children. Imposing exile on himself, Heracles went to the Oracle of Delphi to inquire where he should settle. The Pythia ordered him to live at Attiryns and to serve Eurystheus for the next 12 years. He was told that he would become immortal after this. Eurystheus, being afraid of the presence of such a legendary and powerful man as Heracles, sent him to perform the 12 most difficult tasks that he could think of, commonly known as the 12 labors of Heracles. Before Heracles began his labors, he was armed by the gods: Minerva provided his helmet; Mercury, his sword; Neptune, his horse; Apollo, his bow and arrows; Vulcan, his cuirass; and Zeus, his shield. Heracles then proceeded on the following labors:

1. **The Lion of Nemea**: Heracles strangled the lion raging in Mycenae and then wore its skin.

2. **The Hydra of Leyna**: Heracles ripped out the hydra's belly, dipped his arrows in its gall, and then fatally wounded it with an arrow.

3. **The Stag of Eurystheus**: Heracles spent a year pursuing the stag near Oenoe before catching it in a trap.

4. **The Boar of Eryman**: Heracles caught the boar near Erymanthus by tracking it through the snow.

5. **The Stable of Augeas**: Heracles cleaned out a stable that 3,000 oxen had used for several years.

6. **The Birds of Stymphalus**: Heracles killed flesh-eating birds near lake Stymphalus, in Arcadia.

7. **The Cretan Bull**: Heracles killed a wild bull in Crete.

8. **The Mares of Diomedes**: These were horses who fed on human flesh. Heracles killed Diomedes and fed him to his mares. He then took the horses to Mt. Olympus, where they were eaten by wild animals.

9. **The Girdle of the Amazon Queen**: Heracles stole the girdle of the Amazon queen, Hippolyte.

10. **The Oxen of Geryon**: Heracles captured the oxen of Geryon and then killed the Geryon, a monster with three bodies, and Orthus, a two-headed dog.

11. **The Cerberus**: Heracles entered Hades through Laconia. After freeing Theseus from his eternal torment, Heracles carried off the monster Cerberus to the upper world without using weapons.

12. **The Apples of the Hesperides**: Heracles obtained an apple from a tree guarded by a dragon at the world's end.

Heracles also had several other notable adventures. He killed Laomedon, the king of Troy, and sacked the city. (Laomedon's legendary son Priam survived to defend Troy against Agamenon's attack during the Trojan War.) He also accompanied the Argonauts on part of their journey in search of the golden fleece. However, when Hylas, the boy he loved, was pulled down into the water by a nymph at Cios, in Mysia, Heracles left the expedition to look for him. Heracles also assisted the gods in their war against the giants and made possible Zeus' victory over them.

Heracles married Deianeira, the daughter of Oeneus. Three years after their marriage, Heracles accidentally killed a boy at a banquet in the house of Oeneus and was exiled. He took Deianeira with him, and when they came to the Evenus River, he had the centaur Nessus carry her across while he swam. Upon hearing Deianeira's screams and finding that Nessus had manhandled her, Heracles shot an arrow into his heart. Before dying, Nessus gave Deianeira some of his blood, telling her that it was a powerful love charm.

Years later, when Heracles again pursued Iole, Deianeira, in an attempt to regain his lost love, soaked one of his garments in the blood that Nessus had provided to her and sent it to him. The blood turned out to be a poison, and when Heracles put on the garment it clung to him and burned his flesh. In agony, Heracles leaped into the water to cool his body. Such was the heat generated that the water boiled. (The resulting hot springs gave its name to the nearby pass, which was later known as the "Hot Gates" or Thermopylae.) Unable to obtain relief in the water from the heat, Heracles began to rip off the garment, removing pieces of his flesh along with it. He then climbed Mt. Oeta, placed a pile of wood atop it, and ordered himself set afire. Amid a crack of thunder, a cloud descended and carried him off to Olympus, where he received his immortality. After Heracles' death, a decree was issued by the oracle at Delphi that he was to be honored as a god.

Heracles exerted a powerful influence on Alexander the Great throughout his life. When the Tyrians refused to allow him to sacrifice in their temple identified with his ancestor Heracles, Alexander used this refusal as an excuse to besiege the city. From Egypt, Alexander set out to visit the temple at Siwah, in part because Heracles had done so. Heracles' failure to capture the Rock of Aornos largely prompted Alexander's siege against the position. Alexander felt obliged to either duplicate or surpass any feat that Heracles had attempted. (Arrian IV:11; Hammond and Scullard 1970, 498–99; Lempriere [1788] 1987, 274–76; Plutarch, 541; Radice [1971] 1973, 128–29; Tarn [1948] 1978, 51, 353; Warrington [1961] 1978, 266)

Hero A being between man and god, a sort of supernatural human. The cult of heroes originated in the eighth century B.C. in the aftermath of the Homeric poems. A hero's life consisted of glory and achievement. The respect that he received was predicated upon his deeds being unsurpassed. It was thought that by making sacrifices at a hero's tomb, the living would be able to enlist his aid.

Upon Hephaestion's death, Alexander sent a delegation to Siwah to inquire how he was to honor his friend. He received the answer that it was proper to acknowledge Hephaestion as a hero, and this was done. (Bosworth 1988, 278; Hammond and Scullard 1970, 505; Lempriere [1788] 1987, 279; Radice [1971] 1973, 133)

Hetairoi A Greek name for the Companion cavalry. (Hamilton 1973, 24)

Hipparch A commander of a Macedonian Companion cavalry hipparchy that numbered 1,000 troopers.

Hogging The sagging of a ship's hull from extreme length, causing it to buckle upwards in the center and droop downward at the ends. This was a situation prevalent with the trireme because the two 1.5-foot gangways running along the sides of the ship did not connect into a full deck. (Morrison and Coates 1986, 240)

Homosexuality Homosexual relations between men were a part of Greek culture. It was believed that the older man would inspire the younger to excel and each would encourage the other to serve the public good.

The most widely known homosexual military unit in ancient times was the legendary Theban "Sacred Band." This was a hoplite unit composed of 150 pairs of homosexual lovers who swore to die rather than retreat. True to their word, at the battle of Chaeronea the Sacred Band was virtually eliminated by Alexander the Great, only 46 of the unit's 300 members surviving.

Both Philip and Alexander were said to have homosexual lovers. Two of Philip's were both named Pausanias, while Alexander's were probably Hephaestion and the eunuch Bagoas. (Savill 1993, 279)

Hot Gates A reference to the pass at Thermopylae.

Hydaspes River An Indian river also known as the Jhelum.

Hydraotes River An Indian river also known as the Ravi. (Savill 1993, 117)

Hypaspists (Shield-bearers) Elite peltasts used extensively by Alexander on missions of special difficulty requiring a forced march or exceptional tactical agility. They were originally the shield-bearers and then the bodyguards of the Macedonian kings. They were frequently referred to as the Guards. (Hammond 1981, 28)

Hyphasis River An Indian river also known as the Beas.

Hypozomata (Undergirds) Two cables that ran the length of a trireme to prevent the ship from hogging or sagging. They were tightened when the trireme was put in the water and loosened when it was in dry dock. (Casson 1994, 66)

Ilai A Companion cavalry squadron of 200 troopers. (Hackett 1989, 104)

Illyrians A general reference to Balkan tribes inhabiting modern Yugoslavia and Albania.

Inheritors see **Epigoni**

Ionia An area along the western coast of Asia Minor. The principal cities of Ionia were Clazomenae, Colophon, Erythrae, Lebedus, Phocaea, and Teos. (Bosworth 1980, 134)

Ister The ancient name for the Danube River.

Javelin A six- to seven-foot spear typically used by Greek peltasts, Persian infantry, and light cavalry. It could either be thrown from a standing position to a range of 20 yards or retained for hand-to-hand combat. The javelin was inferior to both the 9-foot-long spear of the Greek hoplite and the 21-foot-long sarissa of the Macedonian phalanx.

Jaxartes River The word means "great river." (Dodge [1890] 1993, 464)

Jhelum River An Indian river also known as the Hydaspes.

Judea The southern area of modern Israel. (Warrington [1961] 1978, 301)

Kausia A broad-brimmed Macedonian hat. (Head 1982, 105)

Khamsin A strong wind blowing in Egypt in April, during which wind velocities often reached gale force. Temperatures rose 40°F, humidity fell to 10 percent or less in a matter of minutes, and severe lightning frequently occurred. During Alexander's trip to Siwah, a Khamsin blew up and obliterated all traces of the route there. (Engels 1978, 62)

Killed to Wounded Ratio In Alexander's time, the number killed to wounded ranged from 1:5 to 1:20, depending on several factors, including the intensity of the assault, type of troops attacking and defending, and the terrain. (Delbruck 1990, 189; Dodge [1890] 1993, 129, 248)

King's Castle One of three citadels at Halicarnassus. It was located along the seashore at the entrance to the city's harbor.

King's Journal see **Daily Record**

Kypsela The Odrysian Thracian capital. (Casson 1926, 196, 201)

Lancers see **Scouts**

Larisa One of the major cities in Thessaly; it was ruled by an aristocratic family known as the Aleuadae. They were overthrown by Philip II of Macedonia, who then assumed control of the city. (Avery 1972, 173)

League of Corinth After his victory in the battle of Chaeronea, Philip was able to coerce the Greeks into establishing a common peace. The ancient Greeks called the League the "Hellenes," but modern historians gave it the name of its first meeting place, and it is generally known as the League of Corinth. The League's members included Acarnania, Achaea, Aeniania, Aetolia, Ambracia, Arcadia, Argos, Athamania, Athens, Boeotia, Cephallenia, the Chalcidice, the Chersonese, Corcyra, Corinth, the Cycladic islands, Dolopia, Doris, Elis, Euboea, Locris, Magnesia, Malis, Megara, Oetaea, Perrhaebia, Phocis, Phthiotis, Samothrace, Thasos, the Thessalian islands, Thessaly, Thrace, and Zacynthus. With the exception of Sparta, it was an offensive and defensive alliance between Macedonia and the states of Greece, who were united in a single federation. Sparta had refused to join the League for two reasons: it considered itself to be the natural leader of the Greeks and refused to concede that right to the Macedonians and objected to Massena being declared independent of Sparta by Macedonia and the members of the League.

Each signer of the treaty establishing the common peace was theoretically protected by the combined strength of the League. If an individual city were threatened, all states of the League were supposed to take united action. Citizens of any allied state who took service with a foreign power against either Macedonia or the League were to be banished as traitors and have their possessions confiscated. All decisions were to be made by a council where each state would be represented according to its size and military significance. A total of 100 delegates were sent from all the member cities. The council would gather together four times a year at the Pan-Hellenic festivals at Olympia, Delphi, Nemea, and the Isthmus, but the hegemon could always convene an extraordinary meeting of the League at any time to consider whatever issues he believed important.

A smaller steering committee of five members would sit permanently at Corinth to monitor the peace continually. Its members were chosen by lot from among the delegates, no single city being allowed to assume more than one position on the committee at any one time. The steering committee would pass legislation for action when necessary and act as a court to arbitrate disputes between both individuals and cities. A simple majority of its vote decided any issue. Macedonia could always address the steering committee, whereas other states would have to present theirs through their council delegates for consideration. It was obvious that any transgressions against the peace by Macedonia were not subject to the decisions of the League. This was because Macedonia was technically not a member of the League but only had a treaty with it. Also, as the majority of the members of the League were controlled by Macedonia, it was not likely to vote through measures contrary to Macedonia's wishes. The League was empowered to impose sanctions or call upon the support of the hegemon to initiate military action against any offenders.

Philip II was appointed hegemon, or commanding general, of the League for life and would command their combined military forces in the field. In this position, he would execute any requests for military action passed by the League. In the field, however, it was the hegemon's discretion alone which determined the scope of military operations. The forces to be made available to the hegemon for any military operation were always determined in advance. Although the full military levy of the League was estimated by the ancients at 15,000 cavalry and 200,000 infantry, it is unlikely that any more than a fraction of this force could have been fielded at any one time. The ability to pay the wages of 1,150 talents a month for such a force or to supply it in the field with the 400 tons of grain per month required for both men and horses was clearly beyond the ability of Greece at that time.

Existing forms of government were to remain in place. A city was protected against any radical changes in its constitution and interference or subversion in its internal affairs. Cities were to be protected against any land encroachment of an exile's backed attack on their homeland. A city could not be coerced into accepting back exiles, redistributing land, canceling debts, or freeing slaves. Every city-state was guaranteed internal freedom and autonomy. The exceptions to this were Corinth, Chalcis, and Thebes, each of which had Macedonian garrisons stationed in them. All three cities were in strategic locations that had to be occupied to prevent the Greeks from joining forces.

At the second meeting of the League, Philip submitted his request for a war against Persia. His stated justification for the war was that it was in revenge for the desecrations Xerxes had committed against the temples of the gods during his invasion of Greece 159 years earlier. Philip had hoped that his religious crusade against the "barbarians" would appeal to all Greeks and unite them in a common purpose. It didn't, but the Greeks had little choice but to cooperate. Philip's proposal was passed, and Philip was appointed supreme commander of the League forces to be raised against the Persians.

With the establishment of the League of Corinth, Philip had taken the first step to unify Greece. Most of the city-states in Greece did not want to be part of a federation, however, and had no inclination to make Philip's plan work. They looked upon their separateness as a guarantee of their freedom and largely regarded the League as a temporary and unwelcome instrument of coercion by a foreign power. Philip's plan to force the Greek city-states to begin thinking collectively as a national entity was far ahead of its time, but the concept was so alien to the Greeks that it could only be imposed on them by the force of Macedonian arms. Thus it was assured not to last. During the short time Philip had left to live, he at least gave the appearance of dealing with an independently functioning League, although we can be sure that he was always engaged in considerable stage managing behind the scenes to make things come out to his satisfaction.

Although Alexander attempted to placate the League in the very beginning, when he thought it useful, as time passed, its members were quickly relegated to the status of conquered subjects. This was clearly illustrated by his imposition on Greece of the hated Exile's Decree that clearly violated one of the basic tenets of the League — that no forcible changes would be made to destabilize the governments of member states. It was obvious to the Greeks that Alexander held their rights in contempt, and they only awaited the day when they would be able to throw off his hated rule. (Bradford 1992, 154; Curtius I; Ellis 1976, 205–6, 228; Fine 1983, 677–78; 682 Green 1991, 86; Hammond and Griffith 1979, 635; Westlake 1935, 215)

Levies The term refers to Persian peasant militia impressed into military service. Typically this infantry was untrained, poorly armed, undisciplined, and of low morale. They were almost a totally ineffective against any Greek or Macedonian troops.

Library of Alexandria The famous Library of Alexandria was part of the museum founded by Ptolemy I. Its mission was to assemble all works in Greek and to translate major foreign works into Greek. By 250 B.C. the library contained 500,000 scrolls of ancient writers; eventually the library contained 750,000 scrolls, although a large number of these must have been duplicate copies. Typically, the work obtained was copied and the copy returned to the owner, the original being retained by the library. Anyone visiting the city had any books in their possession taken from them for copying.

The Library of Alexandria was clearly the largest such facility in the world at that time. During Ptolemy's siege of Caesar's force in the palace, the Egyptian fleet was set afire in the harbor. The fire spread to the docks and burned 40,000 scrolls that were awaiting export to Rome and other cities. Anthony later transferred 200,000 scrolls to the Library of Alexandria from the library at Pergamum. The Library of Alexandria was damaged by revolts in A.D. 272, A.D. 295, and A.D. 391. Its remaining scrolls were destroyed when Caliph Omar captured the city in A.D. 642. During his reign the library's scrolls supplied the fuel for the 4,000 baths of Egypt for six months. (Canfora [1989] 1990, 20, 69–70, 99; De Camp 1972, 294; 1974, 35; Hammond and Scullard 1970, 607; Lempriere [1788] 1987, 33; Toynbee 1967, 113)

Lochagos The commander of a phalanx file. (Connolly [1977] 1978, 58)

Lochoi A military unit of the phalanx consisting of a file of 16 men.

Locked Shields A Macedonian phalanx formation with a file frontage of 1.5 feet.

Lydia A powerful ancient kingdom ruling eastern Asia Minor south of the Halys River. The kingdom's capital was Sardes.

After the defeat of Croesus, Lydia's last king, the Lydian kingdom became a satrapy of the Persian Empire. (Hammond and Scullard 1970, 629)

Magi A religious sect founded by Zoroaster that was probably comprised of Medians. The Magi had great political and religious influence' they led religious processions, provided libations, chanted incantations, and specialized in interpreting dreams. Their understanding of mathematics, philosophy, and astronomy allowed them to astound members of their audiences, who applied the name *magician* to the members of the sect and the word *magic* to the impressive display of their knowledge.

The Magi wore white robes and lived a Spartan lifestyle. They worshiped fire, believing that it was able to purify all things. They would also spend several hours a day gazing into the sun for inspiration. (Cook 1993, 155; Lempriere [1788] 1987, 349)

Magnesia A district in eastern Thessaly comprised primarily of a mountain range running from north to south. Its coastline contained no suitable sites for harbors. (Ellis 1976, 85)

Mahout A trainer and driver of Indian elephants. The mahout's association with his elephant was close, and in his absence the elephant would frequently become confused, frightened, and unmanageable.

Makran A desert in the satrapy of Gedrosa.

Mantelets A large and heavy shield that gave the user protection against missile fire. Mantelets were usually rolled in place on wheels and braced to stand upright by themselves. Javelins and arrows were usually unable to penetrate the heavy mantelets.

Maracanda A city in the satrapy of Sogdiana. It was surrounded by a wall nine miles long and had an inner citadel. (Curtius VII:6)

Marduk, Temple of The sacred Temple of Marduk in Babylon was an L-shaped building about 500 feet in length on each side. The structure rose up seven stories in the form of a ziggurat. Included on the grounds were living quarters for the priests and visiting pilgrims and extensive enclosures for the animals regularly sacrificed at temple services. (de Camp 1974, 70–71)

Massagetae A Scythian tribe living north-west of Sogdiana. Its territory contained no iron or silver but had large deposits of gold and brass. Members of the tribe did not engage in agriculture, instead living on their herds and any fish they were able to catch.

The Massagetae fought both mounted and on foot. They were typically armed with a bow, lance, and battle-axe. The helmets, girdles, and accouterments for their horses were said to be made of gold and their breastplates of brass.

Although each man had a wife, all women were held in common. When a man grew old, his relatives reputedly sacrificed him by boiling and eating him. Those dying of disease were directly buried, much to the regret of their relatives, who bemoaned the fact that the person had been deprived of being properly sacrificed.

Mauryan Empire (321 B.C.–296 B.C.) After the death of Alexander the Great, the Indian Chandragupta expelled the Greeks from the Punjab and then went on to conquer the Nanda Empire of the Ganges valley. His empire at its height extended from the Bay of Bengal to the Arabian Sea. Chandragupta's harsh rule, however, led to continuing revolts by his subjects. His reign lasted for 24 years, ending with his death circa 299 B.C. (Hammond and Scullard 1970, 950; Sastri 1957, 6; Savill 1993, 179)

Mausoleum of Halicarnassus The Mausoleum of Halicarnassus was built between 353 and 350 B.C. by Artemis as a tomb for her recently deceased husband, Mausolus, the king of Caria. The structure was not intended to be the largest tomb ever built, but it was among the most beautiful. A flight of marble stairs flanked by sculptured lions rose up from a walled courtyard. The mausoleum was then surrounded by another wall, atop which were mounted statues of gods and goddesses. At each corner of the wall were stone warriors on horses. The tomb itself was rectangular, measuring 100 feet by 120 feet and being 140 feet tall. Relief sculptures decorated all sides of it. A total of 36 Ionic columns supported a second-story pyramid roof whose 26 stepped-levels led to a platform. On this platform stood a four-horse chariot occupied by Mausolus and a woman representing either the goddess Athena or Artemisia, his wife.

The mausoleum survived for over 1,700

years. In the thirteenth century the upper part of the structure, including the roof, collapsed as the result of an earthquake. In A.D. 1402, the Knights of St. John of Jerusalem acquired possession of Halicarnassus and proceeded to build a castle nearby, using material from the mausoleum. In A.D. 1522, the remains of the mausoleum were dismantled to repair the castle. (Clayton and Price, 1988, 100, 103–5; Cottrell 1962, 69–71; Hammond 1970, 657; Hammond and Scullard 1970, 656)

Medimmus A Greek measure of weight equal to one an a half bushels, 104 pounds, or six modi. (Micelle [1952] 1964, 288; Scullard 1974, 46; Tarn [1948] 1979, 88)

Megalopolis The name means "Great City." It was founded as the capital of Arcadia by Epaminondas after the battle of Leuctra in 371 B.C. Forty villages were consolidated to form the city that lay in a plain along a strategic communications route. Megalopolis was a link in a chain of strong cities intended to form a barrier against Spartan expansion. It was one of the largest cities of the Peloponnesus and the most heavily fortified, being surrounded by a double wall 5½ miles in circumference. (Avery 1972, 197; Bury, 584, 596; Hammond and Scullard 1970, 665; Michell [1952] 1964, 315; Warry 1993, 64)

Melkart The chief god of Tyre, who was widely identified with Alexander's ancestor, Heracles. (Bosworth 1988, 281)

Mercenaries Professional Greek soldiers who hired out for wages. Mercenaries were generally more effective in battle than city-state troops because of their superior training, armament, discipline, and leadership.

Merchant Ships The largest merchant ships during the Macedonian Empire carried about 250 tons, or 10,000 talents, of cargo. Merchant ships were too broad to be rowed efficiently by oars and instead used the sail for mobility. However, a limited number of oars, possibly as many as 20, were carried aboard for maneuvering the ship in close quarters, as in docking. (Torr 1964, 20, 25)

Methone A city along the Macedonian coast that served as a base of operations against Macedonia in the fifth century. Methone was besieged, captured, and razed by Philip in 353 B.C., and its territory was distributed to Macedonians. (Cawkwell 1978, 37)

Mina A Greek unit of money equal to 100 drachmas or 60 staters. A mina weighed almost four pounds avoirdupolis. (Hammond and Scullard 1970, 260)

Mixed Array An Indian army formation, with infantry and chariots deployed in the center, cavalry on the flanks, and elephants on the wings. This was an all-purpose formation used to break through the enemy center with the chariots or to shatter its wings with the elephants. (Head 1982, 53)

Modi A Greek unit of measure weighing about 17 pounds. Six modi were equal to one medimni.

Mole A land bridge built over water to enable siege operations to be conducted against an island. Alexander's famous mole at Tyre was a half-mile long and 200 yards wide. After Alexander's time, the construction of moles was largely abandoned in preference to seaborne amphibious assaults.

Motya A fortified city on Sicily. It was built on a small island separated from the mainland by a narrow channel. In a precursor of Alexander's siege of Tyre, Dionysius, ruler of Sicily, built a mole across the channel, at the end of which he constructed movable six-story towers. Arrow-shooting catapults cleared Motya's walls of defenders, enabling Dionysius to move battering rams up to the walls to effect a breach. The city fell by storm. (Fuller 1958, 43–4)

Mound A hill built by a besieger against an elevated position that would allow the deployment of siege artillery, siege towers, and rams against that position.

Museum (Shrine of the Muses) The common ancient reference to the Museum of Alexandria, renowned throughout the ancient world as the center of scientific inquiry. The Museum was the closest thing to a university in the ancient world. Being generously funded by the Ptolemies and exempted from all taxes, its facilities, resources, and gardens had no equal in the ancient world. The Museum supported a large group of scholars who engaged in extensive scientific research. The lectures that they gave were often attended by the king of Egypt.

In 146 B.C., political instability in Egypt forced the resident scholars to flee from Alexandria. Although some of them eventually returned to the Museum, it did not recover its former supremacy, being now rivaled by similar institutions established in Antioch, Athens, Berytus, Rhodes, and Rome. The first Roman emperors visited the Museum and expanded it. In A.D. 230 the Museum was destroyed by Zenobia. Although eventually reopened, it was permanently eclipsed by a similar institution established at Constantinople. (Clayton and Price [1988] 1989, 142; de Camp 1974, 36; Hammond and Scullard 1970, 704–5)

Nicaea A city founded by Alexander near the battlefield of Hydaspes River to commemorate his victory over Porus there. (Arrian V:19; Bury, Cook, and Adcock [1927] 1978, VI:409)

Nineveh The capital of the Assyrian Empire. (Avery 1972, 229)

Nysa An Indian city located between the Cophen and Indus rivers. Allegedly founded by Dionysus, the city was named in honor of his nurse. The alleged proof of Dionysus' connection with the city was the presence of ivy there that grew nowhere else in India. (Arrian V:1; Bosworth 1988, 121; Curtius VIII:10)

Nisaean Plain A plain in Media, near Ecbatana, where the Persian royal mares were pastured. It was estimated that at one time 150,000 horses were being raised there. When Alexander arrived at the plain in 324 B.C., however, only 50,000 of the horses remained. The rest were thought to have been driven off by local thieves, possibly the Cossaeans. (Arrian VII:12)

Obol A unit of Greek money, six of which were equal to a drachma. (Morrison and Coates 1986, 240; Grote 1900 XI:313)

Oligarchy The concentration of political power in the hands of those of noble birth or wealth. Under such a government, the vast majority of citizens had no political rights. (Hammond and Scullard 1970, 749)

Odrysiang A powerful Thracian tribe ruled by the Odrysian royal house in Thrace. (Hammond and Walbank 1988, 38)

Ouragos The rear-ranked man in a Macedonian phalanx file. (Connolly [1977] 1978, 58)

Pace A linear distance of approximately 2.5 feet.

Paeonia An area in the Balkans located between the Strymon and Axius rivers . Its inhabitants claimed descent from Trojan immigrants and believed their ancestors had fought in the Trojan War in behalf of Troy. Philip invaded Paeonia on the death of its king, Agis, in 358 B.C. and subjugated that area to his rule. (Avery 1972, 242; Bosworth 1980, 66)

Pagasae The sole port of Thessaly. Pagasae was a large city whose walls occupied a greater circumference than those of Athens. (Hammond and Griffith 1979, 278)

Pages Adolescent sons of Macedonian noblemen who served the Macedonian king. They guarded the king while he slept, brought his horse to him, and accompanied him on the hunt and in battles. The king personally supervised their education and was the only one allowed to discipline them. The pages became companions of the king and were frequently appointed to high future military and civil positions.

Pangaeus Mountain A mountain southwest of the town of Crenidas in western Thrace. The position contained rich gold and silver deposits. (Bosworth 1988, 8)

Pasargadae A city in the satrapy of Persis founded by Cyrus the Great at the site of his victory over Astyages in 549 B.C. It became the place where the Persian kings were usually crowned. Cyrus' tomb, which can still be seen today, was located there. Pasargadae was one of the treasury cities of the Persian Empire, and Alexander the Great obtained 6,000 talents in silver there when he captured the city in 331–30 B.C. (Curtius V:6; Warrington [1961] 1978, 384)

Paura The capital of Gedrosa. (Arrian VI:24; Dodge [1890] 1993, 625)

Pella The capital and largest city of Macedonia. (Lane Fox 1974, 31)

Peltasts Greek skirmishing troops whose name was derived from the pelte, a small, round shield that they carried. The peltast was usually armed with a javelin, which they could either throw or retain to engage the enemy in hand-to-hand combat. They were lightly armored to retain their exceptional battlefield mobility.

The elite Balkan peltasts, the Agrianians, frequently supported Alexander's Companions, where their presence served to disorder enemy horses. After the Macedonian Empire, the use of peltasts dramatically declined. (Hammond and Scullard 1970, 797)

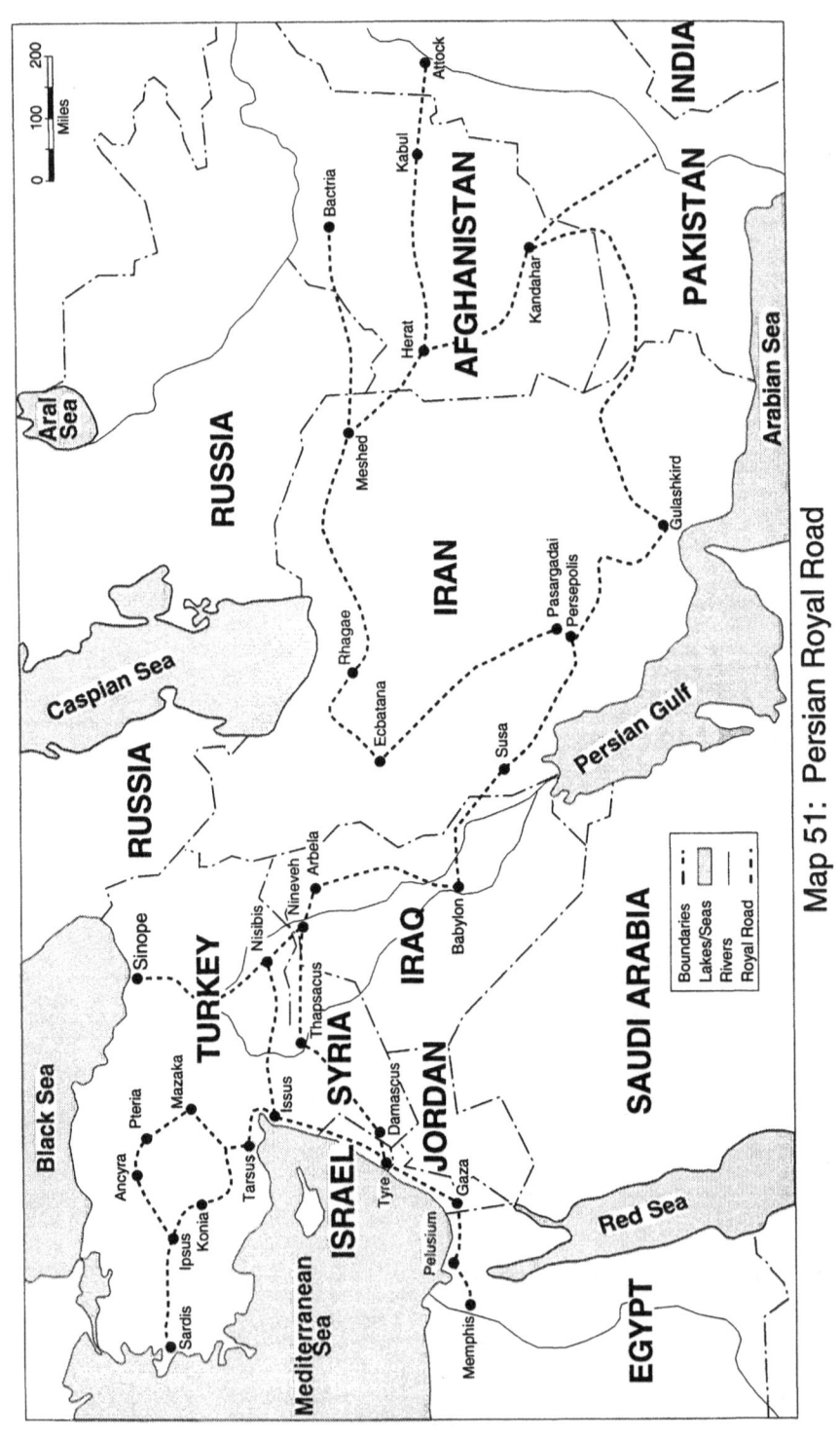

Map 51: Persian Royal Road

Pelte A small, round shield carried by Greek skirmishing troops. They were referred to as peltasts.

Pentakosiarchy A Macedonian Companion cavalry unit of 500 men.

Pentaconter A 125-foot-long Greek warship invented about 700 B.C. It was otherwise known as a "fifty-er" because there were 25 rowers on a side. The pentaconter was rendered obsolete by the trireme after 500 B.C. (Casson 1994, 53, 58; Morrison and Coates 1986, 240; Torr 1964, 147)

Perhaebia A district in northern Thessaly containing two strategic passes leading into southern Macedonia. The area was captured and occupied by Philip during the Third Sacred War. (Ellis 1976, 85)

Periplous (Sailing Around) An Athenian naval ramming technique used by the side outnumbering its opponent in ships. The longer line would allow a number of triremes to sail around the shorter opposing line of ships in order to attack them from the beam or stern. (Casson 1994, 75)

Persepolis The official residence of the Achaemenid kings and the capital of the Persian Empire. The name means "Persian city." Persepolis was considered to be a holy city by the Persians and was said to have exceeded all other cities of the empire in prosperity. The city's citadel was surrounded by triple walls. The first wall was 24 feet high; the second, 48 feet high; and the third, allegedly 90 feet high. In 331 B.C., Alexander captured, looted, and burned the city, supposedly at the instigation of an Athenian prostitute named Thais. (Avery 1972, 256; De Camp 1974, 75; Green [1974] 1991, 314; Hammond and Scullard 1970, 803)

Persia An area of one million square miles bounded on the west by the valleys of the Tigris and Euphrates rivers, on the east by the Indus River, and on the north by the Caspian Sea. (Hammond and Scullard 1970, 804)

Persian Empire The Persian Empire included the modern-day areas of Afghanistan, Egypt, India west of the Indus River, Iran, Iraq, Israel, Pakistan, Syria, and Turkey. The empire was founded by Cyrus I and came to an end during the reign of Darius III.

Persian Royal Road A military highway running 1,500 miles through the Persian Empire from Asia Minor as far south as Egypt and as far east as the Indus River. The road was constructed to facilitate rapid troop movement throughout the strategic areas of the Persian Empire.

Pezetairoi (Foot Companions) The Macedonian name for the soldiers of the phalanx. (Ellis 1976, 27)

Phaedriades (Shining Ones) A reference to the two bare gray rocks above the Oracle of Delphi. (Avery 1972, 117)

Phalanx A close-order Macedonian heavy infantry formation developed by Philip II. It consisted of six taxies of 1,500 heavy infantry soldiers for a total force of 9,000. Files usually had a frontage of three feet. The phalanx had a normal depth of 16 ranks in Philip's time and 8 ranks in Alexander's. The phalanx's combat effectiveness was achieved by shock impact momentum in an attempt to literally push its front rank through the opposing formation. The 21-foot-long sarissa allowed the first five ranks of the formation to project their sarissas out in front of the first rank. The remaining unengaged ranks would supply additional momentum by pushing their shields up against the back of the man in front of them with their shoulders to supply additional pushing momentum. (Dodge [1890] 1993, 142)

Pharos A three-mile-long island that protected Alexandria, in Egypt, against the effect of rough seas. The island's name was derived from the word *pharaoh*. The famous lighthouse known as the Pharos of Alexandria was built on the island lying about a mile offshore of Alexandria, in Egypt, between 285 B.C. and 246 B.C. It was one of the seven wonders of the world. The structure was not only a lighthouse but a fortress, its 300 rooms holding a large garrison that protected the city from pirates and any invasion from the sea.

Construction of the Pharos was begun by Ptolemy I and completed by his son Ptolemy II (Philadelphus) at a cost of 800 talents. The lighthouse was between 380 feet and 400 feet tall and encased in white marble. It was built like a ziggurat, the lower levels being square, the upper ones rounded. A ramp led up to the Pharos on an incline so gradual that even wagons could be driven up it without difficulty. At the top of the ramp, a windlass lifted up fuel for the fire that illuminated a giant reflecting mirror. It is said that the light from the beacon of the

Pharos could be seen 100 miles away at night. By day, the smoke from the beacon's fire could be seen at a distance of 30 miles. It was somewhat fancifully believed that Byzantium could be seen in the reflecting mirror of the Pharos, despite the fact that the city was hundreds of miles away to the northeast.

The Pharos stood for over 1,500 years and was the model for lighthouses later constructed throughout the Roman Empire that were also called Pharos in honor of the original. The Arabs captured the Pharos during the seventh century. Deceived by the emperor of Constantinople into believing that treasure was buried beneath it, they dismantled its beacon and part of the structure. Finally, realizing that they had been made fools of, they attempted to rebuild the Pharos, but the task was clearly beyond their ability. During the rebuilding process, the Arabs dropped the giant reflecting mirror and it was shattered. What remained of the Pharos was turned into a mosque. In A.D. 1375, a severe earthquake struck Alexandria, and the Pharos was leveled. (Clayton and Price [1988] 1989, 142–43, 145, 147; De-Camp 1974, 128–29; Toynbee 1967, 112; Warrington [1961] 1978, 30, 399)

Pharsalians An elite ilai of the Thessalian cavalry that acted as Parmenio's personal guard. The unit's fighting effectiveness was comparable to that of the Agema of the Companions.

Pherae A Thessalian city located on a hill commanding a fertile area near the southern edge of the plain of Pelasgiotis. It lay near important trade routes, and its location along the coast gave Thessaly its only access to the sea. The city controlled Thessalian corn exports. Pherae was the seat of power of a line of tyrants who controlled eastern Thessaly. They were constantly at odds with the Thessalian League of eastern Thessaly. (Hammond 1994, 29; Hammond and Scullard 1970, 811)

Philippi A city in western Thrace originally named Crenidas. In 356 B.C., Philip consolidated a number of towns around the site into a single city that he named Phillipi, after himself. The occupying Thasians were driven out by a subsequent massive influx of Macedonian colonists. (Hammond and Scullard 1970, 816)

Plethra A Greek linear unit of measure equal to about 100 feet. (Curtius V:1)

Polemarch A Thessalian war ruler whose primary function was military command.

Pontus Sea (Black Sea) When the Greeks crossed the Bosporus into the modern-day Black Sea, they were convinced that they were entering an endless sea. Thus they named the Black Sea, the "Pontus (Main) Sea." Because sailing in the Pontus was hazardous, even for experienced sailors, the Greeks referred to it as the "Euxine Sea." The word *Euxine* meant "hospitable" and was an ironic reference to the treacherous sailing conditions in the Pontu Sea. (Bury 1982, 82)

Pothos An irresistible longing. This term was frequently used to refer to Alexander's lifelong desire to outdo the deeds of mortal man, especially his ancestor Heracles and the Persian conqueror Cyrus the Great. (Cawkwell 1981, 164; Hammond and Walbank 1988, 36)

Prodromoi (Forerunners) The Prodromoi were frequently referred to as the Scouts. Their strategic mission was to perform reconnaissance in advance of Alexander's army. On the battlefield, they served in a shock role with the Companions. (Abbott, 93; Ellis 1976, 27)

Prophthasia (Anticipation) Alexander's new name for the capital of Drangiana. The name means "Anticipation." (Bosworth 1988, 100, 104].

Proskynesis Proskynesis was Persian court protocol establishing the relationship between the Great King and his nobility. Near equals of the king — the Persian king considered no one to be his equal — were allowed to kiss him on the mouth; high-ranking or particularly favored subordinates, on the cheek; and all other inferiors were required to bow, the depth of their bow indicating the degree of their inferiority. The Persians considered this normal court etiquette. It was one of their duties to their king, and it was unthinkable not perform it. It had nothing to do with the worship of the Great King as a god; it merely differentiated degrees of social status. To the Greeks, however, proskynesis meant something entirely different. They believed the act to be reserved exclusively to honor a god, and they thought it a sacrilege to perform it to a man. When the Greeks and Macedonians saw the Persians perform proskynesis at

Alexander's court, many racted to it, either with laugher or silent contempt at their fanaticism.

Alexander began wearing the blue and white royal diadem, a purple tunic with a white band, and a girdle, all, of course, Persian conventions. He also started observing Persian protocol and introduced Asian court chamberlains into his court. Alexander was, however, in a dilemma. He could not forbid the Persians to perform proskynesis without having them doubt his right to rule, nor could he order the Macedonians to perform it without risking the humiliation of their rejection of it. So in the late spring of 327 B.C., Alexander decided to entrust Hephaestion with the task of obtaining the advance agreement of a select group of influential Macedonians to perform proskynesis at the next banquet. That way, once the majority of Macedonians there saw its acceptance by this respected group, they might be more inclined to go along with it themselves. Unfortunately, the Greeks refused to cooperate.

The day of the banquet arrived, and the plan for introducing proskynesis was ready to be implemented. When the loving-cup was passed round, those in on the ruse were to drink, stand, and bow slightly forward before Alexander. They would then, in return, receive a kiss from him. It was hoped that the other Macedonians, if only out of deference to their superiors, would then join in. Hephaestion thought that he had an understanding with Callisthenes. When the cup was passed to him, however, Callisthenes apparently could not bring himself to bow to Alexander. Perhaps it was because he was Aristotle's nephew and had been taught by him that Persians were barbarians and slaves by nature or possibly it was because as a Greek he truly believed that the act was to be used only for a god and, notwithstanding his earlier statements, did not really believe Alexander to be one. Whatever the reason, he omitted the bow and walked directly up to Alexander, who was just then talking with Hephaestion. When Demetrius, a Companion, pointed out to Alexander that Callisthenes had neglected to bow, Alexander refused to kiss him. At that, Callisthenes deliberately mocked Alexander by announcing that he had to go back to his seat "short of a kiss."

The ritual continued, however, and it was now the turn of a high Persian official to perform it. Apparently he did it in such an exaggerated manner that Leonnatus, a high-ranking Macedonian officer, burst out laughing. Alexander, of course, was both furious and humiliated. He now realized that Callisthenes had turned the ceremony into comical entertainment. Nothing more is heard about introducing the Macedonians to the practice of proskynesis, and in the future the protocol was confined solely to Alexander's Persian subjects. (Arrian IV:12; Green [1974] 1991, 272–73; Griffith 1966, 373–79; Hamilton 1973, 105–6)

Psiloi A Greek term denoting light infantry. This class of troops were usually missile troops, archers and slingers whose lack of arms or a shield precluded them from fighting hand-to-hand with their opponents. When confronted by an enemy advance, the psiloi invariably took shelter behind heavier troops. The Cretan archers, who were armed with a shield, appear to be the sole exception to this; they were apparently prepared to fight hand-to-hand with any enemy light troops.

Pura The capital of the satrapy of Gedrosa.

Push-back The pushing back of a hoplite formation by an enemy force. A push-back would result in confusion and disorder in a unit's ranks because hoplites would be forced backwards into ranks continuing to advance behind them. This would invariably leave gaps in the formation that could be penetrated by the enemy in an attempt to destroy the formation's cohesion.

Quadrireme An ancient warship with four rows of oarsmen on each side of the ship. (Morrison and Coates 1986, 239, 241)

Quinquereme An ancient warship with five files of oarsmen on each side of the ship. (Morrison and Coates 1986, 239, 241)

Ram A device used in sieges of cities to create a breach in walls that troops could assault through. A ram was usually a pointed log with an armored tip suspended from a frame with chains. The frame had wheels for mobility and was usually covered with hides as protection against combustion and missile fire. The ram was typically moved up to an enemy wall, and the log was repeatedly swung against a point on the wall until a breach, or hole, was created.

Ram Ships Two merchantmen lashed together with a platform suspended across them. On the platform a ram was mounted. The ram ship would usually lie up against a wall along the shoreline, anchor itself, and proceed to strike the wall repeatedly with its ram to create a breach, or hole. These ships were relatively unseaworthy and usually suffered extensive damage in heavy seas.

Rank A single row of soldiers extending laterally across the front of the unit.

Ravi River An Indian river also known as the Hydraotes. (Savill 1993, 117)

Rhomboid A four-sided cavalry formation used by the Thracian cavalry. It could quickly be maneuvered in any direction and still be able to conduct a wedge attack. The narrow widths of each of the points made it ideal for breaking into an enemy line. (Hackett 1978, 107; Head 1981, 48)

Saca A Scythian tribe. (Arrian III:8)

Sacred Band An elite Theban hoplite unit of 150 pairs of homosexual lovers chosen from the ranks of the nobility. They had taken a vow to die rather then to retreat. True to their word, all but 46 of the 300 hoplites of the Sacred Band perished on the battlefield of Chaeronea fighting against Philip II's army. The Sacred Band was originally the guard of Thebes' Cadmea. (Bury, 551; Connolly 1981, 50; Warry 1980, 69)

Sacred Mountain A stronghold in eastern Thrace at Hieron Oros. This was the site of Cersobleptes' treasury and royal residence. It was captured by Philip II.

Sacred War, Third (355 B.C.–346 B.C.) A religious war that broke out between the Amphictyonic Council and Phocis in 355 B.C. It began over Phocia's cultivation of a small plot of land dedicated to the oracle of Delphi. Some 10 years later the war ended in a Phocian defeat. (Warrington [1961] 1978, 449)

Sacred War, Fourth (339 B.C.–338 B.C.) A religious war that broke out in 339 B.C. between the Amphictyonic Council and Amphissa over the city's expansion of cultivation on the sacred Crissia plain. The Council called on Philip II of Macedonia for assistance. He captured Gravia Pass by a stratagem and then occupied Amphissa, which lay just beyond it.

Samacis One of three citadels of Halicarnassus. It was located in the southwest corner of the city along the seashore.

Samarkand A modern reference to the city of Maracanda, in Sogdiana. (Fuller 1958, 65)

Sandracottus The Greek name for Chandragupta, the ruler of the Indian Mauryan Empire. See also **Chandragupta**.

Sangala The capital of the Cathaeans, an Indian tribe in the Punjab. (Dodge [1890] 1993, 571; Hamilton 1971, 116)

Sardis The capital of the kingdom of Lydia and the subsequent Persian satrapy. The city was also the capital of all Persian provinces in Asia Minor along the sea. (Dodge [1890] 1993, 252; Fuller 1958, 92; Warrington [1961] 1978, 454)

Sarissa A 21-foot lance used by the troops of the Macedonian phalanx. A smaller 14 foot version of the weapon was used by the Lancers. (Polybius XVII:29)

Sarissophoroi The Greek name for Alexander's Lancers. They were also known as the Scouts. (Ellis 1976, 27)

Satraps Persian civilian administrators of satrapies. Their functions included collecting tribute, maintaining order, securing communications, and raising military levies when commanded to do so. Persian satraps combined the powers of military, financial, and civil administration and could issue their own coin. Although the satraps were men of high birth and sometimes even members of the royal family, their positions were not hereditary.

Alexander continued the satrapal system but restricted the satraps' authority to civil administration only. All other functions were assumed by appointed Macedonians. Alexander initially reappointed Persian satraps to the office of satrap, but when they proved unsatisfactory, he began appointing Macedonian generals to the positions. (Bury, Cook, and Adcock [1927] 1978, 369–70; Cook 1983, 171; Fuller 1958, 75, 92)

Satrapy The largest political division of the Persian Empire. Initially, the satrapies were based on the boundaries of conquered nations, but later they were reorganized by Darius into 20 administrative areas. At the end of his reign, Alexander began to break the former Persian satrapies he had conquered up into smaller districts. (Fuller 1958,

75)

Scaling Ladders A ladder used by assault troops to climb up a city wall.

Scouts Macedonian light cavalry. They were sometimes referred to as the Lancers.

Scythed Chariots A Persian vehicle drawn by from two to four horses and containing an armored driver. They were used to crash through an enemy formation in an attempt to disorder it. The 27-foot-long rotating blades, or scythes, attached to the hubs of the wheels would cause horrible debilitating injuries to anyone coming into contact with them, usually resulting in an agonizing death. However, against trained troops who would open up lanes in their ranks for the vehicles to pass harmlessly through, the scythed chariots proved to be almost totally ineffective. They were also extremely vulnerable to both heavy missile fire and enemy light troops. (Head 1982, 178)

Scythia An area of southern European Russia, Hungary, and Rumania inhabited by the Scythians. (Avery 1972, 301; Lempriere [1788] 1987, 568)

Scythians The Scythians were nomadic, having no cities in their territory. All their possessions were carried with them in wagons, in which they also lived. They were accustomed to fighting on horseback, firing their bows both on the attack and retreat. The Dahae, Massagetae, and the Saca were all Scythian tribes.

When Darius invaded Scythia, the Scythians consistently withdrew, always staying one day ahead of his army. Being unable to close with them, Darius was eventually forced to withdraw from their territory, abandoning his sick, wounded, and baggage animals. Both Philip and Alexander, however, were able to defeat the Scythians in straight-up fights. (Avery 1972, 301–2; Herodotus IV:64–65, 120; Lempriere [1788] 1987, 568; Rolle [1980] 1989, 82; Warrington [1961] 1978, 461)

Seistan A reference to the area of southern Drangiana.

Shock Impact A tactic of colliding with an enemy formation in an attempt to disorder its ranks. It was commonly used by Greek heavy cavalry and heavy infantry during the classical Greek, Macedonian, and Hellenistic eras.

Sidon Sidon was the oldest city of Phoenicia. Its citizens were widely known for their dishonesty, skill in trading and industry, and knowledge of mathematics and astronomy. Like Tyre, Sidon also had two harbors. Although later superseded by Tyre, Sidon remained commercially powerful. In 351 B.C., Sidon was destroyed in a revolt against Artaxerxes III, but it was soon rebuilt. (Avery 1972, 310; Fuller 1958, 207; Lempriere [1788] 1987, 583)

Siege Tower A multi-story wooden tower that was wheeled up to overlook an enemy held wall. The tower was filled with missile troops whose purpose was to either clear the wall of defenders by heavy missile fire or to draw the defender's fire to the towers. The completion of either mission would allow the rams to safely approach the walls to begin their breaching operations. The tower usually contained a drawbridge that could be dropped either over the wall or into any breach to provide a means of disembarking the assault troops sheltering inside the structure.

Siege Train The military organization used for transporting the catapults. Typically, only the key parts of the catapults were carried. Most of the wood needed to construct the catapult was procured on the site of the siege.

Sigloi A unit of Persian money, 20 of which were equal to one gold daric. (Bury, Cook, and Adcock [1927] 1978, VI:427; Tarn [1948] 1967, 130)

Sindimana The capital of Sambus' territory in India. (Arrian VI:16)

Slaves The usual price of a slave during the Macedonian era was between three and four mina. (Tarn [1948] 1967, 7)

Sling The sling was a pouch attached to two leather thongs. A one-ounce lead bullet was typically inserted in a pouch that was then swung round and round over the head to achieve the desired momentum. When one of the thongs was released, the lead bullet would be propelled towards its intended target. The weapon could kill, stun, or badly bruise an enemy, depending on how heavily he was armored. It was said that only if trained from youth could a slinger achieve the full proficiency of the weapon. Rhodians and Balaeric islanders were widely considered to be the most effective slingers.

Slingers Missile troops who fired slings.

Social War (357–355 B.C.) A war that

began in 357 B.C. between Athens and three of her allies — Chios, Cos, and Rhodes. Byzantium, which had previously revolted from Athens, soon joined with the rebels. The Athenian naval defeat at Embatum in 356 B.C. and the threat of Persian naval intervention led Athens to end the war in 355 B.C. by recognizing the independence of her former subjects. (Cawkwell 1978, 77; Diodorus XVI:22; Hammond and Scullard 1970, 997)

Soma (The Body) The mausoleum at Alexandria where Alexander the Great's sarcophagus lay. It also later contained the sarcophagi of the Ptolemaic kings of Egypt. The Soma was part of the royal palace. (Bosworth 1988, 180; Canfora [1989] 1990, 75; Warrington [1961] 1978, 32)

Somatophylakes A Macedonian reference to the Bodyguards. (Ellis 1976, 53)

Span An ancient unit of measure approximately 27 inches long. (Diodorus XVII:53)

Stability The ability of a ship to return to an upright position. (Morrison and Coates 1986, 241)

Stade A linear measurement of one eighth of a mile. (Tarn [1948] 1979, 16)

Stadium An ancient linear distance of 125 paces.

Stasis A Greek word indicating a state of endless civil/social discord. This was a situation especially prevalent in many of the city-states in classical Greece. (Fine 1983, 681; Fuller 1958, 16; Michell [1952] 1964, 213)

Stater An Athenian unit of money equal to 24 silver drachmas in Philip's reign and 20 drachmas in Alexander's. (Bury, Cook, and Adcock [1927] 1978, VI; 427–28; Tarn [1948] 1967, 130; Warrington [1961] 1978, 154)

Strategos The military title for a commander of a taxies. The strategos was the equivalent of a modern-day general.

Supply Requirements Men: 3 pounds of grain and 2 quarts (5 pounds) of water per day.

Horse/mule: 10 pounds hay/straw, 10 pounds grain, and 8 gallons (80 pounds) of water per day. (Engels 1978, 145)

Susa Susa was a capital of the Persian Empire and the winter residence of the Persian kings. The city was located 375 miles southeast of Babylon and 62 miles from the mouth of the Tigris River. A considerable portion of Susa's wealth came from the Persian Gulf trade and their location along the Persian royal road between Babylon and Persepolis. The city was about 20 miles in circumference and had no defensive walls. It had been occupied since prehistoric times, and a mound had gradually been built up from the ruins of former cities. By Darius' time, Susa sat atop a hill that rose up almost 100 feet above the surrounding plain.

The city stood in a fertile plain surrounded by mountains, making the area a virtual oven for nine months of the year. So intense was the heat from the hot and dry southern winds that at midday snakes and lizards attempting to cross the streets were burned alive. All vegetation withered from the intense summer heat, and bath water was placed outside to be heated to the correct temperature by the sun. In November, the winds shifted and the temperature at Susa began to drop. By the middle of the month, the first rain began to fall. Two weeks later, the temperature would drop below freezing at night, and ice would usually cover the ground at dawn. During the day, snow flurries might occur or, more commonly, hail would fall. During January and February, heavy rains from the Indian Ocean fell, but these rains were usually insufficient to provide adequate water for the crops. A number of reservoirs were built to store the runoff from the mountain snows, which was then distributed to the crops by an extensive irrigation system. By the end of March, the rains ended, and a month later the crops were harvested. (Avery 1972, 321; Dodge [1890] 1993, 391; Hammond and Scullard 1970, 157; Lane Fox 74, 253)

Synhedrion The ruling body of the Amphictyonic League. (Green 1991, 86)

Syntagma A military unit of the Macedonian phalanx comprising two taxiarchias, or 256 men. The formation was 16 ranks deep in Philip's reign and eight ranks deep in Alexander's. (Connolly [1977] 1978, 58; Dodge [1890] 1993, 141)

Syntagmatarch The title of a commander of a Macedonian syntagma. (Connolly [1977] 1978, 58; Dodge [1890] 1993, 141)

Syrian Gates see **Beilan Pass**

Tagus The title of the military and civilian leader of Thessaly. In the 360s B.C., the office became hereditary to the rulers of Pherae. (Cawkwell 1978, 61; Hammond and

Scullard 1970, 1036)

Talent A Greek unit of money equivalent to 6,000 drachma or 300 gold darics. A talent weighed about 57 pounds and was said to represent the maximum load that an average man was able to carry comfortably. The term was also used in reference to the weight of a stone thrown by a catapult. (Morrison and Coates 1986, 244)

Tanais River The ancient name for the lower stretch of the Don River, which was considered at the time to be the boundary between Asia and Europe. (Bosworth 1988, 109; Hammond and Scullard 1970, 1036)

Tarus The capital of Cilicia in Asia Minor. (Avery 1972, 329)

Taulantians A warlike Balkan tribe occupying modern Albania. (Hammond 1981, 56)

Taxiarchia A military unit of the phalanx comprising two tetrarchies, or 128 men.

Taxies A military unit of the phalanx comprising four syntagmas, or 1,024 soldiers. During Alexander's reign a taxies contained approximately 1,500 men.

Tetradrachma A Greek unit of money equivalent to four drachma. (Warrington [1961] 1978, 154)

Tetrarch The title of the commander of a tetrarchia.

Tetrarchia A military unit of the phalanx comprising four lochoi, or 64 soldiers.

Tetrarchy A reference to the four political areas into which Philip II of Macedonia divided Thessaly in 342 B.C. (Hammond and Scullard 1970, 1047-8)

Thebes The ancient capital of Egypt. Thebes was the most important city in Boeotia and the reputed birth place of Dionysus. For details on the founding of Thebes, see **Cadmus**. The Thebans originally settled in the Cadmea. They soon expanded it out to an area of about 61 square acres and surrounded it with a wall. A second outer wall was built when the city's population exceeded 10,000. It enclosed an area ten times the size of the original settlement. When Cadmus was conquered by Amphion and Zethus, the area enclosed by the inner wall was named the Cadmea and the area between the inner and outer wall was named Thebes, in honor of the nymph Thebe, daughter of the river god Asopus and the wife of Zethus. Although the area enclosed by the outer wall was able to accommodate over 100,000 persons, the population of the city never exceeded 25,000.

Thebes was located on a low ridge that formed the southern boundary of the agricultural land of northern Boeotia. The flat plains there forced the city to develop a large and effective cavalry force to combat frequent raids by the Thessalian cavalry.

The various cities of Boeotia were later united into a Boeotian League under the leadership of Thebes, the dominant city there. The site of that city lay at the center of a road network extending out in all directions across Boeotia. (Avery 1972, 336-7; Lempriere [1788] 1984, 114; Radice [1971] 1973, 80; Symeonoglou 1985, 118-19, 122; Warrington [1961] 1978, 110)

Theoric Fund An Athenian fund into which unspent allocations from the state budget were deposited. The purpose of the Theoric Fund was to enable the poor to attend state festivals and functions, to provide for the construction of public works, and to promote trade. Each citizen was given two obols to ensure that they would be able to pay proper homage to the gods. The fund helped to reduce the friction between the poor and the rich of Athens by funding work programs for the poor, especially out-of-work rowers, and providing some tax relief for the rich. The Theoric Fund surpluses were unlikely to have exceeded 15 talents a year, but any unspent amounts were accumulated year after year.

In 339 B.C., the Assembly passed a law allowing the diversion of state surpluses from the Theoric Fund into the military fund. This had the effect of making the Assembly reluctant to authorize expensive military operations because the Theoric Fund would thereby be reduced. Sometime later this law was declared illegal because the financing of it was at the expense of the poor. (Bosworth 1988, 15; Cawkwell 1978, 78; Fine 1983, 623; Grote 1900, XI: 353)

Thermopylae A key pass between Thessaly and Locris that gave access into central Greece from the north. It was located between Mt. Oeta and a swamp bordering the Gulf of Lamia. The name means "Hot Gates" and refers to the nearby hot springs. At its narrowest, Thermopylae was only 50 feet wide.

For additional details on how Thermopylae derived its name, see **Heracles**. (Avery 1972, 341)

Thessalian League A league of Thessalian cities of the inland plain led by the city of Larisa. They were opposed by eastern Thessaly, which was controlled by the tyrants of Pherae. To combat Pherae more effectively, in 360 B.C. the League transferred its allegiance from Thebes, its founder, to Athens. In 358 B.C., with the death in Thessaly of Alexander, the successor to Jason, the League sought and received assistance from Philip II of Macedonia. For additional information, see **Thessaly**. (Hammond 1994, 29)

Thessaly A district in northern Greece that was allegedly the original territory of the Achaeans. The tribe migrated to Crete and other areas of Greece to establish a highly developed civilization, which unfortunately did not continue in Thessaly. The mountains there severely restricted overland communications and apparently inhibited any interaction between the tribes there. The Thessalian plains provided both the room and grain for an extensive horse-raising industry.

A few large families dominated Thessaly. Late in the fifth century, Lycophron established a tyranny at Pherae and initiated a struggle between the western area of the state, organized into a political and military entity known as the Thessalian League, and the eastern area of the country, which was under his domination. The Thessalian League called in Philip II of Macedonia to assist them initially against Lycophron and then to support them in the Third Sacred War. The state became subject to Macedonia politically, militarily, and economically during both Philip and Alexander's reigns. (Avery 1972, 343; Hammond and Scullard 1970, 1063)

Thrace A nation of loosely affiliated tribes located east of Macedonia. It derived its name from Thrax, the son of Mars. The Thracians were widely held to be a cruel and warlike people. The first Thracians lived on plunder acquired from raids. Because of their large population and strong economy, it was thought that the Thracians would have been a significant military threat if they had been united under a single king.

Although the Thracians resisted Greek influence, beginning in the eighth century the coast of Thrace was colonized by Greeks at Abdera, Aenus, Apollonia, Byzantium, Maronea, Mesambria, and Perinthus. The first king of the Ordysians attempted to unite the independent tribes between Macedonia and the Euxine Sea. Afterwards, the kings of the Ordysae began calling themselves the king of Thrace. In 382 B.C., Cotys succeeded to the Ordysae throne. He began to bring the various Thracian tribes under his rule but was assassinated in 358 B.C. before he could complete the task. His kingdom was divided between his sons, Amadocus, Berisades, and Cersobleptes. Although Cersobleptes tried to reunite his father's kingdom, he was defeated by Philip of Macedonia before he could do so and had his kingdom taken from him. (Bosworth 1988, 12; Hammond and Scullard 1970, 1065; Lempriere [1788] 1984, 627–8)

Tigris River The word *tigris* means "arrow" in Persian.

Torsion Catapult A catapult which derived its torque from the tension of human hair. The first recorded use of a torsion catapult to shoot bolts (arrows) was at Philip's siege of Perinthus in 340 B.C. The first use of the torsion catapult as a rock thrower was in 322 B.C. at Alexander the Great's siege of Tyre. For additional details on torsion catapults, see Chapter 2, **Catapults**.

Tower of Babel The structure was located within the walls of Babylon, rising up seven tiers to a height of 300 feet. (Roux [1964] 1992, 395)

Triaconter An ancient warship known as a "thirty-er" or a "30-oared," indicating that the ship had 15 rowers on a side. The triaconter was 75 feet long. (Casson 1994, 53–55; Morrison and Coates 1986, 242)

Triballians Reputed to be the fiercest of all Balkan tribes. (Errington 1990, 57)

Tridrachma A unit of money equivalent to three drachma. (Warrington [1961] 1978, 154)

Trireme The main combat ship of classical Greece. The name was derived from the Latin *triremis* which meant "three-oared." The trireme was invented about 650 B.C. by either Corinth or Phoenicia. It was a shallow, narrow vessel that was highly maneuverable in the hands of a skillful crew. For additional information on triremes, see Chapter 4. (Casson 1994, 60–61)

Troad The region in the northwest corner of Asia Minor. It surrounded Troy, which was its capital. (Avery 1972, 352)

Tylus Modern-day island of Bahrain. (Bosworth 1988, 169)

Tyrant A ruler who had come to power either by force or as a member of a dynasty. Greeks frequently associated tyrants with cruel and arbitrary rule. (Warrington [1961] 1978, 522)

Tyre The leading commercial city in Phoenicia and next to Sidon, the second oldest city there. The city lay alongside trade routes between Asia Minor, Cyprus, Egypt, Rhodes, and Syria. Tyre was an island city measuring 1,000 yards long and 500 yards wide and lying a half mile offshore.
Tyre established colonies in Africa (Carthage), Brittany, India, Sardinia, Sicily, and Spain. The city withstood a 13-year siege (585–572 B.C.) by Nebuchadnezzar but fell to Alexander the Great in 332 B.C., after a siege of seven months. The city's surviving population was then enslaved. (Avery 1972, 355; de Camp 1972, 108)

Wages Allied cavalryman, 250 drachma per month; Athenian cavalryman, 20–40 drachma per month; Athenian foot soldier, 10 drachma per month; Athenian hoplite, 60 drachma per month (Delbruck) or 10 drachma per month (Dodge); Athenian rower, 30 drachma per month; Athenian seaman, 10 drachma per month; Horseman, 30 drachma per month; Hypaspist, 30 drachma per month; Macedonian cavalryman, 300 drachma per month (Dodge) or 60 drachma per month (Hammond); Macedonian hypaspist, 30 drachma per month; Macedonian light infantryman, 84 drachma per month; Macedonian pezetairoi, 100 drachma per month; Mercenary, 20 drachma per month (Hammond) or 30 drachma per month (Rodgers); Mercenary hoplite, 30 drachma per month (Griffith) or 45 drachma per month (Parke); Phalangist, 25 drachma per month; Spartan rower, 15 drachma per month; Thracian peltast, 30 drachma per month; Unskilled laborer, 45 drachma per month. (Sources: Delbruck 1990, 147; Dodge [1890] 1993, 70, 158; Ellis 1976, 54; Hammond 1981, 155–56; Morrison and Coates 1986, 119; Parke 1933, 140; Griffith 1935, 297–8; Grote 1900, XI:313; Rodgers [1937] 1977, 262; Snodgrass 1967, 106)

Weapons Cost In 415 B.C., at the time of the Peloponnesian War, the following weapons costs were recorded: corselet, 1,000 drachma; helmet, 100 drachma; javelin, 2 drachma; spear, 1.75 drachma (Snodgrass 1967, 107).

Wedge A close-order, triangular-shaped cavalry formation used by the Companions. The formation's narrow tip made it ideal for penetrating an enemy formation, and its triangular shape facilitated the rapid expansion of the penetration. The formation was so tightly aligned as to preclude any penetration by enemy horsemen.

Weirs Damlike obstructions Darius III constructed on the Tigris River. They were designed to impede navigation of the river by an enemy force. Alexander dismantled them on his return to Babylon from the Gedrosian campaign in order to facilitate the development of a waterborne trade route from Babylon and Egypt to India. (Arrian VII:7)

Xenagia A syntagma.

Xenagos The title of the commander of a syntagma.

Zadracarta The capital of Hyrcania and the largest city in the satrapy. (Arrian III:25; Dodge [1890] 1993, 429; Savill 1993, 63)

Zariaspa The capital of Bactria. Otherwise known as Bactria. (Fine 1983, 623)

Notes

Introduction

1. Hammond 1981, 33.
2. Hammond 1994, 40.
3. Hammond and Griffith 1979, 670.
4. Cawkwell, 1978, 48.
5. Ibid., 48.
6. Hammond 1994, 135.
7. Bosworth 1988, 250. In point of fact, the Greek mercenaries Alexander had settled in the eastern Persian Empire had been sent there unwillingly. They had no desire to be the linchpin of the economic and social development of a race they despised. Alexander saw that the Greek mercenaries' unruliness and their disdain for the Persians mitigated against the stability of his newfound empire. As a result, he was forced to announce his Exile's Decree, requiring the return of all the mercenaries to their home cities. At Alexander's death, several thousand of the Greek mercenaries abandoned their settlements in the east and marched west. Troops from Babylon, however, were sent out against them, and they were forced back to the cities in which Alexander had settled them. Later Alexander's successors would eagerly conscript them into the armies they raised for the upcoming power struggle between them.

Chapter 1: The Armies

1. Thucydides VI:13.
2. Dodge [1890] 1993, 82; Head 1982, 7.
3. Head 1982, 7.
4. Ibid.
5. Dodge [1890] 1993, 81.
6. Buck 1979, 158; Head 1982, 5; Warrington [1961] 1978, 101.
7. Buck 1979, 159.
8. Bosworth 1988, 14.
9. Diodorus XVII:11.
10. Head 1982, 4–5.
11. Buck 1979, 158.
12. Ibid.
13. Head 1982, 5.
14. Warry, 1993, 64.
15. Ibid., 69.
16. Head 1982, 29.
17. Ibid.
18. Ibid., 52.
19. Ibid., 130.
20. Ibid., 52.
21. Ibid.
22. Ibid.
23. Ibid., 29, 129.
24. Ibid., 32.
25. Ibid.
26. Ibid., 53.
27. Ibid.
28. Ibid.
29. Ibid.
30. Ibid., 139.
31. Ibid., 54.
32. Ibid., 53.
33. Arrian VIII:16; Head 1982, 139.
34. Head 1982, 139.
35. Warry 1993, 84.
36. Head 1982, 136; Warry 1993, 84.
37. Arrian VIII:16; Head 1982, 136.
38. Arrian VIII:16.
39. Head 1982, 53.
40. Ibid., 136.
41. Ibid., 54.
42. Ibid., 53.
43. Arrian (VIII:16) indicates that the Indians used a four-and-a-half-foot-long arrow; Curtius (IX:5), that the Indian arrow which wounded Alexander was three feet long.
44. Dodge [1980] 1993, 554; Head 1982, 136.
45. Head 1982, 136.
46. Arrian VIII:16.
47. Arrian V:15. Although Porus had selected a sandy battlefield solid enough for cavalry charges, there were probably still enough wet areas around from the recent storm to hamper the effectiveness of the Indian archers.
48. Arrian VIII:16; Head 1982, 136.
49. Arrian VIII:16.
50. Head 1982, 32.
51. Curtius VIII:14; Dodge [1890] 1993, 551, 554.

52. Arrian (V:14) indicates that Aristobulus had 120 chariots and 2,000 cavalry at his disposal; Curtius (VIII:13), that he had 100 chariots and 4,000 cavalry; and Plutarch (569), that he had 60 chariots and 1,000 cavalry.
53. Arrian (V:15) and Curtius (VIII:13) indicate that Porus had 300 chariots with him for the battle; Diodorus (XVII:87), that he had more than 1,000 chariots.
54. Scullard 1974, 19, 23.
55. Ibid., 20.
56. Ibid., 17, 20.
57. Lane Fox 1974, 338.
58. Scullard 1974, 19–20.
59. Ibid., 16.
60. Lane Fox 1974, 338.
61. Scullard 1974, 22.
62. Lane Fox 1974, 338.
63. Scullard 1974, 19, 22.
64. Head 1982, 50; Scullard 1974, 22.
65. Head 1982, 53, 246.
66. Ibid., 53.
67. Ibid., 32.
68. Ibid., 54.
69. Scullard 1974, 70, 240. Soldiers did not sit atop an elephant because the difficulty of keeping a firm seat made accurate missile fire virtually impossible.
70. Connolly 1981, 75; Scullard 1974, 240.
71. Head 1982, 50.
72. Scullard 1974, 16. An elephant will not trample a man with the soles of its tender feet but will crush him by kneeling on him with its forehead or its trunk.
73. Head 1982, 32.
74. Hammond and Griffith 1979, 205.
75. Ferrill [1985] 1988, 155.
76. Hackett 1989, 75.
77. At the battles of Issus and Gaugamela, Alexander kept his Greek allied and Greek mercenaries in general reserve, while at Gaugamela he kept his Companions in reserve.
78. Ellis 1976, 79.
79. Ferrill [1985] 1988, 183.
80. Engels 1978, 47, 55.
81. Engels 1978, 155; Ferrill [1985] 1988, 183.
82. Engels 1978, 15.
83. Ibid.
84. Engels 1978, 12; Lane Fox 1974, 72.
85. Hammond and Walbank 1988, 3.
86. Dodge [1890] 1993, 168; Hammond 1981, 16.
87. Hammond 1981, 16.
88. Hammond 1994, 41.
89. Hammond and Walbank 1988, 14.
90. Dodge [1890] 1993, 168.
91. Arrian VI:28.
92. Hackett 1978, 105; Head 1982, 104.
93. Hackett 1978, 106.
94. Bosworth 1988, 262; Ferrill [1985] 1988, 176; Hammond 1981, 32; Head 1982, 104. Ferrill speaks of a nine-foot-long cavalry sarissa, but I am inclined to think that nine feet was the length of the spear that the Companions sometimes used, not the length of their sarissa. We are told that their sarissa was pointed on both ends and was a danger to the rear ranks. A nine-foot-long sarissa gripped in the middle would not extend beyond the rear of the horse to endanger anyone coming up from behind. Also, we are told that the cavalry sarissa vibrated extensively. This would have been unlikely with a short nine-foot length only projecting out four and a half feet out in front of the rider. Therefore it appears more likely that the cavalry sarissa was 14 feet in length.
95. Bosworth 1980, 59.
96. Ellis 1976, 56; Hammond 1981, 30, 32; Head 1982, 100.
97. Hammond 1981, 31; Head 1982, 104; Lane Fox 1974, 74; Warry 1991, 14.
98. Head 1982, 172.
99. Hammond 1981, 31.
100. Head 1982, 48.
101. Dodge [1890] 1993, 150; Warry 1980, 82.
102. Head 1982, 48.
103. Dodge [1890] 1993, 156.
104. Connolly 1981, 171–72; Head 1982, 48.
105. Hackett 1989, 104; Head 1982, 14; Tarn [1948] 1978, 156.
106. Curtius V:2; Head 1982, 14; Hackett 1989, 104.
107. Bosworth 1988, 268; Curtius V:2.
108. Arrian VII:6.
109. Head 1982, 14.
110. Hammond 1981, 188–89.
111. Tarn [1948] 1979, 166.
112. Dodge [1890] 1993, 153.
113. Arrian III:27.
114. Warry 1993, 58.
115. Hackett 1978, 107; Head 1981, 48.
116. Hammond 1981, 31; Head 1982, 101. When engaged in close combat, the Thessalian cavalry soldiers seem to have been unusually proficient at stabbing their opponents in the face.
117. Hammond 1981, 31.
118. Ibid., 32.
119. Hackett 1978, 107; Head 1982, 12.
120. Tarn [1948] 1978, 159.
121. Arrian I:14.
122. Ibid., III:11.
123. Ibid., III:19.

NOTES — CHAPTER 1   443

124. Ibid., III:29.
125. Bosworth 1988, 262; Head 1982, 14.
126. Hackett 1989, 107–8.
127. Arrian III:12.
128. Bosworth 1988, 262; Hackett 1989, 107.
129. Hackett 1989, 105.
130. Head 1982, 49.
131. Ibid., 48.
132. Hackett 1989, 198.
133. Arrian III:19.
134. Ibid., I:14., III:6.11.
135. Hackett 1989, 107–8.
136. Hackett 1978, 107; Head 1982, 14.
137. Hammond 1981, 31.
138. Ibid.
139. Arrian II:9.
140. Hackett 1989, 108.
141. Hackett 1978, 108; Head 1982, 14.
142. Head 1989, 14.
143. Tarn [1948] 1979, 160.
144. Bosworth 1988, 265.
145. Hammond 1981, 31.
146. Hackett 1989, 108.
147. Arrian III:12.
148. Ibid.
149. Bosworth 1988, 271.
150. Dodge [1891] 1994, 109–16. The city of Tarentum in southern Italy requested the assistance of Phyrrhus, king of Epirus, against Rome. At the battles of Heraclea (280 B.C.) and Ascula, the Roman legions were defeated by Phyrrhus' elephants. At the battle of Beneventum (275 B.C.), the Roman legionaries were able to drive Phyrrhus' elephants back into Phyrrhus' phalanx, disordering it and, resulting in Phyrrhus' defeat.

It should be kept in mind, however, that Phyrrhus' heterogeneous phalanx had never fought together, and the morale of the troops does not seem to have been particularly high. Alexander's Macedonian phalanx would have put in a much stronger showing, but they never fought the Romans. A phalanx was to engage the Romans in battle on only one other occasion, that being at the battle of Pydna in 168 B.C. There, unfortunately for the Greeks, the phalanx was disordered by rough ground and was then not unexpectedly defeated by the legions.

151. Head 1982, 107.
152. Fuller 1958, 51.
153. Grote 1899, XII:58; Snodgrass 1967, 117–18. As the sarissa required the use of both hands, the shield had to be small enough not to impede the use of it. Consequently, in battle, the shield was either looped around the forearm or slung over the shoulder.
154. Connolly, 1981, 80; Ferrill [1985] 1988, 178; Head 1982, 105.
155. Snodgrass (1967, 117) raises an interesting point relating to the possibility of the sarissas of the first few ranks of the phalanx being shorter than those of the rear ranks. Although there appears to be no indication of this, it would have been a sensible modification that would have increased the endurance of the critical front ranks without significantly compromising the combat effectiveness of the formation.
156. Connolly [1977] 1978, 58; Dodge [1890] 1993, 140; Grote 1899, XII, 58; Hackett 1989, 106; Polybius XVIII:29; Snodgrass 1967, 118. Polybius gives convincing detail of the length and use of the Macedonian sarissa. The three foot distance he gives per rank appears to be accurate. Allowing one foot as the vertical space occupied by a phalangite, this would leave two feet for him to take his step. As we know that Alexander's phalanx was fast-moving, as evidenced by their lack of armor, any smaller stepping space would have been awkward and would have dramatically slowed their pace. Given that the phalanx troops projected their weapons forward out front of the formation from the fifth rank, the sarissa could not have been much less than 21 feet long. The 14-foot length or even 18-foot length are clearly inadequate to project the necessary distance and are indefensible because no logical support is presented by any of the authors for those particular choices.
157. Connolly 1981, 69; Hackett 1989, 105.
158. Bosworth 1980, 62; Connolly 1981, 69; Ferrill [1985] 1988, 178; Hackett 1989, 106.
159. Bosworth 1988, 260; Hackett 1989, 106.
160. Dodge [1890] 1993, 140; Hackett 1989, 106.
161. Dodge [1890] 1993, 146–47; Grote 1899, XII:251; Polybius XVIII:29; Warry 1993, 73.
162. Connolly [1977] 1978, 58; Dodge [1890] 1993, 140, 146; Ferrill [1985] 1988, 178; Hackett 1989, 119; Lane Fox 1974, 76.
163. Bosworth 1980, 55.
164. Polybius XVIII:31.
165. Hanson 1989, 30.
166. Head 1982, 47.
167. Snodgrass 1967, 119.
168. Bosworth 1980, 55; Dodge [1890] 1993, 146–47; Grote 1899, XII:57; Head 1982, 46; Polybius XVIII:29; Warry 1993, 73.
169. Hackett 1978, 105; Hammond 1981, 103; Head 1982, 140.
170. Connolly [1977] 1978, 58.

171. Dodge 1993, 138, 141.
172. Head 1982, 13.
173. Ibid.
174. Head (1982, 13) and Hackett (1989, 105) indicate that a seventh taxis was created in 330 B.C.
175. Dodge [1890] 1993, 141–42; Tarn [1948] 1978, 142.
176. Arrian VII:23.
177. Ibid.
178. Hammond 1981, 28.
179. Delbruck 1990, 179; Head 1982, 107.
180. Bosworth, 1988, 270; Lane Fox 1974, 78–79. Although the age of the hypaspists might have been slightly exaggerated, the information was supposedly based on eyewitness observations made in 317 B.C.
181. Head 1982, 107.
182. Dodge [1890] 1993, 138; Fuller 1958, 49; Hackett 1978, 105; Head 1982, 13; Tarn [1948] 1978, 150.
183. Bosworth 1980, 171.
184. Ibid., 270.
185. Arrian I:61.
186. Ibid., V:13.
187. Hanson 1989, 30; Head 1982, 46.
188. Hammond 1981, 33; Head 1982, 46.
189. Hanson 1989, 30.
190. Head 1982, 46.
191. Hanson 1989, 56, 81.
192. Ibid., 76–79. The bell corselet consisted of molded front and rear bronze pieces connected at the shoulders. Above the hip the corselet curved outward, giving it its characteristic bell shape. The groin and neck were left unprotected to give the wearer some mobility in the hips. The corselet basically provided protection to the chest and lower stomach. If the momentum behind the missile weapon or the blow that was struck was great enough, however, a corselet could be cracked. Estimates have been made that the corselet weighed somewhere between 30 and 40 pounds and required considerable assistance to put on. Because of the lack of ventilation in the corselet, the wearer quickly became soaked with perspiration on a hot day and would rapidly dehydrate.
Connolly 1981, 54–58. By Alexander's time, the linen corselet was proving to be extremely popular because of its relative inexpensiveness, compared to the bell corselet, its light weight, and its defensive effectiveness. This corselet was comprised of numerous linen layers glued together. It extended down past the waist, with several slits on the bottom to allow the wearer to easily bend forward. The corselet provided an unexpectedly effective defense against the edged weapons of the time.

193. Connolly 1981, 60–61; Hanson 1989, 71–73; Snodgrass 1967, 94. The bronze Corinthian helmet was most commonly used by the hoplite. This headpiece protected both the head and neck, extending in the rear down to the collarbone. The cheek pieces and nose guards met in the center, protecting the face from both slashing and thrusting blows. Because there was no padding to absorb the force of the blows to the helmet, however, the wearer could suffer severe concussions from head blows. As campaigning in Greece was confined almost exclusively to the summer months, when temperatures frequently exceeded 90°F, significant heat was generated on the neck and around the eyes, mouth, nose, and ears of the wearer, making the five-pound helmet extremely uncomfortable to wear. Also, since there were no holes for the ears, it was virtually impossible to hear spoken commands. When not in use, the helmet could be propped up on the wearer's head, being held in place by the flexible cheek guards.
Connolly 1981, 61. The Chalcidian helmet evolved from the Corinthian helmet. Its big advantage was a cutout around the ears that enabled the wearer to hear what was happening around him. The helmet had either fixed or hinged cheek pieces but had no nose guard.
194. Connolly 1981, 59; Hanson 1989, 75; Head 1981, 92. The thin bronze greaves provided the legs with some protection against enemy missile fire and were able to deflect a glancing sword blow. Initially greaves covered only the lower leg, but they were later extended to cover as high up as the knee.
195. Hackett 1989, 55; Hanson 1989, 65, 68, 70, 144; Head 1982, 92; Snodgrass 1967, 53. The hoplite derived his name from his three-foot-diameter round shield called the hoplon. Its face was comprised of a one-and-a-half-inch-thick wooden frame encircled by a metal rim. The front of the shield was covered with leather that was then overlaid with a thin bronze plate. The shield weighed about 16 pounds. It had two grips, one that the left arm slipped through and another held by the left hand. Although the grips distributed the weight of the shield along the arm rather than concentrating it at the hand and wrists, the shield still could not be held up more than a few minutes at a time without exhausting the holder. The shield's curvature made it possible to rest it occasionally on the left shoulder, which facilitated push-support to the rank in front. The holder's shoulder and chest were pushed into the shield, which was pressed

against the back of the soldier directly in front. In a hand-to-hand fight where the momentum of the blows was not great, the shield was effective in deflecting them. The shield could be penetrated by missile weapons, however, and was likely to crack apart in the force of the initial collision of the charge. In Asia, a leather apron was sometimes hung from the bottom of the shield as an additional defense against Persian and Indian arrows.

The round shape of the Greek shield gave poor protection to the body compared to the rectangular shield of the later Roman legionaries. Since the shield was held by the left arm, it offered no protection to the right side of the holder, and he was thus forced to close up to his neighbor on the right to come behind his shield. This led to a noticeable tendency of hoplite formations to drift to the right flank. It was widely believed by the hoplites that the more closely the shields were locked together, the greater their protection.

196. Fuller 1958, 50; Head (1982, 92) indicates that the spear was nine feet long and weighed between two and four pounds. The shaft was made from cornel wood and was about one inch in diameter. It had an iron or bronze butt-spike that could be turned around to fight with in the event the spear point broke off or could be jammed into the ground to absorb the impact of a cavalry attack. It was fairly common for the men in the front two ranks of the hoplite formation to have their spear shafts shattered in the initial impact of their charge. I am inclined to think that the spear was nine feet long, as this would more logically accommodate the manner in which it was used. For a more detailed discussion on the length of the spear, see note 201.

197. Connolly 1981, 77; Head 1988, 92; Snodgrass 1967, 58. The sword was very much a secondary weapon for the hoplite. The weapon had a single-edged curved blade used for stabbing. The blade was short so that it might be drawn in a hurry and used effectively in the limited lateral space available.

198. Head 1989, 31.
199. Ibid., 92.
200. Hanson 1989, 162–63; Head 1982, 92.
201. Although Hanson (1989, 28, 84) states that the first three ranks of hoplites were able to project their spears out in front of the formation, this was unlikely to have been the case. Despite the considerable disagreement over the length of the hoplite spear, the evidence appears to indicate that it was nine feet long, this being substantiated by ancient references to the weapon's length advantage over the Persian six-foot javelin and to the extension of the spears of the second rank out in front of the hoplite formation.

A hoplite's formation depth is stated to be three feet. Considering a normal pace is not less than two feet, it is not possible that the distance between hoplite ranks would be less than this and there is every indication that it might have been more because the hoplites were known to break into a full run just before crashing into the enemy line. This would call for an elongated step to preclude the risk of stumbling.

We are told that the spear was pointed at both ends. Therefore, for the weapon to be properly balanced, it would have had to have been held in the middle, which in a nine-foot-long spear would have been four and a half feet up from the butt. As a rank occupied a depth of three feet, the weapon of the second rank would have projected only one and a half feet out in front of the first rank. An eight-foot-long spear would only extend out six inches beyond the first rank, while a seven-foot-long spear would not extend out at all beyond the front rank.

202. Hackett 1989, 54–55; Hanson 1989, 45; Head 1982, 46.
203. Hanson 1989, 31.
204. Ibid., 58.
205. Ibid., 63.
206. Curtius II.
207. Bosworth 1988, 264.
208. Arrian III:19.
209. Ibid., I:29.
210. Ibid.
211. Ibid., III:5.
212. Griffith (1935, 21) indicates that Alexander employed over 60,000 mercenaries during his reign; Parke (1933, 198), that a minimum of 48,000 were employed.
213. Bosworth 1988, 266; Griffith 1935, 12; Hackett 1989, 108; Head 1982, 13.
214. Griffith 1935, 23.
215. Ferrill [1985] 1988, 161–62.
216. Griffith (1935, 283) states that the typical campaigning season of the Greek citizen militia was about seven to eight months because the soldiers had to be home for the planting and harvest seasons. Since the Greeks did not normally campaign, however, during the inclement weather of the winter, this left only about three months during the summer for them to participate in military operations.
217. Head 1982, 5.
218. Ibid.
219. Arrian III:12.
220. Parke 1933, 192.

221. Curtius VII:3.
222. Arrian IV:13.
223. Connolly 1981, 48; Dodge [1890] 1993, 63; Head 1982, 97–98.
224. Head 1982, 98.
225. Ibid., 47. In most cavalry battles, the horse was usually the target of the attack. The object was to dismount the rider, who would then be vulnerable to attack by supporting peltasts.
226. Head 1982, 97; Warry 1993, 61.
227. Warry 1993, 50.
228. Dodge [1890] 1993, 143.
229. Head 1982, 98.
230. Arrian IV:26.
231. Hammond 1981, 30.
232. Hackett 1989, 108; Head 1982, 13.
233. Hackett 1989, 108.
234. Ibid.
235. Arrian III:9, III:12.
236. Hackett 1989, 108.
237. Hammond 1981, 30.
238. Hackett 1989, 108.
239. Arrian VI:15.
240. Ibid., I:28, II:19, III:12.
241. Head 1982, 48.
242. Delbruck 1990, 125; Snodgrass 1967, 79.
243. Snodgrass 1967, 84.
244. Head 1982, 48.
245. Snodgrass 1967, 80–81.
246. Head 1982, 100.
247. Ibid., 13.
248. Ibid.
249. Ibid., 100.
250. Snodgrass 1967, 83; Warry 1993, 62.
251. Snodgrass 1967, 108.
252. Head 1982, 100.
253. Ibid.
254. Arrian I:8.
255. Ibid., I:28.
256. Ibid., III:5.
257. Ibid., I:14.
258. Head 1982, 99.
259. Head 1982, 99; Snodgrass 1967, 84; Warry 1993, 62; Xenophon III:3.
260. Curtius VIII:4; Diodorus XVII: 108; Plutarch, 574.
261. Arrian VII:12.
262. Head 1982, 14.
263. Bradford 1992, 40; Ellis 1976, 79. Onomarchus of Phocis was the first recorded commander to use catapults tactically on the battlefield; he used them against Philip II in Thessaly.
264. Head 1982, 44.
265. Curtius III:3.
266. Ibid.
267. Lane Fox 1974, 193.
268. Curtius (III:3) indicates that it was the custom of the Persians not to begin a march before sunup.
269. Curtius (I) and Justin (IX:5) indicate that the combined military of the League of Corinth was 15,000 cavalry and 200,000 infantry. Although this may well have been the theoretical strength that could have been mobilized, logistical and command control limitations would preclude a force of this size from ever taking to the field at one time.
270. Head 1982, 3.
271. Ibid., 3.
272. Ibid.
273. Ibid., 44.
274. Hackett 1989, 83–84; Head 1982, 44.
275. Head 1982, 88.
276. Ibid.
277. Fuller 1958, 148; Head 1982, 86.
278. Head 1982, 86.
279. Ibid.
280. Ibid.
281. Snodgrass 1967, 108.
282. Hammond and Griffith 1979, 442. Although Persian kings had almost unlimited funds with which to pay mercenaries, they were slow in settling accounts.
283. Tarn [1948] 1979, 81; Head 1982, 3.
284. Tarn [1948] 1979, 180.
285. Head 1982, 88.
286. Ibid.
287. Ibid.
288. The shield was usually pushed into the ground and held up by a brace, allowing the user to shoot his bow without impediment from behind its protection.
289. Herodotus VII:61.
290. Ibid.
291. Head (1982, 89) indicates that the Persian bow was of composite construction and was able to outrange the Cretan bow. This increased range was probably achieved by the use of a longer arrow that allowed the bowstring to be drawn farther back.
292. Head 1982, 44.
293. Warry 1980, 62.
294. Head 1982, 89; Warry 1993, 62.
295. Head 1982, 90; Snodgrass 1967, 84; Xenophon III:3.
296. At Gaugamela, Alexander's missile troops decimated Darius' chariot crews upon their approach, while at Hydaspes River his horse archers destroyed Porus' chariot force in their deployment areas.
297. Head 1982, 178–79.
298. Ibid., 90.
299. Ibid., 178.

300. Ibid., 45.
301. Hackett 1989, 84–85; Herodotus I:80. In 546 B.C., at the battle of the Plain of Cyrus, just east of Sardis, Cyrus the Great used the camels of his baggage train to screen an advance of his infantry against the Lydian cavalry. The Lydian horses became unmanageable in the presence of the camels, forcing their riders to dismount and fight on foot. The Lydians lost the battle and retreated to Sardis, where they were besieged. The city subsequently fell, and the kingdom of Lydia was incorporated into the Persian Empire.
302. Head 1982, 8.
303. Diodorus XVI:59.
304. Ibid., XVI:56, 60.
305. Rolle [1980] 1989, 82.
306. Ibid., 83.
307. Head 1982, 132.
308. Ibid., 30.
309. Ibid., 131.
310. Snodgrass 1967, 83.
311. Connolly 1981, 48–49.
312. Rolle [1980] 1989, 65.
313. Ibid.
314. Head 1982, 131.
315. Rolle [1980] 1989, 66; Head 1982, 131.
316. Rolle 1980, 68.
317. Ibid., 67.
318. Michell [1952] 1964, 165.
319. Ibid., 171.
320. Connolly 1981, 39; Michell [1952] 1962, 172.
321. Michell [1952] 1964, 173.
322. Fine 1983, 68.
323. Michell [1952] 1964, 172.
324. Forrest 1969, 134.
325. Lane Fox 1974, 199.
326. Bosworth 1988, 13.
327. Michell [1952] 1964, 258.
328. Head 1982, 6.
329. Connolly 1981, 40; Michell [1952] 1964, 262.
330. Hackett 1989, 77; Head 1982, 6.
331. Michell [1952] 1964, 249.
332. Ibid., 239, 250.
333. Ibid., 249.
334. Connolly 1981, 45.
335. Chrimes [1949] 1971, 388; Hackett 1989, 63.
336. Hackett 1989, 63.
337. Head 1982, 46.
338. Chrimes [1949] 1971, 361; Head 1982, 93.
339. Michell [1952] 1964, 362.
340. Chrimes [1949] 1971, 388.
341. Michell [1952] 1964, 249–50.
342. Bury 1913, 120.
343. Michell [1952] 1964, 251.
344. Forrest 1969, 52.
345. Michell [1952] 1964, 257.
346. Head 1982, 12.
347. Ibid.
348. Ibid., 51.
349. Ibid.
350. Bury 1913, 470.
351. Head 1982, 51.
352. Ibid.
353. Ibid.

Chapter 2: Siege Operations

1. Head 1982, 187.
2. Cawkwell 1978, 162.
3. Head 1982, 190.
4. Head 1982, 190; Warry 1980, 78.
5. de Camp 1974, 199.
6. Ibid., 109.
7. Ibid.
8. de Camp 1974, 109; Dodge [1890] 1993, 177; Fuller 1958, 212.
9. Dodge [1890] 1993, 177.
10. de Camp 1974, 109–10; Dodge [1890] 1993, 175–76.
11. de Camp 1974, 111.
12. Ferrill 1986, 171.
13. Warry 1980, 78.
14. Ferrill [1985] 1988, 172; Hammond and Griffith 1979, 446.
15. Warry 1993, 78.
16. de Camp 1974, 108.
17. Lane Fox 1974, 183; Warry 1993, 78.

Chapter 3: Logistics

1. Arrian I:11.
2. Ibid.
3. Bradford (1992, 10), Connolly (1981, 69), Dodge ([1890] 1993, 152), and Engels (1978, 12) indicate that Philip allowed his cavalrymen only one servant each.
4. Bradford (1992, 10), Connolly (1981, 68), Engels (1978, 12), and Lane Fox (1974, 72) indicate that Philip allowed only one servant to each 10 heavy infantrymen.
5. Engels (1978, 13) indicates that Alexander's army on the average had one camp follower for every three combatants.
6. Ibid., 38.
7. Ibid., 31–32.
8. Ibid., 18.
9. Ibid., 125.
10. Engels (1978, 18) indicates that a working horse or mule has a minimum daily requirement of 10 pounds of straw or chaff, 10

pounds of grain, and 8 gallons of water, for a total weight of 100 pounds.
11. Ibid., 14,15, 26.
12. Ibid., 16.
13. Ferrill [1985] 1988, 184.
14. Engels 1978, 20.
15. Lane Fox (1973, 72) and Rogers ([1937] 1977, 116) indicate that servants were considered necessary because the heavy infantryman needed considerable assistance in putting on his armor, taking it off, and caring for it when it was not being worn.
16. Engels 1978, 12; Hammond 1981, 72; 1994, 26; Lane Fox 1973, 72.
17. Bradford 1992, 10; Connolly 1981, 69.
18. Abbott, 116; Curtius III:3.
19. Curtius III:13.
20. Lane Fox 1974, 103.

4. Naval Operations

1. Torr 1964, 3.
2. Ibid., 50, 56. The trireme's deck did not extend across the sides of the ship. Instead, it consisted of two unconnected gangways, perhaps 18 inches wide, running along both sides of the ship. Both the stem and stern of the ship, however, did contain a small deck anchored against both sides of the ship.
3. Casson 1994, 63.
4. Morrison and Coates 1986, 196. If the hull of the trireme had been any lower, it would have been necessary to raise the thalamian holes higher for the second level of rowers. The resulting steeper angle of the oars would had decreased rower performance, and the moving of the second and third level of rowers higher above the waterline would have raised the center of gravity and increased the tendency of the hull to roll. To stabilize the ship would have required a widening of its beam, which would have increased water resistance and lowered its maximum possible speed and maneuverability.
5. Torr 1964, 205.
6. Morrison and Coates 1986, 128; Starr 1989, 22.
7. Torr 1964, 63. The ram was a wooden structure covered with bronze and weighing about 170 pounds.
8. Ibid., 41, 50–51.
9. Casson 1994, 66; Morrison and Coates 1986, 220; Torr 1964, 41–42.
10. Morrison and Coates (1986, 185) indicate that Greek ships were not caulked, while Torr (1964, 34) indicates that they were.
11. Morrison and Coates 1986, 183; Torr 1964, 34.
12. Morrison and Coates 1986, 155–56.
13. Casson 1994, 73; Morrison and Coates 1986, 94, 225–56; Torr 1964, 14.
14. Morrison and Coates 1986, 226.
15. Casson 1994, 67.
16. Torr 1964, 96.
17. Ibid., 97.
18. Casson 1994, 67.
19. Torr 1964, 67.
20. Ibid., 96.
21. Casson 1994, 65.
22. Ibid.
23. Morrison and Coates 1986, 151.
24. Casson 1994, 66.
25. Ibid., 72.
26. Morrison and Coates 1986, 219; Torr 1964, 74, 76.
27. Morrison and Coates 1986, 95.
28. Ibid., 96.
29. Ibid., 162, 225.
30. Ibid., 161–62.
31. Starr 1989, 22.
32. Lane Fox 1974, 143; Morrison and Coates 1986, 103. Assume, for example, that on a long 18-hour day, the trireme set out at sunup and returned to camp at dusk. Allowing two hours to purchase, cook, and eat the noontime meal, this would leave two eight-hour periods for rowing, one of them occurring before lunch and the other after. At an average speed of 8.6 knots, it would take the trireme about three hours to row 30 miles from its base, allowing it to remain on blockade station for only two hours in the morning and two hours in the afternoon. Obviously this was the maximum distance a trireme could be based away from its blockading station and still be able to conduct a minimal blockade. A location closer to the port would allow the ships to remain on station longer, thereby greatly increasing the effectiveness of the blockade.
33. Morrison and Coates 1986, 231.
34. Ibid., 231–32.
35. Ibid.
36. Rodgers [1937] 1977, 232, 262.
37. Gardiner 1995, 63. Each oarsman had about a three-foot-square area of space available to him.
38. Bosworth 1980, 245.
39. Diodorus XVII:21.
40. Ibid., XVI:21.
41. Ibid.
42. Ibid.
43. Bosworth 1988, 148; Parke 1933, 122.
44. Grote 1900, XI:230; Parke 1933, 122.

NOTES — CHAPTER 4   449

45. Grote 1900; XI:231; Parke 1933, 24.
46. Diodorus XVI:22.
47. Ibid., XVI:34.
48. Ellis 1976, 95; Grote 1900, XI:349.
49. Ellis 1976, 98; Grote 1900, XI:349.
50. Ellis 1976, 99; Grote 1900, XI:350.
51. Cawkwell 1978, 75.
52. Cawkwell 1978, 77; Hammond 1974, 50; Hammond and Griffith 1979, 283.
53. Cawkwell 1978, 75; Hammond 1994, 46.
54. Cawkwell 1978, 95; Hammond 1994, 85.
55. Ellis (1976, 179) and Hammond (1994, 132) indicate that the corn fleet consisted of 230 ships; Justin (IX:1), that it consisted of 170 ships.
56. Ellis 1976, 179; Hammond 1994, 132.
57. Curtius I.
58. Lane Fox 1973, 92.
59. Diodorus XVII:22.
60. Arrian I:11.
61. Arrian I:18; Curtius II.
62. Arrian I:18.
63. Ibid.
64. Dodge [1890] 1993, 261; O'Brien 1992, 67.
65. Engels 1978, 111; Morrison and Coates 1986, 119. The 160 triremes in the Macedonian navy were manned by 32,000 rowers, each of whom was paid a daily wage of one drachma. Total monthly wages for the rowers of Alexander's fleet would therefore have equaled 160 talents.
Rodgers ([1937] 1977, 221) indicates that the wages of Alexander's fleet of 160 ships were 250 talents a month, and Dodge ([1890] 1993, 261), that 50 talents were paid monthly in wages to the fleet and another 50 talents in rations were provided.
66. Bosworth 1980, 142; Curtius II, IV:7. Although, as Bosworth correctly points out, Curtius indicates that at Gordium Alexander disbursed 500 talents for the raising of a fleet and 600 talents to defray the expenses of garrisons in Greece, this does not necessary mean he was awash in money. Being careful not to alienate either the Persian satraps in Asia Minor or the citizens, it is quite likely that Alexander generally refrained from looting cities that willingly surrendered to him in the hope that other cities would thereby be encouraged to do the same. This all but precluded him from acquiring any significant revenues from looting. Although it is likely that he received some income from city treasuries being turned over to him, this probably did not amount to much or ancient writers would have commented on it.

It is well to keep in mind that even the Egyptian treasury only amounted to 800 talents. Therefore very little in the way of significant funds was likely to have been available to Alexander until he captured Babylon.
The 5,000 mercenaries, 7,000 Balkan levies, and 10,000 Greek mercenaries serving with Alexander's army required a monthly payment of 110 talents in wages and his 15,000 Macedonian troops an equal amount. With such heavy expenses and no clear indication of when any significant revenue might be obtained, it seems clear that Alexander's disbursement of 1,100 talents for naval purposes was more in recognition of an extremely dangerous military situation than an indication of excess funds.
67. Hammond 1981, 82.
68. Arrian II:20.
69. Ibid.
70. Ibid.
71. Bury, Cook, and Adcock [1927] 1978, VI:375.
72. Arrian II:21.
73. Ibid., II:22.
74. Curtius III:1.
75. Ibid.
76. Arrian II:2.
77. Ibid.
78. Curtius IV:5.
79. Arrian III:2.
80. Curtius IV:5.
81. Arrian III:6.
82. Ibid., III:16.
83. Ibid., V:8.
84. Ibid., V:20.
85. Ibid., VI:4.
86. Ibid., VI:2.
87. Bury, Cook, Adcock [1933] 1978, VI: 411; Hamilton 1973, 119.
88. Bury, Cook, and Adcock [1927] 1978, 411.
89. Hammond 1981, 219.
90. Arrian VI:4.
91. Ibid., VI:5.
92. Ibid., VI:14.
93. Ibid., VI:18.
94. Ibid., VI:19.
95. Engels 1978, 111–12.
96. Ibid., 111. The average crew of a trireme crew was 200; a triaconter, 30; and a merchant ship, 8.
97. Arrian VIII:19.
98. Bosworth 1988, 140.
99. Arrian VIII:21.
100. Ibid.
101. Ibid.
102. Arrian (VIII:21) indicates that Near-

chus waited 33 days in port for the wind to change.

103. Ibid., VIII:23.
104. Curtius IX:10.
105. Arrian VIII:23.
106. Ibid.
107. Ibid. VIII:23.
108. Ibid., VIII:24.
109. Ibid.
110. Ibid.
111. Ibid., VIII:25.
112. Ibid., VIII:27.
113. In his book *Alexander the Great and the Logistics of the Macedonian Army*, Donald Engels works backwards in determining the supply for the fleet. Engels (1978, 111–12) states that Nearchus' fleet contained 24 triremes, 80 triaconters, and 400 merchantmen. He then estimates that the fleet consisted of 6,800 crew members and perhaps 8,000 soldiers, a total which would fully crew all the ships. At Pattala, Engels indicates that Alexander stored about a four-month supply of dry provisions, which he estimates at 52,600 tons. He then states that almost all of the those provisions were stored aboard the fleet, distributed at an average of about 131 tons per merchant ship. The triremes and other warships were able to carry little in the way of supplies because they had almost no storage space.

It took Nearchus about seven days to sail from Pattala down the Indus to Bibacta, located on the Arabian Sea. There he spent 33 days waiting for the wind to change. At a dry ration of about three pounds per man per day, the fleet would have consumed about 888 tons in dry supplies. It was 1,320 stades, or 165 miles, by Arrian's reckoning, between Bibacta and Crocala. With a good wind, a merchant ship might make a steady five knots an hour and cover this distance in six days, eight if stops were made along the way. This would use up another 177 tons of supplies. At Crocala, Nearchus received 10 days worth of supplies from Leonnatus, adding 180 tons to inventory. Sailing for another 5,600 stades, or 800 miles, Nearchus landed at a small town inhabited by the fish-eaters. This journey would have taken about 25 days, perhaps 35 days with stops, and consumed another 777 tons of supplies. At this point, Nearchus' desperation for supplies would indicate that his inventory was near exhaustion. He had consumed only about 1,842 tons of those supplies, however, and had received 227 tons of provisions at Crocala. If the fleet had indeed carried over 52,000 tons of supplies, there clearly should have been no shortage, as over 50,000 tons would have still remained.

Water cannot have made up the difference in cargo tonnage because we are told by Arrian that the fleet only carried a five-day supply. At a half gallon of water per man per day, this ration would weigh five pounds per man. A five-days supply for the fleet would, consequently, weigh only 185 tons. The only logical explanation appears to be that the fleet was only able to carry about 2,000 tons of both dry and wet supplies because the so-called merchantmen were extremely small ships, only having a cargo capacity of about five tons each. The only alternatives to this theory are that additional merchantmen or larger ones accompanied the fleet. If that was the case, however, this does little to explain why Nearchus ran out of provisions when he did. It was not a question of the quantity of provisions available at the Pattala depot but the inability to transport more than a small portion of them. This would clearly indicate a shortage of merchant ships, not an abundance of them. As to Engels' alleged 52,600 tons of supplies laid in at Pattala, this appears to have been a greatly exaggerated figure, no doubt based on a vastly larger force than Alexander actually ever had.

114. Arrian VIII:32.
115. Ibid., VIII:37.
116. Ibid., VIII:40.
117. Ibid., VIII:42.
118. Ibid., VII:7.
119. Ibid., VIII:9.
120. Ibid., VII:19.
121. Ibid.
122. Morrison and Coates 1986, 49, 155.
123. Ibid., 110.
124. Ibid., 154.
125. Hackett 1978, 85.
126. According to Herodotus (VII:89, 95), the Persian fleet at the time of Xerxes' invasion of Greece contained 1,207 triremes provided by the following areas: Aegean Islands (17); Aetolia (60); Caria (70); Cilicia (100); Cyprus (150); Dorians of Asia (30); Egypt (200); Hellespont (100); Ionia (100); Lycia (50); Palestine, Phoenicia, and Syria (300); and Pamphylia (30).
127. The 80,000 crew members of the 400 Persian ships consumed 840 tons of grain a week.
128. Arrian I:18.
129. Ibid.
130. Arrian II:1; Diodorus XVII:31.
131. Arrian II:1; Curtius II.
132. Arrian II:2.
133. Ibid., II:13.

NOTES — CHAPTER 5　451

5. Campaigns of Philip II

1. Diodorus XVI:2.
2. Ibid., XVI:4.
3. Ellis 1976, 58.
4. Hammond 1994, 27.
5. Diodorus XVI:4.
6. Ellis 1976, 58.
7. Hammond 1994, 136.
8. Hammond and Scullard 1970, 54. The Amphictyonic Council was a religious association responsible for the maintenance of the temple at Delphi. Its members included the Aenianes, Boeotians, Dolopians, Dorians, Ionians, Locrians, Magnesians, Malians, Perrhaebians, Phocians, Phthiotic-Achaeans, and Thessalians. Although each of the members had two votes, the association was largely dominated by Thebes.
9. Diodorus XVI:23, 29. During the Leuctrian War in 382 B.C. with the Boeotians, Sparta had occupied the Cadmea of Thebes during a time of peace. Thebes brought charges against Sparta for this action after the battle of Leuctra. The Amphictyonic Council subsequently levied a fine on Sparta of 500 talents. When Sparta refused to pay it, the Thebans obtained another decree from the Council that doubled the fine to 1,000 talents. The Spartans then used arguments in her defense that were similar to those the Phocians would later use, claiming that the amount of the fine was unjust for the offense.
10. Diodorus XVI:24.
11. Ibid.
12. Ibid.
13. Ibid.
14. Ibid., XVI:25.
15. Ibid.
16. Ibid., XVI:30.
17. Ibid.
18. Ibid.
19. Ibid., XVI:33.
20. Ibid., XVI:34.
21. Ibid., XVI:35.
22. Hammond 1994, 47.
23. Ellis 1976, 79. The ground may have been too rough for Philip's cavalry to have performed an effective reconnaissance.
24. Ibid., 80–81. Philip's defeat had some important repercussions. In the early summer of 353 B.C., the Athenian general Chares sailed to the Chalcidice peninsula and captured Sestos. Cersobleptes, upon hearing of Philip's defeat by Onomarchus in the autumn, decided to come to terms with Athens, as did most Chalcidian cities. The Olynthians, who led the Chalcidice League, subsequently approached Athens with an offer of an alliance.
25. Hammond and Griffith 1979, 272.
26. Diodorus XVI:35.
27. Ibid.
28. Ibid.
29. Ellis 1976, 83.
30. Ibid., 87.
31. Grote 1900, XI:296; Hammond and Griffith 1979, 279.
32. Diodorus XVI:36.
33. Ibid., XVI:37.
34. Ibid.
35. Ibid.
36. Ibid., XVI:38.
37. Bury, Cook, and Adcock [1927] 1978, 227.
38. Hammond and Griffith 1979, 486; Parke 1933, 138. This revenue, however, appears to have been little more than a bribe to obtain the use of 1,000 Theban hoplites by Artaxerxes III for an expedition to recover Egypt.
39. Hammond and Griffith 1979, 482.
40. Diodorus XVI:58.
41. Ibid., XVI:56.
42. Ibid.
43. The only other road into central Greece ran through the mountains past Amphissa.
44. Cawkwell 1978, 95; Hammond 1994, 85.
45. Grote 1900, XI:374, 418.
46. Diodorus XVI:56.
47. Hammond and Griffith 1979, 336.
48. Diodorus (XVI:59) states that 8,000 mercenaries departed to the Peloponnese; Parke (1933, 139), that they departed without weapons and horses.
49. Ellis 1976, 75.
50. Diodorus XVI:34.
51. Hammond and Griffith 1979, 356.
52. Ibid., 357.
53. Bradford 1992, 28; Ellis 1976, 80.
54. Grote 1900, XI:347; Hammond and Griffith 1979, 316, 370.
55. Ellis 1976, 95.
56. Cawkwell 1978, 82.
57. Ibid., 31.
58. Hammond and Griffith 1979, 316.
59. Ellis 1976, 95; Grote 1900, XI:349.
60. Ellis 1976, 98; Grote 1900, XI:349.
61. Diodorus XVI:53.
62. Grote 1900, XI:350.
63. Diodorus XVI:53.
64. Ellis 1976, 99; Grote 1900, XI:350.
65. Hammond and Griffith 1979, 330–31.
66. Diodorus XVI:14.
67. Cawkwell 1978, 60.

68. Hammond and Griffith, 1979, 292.
69. Ellis 1976, 86.
70. Hammond and Griffith 1979, 268.
71. Cawkwell 1978, 61.
72. Westlake 1935, 175.
73. Ellis 1976, 84. Pagasae was Thessaly's only port on the Thracian coast. Philip obviously wanted to capture it to prevent Athens from landing troops in Thessaly while he conducted operations there.
74. Hammond and Griffith 1979, 336.
75. Hammond and Griffith 1979, 224. Griffith, Grote, Hammond, and Schaefer place the capture of Pagasae after that of Pherae, as if Pherae would have been a major threat to Philip's campaign in Thessaly had it been bypassed. This is hardly tenable because Lycophron evacuated Pherae with a force of only 2,000 mercenaries in the midst of an otherwise hostile population. Such a force would have posed no serious threat to Philip's army, and any attempt by it to engage him in a field battle would have been suicidal. Also, had the mercenaries left Pherae, it is quite likely that the city would have revolted in their absence.
76. Ellis 1976, 138.
77. Grote 1900, XI:235.
78. Hammond and Griffith 1979, 232–33.
79. Cawkwell 1978, 71.
80. Hammond and Griffith 1979, 236.
81. Ibid., 72–73. There was another crossing between Lakes Cercinitis and Prasias, but it was usually submerged in swamp and only infrequently used.
82. Diodorus XVI:8.
83. Hammond and Griffith 1979, 249.
84. According to Ellis (1976, 104), the forts were apparently solely occupied by Thracian troops.
85. Ellis 1976, 87.
86. Grote 1900, XI:450; Hammond and Griffith 1979, 571.
87. Hammond and Griffith 1979, 564.
88. Ellis 1976, 67.
89. Diodorus XVI:76.
90. Hammond and Griffith 1979, 572.
91. Grote 1900, XI:458.
92. Hammond and Griffith 1979, 563.
93. Ellis (1976, 179) and Hammond (1994, 132) indicate Philip captured 230 corn ships; Justin (IX:1), that he captured only 170.
94. Ellis 1976, 179; Hammond 1994, 132.
95. Ellis 1976, 179; Hammond 1994, 132.
96. Cawkwell 1978, 139–40.
97. Ibid., 140.
98. Cawkwell 1978, 88. The strait at the bridge had been intentionally narrowed so that it was only wide enough to admit a single trireme at a time.
99. Bury, Cook, and Adcock [1927] 1978, VI:231.
100. Grote 1900 XI:341.
101. Hammond 1994, 51.
102. Fine 1983, 634.
103. Ellis 1976, 164; Grote 1900, XI:450; Hammond 1994, 126.
104. Ellis 1976, 186.
105. Justin (IX:2) indicates that 20,000 young Scythian men and women and 20,000 mares were taken by Philip.
106. Hammond 1994, 136.
107. Hammond and Griffith 1979, 585.
108. Grote 1900, XI:479.
109. Hammond 1994, 144.
110. Because the Thebans occupied Nicaea, which controlled the pass at Thermopylae, the Macedonian force was unable to do more than establish a blocking position there.
111. Hammond 1994, 147.
112. Bury, Cook, and Adcock [1927] 1978, VI:259; Grote 1900, XI:495–96.
113. Grote 1900, XI:495–96.
114. Bury, Cook, and Adcock [1927] 1978, VI:259.
115. Hammond 1994, 145.
116. Curtius I.
117. Hammond 1994, 147.
118. Hammond 1973, 544.
119. Diodorus XVI:85.
120. Hammond 1994, 149.
121. It is extremely unlikely, as some historians claim, that a close-order formation like the phalanx could have moved backwards for more than a few feet and continued to maintain its alignment. Any attempt to do so would have resulted in such confusion as to break up the cohesion of the formation. Much more likely, they simply reversed direction and marched to the rear.
122. Hammond 1973, 544; Hammond and Griffith 1979, 602.
123. Curtius I; Diodorus XVI:88.
124. Hammond 1994, 155; Hammond and Griffith 1979, 605.
125. Hammond 1994, 155.
126. Hammond and Griffith 1979, 605.
127. Fine 1983, 675.
128. Hackett 1978, 81.
129. Diodorus XVII:11. The Theban hoplites were able to fight Alexander's phalanx to a standstill outside of Thebes, apparently compensating for their inferiority in weaponry and formation with a greater body strength that they had developed through strenuous and regular athletic exercise.

130. Bury, Cook, and Adcock [1927] 1978, VI:253.
131. Diodorus XVI:39.
132. Ibid.
133. Ibid.
134. Grote 1900, XI:301.
135. Hammond and Griffith 1979, 617.
136. Parke 1933, 78.
137. Hammond 1994, 168.
138. Ibid.
139. Diodorus XVII:7.

Chapter 6

1. Curtius I.
2. Ibid.
3. Bosworth 1988, 29.
4. Bosworth 1980, 54; 1988, 29; Hammond 1981, 46.
5. Arrian I:1.
6. Ibid.
7. Arrian I:1; Curtius I.
8. Arrian I:2.
9. Ibid.
10. Green [1974] 1991, 127. This was the same island that Darius I had laid a bridge over when he crossed the Danube to begin his campaign against the Scythians. Hammond and Walbank (1988, 35) indicate that Peuce Island was known as Pine Tree Island.
11. Arrian I:2.
12. Ibid.
13. Arrian I:2; Curtius I.
14. Arrian (I:2) indicates a total loss for the Macedonians of 51; Curtius (I), a loss of 50.
15. Arrian I:3.
16. Ibid.
17. Ibid.
18. Bosworth 1980, 62. The corn probably exceeded the height of a man standing and would have provided ideal concealment for Alexander's force.
19. Arrian I:4.
20. Green 1974, 91, 129.
21. Arrian I:4.
22. Bosworth 1980, 65. Cleitus was probably the son of Bardylis.
23. Hammond 1981, 49.
24. Dodge [1890] 1993, 200.
25. Arrian I:5.
26. Ibid., I:6.
27. Ibid.
28. Ibid.
29. Ibid.
30. Ibid.
31. Ibid.
32. Ibid., I:7.
33. Bosworth 1980, 91.
34. Fuller 1958, 86.
35. Arrian I:7; Curtius I.
36. Although Arrian (I:7) and Curtius (I) indicate that Alexander marched through the gates at Thermopylae, Bosworth (1988, 32) rightly indicates that this was unlikely because the Thebans would have occupied the pass in force. Had Alexander attempted this, he might have been stalemated at the gates with all Greece mobilizing in safety behind them.
37. Bosworth 1988, 32.
38. Bosworth 1980, 77. Boeotia was divided into 11 military districts, each being required to provide a force of 100 cavalry and 1,000 hoplites.
   Diodorus (XVII:9) indicates that Alexander's army consisted of 3,000 cavalry and 30,000 infantry.
39. Arrian I:7; Curtius I.
40. Hammond 1981, 309.
41. Ibid.
42. Arrian I:8; Curtius I.
43. Bury, 425. The Thebans, apparently, regularly engaged in strenuous exercise designed to improve their strength and endurance.
44. Arrian I:8.
45. Ibid.
46. Curtius I. Evidence of the Macedonian discipline was clearly demonstrated in an incident that occurred during the sacking of the city. A women was brought before Alexander by some Thracian troops and charged with killing one of their officers. She freely admitted it, indicating that the officer had broken into her house, raped her, and demanded her valuables. She then showed him a well, into which she indicated she had thrown her valuables. When he looked down it, she pushed him in and then filled the well up with rocks. Alexander told the Thracians that their officer had gotten what he had deserved and freed the woman and all her relatives. If the Thracians, who were regulars in Alexander's army, had been out of control, they would have taken revenge for the death of their officer by immediately killing the woman, instead of bringing her before Alexander for judgment.
47. Curtius I; Diodorus XVII:14.
48. Arrian I:9. Alexander's allies believed that they were justified in their harsh treatment of Thebes. During the Persian Wars, the city had betrayed Greece by allying herself with Persia. Just prior to the Peloponnesian Wars, Thebes had attempted to capture Plataea during a time of peace. Later, during the war, although the Plataeans had surrendered to

Sparta, they were nevertheless massacred by the Thebans. At the conclusion of the Peloponnesian War, the Thebans strongly urged that the Athenians should be sold into slavery.

49. Diodorus (XVII:14) and Plutarch (545) indicate that 30,000 Thebans were enslaved. Curtius (I) and Diodorus (XVII:4) indicate that 440 talents of revenue was derived from the sale of the Thebans.
50. Curtius I.
51. Arrian I:10.
52. Ibid. I:1.
53. Warry 1993, 64.
54. Curtius (IV:1) indicates the Spartan army at Megalopolis comprised 2,000 cavalry and 20,000 infantry, of which 8,000 were Greek mercenaries; Diodorus (XVII, 47), that the Spartan army contained 8,000 mercenaries. Parke (1933, 201) indicates that 10,000 of Sparta's force were mercenaries.
55. Curtius VI:1; Diodorus XVII:63.
56. Diodorus (XVII:63) indicates that Antipater's losses were 1,000; Curtius (VI:5), that they were 3,500. For such a hard-fought battle, Curtius' figure appears to be the more believable.
57. Diodorus XVII:47.
58. Curtius VI:1.

Chapter 7

1. In ancient times, modern-day Turkey was known as both Asia Minor and Anatolia.
2. Hammond 1981, 82.
3. Arrian (I:11) indicates that Alexander's army crossing over into Asia Minor consisted of 5,000 cavalry and 30,000 infantry; Curtius (II), 3,300 cavalry and 30,000 infantry; Diodorus (XVII:17), 5,100 cavalry and 32,000 infantry; and Justin (IX:6), 4,500 cavalry and 32,000 infantry.
4. Curtius (II) indicates that components of Alexander's cavalry force consisted of 1,800 Companions, 600 allied Greeks, and 900 Thracians/Paeonians.
5. Curtius (II) indicates 5,000 Greek mercenaries.
6. Arrian I:11.
7. Bosworth 1980, 100; Bosworth 1988, 38. The waterway at this point was seven-eighths of a mile wide.
8. Arrian (I:11) and Curtius (II) indicate that Alexander's fleet consisted of 160 triremes; Justin (XI:6), that it consisted of 182 ships.
Diodorus (XVII:17) indicates that a force of 60 triremes was detached from the Macedonian fleet for Alexander's sightseeing excursion to Troy.
9. Arrian II:20. The Cyprians supplied 120 ships to the Persian fleet, and the Phoenicians, including Aradus, Byblos, and Sidon, supplied 80 ships.
10. Curtius (II) indicates that Alexander took 50 ships.
11. Arrian I:11.
12. Ibid., I:12. It is thought that this action by Alexander was symbolic in demonstrating the "special," or homosexual, relationship between himself and Hephaestion. Achilles and Patroclus were widely known to have had such a relationship.
13. Arrian I:12.
14. Arrian (VII:9) and Curtius (II) indicate that Alexander had 60 talents in his treasury; Plutarch (546), 70 talents. Curtius (II) indicates that Alexander had supplies for not more than 30 days. Lane Fox (1974, 116) indicates that Alexander's treasury was only able to pay the army's wages for two weeks.
15. Curtius II.
16. Arrian I:12.
17. Fuller 1958, 148.
18. Arrian I:13.
19. Fuller 1958, 148. Lake Edje Gol precluded any turning movement to the south, while rising foothills leading to the Sea of Marmara negated any turning move to the north.
20. Bosworth 1988, 40.
21. In ancient armies, close-order troops had to keep their alignment to prevent any gaps that an opponent might use to penetrate the formation. Crossing rough ground or an obstacle would disorder the formation and dislocate its alignment, creating such gaps.
22. Arrian I:12. The heavy cavalry that comprised the offensive arm of the Persian army was extremely vulnerable to surprise attack at night because of the Persian practice of hobbling their horses. That was done to prevent them from wandering away or being led off by the enemy. To guard the horses properly against a surprise attack at night required infantry. The only effective infantry soldiers in the Persian army were the Greek mercenaries, but their numbers were usually too small for the task. Parmenio therefore rightly believed that the Persians would withdraw at least two to three miles from the river to establish a minimum buffer between themselves and an enemy force at night.
23. It usually took well over a year or more to raise a Persian army from scratch.
24. Although Diodorus (XVII:19) states that the Persian strength at the battle on the

Granicus River was 10,000, the figure of 20,000 given by Arrian (I:14) and Curtius (II) appears to be far more realistic. Alexander's frontline strength was known to be about 20,000, which was deployed across a frontage of approximately one-and-three-quarter miles. As Persian cavalry normally deployed in a depth of 10 ranks, 10,000 horses would only occupy a frontage of half that distance, allowing Alexander to overlap them considerably on both flanks, and there is no historical evidence of this occurring. A Persian deployment of 20,000, however, would closely approximate Alexander's frontage.

25. Most of Alexander's Greek and Balkan troops were unwilling draftees who were only there as hostages for their homeland's continued good behavior. Not only was their enthusiasm for Alexander's cause lacking, but many of them clearly resented their situation. Only in extreme emergencies was Alexander ever to use them en masse on the battlefield. For the most part, these troops either performed secondary escort missions or were assigned to garrison duty.

26. Curtius II.
27. Curtius II; Diodorus XVII:19.
28. Bosworth 1988, 40.
29. Arrian I:14. For all practical purposes, Philotas' command was probably restricted to just that portion of the phalanx serving on the right wing. Alexander appears to have exercised de facto tactical command over all the elite units stationed there.
30. Arrian (I:15) indicates that Mithridates led the charge; Diodorus (XVII:20), that Spithrobates did so.
31. Arrian I:16.
32. Both horse and rider were fully armored.
33. Arrian I:16; Curtius II.
34. Arrian I:16.
35. Arrian (I:16) indicates that Alexander lost 25 Companions, 60 other cavalry, and 30 infantry; Curtius (II), that he lost 75 cavalry and 30 infantry.
36. Arrian (I:16) indicates that 1,000 Persian cavalry were killed; Curtius (II) and Diodorus (XVII:20), that 2,000 Persian cavalry were killed; and Plutarch (1962, 548), that 2,500 Persian cavalry were killed.
37. Arrian I:16; Curtius 2.
38. Diodorus XVII:21.
39. Arrian I:16.
40. This tactic is a complete devastation of the land in which nothing is left behind that might aid the enemy: fields were burned, livestock driven off or killed, cities evacuated, and wells poisoned.

41. It was axiomatic at this time that cavalry could not penetrate the ranks of steady close-order infantry. The horses simply could not be forced to ride through a steady spear line.
42. It was unlikely that the Persians had the ability to defeat Alexander, even if he had suffered a heavy defeat in attempting to force the Granicus River line. In selecting a position where both their flanks were anchored, the Persians protected Alexander's flanks there as well as their own. Any attempt to attack Alexander's flank would have resulted in the Persians incurring the same disorder to which they intended to subject Alexander. If the Persians had attempted to convert their defense into a frontal attack, they would have been disordered by two obstacles and been met head-on on level ground by the phalanx, which their cavalry force would have been unable to engage.
43. Although the open plain might have better facilitated the escape of the Persian cavalry, this possibility must be offset against the fact that the weight of their armor would have slowed their withdrawal speed, thereby allowing the less encumbered Macedonians to run them down quickly.
44. Although several large cities had submitted to Alexander in Asia Minor, he apparently captured little income from them. Evidence of this is was his demobilization of his fleet, a decision, in large part, based on a shortage of funds with which to pay their wages. Most of the vast Persian treasure was housed well to the east of Phoenicia, at Susa, Persepolis, and Pasargadae. We are not told of any extensive funds that Alexander acquired from either Asia Minor, Syria, or Phoenicia. As a result, it must be concluded that Alexander was tightly controlling his troops from looting at the time in order not to alienate any of the cities there. This would allow him to pose as a liberator rather than a conqueror in the hopes that cities along his line of march would willingly open their gates to him, which, for the most part, they did.
45. Bosworth 1988, 44.
46. Arrian I:17.
47. Ibid. Bosworth (1980, 129) indicates that the citadel at Sardis was reputed to be impregnable to assault. It was situated on a hill that rose 650' above the city, was surrounded by triple walls, and was connected to the city by a single narrow path.
48. Arrian I:17.
49. Ibid.
50. Ibid.
51. Ibid.

52. Ibid.
53. Ibid., I:18.
54. Ibid.
55. Ibid.
56. Ibid.
57. Ibid.
58. Ibid.
59. Ibid.
60. Ibid., I:19.
61. Arrian I:19; Curtius II.
62. Arrian I:20.
63. Curtius (II) indicates that Alexander encamped five-eighths of a mile away.
64. Arrian I:20.
65. Ibid.
66. Diodorus XVII:26. Ephialtes was chosen to lead the sortie because of his ambition, courage, and great physical strength.
67. Ibid.
68. Ibid.
69. Arrian I:22.
70. Ibid.
71. Ibid.
72. Arrian (I:23) and Diodorus (XVII:27) pointed out that Halicarnassus was to be the capital of the satrapy Alexander had just given his adopted mother, Queen Ada. Under these circumstances, it is unlikely that he would have intentionally burned the city down. Any fire damage to the city was probably caused by the Persians in an attempt to cover their withdrawal from it.
73. Arrian II:5.
74. Ibid. I:24.
75. Ibid.
76. Plutarch, 548.
77. Savill 1993, 30.
78. Arrian I:26; Curtius I.
79. Arrian I:27.
80. Ibid.
81. Ibid., I:28.
82. Ibid.
83. Ibid.
84. Ibid.
85. Arrian I:29; Curtius II.
86. Arrian I:29.
87. Curtius III:1.
88. Arrian I:29.
89. Ibid., II:4.
90. Ibid.
91. Tarn [1948] 1978, 177–78.
92. Curtius III:4; Dodge [1890] 1993, 289–90.
93. Curtius III:4.
94. Arrian (II:4) indicates that Alexander took his archers, Agrianians, and hypaspists on the march; Curtius (III:4), that the Thracians were sent in advance of the force to reconnoiter the pass.
95. Curtius III:4.
96. Arrian II:5; Curtius III:7.
97. Arrian II:5.
98. Ibid.
99. Ibid.
100. Ibid., II:12.
101. Ibid., II:6.
102. There seems to be little doubt that Alexander fully intended to engage Darius wherever he was located, be it on the plain of Sochi or anywhere else. To doubt this is to admit to a complete lack of understanding of Alexander's temperament. In no case throughout his 12-year reign did he ever willingly allow his opponent the initiative. Alexander always assumed it himself, despite the apparent disadvantage it sometimes placed him in, Gaugamela being a good case in point.
103. Arrian II:5; Hammond 1981, 93.
104. The Persian army's rate of march was about 6.5 miles per day, only half the normal marching rate of the Macedonian army.
105. Fuller 1958, 98.
106. Large ancient armies could not linger long in any one place unless it was located near a waterway. This was because ancient agricultural production was not particularly efficient and did not ordinarily produce large surpluses. The continued presence of a large army would therefore quickly exhaust local food supplies. Although waterborne transport might deliver an adequate supply of provisions, animals were not capable of transporting supplies over long distances because they often consumed a significant portion of the supplies that they carried. This meant that the greater the distance supplies were transported overland, the fewer supplies would be delivered to the destination. Merchant ships, however, were capable of delivering large quantities of supplies over great distances with little diminution of their cargoes. For additional information on logistics, see Chapter 2.
107. Instead of supporting Persian land operations directly against Alexander, the Persian navy was campaigning along the upper west coast of Asia Minor and among the northern Aegean islands.
108. Bosworth 1980, 200; Hammond 1981, 94.
109. Bosworth 1989, 59. This pass, known as the Amanian Gates, was not screened by the Macedonians because Alexander was apparently unaware of its existence.
110. Arrian II:6. Some historical controversy has been raised about the timing of Darius' and Alexander's marches. This is probably explained by the fact that Darius, being detached

from a large portion of the baggage train he had previously sent to Damascus, probably marched faster than usual, while Alexander, being confined to the narrow Pillars of Jonah Pass and being held up several days by violent storms raging over it, probably marched much slower than usual.

111. Engels 1978, 131–32. The narrowest portion of the Pillars of Jonah Pass was only wide enough to allow the passage of four infantrymen or two cavalry marching abreast. It would thus have taken Alexander's army about eight hours to march back through the mile-high pass.

112. Delbruck 1990, 206–7; Hackett 1989, 113.
113. Delbruck 1990, 204.
114. Ibid., 206–7.
115. It is unlikely that Darius could have recruited an army much larger than Alexander's successor, Antigonus. When he was king of all Asia west of the Euphrates, he was only able to raise an army of 88,000, and part of his troops were recruited outside Asia.
116. Arrian (II:8) indicates that 20,000 Persian troops were stationed off Alexander's right flank.
117. Arrian II:9.
118. Ibid.
119. Hammond 1981, 104. Because of the rocky stream bed and the presence of only two small fords opposite the Persian left flank, it is quite likely that Alexander's hypaspists spearheaded the attack. Their open-order formation would have allowed them to cross the stream quickly on a wide front and rapidly close with the Persian archers. Had the Companions attempted to lead the attack, their advance would have been funneled through the two fords and their pace would have been necessarily slow, because any attempt to gallop across the rocky steam bed would have seriously injured the horses.
120. Arrian II:10.
121. Ibid.
122. Ibid., III:11.
123. The left flank of Parmenio's cavalry was anchored by the Mediterranean, while the phalanx anchored its right flank.
124. Diodorus XVII:37.
125. Arrian II:11; Curtius II:11; Diodorus II:34.
126. Curtius (III:11) and Diodorus (XVII:36) indicate Macedonian losses at 150 cavalry and 300 infantry killed; Justin (XI:9), that 50 cavalry and 130 infantry were killed.
127. Delbruck (1990, 201) indicates between 2,000 and 4,000 were wounded; Hackett (1976,116), that 4,500 were wounded.

128. Hackett 1978, 116.
129. Lane Fox 1974, 178.
130. Arrian (II:13) indicates that 8,000 Greek mercenaries sailed to Egypt; Curtius (IV:1), that 4,000 mercenaries sailed to Egypt and 8,000 to Cyprus and then Egypt; and Diodorus (XVII:48), that 8,000 mercenaries sailed to Crete and 4,000 to Egypt.
131. Arrian II:11.
132. Curtius II.
133. Plutarch 1952, 550.
134. Curtius III:11.
135. Hammond 1981, 100.
136. It would be unbelievable if Darius had not known about this geographical feature, considering the amount of time that he had occupied the battlefield prior to Alexander's arrival.
137. Alexander would use essentially the same tactic at the battle of the Hydaspes River.
138. Curtius II:14.
139. Arrian II:15.
140. Diodorus refers to Ballonymus as Abdalonymus.
141. Rodgers 1977, 219.
142. Although it is unlikely that Alexander's fleet would have ever exceeded the Persian fleet in sheer numbers as long as the Phoenician contingents served with them, his fleet could have been much larger than it was had the Athenians given him their full support. Instead, they contributed only 20 triremes, despite the fact that their naval inventory included about 300 ships. Admittedly, the Athenians had not been able to maintain all their ships in seaworthy condition, but they obviously could have put a minimum of 100 to sea at any one time had they so desired.
143. Arrian II:18. The Temple of Melkart was extremely old, even in Alexander's time. According to Herodotus, sacrifices were said to have been performed at the temple for over 2,300 years.
144. Curtius IV:2.
145. Bosworth 1980, 239; 1988, 65.
146. Arrian II:18.
147. Diodorus XVII:41.
148. Curtius IV:2; Diodorus XVII:41. The Carthaginian ambassadors, who happened to be at Tyre at this time celebrating the annual festival, encouraged the Tyrians to resist Alexander and promised them assistance from their home city.
149. Bosworth 1980, 247. Although Arrian (II:20) claims that Tyre's walls opposite the mole Alexander constructed were 150 feet high, this is extremely unlikely. Demetrius' huge Heliopolis, reputed to be the largest siege tower

ever constructed in antiquity, was about nine stories tall, with sloping sides of 150 feet. Since Alexander's siege towers overlooked Tyre's 60-foot-high walls and the Tyrians were able to overlook his towers with wooden extensions they built on the walls, a reasonable estimate of the towers' height would be about 70 feet.

150. Fuller 1958, 101; May, Stadler, and Votaw 1984, 34.

151. Bosworth 1980, 239–40. The original mole appears to have been about 100 feet wide and a half mile long. In the aftermath of severe storm damage, a new mole was constructed at twice the width of the initial one.

152. Curtius IV:3.
153. Arrian II:20.
154. Ibid.
155. Arrian II:20; Curtius IV:3.
156. Bury, Cook, and Adcock [1927] 1978, VI:375.
157. Arrian II:20. The naval tactics in vogue at this time were based on boarding actions, the naval battle being decided by a hand-to-hand infantry fight on the decks of the ships. This was despite the fact that the trireme was built for maneuverability and speed and was largely unsuitable for this kind of action. The ship's narrow beam and shallow draft made it a relatively unstable fighting platform. Also, the narrow gangways along each side of the ship greatly restricted available deck space for fighting troops. Any large number of troops standing upright were liable to upset the trim, or stability, of the vessel. Nevertheless, the nautical inexperience of the Macedonians and many of their allies mandated that their ships conduct their naval battles like a land campaign in which their hand-to-hand fighting skills could predominate.

158. Bury, Cook, and Adcock [1927] 1978, VI:375; Hackett 1989, 117.

159. It was not possible for the crew to cook or eat meals aboard the narrow and crowded triremes. Crews were jammed in so close together that their noses literally touched the rowers sitting in front of them, and storage space aboard the ship for either food or water was virtually nonexistent.

160. Arrian II:21.
161. Ibid., II:22. One of the ships sunk was the flagship of the Cyprian king, Pnytagoras.
162. Ibid.
163. Bosworth 1980, 247.
164. Curtius IV:3.
165. Ibid.
166. Diodorus XVII:43.
167. Curtius IV:3.
168. Arrian II:23.
169. Curtius IV:4.
170. Ibid.
171. Arrian (II:24) indicates that 8,000 Tyrians were killed in defending their city; Diodorus (XVII:46), 7,000; and Curtius (IV:4), 6,000.
172. Arrian (II:24) indicates that 30,000 Tyrians were sold into slavery; Diodorus (XVII:46), 13,000. Both Curtius (IV:4) and Diodorus (XVII:46) indicate that 2,000 Tyrians were crucified.
173. Bosworth 1980, 254. Although Arrian (II:24) indicates that Macedonian losses were 400 at Tyre, this is undoubtedly much too low for such a lengthy and hard-fought siege. It is far more likely that these losses were, in fact, only those killed in battle, the wounded, ranging between 10 and 20 times the number killed.
174. Arrian II:25.
175. Arrian (II:26) indicates that Gaza was two and a half miles inland from the sea; Fuller (1958, 216), that Gaza was located 150 miles south of Tyre.
176. Weigall 1933, 91.
177. Bosworth 1980, 259. Arrian (II:27) claimed that Gaza stood on a mound 250 feet high and that Alexander had completely surrounded the city by a mound 1,300 feet wide, which reached up to the base of the walls. In the two-month period that the siege of the city lasted, a construction effort of such magnitude was clearly impossible. Considering that the height of the modern hill Gaza rests on is less than 100 feet tall, Arrian's source apparently chose to exaggerate the mound's height in order to glorify Alexander's accomplishment. It seems likely that the hill that Gaza sat on was about half its present height and that Alexander constructed a mound only along one side of the city.
178. Arrian II:26.
179. Curtius IV:6.
180. Ibid.
181. Ibid.
182. Diodorus XVII:48.
183. Curtius IV:6.
184. Arrian III:1; Curtius IV:7.
185. Curtius IV:7.
186. Arrian III:1.
187. Toynbee 1967, 112.
188. Ibid.
189. Ibid.
190. Arrian III:3.
191. Plutarch 1952, 553.
192. Diodorus XVII:49.
193. Weigall 1933, 201.
194. Bosworth 1988, 73.
195. Diodorus XVII:50.

196. Arrian III:4; Bosworth 1980, 274; Bosworth 1988, 74. If Alexander had taken the well-used inland route, it is quite likely that the ancient writers would have commented on it, especially as Cambyses had earlier allegedly lost an entire army while marching along it.
197. Arrian III:5.
198. Curtius IV:8.
199. Arrian (III:7) indicates that Mazaeus' force consisted of 3,000 cavalry, which included 2,000 Greek mercenaries; Curtius (IV:9), that he had 6,000 cavalry at his disposal.
200. Arrian III:7; Marsden 1964, 16. Alexander's march to the north did not disclose any critical shortage of food and fodder as some current writers have indicated, quite to the contrary. Not only did Alexander rest his army for a full two days after crossing the Tigris, but his cavalry was capable of fighting a strenuous battle, and then conducting a lengthy pursuit of Darius after the battle. If the area Alexander had marched through had truly been devastated of provisions, he would have forced to continue on almost immediately after crossing the river because he would have largely exhausted his supplies on his approach. It is not likely that Mazaeus had devastated the area to the north because Darius had fully expected Alexander to turn south, not north, upon crossing the Euphrates River.
201. Arrian III:7.
202. Marsden 1964, 18. The four possible fords Alexander could use were Abu Dhahir, Abu Wajnam Am, Jazirat-Ibn-Omar, and Mosul (Nineveh).
203. Engels 1978, 64. There is some historical controversy over the fact that since Darius' army was unable to keep pace with Alexander's normal rate of march he would have had to have planned out his move to Mosul ford well beforehand and have started his march towards there even before Alexander reached Thapsacus. As Darius had expected to give battle to Alexander on the Cunaxa plain, he clearly had not expected Alexander to march north along the Tigris River. He would therefore not have been able to prepare "carefully" a reaction to an event he had obviously not anticipated.
While it is true that Alexander's army normally was able to march about twice as fast as the Persian army, Darius had several compensating advantages in his march to Gaugamela. The Persians were able to use the Royal Road to march directly north along an interior line, while Alexander marched along a rough road on a significantly longer exterior line. Also, Darius did not have to undergo the five-day delay in fording a major river that Alexander did. In fact, the crossing was so exhausting that Alexander was forced to rest his army for two full days before pushing on. This undoubtedly evened up the differing march rates and made it possible for Darius to arrive at Gaugamela before Alexander, although he was unable to reach the site of Alexander's crossing of the Tigris.
204. Curtius IV:9. The depth of water in the Tigris was above a man's breast, and the force of it was so strong that when it struck a shield it frequently caused a soldier to lose his balance on the slippery stones in the riverbed and be swept away. The loot that the men carried also greatly hampered their crossing. Not only was the additional weight a handicap, but the strenuous efforts that were sometimes made to save the packs resulted in a heavy loss of life. The men were able to effect the crossing only by locking arms and constructing, in effect, a human bridge across the water.
Curtius (IV:10) indicates that Alexander rested his army for two days; Arrian (III:7), that Alexander rested his army, but not for how long; and Diodorus (XVII:55), that he rested it for a day.
205. Plutarch, 555. *Gaugamela* means, "The Camel's House."
206. Arrian III:7.
207. Ibid.
208. Arrian (III:9) indicates that the distance from Alexander's camp to Gaugamela was about seven miles; Curtius (IV:10), that it was 19 miles.
209. Arrian III:9; Curtius IV:10.
210. Against untrained troops with low morale, the chariots could be highly effective in breaking a shaky line, many times even before contact was made. Against the experienced Macedonians, however, the chariots were to prove almost totally ineffective. The vehicles were quickly disabled by massed missile fire on their approach, and those few that did reach the front line passed harmlessly through lanes opened for them and were dispatched by rear area troops.
211. Arrian (III:8) indicates the presence of elephants on the battlefield; Arrian (III:15), their presence with the Persian baggage train.
212. Marsden 1964, 32.
213. The Persian effective infantry only consisted of 2,000 Greek mercenaries and the Persian Royal Foot Bodyguard, which numbered 1,000.
214. Arrian III:9.
215. Although Arrian (III:9) indicates that

Parmenio warned Alexander against Persian entanglements, it is doubtful that they existed. The best support of this conclusion was the charge of the Persian and Indian cavalry against the center of the phalanx. Had any entanglements been deployed opposite the Persian center, as some historians have indicated, it would have been impossible for the Persians to have executed a cavalry charge across the ground, but they did.

216. Arrian III:11.
217. Curtius IV:14.
218. Arrian III:14.
219. Curtius IV:14.
220. Arrian III:15.
221. Ibid.
222. Arrian (III:15) indicates that Arbela was 75 miles from Gaugamela, while Bury, Cook, and Adcock ([1927] 1978, VI:382) indicate that 56 miles separated the two locations.
223. Arrian III:16.
224. Arrian (III:15) indicates Alexander's casualties were 100; Curtius (IV:16), that they were less than 300.
225. Arrian III:15.
226. Arrian III:15; Curtius IV:16.
227. Curtius (V:1) indicates Alexander captured 4,000 talents of silver in the Persian baggage train; Diodorus (XVII:64), that the amount was 3,000 talents.
228. Arrian (III:16) indicates that Alexander captured 50,000 talents in silver at Susa.
229. Arrian III:16.
230. Ibid.
231. Curtius V:2.
232. Diodorus XVII:66.
233. Curtius (V:3) indicates that Alexander's force consisted of 9,000 infantry, the Agrianians, archers, 3,000 Greek mercenaries, and 1,000 Thracians; Arrian (III:17), that his force included the hypaspists and some 8,000 troops of the rest of the army.
234. Diodorus XVII:67.
235. Curtius V:3.
236. Arrian III:17.
237. Ibid.
238. Ibid., III:18. Although the route through the Persian Gates was used extensively during early antiquity, in Alexander's time it was more common to travel to Persepolis by the longer but easier route running through Shiraz.
239. Curtius (V:3) and Diodorus (XVII:68) indicate that Ariobarzanes' force consisted of 3,000 cavalry and 25,000 infantry; Arrian (III:17), that it consisted of 700 cavalry and 40,000 infantry.
240. Dodge [1890] 1993, 402.

241. Curtius V:7. The Lycian was later paid the huge sum of 30 talents for his services.
242. Arrian (III:18) indicates that Craterus' force consisted of his and Meleager's taxies of the phalanx, some archers, and 500 cavalry; Curtius (V:4), that his force consisted of his and Meleager's taxies of the phalanx and 1,000 mounted bowmen.
243. Arrian III:18.
244. Arrian III:18; Curtius V:4.
245. Arrian III:18; Curtius V:4. Although Arrian states that three taxies of the phalanx were detached to repair the bridge over the Araxes River, this was unlikely. It is doubtful whether Alexander would have detached so many men from his already small force, especially in light of the fact that the size of the Persian force that he would be confronting was unknown. Also, it seems unlikely that 4,500 men would be sent merely to build a bridge. In this case, Diodorus' story of the Amyntas group forming an additional assault force is much more credible than Arrian's.
246. Arrian III:18.
247. Curtius V:4.
248. Ibid. V:6.
249. Ibid. V:6.
250. Diodorus XVII:71.
251. Curtius V:6.
252. Ibid. VI:3.
253. Bosworth 1980, 335. Arrian gives Darius' infantry force as 6,000, which is probably too few, while both Diodorus (XVII:73) and Curtius (V:8) indicate it was 30,000, which was probably too many. Considering the fact that Darius had six months after Gaugamela in which to recruit infantry from nearby satrapies, Bosworth is correct in stating that a figure somewhere between the two is probably more realistic.
254. Arrian III:19.
255. Ibid. III:19.
256. Arrian (III:19) indicates that Darius' force consisted of 3,000 cavalry and 6,000 infantry; Curtius (V:8), that it consisted of 3,300 cavalry, 4,000 Greek mercenaries, and 26,000 Persians; and Justin (XI:15), that it consisted of 4,000 slingers and archers.
257. Arrian III:19.
258. Ibid.
259. Engels (1978, 35, 79) indicates Alexander's treasury was transported by 20,000 mules and 5,000 camels; Lane Fox (1974, 260), that 10,000 baggage animals and 5,000 camels were used.
260. Arrian III:19.
261. Ibid.
262. Ibid., III:21.

263. Ibid.
264. Ibid.
265. Dodge ([1980] 1993, 424) indicates that Darius died at Damghan; Bosworth (1988, 66), that he died at Hecatompylus.

Chapter 8

1. Curtius V:13.
2. Arrian III:23.
3. Ibid.
4. Ibid.
5. Arrian III:23; Curtius VI:5.
6. Diodorus XVII:76.
7. Arrian III:24.
8. Ibid., III:25.
9. Ibid.
10. Ibid.
11. Ibid.
12. Curtius VI:6.
13. Ibid.
14. Diodorus XVII:78.
15. Arrian III:28; Diodorus XVII:78.
16. Curtius VII:3.
17. Ibid., VIII:2.
18. Ibid.
19. Diodorus XVII:81.
20. Curtius VII:3.
21. Diodorus XVII:81.
22. Curtius VII:3.
23. Ibid.
24. Arrian III:28.
25. Curtius VII:4.
26. Arrian (II:28) indicates that Bessus had a force of 7,000 Bactrians under arms; Curtius (VII:4), that the force totaled 8,000.
27. Engels 1978, 95.
28. Ibid.
29. Curtius VII:10.
30. Ibid., IV:22.
31. Arrian IV:16.
32. Ibid.
33. Arrian (IV:16) indicates that Spitamenes was able to recruit 600 cavalry; Curtius (VIII:1), that he was able to recruit 900 cavalry.
34. Curtius VIII:1.
35. Arrian IV:16.
36. Ibid.
37. Ibid.
38. Arrian (IV:16) indicates that Spitamenes incurred 150 casualties; Curtius (VIII:1), that he incurred 1,000.
39. Arrian IV:17.
40. Ibid.
41. Ibid.
42. Ibid.
43. Ibid., IV:22.
44. Ibid., III:29.
45. Curtius VII:5.
46. Green [1974] 1991, 355.
47. Arrian III:29.
48. Ibid.
49. Curtius VIII:2.
50. Ibid.
51. Ibid.
52. Ibid.
53. Ibid., VII:6.
54. Arrian III:30.
55. Curtius VII:6.
56. Ibid.
57. Arrian IV:3.
58. Ibid.
59. Ibid.
60. Ibid.
61. Curtius VII:6.
62. Ibid.
63. Arrian (IV:3) indicates that Pharnuches' force consisted of 60 Companions, 800 mercenary cavalry, and 1,500 mercenary infantry; Curtius (VII:6), referring to Pharnuches as Menedemus, gives his force as 800 cavalry and 3,000 infantry.
64. Arrian (IV:3) indicates that Pharnuches was a Lycian interpreter who spoke the language of the area and was skilled in conducting negotiations. Parke (1933, 193) gives the command structure of Pharnuches' force.
65. Arrian IV:5.
66. Arrian (IV:6) indicates that only 40 cavalry and 300 infantry were reputed to have escaped; Curtius (VII: 7, 9), that a force under Menedemus, Pharnuches as he is known by Arrian, lost 300 mercenary cavalry and 2,000 mercenary infantry.
67. Arrian IV:6.
68. Arrian (IV:6) indicates that Alexander marched 187 miles to the Jaxartes River in three days. Although Engels (1978, 155) indicates that a small light force of Alexander's was capable of marching as much as 50 miles a day, it is unlikely that Alexander would have been able to march an average of 63 miles a day for three straight days. It is thus likely, as Engels has correctly observed, that his march would have taken an additional day.
69. Curtius VII:10.
70. Ibid., VII:11.
71. Ibid.
72. Arrian IV:18; Curtius VII:11.
73. Arrian IV:19; Curtius VII:11.
74. Arrian (IV:18) indicates that the first of the climbers to reach the top would receive 12 talents; Curtius (VII:11), that the first up would receive 10 talents.
75. Morrison and Coates 1986, 244. A tal-

ent equaled 6,000 drachmas.
76. Curtius VII:11.
77. Arrian (IV:19) indicates that Alexander's force climbing up the Rock of Sogdiana lost 30 of their number; Curtius (VII:11), that the loss was 32.
78. Arrian IV:19. Since Darius' wife had given birth to several children and was clearly well into middle age, either her beauty must have been greatly exaggerated or she truly must have been one of the most beautiful women of all time.
79. Ibid., IV:21.
80. Ibid.
81. Ibid.
82. Ibid., IV:22.
83. Ibid.
84. Arrian (IV:4) indicates that Alexander had been constructing the walls of this city for 20 days; Justin (XI:5), that Alexander had constructed six miles of wall round the city in 17 days.
85. Curtius VII:8.
86. Arrian IV:4.
87. Ibid.
88. Ibid.
89. Ibid.
90. Curtius VII:9.
91. Arrian IV:4; Curtius VII:9.
92. Curtius VII:9.
93. Ibid.

Chapter 9

1. Sedlar 1980, 33.
2. Arrian VIII:8.
3. Ibid., IV:22.
4. Ibid., IV: 23.
5. Ibid.
6. Ibid. Alexander's wound was not serious because his breastplate had prevented the arrow from penetrating his shoulder. Ptolemy and Leonnatus were also wounded in the same action.
7. Arrian IV:24.
8. Ibid.
9. Ibid., IV:25.
10. Ibid., IV;22.
11. Ibid., IV:25.
12. Ibid.
13. Ibid.
14. Ibid.
15. Arrian (IV:26) indicates that 7,000 mercenaries were added to the city's original garrison; Curtius (VIII:10), that the city's total garrison consisted of 38,000 infantry.
16. Curtius VIII:10.
17. Ibid.
18. Arrian (IV:25) indicates that the distance was seven-eighths of a mile.
19. Arrian IV:26.
20. Ibid.
21. Ibid.
22. Ibid., IV:27.
23. Ibid.
24. Ibid.
25. Arrian (IV:28) indicates that the circumference of Aornos was 25 miles.
26. Arrian IV:28.
27. Ibid.
28. Curtius VIII:11.
29. Ibid., VIII:35.
30. Arrian IV:29.
31. Arrian (IV:30) indicates that Alexander was accompanied by 700 hypaspists on his climb; Curtius (VIII:11), that only 30 soldiers accompanied him.
32. Curtius VIII:11; Diodorus XVII:85.
33. Arrian IV:30.
34. Diodorus XVII:86.
35. Arrian V:3.
36. The Hydaspes River formed the western border of Porus' territory.
37. Arrian V:8. The boats were separated in pieces, the smaller ones into two sections and the larger into three. They were then transported overland by wagons to the Hydaspes River, where they were reassembled.
38. Curtius (VIII:13) indicates Porus fielded 30,000 infantry, 300 chariots, and 85 elephants; Diodorus (XVII:87), that Porus fielded 3,000 cavalry, 50,000 infantry, 1,000 chariots, and 130 elephants.
39. Arrian (V:14) indicates that Alexander disembarked about 5,000 cavalry and 6,000 infantry. Although Arrian's strength for the cavalry is fairly accurate, his strength for the infantry is at least 2,000 too low. The two taxies of the phalanx would total 3,000; the hypaspists, 3000; the Agrianians, 1,000; and the archers, 2,000.
40. Arrian V:12.
41. Ibid.
42. Ibid.
43. Ibid., V:11.
44. Ibid.
45. Diodorus XVII:87. When the battle began, Abisares' army was reputedly 50 miles distant from the battlefield.
46. Arrian V:11.
47. Alexander's troops had perfected the technique of constructing floats on the Danube River in his Balkans campaign; on the Oxus River in his Sogdiana campaign; and on the Jaxartes River in his Scythian campaign. His

NOTES — CHAPTER 9

soldiers undoubtedly knew the procedure well and would need only an hour or two to construct the floats.
48. Arrian V:13.
49. Ibid.
50. Ibid.
51. Arrian (V:14) indicates that Aristobulus had 120 chariots and 2,000 cavalry at his disposal; Curtius (VIII:13), that he had 100 chariots and 4,000 cavalry; and Plutarch (569), that he had 60 chariots and 1,000 cavalry.
52. Arrian V:15; Plutarch 569.
53. Arrian (V:2,15) indicates that Porus' army consisted of 200 elephants, 300 chariots, 4,000 cavalry, and 30,000 infantry; Curtius (VIII:13), that he had 85 elephants, 300 chariots, and 30,000 infantry; and Diodorus (XVII:87), that he had 130 elephants, 1,000 chariots, 3,000 cavalry, and 50,000 infantry available.
54. Arrian V:15; Scullard 1974, 68.
55. Arrian V:15.
56. Ibid.
57. Delbruck 1990, 221–22; Lane Fox 1974, 358. Horses were generally extremely agitated in the presence of elephants and could not be induced to remain in close proximity to them for any length of time.
58. Hackett (1978, 126) indicates that the horse-archers were 1,000 strong.
59. Lane Fox 1974, 338. Elephants usually moved along at about 6 miles per hour, although they were capable of charging at 20 miles per hour.
60. Curtius VIII:14
61. Head 1982, 136. The extreme length of the Indian bow, which was reputed to be as tall as a man, required that it be braced for stringing and shooting on the ground by the firer's foot. The slipperiness of the ground at the battle of Hydaspes River from the recent rain made this extremely difficult.
62. Green [1974] 1991, 400; Lane Fox 1974, 360. Porus had been wounded in the right shoulder by a javelin.
63. Arrian (V:18) indicates Porus' casualties were 3,000 cavalry, 20,000 infantry, and all the chariots; Diodorus (XVII:89), that he suffered 12,000 casualties.
64. Diodorus XVII:89.
65. Arrian V:18; Diodorus XVII:88.
66. Arrian (V:18) and Diodorus (XVII:89) both indicate that Macedonian casualties were 280 cavalry and 700 infantry.
67. Diodorus XVII:89.
68. Curtius (VIII:14) indicates that the massive Indian chariots were pulled by four horses and contained as many as six crew members: two armed with shields, two archers, and two drivers. In effect, the vehicles were more like small wagons than chariots. Head (1982, 179) disagrees, indicating that Chandragupta's chariots had only a single driver and two crewmen. Since almost two decades occurred between the two events, it may well have been that the larger chariots, having proved themselves so ineffective against Alexander at the battle of Hydaspes River, were discarded sometime after the battle for the lighter ones.
69. Arrian V:19; Curtius IX:3. The city of Nicaea was named in honor of Alexander's victory at the Hydaspes River, Bucephala after Alexander's horse, which had been fatally wounded in the battle of Hydaspes River.
70. Arrian V:20.
71. Ibid.
72. Ibid.
73. Ibid.
74. Ibid., V:21.
75. Ibid.
76. Diodorus XVII:91.
77. Arrian V:22.
78. Ibid.
79. Ibid.
80. Ibid.
81. Ibid., V:23.
82. Ibid., V:24.
83. Ibid.
84. Ibid.
85. Ibid.
86. Ibid.
87. Ibid.
88. Ibid., VI:2.
89. Ibid.
90. Curtius IX:1; Diodorus XVII:93.
91. Diodorus, XVII:93.
92. Curtius (IX:2) indicates that Ding Xandrames' force consisted of 3,000 elephants, 2,000 chariots, 20,000 cavalry, and 80,000 infantry; Diodorus (XVII:93), that his army consisted of 4,000 elephants, 2,000 chariots, 20,000 cavalry, and 200,000 infantry.
93. Diodorus XVII:95.
94. Diodorus (XVII:98) indicates that the Malli and Oxydracae fielded a combined force of 700 chariots, 10,000 cavalry, and 80,000 infantry; Curtius (IX:4), that their army consisted of 900 chariots, 10,000 cavalry, and 90,000 infantry.
95. Arrian (VI:2) indicates that Nearchus' fleet consisted of 2,000 ships; Diodorus (XVII:95), that the fleet consisted of 200 galleys and 800 service ships.
96. Arrian VI:5.
97. Ibid.
98. Ibid.
99. Ibid.

100. Ibid., VI:6.
101. Ibid.
102. Ibid.
103. Ibid.
104. Ibid.
105. Ibid., VI:7.
106. Ibid.
107. Ibid.
108. Ibid., VI:8.
109. Ibid.
110. Ibid.
111. Ibid., VI:9.
112. Ibid.
113. Arrian VI:9; Curtius IX:5.
114. Curtius IX:5.
115. Arrian VI:14.
116. Ibid.
117. Ibid.
118. Ibid.
119. Ibid., VI:15.
120. Hammond 1981, 223. This capital city was located near the modern city of Rohri.
121. Arrian VI:15.
122. Curtius IX:8.
123. Ibid.
124. Ibid., IV:8.
125. Curtius IX:8; Diodorus XVII:102.
126. Arrian VI:17.
127. Ibid., VI:20.

Chapter 10

1. Arrian VI:24.
2. Fox Lane 1974, 392.
3. Hamilton 1973, 127.
4. Bury, Cook, and Adcock (1927) 1978, VI:415; Savill 1993, 125.
5. Lane Fox 1974, 392.
6. Hammond (1981, 230–31) indicates that Alexander's military force was estimated to consist of 1,000 horse-archers, 1,000 Agrianians, 1,000 hypaspists, 1,500 archers, 4,500 phalanx infantry, and 4,000 Companion cavalry; Bury, Cook, and Adcock ([1927] 1978, 415), that his force was between 12,000 and 15,000; Bosworth (1988, 142), that his force was not less than 30,000; and Fox Lane (1974, 392), that his force contained 30,000 combat troops, of which 8,000 were Macedonians.
7. Lane Fox 1974, 392. Craterus' force totaled 4,500 infantry of the phalanx, 2,000 hypaspists, and 500 archers. It is not known how many Macedonians whose length of service had expired accompanied his force.
8. The Arabius River marked the eastern boundary of Oreitan territory.
9. Arrian VI:22.
10. Ibid.
11. Bosworth 1988, 143; Curtius IX:10.
12. Apollophanes' death has been alleged to have had tragic consequences for Alexander's march through the Makran Desert. Supposedly, when he died the supply trains from the Oreitae territory stopped coming to Alexander, and, as a consequence, his army was reputed to have gone on starvation rations. This, of course, was hardly true. The maximum range that Apollophanes could have supported Alexander from Oreitae territory was nine days away, and then only with minimal supply deliveries. Because pack animals, mainly horses and mules, could only carry 300 pounds of provisions and since the animal and any accompanying handlers and military guard all had to be fed daily from the supplies carried, those provisions were steadily diminished through consumption. In 10 days all the supplies that could be carried on the animals would be completely consumed. Considering that Alexander's march lasted 60 days, it would be ludicrous to attribute his logistics disaster to the failure of supplies to arrive from the Oreitae. Although it is true that in the early part of his march those supplies would have helped alleviate the supplies shortage, it is well to keep in mind that Alexander did not begin suffering severe logistical problems until he left Jhau, which was approaching the extreme limit of any supplies that could have been delivered from Oreitae territory.
13. Green 1991, 433.
14. Arrian VI:25.
15. Engels 1978, 115.
16. Arrian VI:26.
17. Bosworth 1988, 138. Craterus had taken the inland route over Mullah Pass and through Kandahar, Lake Seistan, Arachosia, and Drangiana.
18. Arrian VI:24.
19. Bosworth 1988, 144. In A.D. 711, Muhammed Ibn Qasim crossed the Makran during the same time of year as Alexander had. His army was smaller than the Macedonian army and more mobile; an advance force also secured his line of march. The result was that Muhammed was able to cross the Makran with small losses and immediately embark on a major campaign in the Sind. Alexander's men, in comparison, concluded their march in an exhausted and totally demoralized condition, suffering heavy casualties in the crossing.
20. Arrian VI:27.
21. Ibid.

Chapter 11

1. Arrian VI:28.
2. Curtius X:1.
3. Arrian VII:4.
4. Ibid., VII:5.
5. Ibid.
6. Ibid.
7. Ibid., VII:7.
8. Ibid. The "weirs" were damlike obstructions along a river that made navigation along it next to impossible.

Chapter 12

1. Arrian VII:20.
2. Hamilton 1973, 149.
3. Arrian VII:19.
4. Ibid.
5. Ibid.
6. Ibid.
7. Ibid., VIII:23.

Appendix

1. Grote 1900, XI:380.
2. Ibid.
3. Ellis 1976, 108.
4. Grote 1900, XI:382.
5. Hammond 1994, 87.
6. Grote 1900, XI:408.
7. Ibid., XI:403.
8. Ellis 1976, 116.
9. Hammond 1994, 100.
10. Arrian I:25; Curtius II. Alexander of Lyncestis' brothers, Heromenes and Arrabaeus, were convicted and executed by Alexander for their part in the murder of his father Philip. Lyncestis was spared because he had been one of the first to rally to Alexander's support immediately after Philip's death.
11. Arrian I:25; Curtius II.
12. Curtius II; Diodorus XVII:80.
13. Curtius VIII:6.
14. Ironically, the army was to endure its two most debilitating campaigns in moving south: the march against the Malli, in the Punjab, and the march across the Makran Desert, in Gedrosa.
15. Curtius X:4.
16. Bosworth (1988, 161) indicates that 1,500 cavalry and 10,000 infantry were mustered out; Curtius (X:4), not fewer than 10,000 soldiers.
17. Lane Fox 1974, 427.
18. Diodorus XVII:115.
19. Curtius X:4.
20. Bosworth 1988, 205.
21. Cawkwell 1978, 75; Hammond and Griffith 1979, 11.
22. Ellis 1976, 167; Hammond 1994, 137.
23. Hammond 1994, 113.
24. Curtius II; Diodorus XVI:8.
25. The army Alexander took with him into Asia Minor totaled 5,000 cavalry and 30,000 infantry. He had left behind in Greece with Antipater 1,500 cavalry and 12,000 infantry. At a wage of two drachma per day for the cavalry and one drachma per day for the infantry, it would have cost Alexander approximately 3,300 talents a year to maintain the two armies.
26. Curtius II; X:2.
27. Justin (XI:1) indicates that Alexander granted the Macedonians relief from all burdens except military service.
28. Arrian VII:9.
29. Arrian VII:9; Curtius II.
30. Curtius II.
31. Ibid., II: X:2.
32. Herodotus (III:90-95) indicates that Alexander's annual revenue from the Persian Empire was about 16,000 talents.
33. Bury, Cook and Adcock (1927) 1978, XIII:429; Fuller 1958, 274; Lane, Fox 1973, 437.

Bibliography

Abbott, Jacob. *Makers of History: Alexander the Great*. Akron, Ohio: Werner, n.d.
Arrian. *History of Alexander and Indica*. Translated by E. Iliff Robson. 1933. Reprint. Loeb Classical Library. London: William Heinemann, 1966.
Avery, Catherine B. *The New Century Handbook of Classical Geography*. New York: Meredith, 1972.
Borza, Eugene N. *In the Shadow of Olympus: The Emergence of Macedon*. Princeton: Princeton University Press, 1990.
Bosworth, A.B. *Conquest and Empire: The Reign of Alexander the Great*. Cambridge: Cambridge University Press, 1989.
———. *A Historical Commentary on Arrian's History of Alexander*. Vol. I. Oxford: Clarendon, 1980.
Bradford, Alfred S. Compiler, editor, and translator. *Philip II of Macedon: A Life from the Ancient Sources*. Westport, Conn.: Praeger, 1992.
Buck, Robert J. A. *A History of Boeotia*. Alberta, Canada: University of Alberta Press, 1979.
Bury, J. B. *A History of Greece to the Death of Alexander the Great*. New York: Modern Library, 1913.
Bury, J. B., S. A. Cook, and F. E. Adcock, eds. *The Cambridge Ancient History: Macedon 401–301 B.C.* Vol VI. 1927. Reprint. Cambridge: Cambridge University Press, 1978.
Canfora, Juciano. *The Vanquished Library: A Wonder of the Ancient World*. Translated by Martin Ryle. 1989. Reprint. Berkeley: University of California Press, 1990.
Casson, Lionel. *Ships and Seafaring in Ancient Times*. Austin: University of Texas Press, 1994.
Casson, Stanley. *Macedonia, Thrace, and Illyria: Their Relations to Greece from the Earliest Times Down to the Time of Philip of Amyntas*. Oxford University Press, 1926.
Cawkwell, George. *Philip of Macedon*. Boston: Farber & Farber, 1978.
Chrimes, K. M. T. *Ancient Sparta: A Re-examination of the Evidence*. 1949. Reprint. Westport, Conn.: Greenwood, 1971.
Clayton, Peter A., and Martin J Price. *The Seven Wonders of the Ancient World*. New York: Dorset, [1988] 1989.
Connolly, Peter. *Greece and Rome at War*. Englewood Cliffs, N.J.: Prentice-Hall, 1989.
———. *The Greek Armies*. 1977. Reprint. Aylesbury: Hazell, Watson & Viney, 1978.
Cook, J. M. *The Persian Empire*. New York: Barnes & Noble, 1993.
Cottrell, Leonard. *Wonders of the World*. New York: Grossett & Dunlap, 1962.
Curtius, Quintus Rufus. *The History of Alexander*. Translated by John Yardley. Loeb Classical Library. London: Penguin, 1984.
De Camp, L. Sprague. *The Ancient Engineers*. New York: Ballantine, 1974.
———. *Great Cities of the Ancient World*. New York: Doubleday, 1972.
Delbruck, Hans. *A History of the Art of War: Warfare in Antiquity*. Vol. 1. Translated by Walter J. Renfroe, Jr. Lincoln: University of Nebraska Press, 1990.
Demand, Nancy H. *Thebes in the Fifth Century: Heracles Resurgent*. London: Routledge & Kegan Paul, 1982.
Diodorus. *Diodorus of Sicily*. Vols. XVI, and XVII. Translated by Charles L. Sherman. Loeb Classical Library. London: William Heinemann, 1952.
Dodge, Theodore A. *Alexander: A History of the Origin and Growth of the Art of War From the Earliest Times to the Battle of Epsus, 301 B.C., with a Detailed Account of the Campaigns of the Great Macedonian*. Vols. land II. 1890. Reprint. India: Greenhill Books, 1993.
———. *Hannibal: A History of the Art of War Among the Carthaginians and Romans Down to the Battle of Pydna, 168 B.C., with a Detailed Account of the Second Punic War*. 1891. Reprint. London: Greenhill Books, 1994.

Ellis, J. R. *Philip II and Macedonian Imperialism.* London: Thames and Hudson, 1976.
Engles, Donald W. *Alexander the Great and the Logistics of the Macedonian Army.* Berkeley: University of California Press, 1978.
Errington, R. Malcolm. *A History of Macedonia.* Translated by Catherine Errington. New York: Barnes & Noble, 1990.
Ferrill, Arthur. *The Origins of War: From the Stone Age to Alexander the Great.* 1985. Reprint. New York: Thames and Hudson, 1988.
Fine, John V. A. *The Ancient Greeks: A Critical History.* Cambridge: Belknap Press of Harvard University Press, 1983.
Forrest. W. G. *A History of Sparta: 950–192 B.C.* New York: W. W. Norton, 1969.
Fuller, J. F. C. *The Generalship of Alexander the Great.* New Brunswick, N.J.: Rutgers University Press, 1958.
Gardiner, Robert, ed. *The Age of the Galley: Mediterranean Oared Vessels Since Pre-classical Times.* Annapolis, MD: Naval Institute Press, 1995.
Green, Peter. *Alexander of Macedon: 356–323 B.C.: A Historical Biography.* 1974. Reprint. Berkeley: University of California Press, 1991.
Griffith, G. T, ed. *Alexander the Great: The Main Problems.* New York: Barnes & Noble, 1966.
_____. *The Mercenaries of the Hellenistic World.* New York: Cambridge University Press, 1935.
Grote, George. *Greece: Greecian History to the Reign of Peisistratus of Athens.* Vols. XI and XII. New York: Peter Fenelon Collier & Son, 1900.
Hackett, Sir John, ed. *Warfare in the Ancient World.* New York: Facts on File, 1989.
Hamilton, J. R. *Alexander the Great.* London: Hutchinson University Library, 1973.
Hammond, N. G. L. *Alexander the Great: King, Commander and Statesman.* London: Chatto & Windus, 1981.
_____. *Philip of Macedon.* Great Britain: Duckworth, 1994.
_____. *Studies in Greek History.* Oxford: Clarendon Press, 1973.
_____, and G. T. Griffith. *A History of Macedonia: 550–336 B.C.* Vol. II. Oxford: Clarendon Press, 1979.
_____, and H. H. Scullard, eds. *The Oxford Classical Dictionary.* Oxford: Clarendon Press, 1970.
_____, and F. W. Walbank. *A History of Macedonia: 336–167 B.C.* Vol. III. Oxford: Clarendon Press, 1988.
Hanson, Victor Davis. *The Western Way of War: Infantry Battle in Classical Greece.* New York: Alfred A. Knopf, 1989.
Head, Duncan. *Armies of the Macedonian and Punic Wars: 359 B.C. to 146 B.C.* Wargamer's Research Group,1982.
Herodotus. *The History of Herodotus.* Great Books of the Western World. Vol. 6. Translated by George Rawlinson. Chicago: Encyclopaedia Britannica, 1952.
Hooker, J. T. *The Ancient Spartans.* London: J. M. Dent and Sons, 1980.
Lane Fox, Robin. *Alexander the Great.* Great Britain: Dial, 1974.
Lempriere, John. *Lempriere's Classical Dictionary of Proper Names Mentioned in Ancient Authors.* 1788. Reprint. London: Routledge & Kegan Paul, 1987.
Livy. *Rome and the Mediterranean.* Translated by Henry Bettenson. London: Penguin, 1976.
Marsden E. W. *The Campaign of Gaugamela.* Liverpool: Liverpool University Press, 1964.
May, Elmer C., Gerald P. Stadler, and John F. Votan. *Ancient and Medieval Warfare.* Series editor, Thomas E. Griess. Wayne, N.J.: Avery, 1984.
M'Crindle, J. W., trans. *The Invasion of India by Alexander the Great as Described by Arrian, Qcurtus, Diodoros and Justin.* Westminster: Archibald Constable, 1896.
Michell, H. *Sparta.* 1952. Reprint. Cambridge: Cambridge University Press, 1964.
Mondadori, Arnoldo, ed. *The Life and Times of Alexander the Great.* Italy: Mondadori Verona, 1972.
Morrison, J. S., and J. F. Coates. *The Athenian Trireme: The History and Reconstruction of an Ancient Greek Warship.* Cambridge: Cambridge University Press, 1986.
O'Brien, John Maxwell. *Alexander the Great: The Invisible Enemy: A Biography.* London: Routledge,1992.
Olmstead. A. T. *History of the Persian Empire:* 1948. Reprint. Chicago: University of Chicago, 1970.
Parke, H. W. *Greek Mercenary Soldiers: From the Earliest Times to the Battle of Ipsus.* Oxford: Clarendon, 1933.

BIBLIOGRAPHY 469

Plutarch. *The Lives of the Noble Grecians and Romans.* Dryden translation. Chicago: Encyclopaedia Britannica, 1952.
Polybius. *The Rise of the Roman Empire.* Translated by Victoria Scott-Kilvert. London: Penguin, 1979.
Radice, Betty. *Who's Who in the Ancient World.:A Handbook to the Survivors of the Greek and Roman Classics.* 1971. Reprint. Middlesex: Penguin, 1973.
Rodgers, W. L. *Greek and Roman Naval Warfare: A Study of Strategy, Tactics, and Ship Design from Salamis (480 B.C.) to Actium (31 B.C.).* 1937. Reprint. Annapolis, Md.: Naval Institute Press, 1977.
Rolle, Tenate. *The World of the Scythians.* Translated by F. G. Walls. 1980. Reprint. Berkeley: University of California Press, 1989.
Roux, George. *Ancient Iraq.* 1964. Reprint. London: Penguin, 1992.
Sastri, K. A. *A Comprehensive History of India: The Mauryas and Satavahans, 325 B.C. to A.D. 300.* Vol. 2. Bombay: Orient Longmans, 1957.
Savill, Agnes. *Alexander the Great and His Time.* New York: Barnes & Noble, 1993.
Scullard, H. H. *The Elephant in the Greek and Roman World.* Ithaca: Cornell University Press, 1974.
Sedlar, Jean W. *India and the Greek World.* Totowa, N.J.: Rowman and Littlefield, 1980.
Snodgrass, A. M. *Arms and Armor of the Greeks.* Ithaca: Cornell University Press, 1967.
Starr, Chester G. *The Influence of Sea Power on Ancient History.* New York: Oxford University Press, 1989.
Strabo. *The Geography of Strabo.* Vols. II–IV. Translated by Horace Leonard Jones. Loeb Classical Library. London: William Heinemann, 1923.
Symeonoglou, Sarantis. *The Typography of Thebes from the Bronze Age to Modern Times.* Princeton: Princeton University Press, 1985.
Talbert, Richard J. A., ed. *Atlas of Classical History.* New York: Macmillan, 1985.
Tarn, W. W. *Alexander the Great.* 1948. Reprint. Boston: Beacon, 1967.
———. *Alexander the Great: Sources and Studies.* Vol II. 1948. Reprint. London: Cambridge University Press, 1979.
Thucydides. Translated by Richard Crawley, revised by R. Feetham. *The History of the Peloponnesian War.* Chicago: Encyclopedia Britannica, 1952.
Torr, Cecil. *Ancient Ships.* Chicago: Argonaut, 1964.
Toynbee, Arnold, ed. *Cities of Destiny.* New York: McGraw-Hill, 1967.
Warrington, John. *Everyman's Classical Dictionary: 800 B.C.–A.D. 337.* 1961. Reprint. London: J.M. Dent and Sons, 1978.
Warry, John. *Alexander 334–323 B.C.: Conquest of the Persian Empire.* London: Osprey Publishing, LTD. 1991.
Warry, John. *Warfare in the Classical World.* New York: Barnes & Noble, 1993.
Weigall, Arthur. *Alexander the Great.* Garden City, N.Y.: Garden City Publishing, 1933.
Westlake, H. D. *Thessaly in the Fourth Century B.C.* London: Methuen, 1935.

Index

Abadeh 278
Abae 116, 121–122, 363, 396
Abastani 339
Abbasabad 288
Abdalonymus 391
Abdera 134, 137, 395
Abisares 52, 313, 387
Abreas 337
Abulites 270–1, 279, 351, 388
Abydos 91, 160–1, 185, 187–8, 190
Acanthus 127–8
Acarnania 151
Acesines River 52, 54, 96–7, 316, 329–30, 334, 338
Achaea 120–1, 133, 151, 153, 160
Achaeans 118, 120, 158, 182
Achaemenid 31
Achilles 187, 189, 374
Acraiphnion 178
Acronnesus Island 205
Acte 127
Acuphis 390
Ada (daughter of Hecatomnus) 386, 401
Adad Gate 270
Adad Street 270
Addaeus 209
Admana Island 96, 319–20, 326, 328
Admetus 246
Adrasteia 191
Aegean Islands 106, 162
Aegean Sea 112, 116, 131, 166, 204, 211
Aegospotami 156, 243
Aenianians 117, 150
Aeropus 203, 211, 401
Aeschines 149–50, 361, 363
Aeschylus 255, 386
Aetolia 158, 175, 183
Aetolians 150, 180
Agamemnon 392
Agathocles 203
Agathon 194, 259–60, 270
Agema 30–1, 40, 103
Agenor 340

Agenorium 247
Agesilaus 107
Aggrammes 389
Agis (king of Paeonia) 137, 182–3, 389, 393
Agis (king of Sparta) 107, 181, 402
Agrianes 168
Agriania 171
Agrianians 40, 45–6
Akontion, Mt. 153–5
Albania 17, 171
Alcetas 39, 303, 312, 318
Aleppo 255–6
Aleuadae 130, 133, 398
Alexander (son of Aeropus) 32, 176, 203, 211, 365, 401
Alexander I 35
Alexander IV 9, 404
Alexander of Epirus 400
Alexander of Lyncestis 365
Alexander of Molossus 144–5, 393, 401
Alexander the Great 165, 376, 399–400; battles of *see* Gaugamela, Granicus River, Hydaspes River, Issus, Thebes; birth of 394; burial of 383; death of 355–6, 358, 368, 404; divinity of 253–4, 404; generalship of 1, 8, 24–6, 46, 66, 174, 180, 201, 229, 234, 247–8, 251, 268–9, 274, 276–7, 293, 299–303, 311, 315, 317, 326–8, 340–1, 348, 355; illnesses of 403; Orientalization policies of 49; as pharaoh 252, 401; and Sacred Band 16; sieges 74 (*see also* Halicarnassus, Rock of Aornos, Rock of Chorienes, Rock of Sogdiana, Tyre); statesmanship of 9; and Tagus of Thessaly 130, 392–3; wounds sustained 251, 295, 297, 312, 335, 401, 403
Alexander's ladders 165
Alexandria 186, 250, 253
Alexandria-Eschate 54, 66, 284, 290, 296, 303
Alexandros 388
Alor 284, 334, 339
Alponus 90, 116, 122–3

471

Amadocus 134–5, 137–8, 395–6, 398
Amanic Gates 218–9, 221
Amanus Mountains 218, 221–2, 232
Amastrine 352
Amazons 65, 287
Ambracia 158
Amedines 389
Amik Plain 218–9, 221
Amminaspes 387–8
Ammon 253–4, 371
Amphictyonic Council 64, 115, 118, 123, 131, 149–50, 362, 364, 394, 400
Amphictyonic League 115, 363
Amphion Hill 178–9
Amphipolan cavalry 170
Amphipolis 112–3, 123, 127–8, 135–6, 137, 166–8, 186, 361, 363, 392–4
Amphissa 16, 116, 119, 149–51, 395, 400
Amphoterus 96, 365, 380
Amritsar 316
Amul 286
Amyntas 39, 135, 160, 162, 194–6, 202, 206, 224–6, 228–30, 232, 235, 254, 279, 283, 285, 293, 295, 367, 386, 393
Amyntas (son of Andromenes) 51, 177, 203
Amyntas (son of Antiochus) 203, 221
Amyntas (son of Arrabaeus) 187, 213
Amyntas (son of Nicolaus) 292, 385
Amyntas (son of Perdiccas III) 400
Amyntor 28
Anabasis of Alexandri 1
Anatolian Plateau 185
Anaxicrates 357
Anaxippus 285
Anchialus 218–9
Ancyra 50, 185–6, 214–6
Andaca 308, 310
Andromachus 34, 51, 94, 243, 260, 297, 300, 388, 389, 401
Andromenes 51, 177, 203
Andronicus 95
Andros 107
Androsthenes 103, 357
Anteas 28
Anthemus 127, 136, 393
Antibelus 280
Antigonus 39, 217, 322, 323, 324, 340, 343, 387, 399
Antigonus (son of Philip) 42, 215, 388
Antioch 255–6
Antiochus 34, 48, 203, 221, 224, 317
Antipater 52–3, 67, 95, 160, 176, 182–3, 356, 367–8, 400, 402, 404

Aornos 96, 284, 290, 313–5, 317, 403
Aphrices 52
Aphrodite 102
Apollo 122
Apollodorus 380
Apollonia 127–8, 394
Apollonides 95
Apollonius (son of Charinus) 254, 385, 387
Apollophanes 100, 345, 386, 389
Apple-bearers 59
Apsus River 172
Arabia 103–4, 250, 254, 357, 373
Arabian Sea 99–100, 284, 342, 344, 347, 352, 404
Arabis River 343
Arabitae 342–3, 344–5
Arachosia 52, 287–9, 340, 402–3
Aradan 286
Aradus 93, 107, 235–6
Arak 278
Araxes River 272, 276
Arbela 256–7, 265
Arbupales 189, 193, 198
Arcadia 152, 159–60, 175
Arcadians 159, 180
Archelaus 391
Archelaus (son of Theodorus) 270–1
Archers 47, 63
Archias 103, 357
Archidamus 117, 122, 159–60
Archon 125, 166, 396
Ardiaioi 114, 398
Areia 28, 52, 284–5, 287–8, 343
Aretes 32, 260
Arethusa 127–8
Argaeus 393
Argead 9, 252
Argives 42, 159, 203, 396
Argolas Ridge 118, 131, 394
Argos 159–60, 165, 175, 398–9
Argyraspids 40
Ariaspians 344
Arigaeum 308
Arimaspians 287
Arimmas 388
Ariobarzanes 273–7, 283, 388, 392
Aristander 249, 304
Aristobulus 1, 20, 321, 326, 328
Aristodemus 361
Ariston 31, 224, 259–60, 263
Aristonicus 95
Aristonous (son of Pisaeus) 28
Aristotle 7, 306, 368, 381, 397, 399, 404

INDEX 473

Aristronicus 390
Arrabaeus 187, 213
Arrhidaeus 9, 129–30, 393, 396–7, 404
Arrhybas 28
Arrian 1
Arsaces 52, 387
Arsames (son of Artabazus) 189, 193–6, 283, 285, 287, 385–6
Arsites 193–4, 196, 198, 386, 388
Artabazus 88–9, 119, 283, 287, 291, 292, 385, 393–5, 401, 403
Artacana 52
Artacoana 285, 288, 352
Artaxerxes II
Artaxerxes III (Ochus) 88, 121, 143, 185, 198, 255, 279, 393, 396, 398–400
Artemis Temple 203
Artemisia 396
Artonis 352
Arybbas 144–5, 393, 396, 399
Asander 387
Asandrus (son of Philotas) 203, 209, 387
Asclepiodorus (son of Eunicus) 51, 388
Asclepiodorus (son of Hegesandros) 51
Asia Minor 26, 112, 140, 160–2, 166, 184–6, 188, 192, 199, 206, 210–1, 214, 216, 401, 404
Asiatic infantry levies 231
Aspasians 308–10
Aspendus 211–2
Assacenians 308, 311–2, 329, 389
Assault ships 94
Astaspes 386
Astes 311, 390
Atarrhias 365
Ateas 148
Atheas 390
Athenian army 15, 46
Athenian Confederacy 146
Athenian fleet 141, 144, 243
Athenian Maritime League 156
Athens 6, 15–6, 53, 86, 89–90, 112, 120, 122, 124, 128, 133, 136–7, 156, 165–6, 179–80, 183, 362–3, 378, 393–8, 400
Atintani 145
Atizues 229, 388
Atropates 352, 387
Attalus 39, 160, 162, 194, 224, 260, 292, 298, 303, 310, 312–3, 318, 340, 343, 400
Attica 145, 150, 152, 361
Attock 96, 308, 313, 316–7
Audata 112, 393
Augustus, Octavius 384
Austane 303

Autaratians 168, 171, 173
Automedon 146
Autophradates 106–7, 389–90
Axios River 108, 113, 168
Axios Valley 171
Azemilcus 391
Azemilk 238, 243

Babel Tower 270
Babylon 51, 53, 102–4, 184, 186, 220, 235, 256, 269–70, 272, 284, 354–6, 357, 368, 380, 402, 404
Babylonia 26, 53–4, 255, 265, 272, 354, 375, 381
Bactria 34, 51, 54, 279, 282, 284–5, 289–91, 294, 298, 303, 305, 309, 402–3
Bactrian army 290
Bactrian light cavalry 34
Badis 101, 344
Bagae 290
Baggage train 56, 220–1, 230, 346
Baghdad 256, 269
Bagisara 344
Bagistanes 280
Bagoas 97, 352, 400
Bagophanes 269
Bahrain 103, 357
Bajaur 52, 54, 308–9, 311, 403
Balacrus 43, 260, 304, 310
Balacrus (son of Amyntas) 254
Balacrus (son of Nicanor) 28, 386
Balaeric slingers 43, 48
Balkans 13, 113, 166, 168
Ballonymus 237, 391
Bampur 284, 344, 347, 351, 354
Bandar Abbas 347
Bardylis 5, 17, 112–4, 389, 392–3
Bargylia 206
Barsaentes 281, 287, 385–6
Bar-sar Ridge 314–5
Barsine 9, 352, 401, 403
Baryaxes 387
Barzanes 388
Batis 249, 390, 401
Battering rams 79
Bazira 308, 312–3
Beas River 52, 284, 306, 316, 333–4, 341, 369–70, 372, 403
Beilan Pass 212, 218–20
Bela 284, 344–5, 349
Belbinatis 159–60
Beldibi 212
Belly-bows 77

Benefactors 287–8
Beqaa Valley 240
Berisades 134–5, 137, 393–5
Bessus 55, 258, 260, 262–3, 265–6, 268, 279–82, 291, 293, 294–5, 385, 402
Bibacta 100
Bistanes 279
Bisutun 354
Black Sea 103, 112, 134, 138, 142–3, 166, 170, 186, 399–400
Bodyguards 28
Boeotia 15–6, 116, 118–9, 121–2, 131, 150–3, 156, 167, 176, 364, 395, 397
Boeotian army 16–7
Boeotian cavalry 170
Boeotian League 16, 121, 156, 362, 364, 395
Boeotians 117, 179, 364
Bolan Pass 335, 343, 367
Bosporus 142–3
Bottice 89, 127, 129
Brahmans 309, 339–40
Breaking array 19
Brison 48, 260
Broadswords 19–20, 22, 323, 327
Brucida 145
Bucephala 333
Bucephalas 321, 329, 403
Bukhara 290
Burimar 314
Byblos 93, 107, 236–7, 401
Byzantium 88, 90, 112, 134–5, 138, 141–3, 148, 156–7, 166, 206, 395–6, 399

Cabeiron 178
Cadmea 16–7, 156, 175, 177–8, 392
Caesar, Julius 384
Cairo 250
Calamus 43
Calas (son of Harpalus) 32, 34, 162, 194, 203, 217, 386–7, 388
Callias 146
Callisthenes 1, 366, 368, 400, 403
Caltrops 22
Cambyses 252
Camels 64, 101
Canasis 101
Canate 344
Cappadocia 216–7
Cappadocian Plateau 185
Caranus 297–8, 300
Cardaces 61–2, 233–4
Cardia 134, 138–9, 398–9

Caria 162, 204, 206, 209
Carians 215
Carmania 53, 101–2, 340, 344, 348, 351, 354–5, 404
Carthage 86, 239, 245–7
Carthaginians 241
Carthasis 303
Carts 26–7, 81, 169, 331
Caryae 159–60
Carystus 116, 145–6, 397
Caspian Gates 278–80, 286
Caspian Sea 103, 186, 283–4, 286
Cassander 368, 404
Cataea 102
Catane 303
Catapults 14, 25, 50, 77
Cathaeans 330–1
Caucasus Mountains 289
Cebalinus 366–7
Celeanae 43, 211, 214
Cephision 159
Cephissus River 121, 153–5, 395–6
Cercinitis, Lake 135
Cerdimmas 389
Cersobleptes 89, 134–5, 137–40, 362, 393–99
Cetriporis 137–8
Chabrias 87–8
Chaeronea 6, 7, 15, 23, 108, 116, 119, 152–7, 159, 395–6, 400
Chakwal 316
Chalcidian League 126–129, 136, 393, 397, 396–7
Chalcidians 392
Chalcidice 6, 112, 126–7, 148, 377, 396–7
Chalcidice peninsula 127, 130, 397
Chalcis 116, 128, 145–7, 363, 398–9; road 178
Chaldaeans 356
Chandragupta 307
Chares 88–90, 96, 120, 136, 138, 142–3, 150, 152–3, 157, 180, 187, 394–5, 399, 404
Charidemus 89–90, 129, 180, 396, 401
Charinus 254, 387
Chariots 20, 56, 63–4, 263–4, 267, 269, 321, 328
Charsadda 311
Chenab River 96–7, 316
Chersonese 89, 123, 138, 362, 377, 395
Chilarch 283
Chilluta 98
Chios 87, 95, 106–7, 143, 162, 361, 393
Chitarchus 399

Choaspes River 271
Choes River 309
Chorasinians 51
Chorienes 302-3, 388
Chorienes, Rock of 284, 290, 302-3, 403
Cilicia 26, 28, 186, 217-9, 221, 401
Cilician Gates 185, 216-7, 219, 401
Cimon 361
Circumnavigation 86
Cirrha 116, 149
Cirrhan plain 115
City-states 6
Cleander (son of Polemocrates) 44, 50-1, 53, 259-60, 363, 380, 351
Cleandrus 47, 215
Clearchus 44, 194, 209, 399
Cleitarchus 1, 2, 146-7, 397
Cleitus, king of the Dardanians 171, 173
Cleitus the Black (son of Dropidas) 31, 197, 260, 290, 309, 336, 318, 385, 389, 403
Cleitus the White 39, 372
Cleomenes 254, 385
Cleopatra (daughter of Olympias) 9, 394, 400
Cleopatra (niece of Attalus) 400
Cleruchs 128, 136, 139, 141, 205, 392, 295
Climax Mountain 211-2
Closed-shields formation 36
Cocala 344
Coenus (son of Polemocrates) 31, 39, 50, 96, 173, 194-6, 224, 226-7, 246, 259-60, 262, 265, 275, 280, 285, 290, 292-3, 310-13, 318, 321-5, 327, 330, 367, 370, 400, 402-3
Coeranus 259-60
Colossus of Rhodes 75
Companion cavalry 5, 23-5, 28-30, 55, 59, 130
Contravallation 14, 73
Cophen (son of Cophen) 237, 283
Corcyra 151, 158
Corinth 112, 153, 158, 160, 166, 180
Corinth, Gulf of 116, 152, 160
Corinth, Isthmus of 180
Corn fleet 399
Corn ships 90
Coronea 116, 119, 121-2, 364, 395-7
Coroneia 123
Corsia 116
Corsiae 119, 121-3, 364-5
Cos 87-8, 96, 106-7, 143, 209, 219
Cossaea 53

Cossaeans 353-5, 404
Cottyphus 150, 400
Cotys 135, 392
Counter wall 14, 73
Craterus 39, 93, 97-8, 194-6, 224-6, 242, 259-60, 262, 264, 271, 275, 279-80, 283, 287, 290, 296-7, 303, 310-1, 313, 318-20, 322, 326, 328-9, 332-3, 335, 339, 343-4, 347, 352, 267, 372, 385, 402-4
Crateuas 28
Crenidas 6, 127, 137, 377, 393-4
Crescent Wall 208
Cretan archers 43, 47
Crete 107, 230, 401
Crobyle 139
Crocala 100
Crocus Field 65, 119-20, 125, 131, 396
Crocus Plain 132
Crowns, golden 381
Ctesiphon 361
Cunaxa 23, 55, 255, 256-7, 392
Curtius 1
Cyclades 107
Cydnus River 217
Cyiza 100, 344
Cynna 393
Cynuria 159
Cyprian fleet 94-5, 241, 243-4, 247-8
Cyprus 86, 93, 107, 186, 230, 236
Cyropolis 290, 296, 297
Cyrus the Great 287, 297, 306, 342, 352, 404
Cyrus the Younger 255, 392
Cythnus 95
Cytinium 116, 150-1
Cyzicus 161-2, 188

Dacia 170
Damascus 221, 237, 255-6, 401
Damghan 281, 286, 402
Danthaletae 143
Danube River 112-3, 148, 166-70, 174
Daochidai 131
Dardanelles 105, 185
Dardanians 5, 17, 108, 112-4, 168, 171, 173
Darius I 193, 392
Darius III 55-6, 66, 184, 187-9 227, 231-4, 266-7, 279, 400, 402
Dascylium 188, 203
Dashatiari plain 347
Datames 95, 107

Daulis 116
Dead ground 235
Decadarchies 133
Deh Bid 278
Deli Cay River 218, 232
Delos 156
Delphi 65, 112, 115–8, 120, 122–5, 149–50, 166, 362–4, 394
Demaratus the Corinthian 197
Demetrius 28, 31, 312, 318, 321–4, 330, 336
Demosthenes 15, 124, 150–2, 158, 361–3, 392, 404
Denthaliatis 159–60
Dercyllus 361
Diekplous 86
Diodorus 1, 2
Diogenes 106, 404
Dionysius I of Syracuse 73, 77, 392
Dionysus (Greek god) 306, 374, 386
Diopeithes 139
Diotimus 180
Dirke River 178
Dobrudja 148
Dodona 112, 144–5, 166
Doloaspis 254, 386
Dolopians 117, 150
Dorians 117
Doris 116, 119, 176, 395
Doriscus 134, 138
Drangiana 39, 287–8, 340, 343–4, 347–8, 403–4
Drangians 402
Drilon Valley 114
Drypetis 352
Durazzo 173
Dymnus 366–7
Dyrta 52, 96, 308, 317

Eastern Harbor 253
Eastern Ocean 306, 370
Ecbatana 28, 32–3, 44, 51, 54, 103, 184, 186, 276, 278–80, 284, 292, 297, 353–5, 357, 380, 402, 404
Egypt 26, 54, 86, 186, 230, 238–9, 250, 252–5, 378, 398–9, 401
Egypt, Gulf of 103
Egypt, lower 250
Egypt, upper 250
Egypt Harbor 95, 239, 243–4, 247
Egyptian quarter 253
Elasson 131
Elatea 150–2, 400

Elbruz Mountains 283, 286
Eleans 182
Elephants 21, 49, 52, 64, 258, 323, 325, 328–9
Eleutherae Gate 177
Elis 152, 159–60, 175, 398
Embolima 308, 313
Engineers 49, 64
Enil Gate 270
Enil Street 270
Enomotia 69–70
Enylus 242
Eordaicus River 145, 171
Epaminondas 5, 16, 22, 67, 392
Ephesus 162, 203–4, 400
Ephialtes 180, 206–10
Epirus 108, 112, 144–5, 393, 396, 399, 402
Epocillus 51–2
Eretria 116, 146–7, 397–9
Ergiske 138
Erices 317
Erigon River 113
Erigon Valley 112–4, 171
Erigyius 28, 34, 44, 260, 283, 287, 289, 385, 402–3
Esagila 270
Etesian Winds 89, 127, 129, 136, 377
Euboea 95, 116, 123, 128, 131, 145–8, 152, 361–3, 393–4, 397–400, 404
Euboean League 146
Euboic Gulf 116
Eudamidas 182
Eudamus 387
Eulaeus River 103, 272, 353
Eumenes 331, 352
Eunicus 51, 388
Euphraeus 147, 398
Euphrates River 102, 186, 221, 249, 255–6, 272, 284, 354, 357
Eurotas River 181
Eurydice 404
Eurylochus 147, 366, 399
Eurymedon River 212
Euryotas 47
Euylos 390
Exile's Decree 44, 181, 404

Fish-eaters 101, 344
Flexion catapults 74, 77
Floats 96, 294, 303, 304
Foot Companions 35
Fuller, J.F.C. 1

INDEX

Ganges River 332
Gangways 84
Ganos 134
Gaugamela 23–4, 26, 31, 33, 55, 184, 186, 256–7, 260, 378, 380, 402
Gaza (Phoenicia) 51, 74, 186, 236–7, 249–50, 256, 401
Gaza (Sogdiana) 296, 402
Gedrosa 284, 340, 342–4, 347
Gerostratus 235, 242, 390
Gerrhaean coast 103
Getae 139, 149, 168, 170–1, 174, 399
Geyser 211
Ghazni 288
Glaucias 31, 171–3, 390
Glaucippus 205
Glausae 52, 316, 329
Gobares 390
Gomphi 131–2
Gordian knot 215
Gordium 32, 53, 214–5, 380
Gordyaean Mountains 257
Gorgias 39, 292, 298, 309, 318
Grabaioi 137
Grabos 136–7, 393–4
Granicus River 24, 26, 31, 60, 188–9, 190–6, 401
Gravia Pass 150, 152, 400
Great King 55
Greece 6, 112, 116, 166, 176
Greek allied fleet 87, 204, 238
Greek allies 54, 203
Greek army 26
Greek light cavalry 33
Greek quarter 253
Grynium 161
Gujrat 26, 316, 318, 330
Gulpaigan 278
Guraea 308
Guraeans 311
Guraeus River 311
Gwadar 284, 344, 347

Hab River 344
Haemus Mountains 113, 115, 148, 168
Haliacmon River 126
Haliacmon Valley 144
Halicarnassus 50, 74, 106–7, 186, 204, 206–10, 219, 401
Halus 123–5, 133, 361–2, 398
Halys River 186, 216–7
Hanging Gardens 270
Haranpur 96, 316, 318, 327, 334

Harmozia 101, 354
Harpalus 28, 52, 203, 381, 385–8, 402, 404
Harrian Pass 343
Hebrus River 113, 135, 168
Hebrus Valley 134, 138–9, 399
Hecatomnus 386
Hecatompylus 283, 286
Hector (son of Parmenio) 251
Hedylium 152–397
Hegesandros 51
Hegelochus 31, 95, 191, 380
Hegemon 7, 400
Hegesistratus 204, 390
Helissus 159
Hellanicus 207
Hellenistic culture 10
Hellenistic era 373
Hellenistic kingdoms 9–10
Hellespont 89–90, 95, 136, 139, 142, 144, 160, 184–5, 187, 398–400
Hellespontine Phrygia 161, 188–9, 203, 210, 215
Helmund Valley 343
Helots 70
Hephaestion (son of Amyntor) 28, 31, 54, 96–7, 103, 187, 265, 292, 309, 311, 317–8, 321–4, 330, 332, 335, 340, 343, 345, 352–3, 355, 374–5, 381, 402, 404
Heptastadion 253
Heracleides 31, 103, 170
Heracles (god) 9, 148, 252, 306, 313, 403
Heracles (island) 241
Heracles, temple of 238, 241
Heraion Teichos 89, 134, 138, 395–6
Herat 288
Hermes 102
Hermolaus 365–6, 403
Hermotus 187–8
Hermus 215
Herodotus 1–2
Heroopolis 254
Herzegovina 173
Hetairoi 28
Hieron, port of 142
Hieron of Oros 134, 138, 398
Hieron of Soli 103, 357
Himalayan Mountains 318
Hindu Kush 290, 402
Hindu Kush Mountains 289, 291, 293–4, 306
Hipparch 30
Hipparchies 30, 35, 48
Hipparchus 146

Hipponicus 147, 399
Histriani 148–9
Homer 83
Homeric hero 337
Homosexuality 117
Hoplites 14, 17, 33, 40–2, 157, 180
Horse-archers 35, 296, 321
Horse transports 84
Horses 26, 29, 81
Hya 121
Hyampolis 122, 397
Hydarnes 390
Hydaspes River 20–2, 26, 96–7, 284, 309, 316–20, 322, 324, 334, 371, 403
Hydraotes River 96, 316, 330, 336–7
Hypani 210
Hypaspists 24, 39–40, 96
Hypereides 180
Hypozomata 83
Hyrcania 51, 54, 282–4, 286, 378, 380, 402

Iatrocles 361
Ida, Mt. 162
Ilai 30, 31, 32, 34, 71
Iliad 337
Illyria 17, 115, 396
Illyrian army 17
Illyrians 18, 185
Imbros 88, 156
India 18, 305, 307, 379, 403
Indian army 13
Indica 1
Indus River 52, 54, 98, 284, 308–9, 316–8, 334, 339, 342, 381
Ioannina 145
Iollas 368
Ionia 204
Ionian Sea 112, 160, 166
Iphicrates 88
Iranian plateau 335
Isaurians 217
Isfahan 278
Iskenderun 218
Iskur River 113, 168
Issus 26, 31, 55, 186, 218, 224, 226, 378, 401
Istar Gate 270
Italy 401

Jabal Maqlub massif 257
Jalalabad 308

Jalalpur 97, 316
Jason, tyrant of Pherae 130, 392
Javelin-men 44, 46
Javelins 22, 35, 60
Jaxartes River 25, 50, 66, 291, 295–8, 303
Jazrat-ibn-Omar 256
Jewish quarter 253
Jhau 345, 350
Jhelum 316
Jhelum River 96, 316
Judea 239
Justin 1, 2
Justinus, M. Junianus 1

Kabul 288, 308
Kabul River 284, 290, 309
Kabul Valley 284, 308, 402
Kalamata, Gulf of 159
Kandahar 288
Karachi 284, 334, 344, 349
Kashmir 316
Kazerun 272
Kelif 290, 294
Kerata Pass 153, 155
Kerdimmas 387, 389
Kerman 354
Ketriporis 134
Khabur River 256
Khamsin 253
Khawak Pass 81, 290–1, 402
King of the Lands 269
Kotai-i Sangar 273
Kothelas 139, 399
Kumbh Pass 344–5
Kumdoz 290
Kurdish Mountains 257
Kyber Pass 308
Kytinion 400

Laconia 70, 159–60, 181
Lade 105, 204–5
Lagus 28, 209, 292, 295
Lamia 112, 116, 124, 131, 150, 166, 176
Lamian Gulf 204
Lampsacus 187–8
Lancers 32–3
Langaros 171, 173, 389
Laomedon 28
Larisa 130–3, 166, 176, 361, 394, 398
Las Bela 343
Lasthenes 130

League of Corinth 33, 95, 126, 157, 179, 400
Lebanon 240
Lemnos 88, 156
Leonidas 183
Leonnatus (son of Anteas) 28, 34, 100, 310, 337, 343, 345 349, 353, 403–4
Lesbos 96, 106–7, 161–2, 188, 204
Lesgard 286
Leucas 152, 158
Leuctra 7, 16, 67, 135, 181, 392
Leuctrian War 117
Libya 250, 253–4, 401
Light Infantry 46–7
Little Zab River 256
Lochagos 38
Lochoi 17, 30–31, 48, 69–70
Lochos 38, 69
Locrians 117, 149, 151
Locris 116–9, 121, 150, 153, 394–6
Lugalgirra Gate 270
Lychnitis, Lake 112–4, 145
Lycia 106–7, 210–2, 242, 401
Lycian coast 106
Lycidas 254
Lycomedes of Rhodes 106
Lycophron 118–20, 130–3, 159, 393–5
Lycurgus 180
Lydia 161, 188–9
Lyginus River 169
Lyppeius 137, 394
Lysicles 153, 157
Lysimachus 28, 403

Macartatus 254
Macedonia 6, 7, 13, 15–6, 29, 112–3, 145, 168, 377, 395; army 7, 48, 175, 193; navy 107
Machatas 335, 387, 389
Maeander River 205
Maedi 113
Magarsus 218, 220
Magi 352
Magnesia 131, 133, 161–2, 203–4, 396
Magnesians 117
Maiameh 288
Maidoi 143, 399
Makran Desert 35, 342–3, 345, 348–51
Malakand Pass 313
Malis 116
Malli 52, 333–5, 337–8, 371
Malli River 97
Mallus 54, 107, 218, 220

Mandrodorus 343, 389
Mantineia 16, 67, 159–60, 392, 396
Maracanda 290, 296–9, 403
Marathon 190
Marathus 236–7, 401
Marcanda 44, 284, 292
Mardi 283, 285–6
Marduk (god) 355
Marduk Gate 270
Marduk Street 270
Marduk Temple 270
Marduk Tower 270
Mareotis Lake 252–3
Margiane 284, 290–1
Maronea 135, 137, 166, 395
Marsyas of Pella 1
Marsyas River 215
Mashlun Spur 314
Massaga 52, 308, 311–3, 317, 403
Massagetae 290, 292–3
Mauryan Empire 307
Mausolus 87, 395–6
Mazaces 230, 251–2, 378, 390
Mazaeus 224, 226, 255, 257, 260, 262–4, 269, 385, 387–9
Mazenes 102
Mecyberna 129
Meda (daughter of Kothelas) 399
Medates 271–4, 390
Media 34, 42, 51, 54, 139, 186, 278–9, 292, 351, 354, 378 380, 402
Mediterranean Sea 186, 216, 218, 250, 256
Medius 368
Megacles 254
Megalopolis 26, 67, 112, 159–60, 166, 181–2, 392, 396, 399, 402
Megara 152–3, 158, 160, 180, 361
Melanidas 51
Meleager (son of Neoptolemus) 31, 39, 171, 194–6, 206, 224–7, 259–60, 262, 275, 292–3, 309, 318, 340, 343
Melkart Island 247
Melkart temple 238, 247
Memnon of Rhodes 162, 185, 189, 193–4, 196, 199, 206–7, 209, 217, 237, 395, 400–1
Memphis 51, 54, 186, 250–2, 254–5, 380, 401
Menedemus 297
Menelaus 51, 129–30, 396–7
Menes (son of Dionysius) 96, 380, 386
Menes (son of Parmenio) 28
Menestratus 146

Menidas (son of Hegesandros) 34–5, 51–3, 259–60, 263, 265, 280
Menoetius 187
Menon (son of Cerdimmas) 43, 289, 385–6, 388–9
Mercenaries 16, 24, 37, 42–4, 50–1, 53–4, 57, 61–2, 104, 117, 120, 124, 132–3, 136, 153, 159, 162, 181, 184–5, 189, 192, 198, 201–2, 204–7, 210, 215, 223, 225, 258, 282; Old Guard 44
Merv 290
Meshed 288
Mesopotamia 26, 186, 256, 265, 402
Messenia 68, 152, 157, 159–60
Methone 126–7, 165, 394–5
Miccalus of Clazomenae 104, 357
Miletus 50, 91–2, 105–6, 204–5, 401
Mining 76
Minithya 389
Mithankot 334
Mithridates 189, 197–8
Mithrines 203, 385, 390
Mithobuzanes 198, 385
Mitylene 96, 401
Mixed array 19
Mnaseas 121, 396
Moerocles 180
Moles 76, 240–2, 248
Molossus 146–7, 397
Monsoon 100, 346, 404
Mophis 387
Mora 70
Mosul 356–7
Motya 73, 392
Mounds 76
Mules 26, 81
Mulla Pass 343
Multan 97, 284, 334, 338, 403
Musicanus 98, 334, 339–40
Mycale 91, 204–5
Mycale, Mt. 105
Mycalassus 71
Mylasa Gate 206, 208
Mylasa Way 207
Myndus 106, 204
Myndus Gate 208
Myriandrus 218, 222, 236
Mytilene 106, 188–9, 238

Nabarzanes 281–3
Narrows 185
Narycara 121, 395
Naryx 116, 121, 396

Nausicles 120, 361
Nautaca 52, 290, 294–5
Neanderthals 100, 344
Neapolis 89–90, 395
Nearchus 1, 28, 51, 97, 99–100, 102–3, 317, 335, 349, 352–3, 355, 357–8, 387, 404
Nebuchadnezzar 239
Nebuchadnezzar's Wall 270
Neiloxenes (son of Satyrus) 289
Neka River 283, 286
Neon 88, 116, 118–9, 131, 394–5, 397
Neoptolemus (king of Epirus) 50, 393
Nesaean fields 355
Nestos River 113, 167–8
Nicaea 90, 116, 122–3, 150, 308, 329, 333, 364, 399
Nicanor (father of Balacrus) 28, 40, 91, 170, 194, 204–5, 224, 259–60, 313, 386–7
Nicarchides 276
Nicesipolis 395–6
Nicolaus 385
Nicomachus 366
Nile River 251–2
Niphates 193, 198
Nisaean Plain 59
Nishapur 288
Northwest frontier 284, 290
Nysa 52, 54, 306, 308
Nyssa 216

Odrysian Thracian cavalry 34
Odrysians 134–5
Ogosta River 113, 168
Oisyme 394
Okhrida Lake 114
Old Guard, Macedonian 367
Oligarchies 162, 367
Olympias (daughter of Neoptolemus) 7, 9, 367, 393, 400
Olympus, Mt. 131, 165
Olynthus 74, 89, 127–30, 137, 396–7
Ombrion 48
Omphalium 145
Omphis 52
Onchestus 176
Onesicritus 353
Onomarchus 25, 118–20, 125, 131–2, 137–8, 144, 190, 395–6
Opis 31, 49, 53–4, 103, 284, 348, 353–4, 371, 381, 404
Ora 308, 312–3

INDEX 481

Orchomenus 116, 119, 121–3, 179, 364, 395–6
Oreitans 100, 342, 349, 351, 404
Orestis 145
Oreus 116, 147, 361–2, 399
Organa 102
Orientalization 366
Orneae 159, 296
Orontes 28
Orontobates 206, 209, 386
Orsines 378
Orxines 352, 388
Ossa, Mt. 131, 165–6
Osum River 113, 168
Othrys, Mt. 131
Oxathres (son of Abulites) 224, 226–7, 279, 288, 351
Oxen 26
Oxodates 280, 387
Oxus River 32, 54, 284, 290–1, 294, 369, 381, 402
Oxyartes 301–2, 317, 385, 387–8
Oxycanus 334, 339
Oxydracae 52–4, 97, 333–5, 338, 371

Pack animals 26, 81
Paeonia 394, 396
Paeonian cavalry 34
Paeonians 5, 35, 108, 113, 137
Pagai 394
Pagasae 120, 125, 131–3, 361, 394, 396
Pagasae, Gulf of 124, 146
Pages 27–8
Pages' Conspiracy 403
Pallene 89, 127, 129, 397
Pammenes 5, 88–9, 119, 137, 395
Pamphylia 50, 210–2, 215, 401
Pantaleon 254
Paphlagonia 215
Paraetacae 278, 279, 290, 302–3
Paraetonium 250
Parapanisadae 208, 402
Parapotamii 116, 151–2
Parauaea 145
Paris (son of Priam) 187
Parmenio 28, 31, 34, 42, 44, 52, 124, 133, 147, 150, 152, 160, 162, 185, 187–8, 191, 193–6, 199–201, 203–5, 214–5, 217, 220, 224–8, 251, 258–62, 264–5, 269, 272, 274, 276–7, 280, 289, 361, 365, 387, 389, 391, 400–2
Parnassus, Mt. 118, 152
Paropamisadae 289–90

Parthia 288
Parysatis 352, 404
Pasargadae 276, 278, 352, 354, 378, 404
Pasitigris River 103, 271–2
Pasni 284, 344, 347
Patara 211
Patroclus 187, 189, 374
Pattala 98, 284, 334, 340, 342–3, 346, 403
Peace of Antalcidas 106
Peace of Philocrates 398
Peace proposal 248
Peasants 14, 62
Peitho (son of Crateuas) 28, 336, 387
Peitholaus 393, 397
Peithon (son of Agenor) 39, 335, 340
Pelinna 176
Pelium 25, 50, 112–3, 145, 165–6, 168, 171–2, 174–6, 186
Pella 112–3, 123, 127, 145, 165–8, 185–6, 270, 361–2, 392
Peloponnese 69, 95, 112, 159–60, 181, 400
Peloponnesian War 15, 46, 69–70, 86, 156, 179
Peltasts 5, 44–6
Pelte 44
Pelusium 186, 250–2, 254
Pentecostyes 70
Percote 187–8
Perdiccas 5, 31, 39, 97, 173, 177, 180, 194–6, 206–7, 224, 226–7, 242, 259–60, 262, 265, 292, 309, 311, 317–8, 321–4, 337, 339, 352–3, 378, 402
Perdiccas III 108, 112, 392–3, 400
Perge 186, 211–2
Perhaebia 396
Perinthus 74, 112, 133–4, 138, 140, 156–7, 166, 206, 395, 399
Perioeci 70
Periplous 86
Perrhaebia 131–3, 395
Perrhaebians 117
Persepolis 184, 186, 272, 274–8, 282, 284, 354, 378, 380, 402, 404
Perseus 252
Persia 13, 141, 143
Persian army 3, 9, 26, 55–7, 192, 199
Persian cavalry 59–61
Persian Empire 9, 58, 186, 211, 282, 306–7, 378
Persian fleet 87, 92–3, 104–7, 184, 187, 204, 230, 237–8
Persian Gates 272, 274, 276–7, 402
Persian Gulf 103–4, 272, 278, 284, 353–4

Persian navy 210, 245
Persian slingers 48
Persians 245
Persis 102, 186, 272, 278, 351, 354
Petines 193, 198
Petisis 254, 386
Petra Pass 131–2
Peuce Island 91, 168–70
Peucelaotis 308–9, 11
Peucestas 48, 53, 255, 257, 337, 351, 353, 386, 404
Peucestas (son of Alexandros) 388
Peucestas (son of Macartatus) 254
Peucestas (son of Orontes) 28
Peucolaus 298
Pezhetairoi 35
Phaedriades 117–8
Phalaecus 90, 121–2, 123–5, 398
Phalangiarch 39
Phalanx 25, 36–9, 49, 158, 178, 180, 182, 190
Pharaoh 252, 401
Pharasmanes 51, 389
Pharcadon 132–3
Pharnabazus 95–6, 106–7
Pharnaces 189, 198
Pharnuches 44, 290, 297–300, 403
Pharos 252–3
Pharsalians 32
Pharsalus 71, 124, 131, 133, 398
Phaselis 211–2, 365
Phayllus 119, 133, 159, 395–6
Phegeus 332
Pherae 112, 120, 130–3, 159, 166, 362, 395, 397–8
Philinna 393
Philip (son of Machatas) 335, 387, 389
Philip (son of Menelaus) 34, 51
Philip II 3, 31, 108, 137, 171, 193–6, 215, 260, 310, 388, 396; battles of (see Chaeronea, Erigon Valley); birth of 392; death of 7–8; generalship of 22, 24, 35, 46, 66, 125, 140–1, 144, 147, 158; illnesses of 396; marriages of 393, 399–400; sieges by (see Byzantium, Perinthus); wounds sustained by 113, 115, 395, 398, 400
Philippi 127
Philippopolis 112–3, 166–8, 394
Philistides 147
Philocrates 361–3, 398
Philomelus 115, 117–8, 394–5
Philon 122
Philotas (son of Parmenio) 37, 39, 172, 193–4, 196, 203, 207, 224, 259, 275, 287, 289, 310, 366–7, 387, 391, 402
Philoxenus 53, 270, 357
Phocian army 64–5
Phocians 120, 133, 179
Phocion (Athenian general) 143, 146
Phocis 115–6, 119, 122–4, 151, 153, 176, 361–2, 364, 394–7, 399
Phoenicia 26, 54, 86, 184, 186, 230, 235, 239, 255, 380, 401
Phoenician fleet 244
Phoenician navy 248
Phradates 387, 389–90
Phrasaortes (son of Rheomithres) 276, 390
Phrataphernes 52, 283, 387–90
Phrygia 189, 211, 214–5, 217
Phrynon 361
Phthiotians 150
Pillar of Jonah Pass 218, 221–2
Pinara 211
Pinarus River 218, 221, 226–7, 232–3, 235
Pindar 179
Pindus Mountains 144–5
Pine Tree Island 169
Pir-sar Ridge 314–5
Pisaeus (father of Aristonous) 28, 156
Pisidians 213, 215
Pitane 161
Pixodarus 28, 400
Plataea 70, 176, 179, 364
Plataeans 179
Plato 397
Platon 51
Pleiads 100
Pleuratus 114
Pleurias 400
Plutarch 1
Plutarchus 146, 397
Pnytagoras 93, 243
Polemarchs 133
Polemocrates 50, 96, 318
Polemon (son of Megacles) 254
Polemon (son of Theramenes) 254–5
Poliorcetes, Demetrius 75, 78
Polybius 1
Polydamas 280
Polyeuctas 180
Polyidus 77
Polysperchon (son of Simmias) 39, 259–60, 262, 275, 292, 298, 303, 311, 318, 335, 343, 372
Poop deck 84
Porthmos 116, 398
Porticanus 339

INDEX

Porus, king of Gujrat 20, 26, 52, 54, 96, 318–29, 330–2, 387, 403
Porus, the Bad 316, 330
Potidaea 127–8, 136–7, 392–3
Practius River 187–8
Praetorian Guard 372
Priam, king of Troy 187
Prodromoi 32
Proexes 286–7, 289
Prophthasia 284, 288
Propontis Sea 134, 162
Proskynesis 290, 403
Proteus (son of Andronicus) 95
Protomachus 224
Proxenus 90, 122–3
Psiloi 5, 46–7
Ptolemy (son of Lagus) 1, 28, 51, 209, 224–6, 292, 295, 310, 315, 331, 335, 352, 367, 403
Ptolemy (son of Seleucus) 39, 50, 227–8
Ptolemy IX 384
Punjab 39, 52, 54, 284, 306–7, 309, 311, 316, 334, 340, 371, 403
Pura 284, 344
Pydna 35, 126–7, 165, 393
Phthophanes 386

Qazvin 278

Ram ships 94, 244
Ras Mussendam 103, 357
Ravi River 96, 316, 330
Red Sea 101, 103, 189, 250
Rhacotis 252
Rhagae 186, 278–80, 284
Rhambacia 284, 344–5
Rheomithres 189, 193–4, 196, 200, 276, 390
Rhodes 75, 78, 87, 93, 107, 143, 204, 242, 361
Rhodian engineers 43
Rhodian slingers 43, 48
Rhoesaces 197–8
Rhoeteum 161–2
Rhomboid formation 30, 32
Rhosaces 193
Roads 27, 81
Roman army 80
Roman Empire 1, 170
Roman legionaries 38
Roman legions 35
Rome 6, 10, 245

Roxane 9, 290, 301–2, 403–4
Royal Guards 59
Royal Harbor 253
Royal Road 215
Rufus, Quintus Curtius 1
Rumania 148

Sabaces 217, 229, 386
Sabiktas 386
Sabistamenes 386
Saca cavalry 34
Sacred Band 5, 16–7, 23, 153, 155, 158
Sacred Mountain 134
Sacred War, Fourth 16, 151, 400; Third 16, 31, 65, 115, 120, 125, 132, 145, 149, 151–2, 159, 361–2, 399
Sagalassus 211, 213, 215
Salmacis 206, 208
Salmus 354
Samarah Lake 99
Samaritans 388–9
Samarkand 290
Sambastae 334
Sambus 334, 339, 403
Samos 74, 88, 105–6, 156, 205, 392
Sangaeus 390
Sangala 52, 54, 284, 316, 330, 330–1, 403
Sangarius River 215
Sardis 42, 161, 186, 188, 203–4, 214, 401
Sardon River 129
Sarisophori 32
Sarissa 22, 29, 33, 35–6, 38, 158, 169
Satibarzanes 44, 285, 287, 289, 385, 402
Satrapal purges 404
Satraps 385–389
Satyrus 289
Scarphe 116
Sciritai 69
Sciritis 159–60
Scouts 30, 32–3
Scyros 156
Scythia 148, 295, 399
Scythian campaign 114
Scythians 65, 113, 290, 292, 297, 303–5, 403
Sebzewar 288
Seer 355
Sehwan 334, 339
Seleucia 256
Seleucus 39, 40, 50, 227–8, 322–3, 352
Selgians 213
Selymbria 90, 134, 141, 157, 399
Semiramis 306, 342

Semnan 286
Serbia 171
Serbonis Lake 251
Serrion 138
Servants 16, 27, 81–2, 185
Sestos 89, 91, 134, 138, 161, 188, 394–5
Shahrud 286, 288
Shamash Gate 270
Shamash Street 270
Shamshirbun Pass 283, 286
Shield-bearers 45
Shield piercer 77
Shipka Pass 113, 168
Shiraz 272–3, 276
Sibyrtius 351, 385–6, 389
Siculus, Diodorus 1
Side 211–3
Sidon 50, 93, 236–7, 242, 247, 398, 401
Sidon Harbor 94–5, 239, 241, 243–4, 247
Siege towers 78
Siege trains 79
Sieges 14
Sigeum 106
Sillyum 211
Silver-shields 40
Simmias 39, 259–60, 262, 264
Sin Gate 270
Sin Street 270
Sind 306
Sindimana 334, 339
Singitic Gulf 127
Sinope 404
Siphnos 95, 107, 230
Sisicottus 329, 389
Sisimithres 295, 390
Sisines 365
Sisygambis 230, 273
Sitalces 46, 53, 72, 224–5, 259–60, 280, 351
Sithonia 127
Siwah 98, 186, 250, 252–4, 383, 401
Slingers 48, 63
Sochi 218–9, 221, 232
Social War 87, 136, 143, 393–4
Socrates 194–5, 386
Soeris 340, 389
Sofia 45, 112, 166
Sogda 98, 334, 339, 344
Sogdian light cavalry 34
Sogdiana 32, 34–5, 54, 284, 290–2, 296, 298, 300–1, 302, 305, 381, 402–3
Soli 93, 107, 218–9, 242
Soma 253, 384
Somatophylakes 28

Sonmiani 343–4, 349–50
Sopithes 54, 316, 332
Sopolis 31, 51–2, 170
Spanish sword 38
Sparta 7, 8, 15, 26, 112, 120–3, 152, 157, 160, 165–6, 179, 181–2, 186, 362, 396, 398, 402
Spartan army 16, 67–8, 181, 401
Spartan cavalry 69
Spartans 159, 230
Spears 29, 35
Spitamenes 34, 44, 290, 292–3, 295–8, 300, 403
Spithridates 189
Staff sling 48
Stagira 127–8, 397
Stamenes 385
Stasanor 289, 351, 385–6
Stateira 9, 230, 402, 404
Statocles 153–4, 157
Statonice 128
Stobi 112–3, 116, 168
Stone-throwing catapults 78
Strabo 1
Strategos 39
Stratonicea 127
Straton (son of Gerostratus) 235, 390–1
Strophia River 178
Strymon River 113, 135, 168
Strymon Valley 45, 143
Suez, Gulf of 357
Sultanabad 278
Supply train 82
Susa 51, 102–3, 107, 184, 186, 270–3, 284, 348, 352–4, 378, 381, 402, 404; marriages 404
Susiana 26, 102, 265, 272, 354
Sutlej River 316
Swat 52, 96, 308, 311, 313, 317, 403
Syllium 212
Syntagma 39
Syntagmatarch 39
Syracuse 46, 77
Syria 218
Syrian Gates 218–21
Syrian plain 220–1
Syrmus 169, 390
Syrphax 203, 390

Taenarum 160
Tagus 130, 392
Talmena 344
Taloi Mountains 99, 343, 349

INDEX 485

Tamynae 116, 146, 397
Tapuria 53, 283
Tarsus 216, 218–9, 401
Tasiaces 386
Tattooing 65
Taulantians 37, 168, 171–4
Tauron 48, 273–4, 321–4
Taurus Mountains 185, 217
Taxiarch(s) 39
Taxiarchia 39
Taxies 36, 39–40, 177
Taxila 52, 54, 316–7, 381
Taxiles 52, 317, 326, 329, 381, 387, 403
Taygetos, Mt. 67
Tegea 159–60
Tegeans 182
Teheran 278
Tejan River 286
Telmissus 46, 204, 211, 213
Tempe 126
Tempe Pass 131
Tempe River 165, 400
Tenedos 50, 95, 106–7, 162
Teres 134, 138–9, 398–9
Terioltes 388
Termessus 211
Tetrarch 39, 133
Tetrarchia 39
Tetrarchies 133, 399
Teutoburger Wald 175
Thais 276
Thalamos 84
Thalestris 389
Thapsacus 103, 221, 255–6, 357
Thasians 137
Thasos 74, 89
Theban army 137, 159
Thebe 393
Thebes 16–7, 26, 88, 112, 116, 123–4, 130, 151–2, 156, 165–6, 175–9, 186, 361–2, 364, 396, 398–400
Theodorus 270–1
Theramenes 254
Thermopylae 90, 116, 119–25, 133, 145, 150, 153, 176, 362–4, 396, 398–9
Thespiae 116, 153, 364
Thessalian cavalry 32, 36, 51, 54, 71
Thessalian League 118–9, 130–3, 165–6, 394–5, 398
Thessalians 150, 152, 394
Thessalonike 396
Thessaly 6, 13, 29, 31, 112, 119–21, 125–6, 130–2, 176, 362, 364, 377, 394–5, 398
Thibron 404

Thisbe 153
Thoas (son of Mandrodorus) 343, 351, 386, 389
Thrace 6, 112, 133–4, 139, 377, 399
Thracian cavalry 71
Thracian Chersonese 134, 138–9, 141, 144
Thracian Sea 113, 134, 168, 176
Thracians 5, 169, 185
Thracians, Free 168
Thracidae 117
Thranites 84
Thronium 90, 119, 122–3, 395
Thymondas 224–6, 228–9
Thyreatis 159–60
Tigris River 103, 186, 255–7, 272, 284, 353–4, 371, 404
Tilphosaion 116, 119, 121, 395
Timotheus 88, 394
Tiridates 275–6, 389–90
Tiristasis 139
Tiryaspes 388
Tisiphonus 130, 393
Tithronium 116
Tlepolemus (son of Phthophanes) 102, 386
Tomerus River 100, 344
Toprakkale 218
Toronaic Gulf 127–9
Torone 89, 129, 397
Torsion catapults 74, 77–8
Tralles 203–4, 210
Triballians 113–5, 168–70, 174, 185, 400
Tricca 112, 131–3, 166, 176
Tridates 386
Trierarchs 97
Triple Gate 208
Tripolis 230
Trireme 83–6, 104
Troad 161–2, 203, 401
Trojan Pass 113, 168–9, 171
Trojan War 187
Troop assault ships 244
Troy 161, 187–9, 392
Tulamba 334
Turbat 284, 344, 347, 350
Turiaspes 388
Tyana 216
Tylus 103–4, 357
Tymphaea 145
Tyre 51, 74, 93–4, 107, 186, 206, 236, 255–6, 401–2; new 240–1; old 238, 241

Uch 334
Una-sar Ridge 314

Upash Gate 270
Uxians 271, 273, 402

Vizier 400
Volustana Pass 131–2

Wazirabad 316
Weddings, at Susa 352, 355
Wedge formation 30
Weirs 103, 353
Welpar 343
Western Harbor 353
Wolf's Pass 171–3

Xandrames, Ding 332
Xanthrians 97
Xanthus 211
Xenippa 295
Xenophilus 271

Xenophon (Athenian General) 23, 394
Xenophon, Flavius Arrianus 1
Xerxes 184–5, 193, 269, 271

Yemen 103–4, 357
Yezd-i-khast 278
Yugoslavia 17, 171

Zababa Gate 279
Zababa Street 270
Zadracarta 283–6
Zahedan 344
Zarangia 366
Zariaspa 289–92, 296, 284
Zeleia 189–90, 193
Zeravshan Valley 292
Zeus 252–4
Zoilus 52
Zyga 84

www.ingramcontent.com/pod-product-compliance
Lightning Source LLC
Chambersburg PA
CBHW051202300426
44116CB00006B/406